MERGERS AND ACQUISITIONS LAW

MERGERS AND ACQUISITIONS LAW

William K. Sjostrom, Jr.
Professor of Law and Director of the Business Law Program
The University of Arizona, James E. Rogers College of Law

CAROLINA ACADEMIC PRESS
Durham, North Carolina

ISBN: 978-1-4224-8329-9 (Print)
ISBN: 978-1-5310-1578-7 (Paperback)
ISBN: 978-1-6304-4772-4 (Looseleaf)
ISBN: 978-0-3271-7967-2 (eBook)

Library of Congress Cataloging-in-Publication Data

Sjostrom, William K., Jr. author.
Mergers and acquisitions law / William K. Sjostrom, Jr., Professor of Law and Director of the Business Law Program, The University of Arizona, James E. Rogers College of Law.
    pages cm
  Includes index.
  ISBN 978-1-4224-8329-9
1. Consolidation and merger of corporations--Law and legislation--United States. I. Title.
  KF1477.S56 2014
  346.73'06626—dc23

                                                                      2014046847

Carolina Academic Press, LLC
700 Kent Street
Durham, North Carolina 27701
Telephone (919) 489-7486
Fax (919) 493-5668
www.caplaw.com

Printed in the United States of America

2019 Printing

Dedication

To Nancy, Liam, Ollie, Simon, and Lulu

Acknowledgements

Thanks to Joseph Baker, Lacee Collins, Joshua Crandell, Mohamed Djenabout, Colleen Ganin, Shruti Gurudant, Jahna Locke, Barbara Lopez, Michelle Moussa, Araceli Rodriguez, David Rosenthal, Cathy Smith, and Mitch Turbenson for their invaluable help on this book.

Preface

This is a transactional, as opposed to litigation, oriented M&A book. M&A lawyers are by definition transactional lawyers, and thus I believe that M&A should be taught with a transactional emphasis. This emphasis is reflected in the following features of the book:

- *Content selected through an M&A lawyer lens*: I worked on many M&A deals during my years in practice, both at a law firm and in-house, and have drawn on this experience in selecting the book's content and topic depth.

- *Emphasis on real-world provisions*: The book is loaded with actual provisions from various M&A documents M&A lawyers draft and review so that students get to see how the covered legal concepts are documented. The provisions also give students a sense for what M&A lawyers do in practice.

- *Teaching through exercises*: The book includes numerous exercises, all of which require students to apply what they've learned from the readings. This involves analyzing deal document language in light of statutory provisions and case law and applying this language in various situations encountered by an M&A lawyer. Some of the exercises involve reviewing a complete document, such as an agreement and plan of merger, and answering questions regarding it. As a result, students get to see how various provisions excerpted or described in the book fit together in a single document. The exercises are designed to reinforce the covered material and help students develop the planning and problem-solving skills of an M&A lawyer as well as expose students to the documents and issues at the heart of an M&A practice.

- *More narrative, fewer cases*: I cover many legal concepts through concise explanatory text instead of judicial opinions. This enables me to keep the book a manageable size while providing more depth in areas central to an M&A practice. It also frees up student preparation and class time for focusing on the exercises instead of case crunching. Each case I do include is followed by a series of straightforward questions to get students to zero in on the key aspects of the case, leading to efficient class discussion. Additionally, unlike most casebooks, the book does not include "notes." Instead, I have integrated the note-type material into the text which enhances readability by making the book flow better.

Note that the provisions and documents included in the book are not meant to serve as model forms. In several instances I have deleted language from the provision or document on which the item is based to shorten or simplify it for pedagogical reasons. With that said, the items do generally serve as examples of good legal drafting as I spent some time cleaning up drafting errors.

William K. Sjostrom, Jr.
November 2014

Table of Contents

Table of Contents

Table of Contents

Table of Contents

Table of Contents

Table of Contents

Chapter 1

INTRODUCTION

This book focuses on the law of mergers and acquisitions (M&A). The quintessential M&A transaction, or deal, is when one business buys another business. M&A law encompasses the myriad of legal rules implicated by such a transaction. There is, however, no distinct body of M&A law. Instead, an M&A lawyer needs to be conversant in corporate law, securities law, contract law, tax law, and antitrust law, to name a few. Hence, this book explores how these and other areas of law apply to an M&A deal so that you gain the basic knowledge needed to be an M&A lawyer.

Chapters 2 through 5 of the book focus on friendly deals. A deal is "friendly" if management of the company to be acquired ("target") is in favor of (or at least not opposed to) being acquired by the pursuing company ("bidder"). The vast majority of deals are friendly. Chapter 6 covers hostile deals. A deal is "hostile" if target's management is against being acquired by bidder. Chapter 7 examines director fiduciary duties in the context of both friendly and hostile deals.

A. DEAL STRUCTURES OVERVIEW

From a legal perspective, an acquisition is typically structured in one of four ways: an asset purchase, stock purchase, merger, or share exchange. While the legal requirements and effects of these structures differ, the end result is the same for each structure: bidder ends up owning target's business. Below I provide a brief overview of each structure. We will focus more on differences between structures in Chapter 4 when we discuss factors that drive the choice of structure for a particular deal. For now, assume that both bidder and target are corporations.

1. Asset Purchase

As the name indicates, in a deal structured as an asset purchase, bidder acquires target's business by buying target's assets. For example, say Sjostrom Gas Co. ("SGC") owns and operates gas stations and has agreed to be acquired by Global Gas Inc. ("GGI") through an asset purchase. This means that SGC will sell its assets (gas stations, real estate, inventory, trademarks, etc.) and assign its contracts (lease agreements, gas supply agreements, etc.) to GGI in exchange for the deal consideration negotiated by SGC and GGI. Deal consideration, regardless of deal structure, can consist of cash, bidder stock, bidder debt, or a combination of any of the foregoing. As part of the deal, GGI may also agree to assume some of SGC's liabilities (such as SGC's bank loan), and this would be factored into the deal price. In other words, if GGI agrees to assume SGC's $1,000,000 bank loan as part of the deal, GGI will pay $1,000,000 less for SGC's assets than it otherwise would have.

The specific assets target is selling to bidder, specific liabilities bidder is assuming from target, and the amount and type of deal consideration will be specified in an "Asset Purchase Agreement" signed by bidder and target. Target remains in existence after the deal, but no longer owns any business assets because it has sold them to bidder. In other words, post-deal target is basically a shell whose only asset is the deal consideration. Thus, following the deal target typically dissolves and distributes the deal consideration to its shareholders.

Below is a diagram of an acquisition structured as an asset purchase. For this and the other diagrams in this chapter, "B" stands for bidder, and "T" stands for target.

ASSET PURCHASE

Transaction

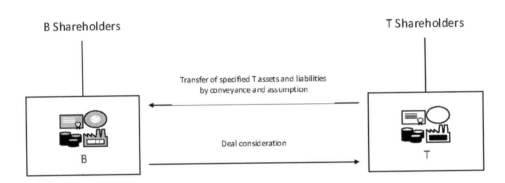

Result

2. Stock Purchase

As the name indicates, in a deal structured as a stock purchase, bidder acquires target's business by buying all of target's outstanding stock. Thus, if the SGC/GGI deal is structured as a stock purchase, GGI would buy all of SGC's outstanding shares from SGC's shareholders. This deal would be reflected in a "Stock Purchase

Agreement" signed by GGI and each of SGC's shareholders, as well as SGC. The agreement will specify the deal consideration, or how much and in what form GGI is paying each SGC shareholder for his or her shares.

Given bidder acquires all of target's outstanding stock; post-deal target ends up as a wholly-owned subsidiary of bidder. A wholly-owned subsidiary is a corporation (or other entity) 100 percent of whose stock is owned by another corporation (or other entity) (often called the "parent" company). In other words, bidder has acquired target's business by acquiring 100 percent stock ownership of target. Target's shareholders pre-deal no longer own any stock in target because they have sold it to bidder in exchange for the deal consideration.

Below is a diagram of an acquisition structured as a stock purchase.

STOCK PURCHASE

Transaction

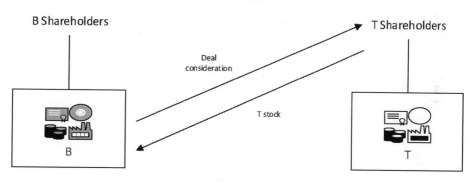

Result

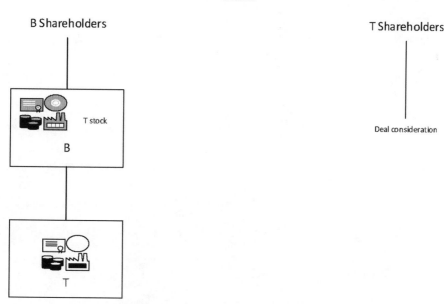

3. Merger

A merger is entirely a function of state corporate law. In other words, a bidder can acquire a target through a merger only because state corporate law statutes include merger provisions. There are three different types of mergers: (1) direct merger, (2) forward triangular merger, and (3) reverse triangular merger. The type of merger the parties have decided on is set forth in an "Agreement and Plan of Merger," as is the deal consideration target's shareholders will receive upon consummation of the merger.

a. Direct Merger

In a direct merger, target merges with and into bidder. Pursuant to the merger statute, upon consummation of the merger: (1) target's assets and liabilities are transferred to bidder by operation of the law, (2) target's outstanding shares are converted into the deal consideration specified in the agreement and plan of merger, and (3) target ceases to exist.

Below is a diagram of an acquisition structured as a direct merger.

DIRECT MERGER

Transaction

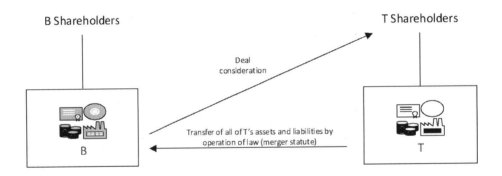

Result

b.   Forward Triangular Merger

In a forward triangular merger, target merges with and into a newly created wholly-owned subsidiary of bidder ("merger sub"). Pursuant to the merger statute and as specified in the agreement and plan of merger, upon consummation of the merger: (1) target's assets and liabilities are transferred to merger sub by operation of the law, (2) target's outstanding shares are converted into the deal consideration specified in the agreement and plan of merger, and (3) target ceases to exist. As a result, target's business ends up in a wholly-owned subsidiary of bidder.

Below is a diagram for a deal structured as a forward triangular merger. In this diagram and the next one, "S" stands for merger sub.

FORWARD TRIANGULAR MERGER

Transaction

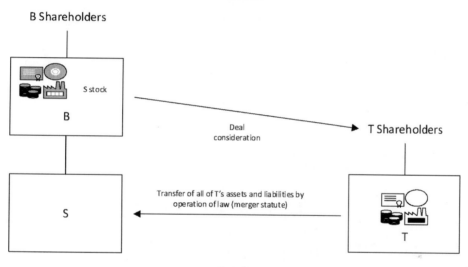

Result

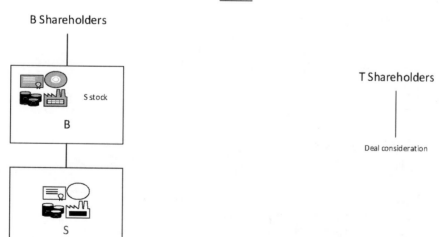

c.   Reverse Triangular Merger

In a reverse triangular merger, merger sub merges with and into target. Pursuant to the merger statute and as specified in the agreement and plan of merger, upon consummation of the merger: (1) target's outstanding shares are converted into the deal consideration specified in the agreement and plan of merger, (2) merger sub's outstanding shares, all of which are owned by bidder, are converted into target common stock, and (3) merger sub ceases to exist. As a result, target ends up as a wholly-owned subsidiary of bidder.

Below is a diagram for a deal structured as a reverse triangular merger.

REVERSE TRIANGULAR MERGER

Transaction

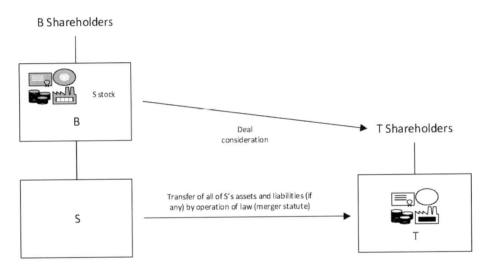

Result

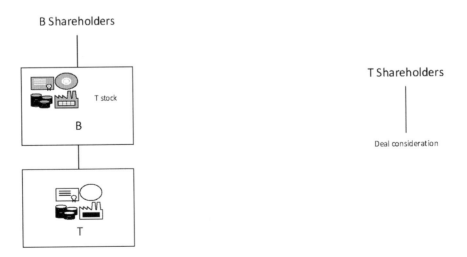

4. Share Exchange

As with a merger, a share exchange is entirely a function of state corporate law. In other words, a bidder can acquire a target through a share exchange only because the Model Business Corporation Act (MBCA), and thus many state corporate law statutes, include share exchange provisions. The Delaware General Corporation Law (DGCL), however, does not provide for a share exchange. Consequently, if either bidder or target is incorporated in Delaware (or some other state that does not provide for a share exchange), the parties cannot structure the deal as a share exchange.

In a share exchange, bidder acquires all of the outstanding stock of target by operation of the law in exchange for the deal consideration which it pays directly to target's shareholders. As a result, target ends up as a wholly-owned subsidiary of bidder. This is very similar to what happens in a stock purchase. The difference between the two is that with a share exchange, instead of each shareholder deciding individually whether or not to sell his or her shares to bidder, target shareholders vote on the deal. If enough shares vote in favor of the deal (the voting requirement under the MBCA is more votes for than against), all shareholders have to participate. In other words, a shareholder cannot refuse to sell his or her shares to bidder.

Following is a diagram for a deal structured as a share exchange.

SHARE EXCHANGE

Transaction

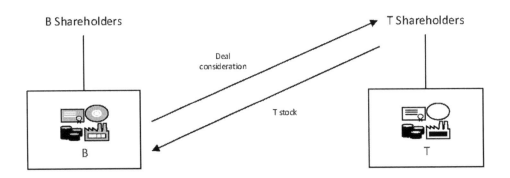

Result

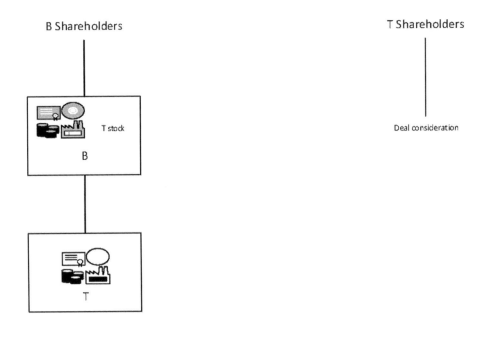

QUESTIONS

1. Under which deal structures does target continue to exist as a legal entity after the deal closes?

2.   In an asset purchase, what happens to target's shares upon consummation of the deal?

3.   In a stock purchase, what happens to target's shares upon consummation of the deal?

4.   In a forward triangular merger, what happens to target's shares upon consummation of the deal? What about merger sub's shares?

5.   In a reverse triangular merger, what happens to target's shares upon consummation of the deal? What about merger sub's shares?

6.   In a share exchange, what happens to target's shares upon consummation of the deal?

B.   DEAL FLOW

To give you a sense for the steps and various parties involved in an M&A transaction, below is an excerpt from a Securities and Exchange Commission ("SEC") filing that describes the events leading up to the acquisition of Zipcar, Inc. by Avis Budget Group, Inc. Zipcar is a car sharing network founded in 2000 that rents out cars by the hour. Its stock was traded on the NASDAQ Global Select Market. Avis Budget owns and operates the Avis and Budget car rental businesses. Its stock is traded on the NASDAQ Global Select Market. Avis Budget and Zipcar signed the agreement and plan of merger on December 31, 2012 and closed the deal on March 14, 2013.

ZIPCAR, INC.
PROXY STATEMENT
(Feb. 4, 2013)

Background of the Merger

The board of directors of the company [Zipcar] . . . regularly reviews and evaluates the company's business strategy and strategic alternatives with the goal of enhancing stockholder value.

At a board meeting on May 31, 2012, the board reviewed various strategic alternatives related to expanding the company's services offerings to address a broader array of mobility services and trip needs. Both prior and subsequent to this meeting, senior executives of the company engaged in discussions with various auto manufacturers, or OEMs, and other potential strategic partners regarding a strategic relationship for the provision of a floating by the minute, or FBM, short trip, one way service offering to complement the company's core car sharing service. During the late summer of 2012, the company approached certain OEMs regarding an exclusive arrangement to be the company's strategic partner regarding this service, which would also involve a significant minority investment in the company to assist the company in meeting the intensive capital requirements of launching this new service. Following discussions with several OEMs, the company received indications of interest from multiple OEMs and eventually received a non-binding letter of intent from one OEM, or the OEM Potential Investor, proposing a strategic relationship regarding the supply of a specific vehicle platform for use in the FBM service, technology integration between the vehicle platform and the company's technology, joint marketing and promotional activities and payment of a program fee by the OEM Potential Investor, and also proposing a significant minority investment in the company by the OEM Potential Investor.

At a board meeting on September 19, 2012, the board discussed the non-binding letter of intent from the OEM Potential Investor as well as other strategic alternatives available to the company. The board authorized the company's management to pursue the relationship with the OEM Potential Investor. The board also discussed the changing competitive landscape, industry dynamics, and various potential next steps for the company in response thereto, including the possibility of pursuing a strategic relationship with a major rental car company to serve longer trip needs and to further bolster the company's balance sheet through a minority investment in parallel to the proposed investment by the OEM Potential Investor. The board also discussed establishing a special committee of the board, or the Committee, for purposes of administrative convenience and effectiveness, to review and assess strategic alternatives that were or might become available to the company and to work with Scott W. Griffith, the company's Chairman and Chief Executive Officer, regarding such alternatives. Following further discussion, the board determined to establish the Committee for purposes of administrative convenience and effectiveness and appointed Messrs. Mahoney (lead director of the board and chairman of the Committee), Kagle, and Davis to the Committee.

From September 19 until late December 2012, Mr. Griffith, Dean J. Breda, the company's General Counsel, and other company representatives continued to meet with the OEM Potential Investor and negotiate the terms of the proposed strategic partnership. As a result of the meetings and negotiations, the OEM Potential Investor indicated to the company its strong desire to consummate the partnership by, or shortly after, the end of calendar year 2012.

On September 27, 2012, Mr. Griffith contacted Ronald L. Nelson, Chairman and Chief Executive Officer of Avis Budget, by telephone. Messrs. Griffith and Nelson discussed the company's plans for exploring methods to enhance the company's value proposition by offering short, medium, and long trip alternatives under a single brand and technology platform offered by the company, including partnerships that Zipcar was exploring or considering, such as an FBM relationship and equity investment with a global OEM. Mr. Griffith also discussed Zipcar's intention to seek a strategic relationship with and equity investment from a major car rental company to complement the company's current offering by better serving longer trip needs and to potentially benefit the company through improved operational efficiencies that may be possible from such a relationship. Mr. Nelson indicated an interest in engaging with the company regarding such discussions or a broader strategic relationship. Messrs. Griffith and Nelson determined to have a follow- up, in- person meeting to further discuss strategic opportunities. An in- person meeting was subsequently scheduled for October 16, 2012.

On September 28, 2012, Mr. Griffith and Party A's Chief Executive Officer spoke by telephone. Mr. Griffith discussed the company's plans for exploring methods to enhance the company's value proposition by offering short, medium, and long trip alternatives under a single brand and technology platform offered by the company, including partnerships that Zipcar was exploring or considering, such as an FBM relationship and equity investment with a global OEM. Mr. Griffith also discussed Zipcar's intention to seek a strategic relationship with and equity investment from a major car rental company to complement the company's current offering by better serving longer trip needs and to potentially benefit the company through improved operational efficiencies that may be possible from such a relationship. Party A's Chief Executive Officer indicated an interest in engaging with the company regarding such discussions or a broader strategic relationship. Mr. Griffith and Party A's Chief Executive Officer determined to have a follow-up meeting to further discuss strategic opportunities. From September 28 through October 16, 2012, Mr. Griffith and Party A's Chief Executive corresponded regarding the logistics and agenda for such meeting, and scheduled such meeting for October 17, 2012.

On October 8, 2012, Party A and the company executed a confidentiality agreement.

On October 15, 2012, Avis Budget and the company executed a confidentiality agreement.

On October 16, 2012, Mr. Griffith and Zipcar representatives met with Mr. Nelson, David Wyshner, Avis Budget's Chief Financial Officer, and Scott Deaver, Avis Budget's Executive Vice President — Strategy. The company's representatives presented an overview of the company's strategic vision to serve a broader array of mobility services and trip types and the representatives of both parties discussed potential strategic alignment and potential strategic relationships between the parties. Avis Budget also indicated that it had interest in a potential business combination and acquisition of Zipcar. Mr. Griffith indicated that a sale of the company had not been the company's or the board's intention when engaging in these discussions but that he would discuss Avis Budget's interest with the Committee.

On October 17, 2012, Mr. Griffith and Zipcar representatives met in person with the Chief Executive Officer and other representatives of Party A. At this meeting, the representatives of the company reviewed the company's strategic vision and representatives of Party A reviewed Party A's strategic vision, followed by discussions between the parties. Party A's Chief Executive Officer also indicated that Party A had interest in a potential business combination and acquisition of Zipcar. Mr. Griffith indicated that a sale of the company had not been the company's or the board's intention in engaging in these discussions but that he would discuss Party A's interest with the Committee.

On October 18, 2012, Mr. Griffith and Party B's Chief Executive Officer had a telephone conversation in which Mr. Griffith discussed the company's plans for exploring methods to enhance the company's value proposition by offering short, medium, and long trip alternatives under a single brand and technology platform offered by the company, including partnerships that Zipcar was exploring or considering, such as an FBM relationship and equity investment with a global OEM. Mr. Griffith also discussed Zipcar's intention to seek a strategic relationship with and equity investment from a major car rental company to complement the company's current offering by better serving longer trip needs and to potentially benefit the company through improved operational efficiencies that may be possible from such a relationship. Party B's Chief Executive Officer indicated an interest in engaging in discussions with the company, but Party B's principal interest would be in a strategic combination with and acquisition of the company. Mr. Griffith indicated that had not been the company's or the board's intention when engaging in these discussions but that he would discuss Party B's interest with the Committee. Party B's Chief Executive Officer suggested an in- person meeting between executives of each company to review strategic alternatives and plans.

During mid to late October 2012, the company and the Committee discussed the benefit of potentially engaging a financial advisor to assist the company in exploring and analyzing the potential strategic alternatives available to the company. Messrs. Griffith and Mahoney, as lead director, discussed engaging Morgan Stanley & Co. LLC, or Morgan Stanley, or another investment banking firm as financial advisor to the Committee. Morgan Stanley and another investment bank also entered into confidentiality agreements with the company.

On October 18, 2012, the Committee and Mr. Griffith met by teleconference and discussed the company's meetings with each of Avis Budget and Party A, as well as Mr. Griffith's conversations with Party B's Chief Executive Officer. In light of the interest expressed by each of the three parties, the Committee authorized Mr. Griffith to engage in further discussions with the three parties to gain a better assessment of the interest level and the potential valuations that the three parties were considering. The Committee also further discussed the potential engagement of a financial advisor and authorized Messrs. Mahoney and Griffith to recommend a financial advisor to the Committee.

On October 19, 2012, Party A's Chief Executive Officer expressed Party A's interest in making a strategic or other investment in the company, and expressed Party A's preference for acquiring all of the company. Mr. Griffith and Party A's Chief Executive Officer scheduled a follow- up meeting on November 5, 2012, to further discuss a potential strategic combination with the company.

On October 19, 2012, by phone, Mr. Griffith and Party B's Chief Executive Officer discussed Party B's interest in a strategic combination with the company and determined to schedule an in- person meeting between executives of the company and Party B to discuss the company's strategic plans and to further explore Party B's interest. Mr. Griffith discussed the need for an executed confidentiality agreement between the parties before the parties could proceed with any further discussion regarding an investment in or sale of the company. On October 24, 2012, Party B executed a confidentiality agreement with the company.

On October 22, 2012, by phone, Messrs. Griffith and Nelson discussed Avis Budget's interest in pursuing a strategic relationship with the company and its preference to consider an acquisition of the company as well as Avis Budget's desire to receive additional information to determine a potential value for a proposal to acquire the company.

On October 26, 2012, Mr. Wyshner requested additional information regarding the company and between October 29, 2012 and November 4, 2012, the company provided limited responses to Avis Budget's request.

On October 30, 2012, the Committee, Mr. Griffith, and Mr. Breda met by teleconference. Mr. Mahoney and Mr. Griffith provided an update of the ongoing discussions and the meetings that had taken place to date with Avis Budget, Party, A and Party B. Mr. Griffith also provided an update regarding the company's ongoing negotiations with the OEM Potential Investor and the likely timeline for potentially closing that transaction. Messrs. Mahoney and Griffith also provided an update regarding the discussions with potential financial advisors (including Morgan Stanley) who might be engaged to advise the Committee. Following such discussion, the Committee determined to engage Morgan Stanley as its financial advisor, with the Committee noting that it had received information from Morgan Stanley about its prior engagements by Avis Budget and other potentially interested parties. Morgan Stanley was chosen, among other reasons, due to its industry experience and expertise and the Committee's determination of its independence from the company and the company's management. In light of the interest shown by Avis Budget, Party A, and Party B in acquiring the company, the Committee also discussed other potential third parties the company may contact in the event that the board chose to pursue a sale of the company.

On October 31, 2012, Messrs. Mahoney, Griffith, and Breda and other company representatives met in person with representatives of the senior management team of Party B. Representatives of the company reviewed its strategic vision and representatives of Party B reviewed Party B's strategic vision for a potential relationship between the parties.

From November 1 to November 5, 2012, Mr. Griffith had further communications with Party B and members of its senior management team and representatives of Party B expressed an intention to provide an indication of interest to acquire the company.

On November 5, 2012, Messrs. Griffith and Breda and other company representatives met in person with Party A's Chief Executive Officer and eight other representatives from Party A. Party A presented its vision for acquiring the company, including integrating the company into Party A and its views on structure, and verbally indicated a preliminary valuation for acquiring the company in the range of $7.00 to $10.00 per share in cash or in some combination of cash and equity. Party A indicated a desire to receive information from the company to further assess a potential acquisition and indicated a desire to enter into exclusive negotiations with the company. Mr. Griffith stated that the company was not prepared to enter into exclusive discussions, particularly at the valuation proposed by Party A.

On November 6, 2012, Party B emailed the company a letter indicating Party B's interest in pursuing further discussions regarding Party B's potential acquisition of the company and requesting access to limited due diligence materials to determine a potential value for a proposal to acquire the company.

From November 6 to November 27, 2012, company representatives and Party B had further communications regarding due diligence.

On November 9, 2012, the Committee met by teleconference with Messrs. Griffith and Breda and representatives of Latham & Watkins LLP, outside counsel to the company. Messrs. Griffith and Mahoney provided an update on the ongoing discussions with Avis Budget, Party A, and Party B, as well as the ongoing discussions with Morgan Stanley regarding Morgan Stanley's engagement. The Committee discussed various strategies regarding further discussions with each of the three primary interested parties, as well as other potential acquirers. The Committee also discussed the company's ongoing discussions with the OEM Potential Investor and the importance of the company continuing to pursue those discussions and to focus on overall company performance and strategy regardless of the current discussions with the OEM Potential Investor, Avis Budget, Party A, and Party B. In light of the ongoing discussions regarding a potential sale of the company, representatives of Latham & Watkins reviewed with the Committee its and the board's fiduciary duties.

On November 11, 2012, the company entered into an engagement letter with Morgan Stanley to be the company's exclusive financial advisor in connection with a potential transaction.

On November 15, 2012, the company communicated to Party A and Party B that, in light of the nature of the ongoing discussions, the company would not facilitate any due diligence investigation by any party without first entering into an appropriate standstill agreement with such party, and provided to, Party A and Party B draft standstill amendments to the confidentiality agreements previously entered into between the company and each of Party A and Party B.

On November 16, 2012, Party B executed a standstill amendment to the confidentiality agreement between the parties.

On November 16, 2012, Messrs. Griffith and Nelson spoke by telephone. Mr. Nelson indicated Avis Budget's interest in acquiring the company and provided a preliminary valuation for acquiring the company in the range of $13.00 to $14.00 per share in cash. Mr. Griffith noted that he would review this preliminary proposal with the Committee and the board.

On November 17, 2012, Avis Budget provided a letter to the company containing a written indication of interest on the terms discussed by Messrs. Griffith and Nelson on November 16, 2012.

On November 18, 2012, the Committee met by teleconference. Also participating in the meeting were Messrs. Griffith and Breda and other Company representatives, representatives of Morgan Stanley, and representatives of Latham & Watkins. The Committee discussed the indication of interest received from Avis Budget and strategies regarding further discussions with Party A and Party B. The representatives of Morgan Stanley discussed with the Committee potential outreach to other potential acquirers of the company. The Committee directed Morgan Stanley to begin contacting other potential parties with regard to a potential change in control transaction. Representatives from Latham & Watkins reviewed again the Committee's and the board's fiduciary duties and reviewed the process followed to date by the Committee, the board, and the company. The Committee also discussed the ongoing discussions with the OEM Potential Investor and the importance of conducting any negotiations with any potential acquirer on a similar year-end timeline.

On November 19, 2012, Mr. Griffith and Party B's Chief Executive Officer spoke by telephone and Mr. Griffith informed Party B's Chief Executive Officer that the company had received an indication of interest from an unnamed party (Avis Budget) that the company would need to seriously consider and which suggested that the unnamed party was prepared to move expeditiously toward the signing of a transaction. Party B's Chief Executive Officer indicated that Party B would also be able to move quickly and that Party B would be providing a written proposal to acquire the company.

On November 19, 2012, Mr. Griffith and Party A's Chief Executive Officer spoke by telephone and Mr. Griffith informed Party A's Chief Executive Officer that the company had received an indication of interest from an unnamed party (Avis Budget) that the company would need to seriously consider and which suggested that an unnamed party was prepared to move expeditiously toward the signing of a transaction. Party A's Chief Executive Officer indicated that Party A would also be able to move quickly. Mr. Griffith noted to Party A's Chief Executive Officer that the indication of interest from the unnamed party was substantially higher than Party A's earlier verbal indication of interest.

Beginning on November 19, 2012 and continuing through December 2012, representatives from Morgan Stanley and Mr. Griffith reached out to seven additional potential acquirers to gauge each party's interest in an acquisition of the company. The potential acquirers included a broad range of possible strategic buyers, including automotive manufacturers, automotive distributors, and technology providers. During this period, the board and the Committee discussed outreach to potential financial acquirers and determined that the company's financial profile would likely preclude a financial acquirer from offering a per-share price comparable to what a strategic acquirer, who would realize value from business synergies, could offer.

On November 20, 2012, Messrs. Griffith and Nelson spoke by telephone to discuss the status of Avis Budget's indication of interest. Mr. Griffith informed Mr. Nelson that the Committee and the board would be meeting during the week of November 25, 2012, to consider and discuss all indications of interest.

On November 21, 2012, Mr. Breda and Party A's General Counsel spoke by telephone. Party A confirmed they would be stepping back from the process, although not withdrawing altogether, indicating that they believed the parties were too far apart on valuation of the company. Party A indicated they were not interested in executing a standstill agreement at this time.

On November 27, 2012, the Committee met by teleconference. Also participating in the meeting were Messrs. Griffith and Breda and other company representatives, representatives of Morgan Stanley, and representatives of Latham & Watkins. Mr. Mahoney, Mr. Griffith, and the representatives of Morgan Stanley provided an update regarding the ongoing discussions with Avis Budget, Party A, and Party B and the preliminary financial analysis conducted by Morgan Stanley to date.

On November 27, 2012, Party B provided the company with an indication of interest in acquiring the company at a valuation of $10.00 per share in cash and proposed that the company and Party B enter into a 30-day exclusivity period for purposes of due diligence and negotiations; the exclusivity period would be automatically extended for so long as the company and Party B were actively negotiating.

On November 28, 2012, Mr. Griffith spoke with a senior executive of Party B regarding any additional details Party B would want the board to consider in connection with Party B's indication of interest.

On November 28, 2012, the board met by teleconference. Also participating were Mr. Breda and other company representatives, representatives of Morgan Stanley, and representatives of Latham & Watkins. The board reviewed the discussions to date with Avis Budget, Party A, and Party B, noting that each had indicated, in response to management's approach to them regarding a strategic relationship, an interest instead in acquiring the company. The board discussed the written indications of interest that had been received from each of Avis Budget and Party B, and the current status of the discussions with Party A. Management also updated the board as to the status of the company's ongoing negotiations with the OEM Potential Investor. The board reviewed the management case financial projections as well as upside financial projections to be shared with potential acquirers. Representatives of Morgan Stanley described the financial analysis conducted to date by Morgan Stanley and discussed its preliminary view with respect to valuation of the company so that the Board could evaluate the indications of interest from Avis Budget and Party B. Representatives of Morgan Stanley and Mr. Griffith also provided an overview of the outreach to other parties who may have an interest in a change of control transaction with the company and the current status of that outreach. Representatives of Latham & Watkins reviewed the board's fiduciary duties. It was the unanimous consensus of the board that the Committee and Morgan Stanley should continue their discussions with each of Avis Budget, Party A, and Party B as well as continue the outreach to other potential acquirers. The board also directed the company to continue its discussions and negotiations with the OEM Potential Investor.

On November 29, 2012, Messrs. Griffith and Nelson spoke by telephone to discuss the willingness of the board to continue discussions with Avis Budget and to engage in a due diligence process, pending execution of a standstill amendment to the existing confidentiality agreement, which the company and Avis Budget subsequently executed on December 4, 2012.

On November 30, 2012, Mr. Griffith and Party B's Chief Executive Officer spoke by telephone. Mr. Griffith noted the board's willingness to pursue further discussions with Party B, but indicated that Party B's current non-binding offer was not competitive with other indications of interest that had been received.

On December 3, 2012, Mr. Griffith and Party B's Chief Executive Officer spoke by telephone. Party B's Chief Executive officer indicated that Party B would not be offering an increased price but expressed that Party B was still interested in pursuing a deal with the company. Mr. Griffith raised concerns about Party B falling behind the company's proposed timeline in relation to other interested parties. Party B's Chief Executive Officer indicated that this was not a concern of Party B as it knew the company's business and would not require significant additional diligence.

On December 3, 2012, Mr. Griffith and Party A's Chief Executive Officer spoke by telephone to discuss the board's decision to authorize further discussions with Party A. Party A's Chief Executive Officer indicated that to have further discussions, Party A wanted Zipcar to agree to a 30- to 90- day exclusivity arrangement, followed by a post-signing go-shop period.

On December 4, 2012, representatives of Morgan Stanley, on behalf of the company, spoke by telephone with a representative of Party A's senior management team to discuss the proposed exclusivity arrangement and Party A's timing concerns. During such discussion, the representative of Party A indicated that it would be challenging for Party A to move quickly and expressed Party A's preference to engage in exclusive discussions with the company rather than participate in a competitive process.

On December 5, 2012, by phone, Mr. Breda and representatives of the company discussed with representatives of Avis Budget the due diligence process, timing, and the introduction of the parties' respective counsel.

On December 5, 2012, Mr. Griffith and Party B's Chief Executive Officer corresponded by email and telephone to discuss the type of additional information Party B would like to receive from the company. Mr. Griffith suggested a call between Morgan Stanley and Party B's financial advisors to facilitate due diligence matters. Accordingly, representatives of Morgan Stanley spoke by telephone with Party B's financial advisors regarding due diligence matters.

In addition, on December 5, 2012, representatives of Morgan Stanley, on behalf of the company, spoke by telephone with a representative of Party A's senior management team to provide limited, high-level guidance regarding a valuation level at which Party A could potentially be competitive.

On December 6, 2012, the company made available an online data site and Avis Budget commenced due diligence.

Between December 6 and 10, 2012, representatives of Morgan Stanley, on behalf of the company, discussed with representatives from Avis Budget timing, process matters, management meetings, and a deadline of December 18, 2012, for submitting a final non-binding offer to the company.

On December 9, 2012, Messrs. Griffith and Nelson spoke by telephone to discuss timing and Avis Budget's efforts to meet the company's timeline.

On December 9, 2012, Latham & Watkins provided a draft merger agreement to representatives of Kirkland & Ellis LLP, outside counsel to Avis Budget.

On December 10, 2012, representatives of Morgan Stanley, on behalf of the company, spoke by telephone with Party B's financial advisors to provide an update on the process timeline and to provide limited, high-level guidance regarding a valuation level at which Party B could potentially be competitive.

On December 10, 2012, representatives of Morgan Stanley, on behalf of the company, spoke by telephone with a representative of Party A's senior management team. The representative of Party A confirmed that Party A would not be continuing with the process, noting that the only scenario where Party A would commit more time and resources to the process would be if the company were to negotiate with Party A on an exclusive basis and if there was better alignment on valuation between the company and Party A.

On December 10, 2012, Morgan Stanley, on behalf of the company, sent a process letter via email to Avis Budget and Party B requesting the submission of final acquisition proposals, including a form of merger agreement the parties would be prepared to execute, by December 18, 2012.

On December 10, 2012, representatives of Morgan Stanley, on behalf of the company, spoke by telephone with Party B's financial advisors to discuss due diligence and timing.

On December 10, 2012, Mr. Griffith and a senior executive of Party B spoke by telephone and the representative of Party B indicated that Party B expected to send a proposal to the company on or about December 18, 2012.

From December 10 to 23, 2012, Avis Budget and Party B engaged in continued due diligence of the company through the company's online data site.

On December 12 and 13, 2012, Avis Budget and the company held in- person meetings on a variety of due diligence topics, including potential synergies and cost savings, financial, business, operational, technology and intellectual property- and legal matters.

On December 14, 2012, the board held a regularly scheduled in- person meeting. During such meeting, representatives of Morgan Stanley and Latham & Watkins each joined the meeting. Representatives of Morgan Stanley provided an update to the board regarding the ongoing discussions with various parties concerning a potential change of control transaction involving the company, including the status of the discussions with each of Avis Budget, Party A, and Party B and the current timeline related to the process. During such discussions, representatives of Morgan Stanley also provided an update as to the status of the discussions with other parties whom Morgan Stanley and Mr. Griffith had contacted on behalf of the company regarding a potential transaction, noting that no other parties had indicated any interest in a transaction with the company. The board authorized the Committee to continue to pursue a potential transaction with Avis Budget and Party B on the timeline discussed. The board members then met in executive session (without Mr. Griffith) and discussed various compensation matters and retention matters related to a potential change of control, including a draft of a proposed bonus plan for the purpose of encouraging certain key employees of the company (excluding named executive officers) to remain employed through and after the date of any change in control transaction that the company may enter into in exchange for a cash bonus for their efforts in connection with any such transaction. The board deemed such plan to be in the best interests of the company and its stockholders and unanimously approved such plan, providing for an aggregate of up to $1.2 million for such purposes.

On December 17, 2012, representatives of Morgan Stanley, on behalf of the company, spoke by telephone with Party B's financial advisors to discuss the status of Party B's due diligence review and other matters with respect to Party B's submission of a final acquisition proposal.

On December 18, 2012, the company held in- person negotiations with the OEM Potential Investor, who indicated a deadline for consummating the transaction by January 4, 2013.

On December 19, 2012, Party B delivered to the company a revised merger agreement, a request for exclusivity, and a proposal for acquiring the company at $11.00 per share in cash.

On December 20, 2012, the Committee met by teleconference with Mr. Griffith, Mr. Breda, representatives of Morgan Stanley and representatives of Latham & Watkins regarding the revised proposal received from Party B and the expected timing for a response from Avis Budget and potential responses to Party B. The Committee authorized Mr. Griffith to contact Party B and discuss an increased valuation as Party B's indication of interest was not competitive with Avis Budget's indication of interest.

On December 20, 2012, representatives of Avis Budget held additional in- person meetings with representatives of Zipcar regarding outstanding diligence items, potential synergies, and related topics.

On December 20, 2012, Mr. Griffith and Party B's Chief Executive Officer spoke by telephone and Mr. Griffith communicated that the valuation proposed by Party B was too low. Party B's Chief Executive Officer indicated that Party B did not intend to raise its offer.

On December 21, 2012, Messrs. Griffith and Nelson spoke by telephone. Mr. Nelson requested additional limited due diligence, noting that Avis Budget was working to comply with the company's request to provide an updated proposal and revised merger agreement as soon as possible. In addition, representatives of Morgan Stanley, on behalf of the company, spoke with representatives of Citigroup Global Markets Inc., financial advisor to Avis Budget, who indicated that Avis Budget would deliver a proposal on December 22, 2012.

On December 22, 2012, Mr. Nelson called Mr. Griffith and stated that Avis Budget was in the process of transmitting a proposal to acquire the company for $12.00 per share in cash, together with a revised merger agreement. Mr. Nelson indicated Avis Budget's willingness and ability to meet the timeline of completing negotiations and signing a definitive agreement by December 31, 2012. Mr. Nelson stated that, due to Avis Budget's determination that the company should be operated on a largely standalone basis, the realization of certain synergies previously identified by Avis Budget would not be realized or would be delayed, which resulted in Avis Budget lowering its offer below the $13 to $14 proposed range provided in its initial indication of interest.

On December 22, 2012, Avis Budget transmitted by email a proposal to acquire the company for $12.00 per share in cash, together with a revised merger agreement and a request for a 14- day exclusivity period. Avis Budget's proposal indicated that there was no financing contingency and that Avis Budget was prepared to move quickly to finalize a transaction.

On December 22, 2012, the Committee met by teleconference with Messrs. Griffith and Breda and other company representatives, representatives of Morgan Stanley, and representatives of Latham & Watkins. The participants discussed responses to both the Avis Budget and Party B proposals and the Committee authorized Mr. Griffith to contact Avis Budget and Party B representatives to seek an improved offer.

On December 23, 2012, Mr. Griffith spoke with Mr. Nelson by telephone and discussed Avis Budget's reduction of price from its earlier indication of interest as well as the extent of the revisions to the terms of the proposed merger agreement. As a result of these discussions, Mr. Nelson stated that Avis Budget was prepared to increase its offer to $12.25 per share in cash, but would not increase its price further. Mr. Nelson also indicated Avis Budget's willingness to negotiate and finalize the merger agreement by December 31, 2012, and reaffirmed that the consummation of the merger with Avis Budget would not be contingent on Avis Budget's ability to secure outside financing.

On December 23, 2012, Mr. Griffith spoke by telephone with Party B's Chief Executive Officer, during which Mr. Griffith advised the representative of Party B that Party B's offer was not competitive. Party B's Chief Executive Officer subsequently indicated that Party B felt that its offer of $11.00 per share reflected a fair valuation of the company and that it would not increase its $11.00 per share non-binding offer.

On December 23, 2012, the Committee, Messrs. Griffith and Breda, representatives of Morgan Stanley, and representatives of Latham & Watkins held numerous telephone conferences regarding the ongoing negotiations.

On December 23, 2012, the board met by teleconference. Also participating in the meeting were Mr. Breda and other company representatives, representatives of Morgan Stanley, and representatives of Latham & Watkins. Messrs. Mahoney and Griffith provided an overview of the ongoing discussions with Avis Budget and Party B regarding a potential acquisition of the company, the non-binding offers that had been received from each of Avis Budget and Party B, the revised merger agreements that had been received from each, and the discussions with the respective Chief Executive Officers of Avis Budget and Party B. The representatives of Morgan Stanley then discussed with the board its valuation analyses. Morgan Stanley's representatives advised the Board that it was prepared to deliver, upon request, its opinion that the $12.25 per share offer price set forth in the Avis Budget proposal was fair, from a financial point of view, to the stockholders of the company. The board also discussed the status of discussions with other parties regarding a potential transaction, none of which had produced any other viable proposals to acquire the company, and the company's ongoing discussions with the OEM Potential Investor, including the fact that the announcement of a change of control transaction involving the company would likely preclude a transaction with the OEM Potential Investor on the terms previously proposed. Following such discussion, the representatives of Morgan Stanley and Latham & Watkins and Mr. Breda and the other company representatives left the meeting. It was the unanimous consensus of the board that it was in the best interests of the company's stockholders to pursue a change of control transaction with Avis Budget on the terms presented to the board and the Committee, based on, among other things, the board's analysis of the risk-adjusted probabilities associated with each of the other alternatives reasonably available to the company and its stockholders, including a transaction with the OEM Potential Investor, as compared to the certainty of value that would be provided to the company's stockholders in a change of control transaction with Avis Budget, and management was authorized to negotiate a definitive merger agreement with Avis Budget on the terms discussed at the meeting, subject to review and approval by the Committee and the board. The board discussed the potential timing for the completion of such a transaction, with the goal to have the merger agreement executed by December 31, 2012, so as not to preclude consummation of the OEM transaction if the change of control transaction was not completed. The board declined to approve the granting of exclusivity to Avis Budget in negotiating the transaction.

On December 28, 2012, the Committee, Mr. Griffith, and representatives from Latham & Watkins held a conference call to discuss Avis Budget's revisions to the merger agreement and open issues and to obtain guidance from the Committee with respect to such matters.

Between December 24 and December 31, 2012, the company and its representatives and Avis Budget and its representatives engaged in extensive negotiations with respect to the merger agreement, Avis Budget's ability to consummate the transaction in a timely manner and its source of funds to consummate the transaction, the voting agreements, and the disclosure schedules to the merger agreement. In particular, during this time period, the company and its representatives and Avis Budget and its representatives negotiated, among other things, provisions of the merger agreement relating to the size of the termination fee and the events that could trigger payment of the termination fee, the circumstances in which Avis Budget and the company could become obligated to reimburse the other party's transaction expenses and whether the payment of any such expenses by the company would be creditable against any subsequent payment of the termination fee, each party's representations and warranties, and the conditions to closing the transaction, including the closing condition relating to regulatory approvals, the outside date by which the merger must be consummated (as it may be extended to obtain regulatory approvals) without giving rise to a termination right of the parties, and the scope of the company's obligations to operate its business in the ordinary course between signing and closing. Messrs. Griffith and Breda and representatives of Latham & Watkins regularly updated the Committee regarding such discussions and held regular telephone conferences with the Committee or Mr. Mahoney as chair of the Committee.

After the closing of trading on December 31, 2012, the board, representatives of Morgan Stanley, and representatives of Latham & Watkins held a telephonic meeting to review and consider the final merger agreement and related documentation. Representatives of Latham & Watkins summarized the terms of the proposed transaction and the material changes to the merger agreement since Avis Budget's non-binding offer to acquire Zipcar was made on December 22, 2012. Representatives of Latham & Watkins reviewed the board's fiduciary duties under Delaware law in connection with the proposed transaction and also summarized the other material terms of the merger agreement and of the voting agreements, including provisions permitting the board to change its recommendation to stockholders or terminate the merger agreement to accept a superior proposal, subject to payment of a termination fee. Also at this meeting, Morgan Stanley reviewed with the board its financial analysis of the merger consideration of $12.25 in cash per share of Zipcar common stock and rendered its oral opinion to the board, which opinion was subsequently confirmed in writing, that, as of December 31, 2012, based upon and subject to the assumptions made, matters considered and qualifications and limitations on the scope of review undertaken by Morgan Stanley, as set forth in its opinion, the $12.25 in cash per share of Zipcar common stock to be received by the holders of shares of Zipcar common stock pursuant to the merger agreement was fair, from a financial point of view, to such holders. The members of the Committee unanimously recommended to the Board that the company move forward with the transaction with Avis Budget on the terms [set] forth in the merger agreement and as described to the board. On a motion made and duly seconded, the board unanimously resolved that the merger is fair to, and in the best interests of, the company and our stockholders and that the merger agreement and the merger are advisable. The board unanimously approved the merger agreement and recommended that our stockholders adopt the merger agreement.

On Monday, December 31, 2012, the company, Avis Budget, and Merger Sub executed the definitive merger agreement following the closing of trading. In addition, Revolution, Greylock, Benchmark, and each of our executive officers and directors entered into definitive voting agreements with Avis Budget.

On Wednesday, January 2, 2013, the company and Avis Budget publicly announced the execution of the merger agreement.

***

QUESTION

Who were the various players involved in the Avis Budget/Zipcar deal?

***

Below is an excerpt from a press release announcing the deal:

AVIS BUDGET GROUP TO ACQUIRE ZIPCAR FOR $12.25 PER SHARE IN CASH

- **Combined company will be the global leader in car sharing and mobility solutions.**
- **Combination expected to produce $50-70 million in annual synergies.**
- **Transaction targeted to close in spring 2013. . . .**

PARSIPPANY, N.J. and CAMBRIDGE, Mass., January 2, 2013 - Avis Budget Group, Inc. (NASDAQ: CAR) and Zipcar, Inc. (NASDAQ: ZIP), the world's leading car sharing network, today announced that Avis Budget Group has agreed to acquire Zipcar for $12.25 per share in cash, a 49% premium over the closing price on December 31, 2012, representing a total transaction value of approximately $500 million. The transaction is subject to approval by Zipcar shareholders and other customary closing conditions, and is expected to be completed in the spring of 2013. The Boards of Directors of both companies unanimously approved the transaction, and Zipcar shareholders representing approximately 32% of the outstanding common stock have agreed to vote their shares in support of the transaction.

Car sharing has grown to be a nearly $400 million business in the United States and is expanding rapidly in major cities around the world. Zipcar has led this industry, leading in innovation and world-class service. Zipcar now has more than 760,000 members, known as Zipsters, with a market-leading presence in 20 major metropolitan areas in the United States, Canada and Europe, and fleet positioned at over 300 college and university campuses. Zipcar has combined leading-edge technology, an outstanding customer experience, and clear brand messaging to develop strong loyalty and advocacy among its customers.

"By combining with Zipcar, we will significantly increase our growth potential, both in the United States and internationally, and will position our Company to better serve a greater variety of consumer and commercial transportation needs," said Ronald L. Nelson, Avis Budget Group chairman and chief executive officer. "We see car sharing as highly complementary to traditional car rental, with rapid growth potential and representing a scalable opportunity for us as a combined company. We expect to apply Avis Budget's experience and efficiencies of fleet management with Zipcar's proven, customer-friendly technology to accelerate the growth of the Zipcar brand and to provide more options for Zipsters in more places. We also expect to leverage Zipcar's technology to expand mobility solutions under the Avis and Budget brands."

Avis Budget expects to generate $50 to $70 million in annual synergies as a result of the transaction. In particular, Avis Budget expects significant cost reductions across the fleet life cycle (from procurement to operations and maintenance to disposition, as well as financing), in addition to savings from eliminating Zipcar's public-company costs. Avis Budget also plans to achieve substantial cost savings by increasing fleet utilization across the two companies. Significant revenue growth opportunities exist, including by leveraging Avis Budget's fleet to meet more of Zipsters' weekend demand, which is currently constrained by fleet availability.

These synergies, combined with the expected growth and rising profitability of Zipcar, are expected to make the transaction accretive to Avis Budget's earnings per share in the second year following the acquisition, excluding certain items and purchase-accounting effects.

"We are delighted to announce our intention to join the Avis Budget Group family of companies, and we believe this combination is a win across the board for our members, shareholders and employees. We will be well positioned to accelerate enhancements to the Zipcar member experience with more offers and additional services as well as an expanded network of locations," said Scott Griffith, chairman and chief executive officer of Zipcar. "As the leading global provider of car sharing services, with a brand that is synonymous with the category, we remain committed to the values and vision that have driven us forward for many years, grounded by our passion for delivering a superior experience to every member for every trip, every day. By combining Zipcar's expertise in on-demand mobility with Avis Budget Group's expertise in global fleet operations and vast global network, we will be able to accelerate the revolution we began in personal mobility."

"Avis Budget's existing infrastructure, scale and experience with managing multiple brands make us uniquely positioned to accelerate the growth and profitability of Zipcar," Mr. Nelson added. "At the same time, we are committed to retaining the elements of the Zipcar brand and culture that have allowed Zipcar to achieve such rapid growth and success over the last twelve years."

Following the acquisition, Zipcar will operate as a subsidiary of Avis Budget Group and will continue with its planned move to new headquarters in Boston, Massachusetts. Avis Budget anticipates that key members of the Zipcar management team, including Mr. Griffith and Mark Norman, president and chief operating officer, will continue to set the overall direction and run day-to-day operations of Zipcar.

Avis Budget Group expects to fund the purchase price primarily with incremental corporate debt borrowings, as well as available cash. As of September 30, 2012, Avis Budget Group had cash and marketable securities of approximately $554 million, and Zipcar had cash and marketable securities of approximately $82 million, or approximately $2 per Zipcar share.

Citigroup is acting as financial advisor, and Kirkland & Ellis LLP is acting as legal counsel, to Avis Budget Group. Morgan Stanley is acting as financial advisor, and Latham & Watkins LLP is acting as legal counsel, to Zipcar.

A lot of work still remains after the parties sign the acquisition agreement. Here is a quick rundown of what typically occurs between signing and closing in a deal such as Avis Budget's acquisition of Zipcar where both bidder and target are public companies, the deal is structured as a merger, the deal consideration consists of cash, and bidder shareholders do not get to vote on the deal.

- The attorneys for bidder and target prepare and file a premerger notification with the Federal Trade Commission and the Department of Justice as required by the Hart-Scott-Rodino (HSR) Antitrust Improvements Act of 1976.

- The attorneys for target prepare and file with the SEC a preliminary proxy statement. This document, once finalized, is used by target in connection with the special shareholders' meeting it will hold to have its shareholders approve the deal.

- HSR waiting period expires (30 days after filing) or the FTC or DOJ notify the parties that they need more information about the deal. (If the latter happens, closing the deal will likely be delayed by a year or more or perhaps scuttled all together.)

- Target receives comments from the SEC on its preliminary proxy statement, revises the document in light of the comments, and refiles it with the SEC.

- Target sets the date for its shareholders' meeting to approve the deal.

- Target holds its shareholders' meeting at which its shareholders presumably approve the deal.

- The deal closes.

The Avis Budget/Zipcar deal took three and a half months from signing to closing which is within the typical time range for a deal of that type. The acquisition of a private company typically takes less than half that amount of time because normally nothing has to be filed and reviewed by the SEC.

C.   WHAT DO M&A LAWYERS DO?

In an M&A deal, bidder and target will each be represented by a team of attorneys with expertise in M&A. Below is a brief description of the various tasks these attorneys handle in a deal, some of which were mentioned in the Zipcar proxy statement excerpt from above. (We discuss these tasks in more detail elsewhere in the book.)

- Negotiate and draft a confidentiality agreement and letter of intent;

- Determine the best legal structure for the deal;

- Negotiate and draft the acquisition agreement and other deal documents;

- Facilitate and perform due diligence;

- Advise the board of directors;

- Navigate corporate formalities;

- Prepare and make regulatory filings; and

- Close the deal.

An M&A deal team will be comprised of attorneys with various years of experience. For example, a team may include a senior partner, junior partner, senior associate, and junior associate from the firm's M&A group. Typically, the most interesting work (high-level advising and negotiations) is done by the senior team members and the most mundane work (facilitating and performing due diligence) is done by the junior team members. The size of the team depends on the size and complexity of the deal and may be as small as two M&A lawyers. Additionally, the team often includes attorneys from specialized areas such as tax, intellectual property, and environmental to handle those discrete aspects of the deal.

D.   WHY DO BIDDERS BUY AND TARGETS SELL?

Bidders buy other companies for a variety of reasons, including the following:

Product Line Expansion. A bidder may buy another company to expand its product line. Bidder can then leverage its existing sales force, distribution network, and/or customer base to increase sales volume. PepsiCo's acquisition of Quaker Oats is a prime example. The deal was largely driven by PepsiCo's desire to obtain the Gatorade sports drink brand which was then owned by Quaker Oats.

Geographic Extension. A bidder may buy another company to extend its reach geographically and thereby grow its customer base. Wells Fargo's acquisition of Norwest is a prime example. Wells Fargo is a bank headquartered in San Francisco and Norwest was a bank headquartered in Minneapolis. At the time, Wells Fargo operated primarily in the Western United States. A key reason for its acquisition of Norwest was to extend its geographic reach to the Midwest.

Lessen Competition. A bidder may buy another company that offers the same products or services in overlapping geographic markets to lessen competition. A prime example is Whole Foods', the premium natural and organic supermarket chain, acquisition of Wild Oats, which was also a premium natural and organic supermarket chain. These types of deal raise antitrust concerns in that they may "substantially lessen competition" and therefore are likely to be scrutinized by regulators. In that regard, the Whole Foods/Wild Oats deal was challenged by the Federal Trade Commission with Whole Foods ultimately having to divest of the Wild Oats chain. We discuss antitrust aspects of M&A deals in the next chapter.

Diversification. A bidder may buy another company in an unrelated business to diversify its operations in an attempt to reduce risk. The basic idea is that a company's financial performance will be less volatile if it owns multiple unrelated businesses because poor performance by one business will be offset by the good performance of another business. Sony's acquisition of Columbia Pictures is an example.

Supply Chain Control. A bidder may buy one of its suppliers to more cheaply obtain supply of a product component. (This is referred to as vertical integration.) For example, Comcast acquired NBCUniversal in part to ensure supply of programming for its cable network.

Technology Acquisition. A bidder may buy a company which has developed a technology the bidder would like to incorporate into its business. For example, in 2003 Google acquired Applied Semantics, a producer of software applications for online advertising. At the time a Google press release stated: "This acquisition will enable Google to create new technologies that make online advertising more useful to users, publishers, and advertisers alike."

Human Capital Acquisition. A bidder may buy a company which has personnel the bidder would like working for it. For example, a major driver of Disney's acquisition of Pixar was reportedly to acquire the services of Pixar's "creative guru," John Lassetter.[1]

Generally, bidder is hoping that the acquisition of target will result in synergy, i.e., that the performance of the two companies combined will be greater than the sum of the parts. Synergy can come from increased revenue, cost savings resulting from economies of scale[2] and economies of scope,[3] lower financing costs, and better

---

[1] *See* Edward Jay Epstein, *The $6 Billion Man*, Slate (Jan. 30, 2006), *available at* http://www.slate.com/articles/arts/the_hollywood_economist/2006/01/the_6_billion_man.html.

[2] Economies of scale is the cost advantage that comes from increased output of a product. Specifically, the average cost of producing a good normally decreases as the volume of its output increases because fixed costs are shared over a larger number of goods.

management of target's business.

Targets sell for many reasons including owner desire for liquidity, access to resources, and desperation.

E.   DEAL TAXONOMY

Deals can be divided into three categories: horizontal integration, vertical integration, and conglomerate. A horizontal integration deal is when bidder acquires a company that is a direct competitor, i.e., one that offers substitutable products or services in overlapping geographic markets. The Whole Foods/Wild Oats deal falls into this category. Advantages of horizontal integration include economies of scale, economies of scope, and increased market power.

A vertical integration deal is when bidder acquires a company within its product chain. Specifically, target may be either an actual or potential "upstream" supplier (backward vertical integration) or "downstream" buyer (forward vertical integration). Comcast's acquisition of NBCUniversal is an example of a backward vertical integration deal. Advantages of vertical integration include improved supply chain coordination, increased control over inputs, capturing upstream or down-stream profit margins, increasing barriers to entry to potential competitors, and gaining access to downstream distribution channels.

Conglomerate deals are subdivided into pure and mixed. A pure conglomerate deal is when bidder acquires a company engaged in an unrelated business. The Sony/Columbia Pictures deal falls into this category. A mixed conglomerate deal is when bidder acquires a company that sells related products or similar products in a different geographic area. In other words, product line expansion and geographic extension deals are considered mixed conglomerate deals.

QUESTIONS

1.   Why did Avis Budget buy Zipcar?

2.   Why did Zipcar sell to Avis Budget?

3.   Where does the Avis Budget/Zipcar deal fit into the above deal taxonomy?

----

[3] Economies of scope refers to factors that make it cheaper to produce a range of goods together rather than individually, for example, by sharing resources common to different products.

Chapter 2

DEAL STRUCTURE MECHANICS

This chapter covers the *basic* corporate, securities, and antitrust law involved in structuring and closing an M&A deal between a *private* bidder and a *private* target. Generally, a company is "private" as opposed to "public" if its securities are *not* traded on a public market such as the New York Stock Exchange or NASDAQ Stock Market. We cover additional issues that arise when one or both of bidder and target is public in the next chapter.

A. STATE CORPORATE LAW REQUIREMENTS

Below we discuss three corporate law issues that must be considered in any M&A deal between corporations: board of director approval, shareholder approval, and appraisal rights. The discussion is divided by deal structure and focuses on provisions of the Model Business Corporations Act (MBCA) and Delaware General Corporation Law (DGCL). The reason we focus on the MBCA is that it serves as the basis for the corporate law statute of 32 states.[1] The reason we look at the DGCL is that Delaware is unquestionably the most important non-MBCA state — it by far attracts the most incorporations by out-of-state businesses and is the state of incorporation for over 50 percent of U.S. publicly traded companies. The discussion in this section assumes that the parties to the deal are incorporated in the same state. We consider multi-jurisdictional deals in Section A.10. Here is a quick overview of the three corporate law issues. We look at these three issues under each deal structure because there is variation by structure.

Board approval. Generally, the board of directors of both bidder and target need to approve the deal. This approval would normally come at a board meeting held shortly after the acquisition agreement is finalized but before it is signed. Here is a sample bidder board resolution approving bidder's acquisition of target through an asset purchase.

---

[1] These states are Alabama, Alaska, Arizona, Arkansas, Connecticut, Florida, Georgia, Hawaii, Idaho, Indiana, Iowa, Kentucky, Maine, Massachusetts, Mississippi, Montana, Nebraska, New Hampshire, New Mexico, North Carolina, Oregon, Rhode Island, South Carolina, South Dakota, Tennessee, Utah, Vermont, Virginia, Washington, West Virginia, Wisconsin, and Wyoming.

> **WHEREAS**, the board of directors of Bidder Co. (the "**Corporation**") deems it to be in the best interests of the Corporation to enter into the Asset Purchase Agreement between the Corporation and Target, Inc. ("**Target**") substantially in the form of Exhibit A attached (the "**Asset Purchase Agreement**"), pursuant to which the Corporation will purchase substantially all of the assets of Target and assume certain liabilities of Target.
>
> **NOW, THEREFORE, RESOLVED**, that the form, terms and provisions of the Asset Purchase Agreement are approved; and
>
> **FURTHER RESOLVED**, that the President, Chief Financial Officer, and Executive Vice President of the Corporation (each such person, an "**Authorized Officer**") be, and each of them hereby is, authorized and empowered to execute and deliver the Asset Purchase Agreement on behalf of the Corporation with such additions, deletions or changes therein as the Authorized Officer executing the same shall approve (the execution and delivery thereof by any such Authorized Officer to be conclusive evidence of his or her approval of any such additions, deletions or changes).

We discuss various aspects involved with board approval in Chapter 6.

Shareholder approval. Generally, target shareholders and sometimes the shareholders of bidder need to approve the deal. This approval often comes at a special shareholders' meeting called by the board when it approves the acquisition agreement. The meeting is held as soon as possible after the acquisition agreement is signed (corporations are required to give at least ten days' notice for a special shareholders' meeting,[2] which means the soonest the meeting can be held is ten days after the acquisition agreement is signed). Alternatively, shareholders can approve the deal through written consent in lieu of a meeting.[3] Written consent is preferable because it is normally faster and easier to obtain than approval through a shareholders' meeting, but it generally only works if target and/or bidder has a small number of shareholders. Here is a sample target shareholder written consent approving the sale of target to bidder.

---

[2] *See* MBCA § 7.05; DGCL § 222.

[3] *See* MBCA § 7.04; DGCL § 228.

WRITTEN CONSENT
OF THE SHAREHOLDERS OF
TARGET, INC.

The undersigned shareholders of Target, Inc. (the "**Corporation**") hereby adopt the following resolution as and for the action of the shareholders without a meeting:

WHEREAS, the Corporation has entered into an Asset Purchase Agreement dated September 22, 2013 by and between the Corporation and Bidder Co. (the "**Asset Purchase Agreement**"), pursuant to which the Corporation will sell substantially all of its assets (the "**Disposition**") to Bidder Co., a copy of which is attached hereto as Exhibit A; and

WHEREAS, the board of directors of the Corporation has approved the terms of the Asset Purchase Agreement and determined that the Disposition is advisable and in the best interests of the Corporation and its shareholders and therefore recommends that the shareholders approve the Disposition.

NOW, THEREFORE, RESOLVED, that the shareholders of the Corporation hereby approve the Disposition as contemplated by the Asset Purchase Agreement.

IN WITNESS WHEREOF, each of the undersigned has executed this written consent effective as of September 23, 2013.

The above document would then have signature lines for each Target, Inc. shareholder to sign and date.

Appraisal Rights. Appraisal rights afford shareholders who vote against specified corporate actions the option of having their shares bought back by the corporation for cash at fair value as determined by a court. The actions triggering appraisal rights for target shareholders under the MBCA include a merger, share exchange, and sale of all or substantially all of the corporation's assets.[4] In contrast, only a merger triggers appraisal rights under the DGCL.[5]

Appraisal rights came into being for historical reasons. Specifically, at one time, state corporate statutes required the proposed sale of a corporation to be unanimously approved by its shareholders. This proved unworkable because it meant a single shareholder could block the sale. Thus, states moved to a majority shareholder voting standard coupled with appraisal rights. The appraisal rights piece was put in to provide shareholders who are against a deal for whatever reason (they think the price is too low, the deal consideration is in stock and they do not want to be a bidder shareholder, etc.) the option of getting cashed out of their investments at a price determined by an objective third party, which may or may not be more than what bidder has agreed to pay for target in the deal.

---

[4] *See* MBCA § 13.02(a).

[5] *See* DGCL § 262(b).

1. Asset Purchase

a. MBCA

1.   Board Approval

For a deal structured as an asset purchase, target board approval is required under MBCA § 12.02(a) if shareholder approval is required (see below). If shareholder approval is not required, target board approval is nonetheless required under agency law if the transaction is outside of the ordinary course of target's business. Bidder board approval is not required under the MBCA but is likewise required under agency law if the transaction is outside of the ordinary course of bidder's business. Regardless, both target's and bidder's attorneys will insist on target and bidder board approval so that there is no question as to whether the officer signing the asset purchase agreement on their behalves had the authority to do so.

2.   Shareholder Approval

a.   Target Shareholder Approval

Shareholder approval of a corporation's disposition of assets is addressed in MBCA Chapter 12. Specifically, § 12.01 specifies when shareholder approval is not required and § 12.02 specifies when shareholder approval is required. Section 12.01 provides as follows:

> No approval of the shareholders of a corporation is required, unless the articles of incorporation otherwise provide:
>
> (1)   to sell, lease, exchange, or otherwise dispose of any or all of the corporation's assets in the usual and regular course of business;
>
> (2)   to mortgage, pledge, dedicate to the repayment of indebtedness (whether with or without recourse), or otherwise encumber any or all of the corporation's assets, whether or not in the usual and regular course of business;
>
> (3)   to transfer any or all of the corporation's assets to one or more corporations or other entities all of the shares or interests of which are owned by the corporation; or
>
> (4)   to distribute assets pro rata to the holders of one or more classes or series of the corporation's shares.

Section 12.02 requires shareholder approval of "[a] sale, lease, exchange, or other disposition of assets" that does not fall under § 12.01 "if the disposition would leave the corporation without a significant continuing business activity." Section 12.02(a) provides the following safe harbor for when a corporation has retained a significant business activity:

> If a corporation retains a business activity that represented at least 25% of total assets at the end of the most recently completed fiscal year, and

25% of either income from continuing operations before taxes or revenues from continuing operations for that fiscal year, in each case of the corporation and its subsidiaries on a consolidated basis, the corporation will conclusively be deemed to have retained a significant continuing business activity.

MBCA Chapter 12 implicitly recognizes that ultimate managerial authority lies in the corporation's board of directors and not its shareholders. Thus, shareholders do not generally get a say on a corporation's decision to dispose of assets, something many corporations are frequently doing, unless the corporation is essentially selling the bulk of its business.

If shareholder approval is required and the corporation seeks it through a meeting (as opposed to by written consent), § 12.02(e) requires a minimum quorum of "a majority of the votes entitled to be cast on the disposition" to be represented at the meeting. Chapter 12 does not specify a voting requirement so that means the general voting requirement of § 7.25 applies. Per § 7.25(c), "[i]f a quorum exists, action on a matter . . . by a voting group is approved if the votes cast within the voting group favoring the action exceed the votes cast opposing the action, unless the articles of incorporation require a greater number of affirmative votes." We refer to this as a "more-for-than-against" requirement.

Note that § 12.02(e) used to impose a voting requirement of a majority of shares entitled to vote, but it was eliminated as part of the 1999 amendments to the MBCA. Many MBCA states, however, still impose this requirement, and some states even impose a two-thirds of outstanding shares entitled to vote requirement. In other words, going with a more-votes-for-than-against requirement has not caught on.

b.   Bidder Shareholder Approval

The MBCA does not explicitly require bidder shareholders to approve bidder's acquisition of target through an asset purchase. However, MBCA § 6.21(f)(1) may essentially give bidder shareholders a vote on the deal if the deal consideration consists of bidder stock or securities convertible into bidder stock. Specifically, under that section, a corporation's shareholders are entitled to vote on an issuance if:

(i)   the shares, other securities, or rights are issued for consideration other than cash or cash equivalents, and

(ii) the voting power of shares that are issued and issuable as a result of the transaction or series of integrated transactions will comprise more than 20 percent of the voting power of the shares of the corporation that were outstanding immediately before the transaction.

In an asset purchase where the consideration is bidder stock, bidder will be issuing shares for consideration other than cash, i.e., target's assets, so (i) is met. Whether (ii) is met depends on the number of shares bidder has outstanding pre-deal and the number of shares it will be issuing in the deal. For example, assume bidder has 1,000,000 shares outstanding pre-deal. If it will be issuing 200,000 shares or less in the deal, (ii) is not met because the shares issued will not "comprise more than 20 percent of the voting power of the shares of the corporation that were outstanding immediately before the transaction" (200,000/1,000,000=20%). Thus, its shareholders will not get to vote on the issuance under § 6.21(f). Conversely, if bidder will be issuing more than 200,000 shares, (ii) is met because the issuance will surpass the 20 percent threshold, and therefore, bidder's shareholders will get to vote under § 6.21(f).

Note that § 6.21(f) comes into play infrequently if bidder is a private company because private company stock is illiquid given there is no established trading market for it. Thus, target generally will not agree to the deal consideration consisting of bidder stock unless bidder is expected to go public within a year or so.

3.   Appraisal Rights

a.   Target Appraisal Rights

MBCA Chapter 13 addresses appraisal rights, and § 13.02 specifies the corporate actions that trigger the rights. The sale of target in a deal structured as an asset purchase is covered by § 13.02(a)(3) which provides as follows:

> (a) A shareholder is entitled to appraisal rights, and to obtain payment of the fair value of that shareholder's shares, in the event of any of the following corporate actions: . . .

> (3) consummation of a disposition of assets pursuant to § 12.02 if the shareholder is entitled to vote on the disposition, except that appraisal rights shall not be available to any shareholder of the corporation with respect to shares of any class or series if (i) under the terms of the corporate action approved by the shareholders there is to be distributed to shareholders in cash its net assets, in excess of a reasonable amount reserved to meet claims of the type described in §§ 14.06 and 14.07, (A) within one year after the shareholders' approval of the action and (B) in accordance with their respective interests determined at the time of distribution, and (ii) the disposition of assets is not an interested transaction.

Hence, the general rule is that if target shareholders get to vote on a deal structured as an asset purchase, they are entitled to appraisal rights. However, if the terms of the deal provide for the liquidation of target within one year after shareholder approval (as is fairly common given that target typically has no operations following closing because it has sold its assets to bidder) and shareholders are to receive cash in accordance with their interests, then target shareholders do not get appraisal rights (so long as the deal is not an interested transaction, for example, where bidder is controlled by target's controlling shareholder). The policy behind this exception is that "[i]n these circumstances, where shareholders are being treated on a proportionate basis in accordance with the corporation's governing documents in an arm's-length transaction (akin to a distribution in dissolution), there is no need for the added protection of appraisal rights."[6] Note

---

[6] MBCA § 13.02, cmt. 1.

that this one-year liquidation exception was added to the MBCA in 2010, so many MBCA states have yet to adopt it.

b. Bidder Appraisal Rights

The MBCA does not provide appraisal rights for bidder shareholders when bidder acquires a target through an asset purchase. This is true even if bidder shareholders are entitled to vote on the deal pursuant to § 6.21(f)(1).

b. DGCL

1. Board Approval

For a deal structured as an asset purchase, target board approval is required under DGCL § 271 if target is selling all or substantially all of its assets. The DGCL does not require target board approval for sales of less than substantially all of target's assets, but it is nonetheless required under agency law if the transaction is outside of the ordinary course of target's business. As is the case under the MBCA, bidder board approval is not required under the DGCL but is required under agency law if the transaction is outside of the ordinary course of bidder's business. Regardless, both target's and bidder's attorneys will insist on target and bidder board approval so that there is no question as to whether the officer signing the asset purchase agreement on their behalves had the authority to do so.

2. Shareholder Approval

a. Target Shareholder Approval

DGCL § 271 requires shareholder approval if target is selling all or substantially all of its assets. Below is a Delaware case on the meaning of "all or substantially all."

HOLLINGER INC. v. HOLLINGER INTERNATIONAL, INC.
Delaware Chancery Court
858 A.2d 342 (2004)

STRINE, Vice Chancellor. . . .

Hollinger Inc. (or "Inc.") seeks a preliminary injunction preventing Hollinger International, Inc. (or "International") from selling the *Telegraph* Group Ltd. (England) to Press Holdings International, an entity controlled by Frederick and David Barclay (hereinafter, the "Barclays"). The *Telegraph* Group is an indirect, wholly owned subsidiary of International and publishes the *Telegraph* newspaper and the *Spectator* magazine. The *Telegraph* newspaper is a leading one in the United Kingdom, both in terms of its circulation and its journalistic reputation.

The key question addressed in this decision is whether Inc. and the other International stockholders must be provided with the opportunity to vote on the sale of the *Telegraph* Group because that sale involves "substantially all" the assets of International within the meaning of 8 *Del. C.* § 271. The sale of the *Telegraph* followed a lengthy auction process whereby International and all of Hollinger's operating assets were widely shopped to potential bidders. As a practical matter, Inc.'s vote would be the only one that matters because although it now owns only 18% of International's total equity, it, through high-vote Class B shares, controls 68% of the voting power.[7]

Inc. argues that a preliminary injunction should issue because it is clear that the sale of the *Telegraph* satisfies the quantitative and qualitative test used to determine whether an asset sale involves substantially all of a corporation's assets. The *Telegraph* Group is one of the most profitable parts of International and is its most prestigious asset. After its sale, International will be transformed from a respected international publishing company controlling one of the world's major newspapers to a primarily American publishing company whose most valuable remaining asset, the *Chicago Sun-Times*, is the second leading newspaper in the Second City. . . .

[International] contends that the sale of the *Telegraph* Group does not trigger § 271. However prestigious the *Telegraph* Group, International says its sale does not involve, either quantitatively or qualitatively, the sale of substantially all International's assets. Whether or not the *Chicago Sun-Times* is as prestigious as the *Daily Telegraph*, it remains a profitable newspaper in a major city. Along with a group of profitable Chicago-area community newspapers, the *Chicago Sun-Times* has made the "Chicago Group" International's most profitable operating segment in the last two years and its contribution to International's profits has been comparable to that of the *Telegraph* Group for many years. Moreover, International retains a number of smaller newspapers in Canada and the prestigious *Jerusalem Post*. After the sale of the *Telegraph* Group, International therefore will quantitatively retain a sizable percentage of its existing assets and will qualitatively remain in the same business line. Although the *Telegraph* sale is admittedly a major transaction, International stresses that § 271 does not apply to every major transaction; it only applies to transactions that strike at the heart of a corporation's existence, which this transaction does not. Only by ignoring the statute's language, International argues, can this court determine that International will have sold substantially all its assets by divesting itself of the *Telegraph* Group.

As an alternative argument, International contends that § 271 is inapplicable for another reason. International argues that none of *its* assets are being sold at all, because the *Telegraph* Group is held through a chain of wholly owned subsidiaries and it is only the last link in that chain which is actually being sold to the Barclays.

In this opinion, I conclude that Inc.'s motion for a preliminary injunction motion should be denied . . . [because] its § 271 [claim has no] . . . reasonable probability of success. . . .

[Here], I address the economic merits of Inc.'s § 271 claim . . . . An application

---

[7] [Normally when a board makes a decision contrary to the wishes of a controlling shareholder, the controlling shareholder will remove the recalcitrant directors and replace them with people who will do the controlling shareholder's bidding. Here, however, as a result of misconduct by Lord Conrad Black, Inc. has agreed, among other things, not to replace International's board. — Ed.]

of the governing test, which was originally articulated in *Gimbel v. Signal Cos.*, to the facts demonstrates that the *Telegraph* Group does not come close to comprising "substantially all" of International's assets. Although the *Telegraph* Group is a very important asset of International's and is likely its most valuable asset, International possesses several other important assets. Prominent among these is its so-called Chicago Group, a valuable collection of publications that, by any objective standard approaches the *Telegraph* Group in economic importance to International. In fact, earlier this year, Inc. based its decision to try to sell itself to the Barclays on advice that the Chicago Group was worth more than the *Telegraph* Group. And the record is replete with evidence indicating that the Chicago Group's recent performance in outperforming the profitability of the *Telegraph* Group was not anomalous and that many reasoned observers — including Inc.'s controlling stockholder, Conrad Black — believe that the Chicago Group will continue to generate EBITDA at levels akin to those of the *Telegraph* Group.

Put simply, after the *Telegraph* Group is sold, International will retain considerable assets that are capable of generating substantial free cash flow. Section 271 does not require a vote when a major asset or trophy is sold; it requires a vote only when the assets to be sold, when considered quantitatively and qualitatively, amount to "substantially all" of the corporation's assets.

Inc.'s inability to meet this economically focused test has led it to place great weight on the greater journalistic reputation of the *Telegraph* newspaper when compared to the *Sun-Times* and the social importance of that newspaper in British life. The problem with this argument is that § 271 is designed as a protection for rational owners of capital and its proper interpretation requires this court to focus on the economic importance of assets and not their aesthetic worth. The economic value of the *Telegraph's* prestige was reflected in the sales process for the *Telegraph* Group and in the cash flows projected for that Group. The Barclays' bid includes the economic value that bidders place on the *Telegraph's* social cachet and does not approach a price that puts the *Telegraph* Group close to being substantially all of International's assets. Nor does the sale of the *Telegraph* Group break any solemn promise to International stockholders. During its history, International has continually bought and sold publishing assets, and no rational investor would view the *Telegraph* Group as immune from the company's ongoing M & A activity. . . .

Because Inc.'s merits-based arguments lack force, its request for a preliminary injunction is denied.

I. *Factual Background*

Because of the subject matter of this motion, it is important to understand what kind of company Hollinger International was, what kind of company it now is, and what kind of company it will become if the *Telegraph* sale is consummated. I will therefore endeavor to set forth the factual conclusions about these issues that I draw from the preliminary injunction record without burdening the reader with exhausting detail.

I will begin with International's origins and its corporate structure and move forward chronologically to the present. Because Inc. has also brought fiduciary duty claims based in equity, I must also discuss the events leading to the International board's decision to sell the *Telegraph* Group, and the facts bearing on the equitable considerations that Inc. contends are at stake.

International's Creation

International cannot be understood without appreciating its relationship with Conrad Black. Black is an accomplished man who, through various entities, came to control a large number of newspaper publications. Over time, he chose to control the holdings he had assembled through the plaintiff in this matter, Hollinger Inc., a publicly traded Canadian company.

Black controlled Inc. through another private company, of which he was the controlling stockholder, The Ravelston Corporation Limited. Ravelston controlled a majority of Inc.'s voting power.

In 1994, Inc. decided to bring American Publishing Company, one of its subsidiaries, public. When American Publishing's initial public offering was made, it owned assets including the *Chicago Sun-Times*, a group of newspapers in the Chicago area, and *The Jerusalem Post*. It did not own the *Telegraph* then.

A year later, American Publishing changed its name to Hollinger International, Inc. ("International"). Inc. then transferred its interests in certain other publications to International. These included the *Daily Telegraph* and related papers in London; a group of prominent Canadian newspapers including *The Ottawa Citizen*, the *Calgary Herald, The Vancouver Sun, The Edmonton Journal*, and *The Gazette* (of Montreal); and various Australian publications, including the *The Sydney Morning Herald, The Age* (of Melbourne), and *The Australia Financial Review*.

The addition of these newspapers to International did not represent a fundamental and lasting commitment to a static and synergistically integrated array of publications. Rather, it merely represented a temporary grouping of publishing assets that would be, as we will now see, subject to a great deal of change over time, as part of the ongoing operations of International. Put simply, International regularly acquired and disposed of sizable publishing assets.

During the years 1995 to 2000, for example, International engaged in the following large transactions:

- The 1996 and 1997 sales of the company's Australian newspapers for more than $400 million.

- The 1998 acquisition of the *Post-Tribune* in Gary, Indiana and the sale of approximately 80 community newspapers, for gross cash proceeds of approximately $310 million.

- The 1998 acquisitions of *The Financial Post* (now *The National Post*), the *Victoria Times Colonist*, and other Canadian newspapers for a total cost of more than $208 million.

- The 1999 sale of 78 community newspapers in the United States, for more than $500 million.

- The 2000 sale of other United States community newspapers for $215 million.

- The 2000 acquisition of newspapers in and around Chicago, for more than $230 million.

- The 2000 sale of the bulk of the company's Canadian newspaper holdings to CanWest for over $2 billion.

The last of the cited transactions is particularly notable for present purposes. As of the year 2000, the so-called "Canadian Newspaper Group" — most of its metropolitan and community newspapers were in Canada — accounted for over 50% of International's revenues and EBITDA.[8] The EBITDA measure is significant because it is a measure of free cash flow that is commonly used by investors in valuing newspaper companies.

Notably, International sold the bulk of the Canadian Newspaper Group to CanWest for $2 billion without a stockholder vote (the "CanWest sale"). And Inc. — then controlled by the same person who controls it now — never demanded one. . . .

International Operating Units After The CanWest Sale

The CanWest sale left International with the set of operating assets it now controls. These operating assets fall into four basic groups, which I label in a reader-friendly manner as: the Canada Group; the Chicago Group, the Jerusalem Group, and the *Telegraph* Group. A brief description of each is in order, beginning with the Group that contributed the least to International's 2003 revenues and working towards the Group that contributed the most. The Groups operate with great autonomy and there appear to be negligible, if any, synergies generated by their operation under common ownership.

The Jerusalem Group

The Jerusalem Group owns four newspapers that are all editions of the *Jerusalem Post*, which is the most widely read English-language newspaper published in the Middle East and is considered a high-quality, internationally well-regarded source of news about Israel. The Jerusalem Group also owns the *Jerusalem Report*, a magazine, and Internet assets associated with its newspapers and magazine.

The Jerusalem Group makes only a very small contribution to International's revenues. In 2003, it had revenues of approximately $10.4 million, a figure amounting to only around 1% of International's total revenues, and its EBITDA was nearly $3 million in the red. This poor performance is attributed by management to economic conditions in Israel, a decrease in that nation's English-speaking population, and the loss of a contract to print Israel's national phone directory. Management has reduced costs in order to address these factors and hopes that the Group will soon return to profitability. Even if that happens, the Group will obviously not

---

[8] [n.6] That is, earnings before interest, taxes, depreciation and amortization.

be a major driver of International's future profitability.

The Canada Group

The Canada Group is the last of the Canadian publishing assets of International. It operates through three main businesses: 1) HP Newspapers, which publishes 29 daily and community newspapers in British Columbia and Quebec; 2) Business Information Group, which publishes dozens of trade magazines, directories and websites in 17 different markets, addressed to various industries (such as the insurance and automotive industries) and professions (such as dentists); and 3) Great West Newspaper Group Ltd., a publisher of 17 community newspapers and shopping guides in Alberta, which is 70% owned by International and its subsidiaries.

The Canada Group is expected to generate over $80 million in revenues this year, a figure similar to last year. But certain retiree benefit issues impair its profitability, and its EBITDA is expected to be slightly negative.

The Chicago Group

The Chicago Group is one of the two major operating asset groups that International controls. The Chicago Group owns more than 100 newspapers in the greater Chicago metropolitan area. Its most prominent newspaper is the *Chicago Sun-Times*, a daily tabloid newspaper that might be thought of as the "Second Newspaper In the Second City." That moniker would not be a slight, however, when viewed from a national or even international perspective.

Even though it ranks behind the *Chicago Tribune* in terms of overall circulation and readership, the *Sun-Times* has traditionally been and remains one of the top ten newspapers in the United States in terms of circulation and readership. Even though it is a tabloid, the *Sun-Times* is not an undistinguished paper. Its sports coverage is considered to be excellent, its film critic Roger Ebert is nationally prominent, and its pages include the work of many well-regarded journalists.

That said, the *Sun-Times* is not the *New York Times* and it fills a niche within the Chicago area similar to the niche filled by tabloids in other areas. Tabloids are useful for commuters, sports fans, and for readers who are interested in a quicker portrayal of news than broadsheets, as well as for folks who care about what's going on in City Hall. For these reasons, the *Sun-Times* actually has a greater weekday readership within the City of Chicago itself than the *Tribune*.

By contrast, its tabloid format and focus leaves the *Sun-Times* more vulnerable in the greater Chicago area, whose affluent suburbs are filled with readers who lean heavily towards the *Tribune* and its broadsheet format. And on Sunday, a day of the week that is important to the profitability of American newspapers, the *Sun-Times* runs behind the *Tribune* even within Chicago.

Regardless of whether it lags the *Tribune*, the *Sun-Times* has generated very healthy EBITDA for International on a consistent basis during the recent past, producing $40 million in EBITDA in 2003, out of a total of nearly $80 million for the entire Chicago Group.

As will be explained in more detail later, the *Sun-Times* recently suffered an embarrassment that could impair its profitability in the short term. In April 2004, the *Sun-Times'* publisher (who had just assumed his duties in late autumn 2003) discovered that the *Sun-Times* had been inflating its circulation numbers through various practices. This discovery, which was promptly investigated and publicly disclosed in June 2004, had a negative effect on International's stock price and credibility. It also came on the heels of an initiative to raise the newsstand price of the *Sun-Times*, a measure that was expected to reduce circulation for some period. Although the best evidence in the record suggests that the *Sun-Times* will weather the storm and not lose its readership's loyalty, this development might stall immediate profit growth as advertisers use it as leverage to resist price increases and as the *Sun-Times* incurs costs to address class action litigation commenced on behalf of certain advertisers as a result of the disclosure.

The *Sun-Times* is only one aspect of the Chicago Group, however. The Chicago Group also owns a valuable group of community newspapers that are published in the greater Chicago metropolitan area. These newspapers include seven daily newspapers, seventy-five weekly newspapers, a magazine, and a variety of shopping guides. Collectively, these publications have a paid daily circulation of over 200,000 copies and even more on Sundays. The geographic coherence of these newspapers is a marketing advantage as advertisers can purchase packages that cover multiple papers in their target markets and get a better rate than dealing with individually owned papers in those markets.

These community papers have important economic value to the Chicago Group and to International. Their revenues and EBITDA, taken together, are roughly equal to that of the *Sun-Times:*

Revenue in millions					
	2000	2001	2002	2003F	2004B
Sun-Times	241.3	222.8	222.7	227.3	239.6
Entire Chicago Group	401.4	442.9	441.8	450.8	473.3
Percentage from *Sun-Times*	60.1%	50.3%	50.4%	50.4%	50.6%

EBITDA in millions					
	2000	2001	2002	2003F	2004B
Sun-Times	33.3	23.2	38.1	40.0	44.2
Entire Chicago Group	59.8	47.6	72.1	78.1	95.1
Percentage from *Sun-Times*	55.7%	48.7%	52.8%	51.2%	46.5%

In recent years, the Chicago Group as a whole has run neck-and-neck with the *Telegraph* Group in terms of generating EBITDA for International. In 2003, it won the race and its over $79 million in EBITDA was the largest contribution to EBITDA of any of International's four operating groups.

The Telegraph Group

The *Telegraph* Group includes the Internet site and various newspapers associated with the *Daily Telegraph*, including the *Sunday Telegraph*, as well as the magazines *The Spectator* and *Apollo*. The *Spectator* is the oldest continually published English-language magazine in the world and has an impressive reputation as a journal of opinion for the British intelligentsia, but it is not an economically significant asset. Rather, the *Telegraph* newspaper is the flagship of the *Telegraph* Group economically.

The *Telegraph* is a London-based newspaper but it is international in importance and readership, with a reputation of the kind that U.S. papers like the *New York Times*, the *Washington Post*, and the *Wall Street Journal* enjoy. It is a high-quality, broadsheet newspaper that is noted for its journalistic excellence, with a conservative, establishment-oriented bent. Its daily circulation of over 900,000 is the largest among English broadsheets but it trails the *London Sunday Times* in Sunday circulation by a sizable margin. Several London tabloids also outsell the *Telegraph* by very large margins. London may be the most competitive newspaper market in the world and that market continues to involve a vigorous struggle for market share that has existed since the early 1990s, when the *Times'* owner, Rupert Murdoch, initiated a price war.

The *Telegraph's* readers are older than the U.K. average but also much more affluent. To capitalize on its reputation and the wealth of its readers, the *Telegraph* Group has initiated businesses that market goods and services to readers. But it also faces the threat that it could lose readership as younger readers have tended to favor tabloids.

The *Telegraph* also faces a business difficulty related to its printing facilities, which are half-owned by Richard Desmond, who owns the *Daily Express*, another newspaper. The *Telegraph* had delayed making a needed investment in a printing facility that will meet its long-term needs and have upgraded color capacity. The cost of that investment is estimated to be over $185 million.

On balance, however, there is no question that the *Telegraph* Group is a profitable and valuable one. In the year 2003, it had over a half billion dollars in revenues and produced over $57 million in EBITDA. . . .

II. Legal Analysis . . .

A. *The Preliminary Injunction Standard*

The standard that a party seeking a preliminary injunction must satisfy is a well-known one. "On a motion for preliminary injunctive relief, the moving party must demonstrate a reasonable probability of success on the merits, that absent injunctive relief irreparable harm will occur, and that the harm the moving party will suffer if the requested relief is denied outweighs the harm the opponents will suffer if relief is granted."[9] The resolution of Inc.'s motion in this case turns largely

---

[9] [n.28] Hubbard v. Hollywood Park Realty Enters., Inc., 1991 WL 3151, at *5 (Del. Ch. Jan. 14, 1991)

on the merits of its claims, which I now discuss.

B. *International's Technical Defense: Does § 271 Apply To A Sale Of Assets By An Indirect, Wholly Owned Subsidiary?*

International argues that the sale of the *Telegraph* Group simply does not implicate § 271 at all. The reason is that the operating assets that the Barclays are buying and that comprise the *Telegraph* Group are actually held by a 6th tier U.K. subsidiary and not by International.

It is undisputed that the chain of subsidiaries through which International controlled the *Telegraph* Group maintained the corporate formalities necessary for it to comply with U.K. and U.S. regulatory requirements. It is also undisputed that these subsidiaries are long-standing parts of the International structure and were formed because they had valuable tax, financial, and liability-insulating purposes. There is no indication that any third parties dealing with the subsidiaries in the ordinary course of business or any tort plaintiff allegedly injured by one of the subsidiaries would have been entitled to pierce their corporate veil and seek recourse directly against International.

On the other hand, the chain of subsidiaries is wholly owned by International. The Strategic Process that resulted in the proposal to sell the *Telegraph* Group was, as a matter of obvious reality, conducted entirely at the International level. None of the subsidiaries, including the ultimate U.K. subsidiary that owned the *Telegraph* Group directly, engaged independent financial or legal advisors. Indeed, the directors of the subsidiaries were employees of International, including Paris. When International needed information and other assistance in preparing for a possible sale of the *Telegraph*, it passed a resolution — that all of the subsidiaries complied with through down-the-line resolutions of their own —"requiring [the subsidiary] to co-operate in the proposed sale of the *Telegraph* Group Limited . . . including the provision of all information required in respect of such sale." . . .

Notably, the contract for sale of the *Telegraph* Group does not run simply between the Barclays and the U.K. subsidiary that directly own the *Telegraph* Group. Instead, International is a direct signatory to that agreement and its lawyers negotiated its terms. In that agreement, International is the guarantor of any breach of warranty claim brought by the Barclays in connection with the sale, promises to cause the subsidiaries to perform their duties under the agreement, and stands to receive payments from claims belonging to the subsidiaries. The reality, of course, is that the Barclays would not have agreed to a contract to which International was not, in substance, required to assume the same risks as the direct seller because the proceeds of the sale will be upstreamed by International for its use, as the intermediate subsidiaries will become inutile once the sale is consummated.

In essence, it is clear to me that the *Telegraph* sale was directed and controlled by International and that its wholly owned subsidiaries did what wholly owned subsidiaries do — the bidding of their sole owner. It is no disrespect to the

(citing Ivanhoe Partners v. Newmont Mining Corp., 535 A.2d 1334, 1341 (Del. 1987)).

employees who populated the subsidiary boards to recognize this obvious reality.

From this, to my view, clear factual picture, the parties draw starkly different legal conclusions. For its part, International contends that it is plain that § 271 does not contemplate ignoring the separate existence of subsidiary corporations unless the stringent test for veil piercing is met. In support of that proposition, they cite the observation of Vice Chancellor Marvel in the case of *J.P. Griffin Holding Corp. v. Mediatrics, Inc.*, that the vote of a parent public corporation in favor of a sale of all the assets of its wholly owned subsidiary satisfied § 271 and (impliedly) that no vote of the parent's own stockholders was therefore required. In further support of this argument, International argues that Delaware law does not lightly ignore the separate existence of subsidiary corporations and that the DGCL has recently been amended in a manner that suggests that the General Assembly knows how to conflate the existence of parent and subsidiary when it wishes. Indeed, International notes that a portion of our primary merger statute — § 251 — explicitly requires that any Delaware corporation that wishes to convert into a holding company insert in the charter of the subsidiary a requirement that the parent's stockholders would have a vote on any transaction that, if undertaken at the parent level, would require their assent. For this court to find that a subsidiary asset sale requires a parent company-level stockholder vote would, International argues, foist upon Delaware corporations a judicial statute that our General Assembly could have adopted, but chose not to. Given these factors, International contends it would be improper and inefficient for this court to now upset the reasonable expectations of transactional planners, who have supposedly relied upon *J.P. Griffin's* plain reading view of § 271 since the toddler days of disco.

Inc. retorts that International exaggerates the importance of *J.P. Griffin*, a decision that does not contain any more than a cursory assertion of the intended scope of § 271. By reference to another decision, *Leslie v. Telephonics Office Technologies, Inc.*, issued by Chancellor Allen, Inc. points out that this court has noted the possibility that a parent-level vote would be required if the court were to conclude that the subsidiary corporation had functioned merely as the instrumentality or agent of the parent in effecting the asset sale. That possibility led the Chancellor to examine the substance of a § 271 claim rather than base his decision on the very argument that International now makes. Furthermore, Inc. also notes that there is case law that finds that a subsidiary was an agent of the parent for purposes of a particular transaction and that does not require that the court find that the subsidiary's separate existence should be ignored for all purposes. Rather than being contrary to Delaware law and tradition, a practical interpretation of § 271 that ignores the separate existence of a subsidiary when it is the mere agent or instrumentality of a parent in an asset sale is consistent with the expectation that our courts will give a sensible interpretation to statutes and not empty them of their utility as important protectors of stockholders.

The policy implications of this debate are interesting. On its side, International has the virtues that accompany all bright-line tests, which are considerable, in that they provide clear guidance to transactional planners and limit litigation. That approach also adheres to the director-centered nature of our law, which leaves directors with wide managerial freedom subject to the strictures of equity, including entire fairness review of interested transactions. It is through this centralized management that stockholder wealth is largely created, or so much thinking goes. But important considerations also weigh in favor of Inc.'s argument.

If International's argument is accepted, § 271's vote requirement will be rendered largely hortatory — reduced to an easily side-stepped gesture, but little more, towards the idea that transactions that dispose of substantially all of a corporation's economic value need stockholders' assent to become effective. An example tied to this case points out this implication. Assume that the CRC decided to sell all four of International's operating groups. Further assume that each is held by subsidiaries that would not be subject to veil piercing but that it is equally clear that International dictated the sale of the assets and was a signatory to and guarantor of the sales contracts. Under International's view, even that sale would not constitute a sale of substantially all of its assets. This would be the case even though the sales would, taken together, result in a de facto liquidation of the firm's operating assets into a pool of cash, a result akin to a sale of the entire company for cash or a liquidation.

Notably, this example and its possible use by transactional planners as a structure is not far-fetched. Rather, it is more unusual than typical for public companies to directly hold their valuable operating assets. They do this for reasons that are perfectly legitimate. These include the desire to limit liabilities to third parties involved in operating certain business lines to those lines and to minimize tax liability. That the law recognizes the separate existence of wholly owned subsidiaries for purposes like this does not necessarily mean that it should recognize their separate existence for all purposes. Yet, that is exactly what International's argument is: that a wholly owned subsidiary is either without any legal dignity at all in the sense that it fails the severe test required to pierce the corporate veil or else its separate existence must be recognized in all contexts. In more human terms, this is like saying that an 18-year old should either be respected in her autonomy to decide all matters in her life (such as whether to drink liquor) or not be permitted any autonomy at all (to decide to leave home and join the military).

The utility of this stark, binary approach is not immediately clear and does not comport with the approach Delaware has taken in other areas of its corporate law. It creates a Hobson's choice that seems unnecessary. At first blush, it is not apparent why the distinctive considerations that apply to the relationship between stockholders and corporations within the corporate family cannot be recognized without doing violence to the wealth-creating value of limiting the ability of third parties who deal with wholly owned subsidiaries to seek recourse against parent corporations.

In drawing lines under § 271 itself, moreover, the facts of this case suggest a possible demarcation point. When an asset sale by the wholly owned subsidiary is to be consummated by a contract in which the parent entirely guarantees the performance of the selling subsidiary that is disposing of all of its assets and in which the parent is liable for any breach of warranty by the subsidiary, the direct act of the parent's board can, without any appreciable stretch, be viewed as selling assets of the parent itself. By its direct contractual action, the parent board is promising to dispose of all of the underlying assets of the subsidiaries by having the parent cause its wholly owned subsidiaries to sell, by promising to bear all the economic risks of the asset sale itself, and by therefore essentially eliminating the subsidiary's purpose and existence and monetizing for itself as parent the value of the assets held by that subsidiary. To find that § 271's vote requirement were implicated by such a contract if it involved the sale of assets that would, if owned directly by the parent, comprise substantially all of the parent's assets would not, despite International's well-stated arguments to the contrary, be an irrational implementation of the legislative intent expressed in that section of our corporation code.

I need not reach that conclusion, or a contrary one, in this case, however. This motion can be resolved without rendering any definitive pronouncement on this area of our law and, given the limited time for reflection on the question presented, prudential considerations counsel in favor of leaving the question to be answered in another case, or at later stage of this one, if that becomes necessary.

C. *As A Matter Of Economic Substance, Does The Telegraph Group Comprise Substantially All Of International's Assets?*

I now discuss the major question presented by this motion: whether the *Telegraph* Group comprises "substantially all" of International's assets, such that its sale requires a vote under § 271.

1. *The Legal Standards To Measure Whether The Telegraph Group Comprises Substantially All Of International's Assets*

Section 271 of the Delaware General Corporation Law authorizes a board of directors of a Delaware corporation to sell "all or substantially all of its property and assets, including goodwill and corporate franchises" only with the approval of a stockholder vote. The origins of § 271 did not rest primarily in a desire by the General Assembly to protect stockholders by affording them a vote on transactions previously not requiring their assent. Rather, § 271's predecessors were enacted to address the common law rule that invalidated any attempt to sell all or substantially all of a corporation's assets without unanimous stockholder approval.

Before 1967, the predecessor to § 271 did not contain an explicit prohibition on selling "substantially all" of the corporation's assets without stockholder approval. Professor Folk's report to the corporate law revision committee noted that it was believed that the statute would nonetheless be interpreted to bar a sale of substantially all the assets without the stockholders' approval, and the comprehensive revision to the DGCL formally incorporated a prohibition on selling substantially all the assets without an affirmative shareholder vote. According to leading commentators, the addition of the words "substantially all" was "intended merely to codify the interpretation generally accorded to the language of the pre-1967 statute that the word 'all' 'meant substantially all,' so that the statute could not be evaded by retaining a small amount of property not vital to the operation of the business."[10]

As I will note, our courts arguably have not always viewed cases involving the

---

[10] [n.44] Ernest L. Folk, III, Report to the Corporate Law Revision Committee 208 (1965–67).

interpretation of § 271 through a lens focused by the statute's plain words. Nonetheless, it remains a fundamental principle of Delaware law that the courts of this state should apply a statute in accordance with its plain meaning, as the words that our legislature has used to express its will are the best evidence of its intent. To analyze whether the vote requirement set forth in § 271 applies to a particular asset sale without anchoring that analysis to the statute's own words involves an unavoidable risk that normative preferences of the judiciary will replace those of the General Assembly.

Therefore, I begin my articulation of the applicable legal principles with the words of the statute itself. There are two key words here: "substantially" and "all." Although neither word is particularly difficult to understand, let's start with the easier one. "All" means "all," or if that is not clear, all, when used before a plural noun such as "assets," means "[t]he entire or unabated amount or quantity of; the whole extent, substance, or compass of; the whole."[11] "Substantially" is the adverb form of "substantial." Among other things, substantial means "being largely but not wholly that which is specified."[12] Substantially conveys the same meaning as "considerably" and "essentially"[13] because it means "to a great extent or degree" and communicates that it is very nearly the same thing as the noun it acts upon.[14] In all their relevant meanings, substantial and substantially convey the idea of amplitude, of something that is "[c]onsiderable in importance, value, degree, amount, or extent."[15] A fair and succinct equivalent to the term "substantially all" would therefore be "essentially everything."

In our jurisprudence, however, words of this kind arguably long ago passed from the sight of our judicial rear view mirrors, to be replaced by an inquiry more focused on the judicial gloss put on the statute than on the words of the statute itself. The need for some gloss is understandable, of course. There are various metrics that can be used to determine how important particular assets are in the scheme of things. Should a court look to the percentage of the corporation's potential value as a sales target to measure the statute's application? Or measures of income-generating potential, such as contributions to revenues or operating income? To what extent should the flagship nature of certain assets be taken into account?

For all these reasons,

> The Supreme Court has long held that a determination of whether there is a sale of substantially all assets so as to trigger section 271 depends upon the particular qualitative and quantitative characteristics of the transaction at issue. Thus, the transaction must be viewed in terms of its overall effect on the corporation, and there is no necessary qualifying percentage.[16]

---

[11] [n.46] OXFORD ENGLISH DICTIONARY ONLINE (2d ed. 1989), http://dictionary.oed.com.

[12] [n.47] MERRIAM-WEBSTER ON-LINE DICTIONARY, http://www.m-w.com.

[13] [n.48] MSN ENCARTA DICTIONARY, http://encarta.msn.com/encnet/features/dictionary/dictionaryhome.aspx.

[14] [n.49] http://www.dictionary.reference.com.

[15] [n.50] AMERICAN HERITAGE DICTIONARY 1727 (4th ed. 2000).

[16] [n.51] Winston v. Mandor, 710 A.2d 835, 843 (Del. Ch. 1997) (footnotes omitted).

In other words,

> Our jurisprudence eschewed a definitional approach to § 271 focusing on the interpretation of the words "substantially all," in favor of a contextual approach focusing upon whether a transaction involves the sale "of assets quantitatively vital to the operation of the corporation and is out of the ordinary and substantially affects the existence and purpose of the corporation." *Gimbel v. Signal Cos., Inc.*, Del. Ch., 316 A.2d 599, 606, *aff'd*, Del. Supr., 316 A.2d 619 (1974). This interpretative choice necessarily involved a policy preference for doing equity in specific cases over the value of providing clear guidelines for transactional lawyers structuring transactions for the corporations they advise. *See* 1 David A. Drexler, et al., *Delaware Corporation Law and Practice* § 37.03 (1999) ("[*Gimbel*] and its progeny represent a clear-cut rejection of the former conventional view that 'substantially all' in § 271 meant only significantly more than one-half of the corporation's assets.").[17]

It would be less than candid to fail to acknowledge that the § 271 case law provides less than ideal certainty about the application of the statute to particular circumstances. This may result from certain decisions that appear to deviate from the statutory language in a marked way and from others that have dilated perhaps longer than they should in evaluating asset sales that do not seem to come at all close to meeting the statutory trigger for a required stockholder vote. In this latter respect, the seminal § 271 decision, *Gimbel v. Signal Cos.*, may have contributed to the lack of clarity. In the heat of an expedited injunction proceeding, the Chancellor examined in some detail whether the sale of assets comprising only 26% and 41% of the Signal Companies' total and net assets was subject to stockholder approval. Although the assets involved the oldest business line of the Signal Companies, the magnitude involved does not seem to approach § 271's gray zone.

In the morass of particular percentages in the cases, however, remain the key principles articulated in *Gimbel*, which were firmly rooted in the statutory language of § 271 and the statute's history. As has been noted, *Gimbel* set forth a quantitative and qualitative test designed to help determine whether a particular sale of assets involved substantially all the corporation's assets. That test has been adopted by our Supreme Court as a good metric for determining whether an asset sale triggers the vote requirement of § 271.

But the *Gimbel* test, as Chancellor Quillen intended it, was not designed to obscure and supplant the statutory language, but to illuminate the meaning of that language. As the Chancellor noted, the definitional test used by our courts in applying § 271 "must begin with and ultimately necessarily relate to our statutory language."[18]

The test that *Gimbel* articulated — requiring a stockholder vote if the assets to be sold "are quantitatively vital to the operation of the corporation" and "substantially affect[ ] the existence and purpose of the corporation" — must therefore be

---

[17] [n.52] In re General Motors Class H S'holders Litig., 734 A.2d 611, 623 (Del. Ch. 1999).

[18] [n.56] *Gimbel*, 316 A.2d at 605.

read as an attempt to give practical life to the words "substantially all." It is for that reason that *Gimbel* emphasized that a vote would never be required for a transaction in the ordinary course of business and that the mere fact that an asset sale was out of the ordinary had little bearing on whether a vote was required.

Indeed, *Gimbel* stressed that "the statute does not speak of a requirement of shareholder approval simply because an independent, important branch of a corporate business is being sold."[19] In that case, the court expressly rejected the argument that Delaware law ought to follow the law of other states that subjected all such major sales to stockholder approval, stating:

> The plaintiff cites several non-Delaware cases for the proposition that shareholder approval of such a sale is required. But that is not the language of our statute. Similarly, it is not our law that shareholder approval is required upon every 'major' restructuring of the corporation. Again, it is not necessary to go beyond the statute. The statute requires shareholder approval upon the sale of 'all or substantially all' of the corporation's assets. That is the sole test to be applied.[20]

To underscore the point that the test it was articulating was tied directly to the statute, *Gimbel* noted that its examination of the quantitative and qualitative importance of the transaction at issue was intended to determine whether the transaction implicated the statute because it struck "at the heart of the corporate existence and purpose," in the sense that it involved the " 'destruction of the means to accomplish the purposes or objects for which the corporation was incorporated and actually performs.' "[21] It was in that sense, *Gimbel* said, that the "statute's applicability was to be determined."[22]

And it is in that sense that I apply the *Gimbel* test in this case.

2. Is The Telegraph Group Quantitatively Vital To The Operations Of International?

The first question under the *Gimbel* test is whether the *Telegraph* Group is quantitatively vital to the operations of International. The short answer to that question is no, it is not quantitatively vital within the meaning of *Gimbel.*

Why?

Because it is clear that International will retain economic vitality even after a sale of the *Telegraph* because it is retaining other significant assets, one of which, the Chicago Group, has a strong record of past profitability and expectations of healthy profit growth.

Now, it is of course clear that the *Telegraph* Group is a major quantitative part

---

[19] [n.58] *Id.* at 605.

[20] [n.59] *Id.*

[21] [n.60] *Id.* at 606 (quoting 6A Fletcher, CYCLOPEDIA CORPORATIONS § 2949.2, at 648 (Perm. Ed. 1968 Rev.)).

[22] [n.61] *Id.*

of International's economic value and an important contributor to its profits. I am even prepared to decide this motion on the assumption that the *Telegraph* Group is the single most valuable asset that International possesses, even more valuable than the Chicago Group.

I base that largely on the results of the auction process. That process ultimately generated a price of $1.2 billion for the *Telegraph* Group. When the bidding on the Chicago Group was halted, the highest bid received was $950 million. I consider these numbers good ones to use, even considering the circulation problems that later emerged at the *Sun-Times*. I do so because it is probable that the $950 million bid was not a final stretch bid as it was not a last round bid, but the ability to extract more from a final bidding round would, in light of the circulation problems that arose, have been doubtful. Unlike Inc., I do not believe that the $950 million bid ought to be discounted by 5% because I do not find it likely that the circulation problems would diminish the value of the Chicago Group to that extent, particularly given that a 15% drop in circulation of the *Sun-Times* had been assumed by the bidders and given that the *Sun-Times* contributes only around half of the profits of the Chicago Group as a whole.

If one were to use the actual high bids received for each of the *Telegraph* and Chicago Groups as a result of the Strategic Process and assume that those were the only assets of International — which is not an accurate assumption — the *Telegraph* Group accounts for 56–57% of International's asset value, while the Chicago Group accounts for only 43–44% of the value. Recognizing that quantitative vitality must be defined in light of the statutory language "substantially all," this breakdown does little to support Inc.'s position. It is less than 60% and the remaining asset is itself a quantitatively vital economic asset, as I will now explain.

Let's consider the relative contribution to International's revenues of the *Telegraph* Group and the Chicago Group. When considering this and other factors the reader must bear in mind that the contribution of the Canada Group dropped steeply after the 2000 CanWest sale. Before that sale, the Canada Group was a larger contributor to the economic value of International in many respects than the *Telegraph* and Chicago Groups combined and it was sold without a stockholder vote. Bearing that fact in mind, a look at the revenue picture at International since 2000 reveals the following:

Revenue ($MM)								
Operating Unit	**2000**	**%**	**2001**	**%**	**2002**	**%**	**Unaudited 2003**	**%**
Telegraph Group	$562.1	26.8	486.4	42.4	481.5	47.9	519.5	49.0
Chicago Group	401.4	19.2	442.9	38.6	441.8	43.9	450.8	42.5
Canada Group	1,065.2	50.8	197.9	17.3	69.6	6.9	80.5	7.6
Jerusalem Group	67.3	3.2	19.1	1.7	13.2	1.3	10.4	1.0
Other	0.0	0.0	0.0	0.0	0.0	0.0	0.0	0.0
Total	2,096.0	100.0	1,146.3	100.0	1,006.2	100.0	1,061.2	100.0

Put simply, the *Telegraph* Group has accounted for less than half of International's revenues during the last three years and the Chicago Group's contribution has been in the same ballpark.

In book value terms, neither the *Telegraph* Group nor the Chicago Group approach 50% of International's asset value because the company's other operating groups and non-operating assets have value:

Book Value of Assets ($MM)								
Operating Unit	2000	%	2001	%	2002	%	Unaudited 2003	%
Telegraph Group	$542.0	19.8	533.2	25.9	568.3	26.0	629.8	35.7
Chicago Group	613.7	22.4	595.9	29.0	557.9	25.5	537.9	30.5
Canada Group	551.6	20.2	448.7	21.8	214.0	9.8	262.0	14.9
Jerusalem Group	61.2	2.2	69.6	3.4	28.9	1.3	30.1	1.7
Other	968.8	35.4	410.5	19.9	819.1	37.4	302.8	17.2
Total	2,737.2	100.0	2,058.0	100.0	2,188.0	100.0	1,762.6	100.0

In terms of vitality, however, a more important measure is EBITDA contribution, as that factor focuses on the free cash flow that assets generate for the firm, a key component of economic value. As to that important factor, the Chicago Group is arguably more quantitatively nutritious to International than the *Telegraph* Group. Here is the picture considering all of International's operating groups:

KBITDA — All Operating Units ($MM)								
Operating Unit	2000	%	2001	%	2002	%	Unaudited 2003	%
Telegraph Group	$106.7	30.3	50.7	85.3	61.4	54.7	57.4	57.4
Chicago Group	59.8	17.0	47.6	80.1	72.1	64.2	79.5	79.4
Canada Group	190.5	54.1	(21.1)	(2.5)	(0.8)	(0.7)	(3.3)	(3.3)
Jerusalem Group	9.6	2.7	(1.5)	(2.5)	(2.8)	(2.5)	(5.3)	(5.3)
Other	(14.3)	(4.1)	(16.3)	(27.4)	(17.5)	(15.6)	(28.3)	(28.3)
Total	352.3	100.0	59.5	100.0	112.4	100.0	100.0	100.0

Here is the picture considering just the *Telegraph* Group and the Chicago Group:

EBITDA — Telegraph Group and Chicago Group Only ($MM)								
Operating Unit	2000	%	2001	%	2002	%	Unaudited 2003	%
Telegraph Group	$106.7	64.1	50.7	51.6	61.4	46.0	57.4	41.9
Chicago Group	59.8	35.9	47.6	48.4	72.1	54.0	79.5	58.1
Total	166.5	100.0	98.3	100.0	133.5	100.0	136.9	100.0

The picture that emerges is one of rough equality between the two Groups with any edge tilting in the Chicago Group's direction. Although in 2000 and earlier years the *Telegraph* Group made a markedly higher contribution, that has not been so since then as continued competition in London holds down its profits.

Importantly, the record evidence regarding the future of both Groups also suggests that their cash flow-generating potential and sale value are not greatly disparate. . . .

The evidence therefore reveals that neither the *Telegraph* Group nor the Chicago

Group is quantitatively vital in the sense used in the *Gimbel* test. Although both Groups are profitable, valuable economic assets and although the *Telegraph* Group is somewhat more valuable than the Chicago Group, International can continue as a profitable entity without either one of them. International is not a human body and the *Telegraph* and the Chicago Group are not its heart and liver. International is a business. Neither one of the two groups is "vital" — i.e., "necessary to the continuation of [International's] life" or "necessary to [its] continued existence or effectiveness." Rather, a sale of either Group leaves International as a profitable entity, even if it chooses to distribute a good deal of the cash it receives from the *Telegraph* sale to its stockholders through a dividend or share repurchase.

3. Does The Telegraph Sale "Substantially Affect The Existence And Purpose Of" International?

The relationship of the qualitative element of the *Gimbel* test to the quantitative element is more than a tad unclear. If the assets to be sold are not quantitatively vital to the corporation's life, it is not altogether apparent how they can "substantially affect the existence and purpose of" the corporation within the meaning of *Gimbel*, suggesting either that the two elements of the test are actually not distinct or that they are redundant. In other words, if quantitative vitality takes into account factors such as the cash-flow generating value of assets and not merely book value, then it necessarily captures qualitative considerations as well. Simply put, the supposedly bifurcated *Gimbel* test may be no more bifurcated in substance than the two-pronged entire fairness test and may simply involve a look at quantitative and qualitative considerations in order to come up with the answer to the single statutory question, which is whether a sale involves substantially all of a corporation's assets. Rather than endeavor to explore the relationship between these factors, however, I will just dive into my analysis of the qualitative importance of the *Telegraph* Group to International.

Inc.'s demand for a vote places great weight on the qualitative element of *Gimbel*. In its papers, Inc. stresses the journalistic superiority of the *Telegraph* over the *Sun-Times* and the social cachet the *Telegraph* has. If you own the *Telegraph*, Inc. notes, "you can have dinner with the Queen." To sell one of the world's most highly regarded newspapers and leave International owning as its flagship the Second Paper in the Second City is to fundamentally, qualitatively transform International. Moreover, after the *Telegraph* sale, International's name will even ring hollow, as it will own only publications in the U.S., Canada, and Israel, and it will own only one paper of top-flight journalistic reputation, the *Jerusalem Post*, which has only a modest readership compared to the *Telegraph*.

The argument that Inc. makes in its papers misconceives the qualitative element of *Gimbel*. That element is not satisfied if the court merely believes that the economic assets being sold are aesthetically superior to those being retained; rather, the qualitative element of *Gimbel* focuses on economic quality and, at most, on whether the transaction leaves the stockholders with an investment that in economic terms is qualitatively different than the one that they now possess. Even with that focus, it must be remembered that the qualitative element is a gloss on the statutory language "substantially all" and not an attempt to identify qualitatively important transactions but ones that "strike at the heart of the corporate existence."

The *Telegraph* sale does not strike at International's heart or soul, if that corporation can be thought to have either one. When International went public, it did not own the *Telegraph*. During the course of its existence, International has frequently bought and sold a wide variety of publications. In the CanWest sale, it disposed of a number of major newspapers in Canada — and diminished its assets by half — all without a stockholder vote. That sale came on the heels of its departure from Australia and an American downsizing. Thus, no investor in International would assume that any of its assets were sacrosanct. In the words of *Gimbel*, it "can be said that . . . acquisitions and dispositions [of independent branches of International's business] have become part of the [company's] ordinary course of business."

Even more importantly, investors in public companies do not invest their money because they derive social status from owning shares in a corporation whose controlling manager can have dinner with the Queen. Whatever the social importance of the *Telegraph* in Great Britain, the economic value of that importance to International as an entity is what matters for the *Gimbel* test, not how cool it would be to be the *Telegraph*'s publisher. The expected cash flows from the *Telegraph* Group take that into account, as do the bids that were received for the *Telegraph* Group. The "trophy" nature of the *Telegraph* Group means that there are some buyers — including I discern, the Barclays, who run a private, not public, company — who are willing to pay a higher price than expected cash flows suggest is prudent, in purely economic terms, in order to own the *Telegraph* and to enjoy the prestige and access to the intelligentsia, the literary and social elite, and high government officials that comes with that control.

Although stockholders would expect that International would capitalize on the fact that some potential buyers of the *Telegraph* would be willing to pay money to receive some of the non-economic benefits that came with control of that newspaper, it is not reasonable to assume that they invested with the expectation that International would retain the *Telegraph* Group even if it could receive a price that was attractive in light of the projected future cash flow of that Group. Certainly, given the active involvement of International in the M & A market, there was no reason to invest based on that unusual basis. It may be that there exists somewhere an International stockholder (other than Mrs. Black or perhaps some personal friends of the Blacks) who values the opportunities that Conrad Black had to dine with the Queen and other eminent members of British society because he was the *Telegraph*'s publisher. But the qualitative element of the *Gimbel* test addresses the rational economic expectations of reasonable investors, and not the aberrational sentiments of the peculiar (if not, more likely, the non-existent) persons who invest money to help fulfill the social ambitions of inside managers and to thereby enjoy (through the ownership of common stock) vicariously extraordinary lives themselves.

After the *Telegraph* Sale, International's stockholders will remain investors in a publication company with profitable operating assets, a well-regarded tabloid newspaper of good reputation and large circulation, a prestigious newspaper in

Israel, and other valuable assets. While important, the sale of the *Telegraph* does not strike a blow to International's heart.

4. *Summary Of § 271 Analysis*

When considered quantitatively and qualitatively, the *Telegraph* sale does not amount to a sale of substantially all of International's assets. This conclusion is consistent with the bulk of our case law under § 271. Although by no means wholly consistent, that case law has, by and large, refused to find that a disposition involved substantially all the assets of a corporation when the assets that would remain after the sale were, in themselves, substantial and profitable. As *Gimbel* noted, § 271 permits a board to sell "one business . . . without shareholder approval when other substantial businesses are retained." In the cases when asset sales were deemed to involve substantially all of a corporation's assets, the record always revealed great doubt about the viability of the business that would remain, primarily because the remaining operating assets were not profitable. But, "if the portion of the business not sold constitutes a substantial, viable, ongoing component of the corporation, the sale is not subject to Section 271."

To conclude that the sale of the *Telegraph* Group was a sale of substantially all of International's assets would involve a determination that International possesses two operating assets, the sale of either of which would trigger a stockholder vote under § 271. That is, because there is no significant distinction between the economic importance of the Chicago and *Telegraph* Groups to International, a conclusion that the *Telegraph* Group was substantially all of International's assets would (impliedly but undeniably) supplant the plain language and intended meaning of the General Assembly with an "approximately half" test. I decline Inc.'s invitation for me to depart so markedly from our legislature's mandate. By any reasonable interpretation, the *Telegraph* sale does not involve substantially all of International's assets as substantial operating (and non-operating) assets will be retained, and International will remain a profitable publishing concern. . . .

IV. *Conclusion*

Inc.'s motion for a preliminary injunction is DENIED. IT IS SO ORDERED.

QUESTIONS

1. What is plaintiff's relationship with defendant, why is it suing, and what is its primary legal argument?

2. What is the test for determining whether a corporation's sale of assets constitutes "substantially all" of its assets?

3. Was the sale of the *Telegraph* Group a sale of substantially all of International's assets? Why or why not?

4. In light of *Hollinger*, the Delaware General Assembly amended § 271 in 2005 to add subsection (c). This subsection provides as follows:

> (c) For purposes of this section only, the property and assets of the corporation include the property and assets of any subsidiary of the corporation. As used in this subsection, "subsidiary" means any entity wholly-owned and controlled, directly or indirectly, by the corporation and includes, without limitation, corporations, partnerships, limited partnerships, limited liability partnerships, limited liability companies, and/or statutory trusts. Notwithstanding subsection (a) of this section, except to the extent the certificate of incorporation otherwise provides, no resolution by stockholders or members shall be required for a sale, lease or exchange of property and assets of the corporation to a subsidiary.

Would *Hollinger* have come out differently if subsection (c) had been in effect at the time of the Telegraph transaction?

5. How would the court's analysis have differed if Delaware was an MBCA state?

The voting standard for shareholder approval under § 271 is "a majority of the outstanding stock of the corporation entitled to vote thereon." We refer to this standard as "majority of outstanding." Section 271 does not specify a quorum requirement for the shareholder meeting at which such approval is sought, which means the general quorum requirement of § 216 applies. This section provides the following default rule: "[a] majority of the shares entitled to vote, present in person or represented by proxy, shall constitute a quorum at a meeting of stockholders." DGCL § 228 provides for written consent of stockholders in lieu of a meeting. Under subsection (a) of that section, the consent must be signed by "the holders of outstanding stock having not less than the minimum number of votes that would be necessary to authorize or take such action at a meeting at which all shares entitled to vote thereon were present and voted . . . ." Hence, a consent approving the sale of all or substantially all of a corporation's assets must be signed by shareholders owning a majority of outstanding shares.

b.   Bidder Shareholder Approval

The DGCL does not require bidder shareholders to approve bidder's acquisition of target through an asset purchase even if bidder will be issuing in the deal shares comprising more than 20 percent of the voting power of the shares of bidder pre-deal. In other words, the DGCL does not have a provision equivalent to MBCA § 6.21(f).

3.   Appraisal Rights

As mentioned above, the DGCL provides appraisal rights only for a deal structured as a merger. Thus, neither target nor bidder shareholders are entitled to appraisal rights in connection with an asset purchase.

EXERCISE 2.1

Bidder and Target are both private companies incorporated in Arizona. Bidder's issued and outstanding stock consists of 1,000,000 shares of common stock; Target's issued and outstanding stock consists of 10,000 shares of common stock. Bidder is acquiring Target for $5 million in cash in a deal structured as an asset purchase. The asset purchase agreement provides that Target will be liquidated shortly after closing with any excess cash left after paying off Target's creditors to be distributed to Target's shareholders pro rata based on the number of shares they own. Assume that the articles of incorporation and bylaws of both Bidder and Target simply track the default provisions of the Arizona corporate code.

1.   Which boards need to approve the deal?

2.   (a) Which shareholders need to approve the deal, (b) how many shareholders constitute a quorum, (c) what is the relevant voting standard, and (d) what is the minimum number of votes required for approval?

3.   Which shareholders have the right to dissent?

4.   Do any of your answers to questions 1 through 3 above change if the deal consideration consists of 220,000 shares of Bidder common stock?

Make sure you explain how you arrived at your answers and provide specific statutory or other cites as support.

2.   Stock Purchase

a.   MBCA

1.   Board Approval

For a deal structured as a stock purchase, target board approval is *not* technically required. In fact, there is no MBCA provision specifically governing a deal structured as a stock purchase. This is because the deal is between bidder and target's shareholders and not target itself. With that said, bidder will insist that target be a party to the stock purchase agreement. Hence, target board approval of target signing the agreement is required under agency law because the transaction is outside the ordinary course of business. Further, both target's and bidder's attorneys will insist on target board approval. A similar analysis applies to bidder board approval, i.e., it is not required under the MBCA but is generally required under agency law and by the parties' attorneys.

2.   Shareholder Approval

a.   Target Shareholder Approval

No formal target shareholder vote is required for a stock purchase. Target shareholders do, however, have essentially an informal vote on the deal — they can refuse to sell their stock to bidder. In other words, unlike all the other deal structures, a target shareholder can holdout even if all other shareholders are in favor of the deal, i.e., have agreed to sell their stock to bidder. In such an event, bidder and target may simply decide to go with a different structure. Alternatively, the deal could still be structured as a stock purchase followed by a squeeze out merger (we discuss squeeze out mergers in Chapter 3).

b. Bidder Shareholder Approval

Bidder shareholder approval would only be required under the MBCA if § 6.21(f)(1) applies, i.e., bidder will be issuing in the deal shares comprising more than 20 percent of its then existing voting power.

3. Appraisal Rights

The MBCA does not provide appraisal rights for target or bidder shareholders when bidder acquires a target through stock purchase. This is true for bidder even if its shareholders are entitled to vote on the deal pursuant to § 6.21(f)(1).

b. DGCL

The board approval, shareholder approval, and appraisal rights analysis under the DGCL is generally the same as the analysis under the MBCA. Specifically:

- Neither target nor bidder board approval is required by the DGCL, but both are generally required under agency law and by the parties' attorneys.

- No formal target shareholder vote is required. Bidder shareholder approval is likewise not required, and unlike under the MBCA, this is true even if bidder will be issuing in the deal shares comprising more than 20 percent of its then existing voting power (the DGCL has no equivalent to MBCA § 6.21(f)(1)).

- The DGCL does not provide appraisal rights for target or bidder shareholders when bidder acquires a target through a stock purchase.

EXERCISE 2.2

Bidder and Target are both private companies incorporated in Texas. Bidder's issued and outstanding stock consists of 1,000,000 shares of common stock; Target's issued and outstanding stock consists of 10,000 shares of common stock. Bidder is acquiring Target for $5 million in cash in a deal structured as a stock purchase. Assume that the articles of incorporation and bylaws of both Bidder and Target simply track the default provisions of the Texas corporate code.

1. Which boards need to approve the deal?

2. (a) Which shareholders need to approve the deal, (b) what is the relevant voting standard, and (c) what is the minimum number of votes required for approval?

3. Which shareholders have the right to dissent?

Make sure you explain how you arrived at your answers and provide specific statutory or other cites as support.

3. Direct Merger

a. MBCA

1.   Board Approval

MBCA § 11.04(a) requires board approval by a corporation that "is a party to a merger . . . ." In a direct merger, both target and bidder are parties to the merger, so board approval of both target and bidder is required under § 11.04(a).

2.   Shareholder Approval

MBCA § 11.04(b) provides the general rule that "the board of directors must submit the plan [of merger] to the shareholders for their approval." Section 11.04(h) provides the following exception to the general rule:

> (h) Unless the articles of incorporation otherwise provide, approval by the corporation's shareholders of a plan of merger . . . is not required [notwithstanding § 11.04(b)] if:
>
> (1)   the corporation will survive the merger . . . ;
>
> (2)   except for amendments permitted by § 10.05, its articles of incorporation will not be changed;
>
> (3)   each shareholder of the corporation whose shares were outstanding immediately before the effective date of the merger . . . will hold the same number of shares, with identical preferences, limitations, and relative rights, immediately after the effective date of change; and
>
> (4)   the issuance in the merger . . . of shares or other securities convertible into or rights exercisable for shares does not require a vote under § 6.21(f).

The way the general rule plus the exception shakes out is that target shareholder approval will always be required. This is because, among other things, by definition target will not survive the merger and therefore (h)(1) will not be met (notice the "and" at the end of (3) which means all four items must be met for the exception to apply). Conversely, bidder shareholders will rarely get a vote on a direct merger unless the deal consideration surpasses the 20 percent threshold of § 6.21(f)(1). Specifically, (h)(1) is met by definition, and it is generally no problem or concern for bidder and target to structure the deal so that (h)(2) and (3) are met. That just leaves (h)(4) which incorporates by reference the 20 percent threshold of § 6.21(f)(1) discussed above.

If shareholder approval is required and the corporation seeks it through a meeting (as opposed to by written consent), § 11.04(e) requires a minimum quorum of "a majority of the votes entitled to be cast on the plan" of merger to be represented at the meeting. Chapter 11 does not specify a voting requirement for a merger so that means the more-votes-for-than-against voting requirement of § 7.25 applies. Note that as with the shareholder vote on the disposition of assets, the MBCA used to impose a majority of outstanding voting requirement for shareholder approval of a merger but changed it to more-votes-for-than-against in 1999. This change, however, has not caught on.

3. Appraisal Rights

MBCA § 13.02(a)(1) provides the following:

(a) A shareholder is entitled to appraisal rights, and to obtain payment of the fair value of that shareholder's shares, in the event of any of the following corporate actions:

(1) consummation of a merger to which the corporation is a party (i) if shareholder approval is required for the merger by § 11.04, except that appraisal rights shall not be available to any shareholder of the corporation with respect to shares of any class or series that remain outstanding after consummation of the merger . . . .

Hence, the general rule is that target shareholders are entitled to appraisal rights in a direct merger because, as discussed above, they get to vote on the deal. There are exceptions to this general rule applicable to public targets (we discuss this exception in Chapter 3) and short-form mergers (we discuss the short-form merger exception in section 9 below).

Conversely, as discussed above, bidder shareholders will rarely be entitled to appraisal rights because their approval of a direct merger is rarely required by § 11.04.

b. DGCL

1. Board Approval

DGCL § 251(b) provides that "[t]he board of directors of each corporation which desires to merge or consolidate[23] shall adopt a resolution approving an agreement of merger . . . and declaring its advisability." In a direct merger, each of target and bidder "desires to the merge" so board approval by both of them is required under § 251(b).

2. Shareholder Approval

DGCL § 251(c) provides the general rule that the shareholders of "each constituent corporation" gets to vote on the merger. A "constituent corporation" is a corporation that will be merged with or into another corporation in the merger. Thus, under the general rule, both target and bidder shareholders get to vote on the merger because in a direct merger target will be merged *into* bidder, and bidder will be merged *with* target. Section 251(f) provides the following exception to the general rule:

---

[23] In this context, a consolidation is when two or more corporations combine, or consolidate, into a new corporation formed by the consolidation as opposed to one corporation merging into another corporation. The MBCA allows for this type of transaction too but refers to it as a merger. The corporate statutory formalities involved for a consolidation under the DGCL are the same as those for a merger, so we do not discuss them.

(f) Notwithstanding the requirements of subsection (c) of this section, unless required by its certificate of incorporation, no vote of stockholders of a constituent corporation surviving a merger shall be necessary to authorize a merger if (1) the agreement of merger does not amend in any respect the certificate of incorporation of such constituent corporation, (2) each share of stock of such constituent corporation outstanding immediately prior to the effective date of the merger is to be an identical outstanding or treasury share of the surviving corporation after the effective date of the merger, and (3) either no shares of common stock of the surviving corporation and no shares, securities or obligations convertible into such stock are to be issued or delivered under the plan of merger, or the authorized unissued shares or the treasury shares of common stock of the surviving corporation to be issued or delivered under the plan of merger plus those initially issuable upon conversion of any other shares, securities or obligations to be issued or delivered under such plan do not exceed 20% of the shares of common stock of such constituent corporation outstanding immediately prior to the effective date of the merger.

As is the case under the MBCA, the way the general rule plus the exception shakes out is that target shareholder approval will always be required. This is because by definition target's stock will not be outstanding after the merger because target will no longer exist, and therefore, § 251(f)(2) will not be met. Conversely, bidder shareholders will rarely get a vote on a direct merger unless the deal consideration surpasses the 20 percent threshold of § 251(f)(3).

The voting standard for shareholder approval under § 251 is a majority of outstanding. Section 251 does not specify a quorum requirement for the shareholder meeting at which such approval is sought, which means the general quorum requirement of § 216 applies.

3. Appraisal Rights

The general rule under DGCL § 262(b) is that target shareholders are entitled to appraisal rights with respect to a direct merger. As is the case under the MBCA, there are exceptions to this general rule applicable to public targets and short-form mergers, which we discuss later in this book.

Bidder shareholders are also entitled to appraisal rights under the general rule of § 262(b). However, as applied to them, the general rule is normally overridden by § 262(b)(1), which provides, among other things, "that no appraisal rights shall be available for any shares of stock of the constituent corporation surviving a merger if the merger did not require for its approval the vote of the stockholders of the surviving corporation as provided in § 251(f) of this title." By definition, bidder survives a direct merger and, as discussed above, it is often the case that bidder shareholders do not get to vote on a direct merger because of § 251(f).

EXERCISE 2.3

Bidder and Target are both private companies incorporated in New York. Bidder's issued and outstanding stock consists of 1,000,000 shares of common stock; Target's issued and outstanding stock consists of 10,000 shares of common stock. Bidder is acquiring Target for $5 million in cash in a deal structured as a direct merger. Assume that the certificate of incorporation and bylaws of both Bidder and Target simply track the default provisions of the New York corporate code.

1.   Which boards need to approve the deal?

2.   (a) Which shareholders need to approve the deal, (b) what is the relevant voting standard, and (c) what is the minimum number of votes required for approval?

3.   Which shareholders have the right to dissent?

Make sure you explain how you arrived at your answers and provide specific statutory or other cites as support.

4.   Forward Triangular Merger

Recall from Chapter 1 that a forward triangular merger involves three parties — bidder, target, and merger sub (a newly created wholly owned subsidiary of bidder). Thus, board approval, shareholder approval, and appraisal rights must be considered with respect not only to bidder and target but merger sub as well.

a.   MBCA

1.   Board Approval

As mentioned above, MBCA § 11.04(a) requires board approval by a corporation that "is a party to a merger . . . ." In a forward triangular merger, the parties to the merger are target and merger sub so board approval of both target and merger sub is required under § 11.04(a). Section 11.04(a) does not require bidder board approval because bidder is not a party to the merger. With that said, target will insist that bidder be a party to the merger agreement (this is not the same as being a party to the merger). Hence, bidder board approval of bidder signing the merger agreement is required under agency law if the transaction is outside the ordinary course of bidder's business (which is likely the case). Further, both target's and bidder's attorneys will insist on bidder board approval. Additionally, bidder board approval will be required if the deal consideration includes bidder stock because MBCA § 6.21 requires board approval of a stock issuance.

2.   Shareholder Approval

MBCA § 11.04(b) provides the general rule that "the board of directors must submit the plan [of merger] to the shareholders for their approval." Per the lead-in to § 11.04, § 11.04(b) only applies to "a corporation that is a party to the merger . . . ." Thus, bidder shareholder approval is not required under § 11.04(b).

Recall that § 11.04(h) provides an exception to the general rule. The way the general rule plus the exception shakes out as applied to target in a deal structured as a forward triangular merger is that target shareholder approval will always be required. This is because, among other things, by definition, target will not survive the merger and therefore § 11.04(h)(1) will not be met. Merger sub's shareholder (bidder) is typically not entitled to vote on the deal because of the subsection (h) exception. Regardless, bidder will vote its shares of merger sub in favor of the deal if merger sub shareholder approval is required, so this vote is a non-issue.

The analysis of the quorum and vote requirement under the MBCA for a shareholder vote on a forward triangular merger is the same as described above for a direct merger.

3.   Appraisal Rights

As discussed above in the direct merger context, a shareholder is generally entitled to appraisal rights if the corporation is a party to a merger and approval of the merger by the corporation's shareholders is required by § 11.04. Thus, the general rule is that target shareholders are entitled to appraisal rights in a forward triangular merger because they get to vote on the deal, subject to exceptions applicable to public targets and short-form mergers. Conversely, a bidder shareholder vote on the deal is not required under § 11.04, so bidder shareholders are not entitled to appraisal rights (this is true even if they get a vote under § 6.21(f)(1)).

As discussed above, merger sub's shareholder (bidder) will rarely be entitled to appraisal rights because its approval of the merger is rarely required by § 11.04. Even if its approval is required, it obviously would not exercise appraisal rights.

b.   DGCL

1.   Board Approval

As mentioned above, DGCL § 251(b) requires board approval by "each corporation that desires to merge . . . ." In a forward triangular merger, each of target and merger sub "desires to the merge" so board approval by both of them is required under § 251(b). Bidder board approval is not required under § 251(b) because bidder is not a party to the merger and therefore does not "desire to merge." But once again, target will insist that bidder be a party to the merger agreement. Hence, bidder board approval of bidder signing the merger agreement is required under agency law if the transaction is outside the ordinary course of bidder's business (which is likely the case). Further, both target's and bidder's attorneys will insist on bidder board approval. Additionally, bidder board approval will be required if the deal consideration includes bidder stock because DGCL § 152 requires board approval of a stock issuance.

2.   Shareholder Approval

As mentioned above, DGCL § 251(c) provides the general rule that the shareholders of "each constituent corporation" get to vote on the merger. The constituent corporations in a forward triangular merger are target and merger sub. Thus, under the general rule, both target and merger sub shareholders get to vote on the merger.

Recall that § 251(f) provides an exception to the general rule. The way the general rule plus the exception shakes out for a forward triangular merger is that target shareholder approval will always be required. This is because the exception only applies to a constituent corporation surviving the merger, and target does not survive. The subsection (f) exception normally applies to merger sub, so its shareholder (bidder) normally does not get a vote on the deal. Regardless, bidder will vote its shares of merger sub in favor of the deal if merger sub shareholder approval is required, so this vote is a non-issue.

The analysis of the quorum and vote requirement under the DGCL for a shareholder vote on a forward triangular merger is the same as described above for a direct merger.

3.   Appraisal Rights

The general rule under DGCL § 262(b) is that target shareholders are entitled to appraisal rights with respect to a forward triangular merger. Again, there are exceptions to this general rule applicable to public targets and short-form mergers, which we discuss later in this book.

Under the general rule, merger sub's shareholder (bidder) is also entitled to appraisal rights. However, as applied to merger sub, the general rule is normally overridden by § 262(b)(1) which provides, among other things, "that no appraisal rights shall be available for any shares of stock of the constituent corporation surviving a merger if the merger did not require for its approval the vote of the stockholders of the surviving corporation as provided in § 251(f) of this title." By definition, merger sub survives a forward triangular merger and, as discussed above, it is normally the case that merger sub's shareholder does not get to vote on a forward triangular merger because of § 251(f). Even if it did get a vote, it obviously would not exercise appraisal rights.

EXERCISE 2.4

Bidder and Target are both private companies incorporated in Illinois. Bidder's issued and outstanding stock consists of 1,000,000 shares of common stock; Target's issued and outstanding stock consists of 10,000 shares of common stock. Bidder is acquiring Target for $5 million in cash in a deal structured as a forward triangular merger. In that regard, Bidder has incorporated Merger Sub in Illinois for purposes of the deal. Assume that the articles of incorporation and bylaws of Bidder, Merger Sub, and Target simply track the default provisions of the Illinois corporate code.

1.   Which boards need to approve the deal?

2.   (a) Which shareholders need to approve the deal, (b) what is the relevant voting standard, and (c) what is the minimum number of votes required for approval?

3.   Which shareholders have the right to dissent?

4.   Do any of your answers to questions 1 through 3 above change if the deal consideration consists of 220,000 shares of Bidder common stock?

Make sure you explain how you arrived at your answers and provide specific statutory or other cites as support.

5. Reverse Triangular Merger

As with a forward triangular merger, a reverse triangular merger involves a bidder, target, and merger sub. Thus, once again we consider board approval, shareholder approval, and appraisal rights for all three.

a. MBCA

1. Board Approval

The board approval analysis is exactly the same as the board approval analysis for a forward triangular merger. Specifically, § 11.04(a) requires board approval by target and merger sub but not bidder. Bidder board approval is generally required by agency law and will be insisted on by the parties' attorneys. Additionally, bidder board approval will be required if the deal consideration includes bidder stock because MBCA § 6.21 requires board approval of a stock issuance.

2. Shareholder Approval

Bidder shareholder approval is not required under § 11.04(b) per the lead-in to § 11.04. Target shareholder approval is required because the § 11.04(h) exception to the general rule requiring shareholder approval will not apply. Specifically, § 11.04(h)(3) will not be met because target shareholders will not "hold the same number of shares, with identical preferences, limitations, and relative rights" that they held before the merger (their shares will be converted into the merger consideration per § 11.07(a)(8)). Likewise, merger sub shareholder approval is required because the § 11.04(h) exception will not apply. Specifically, among other things, § 11.04(h)(1) will not be met because merger sub will not survive the merger.

The analysis of the quorum and vote requirement under the MBCA for a shareholder vote on a reverse triangular merger is the same as described above for a direct merger.

3. Appraisal Rights

As discussed above in the direct merger context, a shareholder is generally entitled to appraisal rights if the corporation is a party to a merger and approval of the merger by the corporation's shareholders is required by § 11.04. Thus, the general rule is that target shareholders are entitled to appraisal rights in a reverse triangular merger because they get to vote on the deal, subject to exceptions applicable to public targets and short-form mergers. Conversely, a bidder shareholder vote on the deal is not required under § 11.04, so bidder shareholders are not entitled to appraisal rights.

Merger sub's shareholder (bidder) will be entitled to appraisal rights because it gets a vote on the deal. However, merger sub's shareholder obviously will not exercise these rights because merger sub is controlled by bidder and bidder is in favor of the deal.

b.　DGCL

1.　　　Board Approval

The board approval analysis is the exact same as the board approval analysis for a forward triangular merger. Specifically, § 251(b) requires board approval by target and merger sub but not bidder. Bidder board approval is generally required by agency law and will be insisted on by the parties' attorneys. Additionally, bidder board approval will be required if the deal consideration includes bidder stock because DGCL § 152 requires board approval of a stock issuance.

2.　　　Shareholder Approval

Under the general rule of DGCL § 251(c), both target and merger sub shareholders get to vote on the merger because they are each a "constituent corporation." Bidder is not a constituent corporation, so its shareholder do not get a vote under § 251(c).

Recall that § 251(f) provides an exception to the general rule. The way the general rule plus the exception shakes out for a reverse triangular merger is that target shareholder approval will always be required. This is because the target stock held by target's shareholders will be converted into the deal consideration (most likely cash), and therefore, § 251(f)(2) will not be met. Merger sub's shareholder (bidder) is entitled to vote on the deal because the subsection (f) exception does not apply. Specifically, it only potentially applies to a constituent corporation that survives the deal, and merger sub does not survive. Bidder will obviously vote its shares of merger sub in favor of the deal, so this vote is a non-issue.

The analysis of the quorum and vote requirement under the DGCL for a shareholder vote on a reverse triangular merger is the same as described above for a direct merger.

3.　　　Appraisal Rights

The general rule under DGCL § 262(b) is that target shareholders are entitled to appraisal rights with respect to a reverse triangular merger. Again, there are exceptions to this general rule applicable to public targets and short-form mergers which we discuss later in this book.

Merger sub's shareholder (bidder) will be entitled to appraisal rights because it gets a vote on the deal. However, merger sub's shareholder obviously will not exercise these rights because merger sub is controlled by bidder and bidder is in favor of the deal.

EXERCISE 2.5

Bidder and Target are both private companies incorporated in California. Bidder's issued and outstanding stock consists of 1,000,000 shares of common stock; Target's issued and outstanding stock consists of 10,000 shares of common stock. Bidder is acquiring Target for $5 million in cash in a deal structured as a reverse triangular merger. In that regard, Bidder has incorporated Merger Sub in California for purposes of the deal. Assume that the articles of incorporation and bylaws of Bidder, Merger Sub, and Target simply track the default provisions of the California corporate code.

1.   Which boards need to approve the deal?

2.   (a) Which shareholders need to approve the deal, (b) what is the relevant voting standard, and (c) what is the minimum number of votes required for approval?

3.   Which shareholders have the right to dissent?

4.   Do any of your answers to questions 1 through 3 above change if the deal consideration consists of 220,000 shares of Bidder common stock?

Make sure you explain how you arrived at your answers and provide specific statutory or other cites as support.

6.   Share Exchange (MBCA)

As mentioned in Chapter 1, the MBCA provides for a share exchange but the DGCL does not. Thus, there is only an MBCA discussion below. Note that the analysis under the MBCA for a share exchange is basically the same as a direct merger because, by their terms, mostly the same statutory provisions apply to both forms.

a.   Board Approval

MBCA § 11.04(a) requires board approval by a corporation that "is a party to a . . . share exchange . . . ." In a share exchange, both target and bidder are parties to the share exchange so board approval of both target and bidder is required under § 11.04(a).

b.   Shareholder Approval

MBCA § 11.04(b) provides the general rule that "the board of directors must submit the plan [of share exchange] to the shareholders for their approval." Recall, however, that § 11.04(h) provides an exception to the general rule. The way the general rule plus the exception shakes out is that target shareholder approval will always be required. Specifically, § 11.04(h)(3) will not be met because target shareholders will not "hold the same number of shares, with identical preferences, limitations, and relative rights" that they held before the share exchange (their shares will be converted into the deal consideration per § 11.07(b)). Conversely, bidder shareholders will rarely get a vote on a share exchange unless the deal consideration surpasses the 20 percent threshold of § 6.21(f)(1). Specifically,

§ 11.04(h)(1) is met by definition, and it is generally no problem or concern for bidder and target to structure the deal so that § 11.04(h)(2) and (3) are met. That just leaves § 11.04(h)(4), which incorporates by reference the 20 percent threshold of § 6.21(f)(1) discussed above.

The analysis of the quorum and vote requirement under the MBCA for a shareholder vote on a share exchange is the same as described above for a direct merger.

c. Appraisal Rights

MBCA § 13.02(a)(2) provides the following:

> (a) A shareholder is entitled to appraisal rights, and to obtain payment of the fair value of that shareholder's shares, in the event of any of the following corporate actions:
>
> > (2) consummation of a share exchange to which the corporation is a party as the corporation whose shares will be acquired, except that appraisal rights shall not be available to any shareholder of the corporation with respect to any class or series of shares of the corporation that is not exchanged . . . .

Hence, the general rule is that target shareholders are entitled to appraisal rights in a share exchange because target is "the corporation whose shares will be acquired." There is an exception to this general rule applicable to public targets (we discuss this exception in Chapter 3). Conversely, bidder shareholders will not be entitled to appraisal rights because bidder is not "the corporation whose shares will be acquired."

EXERCISE 2.6

Bidder and Target are both private companies incorporated in Florida. Bidder's issued and outstanding stock consists of 1,000,000 shares of common stock; Target's issued and outstanding stock consists of 10,000 shares of common stock. Bidder is acquiring Target for $5 million in cash in a deal structured as a share exchange. Assume that the articles of incorporation and bylaws of both Bidder and Target simply track the default provisions of the Florida corporate code.

1. Which boards need to approve the deal?

2. (a) Which shareholders need to approve the deal, (b) what is the relevant voting standard, and (c) what is the minimum number of votes required for approval?

3. Which shareholders have the right to dissent?

4. Do any of your answers to questions 1 through 3 above change if the deal consideration consists of 220,000 shares of Bidder common stock?

Make sure you explain how you arrived at your answers and provide specific statutory or other cites as support.

7. More About Appraisal Rights

Below is an excerpt from the proxy statement of Zipcar, Inc. for its stockholder vote on Zipcar's acquisition by Avis Budget. I include this excerpt because it describes the rather technical requirements a stockholder must fulfill under Delaware law to assert appraisal rights. Zipcar included this section in its proxy statement because it was required by DGCL § 262(d)(1) to notify its stockholders that appraisal rights were available for the deal. Furthermore, SEC proxy rules require a proxy statement to "[o]utline briefly the rights of appraisal or similar rights of dissenters with respect to any matter to be acted upon and indicate any statutory procedure required to be followed by dissenting security holders in order to perfect such rights."[24] We discuss SEC proxy rules in Chapter 3.

Notice the excerpt references Annex D. This Annex consists of a copy of DGCL § 262 and was included by Zipcar because DGCL § 262(d)(1) requires a target to provide its shareholders with such a copy.

ZIPCAR, INC.
PROXY STATEMENT
(Feb. 4, 2013)

APPRAISAL RIGHTS

Under Delaware law, holders of shares of common stock who do not vote in favor of the adoption of the merger agreement and who properly demand appraisal of their shares will be entitled to appraisal rights under § 262 of the General Corporation Law of the State of Delaware, or the DGCL. Stockholders electing to exercise appraisal rights must strictly comply with the provisions of § 262 of the DGCL in order to properly demand and perfect their rights.

The following is a brief summary of the material provisions of the Delaware statutory procedures required to be followed by a stockholder in order to properly demand and perfect the stockholder's appraisal rights. This summary, however, is not a complete statement of all applicable requirements and is qualified in its entirety by reference to § 262 of the DGCL. This summary does not constitute legal advice, nor does it constitute a recommendation that our stockholders exercise their appraisal rights under § 262. If you wish to consider exercising your appraisal rights, you should carefully review the text of § 262 contained in Annex D to this proxy statement because failure to timely and properly comply with the requirements of § 262 will result in the loss of your appraisal rights under Delaware law.

Section 262 requires that, where a merger agreement is to be submitted for adoption at a stockholders' meeting, stockholders be notified not less than 20 days before the meeting to vote on the adoption of the merger agreement that appraisal rights will be available. A copy of § 262 must be included with such notice. This proxy statement constitutes notice to our stockholders of the availability of appraisal rights in connection with the merger and a copy of § 262 is attached hereto

---

[24] Securities Exchange Act of 1934, Schedule 14A, Item 3.

as Annex D in compliance with the requirements of § 262.

If you elect to demand appraisal of your shares, you must satisfy all of the following conditions:

(i) You must deliver to us a written demand for appraisal of your shares before the vote is taken on the adoption of the merger agreement at the special meeting. This written demand for appraisal must be in addition to and separate from any proxy or vote abstaining from or voting against the adoption of the merger agreement;

(ii) You must hold of record the shares on the date that the written demand for appraisal is made and must continue to hold the shares of record through the effective time of the merger, since appraisal rights will be lost if the shares are transferred prior to the effective time of the merger. Voting against or failing to vote for the adoption of the merger agreement itself does not constitute a demand for appraisal under § 262;

(iii) You must not vote in favor of the adoption of the merger agreement. A vote in favor of the adoption of the merger agreement, by proxy or in person, will constitute a waiver of your appraisal rights in respect of the shares so voted and will nullify any previously filed written demands for appraisal. A proxy that is signed and does not contain voting instructions will, unless revoked, be voted in favor of the adoption of the merger agreement, and it will constitute a waiver of the stockholder's right of appraisal and will nullify any previously delivered written demand for appraisal. Therefore, a stockholder who votes by proxy and who wishes to exercise appraisal rights must vote against the adoption of the merger agreement or abstain from voting on the merger agreement; and

(iv) You or the surviving corporation must file a petition in the Delaware Court of Chancery requesting a determination of the fair value of the shares within 120 days after the effective time of the merger. The surviving corporation is under no obligation to file any such petition in the Delaware Court of Chancery and has no intention of doing so.

If you fail to comply with any of these conditions, and the merger is completed, you will be entitled to receive the cash payment for your shares of common stock as provided for in the merger agreement, but will have no appraisal rights with respect to your shares.

All demands for appraisal should be addressed to Zipcar, Inc., Secretary, 25 First Street, 4th Floor, Cambridge, MA 02141, should be delivered before the vote on the adoption of the merger agreement is taken at the special meeting and should be executed by, or on behalf of, the record holder of the shares. The demand must reasonably inform us of the identity of the stockholder and the intention of the stockholder to demand appraisal of his, her or its shares.

To be effective, a demand for appraisal by a stockholder must be made by, or in the name of, such record stockholder, fully and correctly, as the stockholder's name appears on his or her stock certificate(s) and cannot be made by the beneficial owner if he or she does not also hold the shares of record. The beneficial owner must, in such cases, have the record holder submit the required demand in respect of such shares.

If shares are held of record in a fiduciary capacity, such as by a trustee, guardian or custodian, execution of a demand for appraisal should be made in such capacity; and if the shares are held of record by more than one person, as in a joint tenancy or tenancy in common, the demand should be executed by or for all joint owners. An authorized agent, including an authorized agent for two or more joint owners, may execute the demand for appraisal for a stockholder of record; however, the agent must identify the record holder or holders and expressly disclose the fact that, in executing the demand, he or she is acting as agent for the record holder. A record holder, such as a broker, who holds shares as a nominee for others, may exercise his, her or its right of appraisal with respect to the shares held for one or more beneficial owners, while not exercising this right for other beneficial owners. In such case, the written demand should state the number of shares as to which appraisal is sought. Where no number of shares is expressly mentioned, the demand will be presumed to cover all shares held in the name of such record holder.

If you hold your shares in a brokerage or bank account or in other nominee form and you wish to exercise appraisal rights, you should consult with your broker or bank or such other nominee to determine the appropriate procedures for the making of a demand for appraisal by such nominee.

Within 10 days after the effective time of the merger, the surviving corporation must give written notice of the effective time of the merger to each stockholder who has properly submitted a written demand for appraisal and who did not vote in favor of the adoption of the merger agreement. Within 120 days after the effective time of the merger, either the surviving corporation or any stockholder who has complied with the requirements of § 262 may file a petition in the Delaware Court of Chancery demanding a determination of the fair value of the shares held by all stockholders entitled to appraisal. The surviving corporation has no obligation (and has no present intention) to file such a petition in the event there are dissenting stockholders. Accordingly, the failure of a stockholder to file such a petition within the period specified could nullify such stockholder's previous written demand for appraisal.

Within 120 days after the effective time of the merger, any stockholder who has complied with § 262 will be entitled, upon written request, to receive a statement setting forth the aggregate number of shares of common stock not voted in favor of the adoption of the merger agreement and with respect to which demands for appraisal have been received and the aggregate number of holders of such shares. The statement must be mailed within 10 days after a written request therefor has been received by the surviving corporation, or within 10 days after the expiration of the period for delivery of demands for appraisal, whichever is later. A person who is the beneficial owner of shares of common stock held either in a voting trust or by a nominee on behalf of such person may, in such person's own name, file a petition or may request from us the statement described in this paragraph.

If a petition for appraisal is duly filed by a stockholder and a copy of the petition is delivered to the surviving corporation, the surviving corporation will then be obligated within 20 days after receiving service of a copy of the petition to file in the office of the Register in Chancery a duly verified list containing the names and addresses of all stockholders who have demanded an appraisal of their shares and with whom agreements as to the value of their shares has not been reached by the surviving corporation. After notice to stockholders who have demanded an appraisal of their shares, the Chancery Court is empowered to conduct a hearing upon the petition, to determine those stockholders who have complied with § 262 and who have become entitled to the appraisal rights provided thereby. The Chancery Court may require the stockholders who have demanded payment for their shares to submit their stock certificates to the Register in Chancery for notation thereon of the pendency of the appraisal proceedings; and if any stockholder fails to comply with such direction, the Chancery Court may dismiss the proceedings as to such stockholder.

After determination of the stockholders entitled to appraisal of their shares, the Chancery Court will appraise the shares, determining their fair value exclusive of any element of value arising from the accomplishment or expectation of the merger, together with interest, if any, to be paid upon the amount determined to be the fair value. Unless the Court in its discretion determines otherwise for good cause shown, interest from the effective date of the merger through the date of payment of the judgment shall be compounded quarterly and shall accrue at 5% over the Federal Reserve discount rate (including any surcharge) as established from time to time during the period between the effective date of the merger and the date of payment of the judgment. When the value is determined the Chancery Court will direct the payment of such value, with interest thereon accrued during the pendency of the proceeding, to the stockholders entitled to receive the same, upon surrender by such holders of the certificates representing such shares.

In determining fair value, the Chancery Court is required to take into account all relevant factors. In *Weinberger v. UOP, Inc.*, the Supreme Court of Delaware discussed the factors that could be considered in determining fair value in an appraisal proceeding, stating that "proof of value by any techniques or methods that are generally considered acceptable in the financial community and otherwise admissible in court" should be considered, and that "fair price obviously requires consideration of all relevant factors involving the value of a company." The Delaware Supreme Court stated that, in making this determination of fair value, the court must consider market value, asset value, dividends, earnings prospects, the nature of the enterprise and any other facts that could be ascertained as of the date of the merger that throw any light on future prospects of the merged corporation. Section 262 provides that fair value is to be "exclusive of any element of value arising from the accomplishment or expectation of the merger." In *Cede & Co. v. Technicolor, Inc.*, the Delaware Supreme Court stated that such exclusion is a "narrow exclusion [that] does not encompass known elements of value," but which rather applies only to the speculative elements of value arising from such accomplishment or expecta-tion. In *Weinberger*, the Supreme Court of Delaware also stated that "elements of future value, including without limitation the nature of the enterprise, which are known or susceptible of proof as of the date of the merger and not the product of speculation, may be considered."

Stockholders considering seeking appraisal should be aware that the fair value of their shares as so determined could be more than, the same as or less than the consideration they would receive pursuant to the merger agreement if they did not seek appraisal of their shares and that an investment banking opinion as to fairness from a financial point of view is not necessarily an opinion as to fair value under § 262. Although the company believes that the merger consideration is fair, no representation is made as to the outcome of the appraisal of fair value as determined by the Chancery Court, and stockholders should recognize that such an appraisal could result in a determination of a value higher or lower than, or the same as, the merger consideration. The company does not anticipate offering more than the applicable merger consideration to any stockholder of the company exercising appraisal rights, and reserves the right to assert, in any appraisal proceeding, that for purposes of § 262, the "fair value" of a share of common stock of the company is less than the applicable consideration pursuant to the merger agreement, and that the methods which are generally considered acceptable in the financial community and otherwise admissible in court should be considered in the appraisal proceedings. In addition, Delaware courts have decided that the statutory appraisal remedy, depending on factual circumstances, may or may not be a dissenter's exclusive remedy. If a petition for appraisal is not timely filed, then the right to an appraisal will cease. The costs of the action (which do not include attorneys' fees and the fees and expenses of experts) may be determined by the Court and taxed upon the parties as the Court deems equitable under the circumstances. The Court may also order that all or a portion of the expenses incurred by a stockholder in connection with an appraisal, including without limitation reasonable attorneys' fees and the fees and expenses of experts utilized in the appraisal proceeding, be charged pro rata against the value of all the shares entitled to be appraised.

If any stockholder who demands appraisal of shares of our common stock under § 262 fails to perfect, or successfully withdraws the demand or loses, such holder's right to appraisal, the stockholder's shares of common stock will be deemed to have been converted at the effective time of the transaction into the right to receive the merger consideration. A stockholder will fail to perfect, or effectively lose or withdraw, the holder's right to appraisal if, among other things, no petition for appraisal is filed within 120 days after the effective time of the merger or if the stockholder delivers to the surviving corporation a written withdrawal of the holder's demand for appraisal and an acceptance of the merger in accordance with § 262.

Any stockholder who has duly demanded an appraisal in compliance with § 262 will not, after the effective time of the merger, be entitled to vote the shares subject to that demand for any purpose or be entitled to the payment of dividends or other distributions on those shares (except dividends or other distributions payable to holders of record of shares as of a record date before the effective time of the merger).

At any time within 60 days after the effective date of the merger, any stockholder who has not commenced an appraisal proceeding or joined that proceeding as a named party may withdraw his, her or its demand for appraisal and accept the merger consideration by delivering to the surviving corporation a written withdrawal of the stockholder's demand for appraisal. However, any such attempt to withdraw made more than 60 days after the effective date of the merger will require written approval of the surviving corporation. No appraisal proceeding in the Delaware Court of Chancery will be dismissed as to any stockholder without the approval of the Delaware Court of Chancery, and such approval may be conditioned upon such terms as the Delaware Court of Chancery deems just; provided, however, that any stockholder who has not commenced an appraisal proceeding or joined that proceeding as a named party may withdraw its demand for appraisal and accept the merger consideration offered pursuant to the merger agreement within 60 days after the effective date of the merger. If the surviving corporation does not approve a stockholder's request to withdraw a demand for appraisal when that approval is required or, except with respect to a stockholder that withdraws its right to appraisal in accordance with the proviso in the immediately preceding sentence, if the Delaware Court of Chancery does not approve the dismissal of an appraisal proceeding, the stockholder would be entitled to receive only the appraised value determined in any such appraisal proceeding, which value could be more than, the same as or less than the value of the consideration being offered pursuant to the merger agreement.

Failure to comply strictly with all of the procedures set forth in § 262 will result in the loss of a stockholder's statutory appraisal rights. Consequently, any stockholder wishing to exercise appraisal rights is urged to consult legal counsel before attempting to exercise those rights.

The next case discusses various factors a court may and may not take into account in determining fair value in an appraisal proceeding.

PASKILL CORP. v. ALCOMA CORP.
Delaware Supreme Court
747 A.2d 549 (2000)

HOLLAND, JUSTICE:

This appeal relates to a stock appraisal proceeding that was initiated in the Court of Chancery by the petitioner-appellant, Paskill Corporation ("Paskill"), a 14.6% minority shareholder of Okeechobee, Inc. ("Okeechobee"), a Delaware corporation. The impetus for Paskill's petition for an appraisal was Okeechobee's merger with and into Okeechobee, LLC, a Delaware limited liability company wholly owned by Alcoma Corporation ("Alcoma"). Prior to the merger, Alcoma owned approximately 54% of Okeechobee's outstanding stock.

The Court of Chancery determined the fair value of the Okeechobee stock at the time of the merger was $10,049 per share. Paskill contended that the fair value was $13,206 per share. Alcoma argued the fair value was $9,420 per share.

Both sides have appealed from the final judgment that was entered in the appraisal proceeding. Paskill contends that the Court of Chancery's appraisal methodology erroneously included the "speculative" future tax liability that Alcoma attributed to the appreciation of Okeechobee's assets. Alcoma contends that the Court of Chancery's appraisal determination erroneously excluded its estimate of future expenses that would be incurred if and when Okeechobee's appreciated assets were ever sold. . . .

We have concluded that in making its appraisal, the Court of Chancery erroneously valued Okeechobee on a liquidation basis and exacerbated that problem when it calculated Okeechobee's net asset value by deducting speculative future tax liabilities. We have also decided that the Court of Chancery correctly excluded speculative expenses associated with uncontemplated sales when it attempted to compute Okeechobee's net asset value . . . .

Facts

On November 12, 1997, Okeechobee, was merged into a wholly-owned subsidiary of Alcoma Corporation. Alcoma is wholly-owned by The Heckscher Foundation for Children, Inc., a not-for-profit corporation. Immediately prior to the merger, Alcoma held 54%, and Paskill's ownership constituted 14%, of the outstanding stock of Okeechobee.

The Okeechobee stockholders were advised that, pursuant to the proposed Okeechobee/Alcoma merger, the minority stockholders of Okeechobee would receive in cash the "net asset value" of their stock and that Alcoma would receive "the equivalent per-share amount but in kind — the remaining assets after the cash paid to the minority shareholders." Alcoma described how it would calculate "net asset value":

> The net asset value would be determined by valuing the marketable stocks and bonds held by Okeechobee at their trading values on the New York Stock Exchange (or other public markets in which such securities are traded) shortly prior to the effective date of the merger. Any mortgages held by Okeechobee would be valued at full face value. The real estate of Okeechobee would be valued by an independent qualified real estate appraiser. The total of such assets at their fair market values would then be reduced by the liabilities of Okeechobee, *including capital gains tax that would be paid on the unrealized appreciation when such appreciation is realized.* Thus, the full fair market values of the net assets of Okeechobee as described above would be reflected by the net asset value of the shares. (emphasis added).

A special meeting of the stockholders of Okeechobee was held on November 6, 1997, to vote upon the proposed Okeechobee/Alcoma merger. Prior to the vote on the proposed merger, Paskill delivered a written demand for an appraisal of its shares pursuant to 8 *Del. C.* § 262(d)(1) of the Delaware General Corporation Law. Paskill voted its 140.625 shares against the proposed merger. Nevertheless, the merger was approved. Thereafter, Paskill perfected its right to appraisal under Section 262.

In a notice dated November 6, 1997, the Okeechobee's minority stockholder's shares were valued at $9,480.50 per share. The calculation of net asset value was set forth in a "Consolidated Statement of Net Assets" which was attached to the November 6 notice.

According to that Consolidated Statement, Okeechobee had "assets" of $256,909 and "investments" of $7,402,114. The investments were: marketable securities consisting of stock and cash equivalents equal to $5,670,878; an operating parking garage in New York City valued at $6,270,000; unimproved land in Florida valued at $34,100; and a mortgage receivable relating to a Nashua, New Hampshire property valued at $1,098.014. The total value of the two properties and the mortgage receivable as of the valuation date was $7,402,114. The total value of Okeechobee's assets and investments equaled $13,329,901.

According to the same Consolidated Statement of Net Assets, Okeechobee had two liabilities as of the valuation date. Those liabilities consisted of "taxes payable-current" of $87,000 and "accrued expenses-operations" of $36,706. In addition to these two liabilities, Alcoma deducted "additional expenses" that totaled $3,725,700 and consisted of: $568,700 for the "estimated closing costs on sales-commissions, environmental issues, legal, etc." regarding the sale of the New York parking garage and unimproved land in Florida; $569,000 for the "deferred federal, state and other taxes" on the estimated unrealized capital gain on the securities held by Okeechobee; $2,338,000 for the "deferred taxes" on the estimated unrealized gain on the New York City parking garage; $240,000, for the "deferred taxes" on the mortgage receivable; and $10,000 for the "deferred taxes" on the unimproved land in Florida.

Court of Chancery

The Court of Chancery appraised Okeechobee exclusively on the basis of its net asset value. At the time of its merger with Alcoma, Okeechobee's investment assets were not for sale. Under those circumstances, the Court of Chancery determined that Alcoma's deduction of the estimated expenses that Alcoma attributed to those uncontemplated sales of appreciated investment assets was improper. Nevertheless, the Court of Chancery held that it was appropriate to compute Okeechobee's net asset value by deducting the estimated future tax liabilities attributed to those uncontemplated asset sales on the basis of the investment assets' appreciated value. The Court of Chancery distinguished its *allowance* of deductions for possible future tax liabilities from its *disallowance* of deductions for possible future sales expenses as follows:

> First, sales expenses occur only when and if sale of an asset occurs. They are not an accrued, deferred liability such as capital gains tax. Sales expenses represent transaction costs associated with one possible use of an investment. It is a cost difficult to quantify because the seller may be able to reduce or eliminate the expenses. Okeechobee's investments were not sold, but retained by its acquirer at the time of the merger; therefore, sales expenses had not been incurred and the minority shareholders should not front a portion of a cost that might (or might not) be incurred down the road. Instead, the minority are entitled to shareholders' *pro rata* share of the assets' value as a held investment.

The record reflects that a sale of its appreciated investment assets was not part of Okeechobee's operative reality on the date of the merger. Therefore, the Court of Chancery should have excluded any deduction for the speculative future tax liabilities that were attributed by Alcoma to those uncontemplated sales. Conversely, the Court of Chancery properly denied any deduction from Okeechobee's net asset value for speculative expenses relating to future sales that were not contemplated on the date of the merger. The Court of Chancery erred by attempting to appraise Okeechobee exclusively on the basis of its net asset value, however, even if Okeechobee's net asset value had been calculated correctly. Our reasoning is set forth in the balance of this opinion.

Appraisal in Delaware

An appraisal proceeding is a limited statutory remedy. Its legislative purpose is to provide equitable relief for shareholders dissenting from a merger on grounds of inadequacy of the offering price. Several eminent legal scholars have developed theories in an attempt to explain appraisal statutes. The most recent is Professor Peter Letsou's "preference reconciliation" theory of appraisal,[25] which he explains as follows:

> . . . when shareholders lack effective access to capital markets, risk-altering transactions (particularly those that alter the firm's market risk) can make some shareholders better off while leaving others worse off. Appraisal rights require the corporation to compensate shareholders who may be harmed by such transactions and place the net costs of providing that compensation on shareholders who otherwise gain. As a result, shareholders who otherwise gain from appraisal-triggering transactions will only vote in favor of those transactions if their gains more than offset the net costs of compensating objectors. Appraisal rights therefore decrease the probability of risk-altering transactions that result in net losses to shareholders, causing *all* shares to trade at higher prices *ex ante*.[26]

The Delaware appraisal statute affords dissenting minority stockholders the right to a judicial determination of the fair value of their shareholdings. The statutory mandate directs the Court of Chancery to determine the value of the shares that qualify for appraisal by:

> determining their fair value, exclusive of any element of value arising from the accomplishment or expectation of the merger or consolidation, together with a fair rate of interest, if any, to be paid upon the amount determined to be the fair value. In determining such fair value, the Court shall take into account all relevant factors.[27]

In *Tri-Continental Corp. v. Battye*,[28] this Court explained the concept of value contemplated by the statutory mandate:

> that the stockholder is entitled to be paid for that which has been taken from him, *viz.*, his proportionate interest in a going concern. By value of the

---

[25] [n.6] Peter V. Letsou, *The Role of Appraisal in Corporate Law*, 39 B.C.L.Rev. 1121 (1998).

[26] [n.7] *Id.* at 1123–24 (citations omitted).

[27] [n.9] 8 Del. C. § 262(h).

[28] [n.10] Tri-Continental Corp. v. Battye, Del. Supr., 74 A.2d 71 (1950).

stockholder's proportionate interest in the corporate enterprise is meant the true or intrinsic value of his stock which has been taken by the merger.

The underlying assumption in an appraisal valuation is that the dissenting shareholders would be willing to maintain their investment position had the merger not occurred. Consequently, this Court has held that the corporation must be valued as an operating entity. Accordingly, the Court of Chancery's task in an appraisal proceeding is to value what has been taken from the shareholder, i.e., the proportionate interest in the going concern.

Alcoma's Liquidation Argument

In the briefs filed with this Court, Alcoma contends that its proposed net asset valuation constituted the fair value appraisal of Okeechobee's shares because the minority shareholders received "precisely the *same* value as [they] would" if "Okeechobee could have sold all of its assets, paid the applicable tax on the appreciation realized on the sale, and distributed the net cash proceeds after taxes to all shareholders." Alcoma's argument demonstrates a fundamental misunderstanding of Delaware's appraisal jurisprudence. It also conclusively establishes that the Court of Chancery did not properly determine the fair value of Paskill's shares in Okeechobee as a going concern.

Liquidation Value Prohibited

In *Tri-Continental*, the phrase "net asset value" was defined as "simply a mathematical figure representing the total value of the assets of [the corporation] less the prior claims."[29] Accordingly, in *Tri-Continental*, this Court characterized "net asset value" as the "theoretical liquidating value to which the share would be entitled upon the company going out of business."[30] In footnote 2, we acknowledged that theoretical liquidating net asset value could never be obtained in an actual liquidation because of the attendant expenses, *e.g.*, sales costs and taxes.

The seminal importance of *Tri-Continental* is readily apparent fifty years later when the principles it established are applied to the appraisal case *sub judice*. First, "the value of dissenting stock is to be fixed on a going concern basis."[31] Second, "the basic concept of value under the appraisal statute is that the stockholder is entitled to be paid for what has been taken from him, *viz*, his proportionate interest in a going concern."[32] Third, "net asset value is a **theoretical** liquidating value to which the share would be entitled upon the company going out of business."[33] Fourth, because "the value of dissenting stock is to be fixed on a going concern basis, the taking of the net asset value as the appraisal value of the stock is obviously

---

[29] [n.14] Tri-Continental Corp. v. Battye, Del. Supr. 74 A.2d at 74.

[30] [n.15] *Id.*

[31] [n.16] *Id.*

[32] [n.17] *Id.* at 72.

[33] [n.19] *Id.* at 74 (emphasis added).

precluded by the [going-concern] rule."[34] Fifth, since "net asset value is, in reality, a liquidating value, it cannot be made the *sole* criterion of the measure of the value of the dissenting stock."[35]

The Court of Chancery erred, as a matter of law, by relying upon the net asset value as the *sole* criterion for determining the fair value of Okeechobee's stock. It compounded that error when it deducted the speculative future tax liabilities from its net asset value calculation. That deduction was inconsistent with the theoretical nature of the liquidating value that this Court ascribed to the term "net asset value" in *Tri-Continental* and converted Okeechobee's theoretical net asset value into an actual liquidation value. Since it is impermissible to appraise a corporation on the sole basis of its theoretical liquidation net asset value, *a fortiori*, a statutory appraisal can never be made solely on the basis of an actual liquidation net asset value.

Nature of Enterprise

The dissenter in an appraisal action is entitled to receive a proportionate share of fair value in the *going concern* on the date of the merger, rather than value that is determined on a liquidated basis. Therefore, the corporation must first be valued as an operating entity. Consequently, one of the most important factors to consider is the "nature of the enterprise" that is the subject of the appraisal proceeding.

According to Alcoma, Okeechobee was a closed-end investment company. We have assumed the *bona fides* of that contention for the purposes of this appeal. In *Tri-Continental*, one of Delaware's seminal appraisal cases, this Court considered the valuation of a regulated closed-end investment company with leverage that was engaged in the business of investing in a cross-section of the stock market.

Tri-Continental was decided at a time when the Delaware Block Method was the exclusive basis for calculating the value of a corporation in an appraisal proceeding. "The Delaware Block Method actually is a combination of three generally accepted methods for valuation: the asset approach, the market approach, and the earnings approach."[36] Under the Delaware Block Method, the asset, market and earnings approach are each used separately to calculate a value for the entire corporation. A percentage weight is then assigned those three valuations on the basis of each approach's significance to the nature of the subject corporation's business. The appraised value of the corporation is then determined by the weighted average of the *three* valuations.

In *Tri-Continental*, this Court held that in determining what figure represents this true or intrinsic value of the corporation being appraised, the Court of Chancery:

> must take into consideration all factors and elements which reasonably might enter into the fixing of value. Thus, market value, asset value,

---

[34] [n.20] *Id.* at 74.

[35] [n.21] *Id.* at 75.

[36] [n.27] In re Radiology Assocs. Inc. Lit., Del. Ch., 611 A.2d 485, 496 (1991).

dividends, earning prospects, the nature of the enterprise, and any other facts which were known or which could be ascertained as of the date of merger and which throw any light on future prospects of the merged corporation are not only pertinent to an inquiry as to the value of the dissenting stockholders' interest, but must be considered by the agency fixing the value.[37]

That holding has become one of the bedrock principles of Delaware's appraisal jurisprudence over the last fifty years.

In *Tri-Continental*, the factors and elements taken into consideration by the statutory appraiser were: "the nature of the enterprise, i.e., a regulated closed-end investment company; leverage; discount; net asset value; market value; management; earnings and dividends; expenses of operation; particular holdings in the [corporation's] portfolio; and a favorable tax situation."[38] The appraiser found that under the circumstances presented, the factors of management, earnings and dividends, expenses of operation, and the portfolio of the corporation did not merit being debited or credited in arriving at a value for the common stock. The appraiser also found there was no actual market for the corporation's stock at the time of the merger.

Consequently, in *Tri-Continental*, the appraiser focused on the corporation's assets. This Court used three terms to describe that focus: net asset value, full asset value, and fair asset value. We held that the *net* asset value could not be the sole measure of the corporation's common stocks value. We also recognized that "the *full* value of the corporation's assets is not the same as the value of those assets to the common shareholder" because "discount is an element of value which must be given independent effect in the valuing of the common stock of regulated closed-end investment companies."[39] Therefore, given our recognition of the net asset value and the full asset value as polar extremes, this Court approved the appraiser's construction of a "fair asset value" at an intermediate level that included several elements of value over and above the net asset value. This Court then upheld the appraiser's use of Delaware Block Method to value the common stock by applying a discount to that fair asset value.

Methodology Based Corporate Level Discount

The combined argot of law and economics requires periodic explication. *Tri-Continental* has been construed by this Court as standing for the proposition that an appraisal valuation must take into consideration the unique nature of the enterprise. In *Tri-Continental*, this Court held that the Court of Chancery had the authority to discount asset values at the corporate level, in appropriate circumstances, as a means of establishing the fair value of the entire corporation as a going concern. Read in the proper context, *Tri-Continental* was an acknowledgment that the Court of Chancery was vested with the authority to make a discount of the

---

[37] [n.30] Tri-Continental Corp. v. Battye, 74 A.2d at 73.

[38] [n.32] *Id.*

[39] [n.37] *Id.* at 76.

subject corporation's fair asset value at the corporate level because it constituted a proper application of an accepted methodology for arriving at the proper valuation of the unique corporate enterprise, *i.e.*, in *Tri-Continental*, the Delaware Block Method was applied to value a regulated closed-end investment company with leverage that was engaged in investing in a cross-section of the stock market. Similarly, this Court recently upheld the Court of Chancery's conclusion that a corporate level comparative acquisition approach to valuing a company, which included a control premium for a majority interest in a subsidiary, was a relevant and reliable methodology to use in an appraisal proceeding to determine the fair market value of shares in a holding company.

Once the entire corporation has been fairly valued as an operating entity, however, the Delaware appraisal process requires the Court of Chancery to determine the fair value that has been taken from the dissenting shareholder who was forced out of the corporate enterprise, i.e., a proportionate interest in the entire going concern. In *Weinberger*, this Court broadened the process for determining the "fair value" of the company's outstanding shares by including all generally accepted techniques of valuation used in the financial community. As a result of that holding in *Weinberger*, the standard "Delaware block" or weighted average method of valuation, formerly employed in appraisal valuation cases, no longer exclusively controls such proceedings. . . .

In arguing that its liquidated valuation was fair, Alcoma noted that it did not seek a reduction for "the discount normally applied to unmarketable shares not registered with the Securities and Exchange Commission or traded on any public market."[40] Such a discount would have constituted an improper discount at the shareholder level.

Upon remand, the Court of Chancery must ascertain the exact nature of Okeechobee as an enterprise. It must then determine Okeechobee's fair value as a going concern on the date of the merger by any admissible valuation technique that is based on reliable and relevant record evidence. Paskill is then entitled to receive the fair value of its proportionate interest in that operating entity at the time of the merger without any discount at the shareholder level.

QUESTIONS

1. What's the deal involved in this case? How was the deal structured? What was the deal consideration?

2. Who is Paskill Corp.?

3. What's the legal issue in the case? What does the court decide on the issue?

---

[40] [n.49] There was no discount at the shareholder level in *Tri-Continental* even though this Court acknowledged that there was no actual market for the common stock of the corporation that was being appraised. Tri-Continental Corp. v. Battye, Del. Supr., 74 A.2d 71, 74 (1950).

4.   What did the lower court do wrong?

MBCA § 13.01(4) defines "fair value" for purposes of appraisal rights as follows:

(4) "Fair value" means the value of the corporation's shares determined:

(i)   immediately before the effectuation of the corporate action to which the shareholder objects;

(ii) using customary and current valuation concepts and techniques generally employed for similar businesses in the context of the transaction requiring appraisal; and

(iii) without discounting for lack of marketability or minority status except, if appropriate, for amendments to the articles pursuant to § 13.02(a)(5).

Here is what the official comment has to say about the definition:

Subsection (i) of the definition of "fair value" in § 13.01(4) makes clear that fair value is to be determined immediately before the effectuation of the corporate action, rather than, as is the case under most state statutes that address the issue, the date of the shareholders' vote. This comports with the purpose of this chapter to preserve the shareholder's prior rights as a shareholder until the effective date of the corporate action, rather than leaving the shareholder in an ambiguous state with neither rights as a shareholder nor perfected appraisal rights. The corporation and, as relevant, its shares are valued as they exist immediately before the effectuation of the corporate action requiring appraisal. Accordingly, § 13.01(4) permits consideration of changes in the market price of the corporation's shares in anticipation of the transaction, to the extent such changes are relevant. . . .

The definition of "fair value" in § 13.01(4) makes several changes from the prior version. The 1984 Model Act's definition of "fair value" was silent on how fair value was to be determined, except for a concluding clause that excluded from the valuation "any appreciation or depreciation in anticipation of the corporate action, unless exclusion would be inequitable." The Official Comment provided that the section left to the courts "the details by which 'fair value' is to be determined within the broad outlines of the definition." While the logic of the prior Official Comment continues to apply, the exclusionary clause in the prior Model Act definition, including the qualification for cases where the exclusion would be inequitable, has been deleted. Those provisions have not been susceptible to meaningful judicial interpretation and have been set aside in favor of the broader concept in subsection (ii).

The new formulation in paragraph (ii), which is patterned on § 7.22 of the Principles of Corporate Governance promulgated by the American Law Institute, directs courts to keep the methodology chosen in appraisal proceedings consistent with evolving economic concepts and adopts that part of § 7.22 which provides that fair value should be determined using "customary valuation concepts and techniques generally employed for similar businesses in the context of the transaction requiring appraisal." Subsection (ii) adopts the accepted view that different transactions and different contexts may warrant different valuation methodologies. Customary valuation concepts and techniques will typically take into account numerous relevant factors, including assigning a higher valuation to corporate assets that would be more productive if acquired in a comparable transaction but excluding any element of value attributable to the unique synergies of the actual purchaser of the corporation or its assets. For example, if the corporation's assets include undeveloped real estate that is located in a prime commercial area, the court should consider the value that would be attributed to the real estate as commercial development property in a comparable transaction. The court should not, however, assign any additional value based upon the specific plans or special use of the actual purchaser.

Modern valuation methods will normally result in a range of values, not a particular single value. When a transaction falls within that range, "fair value" has been established. Absent unusual circumstances, it is expected that the consideration in an arm's-length transaction will fall within the range of "fair value" for purposes of § 13.01(4). Section 7.22 of the ALI Principles of Corporate Governance also provides that in situations that do not involve certain types of specified conflicts of interest, "the aggregate price accepted by the board of directors of the subject corporation should be presumed to represent the fair value of the corporation, or of the assets sold in the case of an asset sale, unless the plaintiff can prove otherwise by clear and convincing evidence." That presumption has not been included in the definition of "fair value" in § 13.01(4) because the framework of defined types of conflict transactions which is a predicate for the ALI's presumption is not contained in the Model Act. Nonetheless, under § 13.01(4), a court determining fair value should give great deference to the aggregate consideration accepted or approved by a disinterested board of directors for an appraisal triggering transaction.

Subsection (iii) of the definition of "fair value" establishes that valuation discounts for lack of marketability or minority status are inappropriate in most appraisal actions, both because most transactions that trigger appraisal rights affect the corporation as a whole and because such discounts give the majority the opportunity to take advantage of minority shareholders who have been forced against their will to accept the appraisal-triggering transaction.

Subsection (iii), in conjunction with the lead-in language to the definition, is also designed to adopt the more modern view that appraisal should generally award a shareholder his or her proportional interest in the corporation after valuing the corporation as a whole, rather than the value of the shareholder's shares when valued alone. If, however, the corporation voluntarily grants appraisal rights for transactions that do not affect the entire corporation — such as certain amendments to the articles of incorporation — the court should use its discretion in applying discounts if appropriate. . . .

8. Class Voting

The issue of class voting arises when a corporation has more than one class or series of stock outstanding. For instance, a corporation may have common stock and multiple series of preferred stock outstanding. When it comes to an M&A transaction in which the shareholders get a vote, this sort of capital structure raises the issue of whether all shares vote together as a single class or whether one or more types of shares gets to vote as a separate class. For example, say Target, Inc., a Delaware corporation, has the following shares of stock outstanding:

Type of Stock	Shares Outstanding
Common Stock	1,000,000
Series A Preferred Stock	200,000
Series B Preferred Stock	100,000

Figuring out whether all 1,300,000 shares vote together as a single class and whether common, Series A, or Series B gets a separate vote depends on what the corporation's charter says with respect to voting.

For example, let's assume Target's charter is silent on voting rights with respect to the Common Stock (thus by default Common gets one vote per share), states that Series A gets one vote per share and votes with Common as a single class, and states that Series B gets one vote per share and votes as a separate class. Now let's say Target is putting the sale of all of its assets to a vote of its shareholders. Under DGCL § 271, approval of the sale requires an affirmative vote "by holders of a majority of the outstanding stock of the corporation entitled to vote thereon . . . ."[41] This means that the Common, Series A, and Series B would vote as a single class on the sale and of those 1,300,000 shares, at least 650,001 would have to vote in favor of the sale. But that is not the end of the story. A class consisting of Common and Series A would also have to approve the sale because Target's charter says Common and Series A get a separate class vote. Thus, a majority of a quorum of the shares of Common and Series A combined would have to vote in favor of the sale.[42] Finally, Series B would also have to approve the sale because Target's charter says Series B votes as a separate class. Thus, a majority of a quorum of shares of Series B would have to vote in favor of the sale.[43] In other words, there would be three separate votes on the sale, and it would have to carry all three votes to be approved. The need for three votes comes from the language of Target's charter. If it had instead said that Common, Series A, and Series B vote together on all matters as a single class, only one vote (the first one I mentioned) would have been required.

---

[41] DGCL § 271(a).

[42] *See* DGCL § 216(4).

[43] *See id.*

Note that the MBCA refers to what I've been calling, and most lawyers call, "class voting" as "voting by a voting group."[44] MBCA § 1.40(26) defines "voting group" as "all shares of one or more classes or series that under the articles of incorporation or this Act are entitled to vote and be counted together collectively on a matter at a meeting of shareholders."

EXERCISE 2.7

Bidder and Target are both private companies incorporated in Iowa. Bidder's issued and outstanding stock consists of 1,000,000 shares of common stock and 100,000 shares of Series A Preferred Stock. Here is the relevant provision from Bidder's articles of incorporation regarding its capital structure:

3. The total number of shares of capital stock which Bidder has authority to issue is 10,100,000, comprised of 10,000,000 shares of common stock having a par value of $0.01 per share and 100,000 shares of Series A Preferred Stock having a par value of $0.01 per share (the "Series A Preferred"). Each share of Series A Preferred has the following preferences and rights:

(a) Dividends. The holders of the Series A Preferred are entitled to receive preferred dividends in the amount of $50.00 per share annually before any dividends shall be payable on any other class of stock. Dividends on the Series A Preferred shall be cumulative (regardless of whether they were declared or whether the Corporation was legally allowed to pay any dividends).

(b) Voting. The holders of outstanding Series A Preferred shall be entitled to vote with the common stock as a single voting group upon any matter submitted to the shareholders for a vote. Each share of Series A Preferred shall be entitled to 1,000 votes.

Target's issued and outstanding stock consists of 10,000 shares of common stock, 1,000 shares of Series A Preferred Stock, and 500 shares of Series B Preferred Stock. Here is the relevant provision from Target's articles of incorporation regarding its capital structure:

3. The total number of shares of capital stock which Target shall have authority to issue is 1,002,000, comprised of 1,000,000 shares of common stock having a par value of $0.01 per share, 1,000 shares of Series A Preferred Stock having a par value of $0.01 per share (the "Series A Preferred"), and 1,000 shares of Series B Preferred Stock having a par value of $0.01 per share (the "Series B Preferred").

(a) Each share of Series A Preferred has the following preferences and rights:

(i) Dividends. The holders of outstanding Series A Preferred shall be entitled to receive in each year cumulative dividends in cash at a rate per share of $1.00.

---

[44] *See* MBCA §§ 7.25 and 7.26.

(ii) Liquidation Preference. Upon any voluntary or involuntary liquidation, dissolution or other winding up of the affairs of the Corporation, before any distribution or payment shall be made to the holders of Common Stock, the holders of the Series A Preferred shall be entitled to be paid, to the extent possible in cash, $10.00 per share.

(iii) Voting. The holders of outstanding Series A Preferred shall be entitled to vote with the common stock as a single voting group upon any matter submitted to the shareholders for a vote. Each share of Series A Preferred shall be entitled to three votes.

(b) Each share of Series B Preferred has the following preferences and rights:

(i) Dividends. The holders of outstanding Series B Preferred shall be entitled to receive in each year cumulative dividends in cash at a rate per share of $3.00.

(ii) Voting. The holders of outstanding Series B Preferred shall be entitled to vote upon any matter submitted to the shareholders for a vote as a separate voting group. Each share of Series B Preferred shall be entitled to one vote.

Bidder is acquiring Target for 100,000 shares of non-voting Bidder Series B preferred stock, each share of which will be convertible into three shares of Bidder common stock at the option of the holder. The deal will be structured as a forward triangular merger. Bidder has incorporated Merger Sub in Iowa for purposes of the deal. Assume that the articles of incorporation and bylaws of Bidder, Target, and Merger Sub simply track the default provisions of the Iowa corporate code, except as specified above.

1. Which boards need to approve the deal?

2. (a) Which shareholders need to approve the deal, (b) how many shareholders constitute a quorum, (c) what is the relevant voting standard, and (d) what is the minimum number of votes required for approval?

3. Which shareholders have the right to dissent?

Make sure you explain how you arrived at your answers and provide specific statutory or other cites as support.

———

In the next case, the court discusses various provisions of the Iowa corporate code in effect at the time relating to class voting that were implicated by a merger.

SHIDLER v. ALL AMERICAN LIFE & FINANCIAL CORP.
Iowa Supreme Court
298 N.W.2d 318 (1980)

UHLENHOPP, JUSTICE

This proceeding involves construction of Iowa statutory law relating to corporate mergers. The United States District Court for the Southern District of Iowa, Central Division, certified to us a legal question on that subject . . . . Involved is an issue of separate voting by different classes of corporate stock. . . .

Reduced to the basics, the facts certified to us are as follows. In May 1973 an attempt was made to merge General United Group, Incorporated (GUG), a domestic corporation (and its subsidiary, United Security Life Company (USL), which need not be separately considered), into All American Delaware Corporation, a foreign corporation, which would be the surviving entity. At that time GUG had outstanding 105,000 shares of preferred stock, 2,959,650 shares of common stock, and 10,623,150 shares of class B common stock. The preferred and class B common stock had specified conversion rights into common stock. All of the preferred and class B common stock and 67,043 shares of the common stock were owned by another corporation, All American Life & Casualty Company (Casualty), and 2,892,607 shares of the common stock were owned by the public. Casualty also owned all of the stock of All American Delaware, into which GUG was to merge.

The agreement relating to the GUG-All American Delaware merger contained these clauses:

> 4.1 *Cancellation of Certain Shares.* Each share of the GUG Preferred Stock, GUG Common Stock and GUG Class B Common Stock which immediately prior to the Effective Date of the Merger is outstanding and owned by Casualty, shall be cancelled and retired upon the Effective Date of the Merger and by virtue thereof, without any action on the part of the holder or issuer thereof, and all certificates which theretofore evidenced such shares shall be cancelled and no cash or securities or other property shall be issued in the Merger in respect thereof . . . .

> 4.3 *Conversion of Certain Shares.* (a) Except for those shares which are owned by Casualty and therefore subject to Section 4.1, each share of GUG Common Stock, which is outstanding immediately prior to the Effective Date of the Merger, shall, by virtue of the Merger and without any action on the part of the holder thereof, be converted into and exchanged for $3.25 cash . . . .

> 4.5 *Surrender of Certificates.* After the Effective Date of the Merger, each certificate which evidenced ownership of a share or shares of the capital stock of either GUG or USL converted by virtue of the Merger into cash (an " 'Old Certificate' "), shall be surrendered by the holder thereof to O'Hare International Bank, Chicago, Illinois (the " 'Disbursing Agent' "), or such other disbursing agent as shall be designated by the Board of Directors of the Surviving Corporation, as agent for such holders, to effect

the surrender of certificates on their behalf, and each such holder shall upon such surrender receive in exchange therefor the amount to which he is entitled under Section 4.3 as a result of the conversion of the shares of the capital stock of either GUG or USL, as the case may be, into cash. Adoption of this Agreement by the respective stockholders of GUG and USL shall constitute ratification of the appointment of the Disbursing Agent. After the Effective Date of the Merger, the shares of Common Stock of GUG and USL outstanding immediately prior thereto shall cease to be shares of stock of such corporations regardless of whether or not surrendered and the stock transfer books of GUG and USL, shall be closed and there shall be no further transfer or issuance of certificates for the capital stock thereof; provided, however, that a new certificate will be issued in place of any certificate theretofore issued which has been lost or destroyed in accordance with the By-laws of GUG and USL, as the case may be.

Notice of a meeting was given to GUG stockholders. The notice stated that one of the purposes of the meeting was

(t)o consider and vote upon the approval and adoption of an Agreement of Merger dated as of April 20, 1973, pursuant to which GUG will be merged into All American Delaware Corporation ("The New Corporation"), a wholly-owned subsidiary of All American Life and Casualty Company ("All American"). As a result, GUG will become a wholly-owned subsidiary of All American and the holders of Common Stock of GUG other than All American will receive $3.25 in cash in payment for each outstanding share of Common Stock of GUG, all as more fully set forth is the accompanying Proxy Statement and in the copy of the Agreement of Merger attached as Exhibit A to the Proxy Statement.

A proxy statement sent to the stockholders included the following:

The affirmative vote of shares representing at least two-thirds of the Common and Class B Common Stock entitled to vote at the meeting, voting as one class, in person or by proxy, is required to approve the Merger Agreement.

At the time, Iowa had a statute in effect which applied to the merger, § 496A.74, The Code 1973 (references are to that Code). The relevant portion is this:

One or more foreign corporations and one or more domestic corporations may be merged or consolidated in the following manner, if such merger or consolidation is permitted by the laws of the state under which each such foreign corporation is organized:

1. Each domestic corporation shall comply with the provisions of this chapter with respect to the merger or consolidation, as the case may be, of domestic corporations and each foreign corporation shall comply with the applicable provisions of the laws of the state under which it is organized.

Under the statute just quoted, § 496A.70 on mergers thus came into play. The pertinent parts of that section provide:

The board of directors of each corporation, upon approving such plan of merger or plan of consolidation, shall, by resolution, direct that the plan be submitted to a vote at a meeting of shareholders, which may be either an annual or a special meeting . . . .

At each such meeting, a vote of the shareholders shall be taken on the proposed plan of merger or consolidation. Each outstanding share of each such corporation shall be entitled to vote on the proposed plan of merger or consolidation, whether or not such share has voting rights under the provisions of the articles of incorporation of such corporation. The plan of merger or consolidation shall be approved upon receiving the affirmative vote of the holders of at least two-thirds of the outstanding shares of each such corporation, unless any class of shares of any such corporation is entitled to vote as a class thereon, in which event, as to such corporation, the plan of merger or consolidation shall be approved upon receiving the affirmative vote of the holders of at least two-thirds of the outstanding shares of each class of shares entitled to vote as a class thereon and of the total outstanding shares. Any class of shares of any such corporation shall be entitled to vote as a class if the plan of merger or consolidation, as the case may be, contains any provision which, if contained in a proposed amendment to articles of incorporation, would entitle such class of shares to vote as a class.

The reference in this section to a merger containing a provision which, as an amendment to articles, would require class voting also necessitates consideration of portions of § 496A.57 on amendments:

The holders of the outstanding shares of a class shall be entitled to vote as a class upon a proposed amendment, whether or not entitled to vote thereon by the provisions of the articles of incorporation, if the amendment would:

1. Increase or decrease the aggregate number of authorized shares of such class. . . .

3. Effect an exchange, reclassification, or cancellation of all or part of the shares of such class.

At the GUG stockholders' meeting called to consider the merger, the stockholders in control required all classes of stock to vote together on the question. As a result, the merger proposal carried by more than the requisite two-thirds vote of all outstanding stock. Actually, however, the proposal did not carry by two-thirds vote of the outstanding common stock, if that stock is tallied separately.

William F. Shidler and other owners of common stock commenced an action in federal court for themselves and others challenging the merger on several grounds. One of the grounds alleged was noncompliance with §§ 496A.70 and 496A.57 for failure to have the GUG common stock vote separately as a class. The United States District Court for the Southern District of Iowa, Central Division, stating that "it appears there is no controlling precedent (of) the Supreme Court of the State of Iowa," certified the following question of law to us:

Did Iowa law require that the General United Group, Incorporated (GUG) merger into All American Delaware Corporation in May of 1973 be approved by

(a) an affirmative vote of the holders of at least two-thirds (2/3) of the outstanding GUG Common Stock shares voting separately as a class and by at least two-thirds (2/3) of the total outstanding GUG shares; or

(b) an affirmative vote of the holders of at least two-thirds (2/3) of the total outstanding GUG shares (of all classes) voting together as one class?

We called for briefs and oral arguments by the parties, which they provided us. We now answer the certified question.

I. The facts are not in dispute; the controversy relates to construction of corporate merger provisions of chapter 496A of the Iowa Code.

When we construe a statute,

we must look to the object to be accomplished, the evils sought to be remedied, or the purpose to be subserved, and place on it a reasonable or liberal construction which will best effect its purpose rather than one which will defeat it . . . .

We also must ascertain and give effect to the intention of the legislature.

Chicago & Northwestern Railway v. City of Osage, 176 N.W.2d 788, 792 (Iowa 1970). Also when construing a statute, "We consider all its parts together without according undue importance to single or isolated portions." *Osborne v. Edison*, 211 N.W.2d 696, 697 (Iowa 1973).

While this court has not previously passed upon the legal problem now presented, it has considered the corporate merger setting. *Rath v. Rath Packing Co.*, 257 Iowa 1277, 136 N.W.2d 410 (1965). Intervening legislation has changed the specific issue involved in that case, but this court's general view on the merger sections is reflected by that decision. The court quickly looked through the form of the transaction to its substance and granted the stockholders in question their entitlements under the merger statutes. In the light of *Rath* and the provisions of the applicable statutes, we proceed to the present case.

II. GUG, the domestic corporation, had three classes of stock, preferred, common and class B common. All of Casualty's shares in GUG would be cancelled, and paragraph 4.3(a) of the merger plan stated that each share of the public GUG common stock would, "by virtue of the Merger and without any action on the part of the holder thereof, be converted into and exchanged for $3.25 cash . . . ." Paragraph 4.5 stated that the public common certificates "shall be surrendered by the holder thereof" to the disbursing agent for cash. The paragraph also stated:

After the Effective Date of the Merger, the shares of Common Stock of GUG and USL outstanding immediately prior thereto shall cease to be shares of stock of such corporations regardless of whether or not surrendered and the stock transfer books of GUG and USL, shall be closed and there shall be no further transfer or issuance of certificates for the capital stock thereof . . . .

Section 496A.70 provides in part that if a class of stock is entitled to vote on a merger, "the plan of merger . . . shall be approved upon receiving the affirmative vote of the holders of at least two-thirds of the outstanding shares of each class of shares entitled to vote as a class thereon and of the total outstanding shares." It then provides:

> Any class of shares of any such corporation shall be entitled to vote as a class if the plan of merger or consolidation, as the case may be, contains any provision which, if contained in a proposed amendment to articles of incorporation, would entitle such class of shares to vote as a class.

This merger proposal carried by two-thirds of all GUG shares but not by two-thirds of the common stock. Was the common stock entitled to be voted as a class?

Plaintiffs argue that several clauses in § 496A.57 entitled the common to be voted separately. We go no farther than paragraph 3 of that section and specifically to the word "cancellation." Suppose that no merger had been proposed, but an amendment to the articles had been submitted which required that all certificates of GUG common shares be surrendered to a depository for cash, that thereafter the shares of common stock would cease to be stock of the corporation, and that the stock transfer books would be closed. Would not this stock be cancelled in a realistic sense? One day the owner of common stock owns a part of an ongoing enterprise; the next day he does not, he instead has money. His shares are recalled and no further trading is permitted in them; the books are closed. To "cancel" means to "revoke, annul, invalidate." Webster's Third New International Dictionary 325 (1969). Other definitions are, "To revoke or recall; to annul or destroy, make void or invalid, or set aside. To rescind; abandon; repeal; surrender; waive; terminate." Black's Law Dictionary 186 (5th ed. 1979). . . .

The *Rath* decision enjoins us to look at the merger statutes realistically. We think in the first place that if these common shares had been called in for cash by amendment to the articles without a merger, they would have been entitled to be voted as a class under § 496A.57(3). That this stock would be entitled to be voted if its characteristics are altered, but not if it is completely extinguished for cash, does not appear reasonable. Section 496A.57 does not say the cancellation must be "without consideration."

Section 496A.70 provides in the second place that a class of stock is entitled to vote separately if the plan of merger "contains any provision which, if contained in a proposed amendment to articles of incorporation, would entitle such class of shares to vote as a class." We thus conclude that together these section[s] entitled this common stock to be voted separately as a class.

III. Defendants voice several arguments contrary to this construction of the statutes. One is that this was a "cash out" merger. They say the common stock was not changed or reduced; it was eliminated and money was substituted. But we find nothing in §§ 496A.70 and 496A.57 which differentiates cash out mergers from other varieties. Indeed, the cash out merger is drastic: the stockholder is compelled to give up his stock altogether and separate himself from the ongoing organization; he is ejected. Did not the General Assembly intend that such a class of stock should be entitled to vote separately on its fate?

Defendants further contend that if the General Assembly had intended each class of stock to have separate voting rights on mergers, it could have easily so provided as some states have done. But the Assembly did not desire to give each class separate voting rights automatically. It desired to give a class separate voting rights if that stock was affected in ways designated in § 496A.57, one of which is cancellation.

Then defendants urge that the merger plan does not use the word "cancel" or "cancellation" regarding this stock, and they say § 496A.57 does not apply unless the merger plan contains a provision "identical" to one of those in the section. We think this argument flies in the face of the *Rath* rationale of realism. The substance, not the precise words, controls. A merger draftsman cannot avoid § 496A.57 by calling an actual cancellation something else.

Defendants also insist that under § 496A.76 the assets of GUG could have been sold, the proceeds could have been distributed, and GUG could have been dissolved without a separate class vote; the holders of common stock would then have no stock, but money instead. Why then, defendants ask, may not substantially the same thing be done by merger?

We may assume arguendo that a separate class vote would not be required in such a proceeding, and we lay aside the point that a sale, distribution, and dissolution normally have substantially different consequences than a merger. But the controlling point is that for reasons it found sufficient, the General Assembly made the requirements of § 496A.70 on merger and of § 496A.76 on sale of assets materially different. We may not make the sections identical by judicial legislation.

We do not find defendants' arguments against the applicability of § 496A.57(3) to be convincing.

IV. As a separate argument, defendants contend that a section of chapter 496A and a clause of GUG's articles, read together, prohibit class voting of the common stock. Section 496A.138 provided at the time of the attempted merger:

> Whenever, with respect to any action to be taken by the shareholders of a corporation, the articles of incorporation require the vote or concurrence of the holders of a greater or lesser proportion of the shares, or of any class or series thereof, than required by this chapter with respect to such action, the provisions of the articles of incorporation shall control.

(The words "or lesser" were deleted by 1978 Sess., 67 G.A., ch. 1186, s 3.)

GUG's articles stated at the time:

> The holders of the Common Stock and Class B Common Stock shall be entitled at all times to one vote per share and the holders of all classes of common stock of the corporation shall vote together as one class on all matters.

We may assume for the purpose of answering the certified question that during the period § 496A.138 contained the words "or lesser," a clause in corporate articles could lawfully have reduced the two-thirds vote requirement of § 496A.70 to a lesser proportion. The difficulty with defendants' argument, however, is that the quoted portion of the articles on which defendants rely does not deal with the proportion; it does not purport to lessen the two-thirds requirement.

The quoted portion of the articles does however purport to prohibit class voting as between common and class B common. This clause was undoubtedly inserted to give control to Casualty. But the articles cannot override the statutes. Section 496A.138 deals with proportions, not class voting. Its words, "or of any class or series thereof," do not authorize a prohibition of class voting. Rather, they constitute an adjective phrase modifying "shares," and "shares" is in an adjective clause modifying "proportion." On the other hand, § 496A.70 provides that any class of shares "shall" be entitled to vote as a class if the merger contains a provision which, as an amendment to articles, would entitle the class to vote separately; and § 496A.57(3) entitles a class to vote separately upon an amendment to cancel shares, "whether or not entitled to vote thereon by the provisions of the articles of incorporation . . . ."

We are not persuaded by defendants' argument.

V. Finally, defendants urge plaintiffs' claim that the common was entitled to vote as a class is really academic for two reasons. One is that Casualty could have converted its other GUG stock to common and thus obtained a two-thirds affirmative vote by the common on the merger. The other is that under § 496A.138, Casualty could have changed the articles to reduce the two-thirds requirement in § 496A.70 to a lesser proportion and thus carried the merger election.

We lay aside the fact that a conversion of Casualty's other shares to common shares would have involved several other considerations, and that a change in the articles to reduce the two-thirds requirement would today run into the 1978 repeal of the words "or lesser" in § 496A.138. The significant point is that when the vote on the merger actually occurred in May 1973, Casualty had not in fact converted its other stock or reduced the two-thirds requirement. We deal with the election as it occurred, not as it might have occurred. Many corporations have various classes or series of shares which have rights of conversion into other shares. Corporate elections under chapter 496A cannot stand or fall on what would have happened if certain hypothetical conversions had previously taken place or if changes in the articles had previously been made; they must stand or fall on what in fact took place. We do not find merit in defendants' final argument.

We thus answer the question propounded as follows:

The Iowa law required that the General United Group, Incorporated (GUG) merger into All American Delaware Corporation in May of 1973 be approved by an affirmative vote of at least two-thirds (2/3) of the outstanding GUG Common Stock shares voting separately as a class and by at least two-thirds (2/3) of the total outstanding GUG shares. . . .

CERTIFIED QUESTION ANSWERED.

QUESTIONS

1.　What's the deal involved in this case? How was the deal structured? What was the deal consideration?

2.　What capital stock did GUG have outstanding?

3.　Who is Shidler? What is he claiming?

4.　What is the legal issue in the case? What does it turn on?

5.　What does the court decide?

6.　How would the court's analysis have differed under Iowa's current corporate law statute?

9.　"Short-Form" Merger

A short-form merger (also called a parent-subsidiary merger) is a merger effected under a specialized statutory provision (*see, e.g.,* MBCA § 11.05; DGCL § 253) that does not require target board or shareholder approval of the merger. These specialized provisions are available only if the parent owns at least 90 percent of target's stock, i.e., target is an almost "wholly-owned" subsidiary[45] of parent. As explained in the official comment to MBCA § 11.05:

> Approval by the subsidiary's shareholders is not required partly because if a parent already owns 90% or more of the voting power of each class and series of a subsidiary's shares, approval of a merger by the subsidiary's shareholders would be a foregone conclusion, and partly to facilitate the simplification of corporate structure where only a very small fraction of stock is held by outside shareholders. Approval by the subsidiary's board of directors is not required because if the parent owns 90% or more of the voting power of each class and series of the subsidiary's outstanding shares, the subsidiary's directors cannot be expected to be independent of the parent, so that the approval by the subsidiary's board of directors would also be a foregone conclusion.

EXERCISE 2.8

Bidder and Target are both private companies incorporated in Nevada. Bidder's issued and outstanding stock consists of 1,000,000 shares of common stock. Target's issued and outstanding stock consists of 10,000 shares of common stock, 9,000 of which are owned by Bidder. Bidder is acquiring the rest of Target for $1 million in cash in a deal structured as a forward triangular merger. In that regard, Bidder has incorporated Merger Sub in Nevada for purposes of the deal. Assume that the

---

[45] A subsidiary is a company with more than 50% of its voting power controlled by another company. A wholly-owned subsidiary is a company with 100% of its voting power controlled by another company.

articles of incorporation and bylaws of Bidder, Merger Sub, and Target simply track the default provisions of the Nevada corporate code.

1. Which boards need to approve the deal?

2. (a) Which shareholders need to approve the deal, (b) what is the relevant voting standard, and (c) what is the minimum number of votes required for approval?

3. Which shareholders have the right to dissent?

4. Do any of your answers to questions 1 through 3 above change if Target also has 1,000 shares of Series A Preferred Stock outstanding, none of which are owned by Bidder?

Make sure you explain how you arrived at your answers and provide specific statutory or other cites as support.

10. Multi-Jurisdictional Deals

Our discussion of corporate formalities has assumed that bidder, target, and merger sub (if applicable) are all incorporated in the same state. In reality, this is often not the case. For example, assume bidder is acquiring target through a reverse triangular merger and that bidder is incorporated in Ohio, target is incorporated in Minnesota, and merger sub is incorporated in Delaware. Which state's merger statute applies to the deal? The answer is the merger statutes of Ohio, Minnesota, and Delaware. Specifically, pursuant to the internal affairs doctrine,[46] the corporate law statute of Ohio governs bidder, the corporate law statute of Minnesota governs target, and the corporate law statute of Delaware governs merger sub. Thus, to effect the merger between target and merger sub, target must comply with the merger provisions of the Minnesota Business Corporations Act and merger sub must comply with the merger provisions of the DGCL. Likewise, the issues of board approval, shareholder approval, and appraisal rights with respect to bidder, target, and merger sub would be analyzed under the Ohio General Corporation Law for bidder, the Minnesota Business Corporation Act for target, and the DGCL for merger sub.

By necessity, state corporate law statutes address the merger of corporations incorporated in different states. For example, DGCL § 252 provides as follows:

(a) Any 1 or more corporations of this State may merge or consolidate with 1 or more other corporations of any other state or states of the United States, or of the District of Columbia if the laws of the other state or states, or of the District permit a corporation of such jurisdiction to merge or consolidate with a corporation of another jurisdiction. . . .

(b) All the constituent corporations shall enter into an agreement of merger or consolidation. . . .

(c) The agreement shall be adopted, approved, certified, executed and

---

[46] This doctrine provides, among other things, that a corporation is governed by the corporate law statute of the state in which it is incorporated.

acknowledged by each of the constituent corporations in accordance with the laws under which it is formed, and, in the case of a Delaware corporation, in the same manner as is provided in § 251 of this title. The agreement shall be filed and shall become effective for all purposes of the laws of this State when and as provided in § 251 of this title with respect to the merger or consolidation of corporations of this State. In lieu of filing the agreement of merger or consolidation, the surviving or resulting corporation may file a certificate of merger or consolidation . . . .

Thus, for merger sub, the controlling provision is DGCL § 252, since it is merging with a corporation of another state and not § 251. Target would need to comply with the analogous provision of the Minnesota Business Corporation Act.[47]

Note that state corporate statutes often use the phraseology "domestic corporation" and "foreign corporation" in these sorts of provisions. In this context, a domestic corporation is one incorporated under the particular state's corporate law statute;[48] a foreign corporation is one incorporated under some other state's corporate law statute.[49] Thus, in our example, for purposes of the Minnesota statute, target is a domestic corporation and merger sub is a foreign corporation. Conversely, for purposes of the DGCL, target is a foreign corporation and merger sub is a domestic corporation.

EXERCISE 2.9

Bidder and Target are both private companies. Bidder is incorporated in Massachusetts, and Target is incorporated in Pennsylvania. Bidder's issued and outstanding stock consists of 1,000,000 shares of common stock; Target's issued and outstanding stock consists of 10,000 shares of common stock. Bidder is acquiring Target for $5 million in cash in a deal structured as a reverse triangular merger. In that regard, Bidder has incorporated Merger Sub in Michigan for purposes of the deal. Assume that the articles of incorporation and bylaws of Bidder, Merger Sub, and Target simply track the default provisions of their respective states of incorporation.

1.   Which boards need to approve the deal?

2.   (a) Which shareholders need to approve the deal, (b) what is the relevant voting standard, and (c) what is the minimum number of votes required for approval?

3.   Which shareholders have the right to dissent?

4.   Do any of your answers to questions 1 through 3 above change if the deal consideration consists of 220,000 shares of Bidder common stock?

Make sure you explain how you arrived at your answers and provide specific statutory or other cites as support.

---

[47] The analogous provision is Minn. Bus. Corp. Act § 302A.641.

[48] *See, e.g.*, MBCA § 1.40(4).

[49] *See, e.g., id.* § 1.40(10).

11. Inter-Species Deals

Up until now, we have analyzed statutory formalities involved when one corporation acquires another. M&A transactions, however, are not limited to one corporation acquiring another. Corporations acquire or are acquired by limited liability companies (LLCs), limited partnerships (LPs), etc. LLCs, LPs, etc. sometimes acquire non-corporate entities as well. We refer to a deal where bidder and target are different types of legal entities as an inter-species deal.

To give you a flavor for inter-species deals, below we consider statutory formalities for a deal in which bidder is a limited liability partnership (LLP) governed by the Uniform Partnership Act (1997) (RUPA) and target is a Delaware LLC. Similar to what we did above, we go through a deal structured as an asset purchase, ownership interest purchase, and a direct merger (we look at a triangular merger structure in connection with Exercise 2.10 below).

As you may recall from your business organizations or similar class, unincorporated entity statutes are composed largely of default rules that the entity can alter or opt out of through appropriate language in its partnership, LLC, or similar agreement. Thus, for example, the starting point for providing advice to a partnership on partnership law issues is usually a review of the partnership agreement and not the applicable statute. The statute does, however, remain relevant because it provides rules that apply if the partnership agreement is silent on an issue and contains a few rules that partners cannot contract around. You likewise start with the LLC agreement (often called an operating agreement) when advising an LLC.

To simplify things for our purposes, assume that bidder has a barebones partnership agreement which means that it is largely governed by the RUPA default rules. Likewise, assume that target has a barebones LLC Agreement which means it is largely governed by the Delaware Limited Liability Company Act (DLLCA) default rules.

Note that the issues we look at below are different than they were in the corporate context. Specifically, under RUPA default rules, a partnership is managed and owned by its partners. Thus, we consider partner approval as opposed to board and shareholder approval. Likewise, under DLLCA default rules, an LLC is managed and owned by its members. Thus, we consider member approval as opposed to board and shareholder approval. Furthermore, we do not consider appraisal rights at all because neither RUPA nor DLLCA default rules provide for them. (DLLCA § 18-210 does allow an LLC to provide for appraisal rights in its LLC agreement and presumably a partnership could do the same in its partnership agreement even though RUPA does not expressly provide for it.).

a. Asset Purchase

There is no specific RUPA provision addressing a partnership acquiring another business through an asset purchase. Thus, the default RUPA partnership management rule applies. This rule provides that "[e]ach partner has equal rights in the management and conduct of the partnership business."[50] The rule generally translates into partners voting on a proposed course of action. If the matter up for a vote is in the ordinary course of partnership business, it passes if a majority of partners vote in favor of it.[51] Approval of a matter outside of the partnership's ordinary course of business requires unanimous partner approval.[52] Thus, assuming bidder's acquisition of target's assets is outside of the ordinary course, RUPA requires unanimous partner approval. In other words, a single partner can block the deal by refusing to vote in favor of it.

The DLLCA likewise lacks a provision addressing the sale by an LLC of all or substantially all of its assets. Thus, the default general DLLCA limited liability company management rule applies, which provides as follows:

> [T]he management of a limited liability company shall be vested in its members in proportion to the then current percentage or other interest of members in the profits of the limited liability company owned by all of the members, the decision of members owning more than 50 percent of the said percentage or other interest in the profits controlling. . . .[53]

An interest in the profits of an LLC typically equates to, or is called, an LLC interest. Thus, the sale of assets must be approved by members owning a majority of LLC interests. The DLLCA allows an LLC to obtain such approval at a meeting of members or by written consent of the members.[54]

b.   Ownership Interest Purchase

There is no specific RUPA provision addressing a partnership acquiring another business through an ownership interest purchase. Thus, the default general RUPA partnership management rule applies. Hence, if the purchase is in the ordinary course of partnership business, a majority of partners must vote for it. If it is outside of the ordinary course, all partners must vote for it.

The sale of an LLC structured as an LLC interest purchase involves the transfer by targets' members of their ownership interests to bidder. The DLLCA does address the transfer of ownership interests. Specifically, the default rule under the DLLCA is that an LLC interest is freely transferable but, per DLLCA § 18-702(a),

> [t]he assignee of a member's limited liability company interest shall have no right to participate in the management of the business and affairs of a limited liability company except as provided in a limited liability company agreement or, unless otherwise provided in the limited liability company agreement, upon the affirmative vote or written consent of all of the members of the limited liability.

---

[50] RUPA § 401(f).

[51] *See id.* § 401(j).

[52] *See id.*

[53] DLLCA § 18-402.

[54] *See id.* § 18-302(d).

Obviously, bidder will be looking to acquire management rights. Thus, the foregoing language essentially requires unanimous approval by target members of a sale of target structured as an LLC interest purchase.

c. Merger

RUPA does contain provisions addressing mergers, but curiously, they apply only to mergers between partnerships and between a partnership and a limited partnership.[55] Thus, they do not apply to a merger between a RUPA partnership and a Delaware LLC. In adopting RUPA, however, many states have expanded these provisions to apply to LLCs, corporations, etc.[56] Hence, we will assume that the RUPA merger provisions apply to our deal. Thus, per RUPA § 905(c)(1), all of bidder's partners must approve the merger.

The DLLCA also contains provisions addressing mergers. Specifically, § 18-209(b) states as follows:

> (b) Pursuant to an agreement of merger or consolidation, 1 or more domestic limited liability companies may merge or consolidate with or into 1 or more domestic limited liability companies or 1 or more other business entities formed or organized under the laws of the State of Delaware or any other state or the United States or any foreign country or other foreign jurisdiction, or any combination thereof, with such domestic limited liability company or other business entity as the agreement shall provide being the surviving or resulting domestic limited liability company or other business entity. Unless otherwise provided in the limited liability company agreement, an agreement of merger or consolidation or a plan of merger shall be approved by each domestic limited liability company which is to merge or consolidate . . . by members who own more than 50 percent of the then current percentage or other interest in the profits of the domestic limited liability company owned by all of the members . . . .

Thus, owners of more than 50 percent of target's LLC interests would have to approve the deal. Target may secure this approval at a meeting of members or by written consent of the members.[57] As part of closing on the merger, the DLLCA requires bidder to file a certificate of merger with the Delaware Secretary of State.

EXERCISE 2.10

Bidder and Target are both private companies. Bidder is a corporation incorporated in Ohio. Bidder's issued and outstanding stock consists of 1,000,000 shares of common stock. Assume that the articles of incorporation and bylaws of Bidder simply track the default provisions of the Ohio corporate code. Target is an LLP organized in Florida. See below for excerpts from Target's partnership agreement. Bidder is acquiring Target for $5 million in cash in a deal structured as a reverse triangular merger. In that regard, Bidder has formed a new Arizona

---

[55] *See* RUPA §§ 905-907.

[56] *See, e.g.,* Ariz. Rev. Stat. § 29-1085.

[57] *See* DLLCA § 18-302(d).

limited liability company named Merger Sub for purposes of the deal. See below for excerpts from Merger Sub's Operating Agreement.

1. Which boards need to approve the deal?

2. (a) Which shareholders/owners need to approve the deal, (b) what is the relevant voting standard, and (c) what is the minimum number of votes required for approval?

3. Which shareholders/owners have the right to dissent?

4. Do any of your answers to questions 1 through 3 above change if the deal consideration consists of 220,000 shares of Bidder common stock?

Make sure you explain how you arrived at your answers and provide specific statutory or other cites as support.

LIMITED LIABILITY PARTNERSHIP AGREEMENT

THIS LIMITED LIABILITY PARTNERSHIP AGREEMENT (this "**Agreement**") is dated March 11, 2005, between Katrina Y. Appleseed, Walter L. Brunch III, and Ronaldo P. Crusty (each a "**Partner**" and collectively, the "**Partners**").

The Partners agree as follows:

1. Formation, Name and Purpose.

a. The Partners hereby form a partnership (the "**Partnership**") under the Florida Partnership Laws, as amended from time to time. The Partnership shall be a limited liability partnership and shall promptly file a statement of qualification to that effect with the Florida Department of State.

b. The name of the Partnership is Target L.L.P. and all business of the Partnership shall be conducted in such name.

c. The purposes of the Partnership are (i) own, renovate, improve, sell, lease and maintain the premises described in Schedule A (the "**Property**") and (ii) to carry on any and all activities related to the Property. . . .

4. Percentage Interests. Each Partner's percentage interest in the Partnership ("**Percentage Interest**") is as follows:

Appleseed:	65%
Brunch:	25%
Crusty:	10% . . . .

6. Management, Duties, and Restrictions.

a. Except as otherwise provided in this Agreement, each Partner shall have a weighted vote in the management of the business of the Partnership that is equal to the Partner's respective Percentage Interest, and the vote of a Partner or Partners owning a majority of Percentage Interest shall control.

b. Anything to the contrary contained herein notwithstanding, no Partner or the Partnership shall, without the prior written consent of all Partners, (i) borrow or loan money on behalf of the Partnership; (ii) lease, rent, purchase, sell, mortgage, or otherwise create a lien upon any Partnership real estate (including the Property) or any interest therein, or enter into any contract for any such purpose; or (iii) make or incur any expenditure on behalf of the Partnership in excess of $50,000. . . .

9. **Transfer of Partnership Interest.** Except as is otherwise expressly provided herein, no Partner shall voluntarily or involuntarily transfer any part of his interest in the Partnership without the written consent of a majority of Percentage Interest of the other Partners nor shall any Partner cause or allow his interest in the Partnership or its property to be liened, attached, or otherwise encumbered. . . .

OPERATING AGREEMENT
OF
MERGER SUB LLC

This Operating Agreement (this "Agreement") is entered into as of August 11, 2013, by and between Merger Sub LLC, an Arizona limited liability company (the "Company"), and Bidder Inc., an Ohio corporation (the "Member").

ARTICLE 1
ORGANIZATIONAL MATTERS

2.1 Formation of the Company. The Company was formed as a limited liability company under the Arizona Limited Liability Company Act.

2.2 Name. The name of the Company is Merger Sub LLC.

2.3 Purpose of the Company. The Company has been formed for the purposes of engaging in any lawful act or activity for which limited liability companies may be formed under the Act and engaging in any and all activities necessary, convenient, desirable or incidental to the foregoing. . . .

2.6 Membership. The Member shall be the sole member of the Company. . . .

ARTICLE 3
OPERATION OF THE COMPANY

3.1 Designation of the Board of Directors as the Managers of the Company. Management of the business and affairs of the Company is hereby vested in managers who shall be referred to herein as directors (the "Directors"). The Directors shall act collectively as the Board of Directors (the "Board"). The individuals serving as Directors shall be elected or designated by the Member as provided herein, and such Board shall serve as the "Manager" or "Managers" of the Company within the meaning of the Act.

3.2 The Board of Directors.

(a) Rights and Powers. The Board shall have the sole right and power to manage the business and affairs of the Company, except as otherwise specifically required by the Act or this Agreement or as otherwise determined by the Member. . . .

(c) Number and Appointment. The Board shall consist of one or more natural persons. All Directors shall be appointed by the Member. . . .

(e) Initial Board. The persons serving on the Company's initial Board are as follows:

Irene L. Johnson

Andrew G. Estes

Ralph R. Baranowski

(f) Voting Power. Each Director shall have one vote on any matters submitted to the vote of the Board.

(g) Acts of the Board. The Board shall take action by the affirmative vote of a majority of Directors present at a duly held meeting at the time the action is taken. The Board may also take action without a meeting pursuant to a written document signed by a majority of the Directors (or such greater number as may be required to approve the matter at a meeting of the Board). A Board meeting shall not be duly held unless a majority of the Board is present in person or by telephone.

3.3 Officers. The Company shall have one natural person exercising the functions of the office of the President. The Board or the Member may elect or appoint such other officers or agents as it deems necessary for the operation and management of the Company including, but not limited to, a Chairman of the Board, Chief Executive Officer, Chief Financial Officer, Treasurer one or more Vice Presidents, and a Secretary, each of whom shall have the powers, rights, duties and responsibilities as determined by the Board from time to time. Any of the offices or functions of those offices may be held by the same person. . . .

B. SECURITIES LAWS COMPLIANCE

Federal securities laws regulate the offer and sale of securities, among other things. Under these laws:

(1) It is illegal to offer or sell a non-exempt security unless the transaction is registered with the Securities and Exchange Commission (SEC) or falls within a registration exemption (principle 1); and

(2) It is illegal for anyone to misstate or withhold material facts in connection with the purchase or sale of a security (principle 2).

We need to discuss federal securities laws because, as explained below, M&A transactions often involve the offer and sale of securities.

1. Bidder Compliance

Bidder will be offering and selling securities any time the deal consideration consists of or includes bidder stock. This is true regardless of how the deal is structured. In a stock purchase, merger, and share exchange, bidder issues the stock directly to target shareholders. In an asset purchase, bidder issues the stock to target who then typically distributes it to its shareholders.

A private bidder who wants to remain private will rely on a registration exemption to comply with principle 1. Registering the deal with the SEC is not an option because thereafter bidder would have to meet the SEC's periodic reporting requirements applicable to public companies and thus would essentially no longer be private.[58]

The most widely relied on exemption by a bidder in an M&A transaction is § 4(a)(2) of the Securities Act through the safe harbor provided by Rule 506 of Regulation D under the Securities Act. Section 4(a)(2) exempts from registration "transactions by an issuer[59] not involving any public offering." This means that, as a general matter, public offerings must be registered with the SEC, and non-public or private offerings (also called private placements) do not. The Securities Act, however, is silent on what does and does not constitute a public offering, and the case law on the distinction is a bit murky. As a result, in 1982, the SEC adopted Rule 506 under Regulation D of the Securities Act. Rule 506 is a § 4(a)(2) safe harbor; that is, if an offering complies with the conditions specified in Rule 506, the offering will be deemed exempt under § 4(a)(2).

To fall within the safe harbor, the offering must be limited to accredited investors and no more than thirty-five non-accredited investors. Accredited investors include institutional investors (banks, insurance companies, mutual funds, etc.) and individuals with a net worth in excess of $1,000,000 (not including the value of the person's primary residence), annual income in excess of $200,000, or joint annual income in excess of $300,000. Rule 506 also provides that all non-accredited investors in the offering have to be sophisticated, or the issuer has to reasonably believe that they are sophisticated. Sophistication in this context means that the investor "has such knowledge and experience in financial and business matters that he is capable of evaluating the merits and risks of the prospective investment," either in his own right or with the aid of one or more purchaser representatives. Furthermore, Rule 506 requires the issuer to furnish any non-accredited investors that purchase securities in the offering with certain specified information about the issuer and the offering within a reasonable time prior to the purchase.

Thus, as part of the deal process, bidder will ascertain how many shareholders target has and whether they fall under the definition of accredited investor. If target has 35 or fewer non-accredited shareholders (shareholders that do not fall under the definition of accredited investor), bidder will rely on Rule 506 for compliance with principle 1. If target has more than 35 non-accredited shareholders, bidder or target will normally buyout enough of them for cash as part of the deal to get the number to 35 or less so that bidder can rely on Rule 506. Alternatively, bidder and target could structure the deal as an asset purchase because then bidder will be issuing shares to only a single person (target), regardless of how many shareholders target has. Note, however, that the SEC nonetheless treats such issuance as made to target shareholders if, among other things, the asset purchase agreement provides for the dissolution of target

---

[58] Any company who has registered an offering with the SEC in order to comply with principle 1 is thereafter required to file with the SEC the annual, quarterly, and current reports required under the Securities Exchange Act of 1934 (Exchange Act). *See* Exchange Act § 15(d).

[59] "Issuer" refers to the company that is issuing securities, so bidder in an M&A deal.

following the deal or for a pro rata distribution of bidder's stock to target's shareholders.[60]

In light of principle 2, bidder will typically furnish target's shareholders a private placement memorandum, or PPM for short, that describes bidder's business in detail, includes bidder's financial information, and sets forth various "risk factors" facing bidder's business, including those relating to the deal. (Note that Rule 506 essentially requires bidder to furnish target shareholders a PPM if bidder will be issuing shares to any non-accredited target shareholders in the deal.) Here is a sample risk factor:

The failure to successfully integrate [Target]'s business and operations in the expected time frame may adversely affect [Bidder]'s future results.

The success of the merger will depend, in part, on the combined company's ability to realize the anticipated benefits from combining [Bidder] and [Target]. However, to realize these anticipated benefits, [Bidder] and [Target] must be successfully combined. If the combined company is not able to achieve these objectives, the anticipated benefits of the merger may not be realized fully or at all or may take longer to realize than expected.

[Bidder] and [Target] have operated and, until the completion of the merger, will continue to operate independently. It is possible that the integration process could result in the loss of key employees, as well as the disruption of each company's ongoing businesses or inconsistencies in standards, controls, procedures and policies, any or all of which could adversely affect [Bidder]'s ability to maintain relationships with clients, customers, depositors, and employees after the merger or to achieve the anticipated benefits of the merger. Integration efforts between the two companies will also divert management attention and resources. These integration matters could have an adverse effect on each of [Bidder] and [Target].

In this context, the basic idea behind a risk factor section of a PPM (or other disclosure document) is to protect bidder against security fraud suits following the deal. For example, assume that (1) bidder's PPM included the above risk factor, and (2) the deal turned out poorly because key employees left shortly after it closed. Target shareholders will be hard pressed to bring a securities fraud suit against bidder because bidder can simply point to the risk factor and say "we told you this might happen." In other words, detailing various things that might go wrong undercuts an argument that bidder misstated or withheld material facts in connection with the deal when one of those things does go wrong.

---

[60] *See* Securities Act Rule 145(a)(3).

2. Seller Compliance

Target's shareholders will be selling target's shares to bidder (or a subsidiary of bidder), unless the deal is structured as an asset purchase.[61] In other words, if the deal is structured as a stock purchase, merger, or share exchange, target shareholders need to comply with principle one. Here, compliance typically comes through reliance on § 4(a)(1) of the Securities Act. Section 4(a)(1) exempts from registration "transactions by any person other than an issuer, underwriter, or dealer." Target shareholders generally fall outside of these categories, especially in the context of an M&A transaction, so their sales to bidder are generally exempt from registration.

Target shareholders normally do not do anything specific for compliance with principle 2. This is because as part of the deal target will provide bidder with full access to its records and personnel so that bidder can conduct an in-depth "due diligence" investigation. As a result, it will be difficult for bidder to argue that a target shareholder violated principle 2 unless he or she intentionally misstated or withheld material information regarding target. Principle 2 is not the primary reason target allows bidder to perform due diligence. As we discuss later, bidder will require target to provide this access so that bidder can verify it is getting what it is paying for.

C. HART-SCOTT-RODINO COMPLIANCE

Section 7 of the Clayton Antitrust Act of 1914 prohibits an M&A transaction if "the effect of such acquisition may be substantially to lessen competition, or to tend to create a monopoly."[62] To foster enforcement of § 7, the Hart-Scott-Rodino Antitrust Improvements Act of 1976 ("HSR") requires parties to certain M&A transactions to file a Notification and Report Form with the federal government[63] and wait a certain amount of time before closing the proposed transaction.

It is common for an M&A attorney to prepare or have input on the HSR filing for the deal he or she is working on. Hence, you need to have some basic knowledge concerning HSR. In that regard, below are excerpts from two introductory guides prepared by the Federal Trade Commission. Introductory Guide I provides an overview of the premerger notification program and Introductory Guide II provides greater depth on when a party to an M&A transaction is required to file a Report Form. More complicated issues relating to antitrust (for example, if the government raises concerns after reviewing an HSR filing) are normally handled by antitrust counsel and not an M&A attorney and are therefore not covered in detail in this book. However, to give you a sense for some of the issues involved, I've also included excerpts from the federal government's Horizontal Merger Guidelines.

---

[61] Securities laws are not implicated for target's shareholders if the deal is structured as an asset purchase because target is selling its assets; target shareholders are not selling shares.

[62] 15 U.S.C. § 18.

[63] *See* http://www.ftc.gov/bc/hsr/hsr_form_ver_101.pdf for the form.

HART-SCOTT-RODINO PREMERGER NOTIFICATION PROGRAM INTRODUCTORY GUIDE I
What is the Premerger Notification Program?
An Overview
FTC Premerger Notification Office
(Mar. 2009)

AN OVERVIEW

Guide I is the first in a series of guides prepared by the Federal Trade Commission's Premerger Notification Office ("PNO"). It is intended to provide a general overview of the Premerger Notification Program (the "Program") and to help the reader in determining which types of business transactions are reportable under the Hart-Scott-Rodino Antitrust Improvements Act of 1976, 15 U.S.C. § 18a (§ 7A of the Clayton Act or "the Act"). *Guide I* describes the basic reportability requirements and how the program works. It also provides a list of alternative information sources to assist you in deciding whether or not you need to file. This *Guide* will introduce you to certain terminology and concepts regarding the Act and the Premerger Notification Rules (the "Rules"), 16 C.F.R. Parts 801, 802 and 803. . . .

I. INTRODUCTION

The Act requires that parties to certain mergers or acquisitions notify the Federal Trade Commission and the Department of Justice (the "enforcement agencies") before consummating the proposed acquisition. The parties must wait a specific period of time while the enforcement agencies review the proposed transaction. The Program became effective September 5, 1978, after final promulgation of the Rules.[64]

The Program was established to avoid some of the difficulties and expense that the enforcement agencies encounter when they challenge anticompetitive acquisitions after they have occurred. In the past, the enforcement agencies found that it is often impossible to restore competition fully once a merger takes place. Furthermore, any attempt to reestablish competition after the fact is usually very costly for the parties and the public. Prior review under the Program enables the Federal Trade Commission ("FTC" or the "Commission") and the Department of Justice ("DOJ") to determine which acquisitions are likely to be anticompetitive and to challenge them at a time when remedial action is most effective.

In general, the Act requires that certain proposed acquisitions of voting securities, non-corporate interests ("NCI") or assets be reported to the FTC and the DOJ prior to consummation. The parties must then wait a specified period, usually 30 days (15 days in the case of a cash tender offer or a bankruptcy sale),

---

[64] [n.1] The Premerger Notification Rules are found at 16 C.F.R. Parts 801, 802, and 803. The Rules also are identified by number, and each Rule beginning with Rule 801.1 corresponds directly with the section number in the C.F.R. (so that Rule 801.40 would be found in 16 C.F.R. § 801.40). In this Guide, the Rules are cited by Rule number.

before they may complete the transaction. Much of the information needed for a preliminary antitrust evaluation is included in the notification filed with the agencies by the parties to proposed transactions and thus is immediately available for review during the waiting period.

Whether a particular acquisition is subject to these requirements depends upon the value of the acquisition and the size of the parties, as measured by their sales and assets. Small acquisitions, acquisitions involving small parties and other classes of acquisitions that are less likely to raise antitrust concerns are excluded from the Act's coverage.

If either agency determines during the waiting period that further inquiry is necessary, it is authorized by § 7A(e) of the Clayton Act to request additional information or documentary materials from the parties to a reported transaction (a "second request"). A second request extends the waiting period for a specified period, usually 30 days (ten days in the case of a cash tender offer or a bankruptcy sale), after all parties have complied with the request (or, in the case of a tender offer or a bankruptcy sale, after the acquiring person complies). This additional time provides the reviewing agency with the opportunity to analyze the submitted information and to take appropriate action before the transaction is consummated. If the reviewing agency believes that a proposed transaction may violate the antitrust laws, it may seek an injunction in federal district court to prohibit consummation of the transaction.

The Program has been a success. Compliance with the Act's notification requirements has been excellent, and has minimized the number of post-merger challenges the enforcement agencies have had to pursue. In addition, although the agencies retain the power to challenge mergers post-consummation, and will do so under appropriate circumstances, the fact that they rarely do has led many members of the private bar to view the Program as a helpful tool in advising their clients about particular acquisition proposals.

The Rules, which govern compliance with the Program, are necessarily technical and complex. We have prepared *Guide I* to introduce some of the Program's specially defined terms and concepts. This should assist you in determining if proposed business transactions are subject to the requirements of the Program.

II. DETERMINING REPORTABILITY

The Act requires persons contemplating proposed business transactions that satisfy certain size criteria to report their intentions to the enforcement agencies before consummating the transaction. If the proposed transaction is reportable, then both the acquiring person and the person whose business is being acquired must submit information about their respective business operations to the enforcement agencies and wait a specific period of time before consummating the proposed transaction. During that waiting period, the enforcement agencies review the antitrust implications of the proposed transaction. Whether a particular transaction is reportable is determined by application of the Act, the Rules, and formal and informal staff interpretations.

As a general matter, the Act and the Rules require both acquiring and acquired persons to file notifications under the Program if all of the following conditions are met:

1. As a result of the transaction, the acquiring person will hold an aggregate amount of voting securities, NCI [non-corporate interests] and/or assets of the acquired person valued in excess of $200 million (as adjusted)[65], regardless of the sales or assets of the acquiring and acquired persons; or

2. As a result of the transaction, the acquiring person will hold an aggregate amount of voting securities, NCI and/or assets of the acquired person valued in excess of $50 million (as adjusted) but at $200 million (as adjusted) or less; and

3. One person has sales or assets of at least $100 million (as adjusted); and

4. The other person has sales or assets of at least $10 million (as adjusted).

A. Size of Transaction Test

The first step is to determine what voting securities, NCI, assets, or combination thereof are being transferred in the proposed transaction. Then you must determine the value of the voting securities, NCI, and/or assets as well as the percentage of voting securities and NCI that will be "held as a result of the acquisition." Calculating what will be held as a result of the acquisition (referred to as the "size of the transaction") is complicated and requires the application of several rules, including Rules 801.10, 801.12, 801.13, 801.14 and 801.15. Generally, the securities and/or NCI held as a result of the transaction include those that will be acquired in the proposed transaction, as well as any voting securities and/or NCI of the acquired person, or entities within the acquired person, that the acquiring person already holds. Assets held as a result of the acquisition include those that will be acquired in the proposed transaction as well as certain assets of the acquired person that the acquiring person has purchased within the time limits outlined in Rule 801.13.[66]

If the value of the voting securities, NCI, assets or combination thereof exceeds $200 million (as adjusted) and no exemption applies, the parties must file notification and observe the waiting period before closing the transaction.

If the value of the voting securities, NCI, assets or combination thereof exceeds $50 million (as adjusted) but is $200 million (as adjusted) or less, the parties must look to the size of person test.

---

[65] [n.2] The 2000 amendments to the Act require the Commission to revise certain thresholds annually based on the change in the level of gross national product. A parenthetical "(as adjusted)" has been added where necessary throughout the Rules (and in this guide) to indicate where such a change in statutory threshold value occurs. The term "as adjusted" is defined in subsection 801.1(n) of the Rules and refers to a table of the adjusted values published in the Federal Register notice titled "Revised Jurisdictional Thresholds for § 7A of the Clayton Act." The notice contains a table showing adjusted values for the rules and is published in January of each year.

[66] [n.4] The Rules on when to aggregate the value of previously acquired voting securities and assets with the value of the proposed acquisition are discussed in greater detail in *Guide II*.

B. Acquiring and Acquired Persons/Acquired Entity

The first step in determining the size of person is to identify the "acquiring person" and "acquired person." "Person" is defined in Rules 801.1(a)(1) and is the "ultimate parent entity" or "UPE" of the buyer or seller. That is, it is the entity that ultimately controls the buyer or seller. The "acquired entity" is the specific entity whose assets, NCI or voting securities are being acquired. The acquired entity may also be its own UPE or it may be an entity within the acquired person.

Thus, in an asset acquisition, the acquiring person is the UPE of the buyer, and the acquired person is the UPE of the seller. The acquired entity is the entity whose assets are being acquired. In a voting securities acquisition, the acquiring person is the UPE of the buyer, the acquired person is the UPE of the entity whose securities are being bought, and the acquired entity is the issuer of the securities being purchased. In an acquisition of NCI, the acquiring person is the UPE of the buyer, the acquired person is the UPE of the entity whose NCI are being bought, and the acquired entity is the entity whose NCI are being acquired. Oftentimes the acquired person and acquired entity are the same.

In many voting securities acquisitions, the acquiring person proposes to buy voting securities from minority shareholders of the acquired entity, rather than from the entity itself (tender offers are an example of this type of transaction). These transactions are subject to Rule 801.30, which imposes a reporting obligation on the acquiring person and on the acquired person, despite the fact that the acquired person may have no knowledge of the proposed purchase of its outstanding securities. For this reason, the Rules also require that a person proposing to acquire voting securities directly from shareholders rather than from the issuer itself serve notice on the issuer of the shares to ensure the acquired person knows about its reporting obligation.

C. Size of Person Test

Once you have determined who the acquiring and acquired persons are, you must determine whether the size of each person meets the Act's minimum size criteria. This "size of person" test generally measures a company based on the person's last regularly prepared annual statement of income and expenses and its last regularly prepared balance sheet. The size of a person includes not only the entity that is making the acquisition or whose assets or securities are being acquired, but also the UPE and any other entities the UPE controls.

If the value of the voting securities, NCI, assets or combination thereof exceeds $50 million (as adjusted) but is $200 million (as adjusted) or less, the size of person test is met, and no exemption applies, the parties must file notification and observe the waiting period before closing the transaction.

D. Notification Thresholds

An acquisition that will result in a buyer holding more than $50 million (as adjusted) worth of the voting securities of another issuer crosses the first of five staggered "notification thresholds." The rules identify four additional thresholds:

voting securities valued at $100 million (as adjusted) or greater but less than $500 million (as adjusted); voting securities valued at $500 million (as adjusted) or greater; 25 percent of the voting securities of an issuer, if the 25 percent (or any amount above 25% but less than 50%) is valued at greater than $1 billion (as adjusted); and 50 percent of the voting securities of an issuer if valued at greater than $50 million (as adjusted).

The thresholds are designed to act as exemptions to relieve parties of the burden of making another filing every time additional voting shares of the same person are acquired. As such, when notification is filed, the acquiring person is allowed one year from the end of the waiting period to cross the threshold stated in the filing. If within that year the person reaches the stated threshold (or any lower threshold), it may continue acquiring voting shares up to the next threshold for five years from the end of the waiting period. For example, if you file to acquire $100 million (as adjusted) of the voting securities of Company B and cross that threshold within one year, you would be able to continue to acquire voting securities of Company B for a total of five years without having to file again so long as your total holding of Company B's voting securities did not exceed either $500 million (as adjusted) or 50 percent, i.e., additional notification thresholds. Once an acquiring person holds 50 percent or more of the voting securities of an issuer, all subsequent acquisitions of securities of that issuer are exempt.

These notification thresholds apply only to acquisitions of voting securities. The 50 percent threshold is the highest threshold regardless of the corresponding dollar value.

E. Exempt Transactions

In some instances, a transaction may not be reportable even if the size of person and the size of transaction tests have been satisfied. The Act and the Rules set forth a number of exemptions, describing particular transactions or classes of transactions that need not be reported despite meeting the threshold criteria. For example, certain acquisitions of assets in the ordinary course of a person's business are exempted, including new goods and current supplies (e.g., an airline purchases new jets from a manufacturer, or a supermarket purchases its inventory from a wholesale distributor). The acquisition of certain types of real property also would not require notification. These include certain new and used facilities, not being acquired with a business, unproductive real property (e.g., raw land), office and residential buildings, hotels (excluding hotel casinos), certain recreational land, agricultural land and retail rental space and warehouses. In addition, the acquisition of foreign assets would be exempt where the sales in or into the U.S. attributable to those assets were $50 million (as adjusted) or less. Once it has been determined that a particular transaction is reportable, each party must submit its notification to the FTC and the DOJ. In addition, each acquiring person must pay a filing fee to the FTC for each transaction that it reports (with a few exceptions, see IV below).

III. THE FORM

The Notification and Report Form ("the Form") solicits information that the enforcement agencies use to help evaluate the antitrust implications of the proposed transaction. Copies of the Form, Instructions, and Style Sheet are available from the PNO, (202) 326-3100, as well as the FTC website at http://www.ftc.gov/bc/hsr.

A. Information Reported

In general, a filing party is required to identify the persons involved and the structure of the transaction. The reporting person also must provide certain documents such as balance sheets and other financial data, as well as copies of certain documents that have been filed with the Securities and Exchange Commission. In addition, the parties are required to submit certain planning and evaluation documents that pertain to the proposed transaction.

The Form also requires the parties to disclose whether the acquiring person and acquired entity currently derive revenue from businesses that fall within any of the same industry and product North American Industry Classification System ("NAICS") codes,[67] and, if so, in which geographic areas they operate. Identification of overlapping codes may indicate whether the parties engage in similar lines of business. Acquiring persons must also describe certain previous acquisitions in the last five years of companies or assets engaged in businesses in any of the overlapping codes identified. Please note that an acquiring person must complete the Form for all of its operations; an acquired person, on the other hand, must limit its response in Items 5 through 7 to the business or businesses being sold and does not need to answer Item 8. In addition, the acquired person does not need to respond to Item 6 in a pure asset transaction.

B. Contact Person

The parties are required to identify an individual (listed in Item 1(g) of the Form) who is a representative of the reporting person and is familiar with the content of the Form. This contact person is, in most cases, either counsel for the party or an officer of the company. This person must be available during the waiting period.

C. Certification and Affidavits

Rule 803.5 describes the affidavit that must accompany certain Forms. In transactions where the acquiring person is purchasing voting securities from non-controlling shareholders, only the acquiring person must submit an affidavit.

---

[67] [n.17] For information concerning NAICS codes, *see* the *North American Industry Classification System, 2002*, published by the Executive Office of the President, Office of Management and Budget and available from the National Technical Information Service, 5285 Port Royal Road, Springfield VA 22161 (Order Number PB 2002-101430) or online at http://www.ntis.gov/search/product.aspx?ABBR=PB2002101430; and The *2002 Economic Census Numerical List of Manufactured and Mineral Products* published by Bureau of the Census, available from the Government Printing Office or online at http://www.census.gov/prod/ec02/02numlist/m31r-nl.pdf. Information regarding NAICS also is available at the Bureau of the Census website at http://www.census.gov/epcd/www/naics.html.

The acquiring person must state in the affidavit that it has a good faith intention of completing the proposed transaction and that it has served notice on the acquired person as to its potential reporting obligations. In all other transactions, each of the acquired and acquiring persons must submit an affidavit with their Forms, attesting to the fact that a contract, an agreement in principle, or a letter of intent has been executed and that each person has a good faith intention of completing the proposed transaction. These required statements govern when the parties may make a premerger notification filing. The affidavit is intended to assure that the enforcement agencies will not be presented with hypothetical transactions for review.

Rule 803.6 provides that the Form must be certified and the rule specifies who must make the certification. One of the primary purposes of the certification is to preserve the evidentiary value of the filing. It also is intended to place responsibility on an individual to ensure that information reported is true, correct, and complete. Both the certification and the affidavit must be notarized, or may be signed under penalty of perjury.

D. Voluntary Information

The rules provide that reporting persons also may submit information that is not required by the Form. If persons voluntarily provide information or documentary material that is helpful to the competitive analysis of the proposed transaction, the enforcement agencies' review of a proposed transaction may be more rapid. However, voluntary submissions do not guarantee a speedy review. Voluntary submissions are included in the confidentiality coverage of the Act and the Rules.

E. Confidentiality

Neither the information submitted nor the fact that a notification has been filed is made public by the agencies except as part of a legal or administrative action to which one of the agencies is a party or in other narrowly defined circumstances permitted by the Act. However, in response to inquiries from interested parties who wish to approach the agencies with their views about a transaction, the agencies may confirm which agency is handling the investigation of a publicly announced merger.[68] The fact that a transaction is under investigation also may become apparent if the agencies interview third parties during their investigation.

F. Filing Procedures

The parties should complete and return the original and one copy of the Form, along with one set of documentary attachments, to the Premerger Notification Office, Bureau of Competition, Room 303, Federal Trade Commission, 600 Pennsylvania Avenue, NW, Washington, D.C. 20580.

Three copies of the Form, along with one set of documentary attachments, should be sent to the Department of Justice, Antitrust Division, Office of Opera-

---

[68] [n.25] A publicly announced merger is one in which a party to the merger has disclosed the existence of the transaction in a press release or in a public filing with a governmental body.

tions, Premerger Notification Unit, 950 Pennsylvania Avenue, NW, Room 3335, Washington, D.C. 20530 (for non-USPS deliveries, use zip code 20004).

IV. THE FILING FEE

In connection with the filing of a Form, Congress also mandated the collection of a fee from each acquiring person. The filing fee is based on a three-tiered system that ties the amount paid to the total value of the voting securities, NCI or assets held as a result of the acquisition.[69]

VALUE OF VOTING SECURITIES, NCI OR ASSETS TO BE HELD	FEE AMOUNT
greater than $50 million (as adjusted) but less than $100 million (as adjusted)	$45,000
$100 million (as adjusted) or greater but less than $500 million (as adjusted)	$125,000
$500 million (as adjusted) or greater	$280,000

For transactions in which more than one person is deemed to be the acquiring person, each acquiring person must pay the appropriate fee (except in consolidations and in transactions in which there are two acquiring persons that would have exactly the same responses to Item 5 of the Form). In addition, an acquiring person will have to pay multiple filing fees if a series of acquisitions are separately reported.

The filing fee must be paid at the time of filing to "The Federal Trade Commission" by electronic wire transfer, bank cashier's check or certified check. Rule 803.9 contains specific instructions for payment of the filing fee. In addition, information is available at http://www.ftc.gov/bc/hsr/filing2.htm.

V. THE WAITING PERIOD

After filing, the filing parties must then observe a statutory waiting period during which they may not consummate the transaction. The waiting period is 15 days for reportable acquisitions by means of a cash tender offer, as well as acquisitions subject to certain federal bankruptcy provisions, and 30 days for all other types of reportable transactions. The waiting period may be extended by issuance of a request for additional information and documentary material. Any waiting period that would end on a Saturday, Sunday or legal public holiday will expire on the next regular business day.

---

[69] [n.26] The filing fee thresholds are adjusted annually for changes in the GNP during the previous year. The fees themselves are not adjusted.

A. Beginning of the Waiting Period

In most cases, the waiting period begins after both the acquiring and acquired persons file completed Forms with both agencies. However, for certain transactions in which a person buys voting securities from persons other than the issuer (third party and open market transactions), the waiting period begins after the acquiring person files a complete Form. In a reportable joint venture formation, the waiting period begins after all acquiring persons required to file submit complete Forms. It is important to note that failure to pay the filing fee or the submission of an incorrect or incomplete filing will delay the start of the waiting period.

B. Early Termination

Any filing person may request that the waiting period be terminated before the statutory period expires. Such a request for "early termination" will be granted only if (1) at least one of the persons specifies it on the Form; (2) all persons have submitted compliant Forms; and (3) both antitrust agencies have completed their review and determined not to take any enforcement action during the waiting period.

The PNO is responsible for informing the parties that early termination has been granted. The Act requires that the FTC publish a notice in the Federal Register of each early termination granted. Moreover, grants of early termination also appear on the FTC's website at http://www.ftc.gov/bc/earlyterm/index.html.

When it's requested, early termination is granted for most transactions. On the average, requests for early termination are granted within two weeks from the beginning of the waiting period. In any particular transaction, however, the time that it takes to grant a request for early termination depends on many factors, including the complexity of the proposed transaction, its potential competitive impact, and the number of filings from other parties that the enforcement agencies must review at the same time.

VI. REVIEW OF THE FORM

Once a Form has been filed, the enforcement agencies begin their review. The FTC is responsible for the administration of the Program. As a result, the PNO determines whether the Form complies with the Act and the Rules.

The Form is assigned to a member of the PNO staff to assess whether the transaction was subject to the reporting requirements and whether the Form was completed accurately. If the filing appears to be deficient, the staff member will notify the contact person as quickly as possible so that errors can be corrected. It is important to correct the errors as soon as possible because the waiting period does not begin to run until the Form is filled out accurately, all required information and documentary material are supplied and payment of the filing fee is received.

When the PNO determines that the Forms comply with all filing requirements, letters are sent to the parties identifying the beginning and ending of the waiting period, as well as the transaction number assigned to the filing. The conclusion that the parties have complied with the Act and the Rules may be modified later, however, if circumstances warrant.

VII. ANTITRUST REVIEW OF THE TRANSACTION

Initially, both agencies undertake a preliminary substantive review of the proposed transaction. The agencies analyze the filings to determine whether the acquiring and acquired firms are competitors, or are related in any other way such that a combination of the two firms might adversely affect competition. Staff members rely not only on the information included on the Form but also on publicly available information. The individuals analyzing the Form often have experience either with the markets or the companies involved in the particular transaction. As a result, they may have industry expertise to aid in evaluating the likelihood that a merger may be harmful.

If, after preliminary review, either or both agencies decide that a particular transaction warrants closer examination, the agencies decide between themselves which one will be responsible for the investigation. Only one of the enforcement agencies will conduct an investigation of a proposed transaction. Other than members of the PNO, no one at either agency will initiate contact with any of the persons or any third parties until it has been decided which agency will be responsible for investigating the proposed transaction. This clearance procedure is designed to minimize the duplication of effort and the confusion that could result if both agencies contacted individual persons at different times about the same matter. The clearance decision is made pursuant to an agreement that divides the antitrust work between the two agencies.

Of course, any interested person, including either of the parties, is free to present information to either or both agencies at any time. However, if the clearance decision has not yet been resolved, the person must make a presentation, or provide written information or documents, to both agencies. If you are representing a party that wishes to make a presentation, or provide written information or documents, you may inform the PNO of that fact; the PNO will let staff attorneys at both agencies who are reviewing the matter know that persons wish to come in and make a presentation, or provide written information or documents.

VIII. SECOND REQUESTS

Once the investigating agency has clearance to proceed, it may ask any or all persons to the transaction to submit additional information or documentary material to the requesting agency. The request for additional information is commonly referred to as a "second request." As discussed above, although both agencies review each Form submitted to them, only one agency will issue second requests to the parties in a particular transaction.

A. Information Requested

Generally, a second request will solicit information on particular products or services in an attempt to assist the investigative team in examining a variety of legal and economic questions. A typical second request will include interrogatory-type questions as well as requests for the production of documents. A model second request has been produced jointly by the FTC and DOJ for internal use by their attorneys and is contained in *Guide III*. Because every transaction is unique, however, the model second request should be regarded only as an example.

B. Narrowing the Request

Parties that receive a second request and believe that it is broader than necessary to obtain the information that the enforcement agency needs are encouraged to discuss the possibility of narrowing the request with the staff attorneys reviewing the proposed transaction. Often, the investigative team drafts a second request based only on information contained in the initial filing and other available material. At this point, the investigative team may not have access to specific information about the structure of the company or its products and services. By meeting with staff, representatives of the company have an opportunity to narrow the issues and to limit the required search for documents and other information. If second request modification issues cannot be resolved through discussion with staff, the agencies also have adopted a formal internal appeals process that centralizes in one decision maker in each agency the review of issues relating to the scope of and compliance with second requests.

The enforcement agency issuing the second request may have determined that certain data sought in the request can resolve one or more issues critical to the investigation. In such a situation, the agency's staff may suggest use of the informal "quick look" procedure. Under the quick look, the staff will request the parties to first submit documents and other information, which specifically address the critical issues (e.g., product market definition or ease of entry). If the submitted information resolves the staff's concerns in these areas, the waiting period will be terminated on a *sua sponte* basis and the parties will not have to expend the time and cost of responding to the full second request. Of course, if the submitted information does not resolve the staff's concerns on determinative issues, then the parties will need to respond to the full second request.

C. Extension of the Waiting Period

The issuance of a second request extends the statutory waiting period until 30 days (or in the case of a cash tender offer or certain bankruptcy filings, 10 days) after both parties are deemed to have complied with the second request (or in the case of a tender offer and bankruptcy, until after the acquiring person has complied). During this time, the attorneys investigating the matter may also be interviewing relevant parties and using other forms of compulsory process to obtain information.

The second request must be issued by the enforcement agency before the waiting period expires. If the waiting period expires and the agencies have not issued a second request to any person to the transaction, then the parties are free to consummate the transaction. The fact that the agencies do not issue second requests does not preclude them from initiating an enforcement action at a later time. All of the agencies' other investigative tools are available to them in such investigations.

IX. AGENCY ACTION

After analyzing all of the information available to them, the investigative staff will make a recommendation to either the Commission or the Assistant Attorney General (depending on which agency has clearance).

A. No Further Action

If the staff finds no reason to believe competition will be reduced substantially in any market, it will recommend no further action. Assuming that the agency concurs in that recommendation, the parties are then free to consummate their transaction upon expiration of the waiting period. As with a decision not to issue a second request, a decision not to seek injunctive relief at that time does not preclude the enforcement agencies from initiating a post-merger enforcement action at a later time.

B. Seeking Injunctive Relief

If the investigative staff believes that the transaction is likely to be anticompetitive, it may recommend that the agency initiate injunction proceedings in U.S. district court to halt the acquisition. If the Commission or the Assistant Attorney General concurs in the staff's recommendation, then the agency will file suit in the appropriate district court. If it is a Commission case, the FTC is required to file an administrative complaint within twenty days (or a lesser time if the court so directs) of the granting of its motion for a temporary restraining order or for a preliminary injunction. The administrative complaint initiates the FTC's administrative proceeding that will decide the legality of the transaction. If it is a DOJ case, the legality of the transaction is litigated entirely in district court.

C. Settlements

During an investigation, the investigative staff may, if appropriate, discuss terms of settlement with the parties. The staff of the FTC is permitted to negotiate a proposed settlement with the parties; however, it must then be presented to the Commission, accepted by a majority vote, and placed on the public record for a notice and comment period before it can be made final. A proposed settlement negotiated by DOJ staff must be approved by the Assistant Attorney General and also placed on the public record for a notice and comment period before it will be entered by a district court pursuant to the provisions of the Antitrust Procedures and Penalties Act, 15 U.S.C. § 16(b)-(h).

X. FAILURE TO FILE

A. Civil Penalties

If you consummate a reportable transaction without filing the required prior notification or without waiting until the expiration of the statutory waiting period, you may be subject to civil penalties. The Act provides that "any person, or any officer, director or partner thereof" shall be liable for a penalty of up to $16,000 a day for each day the person is in violation of the Act. The enforcement agencies may also obtain other relief to remedy violations of the Act, such as an order requiring the person to divest assets or voting securities acquired in violation of the Act.

B. Reporting Omissions

If you have completed a transaction in violation of the Act, it is important to bring the matter to the attention of the PNO and to file a notification as soon as possible. Even a late filing provides information to the enforcement agencies that assists them in conducting antitrust screening of transactions and antitrust investigations. The parties should include a letter with the notification from an officer or director of the company explaining why the notification was not filed in a timely manner, how and when the failure was discovered, and what steps have been taken to prevent a violation of the Act in the future. The letter should be addressed to the Deputy Director, Bureau of Competition, Federal Trade Commission, 600 Pennsylvania Ave., NW, Washington, D.C. 20580.

C. Deliberate Avoidance

The Rules specifically provide that structuring a transaction to avoid the Act does not alter notification obligations if the substance of the transaction is reportable. For example, the agencies will seek penalties where the parties split a transaction into separate parts that are each valued below the current filing threshold in order to avoid reporting the transaction, but the fair market value of the assets being acquired is actually above the threshold. . . .

XII. OTHER MATERIALS

To make effective use of these guides, you must be aware of their limitations. They are intended to provide only a very general introduction to the Act and Rules and should be used only as a starting point. Because it would be impossible, within the scope of these guides, to explain all of the details and nuances of the premerger requirements, you must not rely on them as a substitute for reading the Act and the Rules themselves. To determine premerger notification requirements, you should consult:

1. Section 7A of the Clayton Act, 15 U.S.C. § 18a, as amended by the Hart-Scott-Rodino Antitrust Improvements Act of 1976, Pub. L. 94-435, 90 Stat. 1390, and amended by Pub. L. No. 106-553, 114 Stat. 2762.

2. The Premerger Notification Rules, 16 C.F.R. Parts 801–803. (2008).

3. The Statement of Basis and Purpose for the Rules, 43 Fed. Reg. 33450 (July 31, 1978); 48 Fed. Reg. 34428 (July 29, 1983); 52 Fed. Reg. 7066.

4. The formal interpretations issued pursuant to the Rules, compiled in 6 Trade Reg. Rep. (CCH) at ¶ 42,475. . . .

HART-SCOTT-RODINO PREMERGER NOTIFICATION PROGRAM INTRODUCTORY GUIDE II
To File or Not to File?
When You Must File a Premerger Notification Report Form
FTC Premerger Notification Office
(Sept. 2008)

III. HYPOTHETICAL TRANSACTION

Throughout this Guide, we will refer to the following hypothetical transaction (italicized in the document). The hypothetical places you in the position of legal counsel to a corporation that is about to be acquired. However, the principles it illustrates should be of use to readers in other circumstances.

The President of Beta Products, Inc., walks into your law office and informs you that the Zed Corporation is acquiring her company. She remarks that Zed Corporation mentioned something about the Hart-Scott-Rodino Act and filing a notification and report form within the next few weeks. Although you have handled certain business transactions for Beta Products in the past, this is the first time that the possibility of a premerger notification filing has been involved. You want to determine, therefore, whether the transaction must be reported, and if so, how.

IV. PRELIMINARY QUESTIONS

In determining whether a particular transaction must be reported, you should begin by answering several preliminary questions:

1) What is being acquired?

2) What are the amount and the nature of the consideration?

3) Who are the parties involved in the transaction?

4) When and under what conditions will the transaction take place?

In exploring these preliminary questions about the hypothetical transaction, you have learned that Zed Corporation has entered into agreements with the shareholders of Beta Products to buy all of Beta Products' outstanding voting stock for $90 million. Further investigation reveals, however, that Zed Corporation does not plan to purchase the voting stock directly; rather, Zed Corporation's wholly-owned subsidiary, Sub Co., will buy the shares from Beta Products' shareholders. You already know who those shareholders are: Mrs. Beta holds 49 percent of the outstanding voting securities and her husband owns one percent, while Mrs. Delta, her sister-in-law, and Mr. Alpha, an unrelated private investor, each own 25 percent. You also know from your previous work that Beta Products holds 4500 shares of common stock, which constitute 25 percent of the voting securities of

Resource Inc. Beta Products is the largest holder of Resource Inc. voting securities.

To clarify the relationships among the parties and the structure of the transaction, it is often helpful to draw a diagram of the transaction such as the one in Figure 1 below. *As you will see later, the Rules treat this transaction as two separate acquisitions, either or both of which may be reportable. In both acquisitions, the acquiring person is Zed Corporation. Mrs. and Mr. Beta, together, are the acquired person in the acquisition of Beta Products, Inc. In addition, because the acquisition of Beta Products will result in Zed Corporation holding voting securities of Resource Inc., the Rules treat this aspect of the transaction as a different acquisition in which Resource Inc. also is an acquired person.*

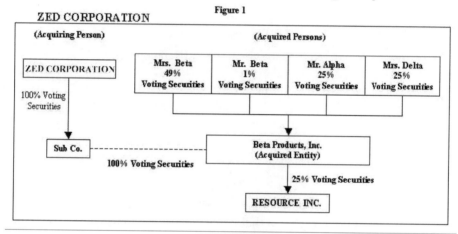

Figure 1

V. STEPS TO DETERMINE REPORTABILITY

Once you have outlined the basic transaction, you are ready to analyze it to determine whether it must be reported. The important steps in this process include:

1) Determining the size of the transaction and the relevant reporting threshold;

2) Identifying the acquiring and acquired persons (the "ultimate parent entity") of each party; and

3) Determining the size of each person involved in the transaction.

A. The Size of Transaction Test

The size of transaction test, as its name suggests, is concerned with the value of what is being acquired. Because the objective of the Program is to analyze the effects of combining once separate businesses, the Rules generally require that assets, voting securities or NCI of the acquired person that have already been acquired must be aggregated with those that will be acquired in the proposed transaction. When what has previously been purchased plus what will be bought in the present acquisition meets the size of transaction criteria, the transaction becomes reportable unless an exemption applies.

1. Value of voting securities, NCI and assets to be held

In order to determine whether a transaction meets the size of transaction test, you must compute the value of the voting securities, NCI and assets, which you will hold as a result of the acquisition. The phrase "held as a result of the acquisition" has a technical meaning under the Rules. It includes not only those securities, NCI and assets that are currently being acquired, but also voting securities, NCI, and, in some circumstances, assets previously acquired from the same person. Rule 801.135 determines what is held as a result of the acquisition, and Rules 801.13 and 801.14 specify how such voting securities, NCI and assets should be aggregated and valued.

a. "Held as a result of the acquisition"

All voting securities, NCI and assets currently being acquired are held as a result of the acquisition. In addition, Rule 801.137 explains when you must aggregate previously-acquired voting securities, NCI or assets with those that you plan to acquire in order to determine what is held as a result of the acquisition. Different principles apply to asset, voting securities and NCI acquisitions.

(1) Aggregating previously-acquired voting securities or NCI

Rule 801.13(a)(1) requires that you add any voting securities that you currently hold of the same issuer to any voting securities that you propose to acquire to determine what voting securities of that issuer will be held as a result of the planned acquisition. There are some special circumstances, however, described in Rule 801.15,9 in which the prior, simultaneous, or subsequent acquisition is exempt from notification and need not be included in the calculation.

Rule 801.14,10 requires that you aggregate the value of all of the voting securities of all of the issuers included within the acquired person that you will hold as a result of the acquisition. Thus, if you hold less than 50% of the voting securities of one subsidiary company and plan to acquire voting securities of the parent or a different subsidiary of the same parent, you would aggregate these holdings to determine the value of the securities held.

Rule 801.13(c)(1)11 requires that you add any NCI that you currently hold of the same non-corporate entity to any NCI that you propose to acquire to determine what NCI will be held as a result of the planned acquisition. Rule 801.14,12 requires that you aggregate the value of all NCI included within the acquired person that you will hold as a result of the acquisition as determined by Rule 801.13(c). Under Rule 801.13(c)(2),13 an acquisition of NCI which does not confer control of the unincorporated entity is not aggregated with any other assets or voting securities which have been or are currently being acquired from the same acquired person.

(2) Aggregating assets and voting securities

In some circumstances, the size of transaction test requires acquiring persons to add the value of an issuer's voting securities that it holds and will hold with the value of assets that have been acquired or will be acquired from that issuer or the person controlling that issuer. Whether the acquisitions of assets and voting securities are both to be considered "held as a result of the transaction" depends on the order of the transactions. If a noncontrolling percentage of voting securities were purchased in a nonreportable transaction and will be held at the time assets are to be acquired, then both the voting securities and assets are held as a result of the transaction.

Their combined value is included to determine if the size of transaction test is satisfied. If, however, the asset transaction precedes the voting securities transaction, then the assets are not held as a result of the later acquisition of voting securities and the value of the assets is not included. The Commission explained the exclusion of assets in the second instance when it promulgated Rule 801.13:14 "once assets are sold, they confer no continuing ability to participate in the affairs of the acquired person, and so prior acquisitions of assets need not be considered for purposes of subsequent acquisitions of voting securities."

(3) Aggregating previously-acquired assets

Generally, the acquisition by an acquiring person of assets from the same acquired person is not aggregated unless: the second acquisition is made pursuant to a signed letter of intent or agreement, and within the previous 180 days the acquiring person has signed a letter of intent or agreement in principle to acquire assets from the same acquired person, which is still in effect but has not been consummated; or the acquiring person has acquired assets from the same acquired person which it still holds; and the previous acquisition (whether consummated or still contemplated) was not subject to the requirements of the Act. If the previous asset acquisition (or aggregated asset acquisitions) was reported properly to the enforcement agencies, aggregation is not required. In addition, if a single agreement calls for multiple closings on purchases of assets from the same person, the purchases must be aggregated to the extent that those closings are within one year.

b. Valuation

Once you have determined what is held as a result of the acquisition, you must value those securities, NCI and assets. Again, different methods are used for valuation, depending on whether voting securities, NCI or assets will be held as a result of an acquisition. i.e., those not traded on a national securities exchange or quoted in NASDAQ. Under the Rules, the value of publicly traded voting securities that are to be acquired is the higher of "market price" or "acquisition price." Thus, if the voting securities are trading at $50 a share, and you have a contract to buy a block for $60 a share, the $60 value is used. If the acquisition price of publicly-traded shares has not been determined, the value is the market price. For non-publicly traded voting securities, the securities are valued at their "acquisition price" or, if the "acquisition price" has not been determined, at "fair market value." Previously acquired securities are valued in similar ways pursuant to Rules 801.10 and 801.13. NCI are valued in the same manner as non-publicly traded voting securities. In an acquisition of assets, Rule 801.10(b)18 provides that the assets must be valued at their "fair market value" or, "if determined and greater than the fair market value," at their "acquisition price."

The terms "market price," "acquisition price," and "fair market value" are defined for premerger notification purposes in Rule 801.10(c). For useful information concerning the "valuation rule", please visit http://www.ftc.gov/bc/hsr/hsrvaluation.shtm and http://www.ftc.gov/bc/hsr/801.10summary.shtm.

(1) Determining market price

In transactions subject to § 801.30, e.g., open market stock purchases, the "market price" is the lowest closing quotation or bid price within 45 days prior to receipt by the issuer of the notice required by Rule 803.5(a) from the acquiring person, which must be delivered to start the waiting period. In transactions to which Rule § 801.30 does not apply, e.g., purchases from a "controlling" stockholder or directly from the issuer, the "market price" is the lowest closing quotation or bid price within the 45 calendar days preceding the closing of the acquisition, but not extending back prior to the day before execution of the agreement or letter of intent to merge or acquire. The "45-day rule" will enable you to determine whether a particular transaction will meet the size of transaction test even though the price of the voting securities may be fluctuating significantly on the open market.

(2) Determining acquisition price

Rule 801.10(c)(2) states that the "acquisition price" includes the value of all consideration for the voting securities, NCI and assets being acquired. This consideration includes any cash, voting securities, tangible assets, and intangible assets that the acquiring person is exchanging with the seller. In an asset transaction, it also includes the value of any liabilities that the acquiring person will assume. Thus, if you will pay $85 million in cash for a factory and, in addition, will assume $10 million in liabilities, the acquisition price is $95 million.

(3) Determining fair market value

"Fair market value" must be determined in good faith by the board of directors of the ultimate parent entity of the acquiring person (or the board's designee). Such a determination must be made within 60 days of filing or, if no filing is required, within 60 days of consummation of the acquisition. Thus, if the parties neither file nor consummate within 60 days of the determination, they cannot rely on it. If a filing is made within the 60 days, however, a new fair market value determination is not required regardless of the consummation date.

(4) Voting securities and assets previously acquired

Voting securities that were acquired in an earlier transaction are valued on the basis of their current worth, not their historical purchase price. If the securities are publicly traded, you should use their current market price, as determined by the 45-day rule under Rule 801.10(c)(1). Otherwise, they are valued at their current fair market value, as determined by Rule 801.10(c)(3). NCI are valued in the same manner as non-publicly traded voting securities. Previously acquired assets should be valued according to Rule 801.10(b) at the greater of their current fair market value or the acquisition price at the time they were acquired.

Since Beta Products, Inc., is a closely-held company and the stock is not publicly traded, the applicable Rule is 16 C.F.R. § 801.10(a)(2). This Rule provides that the value of the voting securities will be the acquisition price, if determined, or, if the acquisition price has not been determined, the fair market value of the voting securities as set by the board of directors of the acquiring person. Sub Co. and Beta Products' shareholders have agreed on a total purchase price of $90 million for 100 percent of the voting securities of Beta Products, Inc. Therefore, you will not have to get the board of directors of Zed Corporation to determine the fair market value of Beta Products' stock. Rather, you can rely on the acquisition price of $90 million to conclude that the acquisition meets the size of transaction test.

To determine whether Zed Corporation and Resource Inc. must report, you will have to calculate the value of the voting securities of Resource Inc. that will be held by Zed as a result of acquiring Beta Products. Because the acquisition price of the Resource securities is not separately identified, the Rules require that the value be determined by the market price. In this transaction, the market price can be determined because the voting securities are publicly traded. Resource shares sell, at the time of your research, for $100 a share; thus, the value of the 4500 Resource shares that Zed will obtain is likely to be about $4.5 million.

If Zed already owned other Resource voting securities, you would add the current market price of those shares to determine if the total value of the voting securities held as a result of the acquisition meets the size of transaction test. After reviewing Zed's holdings, you determine that it does not hold any other Resource securities. Accordingly, the secondary acquisition does not meet the size of transaction test and is not reportable.

c. Calculating percentage of voting securities to be acquired

Rule 801.12 sets out a formula to be used whenever the Act or Rules require calculation of the percentage of voting securities of an issuer to be held or acquired, e.g., in determining control. The Rule is designed to recognize weighted voting rights and different classes of voting securities. As illustrated below, the percentage is derived from the ratio of two numbers: the number of votes for directors of the issuer that the holder of a class of voting securities is presently entitled to cast, or, as a result of the acquisition, will become entitled to cast, divided by the total number of votes for directors which presently may be cast by that class, multiplied by the number of directors elected by that class, divided by the total number of directors.

$$\frac{\# \ of \ Votes \ Class \ A \ Held}{Total \ Votes \ of \ Class \ A} \times \frac{Directors \ Elected \ by \ Class \ A \ Stock}{Total \ \# \ of \ Directors} = \%$$

The resulting percentage should be calculated separately for each class, and then totaled to determine an acquiring person's voting power. You should omit authorized but unissued voting securities or treasury securities, as well as convertible voting securities that have not yet been converted and do not have a present right to vote, unless you are filing notification for their acquisition or conversion.

2. The Notification Thresholds

Rule 801.1(h), 16 C.F.R. § 801.1(h), establishes five notification thresholds for acquisitions of voting securities:

a) $50 million (as adjusted);

b) $100 million (as adjusted);

c) $500 million (as adjusted);

d) 25%, if valued at greater than $1 billion (as adjusted); and

e) 50%, if valued at greater than $50 million (as adjusted).

Because the Rules provide that all voting securities held by the acquiring person after an acquisition are "held as a result of the acquisition," the thresholds are designed to act as exemptions to relieve parties of the burden of making another filing every time additional shares of the same person are acquired. As such, when notification is filed, the acquiring person is allowed one year from the end of the waiting period to cross the threshold it indicated in the filing. If within that year the person reaches the stated threshold or any lower threshold, it may continue acquiring shares up to the next threshold for five years measured from the end of the waiting period. The acquiring person must file again, however, before it can cross that next higher threshold. The 50 percent threshold is the highest threshold regardless of the corresponding dollar value, because it indicates the acquisition of control.

Because Zed is acquiring 100% of the voting securities of Beta Products, it will indicate the 50% filing threshold in its filing regardless of the transaction value.

B. Identifying the Acquiring and Acquired Persons

If the hypothetical transaction were valued in excess of $200 million (as adjusted), the transaction would be reportable unless an exemption applied. But, because the hypothetical transaction is valued at $90 million, you must also turn to the size of person test, as you must for all transactions valued in excess of $50 million (as adjusted) but at $200 million (as adjusted) or less. The first step in determining your size of person is to identify the "acquiring person" and the "acquired person." Under the Act, the obligation to report depends on the size of the "persons" involved. "Person" is defined in Rule 801.1(a)(1) and is the "ultimate parent entity" of the buyer or seller. That is, it is the entity that ultimately controls the buyer or seller.

1. The Ultimate Parent Entity

An ultimate parent entity or "UPE" is the company, individual or other entity that controls a party to the transaction and is not itself controlled by anyone else. For example, the UPE may be a corporate parent of a subsidiary company that has signed a contract to purchase a plant, or it could be a partnership or an individual that owns a majority of the voting securities of the acquiring company. The ultimate parent entity may be separated from the company whose name appears on the sale agreement by many layers of controlled subsidiaries, or the UPE may actually be entering into the transaction in its own name.

2. Control

Identifying the ultimate parent entity involves tracing the chain of "control," a term defined in Rule 801.1(b). Control is established by the "holding" of 50 percent or more of the outstanding voting securities of an issuer. In the case of an entity that has no outstanding voting securities, control is established by the right to 50 percent or more of the profits, or the right, in the event of dissolution, to 50 percent or more of the assets of the entity. Control also is accomplished by having the contractual power presently to designate 50 percent or more of the board of directors of a corporation.

As a result, more than one person may be deemed to control an entity at the same time. For example, one person may hold 50 percent of the voting securities of the entity while another person has the contractual power to appoint 50 percent of the board of directors.

3. "Hold" and "Beneficial Ownership"

To determine control of a corporation you first must identify the individuals or entities that "hold" its voting securities. The holder of voting securities, according to Rule 801.1(c), is the individual or entity that has beneficial ownership. Although the term "beneficial ownership" is not defined in the Rules, the Statement of Basis and Purpose accompanying the Rules provides examples of some indicators of beneficial ownership, including the right to receive an increase in the value of the voting securities, the right to receive dividends, the obligation to bear the risk of loss, and the right to vote the stock. Thus, a person would be the "holder" of voting securities even though the shares were physically held by the person's stockbroker and listed under the broker's street name.

In the hypothetical, Sub Co. is not a UPE because Zed Corporation holds 50 percent or more of its outstanding voting securities. Assume that no one person holds as much as 50 percent of Zed Corporation's voting securities nor does anyone have the contractual power to appoint 50 percent of its board of directors. Under the Rules, therefore, Zed Corporation is not controlled by anyone else, and is the UPE of a "person" consisting of Zed Corporation and any other entities that it controls. In this situation, Beta Products, Inc., does not have a single 50 percent shareholder nor does any person have the contractual power to appoint 50 percent of its board of directors. However, our analysis cannot end here. Under Rule 801.1(c)(2), the holdings of spouses and their minor children must be aggregated. Thus, Mrs. Beta and Mr. Beta hold 50 percent of Beta Products, Inc., (49 percent and one percent, respectively), and together are its ultimate parent entity. Because they are individuals, the Betas cannot be controlled by any other entity.

C. The Size of Person Test

1. The basic test

The next step in the analysis is to determine the size of the persons you have defined as the ultimate parent entities of the parties. The basic "size of person test" established by § 7A(a)(2) of the Act requires a filing in transactions valued in excess of $50 million (as adjusted) but at $200 million (as adjusted) or less only where at least one of the persons involved in the transaction has $100 million (as adjusted) or more in annual net sales or total assets, and the other has $10 million (as adjusted) or more. If these size thresholds are not met, the transaction need not be reported. Thus, for example, filings would not be required for a merger between two $99 million companies.

There is one exception to the basic size of person test. Where an acquired person is not engaged in manufacturing only its total assets (unless its sales are $100 million (as adjusted) or more) are considered in determining its size. In addition, you should be aware that the size of person test is eliminated in transactions valued in excess of $200 million (as adjusted).

2. Calculating annual net sales and total assets

The procedures for calculating the annual net sales and total assets of a person are set out in Rule 801.11. In the majority of cases, you will easily be able to determine whether the size of person test is satisfied. Generally, a person's annual net sales and total assets are as stated on its last regularly prepared annual statement of income and last regularly prepared balance sheet. These financial statements must be as of a date not more than 15 months old, and have been prepared in accordance with procedures normally used by the filing person.

A person should continue to rely on its regularly prepared financial statements until the next regularly prepared statements are available, even if subsequent changes in income or assets have occurred. For example, the most recently prepared statements may show $9 million in annual net sales and $8 million in total assets in the previous year, although the person's sales have increased in the current fiscal year such that its annual revenue will exceed $10 million (as adjusted) when its next statement is issued. For premerger notification purposes, however, the person will not be considered a $10 million (as adjusted) person until the annual income statement reflecting the increased revenue is prepared. The same analysis would be applied, however, if sales in the current fiscal year have decreased. A company's sales and assets may not be relied on until they are reflected in regularly prepared financial statements.

a. Including controlled entities

The size of person test includes the sales and assets of all entities, both domestic and foreign, included within the person. Any entities controlled by the UPE whose sales and assets are not consolidated in its financial statements must be added to determine the total size of the person. Unconsolidated sales and assets should be added, however, only to the extent that such additions are "nonduplicative." If the UPE's interest in the subsidiary is already reflected on the parent's balance sheet as an asset, then adding together the total assets of the subsidiary and the total assets of the parent would result in double counting at least part of the value of the subsidiary's assets. Accordingly, you should add only the subsidiary's total assets after subtracting the value of the interest in the subsidiary as it is carried on the parent's balance sheet.

b. Natural persons

The total assets of a natural person include his or her investment assets (cash, deposits in financial institutions, other money market instruments, and instruments evidencing government obligations), voting securities, and other income-producing property, together with the total assets of any entity he or she controls. Property is income-producing if it is held either for investment or for the production of income, whether or not it actually produces income. You will have to refer to the definitions of "hold" and "control" to determine whether the individual (together with spouse and minor children) "holds" such property and to determine what entities he or she may "control." You may omit from the calculation the value of residences, cars, and personal property not held for the purpose of producing income. The annual net sales of an individual are the sum of the net sales of the entities he or she controls, including proprietorships, as well as income derived from investments.

c. Newly-formed person

A newly formed person, who has not yet prepared financial statements, may need to prepare a special statement of its sales and assets in order to calculate its size. Typically, these entities are formed for the purpose of making an acquisition. Under 801.11(e), a UPE without a regularly prepared balance sheet may exclude funds which will be used to make an acquisition in determining its size. The Rule applies until the UPE, or any entity within it, has a regularly prepared balance sheet.

In the hypothetical, you have already identified Zed Corporation as its own ultimate parent entity and have concluded that Mr. and Mrs. Beta together are the ultimate parent entity of Beta Products, Inc. Assume that you also know that Zed Corporation is a large diversified company which probably has several hundred million dollars in annual sales. To be certain, you can consult Zed Corporation's annual report and refer to the 10-K and 10-Q reports that the company has filed with the Securities and Exchange Commission. In this instance, assume that Zed Corporation's annual report confirms that last year the company had annual revenues of $545 million. Since the current year has not yet ended and Zed Corporation used the calendar year for accounting purposes, there is no more recent annual income figure. Thus, Zed Corporation is clearly a $100 million (as adjusted) person. If it were necessary to consider total assets, you would want to look for the company's most recent regularly prepared balance sheet showing total assets. Note, however, that the balance sheets included in the firm's annual report or SEC filing may not be the company's most recent regularly prepared statements, *since many corporations prepare quarterly or monthly statements of assets apart from those filed.*

Applying the size of person test to Mr. and Mrs. Beta is a bit more involved since neither regularly prepares a financial statement. A good starting point, though, would be to add together the sales and assets of all the companies they control. You would not include the sales and assets of Resource Inc. because the Betas do not control that company but hold only a minority interest with no contractual power to appoint 50 percent or more of the board of directors. Assume here that Beta Products, Inc., is the only company controlled by Mr. and Mrs. Beta. Accordingly, you need not consolidate on one balance sheet the sales and assets of several entities. The minimum annual net sales for Mr. and Mrs. Beta can thus be found in the annual revenue figure from Beta Products' yearly statement of income. Assume that statement shows sales to be $9 million. It also shows total assets to be $9 million. If either figure had been $10 million (as adjusted), you could have stopped there and concluded that the size of person in the case of Mr. and Mrs. Beta was at least $10 million (as adjusted).

In the absence of such a simple solution, however, you must next consider the value of any additional investments owned by Mr. and Mrs. Beta, and any additional revenues these may generate. As provided by Rule 801.11(d), you should not consider Mr. Beta's country residence or the sports car he drives in computing his total assets; similarly, the value of Mrs. Beta's luxury condominium should be omitted from the calculation of her total assets. You should also exclude the value of the Resource Inc. voting securities because, although they are investment assets, their value is already reflected on Beta Products' balance sheet.

However, Mr. and Mrs. Beta also hold in their own names some voting securities in other corporations, a vacation cottage that is rented out during the summer months, and a racehorse. Since these assets are all held to produce income or as investments, you will have to determine their value and include them in your calculation of the value of Mr. and Mrs. Beta's total assets.

You determine that these additional voting securities and income producing properties are worth at least $10 million. Adding this to the total assets of Beta Products, Inc., puts Mr. and Mrs. Beta's total assets over $10 million (as adjusted). You conclude, therefore, that Mr. and Mrs. Beta together satisfy the size of person requirement. Because you have now determined that the acquiring person is a $100 million (as adjusted) person and the acquired person is a $10 million (as adjusted) person (they will need to stipulate to this size of person in their filing), you know that the parties to the proposed transaction meet the size of person test.

Zed's acquisition of Beta is valued at $90 million and the parties meet the size of person test. Thus, unless an exemption applies, the parties in this hypothetical transaction must file and observe the statutory waiting period. . . .

VI. ADDITIONAL CONSIDERATIONS

Note that this Guide does not cover all reporting obligations. The formation of corporate joint ventures and unincorporated entities may be reportable if the parties and the newly-formed entities meet certain criteria. Also, transactions involving foreign businesses are subject to distinct treatment under the Rules.

You also should be aware of Rule 801.90, which is designed to limit the ability of parties to evade the Act's filing requirements. It states that: "Any transaction(s) or other device(s) entered into or employed for the purpose of avoiding the obligation to comply with the requirements of the act shall be disregarded, and the obligation to comply shall be determined by applying the act and these rules to the substance of the transaction."

Finally, it is important to consider the many exemptions provided in the Act and the Rules. The Program is designed to facilitate antitrust review. It, therefore, does not require notification for transactions that have been determined to be unlikely to violate the antitrust laws. For example:

1) Stock splits that do not increase the percentages owned by any person are exempt;

2) Acquisitions of small percentages of an issuer's voting securities solely for the purpose of investment are exempt;

3) Acquisitions of additional voting securities by persons who already hold 50 percent of the voting shares of an issuer are not reportable;

4) Acquisitions in the ordinary course of business, such as purchases of current supplies and used durable goods also are exempt;

5) Acquisitions of several categories of real property, such as unproductive real property, office and residential property, and hotels are not reportable.

6) Acquisitions in regulated industries, whose competitive effects are reviewed by other agencies, may be exempt or subject to modified reporting requirements.

Although the premerger notification Rules tend to be complex and technical, the discussion in this Guide should help you determine whether a particular transaction must be reported. That said, you should not rely on this Guide alone to determine your filing obligation. As indicated earlier, you should refer to the Act, the relevant Rules and the Formal Interpretations of the Rules to understand points that are not discussed in this general introduction. . . .

The HSR thresholds as of February 2014 are as follows:

Original Threshold	Revised Threshold
$10 million	$15.2 million
$50 million	$75.9 million
$100 million	$151.7 million
$110 million	$166.9 million
$200 million	$303.4 million
$500 million	$758.6 million
$1 billion	$1,517.1 million (or $1.517 billion)

EXERCISE 2.11

AngioDynamics, Inc. (traded on NASDAQ under the symbol ANGO) is acquiring Health Tech Consultants, Inc. ("HTCI") for $80 million in cash through a stock purchase. HTCI is a private company. Its stock is owned by four siblings, 25 percent each. Anastasia, the oldest sibling, has the authority to designate three of HTCI's five directors pursuant to a shareholders' agreement between the siblings. HTCI's latest annual income statement indicates it had sales this past year of $25 million, all from providing consulting services. HTCI's latest balance sheet lists $4 million in total assets. Anastasia owns a $6 million residence, a $2 million vacation home which she rents out on occasion, a $1.5 million art collection, and a securities investment portfolio currently valued at $7 million (not including her HTCI stock).

Does an HSR filing need to be made for ANGO's acquisition of HTCI?

EXERCISE 2.12

In addition to the above transaction, in an unrelated transaction, ANGO is acquiring Spine Corp. ("SC") for $70 million in cash through an asset purchase. As part of the deal, ANGO will be assuming SC's $10 million bank loan. SC is a private company. Its stock is owned by ten individuals, 10% each. SC's latest annual income statement indicates it had sales this past year of $1 million. SC's latest balance sheet lists $14 million in total assets. The president of SC owns a securities investment portfolio currently valued at $45 million.

Does an HSR filing need to be made for ANGO's acquisition of SC?

To give you sense for what the DOJ and FTC look at when deciding whether to take a close look at a proposed M&A transaction, below are the most recent Horizontal Merger Guidelines put out jointly by those agencies.

HORIZONTAL MERGER GUIDELINES
U.S. Department of Justice and the FTC
(Aug. 19, 2010)

1. Overview

These Guidelines outline the principal analytical techniques, practices, and the enforcement policy of the Department of Justice and the Federal Trade Commission (the "Agencies") with respect to mergers and acquisitions involving actual or potential competitors ("horizontal mergers") under the federal antitrust laws. The relevant statutory provisions include Section 7 of the Clayton Act, 15 U.S.C. § 18, Sections 1 and 2 of the Sherman Act, 15 U.S.C. §§ 1, 2, and Section 5 of the Federal Trade Commission Act, 15 U.S.C. § 45. Most particularly, Section 7 of the Clayton Act prohibits mergers if "in any line of commerce or in any activity affecting commerce in any section of the country, the effect of such acquisition may be substantially to lessen competition, or to tend to create a monopoly."

The Agencies seek to identify and challenge competitively harmful mergers while avoiding unnecessary interference with mergers that are either competitively beneficial or neutral. Most merger analysis is necessarily predictive, requiring an assessment of what will likely happen if a merger proceeds as compared to what will likely happen if it does not. Given this inherent need for prediction, these Guidelines reflect the congressional intent that merger enforcement should interdict competitive problems in their incipiency and that certainty about anticompetitive effect is seldom possible and not required for a merger to be illegal. . . .

A merger can enhance market power simply by eliminating competition between the merging parties. This effect can arise even if the merger causes no changes in the way other firms behave. Adverse competitive effects arising in this manner are referred to as "unilateral effects." A merger also can enhance market power by increasing the risk of coordinated, accommodating, or interdependent behavior among rivals. Adverse competitive effects arising in this manner are referred to as "coordinated effects." In any given case, either or both types of effects may be present, and the distinction between them may be blurred.

These Guidelines principally describe how the Agencies analyze mergers between rival suppliers that may enhance their market power as sellers. Enhancement of market power by sellers often elevates the prices charged to customers. For simplicity of exposition, these Guidelines generally discuss the analysis in terms of such price effects. Enhanced market power can also be manifested in non-price terms and conditions that adversely affect customers, including reduced product quality, reduced product variety, reduced service, or diminished innovation. Such non-price effects may coexist with price effects, or can arise in their absence. When the Agencies investigate whether a merger may lead to a substantial lessening of non-price competition, they employ an approach analogous to that used to evaluate price competition. Enhanced market power may also make it more likely that the merged entity can profitably and effectively engage in exclusionary conduct. Regardless of how enhanced market power likely would be manifested, the Agencies normally evaluate mergers based on their impact on customers. The Agencies examine effects on either or both of the direct customers and the final consumers. The Agencies presume, absent convincing evidence to the contrary, that adverse effects on direct customers also cause adverse effects on final consumers.

Enhancement of market power by buyers, sometimes called "monopsony power," has adverse effects comparable to enhancement of market power by sellers. The Agencies employ an analogous framework to analyze mergers between rival purchasers that may enhance their market power as buyers. See Section 12.

2. Evidence of Adverse Competitive Effects

The Agencies consider any reasonably available and reliable evidence to address the central question of whether a merger may substantially lessen competition. This section discusses several categories and sources of evidence that the Agencies, in their experience, have found most informative in predicting the likely competitive effects of mergers. The list provided here is not exhaustive. In any given case, reliable evidence may be available in only some categories or from some sources. For each category of evidence, the Agencies consider evidence indicating that the merger may enhance competition as well as evidence indicating that it may lessen competition.

2.1 Types of Evidence

2.1.1 Actual Effects Observed in Consummated Mergers

When evaluating a consummated merger, the ultimate issue is not only whether adverse competitive effects have already resulted from the merger, but also whether such effects are likely to arise in the future. Evidence of observed post-merger price increases or other changes adverse to customers is given substantial weight. The Agencies evaluate whether such changes are anticompetitive effects resulting from the merger, in which case they can be dispositive. However, a consummated merger may be anticompetitive even if such effects have not yet been observed, perhaps because the merged firm may be aware of the possibility of post-merger antitrust review and moderating its conduct. Consequently, the Agencies also consider the same types of evidence they consider when evaluating unconsummated mergers.

2.1.2 Direct Comparisons Based on Experience

The Agencies look for historical events, or "natural experiments," that are informative regarding the competitive effects of the merger. For example, the Agencies may examine the impact of recent mergers, entry, expansion, or exit in the relevant market. Effects of analogous events in similar markets may also be informative.

The Agencies also look for reliable evidence based on variations among similar markets. For example, if the merging firms compete in some locales but not others, comparisons of prices charged in regions where they do and do not compete may be informative regarding post-merger prices. In some cases, however, prices are set on such a broad geographic basis that such comparisons are not informative. The Agencies also may examine how prices in similar markets vary with the number of significant competitors in those markets.

2.1.3 Market Shares and Concentration in a Relevant Market

The Agencies give weight to the merging parties' market shares in a relevant market, the level of concentration, and the change in concentration caused by the merger. See Sections 4 and 5. Mergers that cause a significant increase in concentration and result in highly concentrated markets are presumed to be likely to enhance market power, but this presumption can be rebutted by persuasive evidence showing that the merger is unlikely to enhance market power.

2.1.4 Substantial Head-to-Head Competition

The Agencies consider whether the merging firms have been, or likely will become absent the merger, substantial head-to-head competitors. Such evidence can be especially relevant for evaluating adverse unilateral effects, which result directly from the loss of that competition. See Section 6. This evidence can also inform market definition. See Section 4.

2.1.5 Disruptive Role of a Merging Party

The Agencies consider whether a merger may lessen competition by eliminating a "maverick" firm, i.e., a firm that plays a disruptive role in the market to the benefit of customers. For example, if one of the merging firms has a strong incumbency position and the other merging firm threatens to disrupt market conditions with a new technology or business model, their merger can involve the loss of actual or potential competition. Likewise, one of the merging firms may have the incentive to take the lead in price cutting or other competitive conduct or to resist increases in industry prices. A firm that may discipline prices based on its ability and incentive to expand production rapidly using available capacity also can be a maverick, as can a firm that has often resisted otherwise prevailing industry norms to cooperate on price setting or other terms of competition. . . .

3. Targeted Customers and Price Discrimination

When examining possible adverse competitive effects from a merger, the Agencies consider whether those effects vary significantly for different customers purchasing the same or similar products. Such differential impacts are possible when sellers can discriminate, e.g., by profitably raising price to certain targeted customers but not to others. The possibility of price discrimination influences market definition (see Section 4), the measurement of market shares (see Section 5), and the evaluation of competitive effects (see Sections 6 and 7).

When price discrimination is feasible, adverse competitive effects on targeted customers can arise, even if such effects will not arise for other customers. A price increase for targeted customers may be profitable even if a price increase for all customers would not be profitable because too many other customers would substitute away. When discrimination is reasonably likely, the Agencies may evaluate competitive effects separately by type of customer. The Agencies may have access to information unavailable to customers that is relevant to evaluating whether discrimination is reasonably likely.

For price discrimination to be feasible, two conditions typically must be met: differential pricing and limited arbitrage.

First, the suppliers engaging in price discrimination must be able to price differently to targeted customers than to other customers. This may involve identification of individual customers to which different prices are offered or offering different prices to different types of customers based on observable characteristics.

Example 3: Suppliers can distinguish large buyers from small buyers. Large buyers are more likely than small buyers to self-supply in response to a significant price increase. The merger may lead to price discrimination against small buyers, harming them, even if large buyers are not harmed. Such discrimination can occur even if there is no discrete gap in size between the classes of large and small buyers.

In other cases, suppliers may be unable to distinguish among different types of customers but can offer multiple products that sort customers based on their purchase decisions.

Second, the targeted customers must not be able to defeat the price increase of concern by arbitrage, e.g., by purchasing indirectly from or through other customers. Arbitrage may be difficult if it would void warranties or make service more difficult or costly for customers. Arbitrage is inherently impossible for many services. Arbitrage between customers at different geographic locations may be impractical due to transportation costs. Arbitrage on a modest scale may be possible but sufficiently costly or limited that it would not deter or defeat a discriminatory pricing strategy.

4. Market Definition

When the Agencies identify a potential competitive concern with a horizontal merger, market definition plays two roles. First, market definition helps specify the line of commerce and section of the country in which the competitive concern arises. In any merger enforcement action, the Agencies will normally identify one or more relevant markets in which the merger may substantially lessen competition. Second, market definition allows the Agencies to identify market participants and measure market shares and market concentration. See Section 5. The measurement of market shares and market concentration is not an end in itself, but is useful to the extent it illuminates the merger's likely competitive effects.

The Agencies' analysis need not start with market definition. Some of the analytical tools used by the Agencies to assess competitive effects do not rely on market definition, although evaluation of competitive alternatives available to customers is always necessary at some point in the analysis.

Evidence of competitive effects can inform market definition, just as market definition can be informative regarding competitive effects. For example, evidence that a reduction in the number of significant rivals offering a group of products causes prices for those products to rise significantly can itself establish that those products form a relevant market. Such evidence also may more directly predict the competitive effects of a merger, reducing the role of inferences from market definition and market shares.

Where analysis suggests alternative and reasonably plausible candidate markets, and where the resulting market shares lead to very different inferences regarding competitive effects, it is particularly valuable to examine more direct forms of evidence concerning those effects.

Market definition focuses solely on demand substitution factors, i.e., on customers' ability and willingness to substitute away from one product to another in response to a price increase or a corresponding non-price change such as a reduction in product quality or service. The responsive actions of suppliers are also important in competitive analysis. They are considered in these Guidelines in the sections addressing the identification of market participants, the measurement of market shares, the analysis of competitive effects, and entry.

Customers often confront a range of possible substitutes for the products of the merging firms. Some substitutes may be closer, and others more distant, either geographically or in terms of product attributes and perceptions. Additionally, customers may assess the proximity of different products differently. When products or suppliers in different geographic areas are substitutes for one another to varying degrees, defining a market to include some substitutes and exclude others is inevitably a simplification that cannot capture the full variation in the extent to which different products compete against each other. The principles of market definition outlined below seek to make this inevitable simplification as useful and informative as is practically possible. Relevant markets need not have precise metes and bounds.

Defining a market broadly to include relatively distant product or geographic substitutes can lead to misleading market shares. This is because the competitive significance of distant substitutes is unlikely to be commensurate with their shares in a broad market. Although excluding more distant substitutes from the market inevitably understates their competitive significance to some degree, doing so often provides a more accurate indicator of the competitive effects of the merger than would the alternative of including them and overstating their competitive significance as proportional to their shares in an expanded market.

Example 4: Firms A and B, sellers of two leading brands of motorcycles, propose to merge. If Brand A motorcycle prices were to rise, some buyers would substitute to Brand B, and some others would substitute to cars. However, motorcycle buyers see Brand B motorcycles as much more similar to Brand A motorcycles than are cars. Far more cars are sold than motorcycles. Evaluating shares in a market that includes cars would greatly underestimate the competitive significance of Brand B motorcycles in constraining Brand A's prices and greatly overestimate the significance of cars.

Market shares of different products in narrowly defined markets are more likely to capture the relative competitive significance of these products, and often more accurately reflect competition between close substitutes. As a result, properly defined antitrust markets often exclude some substitutes to which some customers might turn in the face of a price increase even if such substitutes provide alternatives for those customers. However, a group of products is too narrow to constitute a relevant market if competition from products outside that group is so ample that even the complete elimination of competition within the group would not significantly harm either direct customers or downstream consumers. The hypothetical monopolist test (see Section 4.1.1) is designed to ensure that candidate markets are not overly narrow in this respect.

The Agencies implement these principles of market definition flexibly when evaluating different possible candidate markets. Relevant antitrust markets defined according to the hypothetical monopolist test are not always intuitive and may not align with how industry members use the term "market." . . .

Section 4.1 describes the principles that apply to product market definition, and gives guidance on how the Agencies most often apply those principles. Section 4.2

describes how the same principles apply to geographic market definition. Although discussed separately for simplicity of exposition, the principles described in Sections 4.1 and 4.2 are combined to define a relevant market, which has both a product and a geographic dimension. In particular, the hypothetical monopolist test is applied to a group of products together with a geographic region to determine a relevant market.

4.1 Product Market Definition

When a product sold by one merging firm (Product A) competes against one or more products sold by the other merging firm, the Agencies define a relevant product market around Product A to evaluate the importance of that competition. Such a relevant product market consists of a group of substitute products including Product A. Multiple relevant product markets may thus be identified. . . .

4.2 Geographic Market Definition

The arena of competition affected by the merger may be geographically bounded if geography limits some customers' willingness or ability to substitute to some products, or some suppliers' willingness or ability to serve some customers. Both supplier and customer locations can affect this. The Agencies apply the principles of market definition described here and in Section 4.1 to define a relevant market with a geographic dimension as well as a product dimension.

The scope of geographic markets often depends on transportation costs. Other factors such as language, regulation, tariff and non-tariff trade barriers, custom and familiarity, reputation, and service availability may impede long-distance or international transactions. The competitive significance of foreign firms may be assessed at various exchange rates, especially if exchange rates have fluctuated in the recent past.

In the absence of price discrimination based on customer location, the Agencies normally define geographic markets based on the locations of suppliers . . . . In other cases, notably if price discrimination based on customer location is feasible as is often the case when delivered pricing is commonly used in the industry, the Agencies may define geographic markets based on the locations of customers . . . .

5. Market Participants, Market Shares, and Market Concentration

The Agencies normally consider measures of market shares and market concentration as part of their evaluation of competitive effects. The Agencies evaluate market shares and concentration in conjunction with other reasonably available and reliable evidence for the ultimate purpose of determining whether a merger may substantially lessen competition.

Market shares can directly influence firms' competitive incentives. For example, if a price reduction to gain new customers would also apply to a firm's existing customers, a firm with a large market share may be more reluctant to implement a price reduction than one with a small share. Likewise, a firm with a large market share may not feel pressure to reduce price even if a smaller rival does. Market shares also can reflect firms' capabilities. For example, a firm with a large market share may be able to expand output rapidly by a larger absolute amount than can a small firm. Similarly, a large market share tends to indicate low costs, an attractive product, or both. . . .

6. Unilateral Effects

The elimination of competition between two firms that results from their merger may alone constitute a substantial lessening of competition. Such unilateral effects are most apparent in a merger to monopoly in a relevant market, but are by no means limited to that case. Whether cognizable efficiencies resulting from the merger are likely to reduce or reverse adverse unilateral effects is addressed in Section 10.

Several common types of unilateral effects are discussed in this section. Section 6.1 discusses unilateral price effects in markets with differentiated products. Section 6.2 discusses unilateral effects in markets where sellers negotiate with buyers or prices are determined through auctions. Section 6.3 discusses unilateral effects relating to reductions in output or capacity in markets for relatively homogeneous products. Section 6.4 discusses unilateral effects arising from diminished innovation or reduced product variety. These effects do not exhaust the types of possible unilateral effects; for example, exclusionary unilateral effects also can arise.

A merger may result in different unilateral effects along different dimensions of competition. For example, a merger may increase prices in the short term but not raise longer-term concerns about innovation, either because rivals will provide sufficient innovation competition or because the merger will generate cognizable research and development efficiencies. See Section 10.

6.1 Pricing of Differentiated Products

In differentiated product industries, some products can be very close substitutes and compete strongly with each other, while other products are more distant substitutes and compete less strongly. For example, one high-end product may compete much more directly with another high-end product than with any low-end product.

A merger between firms selling differentiated products may diminish competition by enabling the merged firm to profit by unilaterally raising the price of one or both products above the pre-merger level. Some of the sales lost due to the price rise will merely be diverted to the product of the merger partner and, depending on relative margins, capturing such sales loss through merger may make the price increase profitable even though it would not have been profitable prior to the merger.

The extent of direct competition between the products sold by the merging parties is central to the evaluation of unilateral price effects. Unilateral price effects are greater, the more the buyers of products sold by one merging firm consider products sold by the other merging firm to be their next choice. The Agencies consider any reasonably available and reliable information to evaluate the extent of direct competition between the products sold by the merging firms. This includes documentary and testimonial evidence, win/loss reports and evidence from discount approval processes, customer switching patterns, and customer surveys. The types of evidence relied on often overlap substantially with the types of evidence of customer substitution relevant to the hypothetical monopolist test. See Section 4.1.1.

Substantial unilateral price elevation post-merger for a product formerly sold by one of the merging firms normally requires that a significant fraction of the customers purchasing that product view products formerly sold by the other merging firm as their next-best choice. However, unless pre-merger margins between price and incremental cost are low, that significant fraction need not approach a majority. For this purpose, incremental cost is measured over the change in output that would be caused by the price change considered. A merger may produce significant unilateral effects for a given product even though many more sales are diverted to products sold by non-merging firms than to products previously sold by the merger partner.

Example 19: In Example 5, the merged entity controlling Products A and B would raise prices ten percent, given the product offerings and prices of other firms. In that example, one-third of the sales lost by Product A when its price alone is raised are diverted to Product B. Further analysis is required to account for repositioning, entry, and efficiencies.

In some cases, the Agencies may seek to quantify the extent of direct competition between a product sold by one merging firm and a second product sold by the other merging firm by estimating the diversion ratio from the first product to the second product. The diversion ratio is the fraction of unit sales lost by the first product due to an increase in its price that would be diverted to the second product. Diversion ratios between products sold by one merging firm and products sold by the other merging firm can be very informative for assessing unilateral price effects, with higher diversion ratios indicating a greater likelihood of such effects. Diversion ratios between products sold by merging firms and those sold by non-merging firms have at most secondary predictive value.

Adverse unilateral price effects can arise when the merger gives the merged entity an incentive to raise the price of a product previously sold by one merging firm and thereby divert sales to products previously sold by the other merging firm, boosting the profits on the latter products. Taking as given other prices and product offerings, that boost to profits is equal to the value to the merged firm of the sales diverted to those products. The value of sales diverted to a product is equal to the number of units diverted to that product multiplied by the margin between price and incremental cost on that product. In some cases, where sufficient information is available, the Agencies assess the value of diverted sales, which can serve as an indicator of the upward pricing pressure on the first product resulting from the merger. Diagnosing unilateral price effects based on the value of diverted sales need not rely on market definition or the calculation of market shares and concentration. The Agencies rely much more on the value of diverted sales than on the level of the HHI for diagnosing unilateral price effects in markets with differentiated products.

If the value of diverted sales is proportionately small, significant unilateral price effects are unlikely.

Where sufficient data are available, the Agencies may construct economic models designed to quantify the unilateral price effects resulting from the merger. These models often include independent price responses by non-merging firms. They also can incorporate merger-specific efficiencies. These merger simulation methods need not rely on market definition. The Agencies do not treat merger simulation evidence as conclusive in itself, and they place more weight on whether their merger simulations consistently predict substantial price increases than on the precise prediction of any single simulation.

A merger is unlikely to generate substantial unilateral price increases if non-merging parties offer very close substitutes for the products offered by the merging firms. In some cases, non-merging firms may be able to reposition their products to offer close substitutes for the products offered by the merging firms. Repositioning is a supply-side response that is evaluated much like entry, with consideration given to timeliness, likelihood, and sufficiency. See Section 9. The Agencies consider whether repositioning would be sufficient to deter or counteract what otherwise would be significant anticompetitive unilateral effects from a differentiated products merger.

6.2 Bargaining and Auctions

In many industries, especially those involving intermediate goods and services, buyers and sellers negotiate to determine prices and other terms of trade. In that process, buyers commonly negotiate with more than one seller, and may play sellers off against one another. Some highly structured forms of such competition are known as auctions. Negotiations often combine aspects of an auction with aspects of one-on-one negotiation, although pure auctions are sometimes used in government procurement and elsewhere.

A merger between two competing sellers prevents buyers from playing those sellers off against each other in negotiations. This alone can significantly enhance the ability and incentive of the merged entity to obtain a result more favorable to it, and less favorable to the buyer, than the merging firms would have offered separately absent the merger. The Agencies analyze unilateral effects of this type using similar approaches to those described in Section 6.1.

Anticompetitive unilateral effects in these settings are likely in proportion to the frequency or probability with which, prior to the merger, one of the merging sellers had been the runner-up when the other won the business. These effects also are likely to be greater, the greater advantage the runner-up merging firm has over other suppliers in meeting customers' needs. These effects also tend to be greater, the more profitable were the pre-merger winning bids. All of these factors are likely to be small if there are many equally placed bidders.

The mechanisms of these anticompetitive unilateral effects, and the indicia of their likelihood, differ somewhat according to the bargaining practices used, the auction format, and the sellers' information about one another's costs and about buyers' preferences. For example, when the merging sellers are likely to know which buyers they are best and second best placed to serve, any anticompetitive unilateral effects are apt to be targeted at those buyers; when sellers are less well informed, such effects are more apt to be spread over a broader class of buyers.

6.3 Capacity and Output for Homogeneous Products

In markets involving relatively undifferentiated products, the Agencies may evaluate whether the merged firm will find it profitable unilaterally to suppress output and elevate the market price. A firm may leave capacity idle, refrain from building or obtaining capacity that would have been obtained absent the merger, or eliminate pre-existing production capabilities. A firm may also divert the use of capacity away from one relevant market and into another so as to raise the price in the former market. The competitive analyses of these alternative modes of output suppression may differ.

A unilateral output suppression strategy is more likely to be profitable when (1) the merged firm's market share is relatively high; (2) the share of the merged firm's output already committed for sale at prices unaffected by the output suppression is relatively low; (3) the margin on the suppressed output is relatively low; (4) the supply responses of rivals are relatively small; and (5) the market elasticity of demand is relatively low.

A merger may provide the merged firm a larger base of sales on which to benefit from the resulting price rise, or it may eliminate a competitor that otherwise could have expanded its output in response to the price rise.

Example 20: Firms A and B both produce an industrial commodity and propose to merge. The demand for this commodity is insensitive to price. Firm A is the market leader. Firm B produces substantial output, but its operating margins are low because it operates high-cost plants. The other suppliers are operating very near capacity. The merged firm has an incentive to reduce output at the high-cost plants, perhaps shutting down some of that capacity, thus driving up the price it receives on the remainder of its output. The merger harms customers, notwithstanding that the merged firm shifts some output from high-cost plants to low-cost plants.

In some cases, a merger between a firm with a substantial share of the sales in the market and a firm with significant excess capacity to serve that market can make an output suppression strategy profitable. This can occur even if the firm with the excess capacity has a relatively small share of sales, if that firm's ability to expand, and thus keep price from rising, has been making an output suppression strategy unprofitable for the firm with the larger market share.

6.4 Innovation and Product Variety

Competition often spurs firms to innovate. The Agencies may consider whether a merger is likely to diminish innovation competition by encouraging the merged firm to curtail its innovative efforts below the level that would prevail in the absence of the merger. That curtailment of innovation could take the form of reduced incentive to continue with an existing product-development effort or reduced incentive to initiate development of new products.

The first of these effects is most likely to occur if at least one of the merging firms is engaging in efforts to introduce new products that would capture substantial revenues from the other merging firm. The second, longer-run effect is most likely to occur if at least one of the merging firms has capabilities that are likely to lead it to develop new products in the future that would capture substantial revenues from the other merging firm. The Agencies therefore also consider whether a merger will diminish innovation competition by combining two of a very small number of firms with the strongest capabilities to successfully innovate in a specific direction.

The Agencies evaluate the extent to which successful innovation by one merging firm is likely to take sales from the other, and the extent to which post-merger incentives for future innovation will be lower than those that would prevail in the absence of the merger. The Agencies also consider whether the merger is likely to enable innovation that would not otherwise take place, by bringing together complementary capabilities that cannot be otherwise combined or for some other merger-specific reason. See Section 10.

The Agencies also consider whether a merger is likely to give the merged firm an incentive to cease offering one of the relevant products sold by the merging parties. Reductions in variety following a merger may or may not be anticompetitive. Mergers can lead to the efficient consolidation of products when variety offers little in value to customers. In other cases, a merger may increase variety by encouraging the merged firm to reposition its products to be more differentiated from one another.

If the merged firm would withdraw a product that a significant number of customers strongly prefer to those products that would remain available, this can constitute a harm to customers over and above any effects on the price or quality of any given product. If there is evidence of such an effect, the Agencies may inquire whether the reduction in variety is largely due to a loss of competitive incentives attributable to the merger. An anticompetitive incentive to eliminate a product as a result of the merger is greater and more likely, the larger is the share of profits from that product coming at the expense of profits from products sold by the merger partner. Where a merger substantially reduces competition by bringing two close substitute products under common ownership, and one of those products is eliminated, the merger will often also lead to a price increase on the remaining product, but that is not a necessary condition for anticompetitive effect.

Example 21: Firm A sells a high-end product at a premium price. Firm B sells a mid-range product at a lower price, serving customers who are more price sensitive. Several other firms have low-end products. Firms A and B together have a large share of the relevant market. Firm A proposes to acquire Firm B and discontinue Firm B's product. Firm A expects to retain most of Firm B's customers. Firm A may not find it profitable to raise the price of its high-end product after the merger, because doing so would reduce its ability to retain Firm B's more price-sensitive customers. The Agencies may conclude that the withdrawal of Firm B's product results from a loss of competition and materially harms customers.

7. Coordinated Effects

A merger may diminish competition by enabling or encouraging post-merger coordinated interaction among firms in the relevant market that harms customers. Coordinated interaction involves conduct by multiple firms that is profitable for each of them only as a result of the accommodating reactions of the others. These reactions can blunt a firm's incentive to offer customers better deals by undercutting the extent to which such a move would win business away from rivals. They also can enhance a firm's incentive to raise prices, by assuaging the fear that such a move would lose customers to rivals.

Coordinated interaction includes a range of conduct. Coordinated interaction can involve the explicit negotiation of a common understanding of how firms will compete or refrain from competing. Such conduct typically would itself violate the antitrust laws. Coordinated interaction also can involve a similar common understanding that is not explicitly negotiated but would be enforced by the detection and punishment of deviations that would undermine the coordinated interaction. Coordinated interaction alternatively can involve parallel accommodating conduct not pursuant to a prior understanding. Parallel accommodating conduct includes situations in which each rival's response to competitive moves made by others is individually rational, and not motivated by retaliation or deterrence nor intended to sustain an agreed-upon market outcome, but nevertheless emboldens price increases and weakens competitive incentives to reduce prices or offer customers better terms. Coordinated interaction includes conduct not otherwise condemned by the antitrust laws.

The ability of rival firms to engage in coordinated conduct depends on the strength and predictability of rivals' responses to a price change or other competitive initiative. Under some circumstances, a merger can result in market concentration sufficient to strengthen such responses or enable multiple firms in the market to predict them more confidently, thereby affecting the competitive incentives of multiple firms in the market, not just the merged firm. . . .

8. Powerful Buyers

Powerful buyers are often able to negotiate favorable terms with their suppliers. Such terms may reflect the lower costs of serving these buyers, but they also can reflect price discrimination in their favor.

The Agencies consider the possibility that powerful buyers may constrain the ability of the merging parties to raise prices. This can occur, for example, if powerful buyers have the ability and incentive to vertically integrate upstream or sponsor entry, or if the conduct or presence of large buyers undermines coordinated effects. However, the Agencies do not presume that the presence of powerful buyers alone forestalls adverse competitive effects flowing from the merger. Even buyers that can negotiate favorable terms may be harmed by an increase in market power. The Agencies examine the choices available to powerful buyers and how those choices likely would change due to the merger. Normally, a merger that eliminates a supplier whose presence contributed significantly to a buyer's negotiating leverage will harm that buyer.

Example 22: Customer C has been able to negotiate lower pre-merger prices than other customers by threatening to shift its large volume of purchases from one merging firm to the other. No other suppliers are as well placed to meet Customer C's needs for volume and reliability. The merger is likely to harm Customer C. In this situation, the Agencies could identify a price discrimination market consisting of Customer C and similarly placed customers. The merger threatens to end previous price discrimination in their favor.

Furthermore, even if some powerful buyers could protect themselves, the Agencies also consider whether market power can be exercised against other buyers.

Example 23: In Example 22, if Customer C instead obtained the lower pre-merger prices based on a credible threat to supply its own needs, or to sponsor new entry, Customer C might not be harmed. However, even in this case, other customers may still be harmed.

9. Entry

The analysis of competitive effects in Sections 6 and 7 focuses on current participants in the relevant market. That analysis may also include some forms of entry. Firms that would rapidly and easily enter the market in response to a SSNIP are market participants and may be assigned market shares. . . . Firms that have, prior to the merger, committed to entering the market also will normally be treated as market participants. . . .

As part of their full assessment of competitive effects, the Agencies consider entry into the relevant market. The prospect of entry into the relevant market will alleviate concerns about adverse competitive effects only if such entry will deter or counteract any competitive effects of concern so the merger will not substantially harm customers.

The Agencies consider the actual history of entry into the relevant market and give substantial weight to this evidence. Lack of successful and effective entry in the face of non-transitory increases in the margins earned on products in the relevant market tends to suggest that successful entry is slow or difficult. Market values of incumbent firms greatly exceeding the replacement costs of their tangible assets may indicate that these firms have valuable intangible assets, which may be difficult or time consuming for an entrant to replicate.

A merger is not likely to enhance market power if entry into the market is so easy that the merged firm and its remaining rivals in the market, either unilaterally or collectively, could not profitably raise price or otherwise reduce competition compared to the level that would prevail in the absence of the merger. Entry is that easy if entry would be timely, likely, and sufficient in its magnitude, character, and scope to deter or counteract the competitive effects of concern.

The Agencies examine the timeliness, likelihood, and sufficiency of the entry efforts an entrant might practically employ. An entry effort is defined by the actions the firm must undertake to produce and sell in the market. Various elements of the entry effort will be considered. These elements can include: planning, design, and management; permitting, licensing, or other approvals; construction, debugging, and operation of production facilities; and promotion (including necessary introductory discounts), marketing, distribution, and satisfaction of customer testing and qualification requirements. Recent examples of entry, whether successful or unsuccessful, generally provide the starting point for identifying the elements of practical entry efforts. They also can be informative regarding the scale necessary for an entrant to be successful, the presence or absence of entry barriers, the factors that influence the timing of entry, the costs and risk associated with entry, and the sales opportunities realistically available to entrants.

If the assets necessary for an effective and profitable entry effort are widely available, the Agencies will not necessarily attempt to identify which firms might enter. Where an identifiable set of firms appears to have necessary assets that others lack, or to have particularly strong incentives to enter, the Agencies focus their entry analysis on those firms. Firms operating in adjacent or complementary markets, or large customers themselves, may be best placed to enter. However, the Agencies will not presume that a powerful firm in an adjacent market or a large customer will enter the relevant market unless there is reliable evidence supporting that conclusion.

In assessing whether entry will be timely, likely, and sufficient, the Agencies recognize that precise and detailed information may be difficult or impossible to obtain. The Agencies consider reasonably available and reliable evidence bearing on whether entry will satisfy the conditions of timeliness, likelihood, and sufficiency.

9.1 Timeliness

In order to deter the competitive effects of concern, entry must be rapid enough to make unprofitable overall the actions causing those effects and thus leading to entry, even though those actions would be profitable until entry takes effect.

Even if the prospect of entry does not deter the competitive effects of concern, post-merger entry may counteract them. This requires that the impact of entrants in the relevant market be rapid enough that customers are not significantly harmed by the merger, despite any anticompetitive harm that occurs prior to the entry.

The Agencies will not presume that an entrant can have a significant impact on prices before that entrant is ready to provide the relevant product to customers unless there is reliable evidence that anticipated future entry would have such an effect on prices.

9.2 Likelihood

Entry is likely if it would be profitable, accounting for the assets, capabilities, and capital needed and the risks involved, including the need for the entrant to incur costs that would not be recovered if the entrant later exits. Profitability depends upon (a) the output level the entrant is likely to obtain, accounting for the obstacles facing new entrants; (b) the price the entrant would likely obtain in the post-merger market, accounting for the impact of that entry itself on prices; and (c) the cost per unit the entrant would likely incur, which may depend upon the scale at which the entrant would operate.

9.3 Sufficiency

Even where timely and likely, entry may not be sufficient to deter or counteract the competitive effects of concern. For example, in a differentiated product industry, entry may be insufficient because the products offered by entrants are not close enough substitutes to the products offered by the merged firm to render a price increase by the merged firm unprofitable. Entry may also be insufficient due to constraints that limit entrants' competitive effectiveness, such as limitations on the capabilities of the firms best placed to enter or reputational barriers to rapid expansion by new entrants. Entry by a single firm that will replicate at least the scale and strength of one of the merging firms is sufficient. Entry by one or more firms operating at a smaller scale may be sufficient if such firms are not at a significant competitive disadvantage.

10. Efficiencies

Competition usually spurs firms to achieve efficiencies internally. Nevertheless, a primary benefit of mergers to the economy is their potential to generate significant efficiencies and thus enhance the merged firm's ability and incentive to compete, which may result in lower prices, improved quality, enhanced service, or new products. For example, merger-generated efficiencies may enhance competition by permitting two ineffective competitors to form a more effective competitor, e.g., by combining complementary assets. In a unilateral effects context, incremental cost reductions may reduce or reverse any increases in the merged firm's incentive to elevate price. Efficiencies also may lead to new or improved products, even if they do not immediately and directly affect price. In a coordinated effects context, incremental cost reductions may make coordination less likely or effective by enhancing the incentive of a maverick to lower price or by creating a new maverick firm. Even when efficiencies generated through a merger enhance a firm's ability to compete, however, a merger may have other effects that may lessen competition and make the merger anticompetitive.

The Agencies credit only those efficiencies likely to be accomplished with the proposed merger and unlikely to be accomplished in the absence of either the proposed merger or another means having comparable anticompetitive effects. These are termed merger-specific efficiencies. Only alternatives that are practical in the business situation faced by the merging firms are considered in making this determination. The Agencies do not insist upon a less restrictive alternative that is merely theoretical.

Efficiencies are difficult to verify and quantify, in part because much of the information relating to efficiencies is uniquely in the possession of the merging firms. Moreover, efficiencies projected reasonably and in good faith by the merging firms may not be realized. Therefore, it is incumbent upon the merging firms to substantiate efficiency claims so that the Agencies can verify by reasonable means the likelihood and magnitude of each asserted efficiency, how and when each would be achieved (and any costs of doing so), how each would enhance the merged firm's ability and incentive to compete, and why each would be merger-specific.

Efficiency claims will not be considered if they are vague, speculative, or otherwise cannot be verified by reasonable means. Projections of efficiencies may be viewed with skepticism, particularly when generated outside of the usual business planning process. By contrast, efficiency claims substantiated by analogous past experience are those most likely to be credited.

Cognizable efficiencies are merger-specific efficiencies that have been verified and do not arise from anticompetitive reductions in output or service. Cognizable efficiencies are assessed net of costs produced by the merger or incurred in achieving those efficiencies.

The Agencies will not challenge a merger if cognizable efficiencies are of a character and magnitude such that the merger is not likely to be anticompetitive in any relevant market. To make the requisite determination, the Agencies consider whether cognizable efficiencies likely would be sufficient to reverse the merger's potential to harm customers in the relevant market, e.g., by preventing price increases in that market. In conducting this analysis, the Agencies will not simply compare the magnitude of the cognizable efficiencies with the magnitude of the likely harm to competition absent the efficiencies. The greater the potential adverse competitive effect of a merger, the greater must be the cognizable efficiencies, and the more they must be passed through to customers, for the Agencies to conclude that the merger will not have an anticompetitive effect in the relevant market. When the potential adverse competitive effect of a merger is likely to be particularly substantial, extraordinarily great cognizable efficiencies would be necessary to prevent the merger from being anticompetitive.

In adhering to this approach, the Agencies are mindful that the antitrust laws give competition, not internal operational efficiency, primacy in protecting customers.

In the Agencies' experience, efficiencies are most likely to make a difference in merger analysis when the likely adverse competitive effects, absent the efficiencies, are not great. Efficiencies almost never justify a merger to monopoly or near-monopoly. Just as adverse competitive effects can arise along multiple dimensions of conduct, such as pricing and new product development, so too can efficiencies operate along multiple dimensions. Similarly, purported efficiency claims based on lower prices can be undermined if they rest on reductions in product quality or variety that customers value.

The Agencies have found that certain types of efficiencies are more likely to be cognizable and substantial than others. For example, efficiencies resulting from shifting production among facilities formerly owned separately, which enable the merging firms to reduce the incremental cost of production, are more likely to be susceptible to verification and are less likely to result from anticompetitive reductions in output. Other efficiencies, such as those relating to research and development, are potentially substantial but are generally less susceptible to verification and may be the result of anticompetitive output reductions. Yet others, such as those relating to procurement, management, or capital cost, are less likely to be merger-specific or substantial, or may not be cognizable for other reasons.

When evaluating the effects of a merger on innovation, the Agencies consider the ability of the merged firm to conduct research or development more effectively. Such efficiencies may spur innovation but not affect short-term pricing. The Agencies also consider the ability of the merged firm to appropriate a greater fraction of the benefits resulting from its innovations. Licensing and intellectual property conditions may be important to this enquiry, as they affect the ability of a firm to appropriate the benefits of its innovation. Research and development cost savings may be substantial and yet not be cognizable efficiencies because they are difficult to verify or result from anticompetitive reductions in innovative activities.

11. Failure and Exiting Assets

Notwithstanding the analysis above, a merger is not likely to enhance market power if imminent failure, as defined below, of one of the merging firms would cause the assets of that firm to exit the relevant market. This is an extreme instance of the more general circumstance in which the competitive significance of one of the merging firms is declining: the projected market share and significance of the exiting firm is zero. If the relevant assets would otherwise exit the market, customers are not worse off after the merger than they would have been had the merger been enjoined.

The Agencies do not normally credit claims that the assets of the failing firm would exit the relevant market unless all of the following circumstances are met: (1) the allegedly failing firm would be unable to meet its financial obligations in the near future; (2) it would not be able to reorganize successfully under Chapter 11 of the Bankruptcy Act; and (3) it has made unsuccessful good-faith efforts to elicit reasonable alternative offers that would keep its tangible and intangible assets in the relevant market and pose a less severe danger to competition than does the proposed merger.

Similarly, a merger is unlikely to cause competitive harm if the risks to competition arise from the acquisition of a failing division. The Agencies do not normally credit claims that the assets of a division would exit the relevant market in the near future unless both of the following conditions are met: (1) applying cost allocation rules that reflect true economic costs, the division has a persistently negative cash flow on an operating basis, and such negative cash flow is not economically justified for the firm by benefits such as added sales in complementary markets or enhanced customer goodwill; and (2) the owner of the failing division has made unsuccessful good-faith efforts to elicit reasonable alternative offers that would keep its tangible and intangible assets in the relevant market and pose a less severe danger to competition than does the proposed acquisition.

12. Mergers of Competing Buyers

Mergers of competing buyers can enhance market power on the buying side of the market, just as mergers of competing sellers can enhance market power on the selling side of the market. Buyer market power is sometimes called "monopsony power."

To evaluate whether a merger is likely to enhance market power on the buying side of the market, the Agencies employ essentially the framework described above for evaluating whether a merger is likely to enhance market power on the selling side of the market. In defining relevant markets, the Agencies focus on the alternatives available to sellers in the face of a decrease in the price paid by a hypothetical monopsonist.

Market power on the buying side of the market is not a significant concern if suppliers have numerous attractive outlets for their goods or services. However, when that is not the case, the Agencies may conclude that the merger of competing buyers is likely to lessen competition in a manner harmful to sellers.

The Agencies distinguish between effects on sellers arising from a lessening of competition and effects arising in other ways. A merger that does not enhance market power on the buying side of the market can nevertheless lead to a reduction in prices paid by the merged firm, for example, by reducing transactions costs or allowing the merged firm to take advantage of volume-based discounts. Reduction in prices paid by the merging firms not arising from the enhancement of market power can be significant in the evaluation of efficiencies from a merger, as discussed in Section 10.

The Agencies do not view a short-run reduction in the quantity purchased as the only, or best, indicator of whether a merger enhances buyer market power. Nor do the Agencies evaluate the competitive effects of mergers between competing buyers strictly, or even primarily, on the basis of effects in the downstream markets in which the merging firms sell.

Example 24: Merging Firms A and B are the only two buyers in the relevant geographic market for an agricultural product. Their merger will enhance buyer power and depress the price paid to farmers for this product, causing a transfer of wealth from farmers to the merged firm and inefficiently reducing supply. These effects can arise even if the merger will not lead to any increase in the price charged by the merged firm for its output. . . .

Chapter 3

PUBLIC COMPANY DEALS

This chapter covers issues in addition to those we discussed in Chapter 2 that arise when one or both of bidder and target are public. Generally speaking, a company is public if its securities are traded on a public market such as the New York Stock Exchange (NYSE) or NASDAQ Stock Market.[1]

A. STATE CORPORATE LAW REQUIREMENTS

For the most part, the same corporate law rules apply to private and public corporations. Thus, the same analysis we covered in Chapter 2 regarding board approval and shareholder approval of a deal under corporate law applies to a public company deal.

There is, however, a wrinkle when it comes to appraisal rights — both the Model Business Corporation Act (MBCA) and Delaware General Corporation Law (DGCL) include a so-called "market-out" exception. Under this exception (subject to some limited exceptions discussed below), appraisal rights are generally not available for shares that are publicly traded. For example, MBCA § 13.02(b)(1) provides:

> Appraisal rights shall not be available for the holders of shares of any class or series of shares which is:
>
> (i) a covered security under Section 18(b)(1)(A) or (B) of the Securities Act of 1933, as amended; or
>
> (ii) traded in an organized market and has at least 2,000 shareholders and a market value of at least $20 million (exclusive of the value of such shares held by the corporation's subsidiaries, senior executives, directors, and beneficial shareholders owning more than 10% of such shares) . . . .

Section 18(b)(1) of the Securities Act provides:

> A security is a covered security if such security is —
>
> > (A) listed, or authorized for listing, on the New York Stock Exchange or the American Stock Exchange, or listed, or authorized for listing, on the National Market System of the Nasdaq Stock

---

[1] This is a good working definition for our purposes but a securities lawyer would likely tell you it is not technically correct. Securities lawyers generally consider a company public if it has securities registered under the Securities Exchange Act of 1934, which does not necessarily encompass all companies whose shares are traded on a public market. See *infra* note 8 for a brief description of when a company is required to register securities under the Exchange Act.

Market (or any successor to such entities);

(B) listed, or authorized for listing, on a national securities exchange (or tier or segment thereof) that has listing standards that the Commission determines by rule (on its own initiative or on the basis of a petition) are substantially similar to the listing standards applicable to securities described in subparagraph (A).

Notice that § 18(b)(1)(B) contemplates the SEC adding to the list of trading venues whose listed securities fall under the definition of "covered security." The SEC has done so pursuant to Rule 146(b) under the Securities Act, which provides as follows:

(b) *Covered securities for purposes of § 18.* (1) For purposes of § 18(b) of the Act (15 U.S.C. § 77r), the Commission finds that the following national securities exchanges, or segments or tiers thereof, have listing standards that are substantially similar to those of the New York Stock Exchange ("NYSE"), the NYSE Amex LLC ("NYSE Amex"), or the National Market System of the Nasdaq Stock Market ("Nasdaq/NGM"), and that securities listed, or authorized for listing, on such exchanges shall be deemed covered securities:

(i) Tier I of the NYSE Arca, Inc.;

(ii) Tier I of the NASDAQ OMX PHLX LLC;

(iii) The Chicago Board Options Exchange, Incorporated;

(iv) Options listed on the International Securities Exchange, LLC;

(v) The Nasdaq Capital Market; and

(vi) Tier I and Tier II of BATS Exchange, Inc.

(2) The designation of securities in paragraphs (b)(1)(i) through (vi) of this section as covered securities is conditioned on such exchanges' listing standards (or segments or tiers thereof) continuing to be substantially similar to those of the NYSE, NYSE Amex, or Nasdaq/NGM.

So what U.S. equity trading markets do not provide covered securities status? The list includes the OTC Bulletin Board and OTC Link. Securities traded on these markets may nonetheless fall under § 13.02(b)(1)(ii) of the MBCA market out exception.

The MBCA provides the following explanation regarding the market out exception:

Chapter 13 provides a limited exception to appraisal rights for those situations where shareholders can either accept the consideration offered in the appraisal-triggering transaction or can obtain the fair value of their shares by selling them in the market. This provision is predicated on the theory that where an efficient market exists, the market price will be an adequate proxy for the fair value of the corporation's shares, thus making appraisal unnecessary. Furthermore, after the corporation announces an appraisal-triggering action, the market operates at maximum efficiency with respect to that corporation's shares because interested parties and market professionals evaluate the offer and competing offers may be generated if the original offer is deemed inadequate. Moreover, the market exception reflects an evaluation that the uncertainty, costs and time commitment involved in any appraisal proceeding are not warranted where shareholders can sell their shares in an efficient, fair and liquid market. For these reasons, approximately half of the states have enacted market exceptions to their appraisal statutes.[2]

As noted above, the statute provides for limited exceptions to the market out exception (this is sometimes referred to as the "exception to the exception"). Specifically, MBCA § 13.02(b)(3) states:

> Subsection (b)(1) shall not be applicable and appraisal rights shall be available pursuant to subsection (a) for the holders of any class or series of shares (i) who are required by the terms of the corporate action requiring appraisal rights to accept for such shares anything other than cash or shares of any class or any series of shares of any corporation, or any other proprietary interest of any other entity, that satisfies the standards set forth in subsection (b)(1) at the time the corporate action becomes effective, or (ii) in the case of the consummation of a disposition of assets pursuant to § 12.02, unless such cash, shares or proprietary interests are, under the terms of the corporate action approved by the shareholders, as part of a distribution to shareholders of the net assets of the corporation in excess of a reasonable amount to meet claims of the type described in §§ 14.06 and 14.07, (A) within one year after the shareholders' approval of the action, and (B) in accordance with their respective interests determined at the time of the distribution.

Basically, § 13.02(b)(3) excludes from the market out exception transactions that require shareholders to accept anything other than cash or securities that meet one of the liquidity tests of § 13.02(b)(1).

The MBCA also includes an exception to the market-out exception for conflict of interest transactions. Specifically, § 13.02(b)(4) provides: "Subsection (b)(1) shall not be applicable and appraisal rights shall be available pursuant to subsection (a) for the holders of any class or series of shares where the corporate action is an interested transaction." The MBCA defines "interested transaction" in § 13.01(5.1). The official comment to § 13.02 explains:

> The premise of the market out is that the market must be liquid and the valuation assigned to the relevant shares must be "reliable." Section 13.02(b)(1) is designed to assure liquidity. For purposes of these provisions, § 13.02(b)(4) is designed to assure reliability by recognizing that the market price of, or consideration for, shares of a corporation that proposes to engage in a § 13.02(a) transaction may be subject to influences where a corporation's management, controlling shareholders or directors have conflicting interests that could, if not dealt with appropriately, adversely affect the consideration that otherwise could have been expected. Section

---

[2] MBCA § 13.02 Off. Cmt. 2.

13.02(b)(4) thus provides that the market out will not apply in those instances where the transaction constitutes an interested transaction (as defined in § 13.01(5.1)).[3]

The market-out exception under the DGCL appears in § 262(b)(1) which provides:

> . . . no appraisal rights under this section shall be available for the shares of any class or series of stock, which stock, or depository receipts in respect thereof, at the record date fixed to determine the stockholders entitled to receive notice of the meeting of stockholders to act upon the agreement of merger or consolidation, were either (i) listed on a national securities exchange or (ii) held of record by more than 2,000 holders.

The DGCL does not define "national securities exchange." Under federal securities law, a "national securities exchange" is one that has registered with the SEC under § 6 of the Securities Exchange Act of 1934 (Exchange Act). There are currently sixteen exchanges registered as national securities exchanges:

- NYSE MKT LLC (formerly NYSE AMEX and the American Stock Exchange)
- BATS Exchange, Inc.
- BATS Y-Exchange, Inc.
- BOX Options Exchange LLC
- NASDAQ OMX BX, Inc. (formerly the Boston Stock Exchange)
- C2 Options Exchange, Incorporated
- Chicago Board Options Exchange, Incorporated
- Chicago Stock Exchange, Inc.
- EDGA Exchange, Inc.
- EDGX Exchange, Inc.
- International Securities Exchange, LLC
- The Nasdaq Stock Market LLC
- National Stock Exchange, Inc.
- New York Stock Exchange LLC
- NYSE Arca, Inc.
- NASDAQ OMX PHLX, Inc. (formerly Philadelphia Stock Exchange)

The DGCL exception to the exception is found in § 262(b)(2) which provides:

> Notwithstanding paragraph (b)(1) of this section, appraisal rights under this section shall be available for the shares of any class or series of stock of a constituent corporation if the holders thereof are required by the terms of an agreement of merger or consolidation pursuant to §§ 251, 252, 254,

---

[3] *Id.* Off. Cmt. 3.

255, 256, 257, 258, 263, and 264 of this title to accept for such stock anything except:

    a.   Shares of stock of the corporation surviving or resulting from such merger or consolidation, or depository receipts in respect thereof;

    b.   Shares of stock of any other corporation, or depository receipts in respect thereof, which shares of stock (or depository receipts in respect thereof) or depository receipts at the effective date of the merger or consolidation will be either listed on a national securities exchange or held of record by more than 2,000 holders;

    c.   Cash in lieu of fractional shares or fractional depository receipts described in the foregoing paragraphs (b)(2)a. and b. of this section; or

    d.   Any combination of the shares of stock, depository receipts, and cash in lieu of fractional shares or fractional depository receipts described in the foregoing paragraphs (b)(2)a., b., and c. of this section.

As you can see, the DGCL market-out exception and the exception to the exception are similar, though not identical, to those provisions under the MBCA.

EXERCISE 3.1

Bidder is a private company incorporated in Delaware. Target is a public company incorporated in Arizona. Target's shares are traded on the OTC Bulletin Board and are held of record by 2,100 shareholders. Bidder is acquiring Target for $100 million in cash in a deal structured as a reverse triangular merger. Assume that the charter and bylaws of Bidder and Target simply track the default provisions of the corporate codes of their respective states of incorporation.

1.   Are Target shareholders entitled to appraisal rights in connection with the deal?

2.   Would your answer to question 1 be different if the deal consideration consisted of Bidder stock instead of cash?

3.   Would your answer to question 1 be different if Target was incorporated in New Mexico?

Be prepared to explain how you arrived at your answers and provide specific statutory or other cites as support.

B. FEDERAL PROXY REGULATION

As we discussed in Chapter 2, unless a deal is structured as a stock purchase, state corporate law requires target shareholder approval and in some situations bidder shareholder approval too. In the public company context, this shareholder approval almost always takes place at a shareholders' meeting as opposed to through written consent. Recall that a quorum of shares (typically a majority of outstanding shares) must be present, in person or by proxy,[4] before the shareholders may vote on any matter at a shareholders' meeting. For most public company shareholders, in person attendance at a shareholders' meeting is an inefficient use of time — often the meeting site is geographically inconvenient or the shareholder's investment in the corporation represents a small percentage of a diversified portfolio so it does not make sense for the shareholder to attend. Hence, quorum requirements necessitate that public companies solicit shareholder proxies for their shareholders' meetings. As a result, the overwhelming majority of shareholders vote by proxy pursuant to the proxy materials furnished to them by the company. Consequently, these proxy materials are of central importance to shareholder voting at public companies.

Appreciating this importance, Congress empowered the SEC through § 14(a) of the Exchange Act to regulate the solicitation of proxies by public companies. "The purpose of § 14(a) is to prevent management or others from obtaining authorization for corporate action by means of deceptive or inadequate disclosure in proxy solicitation."[5] Thus, SEC rules require a public company to furnish its shareholders with a detailed disclosure document called a proxy statement whenever it solicits proxies. The proxy statement is designed to provide shareholders with relevant information regarding the matters up for vote for which proxies are solicited. Thus, a proxy statement relating to a shareholder vote on an M&A transaction must include, among other things, a description of:

- bidder's business,
- the terms of the deal,
- the deal agreement,
- the events leading up to the deal,
- the board's reasons for approving the deal,
- the required vote,
- the availability of appraisal rights, and
- the federal income tax consequences of the deal.

Attached to the end of the proxy statement (often labeled as "annexes") are normally a copy of the acquisition agreement (but not the schedules) and the fairness opinion for the deal (we discuss fairness opinions in Chapter 7).

A shareholder confers power on a proxy to vote the shareholder's shares at the meeting by filling out a proxy card by hand or electronically over the telephone or internet. Below is Zipcar's proxy card for its shareholders meeting to approve

---

[4] In this context, a proxy is an agent appointed by a shareholder whom the shareholder gives authority to vote the shareholder's shares at a shareholders' meeting. Corporate law statutes specify the rules for a valid appointment of a proxy. *See* MBCA § 7.22; DGCL § 212. Among other things, the appointment must be reflected in a writing or electronic transmission. Note that the term "proxy" is sometimes used to refer to the grant of authority to vote, sometimes to the document granting the authority, and sometimes to the person to whom authority is granted. If you want to be precise, refer to the grant of authority as a proxy appointment, the document as a proxy form or card, and the person as the proxy.

[5] J.I. Case Co. v. Borak, 377 U.S. 426, 431 (1964).

Zipcar's acquisition by Avis Budget Group:

If the deal requires a shareholder vote only by target shareholders, target's counsel takes the lead on drafting the proxy statement with input from bidder's counsel. If the deal requires a vote by both target and bidder shareholders, target and bidder counsel will collaborate on what is called a joint proxy statement that target and bidder will use to solicit proxies for their respective shareholder meetings. In other words, they do not each prepare a separate proxy statement.

Once a draft of the proxy statement is prepared (called a "preliminary proxy statement"), target files it with the SEC. The SEC then notifies counsel within ten days whether it will be reviewing the filing. If the SEC decides not to review it, target then files a "definitive proxy statement." In the "no-review" context, the definitive proxy statement is basically the same as the preliminary proxy statement with the blanks left in the preliminary proxy statement for meeting date, record date, etc. filled in. Target then mails its definitive proxy statement to its shareholders.[6]

If the SEC decides to review target's preliminary proxy statement, it will provide target with comments usually about 30 days after filing via a comment letter. A comment letter typically asks questions based on disclosed information and requests revisions based on the SEC's interpretations of the proxy rules. Target then revises its proxy statement in light of the SEC's comments and refiles. The SEC may have comments on the revised preliminary proxy statement, in which case target again revises and refiles it. At some point, the SEC notifies target that it has no further comments. Once target receives this sign-off, it files the definitive proxy statement and mails it to its shareholders.

EXERCISE 3.2

Pull up the definitive proxy statement for the Avis Budget/Zipcar deal available at www.sjobiz.org/mna and answer the following questions.

1. What was the date, time, and location of Zipcar's special stockholders' meeting?

2. What items were up for a vote at the meeting?

3. How did the board recommend stockholders should vote on the various items?

4. What is Avis Budget's source of funds for the deal?

5. Did any Zipcar stockholders enter into voting agreements with respect to the deal?

6. What are the tax consequences to a U.S. Zipcar stockholder as a result of the deal?

7. What happens to outstanding Zipcar options, warrants, and restricted stock in the deal?

8. What does Morgan Stanley think of the deal?

9. Was there any litigation concerning the deal?

10. Did Zipcar need to make an HSR filing for the deal?

As discussed in the next case, a solicitor's disclosure obligations under the proxy rules are negatively reinforced by Rule 14a-9 under the Exchange Act.

---

[6] SEC regulations that became effective in 2008 allow companies to simply make their proxy materials available on the internet instead of mailing hardcopies to its shareholders. However, doing so is not allowed for a proxy solicitation related to an M&A transaction. *See* Exchange Act Rule 14a-16(m).

VIRGINIA BANKSHARES, INC. v. SANDBERG
United States Supreme Court
501 U.S. 1083 (1991)

JUSTICE SOUTER delivered the opinion of the Court.

Section 14(a) of the Securities Exchange Act of 1934 authorizes the Securities and Exchange Commission (SEC) to adopt rules for the solicitation of proxies, and prohibits their violation. In *J.I. Case Co. v. Borak*, 377 U.S. 426, 84 S.Ct. 1555, 12 L.Ed.2d 423 (1964), we first recognized an implied private right of action for the breach of § 14(a) as implemented by SEC Rule 14a-9, which prohibits the solicitation of proxies by means of materially false or misleading statements.

The questions before us are whether a statement couched in conclusory or qualitative terms purporting to explain directors' reasons for recommending certain corporate action can be materially misleading within the meaning of Rule 14a-9 . . . . We hold that knowingly false statements of reasons may be actionable even though conclusory in form . . . .

I

In December 1986, First American Bankshares, Inc. (FABI), a bank holding company, began a "freeze-out" merger, in which the First American Bank of Virginia (Bank) eventually merged into Virginia Bankshares, Inc. (VBI), a wholly owned subsidiary of FABI. VBI owned 85% of the Bank's shares, the remaining 15% being in the hands of some 2,000 minority shareholders. FABI hired the investment banking firm of Keefe, Bruyette & Woods (KBW) to give an opinion on the appropriate price for shares of the minority holders, who would lose their interests in the Bank as a result of the merger. Based on market quotations and unverified information from FABI, KBW gave the Bank's executive committee an opinion that $42 a share would be a fair price for the minority stock. The executive committee approved the merger proposal at that price, and the full board followed suit.

Although Virginia law required only that such a merger proposal be submitted to a vote at a shareholders' meeting, and that the meeting be preceded by circulation of a statement of information to the shareholders, the directors nevertheless solicited proxies for voting on the proposal at the annual meeting set for April 21, 1987. In their solicitation, the directors urged the proposal's adoption and stated they had approved the plan because of its opportunity for the minority shareholders to achieve a "high" value, which they elsewhere described as a "fair" price, for their stock.

Although most minority shareholders gave the proxies requested, respondent Sandberg did not, and after approval of the merger she sought damages in the United States District Court for the Eastern District of Virginia from VBI, FABI, and the directors of the Bank. She pleaded two counts, one for soliciting proxies in violation of § 14(a) and Rule 14a-9, and the other for breaching fiduciary duties owed to the minority shareholders under state law. Under the first count, Sandberg alleged, among other things, that the directors had not believed that the price offered was high or that the terms of the merger were fair, but had recommended the merger only because they believed they had no alternative if they wished to remain on the board. At trial, Sandberg invoked language from this Court's opinion in *Mills v. Electric Auto-Lite Co.*, 396 U.S. 375, 385, 90 S.Ct. 616, 622, 24 L.Ed.2d 593 (1970), to obtain an instruction that the jury could find for her without a showing of her own reliance on the alleged misstatements, so long as they were material and the proxy solicitation was an "essential link" in the merger process.

The jury's verdicts were for Sandberg on both counts, after finding violations of Rule 14a-9 by all defendants and a breach of fiduciary duties by the Bank's directors. The jury awarded Sandberg $18 a share, having found that she would have received $60 if her stock had been valued adequately. . . .

On appeal, the United States Court of Appeals for the Fourth Circuit affirmed . . . , holding that certain statements in the proxy solicitation were materially misleading for purposes of the Rule . . . .

II

The Court of Appeals affirmed petitioners' liability for two statements found to have been materially misleading in violation of § 14(a) of the Act, one of which was that "The Plan of Merger has been approved by the Board of Directors because it provides an opportunity for the Bank's public shareholders to achieve a high value for their shares." Petitioners argue that statements of opinion or belief incorporating indefinite and unverifiable expressions cannot be actionable as misstatements of material fact within the meaning of Rule 14a-9, and that such a declaration of opinion or belief should never be actionable when placed in a proxy solicitation incorporating statements of fact sufficient to enable readers to draw their own, independent conclusions.

A

We consider first the actionability *per se* of statements of reasons, opinion, or belief. Because such a statement by definition purports to express what is consciously on the speaker's mind, we interpret the jury verdict as finding that the directors' statements of belief and opinion were made with knowledge that the directors did not hold the beliefs or opinions expressed, and we confine our discussion to statements so made. That such statements may be materially significant raises no serious question. The meaning of the materiality requirement for liability under § 14(a) was discussed at some length in *TSC Industries, Inc. v. Northway, Inc.*, 426 U.S. 438, 96 S.Ct. 2126, 48 L.Ed.2d 757 (1976), where we held a fact to be material "if there is a substantial likelihood that a reasonable shareholder would consider it important in deciding how to vote." *Id.*, at 449, 96 S.Ct., at 2132. We think there is no room to deny that a statement of belief by corporate directors about a recommended course of action, or an explanation of their reasons for recommending it, can take on just that importance. Shareholders know that directors usually have knowledge and expertness far exceeding the normal investor's resources, and the directors' perceived superiority is magnified even further by the common knowledge that state law customarily obliges them to exercise their judgment in the shareholders' interest. Naturally, then, the shareowner faced with a proxy request will think it important to know the directors' beliefs about the course they recommend and their specific reasons for urging the stockholders to embrace it.

B

1

But, assuming materiality, the question remains whether statements of reasons, opinions, or beliefs are statements "with respect to . . . material fact[s]" so as to fall within the strictures of the Rule. Petitioners argue that we would invite wasteful litigation of amorphous issues outside the readily provable realm of fact if we were to recognize liability here on proof that the directors did not recommend the merger for the stated reason, and they cite the authority of *Blue Chip Stamps v. Manor Drug Stores*, 421 U.S. 723, 95 S.Ct. 1917, 44 L.Ed.2d 539 (1975), in urging us to recognize sound policy grounds for placing such statements outside the scope of the Rule.

We agree that *Blue Chip Stamps* is instructive, as illustrating a line between what is and is not manageable in the litigation of facts, but do not read it as supporting petitioners' position. The issue in *Blue Chip Stamps* was the scope of the class of plaintiffs entitled to seek relief under an implied private cause of action for violating § 10(b) of the Act, prohibiting manipulation and deception in the purchase or sale of certain securities, contrary to Commission rules. This Court held against expanding the class from actual buyers and sellers to include those who rely on deceptive sales practices by taking no action, either to sell what they own or to buy what they do not. We observed that actual sellers and buyers who sue for compensation must identify a specific number of shares bought or sold in order to calculate and limit any ensuing recovery. *Id.*, at 734, 95 S.Ct., at 1924–1925. Recognizing liability to merely would-be investors, however, would have exposed the courts to litigation unconstrained by any such anchor in demonstrable fact, resting instead on a plaintiff's "subjective hypothesis" about the number of shares he would have sold or purchased. *Id.*, at 734–735, 95 S.Ct., at 1924–1925. Hindsight's natural temptation to hypothesize boldness would have magnified the risk of nuisance litigation, which would have been compounded both by the opportunity to prolong discovery and by the capacity of claims resting on undocumented personal assertion to resist any resolution short of settlement or trial. Such were the premises of policy, added to those of textual analysis and precedent, on which *Blue Chip Stamps* deflected the threat of vexatious litigation over "many rather hazy issues of historical fact the proof of which depended almost entirely on oral testimony." *Id.*, at 743, 95 S.Ct., at 1929.

Attacks on the truth of directors' statements of reasons or belief, however, need carry no such threats. Such statements are factual in two senses: as statements that the directors do act for the reasons given or hold the belief stated and as statements about the subject matter of the reason or belief expressed. In neither sense does the proof or disproof of such statements implicate the concerns expressed in *Blue Chip Stamps*. The root of those concerns was a plaintiff's capacity to manufacture claims of hypothetical action, unconstrained by independent evidence. Reasons for directors' recommendations or statements of belief are, in contrast, characteristically matters of corporate record subject to documentation, to be supported or attacked by evidence of historical fact outside a plaintiff's control. Such evidence would include not only corporate minutes and other statements of the directors themselves, but circumstantial evidence bearing on the facts that would reasonably underlie the reasons claimed and the honesty of any statement that those reasons are the basis for a recommendation or other action, a point that becomes especially clear when the reasons or beliefs go to valuations in dollars and cents.

It is no answer to argue, as petitioners do, that the quoted statement on which liability was predicated did not express a reason in dollars and cents, but focused instead on the "indefinite and unverifiable" term, "high" value, much like the similar claim that the merger's terms were "fair" to shareholders. The objection ignores the fact that such conclusory terms in a commercial context are reasonably understood to rest on a factual basis that justifies them as accurate, the absence of which renders them misleading. Provable facts either furnish good reasons to make a conclusory commercial judgment, or they count against it, and expressions of such judgments can be uttered with knowledge of truth or falsity just like more definite statements, and defended or attacked through the orthodox evidentiary process that either substantiates their underlying justifications or tends to disprove their existence. In addressing the analogous issue in an action for misrepresentation, the court in *Day v. Avery*, 548 F.2d 1018, 179 U.S.App.D.C. 63 (1976), for example, held that a statement by the executive committee of a law firm that no partner would be any "worse off" solely because of an impending merger could be found to be a material misrepresentation. *Id.*, at 70–72, 548 F.2d, at 1025–1027. In this case, whether $42 was "high," and the proposal "fair" to the minority shareholders, depended on whether provable facts about the Bank's assets, and about actual and potential levels of operation, substantiated a value that was above, below, or more or less at the $42 figure, when assessed in accordance with recognized methods of valuation.

Respondents adduced evidence for just such facts in proving that the statement was misleading about its subject matter and a false expression of the directors' reasons. Whereas the proxy statement described the $42 price as offering a premium above both book value and market price, the evidence indicated that a calculation of the book figure based on the appreciated value of the Bank's real estate holdings eliminated any such premium. The evidence on the significance of market price showed that KBW had conceded that the market was closed, thin, and dominated by FABI, facts omitted from the statement. There was, indeed, evidence of a "going concern" value for the Bank in excess of $60 per share of common stock, another fact never disclosed. However conclusory the directors' statement may have been, then, it was open to attack by garden-variety evidence, subject neither to a plaintiff's control nor ready manufacture, and there was no undue risk of open-ended liability or uncontrollable litigation in allowing respondents the opportunity for recovery on the allegation that it was misleading to call $42 "high."

This analysis comports with the holding that marked our nearest prior approach to the issue faced here, in *TSC Industries*, 426 U.S., at 454–455, 96 S.Ct., at 2135. There, to be sure, we reversed summary judgment for a *Borak* plaintiff who had sued on a description of proposed compensation for minority shareholders as offering a "substantial premium over current market values." But we held only that on the case's undisputed facts the conclusory adjective "substantial" was not materially misleading as a necessary matter of law, and our remand for trial assumed that such a description could be both materially misleading within the meaning of Rule 14a-9 and actionable under § 14(a).

2

Under § 14(a), then, a plaintiff is permitted to prove a specific statement of reason knowingly false or misleadingly incomplete, even when stated in conclusory terms. In reaching this conclusion we have considered statements of reasons of the sort exemplified here, which misstate the speaker's reasons and also mislead about the stated subject matter (e.g., the value of the shares). A statement of belief may be open to objection only in the former respect, however, solely as a misstatement of the psychological fact of the speaker's belief in what he says. In this case, for example, the Court of Appeals alluded to just such limited falsity in observing that "the jury was certainly justified in believing that the directors did not believe a merger at $42 per share was in the minority stockholders' interest but, rather, that they voted as they did for other reasons, e.g., retaining their seats on the board."

The question arises, then, whether disbelief, or undisclosed belief or motivation, standing alone, should be a sufficient basis to sustain an action under § 14(a), absent proof by the sort of objective evidence described above that the statement also expressly or impliedly asserted something false or misleading about its subject matter. We think that proof of mere disbelief or belief undisclosed should not suffice for liability under § 14(a), and if nothing more had been required or proven in this case, we would reverse for that reason.

On the one hand, it would be rare to find a case with evidence solely of disbelief or undisclosed motivation without further proof that the statement was defective as to its subject matter. While we certainly would not hold a director's naked admission of disbelief incompetent evidence of a proxy statement's false or misleading character, such an unusual admission will not very often stand alone, and we do not substantially narrow the cause of action by requiring a plaintiff to demonstrate something false or misleading in what the statement expressly or impliedly declared about its subject.

On the other hand, to recognize liability on mere disbelief or undisclosed motive without any demonstration that the proxy statement was false or misleading about its subject would authorize § 14(a) litigation confined solely to what one skeptical court spoke of as the "impurities" of a director's "unclean heart." *Stedman v. Storer*, 308 F.Supp. 881, 887 (SDNY 1969) (dealing with § 10(b)). This, we think, would cross the line that *Blue Chip Stamps* sought to draw. While it is true that the liability, if recognized, would rest on an actual, not hypothetical, psychological fact, the temptation to rest an otherwise nonexistent § 14(a) action on psychological enquiry alone would threaten just the sort of strike suits and attrition by discovery that *Blue Chip Stamps* sought to discourage. We therefore hold disbelief or undisclosed motivation, standing alone, insufficient to satisfy the element of fact that must be established under § 14(a).

C

Petitioners' fall-back position assumes the same relationship between a conclusory judgment and its underlying facts that we described in Part II-B-1, *supra.* Thus, citing *Radol v. Thomas*, 534 F.Supp. 1302, 1315, 1316 (SD Ohio 1982), petitioners argue that even if conclusory statements of reason or belief can be actionable under § 14(a), we should confine liability to instances where the proxy material fails to disclose the offending statement's factual basis. There would be no justification for holding the shareholders entitled to judicial relief, that is, when they were given evidence that a stated reason for a proxy recommendation was misleading and an opportunity to draw that conclusion themselves.

The answer to this argument rests on the difference between a merely misleading statement and one that is materially so. While a misleading statement will not always lose its deceptive edge simply by joinder with others that are true, the true statements may discredit the other one so obviously that the risk of real deception drops to nil. Since liability under § 14(a) must rest not only on deceptiveness but materiality as well (i.e., it has to be significant enough to be important to a reasonable investor deciding how to vote, see *TSC Industries*, 426 U.S., at 449, 96 S.Ct., at 2132), petitioners are on perfectly firm ground insofar as they argue that publishing accurate facts in a proxy statement can render a misleading proposition too unimportant to ground liability.

But not every mixture with the true will neutralize the deceptive. If it would take a financial analyst to spot the tension between the one and the other, whatever is misleading will remain materially so, and liability should follow. *Gerstle v. Gamble-Skogmo, Inc.*, 478 F.2d 1281, 1297 (CA2 1973) ("[I]t is not sufficient that overtones might have been picked up by the sensitive antennae of investment analysts"). Cf. *Milkovich v. Lorain Journal Co.*, 497 U.S. 1, 18–19, 110 S.Ct. 2695, 2705–2706, 111 L.Ed.2d 1 (1990) (a defamatory assessment of facts can be actionable even if the facts underlying the assessment are accurately presented). The point of a proxy statement, after all, should be to inform, not to challenge the reader's critical wits. Only when the inconsistency would exhaust the misleading conclusion's capacity to influence the reasonable shareholder would a § 14(a) action fail on the element of materiality.

Suffice it to say that the evidence invoked by petitioners in the instant case fell short of compelling the jury to find the facial materiality of the misleading statement neutralized. The directors claim, for example, to have made an explanatory disclosure of further reasons for their recommendation when they said they would keep their seats following the merger, but they failed to mention what at least one of them admitted in testimony, that they would have had no expectation of doing so without supporting the proposal. And although the proxy statement did speak factually about the merger price in describing it as higher than share prices in recent sales, it failed even to mention the closed market dominated by FABI. None of these disclosures that the directors point to was, then, anything more than a half-truth, and the record shows that another fact statement they invoke was arguably even worse. The claim that the merger price exceeded book value was controverted, as we have seen already, by evidence of a higher book value than the directors conceded, reflecting appreciation in the Bank's real estate portfolio.

Finally, the solicitation omitted any mention of the Bank's value as a going concern at more than $60 a share, as against the merger price of $42. There was, in sum, no more of a compelling case for the statement's immateriality than for its accuracy. . . .

QUESTIONS

1. What was the deal at issue? How was it structured?

2. Who is Sandberg? Why is she suing?

3. What are Sandberg's legal claims?

4. What were the alleged misstatements in the proxy statement?

5. What test does the Court apply to determine whether the alleged misstatements were material?

6. What is the defendants' primary argument for why there was not a Rule 14a-9 violation?

7. Why did the Court reject this argument?

C. SECURITIES REGISTRATION REQUIREMENTS

As we discussed in Chapter 2, bidder will be selling securities any time the deal consideration includes bidder stock, and these sales must be done in compliance with federal securities laws. If target is public, bidder likely will not be able to rely on a registration exemption for the transaction because target will have too many non-accredited shareholders. Thus, bidder will have to register the transaction with the SEC.

A company registers a securities transaction with the SEC by preparing and filing a registration statement. The contents of a registration statement for securities to be issued in an M&A transaction are dictated by SEC Form S-4. Per the form, bidder's registration statement must contain, or incorporate by reference,[7] detailed information about bidder and the deal. These disclosures include a description of:

- risks associated with bidder and the deal (risk factors),
- bidder's business,
- the terms of the deal,
- the deal agreement,
- the events leading up to the deal,

---

[7] "Incorporate by reference" means that the required information is not actually set forth in the registration statement but instead it contains a cross reference to some other SEC filing by the company that contains (or will contain) the required information.

- the board's reasons for approving the deal,

- the required vote,

- the availability of appraisal rights, and

- the federal income tax consequences of the deal.

As is the case with target's proxy statement, the SEC reviews the registration statement and provides bidder with comments. Bidder then revises the registration statement in light of SEC comments, and at some point the SEC declares the registration statement "effective," which means bidder can then issue the securities covered by the registration statement. In other words, bidder will have to wait until the SEC declares its registration statement effective before it can close on the deal. The policy behind the registration requirement is to provide investors (in this case, target shareholders) with sufficient information concerning an offering so that they can make informed investment decisions. In that regard, the issuer (in this case, bidder) is required to make a "prospectus" available to each investor in a registered offering. A prospectus is a subpart of the registration statement that contains the bulk of the required disclosures about the issuer and the offering.

There is substantial overlap between information required to be in bidder's prospectus and information required to be in target's proxy statement. Thus, SEC regulations allow bidder and target to combine these documents into a single document called a proxy statement/prospectus (if bidder is also soliciting proxies from its shareholders because their approval is required too, the document is called a joint proxy statement/prospectus).

D. DISCLOSURE OBLIGATIONS

1. Current Reports

A public company is required pursuant to the Exchange Act to file a "current report" with the SEC following the occurrence of specified events. The triggering events and contents of current reports are dictated by SEC Form 8-K (see http://www.sec.gov/about/forms/form8-k.pdf), and, as a result, many attorneys refer to the report simply as an "8-K." Two triggering events (what Form 8-K refers to as "Items"), Item 1.01 and Item 2.01, are implicated by an M&A transaction:

Item 1.01 provides as follows:

Item 1.01 Entry into a Material Definitive Agreement.

(a) If the registrant has entered into a material definitive agreement not made in the ordinary course of business of the registrant, or into any amendment of such agreement that is material to the registrant, disclose the following information:

(1) the date on which the agreement was entered into or amended, the identity of the parties to the agreement or amendment and a brief description of any material relationship between the registrant or its affiliates and any of the

parties, other than in respect of the material definitive agreement or amendment; and

(2) a brief description of the terms and conditions of the agreement or amendment that are material to the registrant.

(b) For purposes of this Item 1.01, a *material definitive agreement* means an agreement that provides for obligations that are material to and enforceable against the registrant, or rights that are material to the registrant and enforceable by the registrant against one or more other parties to the agreement, in each case whether or not subject to conditions.

"Registrant" in the above provision refers to a company whose securities are registered under the Exchange Act, which, for the most part, includes all public companies.[8]

Case law has established that a fact, such as entering into an acquisition agreement, is material for purposes of federal securities laws if there is a substantial likelihood that a reasonable investor would consider it important in making an investment decision. Thus, it seems self-evident that target's entry into an agreement for its sale, e.g., a merger agreement, asset purchase agreement, or stock purchase agreement, is material and therefore falls under Item 1.01. The same conclusion is not necessarily the case for bidder. For example, the acquisition by Microsoft Corporation, a $300 billion company, of a small software company for $10 million is likely not material to Microsoft and therefore likely does not trigger a filing obligation for Microsoft under Item 1.01.

Below is what Zipcar included for Item 1.01 in its January 2, 2012 Form 8-K after it entered into the Agreement and Plan of Merger with Avis Budget Group, Inc.

Item 1.01 Entry into a Material Definitive Agreement

On December 31, 2012, Zipcar, Inc., a Delaware corporation ("*Zipcar*"), Avis Budget Group, Inc., a Delaware corporation ("*Avis*"), and Millennium Acquisition Sub, Inc., a Delaware corporation and a wholly-owned subsidiary of Avis ("*Merger Sub*"), entered into an Agreement and Plan of Merger (the "*Merger Agreement*"), pursuant to which, on the terms and subject to the conditions set forth in the Merger Agreement, Avis has agreed to acquire all of the outstanding shares of Zipcar for $12.25 per share in cash, without interest, and pursuant to which Merger Sub will be merged with and into Zipcar with Zipcar continuing as the surviving corporation and a wholly-owned subsidiary of Avis (the "*Merger*").

On the terms and subject to the conditions set forth in the Merger Agreement, which has been unanimously approved by the Board of Directors

---

[8] A company is required to register securities under the Exchange Act if (1) the securities are listed on a national securities exchange; (2) the company has $10 million or more in total assets and a class of equity securities held of record by (a) 2,000 or more persons, or (b) 500 or more persons who are not accredited investors; or (3) the company has filed a registration statement under the Securities Act that became effective.

of Zipcar (the *"Zipcar Board"*), at the effective time of the Merger (the *"Effective Time"*), and as a result thereof, each share of common stock, par value $0.001 per share, of Zipcar (*"Zipcar Common Stock"*) that is issued and outstanding immediately prior to the Effective Time (other than Zipcar Common Stock owned by Avis, Merger Sub or any of their respective subsidiaries, or by Zipcar or any subsidiary of Zipcar, which will be canceled without payment of any consideration, and Zipcar Common Stock for which appraisal rights have been validly exercised and not withdrawn) will be converted into the right to receive $12.25 in cash, without interest (the *"Merger Consideration"*). Each outstanding option to purchase Zipcar Common Stock shall be accelerated, become fully vested and be cancelled prior to the Effective Time (each, an *"Option"*) and each holder of an Option shall be entitled to receive, in cash, the amount by which the Merger Consideration exceeds the exercise price of such Option multiplied by the number of shares of Zipcar Common Stock subject to such Option. Each outstanding warrant to purchase or otherwise acquire Zipcar Common Stock shall be accelerated, become fully vested and be cancelled at the Effective Time (each, a *"Warrant"*) and each holder of a Warrant shall be entitled to receive, in cash, the amount by which the Merger Consideration exceeds the exercise price of such Warrant multiplied by the number of shares of Zipcar Common Stock subject to such Warrant. Each restricted share of Zipcar Common Stock (each, a *"Zipcar Restricted Share"*) shall become fully vested at the Effective Time and shall be converted into the right to receive the Merger Consideration.

Avis and Zipcar have made customary representations, warranties and covenants in the Merger Agreement, including, among others, covenants that: (i) Zipcar will conduct its business in the ordinary course consistent with past practice during the interim period between the execution of the Merger Agreement and the Effective Time, (ii) Zipcar will not engage in certain kinds of transactions during such period without the consent of Avis, (iii) Zipcar will cause a meeting of the Zipcar stockholders to be held to consider adoption of the Merger Agreement, and (iv) subject to certain customary exceptions, the Zipcar Board will recommend adoption of the Merger Agreement by its stockholders. Zipcar has also made certain additional customary covenants, including, among others, covenants not to: (i) solicit proposals relating to alternative business combination transactions or (ii) subject to certain exceptions designed to allow the Zipcar Board to fulfill its fiduciary duties to stockholders of Zipcar, enter into discussions concerning, or provide confidential information in connection with, any proposals for alternative business combination transactions.

Consummation of the Merger is subject to customary conditions, including (i) adoption of the Merger Agreement by the holders of a majority of the outstanding shares of Zipcar Common Stock (the *"Stockholder Approval"*), (ii) the absence of any law or order prohibiting the consummation of the Merger, (iii) expiration or termination of the applicable waiting periods under the Hart-Scott-Rodino Antitrust Improvements Act of 1976 and any other applicable domestic or foreign antitrust or competition laws or regulations, and (iv) the absence of a material adverse effect with respect to Zipcar. The consummation of the Merger is not subject to a financing condition.

The Merger Agreement prohibits Zipcar from directly or indirectly initiating, soliciting or participating in or knowingly or intentionally taking any action to encourage or facilitate any Acquisition Proposal (as defined in the

Merger Agreement); provided, however, that at any time prior to the receipt of the Stockholder Approval, Zipcar may, subject to the terms and conditions set forth in the Merger Agreement, furnish information to, and engage in discussions and negotiations with, a third party that makes an unsolicited Acquisition Proposal that the Zipcar Board determines in good faith constitutes or is reasonably likely to result in a Superior Proposal (as defined in the Merger Agreement). In the event that the Zipcar Board determines that such Acquisition Proposal constitutes a Superior Proposal and Zipcar complies with certain notice and other conditions set forth in the Merger Agreement, including providing Avis with a three (3) business day period to match or improve upon such Superior Proposal, and Avis does not deliver a proposal matching or improving upon such Superior Proposal, Zipcar may either (i) terminate the Merger Agreement to enter into a definitive agreement with respect to such Superior Proposal and pay a termination fee of $16,807,250 (the *"Termination Fee"*), or (ii) effect a Change of Company Board Recommendation (as defined in the Merger Agreement). Zipcar may also effect an Intervening Event Change of Recommendation (as defined in the Merger Agreement), subject to providing Avis with a three (3) business day period to make such adjustments in the terms and conditions of the Merger Agreement as would permit the Zipcar Board not to effect an Intervening Event Change of Recommendation.

The Merger Agreement contains certain termination rights for both Avis and Zipcar, and further provides that, upon termination of the Merger Agreement in certain circumstances, including if the Merger Agreement is terminated by Avis in the event the Zipcar Board effects a Change of Company Board Recommendation or an Intervening Event Change of Recommendation, Zipcar would be required to pay Avis the Termination Fee.

In connection with the parties' entry into the Merger Agreement, the directors, executive officers and three holders of greater than 5% of the issued and outstanding shares of Zipcar Common Stock (the *"Voting Parties"*) have entered into separate voting agreements (the *"Voting Agreements"*) with Avis covering shares of Zipcar Common Stock legally or beneficially owned by the Voting Parties (the *"Voting Party Shares"*), which represent, in the aggregate, approximately 32% of Zipcar's outstanding shares. Under the Voting Agreements, each Voting Party has agreed to vote his or her Voting Party Shares in favor of the Merger and against any Acquisition Proposal and certain other actions, proposals, transactions or agreements that could reasonably be expected to, among other things, result in a breach of any covenant, representation or warranty of Zipcar under the Merger Agreement or such Voting Party under the Voting Agreement or impede, interfere with, delay, discourage, adversely affect or inhibit the timely consummation of the Merger. In addition, each of the Voting Parties has agreed not to make an Acquisition Proposal or initiate, solicit or engage in discussions with any other person regarding an Acquisition Proposal. Each Voting Party has further agreed to certain restrictions on the disposition of its Voting Party Shares, subject to the terms and conditions set forth in the Voting Agreements. The Voting Agreements provide that they will terminate upon the earlier of the effective time of (i) the Merger and (ii) any termination of the Merger Agreement in accordance with its terms.

The foregoing descriptions of the Merger, the Merger Agreement and the Voting Agreements do not purport to be complete and are subject to, and qualified in their entirety by reference to, the full text of the Merger

> Agreement, which is attached hereto as Exhibit 2.1 and incorporated herein by reference, and the full text of the Form of Voting Agreement, which is attached hereto as Exhibit 2.2 and incorporated herein by reference. . . .

The deal was material to Avis Budget Group, Inc. so it filed an 8-K with a similar description on January 2, 2013 as well. SEC regulations generally require that the form be filed within four business days after the occurrence of the event. In this case, the event happened on December 31, 2012, so the parties met the deadline.

Item 2.01 of Form 8-K provides the following:

Item 2.01 Completion of Acquisition or Disposition of Assets.

If the registrant or any of its majority-owned subsidiaries has completed the acquisition or disposition of a significant amount of assets, otherwise than in the ordinary course of business, disclose the following information:

(a) the date of completion of the transaction;

(b) a brief description of the assets involved;

(c) the identity of the person(s) from whom the assets were acquired or to whom they were sold and the nature of any material relationship, other than in respect of the transaction, between such person(s) and the registrant or any of its affiliates, or any director or officer of the registrant, or any associate of any such director or officer;

(d) the nature and amount of consideration given or received for the assets and, if any material relationship is disclosed pursuant to paragraph (c) of this Item 2.01, the formula or principle followed in determining the amount of such consideration;

(e) if the transaction being reported is an acquisition and if a material relationship exists between the registrant or any of its affiliates and the source(s) of the funds used in the acquisition, the identity of the source(s) of the funds unless all or any part of the consideration used is a loan made in the ordinary course of business by a bank as defined by Section 3(a)(6) of the Act, in which case the identity of such bank may be omitted provided the registrant:

(1) has made a request for confidentiality pursuant to Section 13(d)(1)(B) of the Act; and

(2) states in the report that the identity of the bank has been so omitted and filed separately with the Commission . . . .

Per Instruction 2. to the item, the term "acquisition" "includes every purchase, acquisition by lease, exchange, merger, consolidation, succession or other acquisition . . . ." Likewise, the term "disposition" "includes every sale, disposition by lease, exchange, merger, consolidation, mortgage, assignment or hypothecation of assets, whether for the benefit of creditors or otherwise, abandonment, destruction, or other disposition." Thus, an M&A transaction falls within the item regardless of whether it is structured as a merger, asset purchase, stock purchase, etc.

Below is what Zipcar included for Item 2.01 in its March 14, 2013 Form 8-K after closing on its sale to Avis Budget.

Introductory Note

On March 14, 2013, Zipcar, Inc., a Delaware corporation ("*Zipcar*"), announced that Avis Budget Group, Inc., a Delaware corporation ("*Avis Budget*"), has completed its acquisition of Zipcar. Pursuant to the terms of the previously announced Agreement and Plan of Merger, dated as of December 31, 2012 (the "*Merger Agreement*"), by and among Zipcar, Avis Budget, and Millennium Acquisition Sub, Inc., a Delaware corporation and a wholly owned subsidiary of Avis Budget ("*Merger Sub*"), Merger Sub was merged with and into Zipcar, with Zipcar continuing as the surviving corporation (the "*Merger*"). As a result of the Merger, Zipcar became a wholly owned subsidiary of Avis Budget.

Item 2.01 Completion of Acquisition or Disposition of Assets.

On March 14, 2013, Zipcar, Inc., a Delaware corporation ("*Zipcar*"), announced that Avis Budget Group, Inc., a Delaware corporation ("*Avis Budget*"), has completed its acquisition of Zipcar. Pursuant to the terms of the previously announced Agreement and Plan of Merger, dated as of December 31, 2012 (the "*Merger Agreement*"), by and among Zipcar, Avis Budget, and Millennium Acquisition Sub, Inc., a Delaware corporation and a wholly owned subsidiary of Avis Budget ("*Merger Sub*"), Merger Sub was merged with and into Zipcar, with Zipcar continuing as the surviving corporation (the "*Merger*"). As a result of the Merger, Zipcar became a wholly owned subsidiary of Avis Budget.

On March 14, 2013, pursuant to the terms of the Merger Agreement, Merger Sub was merged with and into Zipcar, with Zipcar continuing as the surviving corporation. At the effective time of the Merger (the "*Effective Time*") and as a result of the Merger, Zipcar became a wholly owned subsidiary of Avis Budget and each share of common stock, par value $0.001 per share, of Zipcar (the "*Zipcar Common Stock*") that was issued and outstanding immediately prior to the Effective Time (other than Zipcar Common Stock owned by Avis Budget, Merger Sub or any of their respective subsidiaries, or by Zipcar or any subsidiary of Zipcar and Zipcar Common Stock for which appraisal rights were validly exercised and not withdrawn) was converted into the right to receive $12.25 in cash, without interest (the "*Merger Consideration*"). Each option to purchase Zipcar Common Stock that was outstanding as of immediately prior to the Effective Time was accelerated, became fully vested and was cancelled immediately prior to the Effective Time (each, an "*Option*") and each holder of an Option became entitled to receive, in cash, the amount by which the Merger Consideration exceeded the exercise price of such Option multiplied by the number of shares of Zipcar Common Stock subject to such Option. Avis Budget financed the transaction with incremental borrowings as well as available cash.

The foregoing description does not purport to be complete and is qualified in its entirety by reference to the Merger Agreement, a copy of which is filed as Exhibit 2.1 hereto and is incorporated herein by reference. At the Effective Time, holders of shares of Zipcar Common Stock ceased to have any rights as stockholders of the Company (other than the right to receive the Merger Consideration).

2. No Half-Truths

As a general matter, public companies strive to keep the marketplace informed about material developments regarding their businesses even when not affirmatively required to do so by SEC disclosure rules. They do this through press releases, media interviews, analyst calls, social media, etc. Bidder and target, however, typically prefer to delay disclosure of ongoing M&A discussions until the deal is signed. Bidder does not want another company to find out about the deal and outbid it or drive up the price. Target is worried about being tainted if it announces it is in discussions but bidder pulls out before the deal is signed. The parties can normally keep the deal under wraps until they execute the deal agreement. However, looming in the background is the general principle of securities law prohibiting misstatements or omissions of material facts. The next case explores this issue in the context of an M&A transaction.

BASIC INC. v. LEVINSON
United States Supreme Court
485 U.S. 224 (1988)

BLACKMUN, J.

This case requires us to apply the materiality requirement of § 10(b) of the Securities Exchange Act of 1934 and the Securities and Exchange Commission's Rule 10b-5, promulgated thereunder, in the context of preliminary corporate merger discussions . . . .

I

Prior to December 20, 1978, Basic Incorporated was a publicly traded company primarily engaged in the business of manufacturing chemical refractories for the steel industry. As early as 1965 or 1966, Combustion Engineering, Inc., a company producing mostly alumina-based refractories, expressed some interest in acquiring Basic, but was deterred from pursuing this inclination seriously because of antitrust concerns it then entertained. In 1976, however, regulatory action opened the way to a renewal of Combustion's interest. The "Strategic Plan," dated October 25, 1976, for Combustion's Industrial Products Group included the objective: "Acquire Basic Inc. $30 million."

Beginning in September 1976, Combustion representatives had meetings and telephone conversations with Basic officers and directors, including petitioners here, concerning the possibility of a merger. During 1977 and 1978, Basic made three public statements denying that it was engaged in merger negotiations.[9] On December 18, 1978, Basic asked the New York Stock Exchange to suspend trading in its shares and issued a release stating that it had been "approached" by another company concerning a merger. On December 19, Basic's board endorsed Combustion's offer of $46 per share for its common stock, and on the following day publicly announced its approval of Combustion's tender offer for all outstanding shares.

Respondents are former Basic shareholders who sold their stock after Basic's first public statement of October 21, 1977, and before the suspension of trading in December 1978. Respondents brought a class action against Basic and its directors, asserting that the defendants issued three false or misleading public statements and thereby were in violation of § 10(b) of the 1934 Act and of Rule 10b-5. Respondents alleged that they were injured by selling Basic shares at artificially depressed prices in a market affected by petitioners' misleading statements and in reliance thereon. . . .

[T]he District Court granted summary judgment for the defendants. It held that, as a matter of law, any misstatements were immaterial: there were no negotiations ongoing at the time of the first statement, and although negotiations were taking place when the second and third statements were issued, those negotiations were not "destined, with reasonable certainty, to become a merger agreement in principle."

The United States Court of Appeals for the Sixth Circuit . . . reversed the District Court's summary judgment, and remanded the case. . . . In the Court of Appeals' view, Basic's statements that no negotiations were taking place, and that it knew of no corporate developments to account for the heavy trading activity, were misleading. With respect to materiality, the court rejected the argument that preliminary merger discussions are immaterial as a matter of law, and held that "once a statement is made denying the existence of any discussions, even discussions that might not have been material in absence of the denial are material because they make the statement made untrue." 786 F.2d, at 749. . . .

We granted certiorari . . . to resolve the split . . . among the Courts of Appeals as to the standard of materiality applicable to preliminary merger discussions. . . .

---

[9] [n.4] On October 21, 1977, after heavy trading and a new high in Basic stock, the following news item appeared in the Cleveland Plain Dealer:

"[Basic] President Max Muller said the company knew no reason for the stock's activity and that no negotiations were under way with any company for a merger. He said Flintkote recently denied Wall Street rumors that it would make a tender offer of $25 a share for control of the Cleveland-based maker of refractories for the steel industry." App. 363.

On September 25, 1978, in reply to an inquiry from the New York Stock Exchange, Basic issued a release concerning increased activity in its stock and stated that "management is unaware of any present or pending company development that would result in the abnormally heavy trading activity and price fluctuation in company shares that have been experienced in the past few days."

On November 6, 1978, Basic issued to its shareholders a "Nine Months Report 1978." This Report stated: "With regard to the stock market activity in the Company's shares we remain unaware of any present or pending developments which would account for the high volume of trading and price fluctuations in recent months." Id., at 403.

II

The 1934 Act was designed to protect investors against manipulation of stock prices. See S.Rep. No. 792, 73d Cong., 2d Sess., 1–5 (1934). Underlying the adoption of extensive disclosure requirements was a legislative philosophy: "There cannot be honest markets without honest publicity. Manipulation and dishonest practices of the market place thrive upon mystery and secrecy." H.R.Rep. No. 1383, 73d Cong., 2d Sess., 11 (1934). This Court "repeatedly has described the 'fundamental purpose' of the Act as implementing a 'philosophy of full disclosure.'" *Santa Fe Industries, Inc. v. Green*, 430 U.S. 462, 477–478 (1977), quoting *SEC v. Capital Gains Research Bureau, Inc.*, 375 U.S. 180, 186 (1963). . . .

The Court previously has addressed various positive and common-law requirements for a violation of § 10(b) or of Rule 10b–5. . . . The Court also explicitly has defined a standard of materiality under the securities laws, see *TSC Industries, Inc. v. Northway, Inc.*, 426 U.S. 438 (1976), concluding in the proxy-solicitation context that "an omitted fact is material if there is a substantial likelihood that a reasonable shareholder would consider it important in deciding how to vote." *Id.*, at 449. Acknowledging that certain information concerning corporate developments could well be of "dubious significance," *id.*, at 448, the Court was careful not to set too low a standard of materiality; it was concerned that a minimal standard might bring an overabundance of information within its reach, and lead management "simply to bury the shareholders in an avalanche of trivial information—a result that is hardly conducive to informed decisionmaking." *Id.*, at 448–449. It further explained that to fulfill the materiality requirement "there must be a substantial likelihood that the disclosure of the omitted fact would have been viewed by the reasonable investor as having significantly altered the 'total mix' of information made available." *Id.*, at 449. We now expressly adopt the TSC Industries standard of materiality for the § 10(b) and Rule 10b-5 context.

III

The application of this materiality standard to preliminary merger discussions is not self-evident. Where the impact of the corporate development on the target's fortune is certain and clear, the TSC Industries materiality definition admits straightforward application. Where, on the other hand, the event is contingent or speculative in nature, it is difficult to ascertain whether the "reasonable investor" would have considered the omitted information significant at the time. Merger negotiations, because of the ever-present possibility that the contemplated transaction will not be effectuated, fall into the latter category.[10]

A

Petitioners urge upon us a Third Circuit test for resolving this difficulty. . . . Under this approach, preliminary merger discussions do not become material until "agreement-in-principle" as to the price and structure of the transaction has been

---

[10] [n.9] We do not address here any other kinds of contingent or speculative information, such as earnings forecasts or projections.

reached between the would-be merger partners. . . . By definition, then, information concerning any negotiations not yet at the agreement-in-principle stage could be withheld or even misrepresented without a violation of Rule 10b-5.

Three rationales have been offered in support of the "agreement-in-principle" test. The first derives from the concern expressed in TSC Industries that an investor not be overwhelmed by excessively detailed and trivial information, and focuses on the substantial risk that preliminary merger discussions may collapse: because such discussions are inherently tentative, disclosure of their existence itself could mislead investors and foster false optimism. . . . The other two justifications for the agreement-in-principle standard are based on management concerns: because the requirement of "agreement-in-principle" limits the scope of disclosure obligations, it helps preserve the confidentiality of merger discussions where earlier disclosure might prejudice the negotiations; and the test also provides a usable, bright-line rule for determining when disclosure must be made. . . .

None of these policy-based rationales, however, purports to explain why drawing the line at agreement-in-principle reflects the significance of the information upon the investor's decision. The first rationale, and the only one connected to the concerns expressed in *TSC Industries*, stands soundly rejected, even by a Court of Appeals that otherwise has accepted the wisdom of the agreement-in-principle test. "It assumes that investors are nitwits, unable to appreciate-even when told-that mergers are risky propositions up until the closing." *Flamm v. Eberstadt*, 814 F.2d, at 1175. Disclosure, and not paternalistic withholding of accurate information, is the policy chosen and expressed by Congress. We have recognized time and again, a "fundamental purpose" of the various Securities Acts, "was to substitute a philosophy of full disclosure for the philosophy of caveat emptor and thus to achieve a high standard of business ethics in the securities industry." *SEC v. Capital Gains Research Bureau, Inc.*, 375 U.S. 180, 186 . . . . The role of the materiality requirement is not to "attribute to investors a child-like simplicity, an inability to grasp the probabilistic significance of negotiations," *Flamm v. Eberstadt*, 814 F.2d, at 1175, but to filter out essentially useless information that a reasonable investor would not consider significant, even as part of a larger "mix" of factors to consider in making his investment decision.

The second rationale, the importance of secrecy during the early stages of merger discussions, also seems irrelevant to an assessment whether their existence is significant to the trading decision of a reasonable investor. To avoid a "bidding war" over its target, an acquiring firm often will insist that negotiations remain confidential, . . . and at least one Court of Appeals has stated that "silence pending settlement of the price and structure of a deal is beneficial to most investors, most of the time." *Flamm v. Eberstadt*, 814 F.2d, at 1177.

We need not ascertain, however, whether secrecy necessarily maximizes shareholder wealth-although we note that the proposition is at least disputed as a matter of theory and empirical research — for this case does not concern the timing of a disclosure; it concerns only its accuracy and completeness. We face here the narrow question whether information concerning the existence and status of preliminary merger discussions is significant to the reasonable investor's trading decision. Arguments based on the premise that some disclosure would be "premature" in a sense are more properly considered under the rubric of an issuer's duty to disclose. The "secrecy" rationale is simply inapposite to the definition of materiality.

The final justification offered in support of the agreement-in-principle test seems to be directed solely at the comfort of corporate managers. A bright-line rule indeed is easier to follow than a standard that requires the exercise of judgment in the light of all the circumstances. But ease of application alone is not an excuse for ignoring the purposes of the Securities Acts and Congress' policy decisions. Any approach that designates a single fact or occurrence as always determinative of an inherently fact-specific finding such as materiality, must necessarily be overinclusive or underinclusive. . . .

We therefore find no valid justification for artificially excluding from the definition of materiality information concerning merger discussions, which would otherwise be considered significant to the trading decision of a reasonable investor, merely because agreement-in-principle as to price and structure has not yet been reached by the parties or their representatives. . . .

C

Even before this Court's decision in *TSC Industries*, the Second Circuit had explained the role of the materiality requirement of Rule 10b-5, with respect to contingent or speculative information or events, in a manner that gave that term meaning that is independent of the other provisions of the Rule. Under such circumstances, materiality "will depend at any given time upon a balancing of both the indicated probability that the event will occur and the anticipated magnitude of the event in light of the totality of the company activity." *SEC v. Texas Gulf Sulphur Co.*, 401 F.2d, at 849. Interestingly, neither the Third Circuit decision adopting the agreement-in-principle test nor petitioners here take issue with this general standard. Rather, they suggest that with respect to preliminary merger discussions, there are good reasons to draw a line at agreement on price and structure.

In a subsequent decision, the late Judge Friendly, writing for a Second Circuit panel, applied the Texas Gulf Sulfur probability/magnitude approach in the specific context of preliminary merger negotiations. After acknowledging that materiality is something to be determined on the basis of the particular facts of each case, he stated:

> Since a merger in which it is bought out is the most important event that can occur in a small corporation's life, to wit, its death, we think that inside information, as regards a merger of this sort, can become material at an earlier stage than would be the case as regards lesser transactions-and this even though the mortality rate of mergers in such formative stages is doubtless high." *SEC v. Geon Industries*, Inc., 531 F.2d 39, 47–48 (1976).

We agree with that analysis.

Whether merger discussions in any particular case are material therefore depends on the facts. Generally, in order to assess the probability that the event will occur, a factfinder will need to look to indicia of interest in the transaction at the highest corporate levels. Without attempting to catalog all such possible factors, we note by way of example that board resolutions, instructions to investment bankers, and actual negotiations between principals or their intermediaries may serve as indicia of interest. To assess the magnitude of the transaction to the issuer of the securities allegedly manipulated, a factfinder will need to consider such facts as the size of the two corporate entities and of the potential premiums over market value. No particular event or factor short of closing the transaction need be either necessary or sufficient by itself to render merger discussions material.[11]

As we clarify today, materiality depends on the significance the reasonable investor would place on the withheld or misrepresented information. The fact-specific inquiry we endorse here is consistent with the approach a number of courts have taken in assessing the materiality of merger negotiations. Because the standard of materiality we have adopted differs from that used by both courts below, we remand the case for reconsideration of the question whether a grant of summary judgment is appropriate on this record. . . .

QUESTIONS

1. Who are the respondents and what is their claim?

2. What were the alleged misstatements?

3. Why did the district court conclude the misstatements were immaterial?

4. What test does the Court say applies to determine whether the misstatements were material? Why does the Court go with this test instead of the *TSC Industries* test?

5. In light of this case, what would you advise a client who is involved in preliminary merger discussions to do in response to a media inquiry regarding whether the client is involved in merger discussions?

---

3. Regulation FD

The SEC adopted Regulation FD (stands for "Fair Disclosure") in 2000 to address selective disclosure by public companies. (Selective disclosure is when a public company tells a select group of persons about a new development regarding

---

[11] [n.17] To be actionable, of course, a statement must also be misleading. Silence, absent a duty to disclose, is not misleading under Rule 10b-5. "No comment" statements are generally the functional equivalent of silence. . . .

It has been suggested that given current market practices, a "no comment" statement is tantamount to an admission that merger discussions are underway. . . . That may well hold true to the extent that issuers adopt a policy of truthfully denying merger rumors when no discussions are underway, and of issuing "no comment" statements when they are in the midst of negotiations. There are, of course, other statement policies firms could adopt; we need not now advise issuers as to what kind of practice to follow, within the range permitted by law. Perhaps more importantly, we think that creating an exception to a regulatory scheme founded on a prodisclosure legislative philosophy, because complying with the regulation might be "bad for business," is a role for Congress, not this Court. . . .

the company before informing the public of the development). Regulation FD provides that when a public company discloses material nonpublic information to securities market professionals or the company's securities holders and it is reasonably foreseeable that they may trade on the basis of the information, the company must publicly disclose that information.

If the selective disclosure is intentional, Regulation FD requires the company to simultaneously disclose the same information to the public. If the selective disclosure is unintentional, the company must "promptly" disclose it to the public. Regulation FD defines promptly as follows:

> "Promptly" means as soon as reasonably practicable (but in no event after the later of 24 hours or the commencement of the next day's trading on the New York Stock Exchange) after a senior official of the issuer . . . learns that there has been a non-intentional disclosure by the issuer or person acting on behalf of the issuer of information that the senior official knows, or is reckless in not knowing, is both material and nonpublic.[12]

A company can make the public disclosure by filing a Form 8-K with the SEC (this is contemplated by Item 7.01 of the form) or "through another method (or combination of methods) of disclosure that is reasonably designed to provide broad, non-exclusionary distribution of the information to the public."[13] Below is Item 7.01 disclosure by Avis Budget regarding its acquisition of Zipcar included in a Form 8-K filed by Avis Budget on February 12, 2013.

Item 7.01 Regulation FD Disclosure

On February 12, 2013, Avis Budget Group, Inc., a Delaware corporation ("Avis Budget"), issued a press release announcing that the waiting period under the U.S. Hart-Scott-Rodino Antitrust Improvements Act of 1976, as amended, expired on February 11, 2013, in connection with Avis Budget's previously announced agreement to acquire Zipcar, Inc. A copy of the press release is furnished herewith as Exhibit 99.1 and is incorporated herein by reference.

Note that Regulation FD specifically excludes from its coverage selective disclosure made "[t]o a person who owes a duty of trust or confidence to the issuer (such as an attorney, investment banker, or accountant)" or "[t]o a person who expressly agrees to maintain the disclosed information in confidence . . . ."[14]

---

[12] Regulation FD § 101(d).

[13] Id. (e)(2).

[14] Id. § 100(b)(2).

E. EXCHANGE RULES

A company with shares listed on the NYSE or NASDAQ is required to comply with the rules of such exchange. NYSE rules are set forth in the New York Stock Exchange Listed Company Manual (see http://nysemanual.nyse.com). NASDAQ rules are available at http://nasdaq.cchwallstreet.com. Both NYSE and NASDAQ rules include shareholder approval requirements that may be implicated by an M&A transaction. The relevant rules are below:

NYSE RULES

312.03 Shareholder Approval . . .

(c) Shareholder approval is required prior to the issuance of common stock, or of securities convertible into or exercisable for common stock, in any transaction or series of related transactions if:

1. the common stock has, or will have upon issuance, voting power equal to or in excess of 20 percent of the voting power outstanding before the issuance of such stock or of securities convertible into or exercisable for common stock; or

2. the number of shares of common stock to be issued is, or will be upon issuance, equal to or in excess of 20 percent of the number of shares of common stock outstanding before the issuance of the common stock or of securities convertible into or exercisable for common stock.

However, shareholder approval will not be required for any such issuance involving:

- any public offering for cash;
- any bona fide private financing, if such financing involves a sale of:
    - common stock, for cash, at a price at least as great as each of the book and market value of the issuer's common stock; or
    - securities convertible into or exercisable for common stock, for cash, if the conversion or exercise price is at least as great as each of the book and market value of the issuer's common stock. . . .

Section 312.04(f) defines "voting power outstanding" as "the aggregate number of votes that may be cast by holders of those securities outstanding that entitle the holders thereof to vote generally on all matters submitted to the company's security holders for a vote." As for the voting standard, § 312.07 provides "where any matter requires shareholder approval, the minimum vote which will constitute shareholder approval for such purposes is defined as approval by a majority of votes cast on a proposal in a proxy bearing on the particular matter."[15]

---

[15] Section 312.07 used to also include a requirement that the total vote cast on the proposal must

NASDAQ RULES

5635. Shareholder Approval . . .

(a) Acquisition of Stock or Assets of Another Company

Shareholder approval is required prior to the issuance of securities in connection with the acquisition of the stock or assets of another company if:

> (1) where, due to the present or potential issuance of common stock, including shares issued pursuant to an earn-out provision or similar type of provision, or securities convertible into or exercisable for common stock, other than a public offering for cash:
>
> > (A) the common stock has or will have upon issuance voting power equal to or in excess of 20% of the voting power outstanding before the issuance of stock or securities convertible into or exercisable for common stock; or
> >
> > (B) the number of shares of common stock to be issued is or will be equal to or in excess of 20% of the number of shares of common stock outstanding before the issuance of the stock or securities . . . .

Section 5635(e)(2) defines "voting power outstanding" as "the aggregate number of votes which may be cast by holders of those securities outstanding which entitle the holders thereof to vote generally on all matters submitted to the Company's security holders for a vote." As for the voting standard, § 5635(e)(4) provides as follows:

> Where shareholder approval is required, the minimum vote that will constitute shareholder approval shall be a majority of the total votes cast on the proposal. These votes may be cast in person, by proxy at a meeting of Shareholders or by written consent in lieu of a special meeting to the extent permitted by applicable state and federal law and rules . . . .

EXERCISE 3.3

Bidder is a public company incorporated in Delaware whose stock is traded on NASDAQ. Bidder's issued and outstanding stock consists of 10,000,000 shares of common stock. Bidder is acquiring Target, a private Arizona corporation, for 3,000,000 shares of Bidder common stock in a deal structured as a direct merger.

1. Do Bidder's shareholders need to approve the deal?

2. If so, (a) how many shareholders constitute a quorum, (b) what is the relevant voting standard, and (c) what is the minimum number of votes required for approval?

3. Do Bidder's shareholders have the right to dissent?

---

represent over 50% in interest of all securities entitled to vote on the proposal, but this requirement was dropped in July 2013.

4.   Do any of your answers to questions 1 through 3 above change if the deal is structured as a triangular merger? What about if Bidder's stock is listed on the NYSE instead of NASDAQ?

Be prepared to explain how you arrived at your answers and provide specific statutory or other cites as support.

EXERCISE 3.4

Bidder, Inc. is a corporation incorporated in California. Target Co. is a corporation incorporated in New York. Bidder's common stock is traded on the NASDAQ Global Market. Target is privately held. Bidder and Target have signed a letter of intent whereby Bidder has agreed to acquire Target for 1,500,000 shares of Bidder common stock through a reverse triangular merger. In that regard, Bidder has incorporated in Delaware Merger Sub Inc. ("MS") for purposes of the deal.

Review the corporate documents of Bidder, Merger Sub, and Target available at www.sjobiz.org/mna and answer the following questions with respect to the transaction:

1.   Which boards need to approve the deal?

2.   (a) Which shareholders need to approve the deal, (b) how many shareholders constitute a quorum, (c) what is the relevant voting standard, and (d) what is the minimum number of votes required for approval?

3.   Which shareholders have the right to dissent?

Make sure you explain how you arrived at your answers and provide specific statutory or other cites as support.

F.   TENDER OFFERS

The acquisition of a public target structured as a stock purchase normally falls under the definition of tender offer and is therefore subject to SEC tender offer rules. (Note that a tender offer where the deal consideration consists of bidder stock is sometimes called an exchange offer.). These rules were adopted by the SEC following passage of the Williams Act in 1968 which empowered the SEC to regulate tender offers by amending the Exchange Act to so provide. As discussed below, the rules, among other things, (1) impose on bidder various requirements regarding its offer to target's shareholders, (2) require bidder to file certain documents with the SEC; and (3) require bidder to disseminate specified information to target shareholders.

1. Definition

The term "tender offer" is not defined by statute or SEC rule; instead its definition has been left to the courts. The leading case on the term is *Wellman v. Dickinson*.[16] In that case, the court formulated the following eight-factor test for determining whether a transaction constitutes a tender offer.

1. An active and widespread solicitation of public shareholders for the shares of an issuer;

2. A solicitation is made for a substantial percentage of the issuer's securities;

3. The offer to purchase is made at a premium over the prevailing market price;

4. The terms of the offer are firm rather than negotiable;

5. The offer is contingent on the tender of a fixed number of shares, often subject to a fixed maximum number to be purchased;

6. The offer is open only for a limited period of time;

7. The offeree is subjected to pressure to sell his or her security; and

8. Public announcements of a purchasing program concerning the target issuer precede or accompany a rapid accumulation of large amounts of the target issuer's securities.

The above factors do not all need to be met for a transaction to be considered a tender offer. Courts vary the weight given to the individual factors depending on the facts and circumstances of a particular transaction. All the factors are met in a typical acquisition of a public target through a stock purchase so the parties simply comply with the tender offer rules. It is only an atypical transaction that the parties may try to argue is not a tender offer based on the absence of some of the above factors.

Some courts have applied a "totality of the circumstances" test instead of the *Wellman* test in determining whether a transaction involves a tender offer. Under this test, the court considers whether, in the absence of disclosure and procedures required under the tender offer rules, the offerees will lack the information needed to make an informed decision concerning the offer.[17]

To give you a flavor for a typical negotiated, or friendly, tender offer, below is Item 1.01 from the June 3, 2013 salesforce.com inc. Form 8-K with respect to the tender offer it was launching for shares of ExactTarget, Inc.

---

[16] 475 F. Supp. 783, 823–24 (S.D.N.Y. 1979).

[17] *See, e.g.*, Hanson Trust PLC v. SCM Corp., 774 F.2d 47 (2d Cir. 1985).

Item 1.01. Entry into a Material Definitive Agreement.

Acquisition Agreement

On June 3, 2013, salesforce.com, inc. (the "Company") entered into an Acquisition Agreement (the "Acquisition Agreement") by and among the Company, Excalibur Acquisition Corp., a wholly owned subsidiary of the Company ("Merger Sub"), and ExactTarget, Inc. ("ExactTarget"). Pursuant to the Acquisition Agreement, and upon the terms and subject to the conditions thereof, Merger Sub will commence a cash tender offer (the "Offer") to purchase all of the outstanding shares of common stock, $0.0005 par value per share, of ExactTarget (the "Shares") at a price per share of $33.75 (the "Offer Price"), net to the seller in cash, without interest.

The Offer will be subject to customary conditions, including the valid tender of the number of Shares that would represent more than 50.00% of the outstanding Shares and the expiration or termination of the required waiting period under the Hart-Scott-Rodino Antitrust Improvements Act of 1976. The Offer is expected to be completed in the Company's second fiscal quarter of 2014, ending July 31, 2013.

Under the terms of the Acquisition Agreement, following the completion of the Offer, Merger Sub will be merged with and into ExactTarget, pursuant to which ExactTarget will become a wholly owned subsidiary of the Company (the "Merger"). In the Merger, all then outstanding Shares, other than Shares held by the Company, Merger Sub and ExactTarget, and Shares held by stockholders who have validly exercised their appraisal rights under the Delaware General Corporation Law (the "DGCL"), will be cancelled and converted into the right to receive the Offer Price.

Under the terms of the Acquisition Agreement, if following the consummation of the Offer, the Company and its subsidiaries hold a number of Shares that enable the Company to consummate the Merger under the "short form" merger procedures of § 253 of the DGCL, the Company will take all necessary action to consummate the Merger as soon as reasonably practicable thereafter in accordance with § 253 of the DGCL. Under the terms of the Acquisition Agreement, ExactTarget has granted Merger Sub an irrevocable option, exercisable only upon the terms and subject to the conditions set forth therein, to purchase a number of Shares equal to the lowest number of Shares that, when added to the number of Shares owned by the Company and its subsidiaries after the completion of the Offer, will constitute one share more than 90% of the Shares then outstanding (the "Short Form Merger Threshold") in order to facilitate completion of the Merger under § 253 of the DGCL.

In the event that following the consummation of the Offer, the Company and its subsidiaries do not hold sufficient Shares to enable the Company to consummate the Merger under the "short form" merger procedures of § 253 of the DGCL, and ExactTarget has insufficient authorized Shares to issue the Company a sufficient number of Shares to achieve the Short Form Merger Threshold, then ExactTarget will call and convene a meeting of stockholders to vote on the Merger. In this event, the Company will vote all of the Shares it obtained in the Offer in favor of the Merger, so the Company will control the outcome of the vote on the Merger and guarantee the successful approval of the Merger.

The Acquisition Agreement contains representations, warranties and covenants of the Company, ExactTarget and Merger Sub that are customary for a transaction of this nature, including among others, covenants by ExactTarget concerning the conduct of its business during the pendency of the transactions contemplated by the Acquisition Agreement, restrictions on solicitation of competing acquisition proposals, public disclosures and other matters. The Acquisition Agreement contains certain termination rights of the Company and ExactTarget and provides that, upon the termination of the Acquisition Agreement under specified circumstances, ExactTarget will be required to pay the Company a termination fee of $78.24 million.

The foregoing descriptions of the Acquisition Agreement and the transactions contemplated thereby do not purport to be complete and are qualified in their entirety by reference to the Acquisition Agreement, a copy of which is filed as Exhibit 2.1 hereto and is incorporated herein by this reference. Exhibit 2.1 is filed for purposes of § 18 of the Securities Exchange Act of 1934, as amended (the "Exchange Act"), and therefore may be incorporated by reference into filings made under the Securities Act of 1933, as amended (the "Securities Act"). The Acquisition Agreement, which has been included to provide investors with information regarding its terms and is not intended to provide any other factual information about the Company or ExactTarget, contains representations and warranties of each of the Company, ExactTarget and Merger Sub. The assertions embodied in those representations and warranties were made for purposes of the Acquisition Agreement and are subject to qualifications and limitations agreed to by the respective parties in connection with negotiating the terms of the Acquisition Agreement, including information contained in confidential disclosure schedules that the parties exchanged in connection with signing the Acquisition Agreement. Accordingly, investors and security holders should not rely on such representations and warranties as characterizations of the actual state of facts or circumstances, since they were only made as of a specific date and are modified in important part by the underlying disclosure schedules. In addition, certain representations and warranties may be subject to a contractual standard of materiality different from what might be viewed as material to stockholders, or may have been used for purposes of allocating risk between the respective parties rather than establishing matters of fact. Moreover, information concerning the subject matter of such representations and warranties may change after the date of the Acquisition Agreement, which subsequent information may or may not be fully reflected in the Company's or ExactTarget's public disclosures.

Support Agreements

In order to induce the Company and Merger Sub to enter into the Acquisition Agreement, certain stockholders of ExactTarget entered into support agreements with the Company and Merger Sub (the "Support Agreements") concurrent with the execution and delivery of the Acquisition Agreement. Shares held by these stockholders that are eligible to be tendered into the Offer represent, in the aggregate, approximately 20% of the Shares outstanding on the date of the Acquisition Agreement. Subject to the terms and conditions of the Support Agreements, such stockholders agreed, among other things, to tender their Shares in the Offer and, if required, to vote their Shares in favor of adoption of the Acquisition Agreement. The foregoing descriptions of the Support Agreements do not purport to be complete and are qualified in their entirety by reference to the Support Agreements, a form of which is filed as Exhibit 10.1 hereto and is incorporated herein by this reference.

Commitment Letter

On June 3, 2013, in connection with the Acquisition Agreement, the Company entered into a commitment letter (the "Commitment Letter"), pursuant to which, subject to the terms and conditions set forth therein, Bank of America, N.A. has committed to provide a $300.0 million term loan, the proceeds of which may be used for the payment of the Offer Price contemplated by, and the payment of fees and expenses incurred in connection with, the Acquisition Agreement and the Offer. The term loan facility would be guaranteed by the Company's material domestic subsidiaries and secured by a pledge of the stock of certain of the Company's subsidiaries. The agreement for the term loan facility would contain affirmative covenants, negative covenants and events of default, as well as financial covenants, in each case to be negotiated by the parties. The commitment is subject to various conditions, including consummation of the Offer.

The foregoing descriptions of the Commitment Letter do not purport to be complete and are qualified in their entirety by reference to the Commitment Letter, which is filed as Exhibit 10.2 hereto and is incorporated herein by this reference.

2. Offer Requirements

Described below are the various requirements the tender offer rules impose on a bidder regarding its offer to target's shareholders.

Offer period. Bidder must keep the offer open for at least 20 business days.[18] Further, the offer period must remain open for at least 10 business days following any change by bidder in the percentage of target company shares it is offering to buy or the consideration it is offering to pay.[19] Thus, for example, if bidder initially sets the offer period at 20 business days and then after 15 business days has run it increases its offer price, it is required to extend the offering period by five business days so that it meets the 10-day post change rule.

Withdrawal rights. Tendering shareholders can change their minds and withdraw their tenders at anytime during offering period.[20]

Proration. If the tender offer is oversubscribed, i.e., more shares are tendered than bidder has offered to buy, bidder must buy shares pro-rata from each

---

[18] Exchange Act Rule 14e-1(a).

[19] *Id.* Rule 14e-1(b).

[20] *Id.* Rule 14d-7.

tendering shareholder based on the number of shares tendered.[21] For example, say target has 1 million shares outstanding, bidder makes a tender offer for 51% or 510,000 of these shares, and target shareholders tender a total of 600,000 shares. Say you own and tendered 100,000 of these 600,000 shares. Bidder would thus buy from you 85,000 shares calculated as follows:

$$\frac{100,000}{600,000} \times 510,000 = 85,000$$

In other words, you tendered 16.667% [100,000/600,000] of the total shares tendered so the shares purchased by bidder from you has to equal this same percentage, i.e., 16.667% of 510,000 is 85,000.

All holders. Bidder's offer must be open to all shareholders.[22] In other words, bidder cannot exclude specific target shareholders from being able to participate in the tender offer.

Best price. Bidder must pay all tendering shareholders the highest, or best, price offered by bidder.[23] This requirement comes into play when bidder raises its offering price to get more target shareholders to tender and some shareholders have already tendered at the lower price.

The next case addresses the reach of the best price rule and also discusses when a tender offer commences.

GERBER v. COMPUTER ASSOCIATES INT'L, INC.
United States Court of Appeals, Second Circuit
303 F.3d 126 (2002)

B.D. PARKER, JR., Circuit Judge.

This appeal concerns a transaction in which defendant Computer Associates International, Inc. ("CA"), a computer software company, acquired On-Line Software International, Inc. ("On-Line"), another computer software company, by means of a tender offer and follow-up merger. Plaintiff Joel Gerber, an On Line shareholder, commenced a class action in 1991 on behalf of On-Line shareholders who tendered their stock in CA's tender offer. Gerber alleged that, in acquiring On-Line, CA paid more money per share to Jack Berdy, On-Line's chairman and chief executive officer, than it paid to other On-Line shareholders, in violation of various provisions of the Williams Act . . . .

The United States District Court for the Eastern District of New York . . . denied defendants' motion to dismiss and granted in part and denied in part their motion for summary judgment. Following trial, a jury returned a $5.7 million verdict for the plaintiff class. Judgment was entered on the verdict, and the District

---

[21] *Id.* § 14(d)(6).

[22] *Id.* Rule 14d-10(a)(1).

[23] *Id.* Rule 14d-10(a)(2).

Court . . . denied CA's motion for judgment as a matter of law or, in the alternative, for a new trial. CA and its wholly-owned subsidiary, LWB Merge, Inc. ("LWB"), appeal, and we affirm.

BACKGROUND

CA is in the business of designing and marketing computer software products. In July 1991, CA's chairman, Charles Wang, approached the chairman and chief executive officer of On-Line, Jack Berdy, to discuss the possibility of CA's acquiring On Line. On-Line, which Berdy founded in 1969, was also in the software business. Berdy owned 1.5 million shares of On-Line stock, representing approximately 25% of the company's outstanding shares. Berdy and Wang, as well as Sanjay Kumar, the chief operating officer of CA, negotiated extensively over the price that CA would pay for On-Line's stock.

Negotiations over the terms of a non-compete agreement proceeded concurrently with negotiations over the purchase price. CA insisted that Berdy and other On-Line executives, who would be leaving the company following the acquisition, agree not to compete with CA for a specified period of time, but Berdy initially resisted entering into a non-compete agreement. At one point in the negotiations, CA offered to purchase On-Line's stock (which was then trading at approximately $10 per share on the New York Stock Exchange (the "NYSE")) for $14 per share and to pay Berdy $9 million for a seven-year non-compete agreement. On-Line's Board of Directors felt that CA's offer of $14 per share was too low and that the $9 million offered to Berdy for his agreement not to compete was too high. The On-Line Board sought $16 per share, and the negotiations continued. Negotiations stalled when CA offered $15.50 per share and On-Line insisted on $16. CA and On-Line ultimately agreed that CA would offer to purchase On-Line's stock for $15.75 per share, and that CA would pay Berdy $5 million for a five-year non-compete agreement. The central issue in this litigation is whether the $5 million was compensation for Berdy's non-compete agreement or unlawful additional compensation for his On-Line stock.

On August 15 and 16, 1991, there was an unusually large amount of trading in On-Line stock. On August 15, the stock price rose $1, and the NYSE asked On-Line about the unusual trading activity. On the morning of August 16, when the stock price rose another dollar, On-Line told the NYSE that it was in discussions with CA and that a press release might be issued shortly. Berdy told CA that On-Line was under pressure from the NYSE to issue a press release. Around noon on August 16, On Line and CA reached their agreement at $15.75 per share, On-Line told the NYSE that it would issue a press release, and trading in On-Line stock was halted. Later that day, each company issued a press release announcing that it had reached an agreement with the other. CA's press release stated in relevant part that CA has reached an agreement in principle with the management of [On-Line] whereby CA will acquire all of the outstanding common stock of On-Line for $15-3/4 per share in cash. The transaction is subject to the approval of the Boards of Directors of On-Line and CA, the execution of definitive agreements and regulatory approval.

On-Line's press release was very similar to CA's, except it also noted that "no assurance can be given that a transaction between On-Line and Computer Associates of any sort will occur."

After issuing their August 16 press releases, CA and On-Line continued to negotiate the terms and conditions of their agreement. They agreed that the transaction would take the form of a tender offer and a follow-up merger. On August 20, CA's Board of Directors approved a Merger Agreement, a Stock Purchase and Non Competition Agreement (the "Berdy Agreement"), and several related agreements. The CA Board also authorized the requisite Securities and Exchange Commission ("SEC") filings and the dissemination to On-Line shareholders of an Offer to Purchase. On August 21, On-Line's Board unanimously approved the Merger Agreement, recommended the transaction to On-Line shareholders, and authorized the necessary filings with the SEC.

Pursuant to the Berdy Agreement, which was executed by CA, LWB, and Berdy, LWB purchased Berdy's On-Line stock for $15.75 per share, the same price that CA offered to all other On-Line shareholders. The Berdy Agreement also provided that he could not tender his shares in the tender offer, and that, if another bidder made a better offer, LWB retained an option to purchase Berdy's shares for $15.75 per share. The Berdy Agreement contained a provision prohibiting him from "engaging in any business activities which are competitive with the computer software business activities of CA, [LWB, or On-Line]" for a period of five years, in consideration for which CA agreed to pay Berdy $5 million. Berdy, who in addition to being On-Line's Chairman had been a medical student since 1989, was not restricted from "engaging in the design, development, marketing, licensing or sale of computer software designed for use in the medical industry, in the biological sciences or as a teaching aid for educational purposes." Gerber argues that, because Berdy was disengaging from the business to pursue his medical studies, CA was not genuinely concerned about the possibility of his competing and that the $5 million payment to him-or part of it-was actually additional compensation to ensure that CA acquired Berdy's large block of On-Line shares. CA, on the other hand, insists that it genuinely feared potential competition from Berdy and that the entire $5 million was consideration for Berdy's agreement not to compete.

On August 21, 1991, CA and On-Line executed the Merger Agreement, obligating CA to commence the tender offer "as promptly as practicable," and CA, LWB, and Berdy executed the Berdy Agreement. On August 22, CA and On-Line issued a joint press release announcing that the two companies had entered into an agreement and that CA "will make a tender offer today" and conduct a follow-up merger. The same day, August 22, CA filed with the SEC and disseminated to On-Line shareholders the Offer to Purchase, offering to purchase all shares of On-Line stock not owned by Berdy for $15.75 per share. The Offer to Purchase stated that it would remain open until September 20, 1991. A majority of On-Line shareholders tendered their shares to CA, and CA and LWB completed the acquisition of On-Line with the follow-up merger.

Gerber is an On-Line shareholder who tendered his stock in response to CA's tender offer. He brought this action individually and on behalf of a class of On-Line shareholders (excluding the defendants, their directors, certain On-Line employees, and their immediate families) who tendered On-Line stock to CA in the tender offer.

The complaint alleged that several defendants (including CA, Wang, Kumar, and Berdy) had violated Section 14(d)(7) of the Securities Exchange Act of 1934 . . . and SEC Rule 14d-10, (collectively, the "Williams Act claims"), as well as various other provisions of the federal securities laws, by offering and paying more consideration to Berdy for his On-Line shares than it offered or paid to other On-Line shareholders.

The gravamen of Gerber's Williams Act claims is that the $5 million that CA paid to Berdy, while nominally consideration for Berdy's five-year non-compete agreement, was actually additional consideration for Berdy's On-Line stock. The defendants moved to dismiss the Williams Act claims, arguing that the tender offer did not begin until August 22, 1991 and that the Berdy Agreement, which was executed on August 21, preceded the tender offer. The District Court denied the motion, concluding as a matter of law that the tender offer commenced on August 16, 1991, when CA issued its first press release. . . . The court subsequently certified a class under Fed.R.Civ.P. 23(b)(3) consisting of "all persons who tendered stock of On-Line pursuant to the tender offer announced by Computer Associates on August 16, 1991." . . . Following discovery, the defendants moved for summary judgment. The District Court granted summary judgment in part but, finding genuine issues of material fact, the court denied the motion with respect to the Williams Act claims.

The case went to trial before Judge Wolle. . . . At the close of trial, the District Court instructed the jury, without objection, to "consider whether the payment of 5 million dollars under the so-called Berdy agreement was paid to Dr. Berdy for his On-Line shares, or his agreement not to compete, or partly for the shares and partly for the agreement not to compete." . . . The jury returned a special verdict in favor of the plaintiff class, finding that $2.34 million of the $5 million that CA had paid to Berdy was compensation for Berdy's On-Line shares, while the remainder was legitimate consideration for the non-compete agreement. Judgment was entered in favor of the plaintiff class in the amount of $5,670,507. The District Court awarded the plaintiff class prejudgment interest of $4,646,242.54. CA moved for judgment as a matter of law or, in the alternative, for a new trial, and the District Court denied the motion. CA and LWB appealed.

DISCUSSION

CA and LWB make three arguments on appeal. [I have omitted the discussion of the second argument]. First, they argue that Gerber's Williams Act claims are insufficient as a matter of law because the Berdy Agreement was not executed during the tender offer and because the $5 million was not paid to Berdy during the tender offer. . . . Third, they argue that the District Court erred in permitting the jury to find that part of the $5 million that CA paid to Berdy was compensation for the non-competition agreement and part was additional consideration for Berdy's On-Line shares. We address each of these arguments in turn.

I. Sufficiency of Williams Act Claims

Defendants challenge the legal sufficiency of Gerber's Williams Act claims. Section 14(d)(7) provides:

Where any person varies the terms of a tender offer or request or invitation for tenders before the expiration thereof by increasing the consideration offered to holders of such securities, such person shall pay the increased consideration to each security holder whose securities are taken up and paid for pursuant to the tender offer or request or invitation for tenders whether or not such securities have been taken up by such person before the variation of the tender offer or request or invitation.

. . . Rule 14d-10 provides in relevant part:

(a) No bidder shall make a tender offer unless:

(1) The tender offer is open to all security holders of the class of securities subject to the tender offer; and

(2) The consideration paid to any security holder pursuant to the tender offer is the highest consideration paid to any other security holder during such tender offer.

. . . Section 14(d)(7) and Rule 14d-10 collectively are commonly referred to as the All Holders/Best Price Rule. . . . Rule 14d-10(a)(1) codifies the All Holders Requirement, and Rule 14d 10(a)(2) codifies the Best Price Rule. . . .

A. Whether the Berdy Agreement Was Executed During the Tender Offer

Defendants' arguments regarding the legal sufficiency of the Williams Act claims focus primarily on timing. First, defendants argue that CA's $5 million payment to Berdy could not have violated the Best Price Rule because the Berdy Agreement was executed prior to the commencement of CA's tender offer, and the Best Price Rule is not triggered until a tender offer has begun. According to defendants, the tender offer did not begin until August 22, 1991, when CA disseminated the Offer to Purchase and issued a joint press release with On-Line explicitly announcing a tender offer. Gerber argues that the Best Price Rule was triggered on August 16, 1991, when CA and On Line issued press releases announcing that they had reached an agreement in principle. If defendants are correct, and the tender offer did not commence until August 22, then the Berdy Agreement preceded the tender offer and is not subject to the Best Price Rule. If Gerber is correct, and the tender offer commenced on August 16, then the Berdy Agreement was executed during the tender offer and must satisfy the Best Price Rule.

In order to determine when the tender offer commenced, we turn to SEC Rule 14d-2. . . . In 1991, Rule 14d-2(b) provided:[24]

A public announcement by a bidder through a press release, newspaper advertisement or public statement which includes the information in paragraph (c) of this section with respect to a tender offer in which the consideration consists solely of cash and/or securities exempt from registration under § 3 of the Securities Act of 1933 shall be deemed to constitute the commencement of a tender offer. . . .

---

[24] [n.2] Rule 14d-2 was amended subsequent to the events giving rise to this litigation, but the parties do not urge us to apply the amendment retroactively.

. . . Rule 14d-2(c) provided:

The information referred to in paragraph (b) of this section is as follows:

(1) The identity of the bidder;

(2) The identity of the subject company; and

(3) The amount and class of securities being sought and the price or range of prices being offered therefor.

. . . Under Rule 14d-2(b), if CA's August 16 press release "include[d] the information in [Rule 14d-2(c)]," then the August 16 press release "shall be deemed to constitute the commencement of [the] tender offer." CA's August 16 press release states:

> Computer Associates International, Inc. ("CA") announced today that it has reached an agreement in principle with the management of On-Line Software International, Inc. whereby CA will acquire all of the outstanding common stock of On-Line for $15-3/4 per share in cash. The transaction is subject to the approval of the Boards of Directors of On-Line and CA, the execution of definitive agreements and regulatory approval.

This press release includes all the information listed in Rule 14d-2(c): (1) it identifies CA as the bidder; (2) it identifies On-Line as the subject company; and (3) it identifies "all . . . outstanding common stock" as the amount and class of securities being sought, and "$15-3/4 per share in cash" as the offer price. CA nonetheless contends that its August 16 press release should not be deemed to have commenced a tender offer because the press release was not made "with respect to a tender offer," because the press release states that the transaction is subject to future conditions, and because CA issued the press release to fulfill certain disclosure obligations. For the reasons discussed below, we reject each of these contentions.

In arguing that its August 16 press release was not made "with respect to a tender offer," CA confuses the test for *whether* a tender offer has occurred with the test for *when* a tender offer commences. CA argues that, under the "totality of the circumstances" test of *Hanson Trust PLC v. SCM Corp.*, 774 F.2d 47 (2d Cir. 1985), and the eight-factor test of *Wellman v. Dickinson*, 475 F.Supp. 783 (S.D.N.Y. 1979), the tender offer began on August 22, not August 16, because those tests were not satisfied until August 22. As the District Court correctly found, however, *Hanson* and *Wellman* both involve the issue of *whether* a tender offer has occurred, not *when* a tender offer starts, and the parties here do not dispute that a tender offer occurred. . . . Rather, the only question is when the tender offer commenced, a question which is answered by Rule 14d-2(c), not by *Hanson* or *Wellman*. *See Lerro v. Quaker Oats Co.*, 84 F.3d 239, 246 (7th Cir. 1996) (noting that "our case is about 'when' rather than 'what' "). For the same reason, CA's reliance on *Weeden v. Continental Health Affiliates, Inc.*, 713 F.Supp. 396 (N.D.Ga. 1989), is misplaced. The court in *Weeden* concluded that, although the defendant's press release included all the information listed in Rule 14d 2(c), the press release had not been made "with respect to a tender offer," and therefore did not commence a tender offer, because no tender offer ever occurred. *Weeden*, 713 F.Supp. at 402–03. Here, however, it is undisputed that a tender offer occurred, and CA's August 16 press release announced a transaction that undisputedly was a tender offer. Thus, we have no trouble concluding that CA's August 16, 1991 press release was made "with respect to a tender offer."

CA also argues that its August 16 press release was not made "with respect to a tender offer" because the press release does not contain the words "tender offer." While the August 16 press release does not contain the words "tender offer," Rule 14d-2(c) imposes no such requirement. Because the entire purpose of that rule is to prescribe the information that a public announcement must contain in order to commence a tender offer, we deem it dispositive that the words "tender offer" are not among the Rule's prescriptions. To the extent CA asks us to graft an additional requirement onto Rule 14d-2(c), we decline to do so. "Were the label used by the acquiror determinative, virtually all of the provisions of the Williams Act, including the filing and disclosure requirements[,] could be evaded simply by an offeror's announcement that offers to purchase [ ] stock were private purchases." *Field v. Trump*, 850 F.2d, at 944 (citation omitted).

We also reject CA's argument that the press release did not commence a tender offer because it stated that the transaction was subject to future conditions-i.e., the approval of On-Line's and CA's Boards of Directors, the execution of definitive agreements, and regulatory approval. Nothing in Rule 14d-2 or Rule 14d-10 renders them inapplicable to tender offers that are subject to conditions. Indeed, CA's ultimate Offer to Purchase, which CA contends commenced the tender offer, also states that the transaction is subject to certain conditions. Our conclusion that CA's August 16 press release commenced a tender offer, despite the presence of future conditions, is consistent with the Seventh Circuit's decision in *Lerro*, upon which defendants place considerable reliance. The plaintiffs in *Lerro* contended that a tender offer begins "as soon as a potential bidder opens negotiation with a potential target's management," even if no public announcement has been made. *Lerro*, 84 F.3d at 245. The court rejected this contention, holding that, under Rule 14d-2, " 'the tender offer' means the definitive announcement, not negotiations looking toward an offer." *Id.* Unlike the situation in *Lerro*, CA's August 16 press release did not announce mere "negotiations looking toward an offer"; rather, the release stated that CA and On Line had "reached an agreement in principle." Accordingly, whatever conditions remained after CA's August 16 press release do not prevent that release from marking the commencement of the tender offer.

CA also contends that its August 16 press release did not commence the tender offer because CA issued that release in response to NYSE inquiries and in order to fulfill disclosure obligations. CA argues that it cannot be penalized under one provision of the Exchange Act as a result of its compliance with a disclosure obligation under another provision. We need not reach the merits of this argument for the simple reasons that the NYSE did not make any inquiries of CA on August 16 and CA has not pointed to any particular disclosure obligation that it faced on that date. As CA acknowledges, the NYSE made inquiries of On-Line, not of CA, and did so after "unusual market activity in On-Line stock." On-Line responded to these inquiries by issuing its own press release on August 16, stating that the management of CA and On-Line had "reached agreement at $15.75 per share." Thus, CA's independent press release was not necessary to respond to the NYSE's inquiries. Because there is no evidence that CA issued its August 16 press release in response to any NYSE inquiry or to fulfill any actual disclosure obligation, and for all the reasons discussed above, we conclude that the tender offer commenced on August 16, 1991.

B. Whether Berdy Was Paid During the Tender Offer

Next, CA argues that, regardless of when the tender offer commenced, the $5 million payment to Berdy cannot violate the Best Price Rule because Berdy was paid after, and not during, the tender offer. CA relies on Rule 14d-10(a)(2), which requires a bidder to pay to any security holder pursuant to a tender offer "the highest consideration paid to any other security holder *during such tender offer.*" 17 C.F.R. § 240.14d-10(a)(2) (emphasis added). While Rule 14d-2 governs the determination of when a tender offer commences, no pertinent rule or statute addresses when a tender offer concludes. CA would have us create a rigid rule equating the duration of a tender offer, for purposes of Rule 14d-10(a)(2), with the offer's self-prescribed expiration date. Such a rule would benefit CA, as its tender offer "closed" on September 20, 1991, and Berdy was not paid until September 25, 1991. We believe that the phrase "during the tender offer," however, is flexible enough to include CA's payment to Berdy, which occurred after the shares had been tendered but before any other On-Line shareholder was paid. *See Epstein v. MCA, Inc.,* 50 F.3d 644, 654 (9th Cir. 1995) ("[T]he term 'tender offer,' as used in the federal securities laws, has never been interpreted to denote a rigid period of time.") . . . We deem it significant that Berdy was paid before all other On-Line shareholders, so that, if Berdy was not paid "during the tender offer," then neither was any other On-Line shareholder.

More fundamentally, equating the termination of a tender offer with the offer's self-imposed expiration date, as CA would have us do, would make it all too easy to contract around the Best Price Rule. For example, the Berdy Agreement required CA to pay Berdy for his On-Line stock at a closing which was to occur "as soon as practicable after the expiration of the [tender offer] . . . ." If this agreement removed Berdy's $5 million payment from the ambit of the Best Price Rule, then the Best Price Rule would be rendered toothless. Rule 14d-10 "cannot be so easily circumvented." *Epstein,* 50 F.3d at 655 (noting that the imposition of a rigid timing requirement on the duration of tender offers "would drain Rule 14d-10 of all its force").

In concluding that Berdy was paid during the tender offer, we draw upon our decision in *Field,* 850 F.2d 938, where we looked past the labels that the parties had attached to their transactions. In *Field,* defendants Julius and Eddie Trump commenced a tender offer at a price of $22.50 per share for the stock of Pay'n Save Corporation, withdrew the tender offer four days later, acquired an option to purchase the shares of certain Pay'n Save directors for $25.00 per share ($23.50 per share plus a $900,000 premium for so-called "fees and expenses"), then announced a new tender offer at $23.50 per share. *Field,* 850 F.2d at 940, 942. The plaintiffs argued that the arrangement violated the Best Price Rule, as the Pay'n Save directors received $1.50 more per share than other Pay'n Save shareholders. . . . The defendants argued that their agreement with the directors was not executed during a tender offer, as the agreement was executed after the original tender offer was withdrawn and before the second tender offer commenced. . . . We refused to give effect to the defendants' use of the labels "withdrawal" and "new" tender offer. *Id.* at 944. Instead, we focused on the Trumps' intent. . . . Because the Trumps never abandoned the goal of their original tender offer, we concluded that the second tender offer was a continuation of the first, and that the Trumps had entered into the agreement to purchase the Pay'n Save directors' stock during the tender offer.

Like the defendants in *Field*, CA continuously pursued the goal of its tender offer, the acquisition of On-Line. We have already determined that the Berdy Agreement was executed during the tender offer, and a properly instructed jury determined that CA paid part of the $5 million to Berdy as compensation for his On-Line shares. Far from having abandoned its intent to acquire On-Line, CA paid Berdy in support of its tender offer. In assessing CA's intent, it is significant that Berdy was paid before all other On-Line shareholders. In purchasing a majority of the outstanding common stock of On Line, and in paying the On-Line shareholders for that stock, CA clearly intended to acquire On-Line. Thus, when CA paid Berdy in support of its continuous goal of acquiring On-Line, it did so during the tender offer. We noted in *Field* that "giving effect to every purported withdrawal that allows a discriminatory premium to be paid to large shareholders would completely undermine the 'best-price rule.'" 850 F.2d at 944. Finding that Berdy was paid after, and not during, the tender offer would have the same effect.

In summary, the tender offer commenced on August 16, 1991, the date that CA issued its press release announcing its agreement in principle with On-Line, *see* 17 C.F.R. § 240.14d-2(a), and Berdy was paid "during such tender offer," 17 C.F.R. § 240.14d-10(a)(2). Accordingly, we conclude that Gerber's Williams Act claims are sufficient as a matter of law. . . .

III. Jury's Apportionment of $5 Million Payment

Lastly, CA argues that the District Court erred in instructing the jury that it could find that CA paid $5 million to Berdy "partly for the shares and partly for the agreement not to compete" (Tr. at 825) and that the jury's finding that $2.34 million of the $5 million was compensation for Berdy's shares represents an impermissible compromise verdict. We review the District Court's jury instructions *de novo*. . . .

CA contends that there was no evidentiary predicate for the District Court's apportionment instruction, which permitted the jury to apportion the $5 million between compensation for Berdy's On-Line stock and compensation for Berdy's agreement not to compete. *See Perry*, 115 F.3d at 153 ("A party is not entitled to have the court give the jury an instruction for which there is no evidentiary predicate at trial."). We disagree.

Sufficient evidence was adduced at trial to support the conclusion that some, but not all, of the $5 million was consideration for Berdy's On-Line shares. For example, CA's expert, Ronald Gilson, testified that, as of 1991, the expected loss to CA as a result of Berdy's competing depended on four variables:

    a. the percentage decrease in [CA's] sales resulting from Mr. Berdy's competition;

    b. [CA's] resulting after-tax cash flow loss;

c. the likelihood of Mr. Berdy competing; and

d. when Mr. Berdy begins to compete.

. . . Gilson's report was admitted into evidence, and he testified extensively about its contents. According to Gilson's testimony and report, there were many scenarios in which the expected loss to CA as a result of the risk of Berdy's competing would have been between $0 and $5 million. . . . Thus, CA's own expert provided a sufficient predicate for the District Court's apportionment instruction. In addition, Kumar, who was CA's primary negotiator with On-Line and Berdy, testified that he performed no mathematical analysis in arriving at the $5 million figure, and that he reached that amount by "intuition." . . .

CONCLUSION

For these reasons, we affirm the judgment of the District Court. We have considered all of appellants' other contentions on appeal and have found them to be without merit.

QUESTIONS

1. What is the deal involved? How was it structured?

2. Who is Gerber and what legal claim is he bringing?

3. What is the factual basis for his claim?

4. What arguments does CA make? What does the court decide on these arguments? Why?

Decisions such as *Gerber* caused lawyers to recommend using a deal structure other than a tender offer if the deal involved non-competition, severance, retention or similar payments to target's executive, which deals commonly do. They viewed the post-deal litigation risk of a best price rule violation as too high. In response, the SEC amended the best price rule in 2006 "to alleviate the uncertainty that the various interpretations of the best-price rule by courts have produced" and "reduce a regulatory disincentive to structuring an acquisition of securities as a tender offer, as compared to a statutory merger, to which the best-price rule does not apply."[25] Specifically, the rule now reads as follows (rule marked to show changes from the rule the court applied in *Gerber*):

Rule 14d-10. Equal Treatment of Security Holders

(a) No bidder shall make a tender offer unless: . . .

2. The consideration paid to any security holder ~~pursuant to the~~

---

[25] Amendments to the Tender Offer Best-Price Rule, Exchange Act Release No. 34-54684 (Nov. 1, 2006), 2–3.

~~tender offer~~ for securities tendered in the tender offer is the highest consideration paid to any other security holder ~~during such tender offer~~ for securities tendered in the tender offer.

Thus, the rule now focuses on "securities tendered in" a tender offer instead of "pursuant to" or "during" a tender offer.

The SEC also added a new paragraph (d) to the rule providing as follows:

(d)(1)   Paragraph (a)(2) of this section shall not prohibit the negotiation, execution or amendment of an employment compensation, severance or other employee benefit arrangement, or payments made or to be made or benefits granted or to be granted according to such an arrangement, with respect to any security holder of the subject company, where the amount payable under the arrangement:

   (i)   Is being paid or granted as compensation for past services performed, future services to be performed, or future services to be refrained from performing, by the security holder (and matters incidental thereto); and

   (ii)   Is not calculated based on the number of securities tendered or to be tendered in the tender offer by the security holder.

(2)   The provisions of paragraph (d)(1) of this section shall be satisfied and, therefore, pursuant to this non-exclusive safe harbor, the negotiation, execution or amendment of an arrangement and any payments made or to be made or benefits granted or to be granted according to that arrangement shall not be prohibited by paragraph (a)(2) of this section, if the arrangement is approved as an employment compensation, severance or other employee benefit arrangement solely by independent directors as follows:

   (i)   The compensation committee or a committee of the board of directors that performs functions similar to a compensation committee of the subject company approves the arrangement, regardless of whether the subject company is a party to the arrangement, or, if the bidder is a party to the arrangement, the compensation committee or a committee of the board of directors that performs functions similar to a compensation committee of the bidder approves the arrangement; or

   (ii)   If the subject company's or bidder's board of directors, as applicable, does not have a compensation committee or a committee of the board of directors that performs functions similar to a compensation committee or if none of the members of the subject company's or bidder's compensation committee or committee that performs functions similar to a compensation committee is independent, a special committee of the board of directors formed to consider and approve the arrangement approves the arrangement; or

   (iii) If the subject company or bidder, as applicable, is a foreign private issuer, any or all members of the board of directors or any

committee of the board of directors authorized to approve employment compensation, severance or other employee benefit arrangements under the laws or regulations of the home country approves
the arrangement.

QUESTION

Would *Gerber* have come out differently under the current version of the best
price rule?

---

3.   Disclosure Requirements

The tender offer rules require bidder to file with the SEC a Tender Offer
Statement on Schedule TO "as soon as practicable on the date of the
commencement of the tender offer." The key part of Schedule TO is the offer to
purchase which serves as the principal disclosure document for target
shareholders. This documents includes the identity and background of the parties;
the material terms of the transaction; previous dealings between the parties; the
source and amount of bidder's funding, including a summary of financing
arrangements; and audited financial statements of bidder if its financial condition is
material to target shareholders. The basic idea behind the offer to purchase is to
provide target shareholders with sufficient information for them to make an
informed decision of whether to tender their shares. Bidder typically mails the
offer to purchase, a letter of transmittal detailing the process target shareholders
need to follow to tender their shares, and other tender offer materials to target
shareholders shortly after filing its Schedule TO.

The SEC normally notifies the bidder whether it will review its tender offer
materials within a few days of filing. If the SEC does review the filing, it will
provide bidder with comments via a comment letter usually within a week after
bidder's filing (note that this is a much quicker turnaround than with respect to a
preliminary proxy or S-4 registration statement subject to SEC review). Bidder
then revises its tender offer materials in light of the comments and refiles them. If
bidder makes any material changes to its tender offer materials, it has to promptly
inform target shareholders of the changes. Bidder cannot close on the tender offer
until the SEC has signed-off on its tender offer materials. Sign-off typically
happens before the offering period runs meaning SEC review does not hold up the
deal.

Bidder is also required to publish information regarding a cash tender
essentially on the same day it files its Schedule TO. It must do so "in a newspaper
with a national circulation." In that regard, below is the publication salesforce.com
ran in the Wall Street Journal on the same day it filed its Schedule TO (lawyers
refer to this sort of publication as a summary advertisement or tombstone ad).

This announcement is neither an offer to purchase nor a solicitation of an offer to sell Shares (as defined below). The Offer (as defined below) is made solely by the Offer to Purchase, dated June 12, 2013, and the related Letter of Transmittal and any amendments or supplements thereto and is being made to all holders of Shares. The Offer is not being made to (nor will tenders be accepted from or on behalf of) holders of Shares in any jurisdiction in which the making of the Offer or the acceptance thereof would not be in compliance with the laws of such jurisdictions. In those jurisdictions where the applicable laws require that the Offer be made by a licensed broker or dealer, the Offer will be deemed to be made on behalf of Purchaser by one or more registered brokers or dealers licensed under the laws of such jurisdiction.

Notice of Offer to Purchase for Cash
All Outstanding Shares of Common Stock
of
ExactTarget, Inc.
at
$33.75 Net Per Share
by
Excalibur Acquisition Corp.,
a wholly owned subsidiary of
salesforce.com, inc.

Excalibur Acquisition Corp., a Delaware corporation ("Purchaser") and wholly owned subsidiary of salesforce.com, inc., a Delaware corporation ("salesforce.com"), is offering to purchase all outstanding shares of common stock, par value $0.0005 per share (the "Shares"), of ExactTarget, Inc., a Delaware corporation ("ExactTarget"), at $33.75 per Share (the "Offer Price"), net to the seller in cash without interest thereon, less any required withholding taxes, upon the terms and subject to the conditions set forth in the Offer to Purchase dated June 12, 2013 (which, together with any amendments or supplements thereto, collectively constitute the "Offer to Purchase") and in the related Letter of Transmittal (which, together with any amendments or supplements thereto and the Offer to Purchase, collectively constitute the "Offer"). Tendering stockholders who have Shares registered in their names and who tender directly to Computershare Trust Company, N.A., the depositary for the Offer (the "Depositary"), will not be obligated to pay brokerage fees or commissions or, except as set forth in the Letter of Transmittal, transfer taxes on the purchase of Shares by Purchaser pursuant to the Offer. Stockholders who hold their Shares through a broker or bank should consult with such institution as to whether it charges any service fees or commissions.

THE OFFER AND WITHDRAWAL RIGHTS EXPIRE AT 12:00 MIDNIGHT, NEW YORK CITY TIME, ON WEDNESDAY, JULY 10, 2013 (WHICH IS THE END OF THE DAY ON WEDNESDAY, JULY 10, 2013), UNLESS THE OFFER IS EXTENDED PURSUANT TO THE ACQUISITION AGREEMENT, DATED AS OF JUNE 3, 2013, BY AND AMONG PURCHASER, SALESFORCE.COM AND EXACTTARGET (AS IT MAY BE AMENDED FROM TIME TO TIME, THE "ACQUISITION AGREEMENT").

The purpose of the Offer and the Merger is to acquire control of, and the entire equity interest in, ExactTarget. Pursuant to the Acquisition Agreement, as soon as practicable after consummation of the Offer and subject to the satisfaction or waiver of certain conditions, Purchaser will be merged with and into ExactTarget, and ExactTarget will become a wholly owned subsidiary of salesforce.com (the "Merger").

The Board of Directors of ExactTarget has unanimously (i) determined that the Acquisition Agreement is advisable, (ii) determined that the Acquisition Agreement and the transactions contemplated thereby, including the Offer and the Merger, taken together, are at a price and on terms that are fair to, and in the best interests of, ExactTarget and its stockholders, (iii) approved the Acquisition Agreement and the transactions contemplated thereby, including the Offer and the Merger, and (iv) recommended that ExactTarget's stockholders accept the Offer, tender their Shares to Purchaser pursuant to the Offer, and, to the extent applicable, adopt the Acquisition Agreement in accordance with the applicable provisions of Delaware law.

The Offer is conditioned upon, among other things, the condition that, prior to the expiration date of the Offer (as it may be extended from time to time in accordance with the Acquisition Agreement), there be validly tendered in accordance with the terms of the Offer and not validly withdrawn a number of Shares of ExactTarget, that, together with any outstanding shares of common stock of ExactTarget then owned by salesforce.com and Purchaser, represents more than 50% of all the then outstanding Shares (the "Minimum Condition"). The Offer is also subject to the satisfaction of certain other conditions as described in the Offer to Purchase, including, among other conditions, (i) the expiration or termination of any applicable waiting period under the Hart-Scott-Rodino Antitrust Improvements Act of 1976, as amended (the "Regulatory Condition"), (ii) the performance of ExactTarget in all material respects of its obligations under the Acquisition Agreement that need to be performed before the scheduled expiration of the Offer, (iii) the absence of any material adverse change on ExactTarget that is ongoing as of immediately prior to the scheduled expiration of the Offer, (iv) the delivery to salesforce.com and Purchaser of certain certificates by ExactTarget's chief executive officer or chief financial officer relating to the satisfaction of certain conditions to the Offer, (v) the absence in the United States or in other jurisdictions where salesforce.com, ExactTarget or their respective subsidiaries have material business or operations of (A) any laws prohibiting or making illegal the transactions contemplated by the Acquisition Agreement (including the Offer and the Merger), (B) any governmental orders that are in effect at the scheduled expiration of the Offer that make any of the transactions contemplated by the Acquisition Agreement (including the Offer and the Merger) illegal, or prohibit or prevent them from being consummated or (C) any actions by any governmental authority that would reasonably be expected to have the consequences described in clauses (A)–(D) in the immediately following clause (vi), (vi) the absence of any pending legal proceeding brought by any governmental authority in the United States or in other jurisdictions where salesforce.com, ExactTarget or their respective subsidiaries have material business or operations (A) that seeks to enjoin the acquisition of Shares by Purchaser or restrain or prohibit the making or consummation of the Offer or the Merger or the performance of any of the other transactions contemplated by the Acquisition Agreement or the support agreements (including the voting provisions thereunder) entered into between salesforce.com and certain stock-holders of ExactTarget, (B) that seeks to limit the ability of salesforce.com or Purchaser to accept for payment and pay for the Shares and exercise their rights, including voting rights, with respect to those Shares, (C) that seeks to compel salesforce.com or Purchaser to divest, dispose of or otherwise change any assets or businesses, or restrict the businesses, of salesforce.com, Purchaser or ExactTarget, or any of their subsidiaries or impose any restriction on the operation of the business of salesforce.com, Purchaser or ExactTarget, or any of their subsidiaries, or (D) which otherwise would be reasonably expected to have a material and adverse change on ExactTarget and (vii) the Acquisition Agreement not having been terminated in accordance with its terms prior to the expiration of the Offer. See Section 15 of the Offer to Purchase entitled "Conditions to Purchaser's Obligations" for more details of the terms and conditions of the Offer.

Subject to the applicable rules and regulations of the Securities and Exchange Commission (the "SEC"), if any of these conditions is not satisfied at or prior to the scheduled expiration of the Offer, Purchaser (a) will not be required to accept for payment or pay for Shares that are tendered in the Offer, and (b) may delay the acceptance for payment of, or the payment for, any Shares that are tendered in the Offer.

Purchaser may waive any of the conditions to the Offer, except for the Minimum Condition. The Offer is not subject to any financing conditions or arrangements.

Purchaser may (but is not required to) extend the Offer for one (1) or more successive extension periods of up to ten (10) business days each, if any of the conditions to the Offer are not satisfied or waived as of any then scheduled expiration of the Offer.

Purchaser is required to extend the Offer beyond its scheduled expiration (i) for any period required by any rule, regulation, interpretation or position of the SEC (or its staff) or any rule or regulation of the New York Stock Exchange that is applicable to the Offer, (ii) for successive extension periods of ten (10) business days each in the event that the Regulatory Condition is not satisfied or waived as of any then scheduled expiration of the Offer, or (iii) for two (2) extension periods of ten (10) business days if the Minimum Condition is not satisfied or waived as of any then scheduled expiration of the Offer, but all of the other conditions to the Offer have been satisfied or waived.

Notwithstanding the foregoing, Purchaser is not required to extend the Offer beyond October 4, 2013 (the "Termination Date"); and the ability to extend the Offer does not restrict in any manner the right of salesforce.com to terminate the Acquisition Agreement in accordance with its terms.

Any extension of the Offer will be followed by a public announcement of such extension no later than 9:00 A.M., New York City Time, on the next business day after the previously scheduled expiration date.

After the time at which the conditions to the Offer are met (after giving effect to any applicable extensions of the Offer), Purchaser also may (but is not required to) extend the Offer for a subsequent offering period and one or more extensions thereof, in accordance with Rule 14d-11 under the Securities Exchange Act of 1934, as amended (the "Exchange Act"), for an aggregate duration of not less than three (3) business days nor more than twenty (20) business days (but not beyond the Termination Date). No withdrawal rights apply to Shares tendered in a subsequent offering period, and no withdrawal rights apply during a subsequent offering period with respect to Shares previously tendered in the Offer and accepted for payment.

For purposes of the Offer, Purchaser will be deemed to have accepted for payment, and thereby purchased, Shares validly tendered and not validly withdrawn, if and when Purchaser gives oral or written notice to the Depositary of Purchaser's acceptance of such Shares for payment. In all cases, payment for Shares purchased pursuant to the Offer will be made by deposit of the purchase price with the Depositary, which will act as agent for tendering stockholders for the purpose of receiving payment from Purchaser and transmitting such payment to tendering stockholders. If, for any reason whatsoever, acceptance for payment of any Shares tendered pursuant to the Offer is delayed, or Purchaser is unable to accept for payment Shares tendered pursuant to the Offer, then, without prejudice to Purchaser's rights with respect to the conditions to the Offer, the Depositary, nevertheless, on behalf of Purchaser, may retain tendered Shares, and such Shares may not be withdrawn, except to the extent that the tendering stockholders are entitled to withdrawal rights as described in Section 4 of the Offer to Purchase entitled "Withdrawal Rights" and as otherwise required by Rule 14e-1(c) under the Exchange Act. Under no circumstances will interest be paid on the purchase price for Shares by Purchaser by reason of any delay in making such payment.

Except as otherwise provided below, tenders of Shares made pursuant to the Offer are irrevocable. Shares tendered pursuant to the Offer may be withdrawn at any time prior to the expiration date of the Offer and, unless theretofore accepted for payment pursuant to the Offer, also may be withdrawn at any time after the date that is 60 days from the date of the Offer to Purchase, unless previously accepted for payment pursuant to the Offer to Purchase; ***provided, however*, that there will be no withdrawal rights during any subsequent offering period.** If all conditions to the Offer have been met or waived, Purchaser must pay for all shares validly tendered and immediately accept and pay for all Shares validly tendered and not validly withdrawn prior to the expiration date of the Offer and any Shares tendered during any subsequent offering period pursuant to Rule 14d-11 under the Exchange Act. If the purchase of or payment for Shares is delayed for any reason or if Purchaser is unable to purchase or pay for Shares for any reason, then, without prejudice to Purchaser's rights under the Offer, tendered Shares may be retained by the Depositary on behalf of Purchaser and may not be withdrawn except to the extent that tendering stockholders are entitled to withdrawal rights as set forth in Section 4 of the Offer to Purchase, subject to Rule 14e-1(c) under the Exchange Act, which provides that no person who makes a tender offer shall fail to pay the consideration offered or return the securities deposited by or on behalf of security holders promptly after the termination or withdrawal of the Offer.

For a withdrawal to be effective, a written, telegraphic or facsimile transmission notice of withdrawal must be timely received by the Depositary at one of its addresses set forth on the back cover of the Offer to Purchase. Any notice of withdrawal must specify the name of the person who tendered the Shares to be withdrawn, the number of Shares to be withdrawn and the name in which the certificates representing such Shares are registered, if different from that of the person who tendered the Shares. If certificates for Shares to be withdrawn have been delivered or otherwise identified to the Depositary, then, prior to the physical release of such certificates, the serial numbers shown on such certificates must be submitted to the Depositary and, unless such Shares have been tendered by an Eligible Institution, the signatures on the notice of withdrawal must be guaranteed by an Eligible Institution. If Shares have been tendered pursuant to the procedures for book-entry transfer set forth in Section 3 of the Offer to Purchase entitled "Procedure for Tendering Shares," any notice of withdrawal also must specify the name and number of the account at DTC to be credited with the withdrawn Shares.

All questions as to the form and validity (including time of receipt) of notices of withdrawal will be determined by Purchaser, in its sole discretion, and its determination will be final and binding on all parties. None of Purchaser, the Depositary, MacKenzie Partners, Inc. (the "Information Agent") or any other person will be under any duty to give notification of any defects or irregularities in any notice of withdrawal or incur any liability for failure to give any such notification.

Any Shares properly withdrawn will be deemed not validly tendered for purposes of the Offer but may be tendered at any subsequent time prior to the expiration date of the Offer by following any of the procedures described in Section 3 of the Offer to Purchase entitled "Procedure for Tendering Shares."

The information required to be disclosed by paragraph (d)(1) of Rule 14d-6 of the General Rules and Regulations under the Securities Exchange Act of 1934, as amended, is contained in the Offer to Purchase and the related Letter of Transmittal and is incorporated herein by reference.

The Offer to Purchase and the related Letter of Transmittal will be mailed to record holders of Shares and will be furnished to brokers, banks and similar persons whose names, or the names of whose nominees, appear on the stockholder list or, if applicable, who are listed as participants in a clearing agency's security position listing for subsequent transmittal to beneficial owners of Shares.

The Offer to Purchase and the related Letter of Transmittal contain important information. Stockholders should carefully read these documents in their entirety before any decision is made with respect to the Offer.

Any questions or requests for assistance may be directed to the Information Agent at the telephone number and address set forth below. Requests for copies of the Offer to Purchase and the related Letter of Transmittal and other tender offer materials may be directed to the Information Agent as set forth below, and copies will be furnished promptly at Purchaser's expense. Stockholders also may contact their broker, dealer, commercial bank, trust company or nominee for assistance concerning the Offer. To confirm delivery of Shares, stockholders are directed to contact the Information Agent at the number below.

The Information Agent for the Offer is:

105 Madison Avenue
New York, New York 10016
(212) 929-5500 (Call Collect)
or
Call Toll-Free (800) 322-2885

Email: tenderoffer@mackenziepartners.com

June 12, 2013

Note that if the deal consideration includes bidder securities, it will have to register the transaction with the SEC. Thus, tender offer rules do not require or allow bidder to do a newspaper publication like salesforce.com did. Instead, bidder is required to mail the tender offer materials, including a prospectus, to target shareholders.

EXERCISE 3.5

Review the above summary advertisement and the Offer to Purchase for Cash available at www.sjobiz.org/mna and answer the following questions.

1. Who is making the offer and when does it expire?

2. Why are they making the offer?

3. How much are they offering and for what percentage of shares?

4. How is bidder financing the deal?

5. Does the offer trigger appraisal rights?

6. What happens to shares that are not tendered?

7. What happens to ExactTarget outstanding options in the deal?

8. How does an ExactTarget shareholder go about tendering?

9. How does an ExactTarget shareholder go about withdrawing a tender?

10. What is ExactTarget's business? What about salesforce.com?

11. What are the U.S. federal income tax consequences to an ExactTarget shareholder who tenders?

12. What role does MacKenzie Partners serve in the deal?

13. When did salesforce.com first approach ExactTarget about doing a deal?

14. How many ExactTarget shares are subject to support agreements? What is the purpose of these agreements?

15. Who is the CEO of salesforce.com?

4. Second Step Merger

a. Overview

As demonstrated by the salesforce.com/ExactTarget transaction described above, friendly tender offers almost always involve a second-step, or back-end, merger. The second step merger is necessary for bidder to acquire 100% of targets stock because presumably not all of target's shares will be sold to bidder in the tender offer. Given bidder's tender offer will be contingent on at least a majority of target's shares being tendered, bidder will have sufficient voting power to ensure that the second step merger will receive the requisite shareholder approval required under state corporate law. The only question is whether bidder will have to effect the second step as a regular, or long-form merger, or secured enough shares for it to do a short-form merger. Bidder would prefer a short-form merger because, as we discussed in Chapter 2, no target shareholder approval is required. Thus, target will not have to file and distribute a proxy statement, wait for the minimum notice period to run, and hold a shareholders meeting. In other words, it will be able to close on the second step merger more quickly and cheaply than if it has to do a long-form merger.

Note that bidder is not required to follow a tender offer with a merger but eliminating all target shareholders gives bidder much more flexibility in how it operates target because it won't have to worry about fiduciary duties owed by a majority shareholder to minority shareholders. In other words, if bidder does not take out all of target's shareholders, it will have to ensure all transactions between target and bidder or bidder controlled entities are on an arms-length basis or risk getting sued by target shareholders for breach of fiduciary duty.

b. Top-Up Options

Bidder and target routinely include in the acquisition agreement a provision known as a "top-up option" to increase the chances of bidder being able to structure the second-step merger as a short-form merger. Here is the top-up option provision from the salesforce.com/ExactTarget Acquisition Agreement:

6.14 *Top-Up Option.*

(a) The Company hereby grants to Merger Sub an irrevocable option (the "*Top-Up Option*"), exercisable only upon the terms and subject to the conditions set forth herein, to purchase at a price per share equal to the Offer Price that number of Company Shares (the "*Top-Up Option Shares*") equal to the lowest number of Company Shares that, when added to the number of Company Shares owned by Parent and its Subsidiaries at the time of such exercise, shall constitute one share more than 90% of the Company Shares then outstanding (the "*Short Form Threshold*") (after giving effect to the issuance of the Top-Up Option Shares); *provided, however,* (x) that the Top-Up Option shall not be exercisable unless the Minimum Condition has been satisfied and, immediately after such exercise and the issuance of Company Shares pursuant thereto, the Short Form Threshold would be reached (assuming the issuance of the Top-Up Option Shares); and (y) that in no event shall the Top-Up Option be exercisable for a number of Company Shares in excess of the Company's total authorized and unissued Company Shares (treating any Company Shares held in the treasury of the Company as unissued).

(b) The parties shall cooperate to ensure that the issuance and delivery of the Top-Up Shares comply with all applicable Law, including compliance with an applicable exemption from registration of the Top-Up Shares under the Securities Act. Merger Sub may pay the Company the aggregate price required to be paid for the Top-Up Option Shares either (i) entirely in cash or (ii) at Merger Sub's election, by (x) paying in cash an amount equal to not less than the aggregate par value of the Top-Up Option Shares and (y) executing and delivering to the Company a promissory note having a principal amount equal to the balance of the aggregate purchase price pursuant to the Top-Up Option less the amount paid in cash pursuant to the preceding clause (x) (a "*Promissory Note*"). Any such Promissory Note shall be full recourse against Parent and Merger Sub and (i) shall bear simple interest at the prime rate of Bank of America, N.A. in effect on the date such Promissory Note is executed and delivered, (ii) shall mature thirty (30) days after the date of execution and delivery of such Promissory Note and (iii) shall have no other material terms.

(c) Provided that no Law or Order shall prohibit the exercise of the Top-Up Option or the issuance of the Top-Up Option Shares pursuant thereto, or otherwise make such exercise or issuance illegal, Merger Sub may exercise the Top-Up Option, in whole but not in part, at any one time after the Appointment Time and prior to the earlier to occur of (i) the Effective Time and (ii) the termination of this Agreement pursuant to *Article VII*.

(d) In the event Merger Sub wishes to exercise the Top-Up Option, Parent or Merger Sub shall provide to the Company one (1) Business Day prior written notice (a "*Top-Up Exercise Notice*," the date of which notice is referred to herein as the "*Top-Up Notice Date*") specifying the denominations of the certificate or certificates evidencing the Top-Up Option Shares which such party wishes to receive, and the place, time and date for the closing of the purchase and sale pursuant to the Top-Up Option (the "*Top-Up Closing*"). The Company shall, as soon as practicable after receipt of the Top-Up Exercise Notice, deliver a written notice to Parent and Merger Sub confirming the number of Top-Up Option Shares and the aggregate purchase price therefore (the "*Top-Up Notice Receipt*"). At the Top-Up Closing, Merger Sub shall pay the Company the aggregate price required to be paid for the Top-Up Option Shares, by delivery of cash and, if applicable, a Promissory Note in an aggregate principal amount equal to the amount specified in the Top-Up Notice Receipt, and the Company shall cause to be issued and delivered to Merger Sub a Certificate or Certificates representing the Top-Up Option Shares or, if the Company does not then have certificated shares, the applicable number of Book-Entry Shares. Such Certificates or Book-Entry Shares may include any legends that are required by federal or state securities laws.

(e) Parent and Merger Sub acknowledge that the Top-Up Option Shares that Merger Sub may acquire upon exercise of the Top-Up Option shall not be registered under the Securities Act and shall be issued in reliance upon an exemption from registration under the Securities Act. Parent and Merger Sub represent and warrant to the Company that Merger Sub is, or shall be upon any purchase of Top-Up Shares, an "accredited investor", as defined in Rule 501 of Regulation D under the Securities Act. Merger Sub agrees that the Top-Up Option, and the Top-Up Option Shares to be acquired upon exercise of the Top-Up Option, if any, are being and shall be acquired by Merger Sub for the purpose of investment and not with a view to, or for resale in connection with, any distribution thereof (within the meaning of the Securities Act).

(f) Any impact on the value of the Company Shares as a result of the issuance of the Top-Up Option Shares will not be taken into account in any determination of the fair value of any Dissenting Company Shares pursuant to § 262 of the DGCL.

Basically, the provision gives bidder (through Merger Sub) the option to purchase, following completion of the tender offer, a number of newly issued target shares so that bidder (including its subsidiaries) owns over 90% of target's shares, thereby enabling bidder to structure the second-step merger as a short-form merger.

A top-up option, however, only works if target has sufficient authorized but unissued shares to issue to bidder to bring its ownership over 90%. For example, say target has 100 million authorized shares, 55 million of which are outstanding. Of these 55 million shares, 30 million are tendered to bidder in the tender offer. To get bidder one share over 90%, target would have to issue 195,000,001 shares to bidder. Here's the calculation:

$$\frac{30,000,000 \ + \ 195,000,001}{55,000,000 \ + \ 195,000,001} = 0.9000000004$$

Target would not be able to do this because it only has 45 million authorized but unissued shares, well short of the shares necessary to top up bidder. (This sort of situation is contemplated by (a)(y) of the above top-up provision from the salesforce.com/ExactTarget deal). Thus, historically bidder would have to structure the second-step merger as a long form merger. Alternatively, it could have target amend its charter to increase its authorized but unissued shares by at least 150,000,001, although this would require target to file and distribute a proxy statement, wait for the minimum notice period to run, and hold a shareholders meeting. In other words, it will involve the same time and expense of a long-form merger.

EXERCISE 3.6

Assume that ExactTarget shareholders tendered 64 million shares in the above tender offer out of the 72 million shares ExactTarget had outstanding and thus salesforce.com wants to exercise the Top-Up Option.

1.   What does salesforce.com need to do to exercise the option?

2.   How many shares is ExactTarget required to issue under the option? At what price? To whom?

3.   Does Merger Sub have to pay cash for the shares?

4. Does ExactTarget have sufficient authorized but unissued shares available? What happens if it does not?

5. When is the closing on the issuance to occur?

6. How do you suspect the parties will comply with federal securities laws with respect to the issuance?

The legality of a top-up option under Delaware law was challenged in 2010 and upheld in *In re Cogent, Inc. Shareholder Litigation*, 7 A.3d 487 (Del. Ch. 2010). The case arose out of the proposed acquisition of Cogent, Inc. by 3M Company through a friendly tender offer followed by a second-step merger. The acquisition agreement between 3M and Cogent contained a top-up option provision. Plaintiffs sought to enjoin the deal by, among other things, arguing that Cogent's board breached its fiduciary duties when it agreed to the top-up option provision. Below is the portion of the opinion which discusses the issue.

> The provision to which Plaintiffs devote the most significant amount of their advocacy is the Top–Up Option, which would allow Cogent, subject to certain conditions, to sell to 3M up to 139 million shares at the tender offer price of $10.50 for either cash or a promissory note payable in one year. In arguing that this provision is unreasonable, Plaintiffs first allege that the Board did not properly inform itself as to the effects such a provision would have. Plaintiffs specifically allege that Defendants breached their statutory obligations under the Delaware General Corporation Law ("DGCL") §§ 152, 153, and 157, which require boards to determine the consideration for the issuance of stock and to control and implement all aspects of the creation and issuance of an option. Plaintiffs allege that Defendants failed to make an informed judgment regarding whether to grant the option. In support of this claim, Plaintiffs assert that neither the Cogent Board minutes nor the Recommendation Statement reflects any discussion of the Top–Up Option.

> These allegations are refuted convincingly by the deposition of Defendant Bolger, in which he testified that the Board received legal advice regarding the Top–Up Option provisions and that he understood the general nature of its mechanics, including that: (1) it would make the transaction "a lot more straightforward"; (2) a majority of Cogent shares would have to be tendered before the option would be exercised; and (3) the option would not disadvantage the minority stockholders. While some of the provisions of the Top–Up Option are more expansive than Bolger might have realized, he is correct, as discussed further *infra*, that the Board can prevent 3M from exercising the Top–Up Option if a majority of the shares are not tendered, and that in order for the Top–Up Option to allow for a short-form merger, a majority of the minority stockholders would have to tender. Thus, at the very least, Defendants have proffered credible evidence that they made a reasonable effort to be informed as to the mechanics of the Top–Up Option.

> Plaintiffs next allege that the Top–Up Option would allow 3M to take control of the Company against the wishes of minority stockholders, even

if a majority of shares are not tendered. I find this argument unpersuasive. Top-up options have become commonplace in two-step tender offer deals.[26] Plaintiffs contend, however, that the Top–Up Option in question here is exceedingly broad and, as structured, might well result in minority stockholders being disenfranchised. While Plaintiffs appear to be correct that it technically might be possible for 3M to acquire the Company through the Top–Up Option without acquiring a majority of the shares in the tender offer, this argument depends on the occurrence of more than one highly unlikely event and is far too speculative to warrant injunctive relief.

Under the Merger Agreement, 3M theoretically is able to exercise the Top–Up Option if it acquires even a single share in the tender offer. One condition required in the Minimum Tender Condition, however, is that a majority of shares outstanding be tendered to 3M. As Plaintiffs note, 3M "expressly reserve[d] the right to waive any condition to the Offer," but it cannot waive the Minimum Tender Condition "without the consent of the Company." In a further effort to advance their cause, Plaintiffs urge the Court to recognize that the Company's Board *might* grant such a consent even though it would disenfranchise Cogent's stockholders. Such a theory is far too speculative to take seriously in the context of a preliminary injunction motion and is not sufficient to support interim relief in this case.

Another factor supporting my conclusion that this Top–Up Option is likely reasonable is the fact that, as a practical matter, for 3M to meet the 90% threshold necessary to effect a short-form merger, it effectively would have to acquire a majority of the minority outstanding shares.[27] I therefore

---

[26] [n.56] *See, e.g.,* Am. Bar Ass'n Mergers & Acqs. Mkt. Subcomm., *2009 Strategic Buyer/Public Targets M & A Deal Points Study,* at 106 (Sept. 10, 2009) (reporting that 94% of two-step tender offer cash deals involved a top-up option in 2007 compared to 67% in 2005/2006).

[27] [n.60] There are currently approximately 90 million Cogent shares outstanding. Even if 3M exercised the Top–Up Option to acquire the entire allotment of 139 million shares, this would bring the total number of outstanding shares to 229 million. In order to obtain 90% of 229 million shares, 3M must acquire approximately 206 million shares. Hsieh owns approximately 35 million shares. This means that of the 90 million shares currently outstanding, 55 million shares are in the hands of minority stockholders. Assuming that 3M acquires the 139 million shares under the Top–Up Option and the 35 million that Hsieh owns, it would have 174 million shares. To get to 206 million shares, therefore, it still would have to acquire 32 million (or approximately 59%) of the 55 million shares in the hands of minority stockholders.

Plaintiffs also emphasize that there are no limits on when 3M can exercise the Top–Up Option and how often. Thus, according to Plaintiffs, 3M could acquire a bare majority of the shares in the tender offer and then partially exercise its rights under the option and increase its holdings to, for example, 68%. In that case, Plaintiffs argue that the non-tendering Cogent stockholders would be disadvantaged in that they would not know 3M's intentions or how best to protect their interests. Instead, they would be caught in a state of limbo waiting for 3M's next move. Defendants respond by noting that, if 3M succeeds in obtaining a majority of the Company's shares in the tender offer, it will be bound contractually to proceed with a merger at the same price, either by way of a long form merger, which it would have the votes to approve, or a short form merger, assuming it has the necessary 90% of the shares. Again, I consider the theoretical harms Plaintiffs claim to fear too speculative and attenuated to support a conclusion that Plaintiffs are likely to succeed on the merits of their challenge to the reasonableness of the Top–Up Option.

find it highly unlikely that minority stockholders will be disenfranchised as a result of the Top–Up Option.

Plaintiffs next allege that the Top–Up Option is, in effect, a sham transaction. They foresee a risk that the Company will issue shares one day and shortly thereafter effect a transaction that will cancel them, all for the purpose of inequitably freezing out minority stockholders. In that regard, Plaintiffs argue that the Top–Up Option allows 3M to gain control of Cogent through illusory consideration because under the Merger Agreement, 3M can pay for the top-up shares with a promissory note payable in a year (by which time 3M presumably would own the Company). Essentially, they argue, 3M is buying shares with a promise to pay itself, which is illusory. Thus, Plaintiffs assert that there would be no consideration for the issuance of the top-up stock, and it, therefore, would be invalid.

This argument, too, is not likely to succeed. DGCL § 157 leaves the judgment as to the sufficiency of consideration received for stock to the conclusive judgment of the directors, absent fraud. As no fraud is alleged here, it suffices that the Board entered into the Merger Agreement "in consideration of the . . . representations, warranties, covenants and agreements set forth in this agreement." Moreover, Plaintiffs' argument regarding the illusory nature of the consideration to be paid upon the exercise of the Top–Up Option, likely in the form of a promissory note, is also weak. The Merger Agreement explicitly provides, for example, that the note is a recourse obligation against the parent company, 3M, and its subsidiary, Ventura. Moreover, while it may be true that this obligation likely will be nullified if the two-step transaction closes, this does not change the fact that, giving due respect to the corporate form, when the note is issued, it will be a legally enforceable obligation owed by 3M and Ventura to Cogent.

The last argument Plaintiffs make regarding the Top–Up Option is that the appraisal rights of Cogent stockholders will be adversely affected by the potential issuance of 139 million additional shares. They claim that the value of current stockholder's shares may be significantly reduced as a result of the dilutive effect of a substantial increase in shares outstanding and the "questionable value" of the promissory note. Plaintiffs argue that the Top–Up Option will result in the issuance of numerous shares at less than their fair value. As a result, when the Company's assets are valued in a subsequent appraisal proceeding following the execution of the Top–Up Option, the resulting valuation will be less than it would have been before the Option's exercise. Plaintiffs admit that Defendants have attempted to mitigate any potential devaluation that might occur by agreeing, in § 2.2(c) of the Merger Agreement, that "the fair value of the Appraisal Shares shall be determined in accordance with DGCL § 262 without regard to the Top–Up Option, the Top–Up Option Shares or any promissory note delivered by the Merger Sub." Plaintiffs question, however, the ability of this provision to protect the stockholders because, they argue, a private contract cannot alter the statutory fair value or limit what the Court of Chancery can consider in an appraisal. Because DGCL § 262's fair value standard requires that appraisal be based on all relevant factors, Plaintiffs contend the Merger Agreement cannot preclude a court from taking into account the total number of outstanding shares, including those distributed upon the exercise of the Top–Up Option. In addition, they argue that even if the parties contractually could provide such protection to the stockholders, § 2.2 of the Merger Agreement fails to accomplish that purpose because the Merger Agreement does not designate stockholders as third-party beneficiaries with enforceable rights.

While the issue of whether DGCL § 262 allows merger parties to define the conditions under which appraisal will take place has not been decided conclusively, there are indications from the Court of Chancery that it is permissible. The analysis in the cited decisions indicates there is a strong argument in favor of the parties' ability to stipulate to certain conditions under which an appraisal will be conducted — certainly to the extent that it would benefit dissenting stockholders and not be inconsistent with the purpose of the statute. In this case, I find that § 2.2(c) of the Merger Agreement, which states that "the fair value of the Appraisal Shares shall be determined in accordance with § 262 without regard to the Top–Up Option . . . or any promissory note," is sufficient to overcome Plaintiffs' professed concerns about protecting the Company's stockholders from the potential dilutive effects of the Top–Up Option. Accordingly, I find that Plaintiffs have not shown that they are likely to succeed on the merits of their claims based on the Top–Up Option.

Id. at 504–08.

In 2013, Delaware amended DGCL § 251 to create what's referred to as a "medium form" merger. Specifically, the legislature added subsection (h) which provides as follows:

> (h) Notwithstanding the requirements of subsection (c) of this section, unless expressly required by its certificate of incorporation, no vote of stockholders of a constituent corporation whose shares are listed on a national securities exchange or held of record by more than 2,000 holders immediately prior to the execution of the agreement of merger by such constituent corporation shall be necessary to authorize a merger if:
>
> (1) The agreement of merger, which must be entered into on or after August 1, 2013, expressly provides that such merger shall be governed by this subsection and shall be effected as soon as practicable following the consummation of the offer referred to in paragraph (h)(2) of this section;
>
> (2) A corporation consummates a tender or exchange offer for any and all of the outstanding stock of such constituent corporation on the terms provided in such agreement of merger that, absent this subsection, would be entitled to vote on the adoption or rejection of the agreement of merger;
>
> (3) Following the consummation of such offer, the consummating corporation owns at least such percentage of the stock, and of each class or series thereof, of such constituent corporation that, absent

this subsection, would be required to adopt the agreement of merger by this chapter and by the certificate of incorporation of such constituent corporation;

(4) At the time such constituent corporation's board of directors approves the agreement of merger, no other party to such agreement is an "interested stockholder" (as defined in § 203(c) of this title) of such constituent corporation;

(5) The corporation consummating the offer described in paragraph (h)(2) of this section merges with or into such constituent corporation pursuant to such agreement; and

(6) The outstanding shares of each class or series of stock of the constituent corporation not to be canceled in the merger are to be converted in such merger into, or into the right to receive, the same amount and kind of cash, property, rights or securities paid for shares of such class or series of stock of such constituent corporation upon consummation of the offer referred to in paragraph (h)(2) of this section.

If an agreement of merger is adopted without the vote of stockholders of a corporation pursuant to this subsection, the secretary or assistant secretary of the surviving corporation shall certify on the agreement that the agreement has been adopted pursuant to this subsection and that the conditions specified in this subsection (other than the condition listed in paragraph (h)(5) of this section) have been satisfied; provided that such certification on the agreement shall not be required if a certificate of merger is filed in lieu of filing the agreement. The agreement so adopted and certified shall then be filed and shall become effective, in accordance with § 103 of this title. Such filing shall constitute a representation by the person who executes the agreement that the facts stated in the certificate remain true immediately prior to such filing.

Section 251(h) eliminates the need to include a top-up option provision in an acquisition agreement if target is a Delaware corporation. To date, no other state's corporate code provides for a medium-form merger, so a top-up option provision is still necessary in a tender offer for a non-Delaware target.

Chapter 4

DEAL STRUCTURING CONSIDERATIONS

This chapter covers the primary considerations that drive the choice of deal structure for a friendly M&A deal.

A. TARGET LIABILITIES

1. Overview

All companies incur liabilities in the normal course of operations. Examples include bank loans, accounts payable, wages payable, and taxes payable. Bidder will not be concerned about these liabilities because they will be reflected in the deal price. For example, if post-closing bidder (or a bidder subsidiary) will be liable on a $10 million target loan, bidder will pay $10 million less for target than it otherwise would have.

Conversely, bidder will be concerned about contingent liabilities of target. A contingent liability is a liability that may or may not come into being depending on whether some future event occurs. A pending target lawsuit is a classic example of a contingent liability. Target will be liable for any judgment if it loses the lawsuit, but obviously not if it wins. It is difficult for bidder and target to agree on a price reduction with respect to a contingent liability because it is often hard to estimate the chance of it coming to fruition and how much it will be if it does.

Bidder will also be concerned about unknown liabilities of target. These are liabilities that may emerge in the future from target's past business operations, but it is unknown if they actually will. Thus, they cannot be quantified at the time of bidder's acquisition of target. Examples of unknown liabilities include environmental and product liability claims.

The basic ground rules with respect to target's liabilities are as follows:

- If target merges directly into bidder, that is, the deal is structured as a direct merger, bidder succeeds by operation of law to all target liabilities, known, contingent, and unknown.

- If bidder purchases target's stock (whether through a stock purchase or a share exchange), bidder does not itself assume target's liabilities; but since bidder now owns target, and since target remains subject to all of its pre-existing known, contingent, and unknown liabilities, bidder will be seriously concerned about those liabilities.

- A forward or reverse triangular merger accomplishes the same thing as bidder's acquisition of target's stock, as far as target's liabilities are concerned. Whether target merges into merger sub or merger sub merges into target, target's liabilities wind up in a wholly owned subsidiary of bidder.

- If bidder acquires target's assets, then bidder can list in the asset purchase agreement for the deal the target liabilities it is and is not assuming. Typically, an asset purchase agreement will provide that bidder is not assuming any unknown liabilities of target. Here is the sample language.

Subject to the terms and conditions set forth in this Agreement, at the Closing, Buyer shall assume from Seller and thereafter pay, perform, or discharge in accordance with their terms only those liabilities listed on **Schedule 1.1** (the "**Assumed Liabilities**"). Except for the Assumed Liabilities, Buyer shall not assume, or otherwise be responsible or liable for or obligated with respect to, any liabilities or obligations of Seller, whether actual or contingent, accrued or unaccrued, matured or unmatured, liquidated or unliquidated, or known or unknown, whether arising out of occurrences prior to, on or after the Closing Date (the "**Excluded Liabilities**"). Without limiting the generality of the foregoing, Excluded Liabilities shall include, but not be limited to, the following:

(a)   environmental claims related to, associated with or arising out of the ownership, operation, use or control of the Purchased Assets, or environmental conditions existing on, or as a result of the operations of, the Purchased Assets, before or as of the Closing Date, whether arising under environmental laws, or in any way arising in connection with the presence, release or threatened release of any contaminant at, on, to or from (i) the Purchased Assets, including, but not limited to, surface water, air, soil or groundwater thereon, thereunder or adjacent thereto or (ii) any real property at which contaminants generated by operations of the Purchased Assets were sent prior to the Closing Date;

(b)   warranty and product liability claims related to, associated with or arising out of the ownership, operation, use or control of the Purchased Assets existing on, or as a result of the operations of, the Purchased Assets, before or as of the Closing Date; and

(c)   liabilities in respect of any pending or threatened action arising out of, relating to or otherwise in respect of the operation of Seller's business or the Purchased Assets to the extent such action relates to such operation on or prior to the Closing Date.

Schedule 1.1 referenced in the above language will list the liabilities of target ("Seller" in the above language) bidder ("Buyer" in the above language) is assuming. This list will likely consist only of known liabilities that have been reflected in the purchase price. The disclaimer of liability language is a bit of overkill, but bidder's lawyers will want to make it crystal clear that bidder assumes nothing that is not listed on Schedule 1.1.

If bidder is concerned about target's liabilities but for other reasons it is not feasible to structure the deal as an asset purchase, bidder should at least not merge target directly into itself. In other words, bidder should avoid structuring the deal as a direct merger but should instead use a structure in which target's liabilities end up in a bidder subsidiary. Bidder can achieve this through a stock purchase, share exchange (if available), or a triangular merger. Then, if catastrophic liabilities emerge later, bidder will hopefully at least be able to shield the rest of its business from these liabilities.

2. Successor Liability

As indicated above, the only way for a bidder to potentially avoid unwanted liabilities of target is to structure the deal as an asset purchase and provide in the asset purchase agreement that it is not assuming certain target liabilities. The "potentially" qualifier is included because of the doctrine of successor liability. Under this doctrine, courts have held bidders liable for target liabilities even though the deals were structured as asset purchases. The next case discusses successor liability in the context of a products liability claim.

RAY v. ALAD CORPORATION
California Supreme Court
560 P.2d 3 (1977)

WRIGHT, Associate Justice.

Claiming damages for injury from a defective ladder, plaintiff asserts strict tort liability against defendant Alad Corporation (Alad II) which neither manufactured nor sold the ladder but prior to plaintiff's injury succeeded to the business of the ladder's manufacturer, the now dissolved "Alad Corporation" (Alad I), through a purchase of Alad I's assets for an adequate cash consideration. Upon acquiring Alad I's plant, equipment, inventory, trade name, and good will, Alad II continued to manufacture the same line of ladders under the "Alad" name, using the same equipment, designs, and personnel, and soliciting Alad I's customers through the same sales representatives with no outward indication of any change in the ownership of the business. The trial court entered summary judgment for Alad II and plaintiff appeals. . . .

Plaintiff alleges in his complaint that on March 24, 1969, he fell from a defective ladder in the laundry room of the University of California at Los Angeles while working for the contracting company by which he was employed. . . .

It is undisputed that the ladder involved in the accident was not made by Alad II and there was testimony that the ladder was an "old" model manufactured by Alad I. Hence the principal issue addressed by the parties' submissions on the motion for summary judgment was the presence or absence of any factual basis for imposing any liability of Alad I as manufacturer of the ladder upon Alad II as successor to Alad I's manufacturing business.

Prior to the sale of its principal business assets, Alad I was in 'the specialty ladder business' and was known among commercial and industrial users of ladders as a 'top quality manufacturer' of that product. On July 1, 1968, Alad I sold to Lighting Maintenance Corporation (Lighting) its 'stock in trade, fixtures, equipment, trade name, inventory and goodwill' and its interest in the real property used for its manufacturing activities. The sale did not include Alad I's cash, receivables, unexpired insurance, or prepaid expenses. As part of the sale transaction Alad I agreed "to dissolve its corporate existence as soon as practical and (to) assist and cooperate with Lighting in the organization of a new corporation to be formed by Lighting under the name 'ALAD CORPORATION.'" Concurrently with the sale the principal stockholders of Alad I, Mr. and Mrs. William S. Hambly, agreed for a separate consideration not to compete with the purchased business for 42 months and to render nonexclusive consulting services during that period. By separate agreement Mr. Hambly was employed as a salaried consultant for the initial five months. There was ultimately paid to Alad I and the Hamblys "total cash consideration in excess of $207,000.00 plus interest for the assets and goodwill of ALAD (I)."

The only provisions in the sale agreement for any assumption of Alad I's liabilities by Lighting were that Lighting would (1) accept and pay for materials previously ordered by Alad I in the regular course of its business and (2) fill uncompleted orders taken by Alad I in the regular course of its business and hold Alad I harmless from any damages or liability resulting from failure to do so. The possibility of Lighting's or Alad II's being held liable for defects in products manufactured or sold by Alad I was not specifically discussed nor was any provision expressly made therefor.

On July 2, 1968, the day after acquiring Alad I's assets, Lighting filed and thereafter published a certificate of transacting business under the fictitious name of "Alad Co." Meanwhile Lighting's representatives had formed a new corporation under the name of "Stern Ladder Company." On August 30, 1968, there was filed with the Secretary of State (1) a certificate of winding up and dissolution of "Alad Corporation" (Alad I) and (2) a certificate of amendment to the articles of Stern Ladder Company changing its name to "Alad Corporation" (Alad II). The dissolution certificate declared that Alad I "has been completely wound up . . . (its) known debts and liabilities have been actually paid . . . (and its) known assets have been distributed to the shareholders." In due course Lighting transferred all the assets it had purchased from Alad I to Alad II in exchange for all of Alad II's outstanding stock.

The tangible assets acquired by Lighting included Alad I's manufacturing plant, machinery, offices, office fixtures and equipment, and inventory of raw materials, semifinished goods, and finished goods. These assets were used to continue the manufacturing operations without interruption except for the closing of the plant for about a week "for inventory." The factory personnel remained the same, and identical "extrusion plans" were used for producing the aluminum components of the ladders. The employee of Lighting designated as the enterprise's general manager as well as the other previous employees of Lighting were all without experience in the manufacture of ladders. The former general manager of Alad I, Mr. Hambly, remained with the business as a paid consultant for about six months after the takeover.

The "Alad" name was used for all ladders produced after the change of management. Besides the name, Lighting and Alad II acquired Alad I's lists of customers, whom they solicited, and continued to employ the salesman and manufacturer's representatives who had sold ladders for Alad I. Aside from a redesign of the logo, or corporate emblem, on the letterheads and labels, there was no indication on any of the printed materials to indicate that a new company was manufacturing Alad ladders, and the manufacturer's representatives were not instructed to notify customers of the change.

Our discussion of the law starts with the rule ordinarily applied to the determination of whether a corporation purchasing the principal assets of another corporation assumes the other's liabilities. As typically formulated the rule states that the purchaser does not assume the seller's liabilities unless (1) there is an express or implied agreement of assumption, (2) the transaction amounts to a consolidation or merger of the two corporations, (3) the purchasing corporation is a mere continuation of the seller, or (4) the transfer of assets to the purchaser is for the fraudulent purpose of escaping liability for the seller's debts.

If this rule were determinative of Alad II's liability to plaintiff it would require us to affirm the summary judgment. None of the rule's four stated grounds for imposing liability on the purchasing corporation is present here. There was no express or implied agreement to assume liability for injury from defective products previously manufactured by Alad I. Nor is there any indication or contention that the transaction was prompted by any fraudulent purpose of escaping liability for Alad I's debts.

With respect to the second stated ground for liability, the purchase of Alad I's assets did not amount to a consolidation or merger. This exception has been invoked where one corporation takes all of another's assets without providing any consideration that could be made available to meet claims of the other's creditors or where the consideration consists wholly of shares of the purchaser's stock which are promptly distributed to the seller's shareholders in conjunction with the seller's liquidation. In the present case the sole consideration given for Alad I's assets was cash in excess of $207,000. Of this amount Alad I was paid $70,000 when the assets were transferred and at the same time a promissory note was given to Alad I for almost $114,000. Shortly before the dissolution of Alad I the note was assigned to the Hamblys, Alad I's principal stockholders, and thereafter the note was paid in full. The remainder of the consideration went for closing expenses or was paid to the Hamblys for consulting services and their agreement not to compete. There is no contention that this consideration was inadequate or that the cash and promissory note given to Alad I were not included in the assets available to meet claims of Alad I's creditors at the time of dissolution. Hence the acquisition of Alad I's assets was not in the nature of a merger or consolidation for purposes of the aforesaid rule.

Plaintiff contends that the rule's third stated ground for liability makes Alad II liable as a mere continuation of Alad I in view of Alad II's acquisition of all Alad I's operating assets, its use of those assets and of Alad I's former employees to manufacture the same line of products, and its holding itself out to customers and the public as a continuation of the same enterprise. However, California decisions holding that a corporation acquiring the assets of another corporation is the latter's mere continuation and therefore liable for its debts have imposed such liability only upon a showing of one or both of the following factual elements: (1) no adequate consideration was given for the predecessor corporation's assets and made available for meeting the claims of its unsecured creditors; (2) one or more persons were officers, directors, or stockholders of both corporations. There is no showing of either of these elements in the present case. . . .

We therefore conclude that the general rule governing succession to liabilities does not require Alad II to respond to plaintiff's claim. In considering whether a special departure from that rule is called for by the policies underlying strict tort liability for defective products, we note the approach taken by the United States Supreme Court in determining whether an employer acquiring and continuing to operate a going business succeeds to the prior operator's obligations to employees and their bargaining representatives imposed by federal labor law. Although giving substantial weight to the general rules of state law making succession to the liabilities of an acquired going business dependent on the form and circumstances of the acquisition, the court refuses to be bound by these rules where their application would unduly thwart the public policies underlying the applicable labor law. Similarly we must decide whether the policies underlying strict tort liability for defective products call for a special exception to the rule that would otherwise insulate the present defendant from plaintiff's claim.

The purpose of the rule of strict tort liability "is to insure that the costs of injuries resulting from defective products are borne by the manufacturers that put such products on the market rather than by the injured persons who are powerless to protect themselves." (*Greenman v. Yuba Power Products, Inc.* (1963) 59 Cal.2d 57, 63, 27 Cal.Rptr. 697, 701, 377 P.2d 897, 901.) However, the rule "does not rest on the analysis of the financial strength or bargaining power of the parties to the particular action. It rests, rather, on the proposition that 'The cost of an injury and the loss of time or health may be an overwhelming misfortune to the person injured, and a needless one for the risk of injury can be insured by the manufacturer and distributed among the public as a cost of doing business.' (*Escola v. Coca Cola Bottling Co.*, 24 Cal.2d 453, 462, 150 P.2d 436 [concurring opinion].)" (*Seeley v. White Motor Co.* (1965) 63 Cal.2d 9, 18–19, 45 Cal.Rptr. 17, 23, 403 P.2d 145, 151.) Thus, "the paramount policy to be promoted by the rule is the protection of otherwise defenseless victims of manufacturing defects and the Spreading throughout society of the cost of compensating them." (*Price v. Shell Oil Co.* (1970) 2 Cal.3d 245, 251, 85 Cal.Rptr. 178, 181, 466 P.2d 722, 725.) Justification for imposing strict liability upon a Successor to a manufacturer under the circumstances here presented rests upon (1) the virtual destruction of the plaintiff's remedies against the original manufacturer caused by the successor's acquisition of the business, (2) the successor's ability to assume the original manufacturer's risk-spreading role, and (3) the fairness of requiring the successor to assume a responsibility for defective products that was a burden necessarily attached to the original manufacturer's good will being enjoyed by the successor in the continued operation of the business. We turn to a consideration of each of these aspects in the context of the present case.

We must assume for purposes of the present proceeding that plaintiff was injured as a result of defects in a ladder manufactured by Alad I and therefore could assert strict tort liability against Alad I under the rule of *Greenman v. Yuba Power Products, Inc., supra,* 59 Cal.2d 57, 27 Cal.Rptr. 697, 377 P.2d 897. However, the practical value of this right of recovery against the original manufacturer was vitiated by the purchase of Alad I's tangible assets, trade name and good will on behalf of Alad II and the dissolution of Alad I within two months thereafter in accordance with the purchase agreement. The injury giving rise to plaintiff's claim against Alad I did not occur until more than six months after the filing of the dissolution certificate declaring that Alad I's "known debts and liabilities have been actually paid" and its "known assets have been distributed to its shareholders." This distribution of assets was perfectly proper as there was no requirement that provision be made for claims such as plaintiff's that had not yet come into existence. Thus, even if plaintiff could obtain a judgment on his claim against the dissolved and assetless Alad I he would face formidable and probably insuperable obstacles in attempting to obtain satisfaction of the judgment from former stockholders or directors.

The record does not disclose whether Alad I had insurance against liability on plaintiff's claim. Although such coverage is not inconceivable products liability insurance is usually limited to accidents or occurrences taking place while the policy is in effect. Thus the products liability insurance of a company that has gone out of business is not a likely source of compensation for injury from a product the company previously manufactured.

These barriers to plaintiff's obtaining redress from the dissolved Alad I set him and similarly situated victims of defective products apart from persons entitled to recovery against a dissolved corporation on claims that were capable of being known at the time of its dissolution. Application to such victim of the general rule that immunizes Alad I's successor from the general run of its debts would create a far greater likelihood of complete denial of redress for a legitimate claim than would the rule's application to most other types of claimants. Although the resulting hardship would be alleviated for those injured plaintiffs in a position to assert their claims against an active and solvent retail dealer who sold the defective product by which they were injured, the retailer would in turn be cut off from the benefit of rights against the manufacturer.

While depriving plaintiff of redress against the ladder's manufacturer, Alad I, the transaction by which Alad II acquired Alad I's name and operating assets had the further effect of transferring to Alad II the resources that had previously been available to Alad I for meeting its responsibilities to persons injured by defects in ladders it had produced. These resources included not only the physical plant, the manufacturing equipment, and the inventories of raw material, work in process, and finished goods, but also the know-how available through the records of manufacturing designs, the continued employment of the factory personnel, and the consulting services of Alad I's general manager. With these facilities and sources of information, Alad II had virtually the same capacity as Alad I to estimate the risks of claims for injuries from defects in previously manufactured ladders for purposes of obtaining insurance coverage or planning self-insurance. Moreover, the acquisition of the Alad enterprise gave Alad II the opportunity formerly enjoyed by Alad I of passing on to purchasers of new "Alad" products the costs of meeting these risks. Immediately after the takeover it was Alad II, not Alad I, which was in a position to promote the "paramount policy" of the strict products liability rule by "spreading throughout society . . . the cost of compensating [otherwise defenseless victims of manufacturing defects]" (*Price v. Shell Oil Co.*, *supra*, 2 Cal.3d 245, 251, 85 Cal.Rptr. 178, 182, 466 P.2d 722, 726).

Finally, the imposition upon Alad II of liability for injuries from Alad I's defective products is fair and equitable in view of Alad II's acquisition of Alad I's trade name, good will, and customer lists, its continuing to produce the same line of ladders, and its holding itself out to potential customers as the same enterprise. This deliberate albeit legitimate exploitation of Alad I's established reputation as a going concern manufacturing a specific product line gave Alad II a substantial benefit which its predecessor could not have enjoyed without the burden of potential liability for injuries from previously manufactured units. Imposing this liability upon successor manufacturers in the position of Alad II not only causes the one "who takes the benefit (to) bear the burden" (Civ.Code, s 3521) but precludes any windfall to the predecessor that might otherwise result from (1) the reflection of an absence of such successor liability in an enhanced price paid by the successor for the business assets and (2) the liquidation of the predecessor resulting in avoidance of its responsibility for subsequent injuries from its defective products. By taking over and continuing the established business of producing and distributing Alad ladders, Alad II became "an integral part of the overall producing and marketing enterprise that should bear the cost of injuries resulting from defective products" (*Vandermark v. Ford Motor Co.*, *supra*, 61 Cal.2d 256, 262, 37 Cal.Rptr. 896, 899, 391 P.2d 168, 171).

We therefore conclude that a party which acquires a manufacturing business and continues the output of its line of products under the circumstances here presented assumes strict tort liability for defects in units of the same product line previously manufactured and distributed by the entity from which the business was acquired.

. . .

The judgment is reversed.

QUESTIONS

1. Why is plaintiff suing?

2. What is defendant's argument for why it is not liable?

3. What are the four exceptions the court discusses to the rule that a purchaser of assets does not assume target's liabilities? Do any of them apply in this case? Why or why not?

4. What is the product line exception?

5. In light of this case, what should defendant have done differently in connection with the purchase of Alad I's assets?

The product line exception has been adopted in five other states (Mississippi, New Jersey, New Mexico, Pennsylvania, and Washington). Roughly, 30 states have declined to adopt it, including Arizona, Delaware, Florida, Illinois, New York, and Texas.

Successor liability is not limited to products liability cases. Courts have applied it to hold asset purchasers liable for target environmental liabilities, employment discrimination, and ERISA liabilities, to name a few, sometimes fine tuning the doctrine for specific types of liabilities in the process.

B.   TARGET'S CONTRACTS

A target will normally be a party to a large number of agreements, some of which, while not critical, are on favorable economic terms. The price bidder is willing to pay for target will be impacted by whether bidder will be able to step into the shoes of target on these agreements. Under contract law, the basic default rule is that a contract is assignable. In other words, if the contract is silent on the issue, target will be able to transfer it to bidder in the transaction. Contracts drafted by lawyers, however, typically are not silent on the issue. A standard provision included in the "General" or "Miscellaneous" section of a contract (typically, the last section of a contract) is a non-assignment clause.

Below is an example non-assignment clause from a building lease agreement. Assume that target is the Renter, bidder wants the benefit of the lease, but Owner would like to get out of the lease because it could now charge a much higher rate of rent. In other words, Owner will not consent to the lease being assigned to bidder.

EXAMPLE 1

Renter may not assign any of its rights, duties or obligations under this Agreement without the prior written consent of Owner.

Under this language, bidder will not be able to step into the shoes of target if the deal is structured as an asset purchase. This is because with an asset purchase, for bidder to get the benefit of a target contract, target has to assign the contract to bidder, but here Owner will not consent to the assignment as required by the agreement. (Owner is probably more than willing for bidder to take over the lease if bidder agrees to a higher rent).

The analysis is different if the transaction is structured as a direct or forward triangular merger. As you know, in a merger, all target's assets and liabilities are transferred to bidder (or a subsidiary of bidder) by operation of the law pursuant to the merger statute as opposed to being assigned. This includes target's contractual rights and obligations.[1] Thus, arguably, under the above language bidder (or a subsidiary of bidder) will be able to step into the shoes of target with respect to the Agreement if the deal is structured as a direct or forward triangular merger because the Agreement will not be assigned but instead transferred by operation of the law. Most transactional attorneys are well aware of this nuance and will thus include a reference to an assignment by "operation of law" in their

---

[1] *See, e.g.,* MBCA § 11.07(a) ("When a merger becomes effective: . . . (3) . . . every contract right possessed by . . . each corporation or eligible entity that merges into the survivor is vested in the survivor without reversion or impairment . . . .").

anti-assignment clauses. Here's an example (emphasis added):

EXAMPLE 2

Renter may not assign any of its rights, duties, or obligations under this Agreement, *by operation of law or otherwise*, without the prior written consent of Owner.

The "arguably" modifier was introduced above because, in some situations including "by operation of the law or otherwise," it may still not be enough to prevent a transfer of contractual rights by a merger, as exemplified by the next case.

TENNECO AUTO. INC. v. EL PASO CORP.
Delaware Chancery Court
2002 Del. Ch. LEXIS 26 (Mar. 20, 2002) (unpublished)

NOBLE, Vice Chancellor . . .

Shortly before trial commenced, Newport News Shipbuilding, Inc. ("NNS II") sought to be substituted for an original plaintiff entity, Newport News Shipbuilding, Inc. ("NNS I"). This motion was necessitated by the acquisition of NNS I by Northrop Grumman Corporation ("Northrop"). On January 18, 2002, NNS I, pursuant to an exchange offer, merged into Purchaser Corp. I, a wholly-owned subsidiary of Northrop. Purchaser Corp. I then changed its corporate name to Newport News Shipbuilding, Inc.

NNS I and Defendant El Paso Tennessee Pipeline Co. (collectively with Defendant El Paso Corporation and its related defendants, "El Paso") were among the surviving entities from the deconstruction of Tenneco, Inc. ("Old Tenneco") in 1996. The rights of the surviving entities to Old Tenneco's historical insurance coverage are at the center of this litigation. These entities have been bound by the "Insurance Agreement," which was negotiated in an attempt to allocate the benefits and duties associated with Old Tenneco's historical insurance coverage. NNS I, in bringing this action, asserted its rights under the Insurance Agreement.

The Insurance Agreement (Section 8.6) contains the following provision:

> 8.6 *Successors and Assigns.* Except as otherwise expressly provided herein, no party hereto may assign or delegate, whether by operation of law or otherwise, any of such party's rights or obligations under or in connection with this Agreement without the written consent of each other party hereto. No assignment will, however, release the assignor of any of its obligations under this Agreement or waive or release any right or remedy the other parties may have against such assignor hereunder. Except as otherwise expressly provided herein, all covenants and agreements contained in this Agreement by or on behalf of any of the parties hereto will be binding upon and enforceable against the respective successors and assigns

of such party and will be enforceable by and will inure to the benefit of the respective successors and permitted assigns of such party.

El Paso has opposed the motion to substitute NNS II for NNS I. It contends that the merger of NNS I into Purchaser Corp. I constituted an "assignment . . . by operation of law . . ." of rights under the Insurance Agreement. The parties agree that NNS I did not seek or obtain El Paso's consent to the merger. Thus, El Paso contends that Section 8.6 of the Insurance Agreement, which it characterizes as an "anti-assignment" provision, precludes the transfer of rights covered by the Insurance Agreement to NNS II.

The basic principles governing interpretation of a contract are not in dispute. In interpreting a contract (here, the Insurance Agreement), courts look to the language of the agreement, read as a whole, in an effort to discern the parties' collective intent. Where the language of a contract is clear and unambiguous on its face, the parties' intent is derived by giving the contractual terms their ordinary and plain meaning. Only if the intent of the parties cannot be derived from the plain meaning of the contractual language may a court resort to the use of extrinsic evidence.

Fortunately, the parties agree that the language of the Insurance Agreement is unambiguous. Unfortunately, the parties' readings of that agreement are diametrically opposed. I conclude that the Insurance Agreement, and Section 8.6 thereof in particular, is ambiguous.

El Paso argues that a merger is an "assignment . . . by operation of law" and that the language of the first sentence of Section 8.6 of the Insurance Agreement makes clear that any such transfer must first receive its consent. As a general matter in the corporate context, the phrase "assignment by operation of law" would be commonly understood to include a merger. Indeed, the Delaware Supreme Court has equated an "assignment by operation of law" with a merger. Furthermore, this Court has suggested that the phrase "transfer by operation of law" would, again in the corporate context, be understood to include a merger.

In sum, I would read the first sentence of Section 8.6 of the Insurance Agreement, in isolation, to preclude a transfer of rights under the Insurance Agreement by merger absent prior consent from the other parties to the Insurance Agreement.

The Court's task, however, is to consider the Insurance Agreement as a whole and certainly to consider Section 8.6 as a whole. The second sentence of Section 8.6 provides that an assignment of rights or duties under the Insurance Agreement does not relieve the assignor of responsibility for those duties. The application of this provision in the context of a traditional assignment, accomplished by one party specifically assigning certain rights to another party, is obvious. The application of this provision to an "assignment by operation of law," however, is less transparent. "Assignment by operation of law" can be understood to include the vesting of rights in a receiver or in a trustee. In these cases, the vesting of rights and duties in a receiver or trustee would not *ipso facto* relieve the corporation for which the trustee or receiver was appointed from responsibility under the subject agreement in perpetuity. The corporation for which the receiver or trustee is appointed would resume the rights and duties under the agreement in the event that the receivership or trusteeship were discontinued (assuming that the corporation ever lost such rights or duties). In the context of a merger, however, the second sentence has no apparent purpose. Once the merger is complete, there is no "assignor" remaining because the corporation that was merged (in this case, NNS I) into the second corporation (in this case, Purchaser Corp. I) ceases to exist. Thus, this sentence is consistent with the first sentence of Section 8.6 if it is read as preserving the duties of a surviving assignor. On the other hand, if it is read as in essence requiring that there be a surviving assignor, the scope of the phrase "assignment by operation of law" would be called into question.

The third sentence of Section 8.6 raises other questions. First, it reads in part:

> Except as otherwise expressly provided herein, all covenants and agreements contained in this Agreement . . . will be enforceable by and will inure to the benefit of the respective successors and permitted assigns of such party.

The parties agree that NNS II is a "respective successor" of NNS I and that it is not a "permitted assign." Thus, if read in isolation, this third sentence would appear to allow NNS II, as successor to NNS I, to continue to assert the rights of NNS I under the Insurance Agreement against El Paso. Second, both the first sentence and the third sentence begin with a phrase "[e]xcept as otherwise expressly provided herein." When two of the three sentences in a paragraph begin with this phrase and where the two sentences can plausibly be read as being inconsistent with one another, determining the priority of each or the meaning to be ascribed to the paragraph as a whole becomes more difficult.

If, for example, the introductory language had been omitted from the first sentence, the first sentence could have been viewed as controlling.[2] However, merely because it is the first sentence appearing in the paragraph does not lead to the conclusion that it is the controlling or more important sentence. There are no signals, such as "provided further" or "provided, however," to lead the reader to an understanding that the second and third sentences are subordinate to or merely limitations on the language of the first sentence. In short, the tension between the relatively clear language of both the first and third sentences cannot be resolved based exclusively on the wording of either the Insurance Agreement as a whole or the text of Section 8.6.[3]

Thus, I cannot conclude that the language of the Insurance Agreement can fairly be read to preclude transfer of the rights conferred under the Insurance Agreement by any and all mergers unless consent to the merger is first obtained. Accordingly,

---

[2] [n.9] El Paso is unable to identify any provision in the balance of the Insurance Agreement that would fall within the scope of "otherwise expressly provided." Indeed, El Paso comes close to asking the Court simply to ignore the "[e]xcept as otherwise expressly provided" clause in the first sentence either as without meaning or as boilerplate.

[3] [n.10] It is for this reason that the authorities cited by El Paso for the proposition that a merger is an "assignment by operation of law" are ultimately unhelpful. *See, e.g.*, DeAscanis v. Brosius-Eliason Co., *supra*; In re Asian Yard Partners & Asian Yard Venture Corp., *supra*; Pacific First Bank v. The New Morgan Park Corp., 319 Or. 342, 876 P.2d 761 (Or. 1994); The Citizens Bank & Trust Co. of Maryland v. The Barlow Corp., 465 A.2d 1283 (Md.App. 1983).

it becomes necessary to engage in the analysis employed by this Court in *Star Cellular:*

> Where an antitransfer clause in a contract does not explicitly prohibit a transfer of property rights to a new entity by a merger, and where performance by the original contracting party is not a material condition and the transfer itself creates no unreasonable risks for the other contracting parties, the court should not presume that the parties intended to prohibit the merger.[4]

This requires consideration of the rights and duties arising under the Insurance Agreement, which generally deals with the handling and allocation of claims to Old Tenneco's historical insurance coverage. These claims all arise out of past conduct and do not affect the current insurance held by the parties to the Insurance Agreement.

Those parties are responsible for performing certain obligations under the Insurance Agreement, such as processing claims for historical coverage, not only for themselves, but also for other entities which were former members of the Old Tenneco corporate structure and which were in the same line of business as their respective representatives among the parties to the Insurance Agreement. For example, NNS I represented, as the exclusive agent, the interests of all "shipbuilding" entities, including Newport News Shipbuilding & Dry Dock, Inc. ("Dry Dock"), which was the principal corporate entity engaging in the shipbuilding business both before and after the breakup of Old Tenneco. It is difficult to perceive how a change in the identity of a party charged with this responsibility could be viewed either as a material condition or as creating an unreasonable risk to the other parties to the Insurance Agreement.

The Insurance Agreement, however, imposes other duties on the parties as well. For example, a party exhausting certain historical coverage may be under an obligation to procure replacement coverage for (or to take other steps for the benefit of) the other parties to the Insurance Agreement. The financial wherewithal of such a party, for example, could be a basis for concern. However, there are protective provisions in the Insurance Agreement to mitigate this type of risk. One of those provisions is Section 3.2(d) which may be read to provide for advance notice of impairment of such coverage that would afford the other parties to the Insurance Agreement the opportunity to take appropriate steps to protect their interests in advance of the loss of coverage under a particular policy. In short, the ongoing interactions among the parties required by or anticipated by the Insurance Agreement are relatively limited.

Furthermore, El Paso has not identified any adverse consequences that may befall it from the merger. The only difference that is immediately obvious is that NNS I was owned by public shareholders and NNS II is owned by Northrop. Thus, it does not appear that the merger and the resulting transfer of rights and duties under the Insurance Agreement to NNS II pose any unreasonable risk to El Paso.

---

[4] [n.11] Star Cellular Tel. Co., Inc. v. Baton Rouge CGSA, Inc., Del. Ch., C.A. No. 12507, mem. op. at 15.

In conclusion, and in accordance with the approach adopted in *Star Cellular*, I am satisfied that the parties to the Insurance Agreement would not have intended to preclude the acquisition of rights under the Insurance Agreement by NNS II as the result of the Northrop transaction. Thus, I will enter an order, a copy of which is enclosed, that grants the motion to substitute NNS II for NNS I as a party plaintiff. . . .

QUESTIONS

1. What is the contract involved in this case? Who are the parties to this contract?

2. On what basis is NNS II trying to assert rights under the contract?

3. What do the defendants argue as to why NNS II has no rights under the contract? What contractual language do they point to?

4. Why does the court decide in favor of NNS II?

5. In hindsight, if you represented El Paso, what changes would you make to Section 8.6?

Bidder and target can easily structure around an Example 2-type non-assignment clause. They just have to go with a structure where target survives as a legal entity post-deal, i.e., a reverse triangular merger, stock purchase, or share exchange (if available). This is because, under each of these structures, nothing is being transferred or assigned by target. All of the assets and liabilities of target (including its rights and obligations under its contracts) remain in target. The acquisition is instead affected by the ownership of target changing from its shareholders to bidder.

The next case considers a non-assignment clause in the context of a reverse triangular merger.

MESO SCALE DIAGNOSTICS, LLC v. ROCHE DIAGNOSTICS GMBH
Delaware Chancery Court
62 A.3d 62 (2013)

PARSONS, Vice Chancellor

[Roche Holding Ltd. acquired BioVeris Corp. in order to acquire certain BioVersis intellectual property rights, including those under a global consent agreement ("Global Consent") between BioVersis and the plaintiffs. The deal was structured as a reverse triangular merger. Plaintiffs sued, claiming, among other things, that the reverse triangular merger constituted an assignment of the Global Consent by operation of law that required their consent. The opinion addresses

Roche's motion for summary judgment on the issue.] . . .

b. The Global Consent

[The Global Consent] contained an important provision preventing the assignment of rights of [BioVersis] without the prior written consent of the other parties. Specifically, Section 5.08 stated:

> Neither this Agreement nor any of the rights, interests or obligations under this Agreement shall be assigned, in whole or in part, *by operation of law or otherwise by any of the parties without the prior written consent of the other parties* . . . . Any purported assignment without such consent shall be void. Subject to the preceding sentences, this Agreement will be binding upon, inure to the benefit of, and be enforceable by, the parties and their respective successors and assigns . . . .

D. Parties' Contentions

Roche . . . [contends that] as a matter of law, a reverse triangular merger cannot be an assignment by operation of law. . . .

II. ANALYSIS . . .

3. Did the BioVeris Merger constitute an assignment "by operation of law or otherwise" under Section 5.08?

Roche argues . . . that [it] is entitled to summary judgment. . . . because no assignment by operation of law or otherwise occurred when Roche acquired BioVeris through a reverse triangular merger. Specifically, Roche asserts that BioVeris remained intact as the surviving entity of the merger, and, therefore, BioVeris did not assign anything. Meso, on the other hand, contends that mergers generally, including reverse triangular mergers, can result in assignments by operation of law.

At the motion to dismiss stage, I noted that Section 5.08 does not require Meso's consent for changes in ownership, but prohibits, absent consent from MSD and MST, an assignment of BioVeris's rights and interests *by operation of law or otherwise.* I concluded that no Delaware case squarely had addressed whether a reverse triangular merger could ever be viewed as an assignment by operation of law. I further stated that "Plaintiffs plausibly argue that 'by operation of law' was intended to cover mergers that effectively operated like an assignment, even if it might not apply to mergers merely involving changes of control."

To interpret an anti-assignment provision, a court "look[s] to the language of the agreement, read as a whole, in an effort to discern the parties' collective intent."[5] Roche contends that the language "by operation of law or otherwise" makes clear that the parties did not intend Section 5.08 to cover reverse triangular mergers. I

---

[5] [n.119] Tenneco Automotive Inc. v. El Paso Corp., 2002 WL 453930, at *1 (Del. Ch. Mar. 20, 2002).

find Roche's interpretation of Section 5.08 to be reasonable. Generally, mergers do not result in an assignment by operation of law of assets that began as property of the surviving entity and continued to be such after the merger.

Upon the completion of a merger, Section 259 of the DGCL provides:

> When any merger or consolidation shall have become effective under this chapter, for all purposes of the laws of this State the separate existence of all the constituent corporations, or of all such constituent corporations *except the one into which the other or others of such constituent corporations have been merged*, as the case may be, shall cease and the constituent corporations shall become a new corporation, or be merged into 1 of such corporations . . . the rights, privileges, powers and franchises of each of said corporations, and all property, real, personal and mixed, and all debts due to any of said constituent corporations on whatever account . . . *shall be vested in the corporation surviving or resulting from such merger or consolidation;* and all property, rights, privileges, powers and franchises, and all and every other interest shall be thereafter as effectually the property of the surviving or resulting corporation as they were of the several and respective constituent corporations.

In *Koppers Coal & Transport Co. v. United States*,[6] the United States Court of Appeals for the Third Circuit concluded that "the underlying property of the constituent corporations is transferred to the resultant corporation upon the carrying out of the consolidation or merger as provided by Section 259."[7] Other courts in Delaware have held that Section 259(a) results in the transfer of the *non-surviving corporation's* rights and obligations to the surviving corporation by operation of law. For example, in *DeAscanis v. Brosius–Eliason Co.*,[8] the Delaware Supreme Court associated § 259 with assignments by operation of law. The language in Section 259, "except the one into which the other or others of such constituent corporations have been merged," however, suggests that the surviving corporation would not have effected any assignment. In sum, Section 259(a) supports Roche's position that a reverse triangular merger generally is not an assignment by operation of law or otherwise, and that, therefore, Section 5.08 was not intended to cover reverse triangular mergers.

I also note that Roche's interpretation is consistent with the reasonable expectations of the parties. Pursuant to the widely accepted "objective theory" of contract interpretation — a framework adopted and followed in Delaware — this Court must interpret a contract in a manner that satisfies the "reasonable expectations of the parties at the time they entered into the contract."[9] The vast majority of commentary discussing reverse triangular mergers indicates that a reverse triangular merger does not constitute an assignment by operation of law as to the surviving entity. For example, this Court has recognized that "it is possible that the only practical effect of the [reverse triangular] merger is the conversion of

---

[6] [n.122] 107 F.2d 706 (3d Cir. 1939).

[7] [n.123] *Id.* at 708 (referring to Del. Rev.Code 1935, § 2092, a precursor to 8 *Del. C.* § 259(a)).

[8] [n.125] 533 A.2d 1254, 1987 WL 4628 (Del. 1987) (ORDER).

[9] [n.127] The Liquor Exchange, Inc. v. Tsaganos, 2004 WL 2694912, at *2 (Del. Ch. Nov. 16, 2004).

the property interest of the shareholders of the target corporation."[10] Similarly, in *Lewis v. Ward*,[11] then-Vice Chancellor Strine observed:

> In a triangular merger, the acquiror's stockholders generally do not have the right to vote on the merger, nor are they entitled to appraisal. If a reverse triangular structure is used, the rights and obligations of the target are not transferred, assumed or affected. Because of these and other advantages to using a triangular structure, it is the preferred method of acquisition for a wide range of transactions.[12]

Leading commentators also have noted that a reverse triangular merger does not constitute an assignment by operation of law.[13] Based on the commentary on this subject, I consider it unlikely that the parties would have expected a clause covering assignments by operation of law to have applied to reverse triangular mergers.

Meso disagrees and has advanced three theories in support of its interpretation of Section 5.08, i.e., that the anti-assignment clause was intended to cover reverse triangular mergers. Those theories are: (1) the acquisition of BioVeris was nothing more than the assignment of BioVeris's intellectual property rights to Roche; (2) Delaware case law regarding forward triangular mergers compels the conclusion that a provision covering assignment "by operation of law" extends to all mergers; and (3) this Court should embrace a California federal court's holding that a reverse triangular merger results in an assignment by operation of law.

First, Meso contends that "the acquisition of BioVeris was nothing more than the assignment of BioVeris's intellectual property rights to Roche" because, as a result of the acquisition, Roche Diagnostics effectively owned the ECL patents. Meso's argument, however, is unavailing because it ignores Delaware's longstanding doctrine of independent legal significance. That doctrine states:

> [A]ction taken in accordance with different sections of [the DGCL] are acts of independent legal significance even though the end result may be the same under different sections. The mere fact that the result of actions taken under one section may be the same as the result of action taken

---

[10] [n.128] Wells Fargo & Co. v. First Interstate Bancorp, 1996 WL 32169, at *7 (Del. Ch. Jan. 18, 1996).

[11] [n.129] 2003 WL 22461894 (Del. Ch. Oct. 29, 2003).

[12] [n.130] *Id.* at *4 n. 18.

[13] [n.131] *See, e.g.*, 1 R. Franklin Balotti & Jesse A. Finkelstein, Delaware Law of Corporations and Business Organizations § 9.8 (2013) ("The advantage of this type of merger is that T will become a wholly-owned subsidiary of A without any change in its corporate existence. Thus, the rights and obligations of T, the acquired corporation, are not transferred, assumed or affected. For example, obtaining consents for the transfer of governmental or other licenses may not be necessary, absent a provision to the contrary in the licenses or agreement, since the licenses will continue to be held by the same continuing corporation."); Elaine D. Ziff, *The Effect of Corporate Acquisitions on the Target Company's License Rights*, 57 Bus. Law. 767, 787 (2002) ("One widely-recognized advantage of employing a reverse subsidiary structure is that it purportedly obviates the issue of whether the merger constitutes a transfer of the target company's assets in violation of existing contracts, because the 'surviving company' is the same legal entity as the original contracting party.").

under another section does not require that the legality of the result must be tested by the requirements of the second section.[14]

Indeed, the doctrine of independent legal significance has been applied in situations where deals were structured so as to avoid consent rights. For example, in *Fletcher International, Ltd. v. ION Geophysical Corp.*,[15] this Court noted:

> [T]he fact that one deal structure would have triggered [Plaintiff's] consent rights, and the deal structure in the Share Purchase Agreement did not, does not have any bearing on the propriety of the Share Purchase Agreement or the fact that under that Agreement, [Plaintiff's] consent rights did not apply. This conclusion, for contract law purposes, is analogous to results worked by the "doctrine of independent legal significance" in cases involving similar statutory arguments made under the DGCL.[16]

Here, [merger sub] was merged into BioVeris, with BioVeris as the surviving entity. Under Section 259, the surviving entity continued to "possess[ ] all the rights, privileges, powers and franchises" it had before the merger plus those of each of the corporations merged into it. Thus, no assignment by operation of law or otherwise occurred as to BioVeris with respect to what it possessed before the merger.

Meso also avers that this Court should look to Delaware's forward triangular merger cases for the propositions (1) that a provision covering assignment "by operation of law" extends to *all* mergers and (2) that this Court should assess whether Meso was adversely harmed in construing the parties' intent. Meso relies primarily on two cases for that proposition: *Star Cellular Telephone Co. v. Baton Rouge CGSA, Inc.*[17] and *Tenneco Automotive Inc. v. El Paso Corp.*[18]

In *Star Cellular*, the Star Cellular Telephone Company, Inc. ("Star Cellular") and Capitol Cellular, Inc. ("Capitol Cellular") were limited partners in the Baton Rouge MSA Limited Partnership. Baton Rouge CGSA, Inc., the original general partner, could "transfer" its interest as a general partner only after written notice to all the other partners and a unanimous vote of the other partners. Baton Rouge CGSA, Inc. ultimately was merged into Louisiana CGSA Inc. through a forward triangular merger. Star Cellular and Capitol Cellular sued, alleging that the merger constituted a prohibited "transfer" of Baton Rouge's general partnership interest. The Court of Chancery first noted that "[a]s a general matter in the corporate context, the phrase 'assignment by operation of law' would be commonly understood to include a merger."[19] Nonetheless, the Court held that it "will not attribute to the contracting parties an intent to prohibit the Merger where the transaction did not

---

[14] [n.133] Orzeck v. Englehart, 195 A.2d 375 (Del. 1963).

[15] [n.134] 2011 WL 1167088 (Del. Ch. Mar. 29, 2011).

[16] [n.135] *Id.* at *5 n. 39.

[17] [n.139] 1993 WL 294847 (Del. Ch. Aug. 2, 1993), *aff'd*, 647 A.2d 382, 1994 WL 267285 (Del. 1994) (ORDER).

[18] [n.140] 2002 WL 453930 (Del. Ch. Mar. 20, 2002).

[19] [n.142] *Star Cellular*, 1993 WL 294847, at *2.

materially increase the risks to or otherwise harm the limited partners."[20] The Court also noted that "where an antitransfer clause in a contract does not explicitly prohibit a transfer of property rights to a new entity by a merger, and where performance by the original contracting party is not a material condition and the transfer itself creates no unreasonable risks for the other contracting parties, the court should not presume that the parties intended to prohibit the merger."[21] Thus, the trial court in *Star Cellular* concluded that the challenged merger did not constitute a prohibited transfer.

The Supreme Court affirmed the Court of Chancery's decision and summarized the lower Court's ruling as follows:

> The court found that the term "transfer" in the anti-transfer provision has no "generally prevailing meaning." The court determined that the assets of Baton Rouge, including its General and Limited Partnership Interest, were transferred to Louisiana by operation of law. The trial court rejected a "mechanical" interpretation of the term "transfer," adopting the criticism of such an analysis found in certain legal journals. The Court of Chancery held that there was an ambiguity as a matter of law, and that the Partnership Agreement did not expressly include transfers by operation of law in its anti-transfer provision.[22]

The Supreme Court then summarily held that: "This is a contract case, and we agree that an ambiguity exists in the Partnership Agreement. The Court of Chancery correctly dealt with that ambiguity."[23]

In *Tenneco Automotive*,[24] the Court of Chancery examined the enforcement of an insurance agreement. While that action was ongoing, the plaintiff merged into a successor entity through a forward triangular merger. The original insurance agreement contained an anti-assignment provision which stated that "no party hereto may assign or delegate, whether by operation of law or otherwise, any of such party's rights or obligations under or in connection with this [insurance agreement] without the written consent of each other party hereto."[25] The Court concluded that the anti-assignment provision was ambiguous based on a tension that existed between the language of that provision and that of the whole agreement. Having concluded that the provision was ambiguous, the Court applied the approach adopted in *Star Cellular*, and noted that the defendant "has not identified any adverse consequences that may befall it from the merger."[26] Therefore, the Court found that the parties did not intend to preclude the challenged acquisition of rights under the insurance agreement, and granted a motion to substitute the successor entity as the plaintiff.

---

[20] [n.143] *Id.* at *11.

[21] [n.144] *Id.* at *8.

[22] [n.145] Star Cellular Telephone Co. v. Baton Rouge CGSA, Inc., 647 A.2d 382, 1994 WL 267285, at *3 (Del. 1994) (ORDER).

[23] [n.146] *Id.*

[24] [n.147] 2002 WL 453930 (Del. Ch. Mar. 20, 2002).

[25] [n.148] *Id.* at 1.

[26] [n.150] *Id.* at *4.

Although both *Star Cellular* and *Tenneco* involved a transfer assignment by operation of law, each of those decisions involved a finding that the non-consenting party had not been adversely harmed and that the parties had not intended to require consent to the challenged transaction. It is important to note, however, that the broad statement in *Tenneco* that an assignment by operation of law commonly would be understood to include a merger, appears to rely on *DeAscanis v. Brosius-Eliason Co.* The *DeAscanis* case focused on Section 259 and mergers in connection with which assignments were made by non-surviving constituent entities. Indeed, *Tenneco* acknowledged that, under § 259, the corporation that was merged into the second corporation "cease[d] to exist." Thus, both *Tenneco* and *Star Cellular* are distinguishable because they involved forward triangular mergers where the target company was not the surviving entity, whereas in this case BioVeris was the surviving entity in a reverse triangular merger.

In both cases, after reading the agreement as a whole, the Court found the anti-assignment language at issue to be ambiguous. The anti-assignment provisions on their own indicated that consent might be required because there had been assignments as a matter of law. In light of other inconsistencies, however, the Court ultimately determined the agreements to be ambiguous. In this case, on the other hand, there was no assignment by operation of law or otherwise. Furthermore, upon examination of Section 5.08, the Global Consent, and the related Transaction Agreements, there are no comparable inconsistencies that might support an inference that the parties intended to depart from the principle that a reverse triangular merger is not an assignment by operation of law. To the contrary, there was a recognition that Roche might acquire BioVeris.

As a final argument, Meso suggests that this Court should embrace the United States District Court for the Northern District of California's holding in *SQL Solutions, Inc. v. Oracle Corp.*[27] that a reverse triangular merger results in an assignment by operation of law. There the court stated, "an assignment or transfer of rights does occur through a change in the legal form of ownership of a business."[28] The court in *SQL Solutions* applied California law and cited a line of California cases for the proposition that whether "an assignment results merely from a change in the legal form of ownership of a business . . . depends upon whether it affects the interests of the parties protected by the nonassignability of the contract."[29]

I decline to adopt the approach outlined in *SQL Solutions*, however, because doing so would conflict with Delaware's jurisprudence surrounding stock acquisitions, among other things. Under Delaware law, stock purchase transactions, by themselves, do not result in an assignment by operation of law. For example, in the *Baxter Pharmaceutical Products* case,[30] this Court stated, "Delaware corporations may lawfully acquire the securities of other corporations, and a purchase or change

---

[27] [n.156] 1991 WL 626458 (N.D.Cal. Dec. 18, 1991).

[28] [n.158] *Id.* at *3.

[29] [n.159] *See* Trubowitch v. Riverbank Canning Co., 30 Cal.2d 335, 344–45, 182 P.2d 182 (1947); *see also* People ex rel. Dep't of Pub. Works v. McNamara Corp., 28 Cal.App.3d 641, 648, 104 Cal.Rptr. 822 (1972).

[30] [n.160] Baxter Pharm. Prods., Inc. v. ESI Lederle Inc., 1999 WL 160148 (Del. Ch. Mar. 11, 1999).

of ownership of such securities (again, without more) is not regarded as assigning or delegating the contractual rights or duties of the corporation whose securities are purchased."[31] Similarly, in *Branmar Theatre Co. v. Branmar, Inc.,*[32] the Court held that "in the absence of fraud . . . transfer of stock of a corporate lessee is ordinarily not a violation of a clause prohibiting assignment. . . ."[33]

Delaware courts have refused to hold that a mere change in the legal ownership of a business results in an assignment by operation of law. *SQL Solutions*, on the other hand, noted, "California courts have consistently recognized that an assignment or transfer of rights does occur through a change in the legal form of ownership of a business."[34] The *SQL Solutions* case, however, provides no further explanation for its apparent holding that any change in ownership, including a reverse triangular merger, is an assignment by operation of law. Both stock acquisitions and reverse triangular mergers involve changes in legal ownership, and the law should reflect parallel results. In order to avoid upsetting Delaware's well-settled law regarding stock acquisitions, I refuse to adopt the approach espoused in *SQL Solutions.*

In sum, Meso could have negotiated for a "change of control provision." They did not. Instead, they negotiated for a term that prohibits "assignments by operation of law or otherwise." Roche has provided a reasonable interpretation of Section 5.08 that is consistent with the general understanding that a reverse triangular merger is not an assignment by operation of law. On the other hand, I find Meso's arguments as to why language that prohibits "assignments by operation of law or otherwise" should be construed to encompass reverse triangular mergers unpersuasive and its related construction of Section 5.08 to be unreasonable.

For the foregoing reasons, I conclude that Section 5.08 was not intended to cover the BioVeris Merger and that Roche is entitled to summary judgment in its favor as to Count I. . . .

QUESTIONS

1. What is the doctrine of independent legal significance? How is it relevant to this case?

2. What was the court's holding in *SQL Solutions, Inc. v. Oracle*? Why did the court here decline to follow that case?

---

[31] [n.161] *Id.* at *5 (internal citations omitted) ("The nonassignability clause contains no language that prohibits, directly or by implication, a stock acquisition or change of ownership of any contracting party.").

[32] [n.162] 264 A.2d 526 (Del. Ch. 1970).

[33] [n.163] *Id.* at 528.

[34] [n.164] *SQL Solutions, Inc.,* 1991 WL 626458, at *3. It is not entirely clear whether the *SQL* court intended to distinguish between a change in legal ownership and a "change in the legal form of ownership." As I understand it, the *SQL* court intended the latter phrase to include the former.

3.   In hindsight, if you represented Meso, what changes to the contract would you have recommended in an effort to avoid this litigation?

Good transactional attorneys are well aware that it is easy to structure a deal around an anti-assignment clause, and thus know how to eliminate this possibility, if so desired. They do it by including a change-of-control provision in addition to an anti-assignment provision in the contracts they draft (the *Meso* opinion references this type of provision in the second to last paragraph above). Here is the sample language:

> Owner may terminate this Agreement at any time following a Change of Control of Renter.
>
> A **"Change of Control"** means the occurrence of any of the following events: (i) the consummation of a merger or consolidation of Renter with or into any corporation or other entity; (ii) the sale or other disposition of all or substantially all of Renter's assets; or (iii) any "person" (as such term is used in §§ 13(d) and 14(d) of the Securities Exchange Act of 1934, as amended) becoming the "beneficial owner" (as defined in Rule 13d-3 under said Act), directly or indirectly, of securities of Renter representing fifty percent (50%) or more of the total voting power represented by Renter's then outstanding voting securities.

There is no structuring around the above provision because it is triggered by a "Change of Control" which is defined to encompass any acquisition of Renter, regardless of structure.

C. TAX CONSIDERATIONS

Michael L. Schler,[35] *Basic Tax Issues in Acquisition Transactions*
116 Penn. St. L. Rev. 879 (2012)[36]

I. Introduction

This article discusses basic U.S. tax issues that arise in an acquisition transaction. It is intended primarily for readers who are corporate lawyers rather than tax lawyers. The discussion is written in general terms and does not include every exception to the general rules (and exception to exception, and so on).

Most importantly, it is vital for the corporate lawyer to consult a tax lawyer at

---

[35] [n.1] Partner, Cravath, Swaine & Moore LLP. The views in this article are solely those of the author. This article was originally published in 116 Penn State L. Rev. 879 (2012), and is updated here through July 1, 2013. It is not intended as tax advice in connection with any particular transaction or set of facts.

[36] Copyright © 2012. All rights reserved. Reprinted with permission.

every stage of an acquisition transaction. The tax rules are detailed, often counterintuitive, and always changing. Details that are minor from a corporate point of view, such as which corporation survives a merger, can have vast consequences from a tax point of view. The particular structure of a transaction can mean that one party might achieve a significant tax benefit at the expense of the other party (e.g., your client), or even worse, both parties could end up significantly worse off than if a different corporate structure had been used. In addition, it is not enough merely to rely on the Internal Revenue Code and regulations, because there is a large body of Internal Revenue Service ("IRS") rulings, judicial decisions, and nonstatutory doctrines.

It is also essential that the tax lawyer begin to participate in a transaction at the very beginning. This is usually when the basic structural elements of the transaction are determined. It is much easier to propose a particular structure at the time an initial term sheet is being negotiated than it is to propose a change in structure after both sides (with or without their respective tax lawyers) have agreed to it. Likewise, detailed ongoing participation by the tax lawyer is necessary to be sure that changes in documentation do not change the tax results that are important to the client.

Part II of this article discusses the considerations involved in deciding whether a transaction should be a taxable transaction or a so-called "tax-free reorganization." Part III discusses taxable transactions, including the different tax effects of stock and asset acquisitions and the different structures for achieving either of these tax results. Part IV discusses the requirements for a tax-free reorganization and the structures that can be used in a reorganization. Part V discusses other issues that arise in both taxable and tax-free transactions. Part VI discusses issues that arise when the acquiring entity is a partnership rather than a corporation. Part VII provides conclusions.

This article assumes throughout that one corporation ("Acquiring") intends to acquire the business of another corporation ("Target"). The shareholders of Target are referred to as the "Shareholders." Unless otherwise indicated:

> Target and Acquiring are both taxable as "C" corporations, i.e., they are taxable on their own income.[37] This is in contrast to an "S" corporation, which is a closely held corporation that meets various conditions,[38] that does not pay income tax itself,[39] and whose income is taxed directly to its shareholders.[40]

Acquiring and Target are unrelated before the transaction. They have primarily different shareholders, and Acquiring does not own any preexisting stock in Target.

The Shareholders hold their stock for investment, and are not dealers or in other special tax situations.

---

[37] [n.2] *See* I.R.C. § 11. All references to I.R.C. are to the I.R.C. as in effect on the date referenced in *supra* note 1.

[38] [n.3]*Id.* § 1361.

[39] [n.4] *See id.* § 1363.

[40] [n.5] *See id.* § 1366.

Acquiring will acquire all the business of Target, i.e., there are no retained assets that will go to the Shareholders.

References to tax are to federal income tax.

II. Taxable or Tax-Free Transaction?

If the price being paid by Acquiring is all cash, the transaction can only be a taxable transaction. If a portion of the price being paid by Acquiring is stock of Acquiring, then it may be possible to structure the transaction as a tax-free reorganization in which Shareholders are not taxed on the receipt of Acquiring stock.

A. Is a Tax-Free Reorganization Possible?

In order for a tax-free reorganization to be possible, two basic conditions must be satisfied. First, at least 40% of the value of the total consideration paid to Shareholders must be in the form of stock of Acquiring (or in some cases stock of a parent of Acquiring).[41] In other words, the nonstock consideration, referred to as "boot", cannot exceed 60% of the total consideration. If the boot will exceed 60%, there cannot be a tax-free reorganization, although a more complex structure discussed below[42] that would achieve similar results may be possible.

Second, a reorganization requires that Target be a corporation for tax purposes.[43] If Target is a partnership, a tax free reorganization involving the acquisition of the partnership is not possible, although Acquiring could acquire one or more corporate partners of the partnership in tax-free reorganizations if the usual conditions for a reorganization with a corporate Target are satisfied. It is also not possible for any party to transfer assets to a new or existing corporate Target, and then, as part of the same plan, for those assets to be part of a tax-free reorganization in which Acquiring acquires Target. The so-called "step transaction" doctrine would treat those contributed assets as being transferred directly from the transferor to Acquiring in a taxable transaction, and not as part of the reorganization involving Target.[44]

Third, a reorganization might not be practicable if Target will retain a substantial amount of assets that will be transferred to the Shareholders rather than to Acquiring. While some types of reorganizations would permit Target to transfer some of its assets to the Shareholders before Target is acquired, such a transfer would generally be taxable to both Target[45] and the Shareholders.[46]

---

41 [n.6] Treas. Reg. §§ 1.368-1(e)(1), (2)(v) ex. 1. All regulations are cited as in effect on the date referenced in *supra* note 1.

42 [n.7] *See infra* Part IV.D.

43 [n.8] I.R.C. § 368(a)(1), (b); Treas. Reg. §§ 1.368-1(b), -2(b)(1)(i)(B), -2(b)(1)(ii).

44 [n.9] Rev. Rul. 70-140, 1970-1 C.B. 73.

45 [n.10] I.R.C. §§ 311(d), 361(c)(2) (taxable gain to Target on use of appreciated property to pay dividend, redeem stock, or make a distribution in connection with a reorganization).

46 [n.11] *Id.* §§ 301, 302, 356 (tax to Shareholder on receipt of assets from Target as dividend, payment

On the other hand, a tax-free reorganization is possible if Target is a limited liability company (LLC) that has previously, and not as part of the same plan, elected (through a so-called "check the box" election) to be treated as a corporation for federal income tax purposes.[47] Likewise, Target may be a "Subchapter S" or "S" corporation,[48] which is a closely held corporation that meets certain conditions and is treated similarly to a partnership for tax purposes.[49] In fact, a major benefit of a business choosing to be an S corporation as opposed to a partnership or LLC is the ability of the owners to "sell out" on a tax-free basis through a reorganization as well as to obtain pass-through treatment of income on an ongoing basis.

Additional requirements of a reorganization are discussed in Part IV below. Moreover, if the conditions for a reorganization are satisfied, the transaction is automatically tax-free even if a taxable transaction is desired. Thus, if stock of Acquiring is being issued and a taxable transaction is desired, it is necessary to be sure that the transaction does not inadvertently satisfy all the requirements of a tax-free reorganization.

B. Is a Tax-Free Reorganization Desirable?

Even if a tax-free reorganization is possible, the question remains whether it is desirable in any particular case.

The main benefit of a reorganization is that Shareholders who exchange their Target stock for Acquiring stock are not taxed currently on the exchange.[50] In addition, Target is not subject to tax, even if the particular kind of reorganization is treated (as discussed in Part IV.C below) as a transfer of assets by Target to Acquiring followed by the liquidation of Target.[51]

The nontaxability of Shareholders on the receipt of Acquiring stock is primarily a timing benefit. Each Shareholder receives the same tax basis in the Acquiring stock that it had in the Target stock.[52] Thus, the gain that is not taxed on the exchange will be taxed later when the Acquiring stock is sold.

In some cases, the benefit is more than a timing benefit. The holding period of Acquiring stock received by a Shareholder includes the Shareholder's holding period of the Target stock surrendered.[53] Thus, if the Shareholder has a holding period of less than a year in the Target stock at the time of the closing of the

---

for stock redemption, or as additional consideration in a tax-free reorganization).

[47] [n.12] Treas. Reg. § 301.7701-3(a).

[48] [n.13] I.R.C. § 1371(a) (an S corporation is a corporation for purposes of Subchapter C, which includes the reorganization rules).

[49] [n.14] *Id.* §§ 1361-1368.

[50] [n.15] *Id.* § 354(a)(1).

[51] [n.16] *Id.* §§ 361(a) (no tax to Target on exchange of assets for Acquiring stock), 361(b) (no tax to Target on receipt of boot from Acquiring that is distributed to Target shareholders), 361(c) (no tax to Target on its distribution of Acquiring stock to Target shareholders).

[52] [n.17] *Id.* § 358.

[53] [n.18] *Id.* § 1223(1).

transaction, a taxable sale of the stock will result in short term capital gain,[54] which is taxable at ordinary income tax rates of up to 39.6%.[55] A tax-free exchange will allow the holding period of the Target stock to carry over into the holding period of the Acquiring stock.[56] Then, a sale of the Acquiring stock after the total holding period exceeds one year will result in long term capital gain, currently taxable to an individual at a maximum statutory rate of 23.8%.[57]

Even more significantly, if a former individual Shareholder of Target dies while holding stock of Acquiring, the stock will receive a stepped up tax basis equal to its fair market value on the date of death.[58] Any gain existing in the stock at that time is permanently exempted from tax. This makes a tax-free transaction particularly beneficial to an elderly Shareholder that holds stock of Target with a low tax basis. In that situation, if the Shareholder has a choice, a taxable sale may be simply unacceptable because it results in tax that would be eliminated in the relatively near future.

On the other hand, the advantages of a tax-free transaction should not be overstated. Depending on the facts, but particularly in the public company context, Shareholders may not have much taxable gain in their stock. Even if they do, many of the Shareholders may be charities, pension funds or foreigners, all of whom are not subject to tax, even on a taxable sale. Moreover, in the public context, hedge funds or arbitrageurs may buy up a lot of the Target stock with the intent to exchange it into Acquiring stock and immediately sell the Acquiring stock (or even sell the Acquiring stock short before the transaction closes). They will obtain no benefit from a tax-free transaction. Shareholders with a loss in their stock will also obtain no benefit from a tax-free transaction. If they cannot easily sell their Target or Acquiring stock for cash outside the transaction, they might prefer to obtain their loss in a taxable acquisition.

In addition, future legislation could increase the capital gains rate, perhaps in the context of equalizing the tax rates on capital gains and ordinary income. A Shareholder may prefer to pay tax at the known rate today rather than at an unknown and possibly higher rate in the future.

The advantages of a tax-free transaction will also be reduced if the transaction will involve a significant amount of boot. A Shareholder will be taxed on the *lesser* of the total gain on the Target stock (total value of stock and boot received over tax basis in the Target stock), and the amount of boot received.[59] Thus, if the Shareholder has a tax basis of $10 in each of its shares of Target stock and receives,

---

54 [n.19] *Id.* § 1222(1).

55 [n.20] *Id.* § 1(i)(3)(A)(ii).

56 [n.21] *Id.* § 1223(1).

57 [n.22] *Id.* §§ 1222(3), 1222(11), 1(h)(1)(D) (20% maximum rate); § 1411(a) (3.8% "Medicare" tax on net investment income). The effective marginal tax rate on long term capital gains will often be approximately 1.2% higher, or approximately 25%. This is because every $100 of capital gain causes the disallowance of $3 of itemized deductions, *see* § 68(a)(1), meaning that the taxpayer's ordinary taxable income will increase by $3 and so the tax (at the rate of 39.6%) will increase by approximately $1.19.

58 [n.23] *Id.* § 1014.

59 [n.24] *Id.* § 356(a)(1).

for each such share, Acquiring stock worth $8 and cash of $6, the taxable gain will be $4 per share (lesser of total gain of $4 and cash of $6). This is exactly the same as in a taxable transaction. It may be possible to reduce the total taxable gain by allocating all the Acquiring stock received by a particular Shareholder to some of the Target shares held by the Shareholder, and all the cash received by the Shareholder to other Target shares held by the Shareholder.[60] However, these rules are uncertain in many respects and are in a state of flux.[61] They do not change the basic principle that a Shareholder receives less benefit from a tax-free transaction if the Shareholder also receives cash.

Moreover, in a tax-free reorganization, Acquiring receives the Target assets with a tax basis equal to Target's old tax basis.[62] There is no increase in tax basis for any boot paid by Acquiring in the transaction, as there is in an asset purchase.[63] This is consistent with the fact that Target does not recognize any gain on boot paid by Acquiring that is distributed to the Shareholders.[64] Nevertheless, this is a counterintuitive result, particularly if the reorganization is in the form of an asset acquisition as discussed in Part IV.C below.

A tax-free reorganization is also more complicated from a tax point of view than a taxable stock or asset purchase. The obligation of each party to close a tax-free transaction is almost always conditioned upon that party receiving an opinion from its tax counsel stating that the requirements for a tax-free reorganization are satisfied. Such tax opinions are based on elaborate representation letters by Acquiring and Target indicating that the required conditions are satisfied.

If any difficult issues are raised, it may also be necessary to obtain a ruling from the IRS on those issues. The IRS would previously rule on the overall tax status of a transaction as a reorganization, but it will now only rule on specific "significant issues" on which the law is not clear.[65] As a result, even if an IRS ruling is obtained, it is still necessary for each party to obtain a tax opinion on the overall status of the transaction as a reorganization, based in part on the IRS ruling. As to timing, the IRS used to have an expedited procedure under which rulings on reorganizations would often be issued within 10 weeks after the request was received.[66] However, this procedure is no longer available,[67] and a ruling now generally takes at least 6 months to receive from the time it is submitted.

---

[60] [n.25] Treas. Reg. § 1.358-2. In the example, the result would be that there is no taxable gain on the 8/14 of the Target shares exchanged entirely for Acquiring stock, and gain of $4 per share on the 6/14 of the Target shares exchanged entirely for cash. Because the same gain per share is recognized on fewer shares, the total recognized gain is reduced.

[61] [n.26] *See* Prop. Treas. Reg. §§ 1.354-1(d)(1), 1.356-1(b), 1.356-1(d) ex. 4, 1.358-2, 74 Fed. Reg. 3509 (Jan. 21, 2009).

[62] [n.27] I.R.C. § 362(b).

[63] [n.28] *See infra* Part III.C.

[64] [n.29] I.R.C. § 361(b).

[65] [n.30] Rev. Proc. 2013-32, 2013-2 C.B. 28, § 5.01(1) (effective for ruling requests received after August 23, 2013).

[66] [n.31] Rev. Proc. 2012-1, 2012-1 C.B. 1, § 7.02(4)(a).

[67] [n.32] Rev. Proc. 2013-1, 2013-1 C.B. 1, § 16.

Finally, the representations that Acquiring is required to give for a tax opinion, and depending on the issue for an IRS ruling, will include representations that it does not plan to engage in certain future transactions that, if treated as part of the same plan as the reorganization, would cause the reorganization rules to be violated.[68] Even if the representation is true at the time it is given, as a practical matter Acquiring will not want to engage in any of the specified transactions for one or two years after the acquisition, unless clearly due to a change in circumstances. A transaction that is done sooner may call into question the correctness of the earlier representation about intent and therefore call into question the qualification of the acquisition as a tax-free reorganization. This loss of flexibility to Acquiring is an additional disadvantage to a tax-free transaction.

III. Taxable Transactions

This Part discusses the issues that arise if the parties have decided to do a taxable transaction. The basic question at this point is whether the transaction should be one that is treated as a stock acquisition or an asset acquisition for tax purposes. These alternatives have vastly different tax consequences to Acquiring, Target, and the Shareholders. Once that decision is made, there are various legal forms of transactions, discussed in Parts III.D and III.E below, that can achieve the desired tax result.

A. Transaction Treated as Stock Acquisition for Tax Purposes

In a transaction treated as a sale of Target stock for tax purposes, the Shareholders will have capital gain or loss on the sale, and the gain or loss will be long term if the stock has been held for more than a year.[69] Target will not be subject to tax as a result of the sale. Acquiring will obtain a cost basis in the stock,[70] although that tax basis will not provide any tax benefit until Acquiring sells the stock. Most significantly for Acquiring, the tax basis of the Target assets will remain unchanged, rather than reflecting Acquiring's purchase price for the stock. Assuming the assets have a value in excess of their tax basis, this is an unfavorable result to Acquiring.

B. Transaction Treated as Asset Acquisition for Tax Purposes

In a taxable asset purchase, Acquiring's tax basis in the purchased assets will be equal to the purchase price including assumed liabilities.[71] This is generally the fair market value of the assets. Assuming the purchase price is greater than Target's tax basis in the assets, the tax basis of the assets is "stepped up" to the purchase price. This step-up in tax basis is particularly important to Acquiring if it intends to sell

---

[68] [n.33] *See* Rev. Proc. 77-37, 1977-2 C.B. 568; Rev. Proc. 86-42, 1986-2 C.B. 722, which are outdated but are the most recent published list of representations required by the IRS for a ruling on a reorganization.

[69] [n.34] I.R.C. § 1222(3)-(4).

[70] [n.35] *Id.* § 1012(a).

[71] [n.36] *Id.*

a portion of the acquired assets in the near future, because absent the step-up there could be significant tax on the sale even if the value of the assets is unchanged from the time of the acquisition by Acquiring.

If Acquiring retains the Target assets, the step-up allows Acquiring to obtain greater depreciation and amortization deductions over a period of years in the future. The amortization period for any asset is based on the assumed life of the particular asset.[72] In practice, much of the step up is usually allocable to intangible assets of Target that have a very low tax basis to Target and for which Acquiring is permitted to amortize the new basis over 15 years.[73] If the step-up is amortized over 15 years and Acquiring has a combined 40% federal and state marginal tax rate, then $100 of step-up will result in $40 of tax savings spread over 15 years. At a 10% discount rate, the present value of the tax saving from the step-up is about $20, or 20% of the amount of the step-up.

The relative benefit to Acquiring of an asset purchase as compared to a stock purchase may be offset in part by a different factor. A stock purchase would result in Target continuing to amortize its existing tax basis over the remainder of the statutory lives of its assets. However, an asset purchase would result in all of Acquiring's tax basis being amortized over a new statutory life beginning on the acquisition date. Therefore, even though an asset purchase gives Acquiring "new" asset basis to amortize, the result of the asset purchase may be to slow down the amortization of the "existing" asset basis. Normally, this factor is much less significant to Acquiring than the benefit of the step-up.

As to Target, unless it is an S corporation, it recognizes gain or loss on the sale of its assets.[74] Because corporations do not receive a reduced tax rate on capital gains, all the gain to Target is taxable at the 35% corporate tax rate.[75] This could be a very significant amount of tax unless Target has little or no gain on its assets, or net operating losses to shelter that gain. Assuming the Target liquidates after the asset sale and distributes the after-tax sale proceeds, the Shareholders (except for an 80% corporate Shareholder) recognize gain on the liquidation measured by the excess of the cash and property received over their tax basis in the Target stock.[76] The result is a double tax on a corporate sale of assets and liquidation. This result has existed since the repeal in 1986 of the so-called *General Utilities* doctrine,[77] which had exempted a C corporation from most corporate-level taxation on the sale of its assets followed by a complete liquidation.

---

[72] [n.37] *Id.* §§ 167–68, 197.

[73] [n.38] *Id.* § 197. *See infra* Part III.F.

[74] [n.39] *Id.* § 1001.

[75] [n.40] *Id.* § 11.

[76] [n.41] *Id.* §§ 331 (general rule), 332 (exception for 80% shareholder).

[77] [n.42] *See* Gen. Utils. & Operating Co. v. Helvering, 296 U.S. 200 (1935).

C. Comparison of Taxable Stock and Asset Acquisition

1. Target a Stand-Alone C Corporation

If the Target is a C corporation that is not an 80% subsidiary of another corporation, the double tax on an asset sale makes a stock sale significantly more advantageous to the Shareholders than an asset sale. On the other hand, Acquiring is generally better off from a tax point of view from an asset sale as opposed to a stock sale because of the step-up in tax basis of the assets that only arises on an asset sale.

Because of the tax benefits of an asset purchase, Acquiring will be willing to pay more for an asset purchase than a stock purchase. (Or, as Acquiring would say, its bid price was already based on an asset purchase and will be reduced if a stock purchase is required by Target.) By contrast, the Shareholders will usually retain a significantly smaller amount of cash on an after-tax basis for any given sale price where the transaction is treated as an asset purchase rather than a stock purchase.

The question, then, is which transaction results in less aggregate tax to all parties on a present value basis. Once the aggregate tax liability is minimized, the parties can then negotiate how to divide up the resulting tax benefits and detriments.

In practice, the total tax will almost always be minimized by a transaction treated as a stock sale rather than an asset sale. The reason is that the tax detriment to Target and the Shareholders from an asset sale as compared to a stock sale will usually be significantly more than the tax advantage to Acquiring from an asset purchase as compared to a stock purchase. This is because on an asset sale, Target pays immediate tax on its gain on the assets. The amount of gain is the same as the amount of Acquiring's step-up in tax basis and the increased dollar amount of tax deductions in the future. However, the additional tax deductions are generally spread over a period of up to 15 years.[78] As a result, assuming Target and Acquiring are subject to the same tax rates, the present value of the upfront tax to Target is much greater than the present value of the future tax savings to Acquiring.

Looking at the same point in a different way, assume Acquiring was willing to pay Target, for the opportunity to buy assets rather than stock, an extra amount equal to the full present value of the tax benefit of the step-up in asset basis. Even then, if Target is in the same tax bracket as Acquiring, the extra amount would be less than the cost to the Target and Shareholders of an asset sale as compared to a stock sale. As a result, almost all transactions involving a Target that is a "C" corporation without an 80% shareholder are done in a manner that is treated as a stock sale rather than an asset sale for tax purposes, unless Target has net operating losses to shelter the corporate level gain.

---

[78] [n.43] *See supra* Part III.B.

2. Target an S Corporation

The considerations are different if Target is an "S" corporation. An S corporation is generally not itself taxable,[79] so there is no "double tax" from an asset sale. Rather, the issue is whether the Shareholders will be subject to more tax if Target is treated as selling assets and liquidating than if the Shareholders are treated as selling their stock. Generally, the amount and character of the gain or loss at the Target level will pass through to the Shareholders,[80] will be taken into account on their individual tax returns,[81] and will increase or decrease their tax basis in the stock.[82] In principle, therefore, the Shareholders will have the same total net gain or loss if the Target sells its assets and liquidates, or if the Shareholders sell their Target stock for the same amount. As a result, because there is no harm to the Shareholders and there is a benefit to Acquiring from an asset sale, most sales of S corporations are structured as asset sales for tax purposes.

However, this is not always true. The Shareholders will generally have long term capital gain on a stock sale. On an asset sale, the character of the gain that is passed through to the Shareholders from the Target is determined by the nature of the Target's assets.[83] It is possible that some of the Target-level gain would be ordinary income[84] or short term capital gain, which when passed through to the Shareholders would put them in a worse position than if they had sold their stock. In an extreme case, the Shareholders might have ordinary income passed through from the Target in excess of their total economic gain on the stock, in which case such excess would be offset by a capital loss on the stock when Target liquidates.[85]

As a result, there could still be disadvantages to the Shareholders from an asset sale as compared to a stock sale. In that case, negotiations between the parties are necessary to determine if Acquiring is willing to pay a higher price for an asset purchase to offset the tax disadvantages to the Shareholders from an asset sale.

Finally, Target may owe additional tax if it was formerly a C corporation and if it sells assets within 10 years (or certain shorter statutory periods) after the effective date of the conversion to S status. If Target held any assets on the conversion date with "built-in gain," then Target must pay tax on that gain to the extent the gain is realized upon the asset sale.[86] This rule could also make an asset sale more expensive for the selling Shareholders than a stock sale.

---

[79] [n.44] I.R.C. § 1363(a).

[80] [n.45] *Id.* § 1366.

[81] [n.46] *Id.*

[82] [n.47] *Id.* § 1368.

[83] [n.48] *Id.* § 1366(a), (b).

[84] [n.49] *See, e.g.,* id. §§ 1245 (depreciation recapture is ordinary income), 1221(a)(1) (inventory is not a capital asset, resulting in gain being ordinary income).

[85] [n.50] *Id.* § 331(a).

[86] [n.51] *Id.* § 1374.

3. Target an 80% Subsidiary

If Target is a C corporation and 80% or more of the Target stock is owned by another corporation, no double tax arises from an asset sale. Target recognizes gain on the sale of its assets, but the liquidation of Target is tax free to the 80% Shareholder (although not to a minority shareholder).[87] In this situation, the issue from the Target point of view is the amount of the single tax that arises on either a stock or asset sale. If the Target is considered to sell assets, the taxable gain is based on the Target's tax basis for its assets. If the Shareholder is considered to sell the stock of the Target, the taxable gain is based on the tax basis in that stock. From Acquiring's point of view, an asset purchase is again more favorable because of the stepped-up tax basis it will receive in the assets.

If the Shareholder has the same tax basis in the stock of the Target as the Target has in its assets, the total tax to the selling group should be the same for a stock sale or asset sale. This will usually be the case if Target is a member of a consolidated federal income tax group and was originally formed within the group.[88] In that case, Acquiring will generally insist on buying assets, and the Target will have no reason to refuse. On the other hand, if the Shareholder has a higher tax basis in the stock of the Target than the Target has in its assets, an asset sale will result in more tax to the Target group than a stock sale. This will usually be the case if Target is in a consolidated group and the group had acquired the stock by purchase from a third party. In this case, depending on the difference in tax basis of stock and assets, the parties may or may not be able to agree on an increased purchase price for an asset purchase that will compensate the Target group for its extra tax cost and give Acquiring the benefit of the step up in asset basis. If Acquiring's potential benefit is less than the extra tax cost to the Shareholder, a stock sale will obviously occur.

D. Forms of Taxable Stock Purchase for Tax Purposes

Once the parties have agreed that the transaction should be treated as a taxable stock or asset purchase for tax purposes, the form of the transaction can be determined. This issue is significant because the legal form of the transaction does not necessarily correspond to its treatment for tax purposes.

A transaction intended to be a stock purchase for tax purposes can be accomplished in the following ways:

1. Straight Purchase of All Stock

Acquiring can individually purchase the Target stock from each Shareholder. This of course requires the agreement of each Shareholder. This may not be practicable if there are a significant number of Shareholders.

---

[87] [n.52] *Id.* § 332.

[88] [n.53] Treas. Reg. § 1.1502-32(b)(2) (tax basis in stock of consolidated subsidiary is increased and decreased by income and losses of subsidiary).

2. Reverse Merger

Acquiring can set up a new wholly owned subsidiary in the form of a corporation or LLC ("Newco"). Newco merges into Target, with Target surviving. The Newco stock held by Acquiring is converted into all the Target stock, and the old Target stock is converted into cash. Acquiring ends up owning 100% of the Target stock.[89] This form of merger in which Target survives is often referred to as a "reverse merger." This merger will generally require a vote of the Shareholders, because Target is a party to the merger. A vote of Acquiring shareholders is probably not necessary under state corporate law, because Acquiring is not a party to the merger.

3. Stock Purchase Followed by Merger

The two techniques described above can be combined. Acquiring first sets up wholly owned Newco. Newco purchases as much of the Target stock as it can, either by individual agreements with the Shareholders or, if Target is a public company, through a tender offer. Then, if Newco has acquired enough stock in Target to satisfy the state law requirements for a "short form merger," Newco can merge downstream into Target without a shareholder vote. In that merger, Target survives the merger, Acquiring's stock in Newco is converted into all the stock in Target, and the remaining Shareholders receive cash. Because Target stays alive at all times, this is treated as a taxable stock purchase by Acquiring for tax purposes.[90] If Newco does not acquire enough Target stock in the first step to be eligible for the short form merger statute, it may be possible for Newco to then buy additional Target stock directly from Target in order to meet the threshold ownership requirement, and then do the downstream merger. This would not change the tax result.

Alternatively, if Newco acquires at least 80% of the Target stock in the first step, Target can then merge upstream into Newco, with the minority Shareholders receiving cash from Acquiring. For tax purposes, this is a taxable purchase of some of the Target shares, followed by a liquidation of Target that is tax-free to Target[91] and Newco.[92]

As yet another alternative, Newco can set up a new wholly owned subsidiary, Newco2, after Newco acquires as much Target stock as it can,. Newco2 then merges into Target, with Target surviving and the remaining Shareholders receiving cash. This step would be viewed as an additional purchase of Target stock by Newco.[93] Target could then be merged upstream into its sole shareholder Newco on a tax-free basis.

---

[89] [n.54] *See* Rev. Rul. 79-273, 1979-2 C.B. 125 (treating this structure as a taxable stock purchase by Acquiring).

[90] [n.55] *See* Rev. Rul. 90-95, 1990-2 C.B. 67 (step transaction principles); IRS Field Service Advice 117 (June 25, 1992) (involving facts similar to the facts in the text).

[91] [n.56] I.R.C. § 337.

[92] [n.57] *Id.* § 332.

[93] [n.58] Rev. Rul. 79-273, 1979-2 C.B. 125.

E. Forms of Taxable Asset Purchase for Tax Purposes

A transaction intended to be an asset purchase for tax purposes can likewise be accomplished in a number of different ways.

1. Straight Purchase of All Assets

Acquiring can directly purchase all the assets of Target. Target will have taxable gain on the sale, and can choose to liquidate (with tax to the nonexempt Shareholders except 80% corporate Shareholders) or to keep its cash and stay alive. However, this transaction could result in significant state transfer taxes on the physical transfer of assets. In addition, it may not be easy to physically transfer title to a large number of assets on a single date. As a result, alternative methods of reaching the same result are often utilized.

2. Forward Merger

Target can merge into Acquiring or into Newco (a newly formed subsidiary of Acquiring), with the Shareholders receiving cash in the merger in exchange for their Target stock. This form of merger in which Target goes out of existence is known as a "forward merger." For tax purposes, this is treated as if Target sold its assets to Acquiring or Newco for cash, and then liquidated and distributed the cash to the Shareholders.[94] As a result, the double tax automatically arises unless Target has an 80% corporate Shareholder or is an S corporation. Note that the merger would require the approval of the Shareholders. The Acquiring shareholders would also have to approve a merger of Target into Acquiring, but might not have to approve a merger into Newco. If, as a business matter, Acquiring desires to hold the assets directly, a merger into Newco could be followed by the liquidation of Newco into Acquiring with no tax consequences.[95]

3. Dropdown of Assets to LLC and Sale of LLC Interests

Target can drop down all its assets into a newly formed, wholly owned, LLC. The LLC could also assume any liabilities intended to be transferred to Acquiring. On the closing date, Target would sell 100% of the LLC interests to Acquiring. This procedure gives Target time to transfer title to the assets before the closing. In fact, the transfer will often be done before the purchase agreement with Acquiring is signed, so it is clear to both parties exactly which assets are being sold. From a tax point of view, the LLC is treated as a "disregarded entity," and all its assets are treated as if they were directly owned by Target.[96] As a result, Target is treated as selling the underlying assets, and Acquiring is treated as purchasing the underlying assets. Target can then either liquidate or stay alive with its cash.

---

[94] [n.59] Rev. Rul. 69-6, 1969-1 C.B. 104.

[95] [n.60] I.R.C. § 332.

[96] [n.61] *See* Treas. Reg. § 301.7701-2(c)(2)(i) (entity "is disregarded as an entity separate from its owner" for federal tax purposes).

4. Conversion of Target Into LLC, Then Sale of LLC Interests

The tax consequences of a sale of assets by Target can even be achieved without any physical transfer of the assets. Target would first convert into an LLC under state law. For tax purposes, this is treated as a taxable liquidation of Target. Assuming Target does not have an 80% corporate shareholder and is not an S corporation, Target has taxable gain on its assets[97] and the Shareholders have taxable gain on their stock.[98] Target at that point is treated as a partnership for tax purposes.[99] Immediately thereafter, the Shareholders would sell all the equity of the LLC to Acquiring, using one of the methods for a stock acquisition in Part III.D. The Shareholders, who had recognized taxable gain on the liquidation of Target, would have no additional gain on this sale, and Acquiring would become the sole owner of the LLC. Acquiring would be treated as if it had bought the assets of Target.[100]

5. New Holding Company Followed by Sale of LLC Interests

Under this structure, the Shareholders first transfer all their Target stock to a newly formed corporation, Newco. This step could be accomplished either by a direct transfer of Target stock to Newco in exchange for Newco stock, or by Newco setting up a new subsidiary that merges into Target, with Target shareholders receiving Newco stock in the merger. Next, Target converts into an LLC wholly owned by Newco. Finally, Newco sells all the LLC interests to Acquiring.

For tax purposes, after the first two steps, Newco is considered to be a continuation of the same corporation as Target, and the assets owned by the LLC are treated as being owned by Newco.[101] Then, Newco's sale of the LLC interests to Acquiring is treated as a sale of the assets of the LLC to Acquiring.

This structure has a number of advantages over the other techniques. First, there is no physical transfer of assets to Acquiring. Second, unlike the other cases that avoid a physical transfer of assets, there is no deemed liquidation of Target. Newco could stay alive with the cash proceeds of the sale of LLC interests, and there would be no current tax to the Shareholders. Third, this structure allows Newco to retain assets that will not be sold to Acquiring without any tax on those assets. The reason is that during the period that Target is an LLC wholly owned by Newco, the LLC is treated as part of Newco[102] and therefore can distribute assets to Newco without tax consequences. Newco can then sell the LLC, and is treated as selling the assets held by the LLC.

---

[97] [n.62] I.R.C. § 311(b).

[98] [n.63] *Id.* § 331.

[99] [n.64] Treas. Reg. § 301.7701-3(b)(1).

[100] [n.65] Rev. Rul. 99-6, 1999-1 C.B. 432. This transaction would not work if the stock of Target was publicly traded, because a publicly traded partnership is taxable as a corporation. I.R.C. § 7704.

[101] [n.66] In technical terms, these two steps constitute an "F" reorganization. Rev. Rul. 87-27, 1987-1 C.B. 134.

[102] [n.67] Treas. Reg. § 301.7701-2(c)(2)(i).

6. Section 338(h)(10) Election

If Target is either an S corporation or has an 80% U.S. corporate Shareholder, the parties can agree that Acquiring will buy the stock of Target, but that the parties will jointly elect to have the transaction treated as an asset sale for tax purposes. This election is universally referred to as an "(h)(10) election."[103] If both parties make the election, the transaction is treated as if Target sold its assets to a new corporation ("New Target") for cash, and then liquidated, distributing the cash to the Shareholders.[104] New Target, of course, is the same legal entity as Target, but the corporation at that point is treated for tax purposes as a newly formed corporation. As noted above, if Target is an S corporation, the result will be a single tax at the Shareholder level, while if Target has an 80% U.S. corporate Shareholder, the result will be a single level of tax at the corporate level.

When Target has an 80% U.S. corporate shareholder, it will generally be a member of a selling consolidated group. In that case, Target's gain on the deemed asset sale will be reported on that group's tax return, not in Acquiring's return.[105] However, in the unusual case where Target is not a member of a consolidated group, Target itself will report the gain on its own tax return and will owe the tax on the gain.[106] Thus Acquiring (as the new shareholder of Target) in effect will owe the tax. An (h)(10) election would probably not be made in this situation.

As a practical matter, therefore, any time Acquiring is purchasing a consolidated subsidiary or S corporation, the form of the transaction is almost always a stock sale. The only tax negotiation is over whether or not the seller will agree to an (h)(10) election that is desired by Acquiring. In addition, if Acquiring is only buying some of the assets of Target, and Target is a consolidated subsidiary, the election allows Target to distribute the "unwanted" assets to its parent corporation on a tax-free basis.[107] As a result, if the parties agree to the tax results of a sale of assets of a consolidated subsidiary, a stock sale and (h)(10) election is feasible even when some of the Target assets will be left behind in the selling group.

F. Allocation of Purchase Price

In a transaction intended to be a sale of assets for tax purposes, the purchase price (including assumed liabilities) must be allocated among the purchased assets.[108] This allocation determines the amount of gain or loss that Target has on each asset, and the tax basis that Acquiring receives in each asset. The allocation must be made by placing each asset into one of seven categories (starting with cash equivalents and ending with goodwill and going concern value). The purchase price is allocated to the assets in each category in sequence, up to the value of the assets

---

[103] [n.68] The reason is that it is made pursuant to I.R.C. § 338(h)(10).

[104] [n.69] *Id.*; Treas. Reg. § 1.338(h)(10)-1.

[105] [n.70] Treas. Reg. § 1.338(h)(10)-1(d)(3)(i) (5th sentence).

[106] [n.71] *Id.* (6th sentence); Treas. Reg. § 1.338-2(c)(10).

[107] [n.72] Treas. Reg. § 1.338(h)(10)-1(e) ex. 2.

[108] [n.73] I.R.C. § 1060(a); Treas. Reg. §§ 1.338(h)(10)-1(d)(2), (3).

in each category, until the purchase price runs out.[109] The effect is that to the extent the purchase price exceeds the value of all assets other than goodwill and going concern value, the remaining price is allocated to goodwill and going concern value (the so-called "residual category") and is eligible for 15-year amortization.[110] This method of allocation is referred to as the "residual method." In a typical asset purchase, a significant portion of the purchase price is allocated to the residual category.

The principal factual uncertainty as to the allocation of price among the assets is the value of the assets in each of the categories other than the residual category. There is no legal requirement that Target and Acquiring take consistent positions on their respective tax returns, and therefore each could in principle take a different position favorable to itself. However, if they do so, the IRS is likely to discover this fact[111] and protect itself by challenging the positions taken by both parties. This would be undesirable for both.

To avoid this result, acquisition agreements almost always provide that the parties will attempt to agree on an allocation of price among the assets within a relatively short time after the closing of the transaction. If they cannot agree, the agreement will often require the parties to submit to binding arbitration. The agreement will also generally provide that the allocation that is agreed to by the parties or determined by arbitration will be binding on the parties for purpose of filing their own tax returns.

In reality, the particular allocation often will not matter to Target. Corporations are taxed at the same rate on capital gain and ordinary income, so Target may not care whether a greater amount of purchase price is allocated to an asset giving rise to capital gain or to an asset giving rise to ordinary income. Target may care in some cases, however, such as where it has unrelated capital losses that can only be used to shelter capital gains.[112] In that case, Target will prefer to take the position that the capital assets it is selling have a high value, and the ordinary income assets it is selling have a low value, in order to maximize the resulting capital gain.

The allocation usually matters more to Acquiring, because the allocation determines the speed at which Acquiring can claim depreciation and amortization deductions. Acquiring will prefer to allocate as much purchase price as possible first to inventory where the tax basis can be recovered quickly, next to other assets such as equipment with the shortest depreciable lives, and last to nondepreciable assets such as land. Consequently, Acquiring will try to negotiate for as much flexibility as possible in determining an allocation of purchase price that will be binding on Target.

---

[109] [n.74] Treas. Reg. § 1.338-6 (procedure for § 338(h)(10) election); Treas. Reg. § 1.1060-1(a)(1) (adopting the same procedure by cross-reference for other purchases of the assets of a business).

[110] [n.75] I.R.C. § 197.

[111] [n.76] IRS Form 8594 (Feb. 2006) and IRS Form 8883 (Dec. 2008) must be filled out by both sides to an asset sale and (h)(10) transaction, respectively. Both forms ask for the name and identifying information for the other party, and IRS Form 8594 also asks whether the allocations listed on the form were agreed to by the parties.

[112] [n.77] I.R.C. § 1211(a).

G. Contingent Purchase Price

A stock or asset purchase may involve additional payments to the Shareholders if specified conditions are satisfied, such as the Target business doing well in the hands of Acquiring. For tax purposes, a portion of such a payment will be considered imputed interest, based on the period of time from the closing date to the date of the payment.[113] The remainder of each payment is considered additional purchase price. Acquiring will increase its tax basis in the acquired stock or assets by this amount when each payment is made. In the case of an asset purchase, additional amortization deductions relating to that increase in basis will begin at that time.

The tax treatment of Shareholders in a transaction treated as a stock sale, or of Target in the case of a transaction treated as an asset sale, is more complex. Depending on the circumstances, the Shareholders or Target, as applicable, may be permitted or required to (1) disregard the payments until they are made, and then treat them as additional taxable purchase price,[114] (2) include the expected present value of the payments as additional taxable purchase price at the time the transaction closes,[115] or (3) elect the "installment method" for the sale.[116] Under the first two methods, the seller's tax basis can be used in full to reduce the upfront gain. Under the installment method, each payment is taxable when received, but the seller's tax basis must be allocated to each payment rather than being used in full to offset the initial taxable gain.[117]

H. State and Local Tax Considerations

State and local income and franchise taxes are generally based on federal taxable income. As a result, a transaction will generally be treated in the same manner for state and local purposes as it is for federal purposes. In particular, states will generally respect an (h)(10) election and treat the transaction in accordance with the federal characterization.

However, many state and local jurisdictions impose sales, documentary, or similar transfer taxes on the sale of certain categories of assets. For example, a sales tax might apply to the sale of tangible personal property other than inventory held for resale. In addition, many states impose real property transfer taxes. In general, these state transfer taxes are based entirely on the form of the transaction, and they do not apply to the sale of stock where the legal title to the property does not change. For example, they would not generally apply to an (h)(10) transaction. They might also not apply to a transfer of assets by operation of law pursuant to a merger of Target into Acquiring or a subsidiary of Acquiring.

Nevertheless, some states such as New York now impose a real property transfer

---

[113] [n.78] *Id.* § 1274.

[114] [n.79] Treas. Reg. § 1.1001-3(g)(2)(ii) (allowing this method in the "rare and extraordinary circumstances" where the value of the contingent payment is not readily ascertainable).

[115] [n.80] *Id.*

[116] [n.81] I.R.C. § 453.

[117] [n.82] Treas. Reg. § 15A.453-1(c).

tax, based on the value of real property located in the state, in the event of a transfer of a controlling stock interest in the corporation that owns the property.[118] These taxes would apply to a sale of the Target stock, whether or not an (h)(10) election was made.

IV. Tax-free Reorganizations

This Part discusses the requirements and acquisition structures for tax-free reorganizations. There are several different types of reorganization. Part IV.A describes the requirements that apply to all reorganizations. Parts IV.B and IV.C describe the different types of reorganizations and the additional requirements, if any, that apply to each type. Part IV.D describes a non-reorganization technique that reaches similar results.

It should be emphasized that many of the requirements for a reorganization are quite arbitrary and form-driven. It is impossible to rationalize the different requirements for different types of reorganizations. Nevertheless, the rules are quite specific, and a minor breach of any of the requirements will disqualify a transaction as a reorganization.

A. General Requirements for Reorganizations

1. Continuity of Interest

As noted above,[119] at least 40% of the value of the total consideration issued in a reorganization must consist of stock of Acquiring. If the acquisition agreement provides for fixed consideration for the Target stock, the Acquiring stock must be valued on the day before the acquisition agreement is signed.[120] Consequently, if the 40% test is satisfied on that day, a decline in value of the Acquiring stock thereafter and before the closing will not cause the 40% test to be violated. However, if the acquisition agreement provides for a contingent adjustment to the consideration based on a change in value of Acquiring stock occurring between the signing and closing, in some situations the 40% test will be based on the value of the Acquiring stock at the time of closing.[121]

For stock to count favorably towards the 40% test, Acquiring (or its affiliates) cannot have a plan to buy back that stock after the transaction.[122] If Acquiring is publicly traded, it is allowed to buy back its stock on the open market pursuant to a general stock repurchase program, as long as the program was not negotiated in advance with Target, and as long as Acquiring cannot tell whether it is buying back

---

[118] [n.83] *See, e.g.*, New York Tax Law § 1401(b), (e) (McKinney 2012).

[119] [n.84] *See supra* Part II.A.

[120] [n.85] Treas. Reg. § 1.368-1(e)(2)(i).

[121] [n.86] Treas. Reg. §§ 1.368-1(e)(2)(iii), (v) ex. 10. An adjustment based on changes in value of the Target stock does not generally change the valuation date for the Acquiring stock. *Id.* ex. 11-12.

[122] [n.87] *See* Treas. Reg. §§ 1.368-1(e)(1), (3).

stock from a former Shareholder of Target.[123] There is no restriction on the ability of a Shareholder to have a plan, or even a binding contract, before the acquisition to sell the stock of Acquiring after the acquisition, as long as the sale will not be to Acquiring or an affiliate of Acquiring.[124]

Preferred stock of Acquiring counts towards the 40% continuity test, just like any other stock. However, if the preferred stock is nonparticipating and has either a maturity of 20 years or less, certain put/call features within 20 years, or a floating dividend rate, it will be treated as boot to the Shareholders and taxable to them just like cash.[125] As a result, such preferred stock is rarely used.

2. Continuity of Business Enterprise

Acquiring must intend to continue a significant historic business of Target, or to use a significant amount (e.g., one-third) of Target assets in the same or a different business.[126]

3. Business Purpose

A reorganization requires a corporate level business purpose, as opposed to a purpose primarily to benefit the shareholders of Target or Acquiring.[127] As a practical matter, this test is easily satisfied except in very extreme cases where, for example, the only reason for the transaction is estate planning for a major shareholder of Target.

4. Subsequent Transfers of Assets

In general, Acquiring is permitted to move the Target stock or assets around within its corporate group. These rules have been liberalized in recent years, although it is still generally impermissible to move assets to a less-than-80% owned corporate subsidiary or, in some cases, to a partnership.[128]

Specific kinds of reorganizations have additional requirements. Reorganizations can be divided into two categories, those where Target stays alive and those where Target is merged or liquidated out of existence. These categories are discussed separately below.

---

[123] [n.88] *See* Rev. Rul. 99-58, 1999-2 C.B. 701.

[124] [n.89] Treas. Reg. § 1.368-1(e)(8) ex. 1(i).

[125] [n.90] I.R.C. §§ 351(g), 354(a)(2)(C)(i).

[126] [n.91] Treas. Reg. § 1.368-1(d).

[127] [n.92] Treas. Reg. § 1.368-1(b) (transaction must be "required by business exigencies").

[128] [n.93] Although Treas. Reg. § 1.368-2(k) allows a dropdown of assets to a less-than-80% owned corporate subsidiary, such assets would no longer count towards satisfaction of the continuity of business enterprise requirement in Treas. Reg. § 1.368-1(d). Therefore, the dropdown would not be permissible unless that requirement could be satisfied without taking those assets into account.

B. *Reorganizations Where Target Stays Alive*

1. "(a)(2)(E)" Reorganization

An "(a)(2)(E)" reorganization[129] requires that a first tier corporate subsidiary of Acquiring, usually a newly formed subsidiary, merge into Target, with Target surviving. The Shareholders receive the merger consideration, and Acquiring ends up owning all the stock of Target. At least 80% of the consideration must consist of voting stock of Acquiring.[130] There is no requirement that each new share have the same voting power as other outstanding stock of Acquiring, so "high vote/low vote" structures are permissible.

In addition, Target must retain "substantially all" its assets as part of the transaction.[131] This means in effect that it cannot pay substantial dividends or make substantial stock redemptions before the reorganization that are part of the same plan. IRS ruling guidelines define "substantially all" to mean 90% of the net assets and 70% of the gross assets of Target.[132] If Target sells assets before the transaction, this will not count against the "substantially all" requirement as long as the proceeds of the sale are retained by Target.[133] Likewise, a sale of assets after the transaction does not violate the test as long as Target retains the cash proceeds.[134] Subject to the "substantially all" limit, Target may redeem stock with its own funds prior to the merger, and that stock will be disregarded in determining whether the foregoing 80% test for an "(a)(2)(E)" is satisfied.[135]

2. "B" Reorganization

A "B" reorganization[136] requires that Acquiring acquire the Target stock "solely" for voting stock of Acquiring. It can be accomplished by a direct acquisition of the Target stock by Acquiring, or by a first tier corporate or LLC subsidiary of Acquiring, in exchange for Acquiring stock. Alternatively, Acquiring (or a first tier subsidiary) can set up a new subsidiary that merges into Target, with the Shareholders receiving stock of Acquiring.[137]

A "B" reorganization is stricter than an "(a)(2)(E)" reorganization in that even $1 of boot will disqualify the "B" reorganization. On the other hand, the requirements for a "B" reorganization are more liberal than for an "(a)(2)(E)" reorganization because the stock can be acquired without a merger. In addition, there is no "substantially all" requirement for a "B" reorganization. This allows Target to

---

[129] [n.94] I.R.C. §§ 368(a)(1)(A), (2)(E).

[130] [n.95] *Id.* §§ 368(a)(2)(E)(ii), (c).

[131] [n.96] *Id.* § 368(a)(2)(E)(i).

[132] [n.97] Rev. Proc. 77-37, 1977-2 C.B. 568, § 3.01.

[133] [n.98] Rev. Rul. 88-48, 1988-1 C.B. 117.

[134] [n.99] *See* Rev. Rul. 2001-25, 2001-1 C.B. 1291.

[135] [n.100] Treas. Reg. § 1.368-2(j)(6) ex. 3.

[136] [n.101] I.R.C. § 368(a)(1)(B).

[137] [n.102] *See* Rev. Rul. 67-448, 1967-2 C.B. 144.

redeem stock for cash as part of the reorganization without being limited by the "substantially all" test. As long as the cash does not come directly or indirectly from Acquiring, the "solely for voting stock" requirement for a "B" is not violated.[138] As in an "(a)(2)(E)" reorganization, high vote/low vote structures are allowed.

3. Structuring Issues

These rules demonstrate that, in order for Target to stay alive in a tax-free reorganization, at least 80% of the consideration must be in the form of voting stock of Acquiring. If this condition is not met, the only possibilities for a tax-free reorganization are those discussed below where Target liquidates or is merged out of existence.

If all the consideration paid to Shareholders will be voting stock of Acquiring, the transaction can be done as either a "B" or an "(a)(2)(E)" reorganization. The Shareholders are indifferent between a "B" and an "(a)(2)(E)." However, Acquiring would often prefer that the transaction be a "B" reorganization. This is because in a "B", its tax basis in Target stock will be the same as the tax basis of the former Shareholders in Target stock,[139] but in an "(a)(2)(E)," its basis in Target stock will be Target's net basis in its assets.[140] At least in the public company context, the former is usually higher than the latter.

In this situation, the form of the transaction will almost always be the merger of a subsidiary of Acquiring into Target. That merger might qualify as both a "B" and an "(a)(2)(E)" reorganization.[141] However, if for some reason a small amount of boot is deemed to exist, and so the transaction will not qualify as a "B" reorganization, it can still qualify as an "(a)(2)(E)," because there will likely not be more boot than is permitted in an "(a)(2)(E)" reorganization. This provides a fallback position to protect the Shareholders from taxability even if the transaction fails as a "B" reorganization. This fallback protection would not exist in an attempted "B" reorganization that did not involve a merger, because an "(a)(2)(E)" reorganization requires a merger.

Another important feature of both a "B" and "(a)(2)(E)" reorganization is that if for any reason the transaction fails to qualify as a reorganization, the Shareholders are taxable but there is no corporate level tax. Target stays alive with its own assets, and so there is no transfer of assets that would be taxable in a failed reorganization.

---

[138] [n.103] *See* Treas. Reg. § 1.368-2(j)(6) ex. 5.

[139] [n.104] I.R.C. §§ 362(b), 358(e).

[140] [n.105] Treas. Reg. § 1.358-6(c)(2)(i)(A).

[141] [n.106] In that case, P can choose whichever tax basis it wishes to have in the Target stock. Treas. Reg. § 1.358-6(c)(2)(ii).

C. Reorganizations Where Target Goes out of Existence

1. "A" Reorganizations

An "A" reorganization[142] is a direct statutory merger of Target into Acquiring, or a consolidation of Acquiring and Target into a new corporation.[143] Alternatively, Target may merge into an LLC directly and wholly owned by Acquiring, because the LLC is disregarded for tax purposes and is treated as part of Acquiring.[144]

An "A" reorganization has no requirements in addition to the basic requirements for a reorganization. In particular, it is enough for 40% of the consideration to be stock, the stock does not have to be voting stock, and there is no "substantially all" requirement.[145]

2. "(a)(2)(D)" Reorganizations

An "(a)(2)(D)" reorganization[146] is similar to an "A" reorganization, except that Target merges into a wholly owned first tier corporate subsidiary of Acquiring, or into an LLC wholly owned by a first tier corporate subsidiary.[147] In this case, the usual minimum of 40% stock consideration applies. However, the "substantially all" requirement applies in this case.[148]

3. "C" Reorganizations

A "C" reorganization[149] is a transfer by Target of substantially all its assets to Acquiring, or a subsidiary of Acquiring, in exchange for voting stock of Acquiring, followed by the liquidation of Target and distribution of the Acquiring stock to the Shareholders. Boot of up to 20% may be permissible, depending on the amount of Target liabilities assumed by Acquiring in the transaction.[150]

4. Structuring Issues

A "C" reorganization is rarely used today. The requirements are much more restrictive than those for an "A" reorganization, and the end result is the same. In practice, a "C" reorganization is primarily useful when the transaction requires a transfer of assets from Target to Acquiring without the existence of a statutory

---

[142] [n.107] I.R.C. § 368(a)(1)(A).

[143] [n.108] Treas. Reg. § 1.368-2(b)(1)(ii).

[144] [n.109] *See* Treas. Reg. § 1.368-2(b)(1)(iii) ex. 2.

[145] [n.110] I.R.C. § 368(a)(1)(A).

[146] [n.111] *Id.* §§ 368(a)(1)(A), (2)(D).

[147] [n.112] *See* Treas. Reg. § 1.368-2(b)(1)(iii) ex. 4.

[148] [n.113] I.R.C. § 368(a)(2)(D).

[149] [n.114] *Id.* § 368(a)(1)(C).

[150] [n.115] If the liabilities of Target assumed by Acquiring equal or exceed 20% of the value of the Target assets, no boot is allowed. If such liabilities are less than 20% of the value of the Target assets, boot equal to the difference is allowed. *Id.* § 368(a)(2)(B).

merger or consolidation. In that situation, the only kind of reorganization that is available is a "C" reorganization.

Putting aside "C" reorganizations, an "A" or an "(a)(2)(D)" reorganization, as opposed to a "B" or "(a)(2)(E)" reorganization, is necessary when less than 80% of the consideration will be in the form of voting stock of Acquiring. However, they can be used even if 80% or more of the consideration is in this form.

As to the form of an "A" or "(a)(2)(D)" reorganization, an "A" merger into an LLC owned by Acquiring, or an "(a)(2)(D)" merger into a corporate subsidiary of Acquiring, will often be preferable to an "A" merger directly into Acquiring. Either of the first two alternatives might avoid the need for a vote of the Acquiring shareholders under state corporate law, although a vote might be required anyway under federal securities laws or stock exchange rules on account of the issuance of Acquiring stock in the merger. A merger into a subsidiary of Acquiring also means that Acquiring does not become liable for any liabilities of Target.

As to the choice between merging into an LLC subsidiary of Acquiring or into a corporate subsidiary of Acquiring, the "A" merger into the LLC avoids the need to satisfy the "substantially all" test that is required for an "(a)(2)(D)" merger into a corporate subsidiary. If it is desired that the Target business be conducted through a corporate subsidiary, an "A" merger into an LLC is still practical, because it can be followed by the immediate conversion of the LLC into a corporation, or by the immediate transfer by Acquiring of the LLC to a corporate subsidiary of Acquiring.

It is particularly important to be sure that the reorganization rules are satisfied in an "A" or "(a)(2)(D)" (or "C") reorganization. Such a reorganization is treated for tax purposes as the transfer by Target of its assets to Acquiring, or to an Acquiring subsidiary, in exchange for stock of Acquiring and possibly cash, followed by the liquidation of Target. If the reorganization rules are satisfied, Target is not subject to tax on account of any of these transactions.[151]

However, if one of these transactions fails for any reason to qualify as a reorganization, the potential tax liability is much greater than in a failed "B" or "(a)(2)(E)" reorganization. Absent the protection of the reorganization rules, Target is deemed to sell all of its assets to Acquiring or an Acquiring subsidiary in a fully taxable transaction, and then to liquidate in a taxable liquidation.[152] Thus, not only would the Shareholders be taxable on the deemed taxable liquidation of Target, as in a failed "B" or "(a)(2)(E)," but Target itself could be subject to substantial corporate level tax.

This risk of corporate level tax in a failed "A" or "(a)(2)(D)" reorganization can be avoided by a small change in the structure. First, Acquiring sets up a new corporate or LLC subsidiary that merges into Target, with Target surviving. The Shareholders receive the same consideration in this merger that they would have received in the more typical structure. Second, and immediately afterwards, Target merges into Acquiring (its new parent) or an LLC or corporate subsidiary of Acquiring. The end result is exactly the same as in the "one-step" "A" or "(a)(2)(D)" reorganization.

---

[151] [n.116] *See supra* Part II.B.

[152] [n.117] *See* Rev. Rul. 69-6, 1969-1 C.B. 104.

If the usual conditions for those reorganizations are satisfied, the transaction qualifies as such under step-transaction principles.[153]

However, if for any reason the conditions for an "A" or "(a)(2)(D)" reorganization are not satisfied, the initial merger of the Acquiring subsidiary into Target is treated separately as a taxable purchase by Acquiring of the Target stock, and the second step is treated as a tax-free liquidation or merger of Target within the Acquiring group.[154] As a result, the Shareholders are still taxable if the transaction does not qualify as a reorganization, but Target is not taxable. Thus, there is no risk of corporate level tax for a failed reorganization, just as there is no risk in a "B" or "(a)(2)(E)" reorganization.

This structure is slightly more complicated to accomplish and much more complicated to explain. Some tax counsel believe this structure is a cheap insurance policy against corporate level tax and use it routinely for "A" or "(a)(2)(D)" reorganizations. Others use it only when there is an identified risk, however small, about the qualification of the transaction as a reorganization.

D. Tender Offer Followed By Merger

A tax-free reorganization may be accomplished in the form of a tender offer followed by a merger. Under this approach, Acquiring first tenders for all or part of the Target stock, with the consideration being Acquiring stock and/or cash. Then, assuming the tender offer is successful, Target merges into Acquiring or with an Acquiring subsidiary. In the merger, the Target stock held by the remaining Shareholders is canceled in exchange for specified consideration, often the same consideration that was offered in the tender offer. Normally a condition of Acquiring's obligation to close the tender offer is that enough Target shares are tendered so that Acquiring will be able to accomplish the second-step merger without the risk of a negative shareholder vote on the merger.

For the overall transaction to qualify as a tax-free reorganization, it is necessary that the tender offer and the merger be treated as a single integrated transaction for tax purposes. This condition should be satisfied if Acquiring imposes the foregoing condition on the closing of the tender offer and announces its intent to cause the merger to occur promptly after completion of the tender offer.[155]

Assuming the tender offer and the merger are integrated for tax purposes, the tender offer is in effect disregarded. The qualification or nonqualification of the reorganization is determined on the basis of the form of the merger without regard to the tender offer. Likewise, the consideration received by Shareholders in the tender offer is treated as received by them in the merger, and all the consideration paid in the tender offer and the merger is aggregated in testing whether the

---

[153] [n.118] *See* Rev. Rul. 2001-46, 2001-2 C.B. 321. The ruling involves a second step merger into Acquiring that, combined with the first step, would qualify as an "A" reorganization. The same principles should apply if the second step merger is into an LLC subsidiary of Acquiring (which should likewise be an "A") or into a corporate subsidiary of Acquiring (which should likewise be an "(a)(2)(D)").

[154] [n.119] *Id.*

[155] [n.120] Rev. Rul. 2001-26, 2001-1 C.B. 1297; Rev. Rul. 2001-46, 2001-2 C.B. 321.

consideration meets the requirements for a tax-free reorganization. For example, if the merger consists of a merger of Target into a corporate subsidiary of Acquiring, the aggregate consideration must meet the requirements for an (a)(2)(D) reorganization and all the other requirements for an (a)(2)(D) reorganization must be satisfied.[156]

E. The "Double Dummy" Structure

One additional structure is sometimes used to combine Acquiring with Target. This structure is sometimes used for a "merger of equals," where neither party wants to be viewed as being acquired by the other. Alternatively, because this structure does not require compliance with the rules for tax-free reorganizations, it can be used when a tax-free transaction is desired but the requirements for a tax-free reorganization are not available. For example, it can be used when it is necessary or desirable to keep the Target corporation alive, but less than 80% of the consideration for the Target stock will be voting stock of Acquiring.

While variations on this structure are possible, in the simplest situation, a new parent corporation is created ("New Parent") with a temporary owner. New Parent sets up two new directly and wholly owned corporate or LLC subsidiaries (the "Double Dummies"). One of the Dummies merges into Target, and the other Dummy merges into Acquiring. Target and Acquiring are the surviving corporations, and both are then wholly owned by New Parent. The shareholders of Target and Acquiring receive stock of New Parent and possibly cash in exchange for their stock in Target and Acquiring, respectively.

Often the shareholders of Acquiring will receive solely voting stock of New Parent, and this aspect of the transaction would qualify as a "B" or "(a)(2)(E)" reorganization in which New Parent acquires Acquiring. Depending on the facts, New Parent's acquisition of Target might qualify under the same sections. However, this structure is very flexible in that it works even if the acquisition by New Parent of Target (or even of Acquiring) would not qualify as a reorganization, for example because more than 20% of the consideration payable to the Shareholders is cash.

Under this structure, there is no risk of corporate level tax because Acquiring and Target remain alive. Moreover, even if the acquisition of Acquiring or Target does not qualify as a reorganization, it is nevertheless tax free to the Acquiring shareholders and to the Shareholders on account of § 351.[157] Under that section, transferors who transfer property to a corporation are not taxed on the receipt of stock of the transferee corporation, as long as the transferors own 80% of the transferee corporation after the transfers. Here, the Target and Acquiring shareholders transfer their shares in Target and Acquiring to New Parent, and collectively some or all of those shareholders end up owning 100% of the stock of New Parent, no matter how much cash they also receive. As a result, Section 351 applies, and the transferring shareholders are taxed only on the cash they receive,

---

[156] [n.121] *Id.*

[157] [n.122] *See* Rev. Rul. 84-71, 1984-1 C.B. 106.

up to their gain on the transferred stock.[158]

As noted, this transaction is somewhat complicated, and not every Acquiring will be willing to have a new holding company placed above it, particularly if it is a public corporation. Variations on this structure may also be possible, such as where Acquiring merges into New Parent (or an LLC owned by New Parent) rather than becoming a subsidiary of New Parent.[159] This structure and its variations are useful when the usual rules for a reorganization cannot be satisfied.

F. Foreign Transactions

This article is primarily about a domestic Acquiring corporation acquiring a domestic Target corporation. In general, the same rules apply if both Acquiring and Target are foreign. In that regard, a merger or amalgamation under foreign law is a good merger for purposes of an "A" or "(a)(2)(D)" reorganization.[160] Consequently, a Shareholder that is a U.S. person will not be subject to tax on the receipt of Acquiring stock in a transaction that qualifies under the U.S. reorganization rules.[161] However, a U.S. Shareholder that ends up owning five percent or more of a non-U.S. Acquiring corporation will receive tax-free treatment only if it files a so-called "gain recognition agreement," requiring the Shareholder to pay tax on the initial exchange if Acquiring disposes of the Target business within five years.[162]

Additional rules apply if Acquiring is foreign and Target is domestic. In that case, even if the general requirements for a tax-free reorganization are satisfied, the transaction cannot be a tax-free reorganization unless a number of additional conditions are satisfied.[163] One significant requirement is that Acquiring must have a fair market value at least equal to Target's fair market value on the acquisition date.[164] Market capitalization is usually used in applying this test when Acquiring and Target are public companies. This requirement was designed to prevent tax-free expatriations of U.S. corporations abroad, although it has not always been successful.[165] The rules for gain recognition agreements also apply in this situation.[166]

V. Other Issues Arising in All Transactions

A number of other issues can come up in a taxable or tax-free transaction. Among them are the following.

---

[158] [n.123] I.R.C. § 351(b).

[159] [n.124] *See* Rev. Rul. 76-123, 1976-1 C.B. 94.

[160] [n.125] *See* Treas. Reg. § 1.368-2(b)(1)(iii) ex. 13-14.

[161] [n.126] Treas. Reg. § 1.367(a)-3(b)(1)(i).

[162] [n.127] Treas. Reg. § 1.367(a)-3(b)(1)(ii).

[163] [n.128] Treas. Reg. § 1.367(a)-3(c).

[164] [n.129] Treas. Reg. § 1.367(a)-3(c)(3)(iii).

[165] [n.130] To further prevent expatriation, recent legislation provides that if 80% of the stock of Acquiring is issued to former Shareholders of Target, Acquiring will be treated as a U.S. corporation unless specified conditions are satisfied. *See* I.R.C. § 7874(b).

[166] [n.131] Treas. Reg. § 1.367(a)-3(c)(1)(iii).

A. *Net Operating Losses*

If Target has net operating losses (i.e., losses that cannot be used as current deductions), those losses are subject to a limitation on usage in future tax years if there is a greater-than-50% change in ownership of Target within a three-year period.[167] The annual usage of those losses after such a change in ownership is limited to the value of the Target stock on the change date, multiplied by a tax-exempt, risk-free rate of return, subject to various adjustments.[168] A detailed study is required to determine the annual limit. The annual limit is cumulative, so that if there is not enough income in a future year to allow utilization of losses up to the limit for that year, the unused portion of the limit carries forward to future years.[169]

These rules do not apply if the transaction is treated as an acquisition of Target assets for tax purposes.[170] Then, there is no change of ownership of Target or shifting of losses to Acquiring. Rather, losses of Target can then be used in full to shelter Target's gain on the asset sale. In the case of a transaction treated as a taxable purchase of Target stock for cash, a 50% change in ownership would occur on the purchase date[171] and so the limitations would apply. In the case of a tax-free reorganization, the reorganization would result in a change in ownership of Target to the extent of the reduction in the percentage of direct and indirect ownership held by the Shareholders in Target, taking into account their indirect ownership in Target as a result of their ownership in Acquiring.[172] The reorganization itself would therefore result in a 50% change in ownership of Target if the Shareholders received less than 50% of the total then-outstanding stock of Acquiring.

B. *Prior Spin-offs*

When a parent corporation ("Distributing") distributes the stock of its subsidiary ("Spinco") to the Distributing shareholders, the distribution will be tax-free to both Distributing and Spinco if the requirements of a tax-free spin-off are satisfied.[173] However, (1) the spin-off requirements will likely not be satisfied if, at the time of the spin-off, the Distributing shareholders have a plan to dispose of their Distributing or Spinco stock in a taxable or partially taxable transaction after the spin-off,[174] and (2) even if the spin-off requirements are satisfied, the distribution will be taxable to Distributing, although not the Distributing shareholders, if, as

---

[167] [n.132] I.R.C. §§ 382(a), (g)(1), (i)(1).

[168] [n.133] *Id.* § 382(b)(1); *see also* IRS 2003-2 C.B. 747, Notice 2003-65 (providing rules that usually result in an increase in the limit).

[169] [n.134] I.R.C. § 382(b)(2).

[170] [n.135] *Id.* § 382(g)(1) (defining an ownership change as a change in stock ownership or an equity structure shift).

[171] [n.136] *Id.* § 382(j)(1).

[172] [n.137] Temp. Treas. Reg. § 1.382-2T.

[173] [n.138] I.R.C. § 355(a)(1) (shareholders); *id.* § 355(c) (Distributing).

[174] [n.139] Treas. Reg. § 1.355-2(d)(2)(iii) (subsequent sale a negative factor in applying the "device" test).

part of the same plan as the spin-off, there is a 50% or greater change in ownership of either Distributing or Spinco.[175]

Normally there is a tax sharing agreement between Spinco and Distributing under which Spinco will indemnify Distributing for the Distributing tax liability that would arise under clause (2) if there is a 50% change in ownership of Spinco. Moreover, the agreement may give Distributing unlimited or limited veto rights over corporate transactions of Spinco for a one- or two-year period after the spin-off to avoid any tax risk to Distributing.

It is beyond the scope of this article to discuss the requirements for a tax-free spin-off. However, it is important for Acquiring to know whether Target was either the "Distributing" or the "Spinco" in a spin-off that occurred as part of the same plan as the proposed acquisition. For example, if Spinco had recently been spun off, tax liability would arise on the spin-off if, as part of the same plan, (1) Acquiring paid any material amount of cash for the Distributing or Spinco stock, or (2) Acquiring acquired Distributing or Spinco even solely for Acquiring stock if the Distributing or Spinco shareholders would end up owning 50% or less of Acquiring (and therefore indirectly 50% or less of Distributing or Spinco). Any event in clause (2) would result in a 50% change of ownership of Distributing or Spinco.[176]

This means, in practice, that if Distributing has announced a plan to spin off Spinco, and Acquiring would like to acquire either Distributing or Spinco after the spin-off, then with one exception discussed below, it is critical for Acquiring not to approach Distributing or Spinco before the spin-off, but rather to wait until after the spin-off is completed to begin discussions. This is necessary, and generally sufficient, to assure that Acquiring's acquisition of Distributing or Spinco is not considered part of the same plan as the spin-off, and therefore preserves the tax-free nature of the spin-off.[177] If Acquiring has had discussions with Distributing or Spinco before the spin-off, it is generally necessary for Acquiring to wait six months or one year after the spin-off in order to begin discussions anew without concern that the subsequent transaction might be considered part of the same plan as the spin-off.[178] By contrast, any competing acquiror that did not begin discussions with Distributing or Spinco until the day after the spin-off would not be subject to this limitation.

---

[175] [n.140] I.R.C. § 355(e).

[176] [n.141] Likewise, if Acquiring was the distributing or spun-off corporation in a prior spin-off, and its acquisition of Target was part of the same plan as the spin-off, it is important that the issuance of stock by Acquiring not result in a 50% change of ownership of Acquiring.

[177] [n.142] Treas. Reg. § 1.355-7(b)(2) (no "plan" for subsequent acquisition exists at time of spin-off if no agreement, arrangement or substantial negotiations for a similar acquisition occurred in the two years prior to the spin-off). The "device" test referred to in the third preceding footnote is also generally considered inapplicable if this condition is met.

[178] [n.143] Treas. Reg. § 1.355-7(d)(3) (safe harbor if no understanding at time of spin-off and subsequent negotiations do not begin until a year after the spin-off); id. § 1.355-7(d)(1) (safe harbor if good business purpose for spin-off and no substantial negotiations in period between one year before and six months after the spin-off). If no safe harbor in Treas. Reg. § 1.355-7(d) is available, it is generally advisable to wait for two years after the spin-off to begin discussions in order to avoid the presumption of a plan contained in I.R.C. § 355(e)(2)(B).

On the other hand, the spin-off rules are not violated if Distributing or Spinco is acquired by Acquiring after the spin-off as part of the same plan as the spin-off, where the consideration for the Distributing or Spinco stock is entirely Acquiring stock that represents more than half the then-outstanding stock in Acquiring. In that case, the old Distributing shareholders retain a greater than 50% direct or indirect interest in both Distributing and Spinco, and so there is not a 50% change in ownership of Distributing or Spinco as a result of the acquisition. Therefore, assuming no other "bad" changes in ownership of Distributing or Spinco as part of the same plan as the spin-off, the parties can agree to this transaction before the spin-off is completed.

If Acquiring acquires Distributing in this manner, the transaction is known as a "Morris Trust" transaction (after the name of the case that authorized it).[179] If Acquiring acquires Spinco in this manner, the transaction is known as a "reverse Morris Trust" transaction (for obvious reasons).

VI. Partnership as the Acquiror

The foregoing discussion assumed that Acquiring is taxable as a C corporation. Some of the considerations are different if Acquiring is taxable as a partnership ("Acquiring Partnership"), including an LLC taxable as a partnership. Moreover, the considerations may depend upon whether Acquiring Partnership is an operating partnership that directly engages in business, or a holding partnership that primarily holds stock of corporate subsidiaries.

A. General Structural Considerations

If Acquiring Partnership is a holding partnership, the parties have accepted the double tax on corporate earnings that arises from the structure. In that case, Acquiring Partnership may intentionally avoid engaging directly in business in order to simplify the tax positions of its partners.[180] Acquiring Partnership could maintain its status as a holding partnership by acquiring the stock of Target or by setting up a corporate subsidiary to acquire the assets.

On the other hand, if Acquiring Partnership is an operating partnership, its shareholders have accepted the complexity that arises from being a partner in an operating partnership, and it likely operates as a partnership to avoid the double tax that arises on corporate earnings. Therefore, Acquiring Partnership would normally prefer to acquire the assets rather than the stock of Target. This would result in the tax benefits of the operating partnership being extended to the Target business.

In addition, if Acquiring Partnership intends to integrate the business of Target

---

[179] [n.144] Comm'r v. Morris Trust, 367 F.2d 794 (4th Cir. 1966).

[180] [n.145] A partner in an operating partnership is required to file a federal income tax return that reflects the underlying tax items of the partnership, which can be quite complex, and may be required to file a state tax return in every state in which the partnership does business. In addition, U.S. tax-exempt partners and non-U.S. partners may be subject to tax disadvantages from being partners in an operating partnership.

with its own business, it would want the Target assets to end up in the same tax group as its existing assets. For example, if Acquiring Partnership is an operating partnership, it would normally want to acquire the assets rather than stock of Target. In that way, it will have flexibility in dealing with the assets of Target on an ongoing basis. By contrast, if Acquiring Partnership acquires the stock of Target, then Target remains a separate taxable entity. Acquiring Partnership would then be required to conduct all transactions between Acquiring Partnership and Target on an arm's length basis.

In particular, any purported shifting of value from Target to Acquiring Partnership, either by an underpayment by Acquiring Partnership to Target or an overpayment by Target to Acquiring Partnership, could be viewed for tax purposes as a deemed distribution of assets from Target to Acquiring Partnership. Any deemed distribution of assets by Target would be a taxable sale of the assets by Target, and any deemed distribution to Acquiring Partnership would be a taxable dividend to Acquiring Partnership.

The need to avoid the possibility of such a distribution could considerably restrict the flexibility of Acquiring Partnership in operating the combined business, especially if the goal is to integrate the businesses of Target and Acquiring Partnership. The same issues would arise if Acquiring Partnership is a holding partnership and it directly acquires the stock of Target. Unless it contributes the stock of Target to an existing corporate group, any transactions between Target and either Acquiring Partnership or the existing group would need to be on arm's length terms.

B. Tax-Free Transaction

If a transaction that is tax-free to Target and the Shareholders is desired, Acquiring Partnership could not issue its equity to the Shareholders in reliance on the rules concerning tax-free reorganizations discussed above.[181] Those rules apply only if the acquiring entity is taxable as a corporation. To be sure, Acquiring Partnership could set up a "C" corporation that would issue its stock in exchange for the Target stock or assets in a tax-free reorganization. However, Acquiring Partnership could only obtain its own equity in the corporation by contributing its own cash or assets. This contribution will not be desirable if Acquiring Partnership is an operating partnership, since such a partnership would not want to hold its assets in a "C" corporation.

Alternatively, tax-free treatment to Target and the Shareholders could be obtained on the basis of the rule that contributions of property to a partnership in exchange for partnership interests are generally tax free to both the contributor and to the partnership.[182] As a result, either Target could transfer its assets to Acquiring Partnership in exchange for partnership interests, or the Shareholders could transfer their Target stock to Acquiring Partnership in exchange for partnership interests.

---

[181] [n.146] *See* Part IV.

[182] [n.147] I.R.C. § 721(a).

However, if Target is widely held, it will usually not be possible to have the Shareholders transfer their Target stock to Acquiring Partnership in exchange for partnership interests in Acquiring Partnership. Unless an exception applies, Acquiring Partnership will become a publicly traded partnership taxable as a corporation if its equity is readily tradable on a securities market.[183] This result would be extremely undesirable. Moreover, the definition of trading for this purpose is very broad,[184] and most private partnerships rely on a "safe harbor" against public trading that requires that there be no more than 100 partners.[185]

Finally, even if Acquiring Partnership is eligible for an exception and can remain a partnership even if its equity is publicly traded, Acquiring Partnership is likely not to want to become subject to the very complex rules that apply to publicly traded partnerships. As a result, if Target is widely held, often the only practical method for a tax- free transaction will be for Target to transfer its assets to Acquiring Partnership in exchange for partnership interests, with Target agreeing to restrictions on its transfer of the partnership interests.

C. Taxable Transaction

If a taxable transaction treated as a stock acquisition for tax purposes is desired, Acquiring Partnership could buy the Target stock directly. Alternatively, Acquiring Partnership could set up a wholly owned subsidiary to merge into Target, with Target shareholders receiving cash.[186]

If a taxable transaction treated as an asset acquisition is desired, and if Acquiring Partnership is a holding partnership, Acquiring Partnership would normally desire to hold the Target assets in corporate form.[187] Acquiring Partnership could set up a new corporate subsidiary to acquire the assets in any of the ways discussed above for a corporate purchaser.[188] For example, Target could merge into the corporate subsidiary, or Target could drop its assets into an LLC that would be purchased by the corporate subsidiary.

Finally, a taxable asset acquisition may be desired where Acquiring Partnership is an operating partnership. As noted above,[189] Acquiring Partnership would normally desire to hold the assets in noncorporate form rather than through a corporation after the acquisition. This result could be achieved if either (1) Target converted to an LLC and then Acquiring Partnership acquired the LLC interests,

---

183 [n.148] I.R.C. § 7704(b). The principal exception is for a partnership where 90% of its income is either passive income or income from real estate, minerals, or natural resources. Therefore, the exception might be available if Acquiring Partnership is a holding partnership, since its primary income in that case might be dividends from subsidiaries.

184 [n.149] Treas. Reg. §§ 1.7704-1(c)(1), (2).

185 [n.150] Treas. Reg. § 1.7704-1(h)(1).

186 [n.151] *See* Part III.D.

187 [n.152] *See* Part IV.A.

188 [n.153] *See* Part III.E.

189 [n.154] *See* Part VI.A.

or (2) Acquiring Partnership set up an LLC and then Target merged into the LLC.[190]

Further, if Target is an 80% corporate subsidiary, and an asset acquisition is desired, it would also be possible for Acquiring Partnership to set up a new corporate subsidiary that acquires Target with an (h)(10) election.[191] This might be acceptable if Acquiring Partnership is a holding partnership.

However, if Acquiring Partnership is an operating partnership and the goal is for the assets to be owned by Acquiring Partnership, it would be necessary to liquidate both the new subsidiary and Target, or to convert both of those entities into LLCs. The liquidation or conversion of the new subsidiary would likely invalidate the (h)(10) election, since a corporate purchaser is needed for an (h)(10) election and these steps would likely cause the corporate purchaser to be disregarded as transitory.[192]

This problem can be avoided with a new election (a "§ 336(e) election") that first became available in May 2013. If an acquisition would be eligible for an (h)(10) election except for the fact that there is not a corporate purchaser, the § 336(e) election can be made with substantially the same results.[193] Therefore, if Target is an 80% corporate subsidiary in a consolidated group, Acquiring Partnership could directly acquire the stock of Target, with the selling group agreeing to make the § 336(e) election to treat the transaction as an asset sale for tax purposes. Target would then be treated as a new corporation owned by Acquiring Partnership with a cost basis in its assets.

In this scenario, immediately after Acquiring Partnership purchases the Target stock, Target could liquidate into Acquiring Partnership or be converted into an LLC. In either case, the liquidation would be a taxable transaction to both Target and Acquiring Partnership. However, there should be no taxable gain (1) to Target because it has a stepped up tax basis in its assets, or (2) to Acquiring Partnership because it has a fair market value tax basis in its stock of Target.[194] As a result, the § 336(e) election simplifies the ability of a Acquiring Partnership to obtain direct ownership of the Target assets with a stepped up tax basis.

Note that if Target is a consolidated subsidiary, the § 336(e) election is made unilaterally by the selling consolidated group.[195] Consequently, whether or not an election is desired, if Target is a consolidated subsidiary and Acquiring Partnership buys the Target stock, Acquiring Partnership will need to obtain appropriate

---

[190] [n.155] *See* Part III.E.

[191] [n.156] Part III.E.6.

[192] [n.157] Treas. Reg. § 1.338-3(b)(1).

[193] [n.158] Treas. Reg. §§ 1.336(e)-1, -2.

[194] [n.159] There might be a risk of gain recognition to Acquiring Partnership in this case if it reduced its purchase price for the stock for any contingent liabilities of Target. In that case, the gross value of the Target assets would exceed the tax basis of the stock held by Acquiring Partnership. It might not be possible to reduce the resulting gain to Acquiring Partnership by the amount of contingent liabilities.

[195] [n.160] Treas. Reg. § 1.336(e)-2(h)(1).

representations and covenants from the selling group concerning whether or not group will make the election.[196]

VII. Conclusions

This article only scratches the surface in describing the tax rules applicable to taxable and tax-free acquisitions. These rules are the subject of many lengthy treatises, as well as innumerable articles contained in a large number of daily, weekly, monthly, and quarterly tax publications. In addition, new tax regulations and rulings are issued by the Treasury Department and IRS on an almost daily basis.

A corporate lawyer in most cases would not have the slightest interest in learning all the detailed tax rules and keeping up with the changes in the rules. However, having a general familiarity with the basic underlying tax principles makes it easier to understand the reasons for the structures that the tax lawyer is proposing. It also facilitates discussions with a tax lawyer to develop structures that work from both a corporate and tax point of view. But to close this article where it began, a little knowledge is a dangerous thing, and the corporate lawyer needs to understand most of all the importance of consulting with a tax lawyer at all stages of a transaction.

EXERCISE 4.1

Bidder Inc. has agreed to acquire substantially all of Target Co.'s assets for $45 million in Bidder common stock and $5 million in non-voting Bidder preferred stock. Bidder will also assume $10 million in Target debt in connection with the deal. Does the deal qualify as a tax-free reorganization? If not, what could be changed so it does?

EXERCISE 4.2

1.　Bidder buys Target for $10.00 per share in cash through a forward triangular merger. The deal closed on June 1, 2014. You owned 100 shares of Target stock that you bought in 2011 for $6.00. What are the federal income tax consequences to you of this transaction for tax year 2014?

2.　Bidder buys Target for $10.00 per share in Bidder stock through a forward triangular merger. The deal closed on June 1, 2014. You owned 100 shares of Target stock that you bought in 2011 for $6.00. What are the federal income tax consequences to you of this transaction for tax year 2014?

You sell the Bidder stock you got in the deal in 2016 for $13.00. What are the federal income tax consequences to you of this transaction for tax year 2016?

3.　Bidder buys Target for $10.00 per share comprised of $6.00 of Bidder stock and $4.00 of cash through a forward triangular merger. The deal closed on June 1,

---

[196] [n.161] This concern about a unilateral election by seller does not arise if Acquiring is a corporation, because an election under § 336(e) is not available if an (h)(10) election is available, Treas. Reg. § 1.336(e)-1(b)(6)(ii), and an (h)(10) election must be made by both parties.

2014. You owned 100 shares of Target stock which you bought in 2011 for $6.00. What are the federal income tax consequences to you of this transaction for tax year 2014?

You sell the Bidder stock you got in the deal in 2017 for $13.00. What are the federal income tax consequences to you of this transaction for tax year 2017?

D.   VOTING CONCERNS

As we covered in Chapter 2, with the exception of a stock purchase, target shareholders get to vote on a deal regardless of structure. Even with a stock purchase, each individual shareholder gets to decide whether or not to participate. Thus, there is no structuring around a deal that does not have the support of target shareholders owning a majority of shares.

It is a different story when it comes to the shareholders of bidder, and there is variance between the MBCA and the DGCL. Under the MBCA, whether bidder's shareholders get to vote on the proposed acquisition of target turns on how much stock, if any, bidder will be issuing in the deal. Specifically, MBCA § 6.21(f)(1)(ii) requires a bidder shareholder vote on the deal if bidder will be issuing shares equal to more than 20 percent of its outstanding voting power pre-deal. For example, say bidder has 1,000,000 shares of common stock outstanding and has agreed to acquire target for 250,000 shares of common stock. Bidder's common stock is currently worth $10 per share so 250,000 shares equates to $2,500,000. Bidder shareholders would get to vote on this deal because bidder will be issuing shares equal to more than 20 percent of its pre-deal voting power (250,000/1,000,000=0.25 or 25%). If instead the deal consideration was, for example, 150,000 shares and $1,000,000 in cash, bidder's shareholders would not get to vote on the deal. In other words, under the MBCA, whether bidder shareholder's get to vote depends on the type and amount of deal consideration.

The DGCL has a similar 20 percent rule, but it only applies to a deal structured as a direct merger.[197] It does not apply to a triangular merger because the Delaware merger statute affords a shareholder vote, if at all, only to the shareholders of a corporation party to the merger. With a triangular merger, bidder is not a party to the merger; the parties are target and merger sub. Hence, under Delaware law, there are several ways to structure a deal so that it does not require a bidder vote, including going with an asset purchase, triangular merger, stock purchase, or using cash consideration in a direct merger.

Shareholders, however, may take issue with a deal structure that disenfranchises them and bring suit based on the doctrine of *de facto* merger, as discussed in the next case.

---

[197] *See* DGCL § 251(f).

EQUITY GROUP HOLDINGS v. DMG, INC.

United States District Court, Southern District of Florida
576 F. Supp. 1197 (1983)

ARONOVITZ, DISTRICT JUDGE.

INTRODUCTION

THIS CAUSE was heard by the Court on December 13, 1983, upon Plaintiff's Motion for Preliminary Injunction, in which Plaintiff sought the following relief:

1. A judicial declaration that Section 607.221 of the Florida Corporation Act is applicable to the vote of DMG shareholders with respect to the issuance of approximately 12.5 million (12,500,000) shares of DMG common stock pursuant to the proposed Merger between *DMI and Carlsberg*, and that accordingly a majority of the outstanding shares of DMG must be voted in favor of such transaction if it is to take place at all; and

2. A judicial declaration that the issuance of two million (2,000,000) shares of DMG stock to Carlsberg Resources is an integral part of the aforementioned transaction, thereby rendering the transaction a *de facto* merger between *DMG and Carlsberg*, invoking Florida Corporation Act Section 607.221, which would, if applicable, require the approval of a majority of votes of the outstanding shares of DMG. . . .

The undisputed facts as stipulated by the parties can be summarized as follows: Defendant, DMG, Inc. ("DMG"), a Florida corporation, is a holding company which has no assets or operations. It is the listed (New York Stock Exchange) parent corporation of a wholly-owned subsidiary, Defendant Diversified Mortgage Investors, Inc. ("DMI"), a Florida corporation. DMG was incorporated in 1980 by DMI for the purpose of carrying out a corporate reorganization. At that time, the shareholders of DMI automatically became shareholders of DMG.

DMI is an operating company, in prior years a Real Estate Investment Trust, which is now passively managing a portfolio of real estate holdings. It has an approximate One Hundred Million ($100,000,000) Dollar tax loss carry-forward. It is indebted to its bank in the sum of Twenty-three Million ($23,000,000) Dollars which is due and payable on December 31, 1983 in full.

Defendant Carlsberg Corporation ("Carlsberg"), a Delaware corporation, is the parent corporation of Defendant Carlsberg Resources Corporation ("Carlsberg Resources"), which in turn is wholly owned by Carlsberg. It is a diversified real estate firm, primarily engaged in land development and sale, residential and commercial real estate sites, general contracting, modular housing and real estate management.

Plaintiff Equity Group Holdings is a District of Columbia General Partnership which invests in real estate, real estate companies and manufacturing companies.

DMG had outstanding and issued stock, as of October 27, 1983, in the amount of seven million, four hundred thousand, (7,400,000) shares of common voting stock.

Plaintiff Equity Group Holdings ("Equity" or "Equity Group" and related parties) owned approximately two million (2,000,000) shares of DMG common stock, representing 27.1% of such shares outstanding just prior to October 28, 1983. Equity's shares of DMG were purchased on the open market (the New York Stock Exchange) or in private sales. As of now, Equity may own two million, eight hundred thousand (2,800,000) shares of DMG.

On October 28, 1983, DMG, Carlsberg and Carlsberg Resources Corporation entered into a Stock Purchase Agreement, pursuant to which DMG agreed to issue two million (2,000,000) shares of DMG voting preferred stock, which had been authorized but unissued, in exchange for forty-four thousand, four hundred, forty-four (44,444) of the one hundred twenty-five thousand (125,000) shares of Carlsberg convertible preferred stock then held by Carlsberg Resources.

Also on October 28, 1983, DMG, DMI and Carlsberg entered into an Agreement and Plan of Merger (the "Merger Agreement"). Pursuant to the Merger Agreement, Carlsberg will merge into DMI; outstanding shares of Carlsberg will then be converted into DMG common. To accomplish this plan, approximately 12.5 million new shares of Common will be issued to shareholders of Carlsberg. Thereafter, some 64% of DMG Common Stock will be owned by Carlsberg shareholders.

DMG retained Blyth, Eastman, Paine, Webber, Inc., ("Blyth Eastman") as financial advisor and investment banker to advise DMG concerning the earlier aborted Master Shields acquisition, see *infra*, which had been supported by plaintiff, as well as the negotiations with regard to both the Stock Purchase Agreement between DMG and Carlsberg, and the Merger Agreement among DMG, DMI and Carlsberg. See Affidavit of Donald K. Miller, a managing director of Blyth, Eastman, wherein he opines that the DMI-Carlsberg merger was structured as it was on the basis of business and tax reasons and not with the intent of avoiding the voting requirements of Florida law applicable to mergers. No evidence to the contrary or contradicting same has been presented to this Court. Additionally, Blyth, Eastman delivered an opinion . . . finding the exchange of two million (2,000,000) shares of preferred stock by DMG with Carlsberg for forty-four thousand, four hundred forty-four (44,444) preferred shares of Carlsberg to be a fair transaction in terms of the exchange of the consideration involved, and likewise fair from a financial point of view to DMG. A similar opinion and finding is made with regard to the DMI-Carlsberg Merger Agreement. As of October 29, 1983, Carlsberg Resources Corporation owned some 27% of DMG's voting stock. This transaction increased the total amount of voting stock of DMG by approximately 18.5%.

The New York Stock Exchange, wherein DMG is listed, requires that to validate the issuance of the authorized twelve and one-half million shares of DMG common stock that are to be issued to Carlsberg, a majority of DMG shareholders who are represented in person or by proxy at a meeting of shareholders must so vote. This election is necessary in order to maintain DMG's listing on the Exchange. Consequently, a shareholders' meeting of DMG has been currently scheduled for December 22, 1983, to vote on a corporate resolution approving the issuance by DMG of the 12.5 million shares of DMG common stock to shareholders of Carlsberg. DMG has also announced that officers and directors of Carlsberg will stand for election to the DMG Board of Directors at the shareholders' meeting scheduled for December 22, 1983, and that Carlsberg will seek to fill by election four of the seven directorial seats on the DMG Board.

In July 1983, prior to the Carlsberg/DMI merger talks, DMG had discussed a possible merger between itself or a subsidiary with Master Shield, Inc., an affiliate of Plaintiff. Master Shield, Inc., was to be merged into DMG in exchange for shares of DMG stock and notes. A Letter of Intent was executed, and implementing documents were drafted and exchanged by these parties, but Master Shield, Inc. decided not to proceed on the initially-agreed terms. Thereafter, Plaintiff revised its proposal on terms substantially more favorable to it. On October 27, 1983, DMG's Board of Directors rejected the revised proposal, in part upon the advice of Blyth Eastman. The Carlsberg transactions, it was determined, were more favorable to DMG than Plaintiff's revised merger proposal. . . .

ISSUES ADDRESSED TO THE COURT

On the basis of the foregoing record and stipulated facts, the issues presented to the Court, in the procedural posture of a motion for preliminary injunction, can be summarized as follows:

Plaintiff contends that the two transactions at issue here, i.e., (a) the issuance of two million (2,000,000) voting preferred shares of DMG to Carlsberg, and (b) the merger of DMI and Carlsberg which results in issuance of 12.5 million shares of DMG common to Carlsberg, together constitute a *de facto* merger of *three* corporations: the present DMG, its subsidiary, DMI and Carlsberg; that the real merger is not only that between DMI and Carlsberg, but between DMG, the parent company, and Carlsberg; that, because Carlsberg is approximately three times the size of DMG, it is really Carlsberg which is surviving and DMG which is ceasing to exist after the merger; and that, if in fact these transactions together do constitute a *de facto* merger of DMG into Carlsberg, then Florida Corporation Law § 607.221 requires a full majority of *all outstanding* shares to approve the transaction, rather than a *quorum of shares voted either at the December 22, 1983 meeting or by proxy*, which is all that is required under the rules of the New York Stock Exchange.

Plaintiff concedes that the transactions do not fall within the strict statutory wording of Florida Statute Section 607.221, and that therefore this Court would have to declare the transactions a *de facto* merger in order to find that the statute applies. Plaintiff further argues that if a *de facto* merger were declared in this case, the appropriate relief would be for the Court to issue a preliminary injunction against holding the shareholder vote at which only a quorum, rather than a full majority, would be required to effectuate the merger. . . .

Defendants' central contention is that the Florida Merger Statute is inapplicable to the instant transaction because it does not require that the shareholders of a parent corporation be given the opportunity to vote upon the issuance of already authorized shares; that the merger between DMI and Carlsberg does not constitute a merger of DMG, the parent; and that all of the relevant shareholders — those of DMI and Carlsberg, which are the merging corporations — have been given or will be given the opportunity to vote upon the proposed transaction. Moreover,

Defendants emphasize, it is the business judgment of DMG which is at issue when considering this transaction, either as a whole or in its separate parts. Defendants contend, and Plaintiffs concede, that within the strict construction of the face of the statute, the transaction at issue is not a statutory merger and is not subject to the majority outstanding requirement. Defendants further argue that a preliminary injunction is not necessary at this time, for the following reasons: if an injunction [was] not issued and the vote were to be taken as scheduled at the December 22, 1983 meeting, three alternative outcomes could emerge:

1.   Plaintiff Equity Group could win the election by a majority of outstanding voting shares, which would render this litigation moot;

2.   Defendant Carlsberg could prevail by a majority of the outstanding shares, which would render this litigation moot; or

3.   Defendant Carlsberg could prevail, by a majority of votes cast, but by less than enough votes to satisfy Florida Statute Section 607.221, which would likely result in Plaintiff coming back to this Court for a ruling on the status of the matter.

On this basis, Defendants have argued that the potential harm to Plaintiff is not irreparable at this time, and that no harm might in fact result at all to Plaintiff if Plaintiff prevails at the election by an outright majority.

On the foregoing basis, the Court finds that the Plaintiff has not met its burden of proof sufficiently to support the issuance of a preliminary injunction. This is not to say that, given more facts and further discovery, the Court could not find that the transaction at issue is a *de facto* merger requiring a full majority vote of all the outstanding shares of DMG to be approved. However, in the present procedural posture of this litigation, on the basis of the record now before the Court, the relief requested by Plaintiff must be DENIED at this time.

The parties seem to agree that the DMI-Carlsberg Merger, the second of the two transactions at issue here, is a forward triangular merger: a wholly-owned subsidiary is acquiring the assets, liabilities, and stock of the target, a third-party corporation, after which the parent company and its original subsidiary will survive and the target will become part of the subsidiary. The key question before the Court is whether, as Plaintiff alleges, this requires that the Court treat the two transactions — the issuance of two million (2,000,000) shares of DMG voting preferred shares to Carlsberg, and the issuance of 12.5 million shares of common to effectuate a DMI-Carlsberg Merger — as a single transaction. The reason to do so, Plaintiff alleges, is that in reality, Carlsberg will be taking control of DMG, rather than DMG acquiring Carlsberg as part of its subsidiary, DMI. Plaintiff argues that this is so because: (1) Carlsberg is three times the size of DMG; (2) the Carlsberg family will end up controlling a majority of DMG voting shares; (3) the President of Carlsberg will become the President of DMG; and (4) the DMG Board of Directors will be composed of a majority of persons nominated by, and, essentially, voted in by, Carlsberg. These elements, Plaintiff has repeated in its papers as well as orally, constitute a situation in which, in reality, "the minnow is swallowing the whale".

The Court finds that under these facts and circumstances, on the basis of the record before it, Florida law does not necessarily stop or prevent the minnow from swallowing the whale where the business judgment of both the minnow and the whale is that the event will be mutually beneficial to both parties. Without evidence of a breach of fiduciary duty by the Officers/Directors of DMG or DMI or fundamental unfairness, or without allegations or proof of fraud, misrepresentation, *mala fides* or economic harm resulting from such merger, there is not presented to this Court a basis to invoke its equity jurisdiction. The Court again reiterates that this ruling is premised only on the basis of the facts now before the Court and a failure of Plaintiff to sustain its burden of proof on the four elements necessary to be shown as a predicate for a preliminary injunction.

The reason that the minnow may swallow the whale here is simply that nothing appears to prevent this from occurring. Each gets the opportunity to vote on the transaction. Florida law does not define the dilution of voting rights through the issuance of authorized stock as a matter which requires a full shareholder vote and the Florida legislature has specifically abolished preemptive rights. DMG could go forward with the issuance of every one of its authorized but unissued shares, without asking the shareholders for approval. This is not to say that if this were done for fraudulent reasons or illegitimate business purposes, the shareholders would not have numerous causes of action on which to sue, both under state law and under the Federal Securities Laws. The Court is not precluding such actions, or holding that they would not be recognized, in this very case or any other. However, the parties have not presented these issues to the Court in this case . . . .

Similarly, the consideration for both of these transactions is adequate under Florida law, or more than adequate. No shareholder approval would be required as to the consideration, which, for DMG, comes in the form of valuable shares of a larger, more diversified corporation. In and of itself, there is nothing wrong with DMG's exchange of shares for a ten percent (10%) ownership interest in Carlsberg under the Stock Purchase Agreement which Plaintiff has argued is the first part of a necessarily integrated two-part merger process.

Carlsberg is becoming a party to the use of a One Hundred Million ($100,000,000) Dollar tax loss carry-forward with DMG, a substantial consideration regardless of its enhanced position of control of DMG. Similarly, DMG will be less likely to suffer a possible default and non-renewal of a Twenty-three Million ($23,000,000) Dollar loan from Continental Bank due in full December 31, 1983; if default were to occur, it would seriously jeopardize DMG's continued existence. Equity, as well as other shareholders of DMG, will not be harmed *economically* by the Carlsberg-DMG transaction, since the book value of the shares would be roughly equivalent both before and after the DMI-Carlsberg merger. The pre-merger book value would be Two and 77/100 ($2.77) Dollars per share, while the post-merger *pro forma* value would be Two and 70/100 ($2.70) Dollars. The Court cannot speculate on how the merger would affect the market price of DMG stock, except to note that it is not unlikely that a smaller supply of remaining shares traded could enhance the price of DMG's stock. The Court cannot opine, on the basis of the record now before it, as to whether the opposite effect would result, as Plaintiff contends, because investors would shy away from owning a smaller percentage piece of a bigger, more closely-controlled pie. In the case at bar, it would be a mistake for the Court to substitute its own judgment for the business judgment of the directors of the corporations involved as to the benefits ultimately to inure to shareholders, absent any evidence of breach of fiduciary duty, or fundamental unfairness, or overreaching.

Also worth noting is that even if a large enough number of shares of DMG were issued so as to change its management or its business nature, this alone, as an isolated business transaction, would not require a vote of the majority of shareholders of DMG under the Florida statutes.

STANDARDS FOR INJUNCTIVE RELIEF

The standards for issuance of a preliminary injunction have been defined to require the movant to show:

1. A substantial likelihood of success on the merits;

2. Irreparable injury if the injunction is not issued;

3. The threatened injury outweighs whatever harm the issuance of an injunction may cause the opposing party; and

4. The injunction would not be adverse to the public interest.

These prerequisites shall be addressed in turn.

1. *Likelihood of Success* — As explained more fully above, the Court cannot find at this time on this record that the transactions at issue together constitute a *de facto* merger of Carlsberg and DMG. Thus, the Court should not apply Florida Statute Section 607.221 to the arrangement between DMG, DMI and Carlsberg. The merger between DMI and Carlsberg comes within the ambit of the statute and both said Defendants have indicated an intent to comply therewith. However, nothing in the statute or the relevant case law would require the parent of a merging subsidiary to conduct a full vote of its shareholders. Moreover, the New York Stock Exchange rules are also being followed, and the appropriate voting standards are being applied pursuant thereto.

The Court fully comprehends Plaintiff's argument that, in effect, it is DMG that is being acquired by Carlsberg, which is much larger. Stated another way, Plaintiff has argued that this transaction is somewhat unique, in that it is in reality a reverse triangular merger, the subsidiary of DMG being merged into a third corporation — and the parent being merged therein as well. However, there is no evidence which supports the contention that this is in any way bad or unfair to the shareholders of DMG, or that the substance of the transaction so significantly differs from its form as to call these transactions anything other than what they appear to be, e.g., an exchange of stock and a merger of a third company into a subsidiary. After the transactions are completed, DMG shareholders will hold stock in the same corporate entity as previously, and the stock will continue to be traded on the New York Stock Exchange.

For the Court to apply Florida Statute § 607.221 here, these transactions would have to be considered a "de facto" merger between DMG and Carlsberg. The Court recognizes that the de facto Merger doctrine has occasionally been used in situations in which the parties to a transaction structure it so as to avoid or circumvent the requirements of the applicable statutes. In these cases, it is important to realize, the Courts were faced with two-party transactions only. To apply these cases to the facts at bar would result simply in a finding that DMI and Carlsberg will be merging. This, of course, has been conceded by everyone involved. To bridge the gap in Plaintiff's conceptual analogy, Plaintiff has argued that because Carlsberg is larger than DMG and will essentially "control" DMG after the DMI/Carlsberg merger and the directorial elections, the real acquiror is Carlsberg and the real acquired is DMG. This argument is not without its intellectual appeal, and on a theoretical level it may be quite descriptive; but this is a Court of law and equity rather than one of metaphysics and philosophy. There is simply no basis in the case law to support Plaintiff's contentions sufficiently to constitute a ground for preliminary injunctive relief.

In support of Defendants' arguments, on the other hand, stands a small body of law from outside this jurisdiction. While not binding on this Court, these decisions are insightful and informative. See *Perl v. I.U. International Corp.*, 61 Haw. 622, 607 P.2d 1036 (1980) (notwithstanding that parent formed subsidiary for sole purpose of merger with target, the Hawaii Supreme Court held that parent not a party, so no de facto merger was found with respect to parent); *Allyn Corp. v. Hartford National Corp.*, [1982 Tfr. Binder] Fed.Sec.L.Rep. (CCH) ¶ 98,646 at 93,181 (D.Conn. 1982) ("Under Delaware law, a merger between a wholly-owned subsidiary and a third party is not to be treated as though it is a merger between the parent corporation and the third party."); cf. *Troupiansky v. Henry Disston & Sons*, 151 F.Supp. 609 (E.D.Pa. 1957) (dissenting shareholders of one party to a de facto merger were held entitled to sue the other party, which had become a subsidiary by acquiring the former's assets in exchange for stock, but the parent was dismissed because not a party to the de facto merger); cf. also *Terry v. Penn Central Corp.*, 668 F.2d 188 (3rd Cir. 1981) (under a Pennsylvania statute enacted to minimize the applicability of the de facto merger doctrine, the Court noted: "No allegation of fraud has been advanced, and the only allegation of fundamental unfairness is that the appellants will, if the merger is consummated, be forced into what they consider will be a poor investment . . . Even if appellants' evaluation of the merits of the proposed merger is accurate, poor business judgment on the part of management would not be enough to constitute unfairness cognizable by a court." *Id.* at 194).

The Court also does not find that DMG is in some sense the "alter ego" of DMI or vice-versa. Such a finding would require the Court to infer facts constituting fraud, bad faith, sham, or some other compelling reasons for piercing an apparently legitimate corporate "veil". No such factor appears in the stipulated facts or affidavits. DMG and DMI are separate corporate entities with different functions and different roles and interests, and the Court cannot consider them identical. If there are valid business reasons for so structuring two intimately related transactions, the Court as a matter of equity shall not interfere absent some form of overreaching or foul play which does not appear here.

2. *Irreparable Injury* — In the first instance, it is not certain that the transactions will be approved on December 22, and therefore it is not at all clear that even those injuries asserted by Plaintiff will, in fact, materialize. Even if the merger were to be effectuated and later declared unlawful, the merger could be judicially unwound if the law required such action. See *SEC v. National Securities, Inc.*, 393 U.S. 453, 89 S.Ct. 564, 21 L.Ed.2d 668 (1959) (trial court may return

merged parties to pre-merger status if necessary). However, the crux of why Plaintiff has failed to satisfy the second prong of the injunctive relief test is not the issue of ripeness or mootness or speculation. It is, instead, Plaintiff's failure to articulate any cognizable injury that could not be repaired. Plaintiff's loss of voting power is not an injury which the Florida legislature has sought to define as such, and indeed, preemptive rights have been eliminated under Florida law. Moreover, Plaintiff apparently seeks to block the merger so as to better position itself to accomplish some similar type of transaction. Nothing in the law of Florida gives Plaintiff any absolute right to accomplish a two-party transaction without the assent of the other party. As a Court of equity as well as of law, this Court cannot consider one proposed business transaction better or worse than another; it is the parties to the transaction who must make such decisions. Finally, given Equity Group's not insignificant share ownership in DMG, it is apparent that anything which would strengthen DMG's financial position would ultimately inure to Equity Group's benefit as a shareholder. Plaintiff can always choose to sell its stock on the open market in the same way it was acquired. Thus no real *economic* injury will be sustained by Plaintiff if the transaction is effected [*sic*]. This Court will not declare voting power in a corporation to be a property right worthy of the type of protection Plaintiff seeks here, when the state legislature has declined to do so. The Court does not pass upon the rightness or wrongness of this issue; the Court only observes that it will not judicially create legislation for a state that has chosen not to do so. Moreover, as noted previously, even under the voting standards to which Plaintiff so vehemently objects, it is not certain that the DMI-Carlsberg merger will take place. At present, any injury about which Plaintiff might have a valid claim is purely speculative. The business judgment of the Board of Directors is what is really at issue here at this time.

3. *Balance of Harms* — As explained above, Plaintiff's harms primarily involve the loss of proportionate voting rights, which are not recognized by Florida law in this situation. On the other hand, to grant the preliminary injunction would substantially affect the business interests of Defendants DMG, DMI and Carlsberg. Most immediately, the injunction would seriously jeopardize DMG's financing arrangement with the Continental Illinois National Bank & Trust Company of Chicago. The company has outstanding approximately Twenty-Three Million ($23,000,000) Dollars of debt, which will place DMG in default on December 31, 1983, if the loan is not renewed. The bank has agreed in principle to an extension of DMG's credit if, among other things, the merger is consummated. If the loan were not renewed and DMG were unable to obtain financing elsewhere, DMG would face serious consequences which would inure to the detriment of all its shareholders, including Equity Group. Additionally, the merger between DMI and Carlsberg would increase shareholders' equity from approximately 20.5 million dollars to 54 million dollars; it would lower DMG's debt-to-equity ratio from 1.50:1 to 1.28:1; and it would only minimally affect DMG's book value per share ($2.77 vs. $2.70). Similarly, Carlsberg would benefit by contributing to the use of DMI's One Hundred Million ($100,000,000) Dollar tax loss carry-over. To block the deal would thus frustrate the valid business purposes of the arrangement for the ultimate benefit of no party other than Plaintiff. The Court would nevertheless do so if the law so required, but here it is clear that at this point in time, the law imposes no such requirement.

4. *The Public Interest* — This issue does not come down squarely on either side. The Court does not deny that there is a public interest in corporate democracy at stake here, and that there is merit to Plaintiff's argument that shareholders in a public corporation should be given an opportunity to voice their opinion in a vote on matters of fundamental importance to them. However, it is of importance that the Court is here dealing with shares that were duly authorized by the shareholders of DMG through the 1980 Amendment to DMG's Articles of Incorporation, voted upon by a majority of holders of outstanding stock, which amendments specifically gave the directors the right to issue up to five million (5,000,000) shares of preferred stock *without further shareholder approval.*

The New York Stock Exchange requirement, that a majority of votes cast is required to approve the transaction, also cannot be overlooked. Shareholders are given the right to vote and are free to do so with respect to the DMG issuance of shares to Carlsberg; only the required percentage standard for approval differs between the New York Stock Exchange Rule and the statutory merger standard. The right to vote — or not to do so — is the essence of democracy and is not disregarded in the corporate transactions now before the Court.

Moreover, it cannot be said that corporate suffrage with respect to the shareholders of a parent corporation in a forward triangular merger of its subsidiary with another corporation is a value which the Florida legislature has seen fit to recognize. Florida Statute § 607.221 guarantees voting rights to the shareholders of the merging subsidiary and the third company, the target or non-surviving corporation; but the section does not contemplate the triangular situation with which the Court is herein faced. The Florida statutes permit the use of the parent's shares as merger consideration. Coupled with the tax advantages and tax-free status of the triangular merger under the Internal Revenue Code, and the convenience of a merger by exchange of stock rather than assets, this is just the type of transaction which the legislature cannot be presumed to have overlooked. In fact, it might be inferred that the legislature intentionally did *not* want to discourage such forms of merger by awarding voting or appraisal rights to the shareholders of the parent. It will be noted that commentators familiar with the drafting of provisions authorizing triangular mergers support exactly this position. . . .

On the foregoing basis, this Court cannot surmise from the Florida Corporation Act that Florida intended anything other than to allow the type of transactions at issue in the case at bar to occur without the necessity of a vote of a full majority of shareholders of the parent of the acquiror. Plaintiff has thus not met its burden with respect to establishing that the DMI-Carlsberg merger or the DMG issuance of stock to Carlsberg would be adverse to the public interest, as that term reflects the apparent intent of the Florida legislature. The Court infers that the legislature means what it does not say, as well as what it explicitly has set forth in the laws it has passed. . . .

By reason of the aforegoing, it is

ORDERED AND ADJUDGED that Plaintiff's Motion for Preliminary Injunction be and is hereby DENIED.

QUESTIONS

1. What are the deals involved in this case?

2. What is the *de facto* merger doctrine?

3. What is plaintiff's argument under the doctrine?

4. Why does the doctrine not apply here?

E. APPRAISAL RIGHTS

As we discussed in Chapter 2, appraisal rights afford shareholders who vote against specified corporate actions the option of having their shares bought back by the corporation for cash at fair value as determined by a court. The actions triggering appraisal rights for target shareholders under the MBCA include a merger, share exchange, and sale of all or substantially all of the corporation's assets.[198] In contrast, only a merger triggers appraisal rights under the DGCL.

Under both the DGCL and the MBCA, bidder shareholders generally are not entitled to appraisal rights even if they get to vote on the acquisition. One exception is when the deal is structured as a direct merger and the deal consideration consists of greater than 20 percent of bidder's outstanding stock pre-deal.

Appraisal rights may become a prominent structuring consideration if it appears rights, if available, will be asserted with respect to a significant number of target's shares, especially if bidder is tight on cash. This is because if the deal is structured as anything other than an asset purchase, it will essentially be bidder cashing out target's shareholders following an appraisal proceeding since the proceeding will be concluded post-closing, at which point bidder will be responsible for target's liabilities. Structuring around appraisal rights is easy if target is a Delaware corporation because the DGCL does not afford target shareholders appraisal rights in a deal structured as an asset purchase. The same is not true under the MBCA, but an asset purchase helps in that situation too, since target survives the transaction and is still owned by target's shareholders. Hence, bidder will not be involved in the appraisal proceeding.

Concerns over shareholders exercising appraisal rights also come into play when the deal is to be structured as a tax-free reorganization. This is because cash paid to shareholders who have asserted appraisal rights may count as "boot," and having too much boot can disqualify a transaction from being tax-free.

Note that neither the DGCL nor the MBCA provide for appraisal rights when the deal is structured as a stock purchase. The problem, however, of using a stock purchase when it appears that some target shareholders are not in favor of the deal is that there is a good chance they will not participate, i.e., agree to sell their shares

---

[198] *See* MBCA § 13.02(a).

to bidder. In such a case, target ends up as a less than wholly-owned subsidiary of bidder, which is not ideal for bidder from a legal standpoint because it will then owe these shareholders fiduciary duties since bidder has become a controlling shareholder of target. Bidder can follow up the transaction with a back-end merger but this adds to the transaction costs of the deal and triggers appraisal rights for target's shareholders.

F. MINIMIZING THE GAP PERIOD

M&A lawyers refer to the time between the signing of an acquisition agreement and the closing as the "gap period." From bidder's perspective, among the things that can go wrong during the gap period is someone coming in with a higher, or topping, bid in an effort to win the deal away from bidder. In this situation, bidder will likely have to up its bid or lose the deal. One way for bidder to reduce the risk of a topping bid coming in during the gap period is to minimize the length of the gap period. If target is public, the most effective way to do so is to structure the deal as a tender offer. This is because all other deal structures require a target shareholder vote, which realistically won't occur for at least two or three months after signing (two months if the SEC does not review target's preliminary proxy statement; three months if it does). As an example, below is a timeline from the Avis Budget/Zipcar deal:

> December 31, 2012: Avis Budget and Zipcar sign the Agreement and Plan of Merger
>
> January 22, 2013: Zipcar files its Preliminary Proxy with the SEC (no SEC review)
>
> February 4, 2013: Zipcar files its Definitive Proxy Statement with the SEC
>
> March 7, 2013: Zipcar holds its special stockholders meeting to vote on the deal.
>
> March 14, 2013: The deal closed.
>
> Length of gap period: 74 days

Conversely, a tender offer can potentially close within a month and a half of the parties signing the acquisition agreement because no target shareholder vote is required. As we discussed in Chapter 3, a tender offer does have to remain open for at least 20 business days, but this period normally starts to run within a week of the parties signing the acquisition agreement because no SEC pre-clearance is involved. Furthermore, the HSR waiting period for a cash tender offer is 15 days as opposed to 30 days for most all other deal structures. As an example, below is the timeline from the salesforce.com/ExactTarget tender offer:

> June 3, 2013: salesforce.com and ExactTarget sign the Acquisition Agreement
>
> June 12, 2013: salesforce.com commences its tender offer (files Form TO with the SEC, publishes a Notice of Offer, etc.)

July 10, 2013: offering period ends; approximately 64.2 million shares were tendered (89.7% of ExactTarget's outstanding common stock).

July 11, 2013: salesforce.com accepts the 64.2 million shares thereby completing the tender offer and becoming the majority owner of Exact-Target.

Length of gap period: 39 days

If the second step merger that follows bidder's tender offer has to be done as a long-form merger, a target shareholder vote will be required, triggering the same two- or three-months delay. In such a case, going with a tender offer plus second-step merger ends up taking longer than if the deal had instead been structured simply as a merger. However, bidder will already have majority control of target from the tender offer, and thus it will be too late for any competing bidders. In other words, topping bid risk ends when bidder closes on the tender offer. Incidentally, salesforce.com exercised its top-up option and closed on the short-form merger with ExactTarget on July 12, 2013, less than 48 hours after its tender offer offering period expired.

Bidders who need to quickly complete a deal for reasons other than eliminating topping bid risk, for example, to take advantage of time dependent tax perks, may choose to pursue a dual track, or "Burger King," structure (so named because it was first used in the 2010 acquisition of Burger King Holdings Inc.). Under this structure, bidder commences a tender offer with the minimum tendered shares condition set at the percentage that, when added to the maximum shares that can be issued by target pursuant to a top-up option based on the number of authorized but unissued shares target has available, will ensure that bidder will cross the 90-percent short-form merger threshold. During the pendency of the tender offer, target also prepares and files a preliminary proxy statement for a target share-holder vote on a merger as a backup in case the tender offer fails. If the tender offer is successful, bidder exercises the top-up option, target withdraws the preliminary proxy statement, and bidder completes the deal using a short-form merger. If the tender offer fails, bidder and target instead pursue the merger (assuming at least a majority of shares were tendered), which as you know requires a target shareholder vote, but the fact that target already filed a preliminary proxy statement speeds things along.

EXERCISE 4.3

B Inc. ("B") is a conglomerate incorporated in Nevada. T Co. ("T") is a video game development company incorporated in Delaware. Both B and T are private companies. B has agreed to acquire T for 5,000,000 shares of B Common Stock. T asked for at least a portion of the deal consideration to consist of cash, but B declined because B is currently short on cash.

T was started three years ago by two college roommates and has been financed by venture capitalists. T also has $3 million in bank debt on its books. T's most important asset is a lucrative long term contract with Microsoft for the development of eight games for the X-Box game system over a period of ten years. While the first game developed by T under the contract was a success, the second game was a flop, and as a result, Microsoft has expressed its displeasure with the contract. The contract provides that it may not be assigned by operation of the law or otherwise without Microsoft's prior written consent.

Each T founder owns 2,000,000 shares of common stock, VC Fund I owns 1,000,000 shares of T Series T Preferred Stock, VC Fund II owns 1,000,000 shares of T Series B Preferred Stock and VC Fund III owns 1,000,000 shares of T Series C Preferred Stock. Each share of T preferred stock is entitled to one vote on any matter submitted to the T shareholders. T's board of directors consists of five members — the two founders and a representative of each VC Fund. The VC Fund III board member has indicated that she does not support T's acquisition by B under the above terms and will therefore vote against the deal and assert appraisal rights. B has indicated to you that, given its cash situation, if appraisal rights are asserted by 10 percent or more of T's shares B will not be able to go forward with the deal.

1. How do you recommend B structure the deal?

2. What will be the tax consequences to B and T shareholders if the deal is structured per your recommendation?

EXERCISE 4.4

B Inc. ("B") is a publicly traded computer software company incorporated in Delaware. B's common stock is traded on the NASDAQ Global Market and its current market capitalization is $10 billion. T Corp. ("T") is a privately held computer software company incorporated in Arizona. B has agreed to acquire T in a friendly deal valued at $800 million. You have been retained by B as deal counsel to advise B on the deal. B has provided you with the following facts:

- T's primary product is "Spyware Assassin," the market-leading computer program for removing spyware, adware and malware from personal computers.

- T is party to a software supply agreement with Hewlett Packard Co. (the "HP Agreement"). Under the agreement, HP has agreed to install Spyware Assassin on every personal computer HP sells for the next three years, and T has agreed to supply Spyware Assassin only to HP. Approximately 90 percent of T's revenue for the current year was generated under the HP Agreement.

- The HP Agreement provides that it is not assignable by operation of the law or otherwise. It also provides that the HP Agreement terminates automatically upon the merger of T into another entity unless T obtains HP's prior written consent to the merger.

- T has five shareholders, each of which owns 20% of the outstanding stock of T.

- Jones, one of T's shareholders, is opposed to the deal because he thinks the price is too low. He has indicated that he will assert appraisal rights with respect to his shares.

- The remaining T shareholders have indicated they would prefer a tax free deal given their low basis in T stock.

- T is a defendant in a patent infringement suit relating to a product no longer produced or sold by T. The plaintiff in the suit is seeking $150 million in damages. T's patent litigation counsel gives the suit little chance of success and thinks it could be settled for $5 million or less.

- B has sufficient cash reserves and borrowing capacity to do an all- cash deal but is willing to do a common stock deal. If it is an all common stock deal, closing the deal would involve the issuance by B of common stock representing approximately 19.8 percent of B's pre-deal voting power based on B's current stock price on Nasdaq.

Additionally, B's CEO has provided you with the following prioritized list of some deal objectives (with 1. being the most important objective to B and 4. being the least important).

1. Preserve HP Agreement.

2. Provide T shareholders with tax-free treatment.

3. Avoid potential liability from existing patent infringement litigation.

4. Minimize corporate formalities and legal fees.

B recognizes that it may not be possible to structure a deal that meets all of the above four objectives, and that it may be necessary to approach HP and/or Jones in order to facilitate a particular deal structure. B has indicated that it will cooperate in doing so.

In light of the above list of priorities, advise B on what acquisition structure you recommend for the deal (including the type of consideration) and why. In order to meet as many priorities as possible, your recommendation may include approaching HP and/or Jones, in which case you should specify what would be sought from either of them. You should also provide a fallback recommendation in the event negotiations with HP or Jones fail.

EXERCISE 4.5

B Inc. ("B") is a small publicly traded chemical company incorporated in Texas. B's common stock is traded on the NASDAQ Capital Market and has been trading at around $10.00 per share. B currently has 20,000,000 shares of common stock outstanding. T Corp. ("T") is a privately held insecticide and pesticide manufacturer also incorporated in Delaware. B has agreed to acquire T in a friendly deal valued at $50 million. You have been retained by B as deal counsel to advise B on the deal. B has provided you with the following facts:

- T manufactures a number of its minor products pursuant to various intellectual property license agreements (the "IP Agreements"). All of the IP Agreements state that they are not assignable by operation of the law or otherwise.

- T used to manufacture and sell DDT, an insecticide that was banned in the U.S. in 1972. Plaintiffs' attorneys continue to bring product liability lawsuits against T from time to time relating to T's manufacture and sale of DDT.

- T currently owes $20 million on a loan it received from its CEO. The terms of the loan provide it is non-transferable by operation of the law or otherwise, but T's CEO has indicated he will consent to a transfer. In fact, the $50 million deal price assumes that the loan will be transferred to B (or an B subsidiary) as part of the deal.

- T has 20 shareholders, each of which owns 5% of the outstanding stock of T.

- Five of T's shareholders are opposed to the deal and have indicated that they will vote against it and assert appraisal rights with respect to their shares.

- The remaining T shareholders have indicated they would prefer a tax free deal given their low basis in T stock.

- B has sufficient cash reserves and borrowing capacity to acquire T for up to 50% in cash with the balance paid in B common stock.

Additionally, B's CEO has provided you with the following prioritized list of some deal objectives (with 1 being the most important objective to B and 4 being the least important).

1. Minimize liability exposure relating to T's manufacture and sale of DDT.

2. Close the deal as quickly as possible.

3. Minimize formalities and legal fees.

4. Provide T shareholders with tax-free treatment to the greatest extent possible.

5. Preserve the IP Agreements.

In light of the above list of priorities, advise B on what acquisition structure you recommend for the deal (including the type and mix of consideration) and why.

Chapter 5

DOCUMENTING THE DEAL

This chapter covers the principal legal documents and related issues involved in documenting an M&A deal.

A. ENGAGEMENT LETTER

Fairly frequently, target's board will decide it wants to explore selling the company before being contacted by a potential buyer and will thus retain an investment banking firm to lead the process. Hence, frequently the first legal document involved in a deal is an engagement letter specifying the details of the investment banks retention. Such a letter is typically drafted by the investment banking firm, and the key provisions are the scope of services to be provided, exclusivity, and fees. Below are some sample provisions.

---

1. Retention and Scope of Services.

The Company hereby retains Investment Bank on an exclusive basis to pursue offers for a sale transaction involving a merger, sale of assets or equity interests, or similar transaction with respect to all or a majority of the business, assets, or equity interests of the Company (each a "Transaction"). Investment Bank's services will include, if appropriate or if reasonably requested by the Company: (a) reviewing the Company's financial condition, operations, competitive environment, prospects, and related matters; (b) preparing the information package or confidential information memorandum regarding the Company; (c) soliciting, coordinating, and evaluating indications of interest and proposals regarding a Transaction; (d) advising the Company as to the structure of a Transaction; and (e) providing such other financial advisory and investment banking services reasonably necessary to accomplish the foregoing. The Company hereby authorizes Investment Bank to send prospective purchasers the information package and other pertinent information and legal agreements concerning the Transaction.

The Company agrees that neither it, its shareholders, or other affiliates, nor its management will initiate any discussions regarding a Transaction during the term of this Agreement, except through Investment Bank. In the event that the Company, its shareholders or other affiliates, or its management receives any inquiry regarding a Transaction, Investment Bank will be promptly informed of such inquiry so that it can evaluate such party and its interest in any Transaction and assist the Company in any resulting negotiations. . . .

---

4. Fees.

The Company shall pay Investment Bank a one-time nonrefundable retainer fee of $200,000. Such amount shall be credited against any Success Fee that may be payable as provided below.

Upon closing of a Transaction, the Company will pay Investment Bank a success fee (the "Success Fee"), in cash, equal to the aggregate of:

(a)   a minimum fee of $1,000,000 for the first $50,000,000 of Transaction Value; plus

(b)   1.25% of Transaction Value, if any, greater than $50,000,000 and up to and including $100,000,000; plus

(c)   1.00% of Transaction Value, if any, greater than $100,000,000 and up to and including $250,000,000; plus

(d)   0.75% of Transaction Value, if any, greater than $250,000,000 and up to and including $500,000,000; plus

(e)   0.50% of Transaction Value, if any, greater than $500,000,000.

"Transaction Value" means the total value of all cash, securities, or other property paid at the closing of the Transaction to the Company or its shareholders or to be paid in the future to them with respect to the Transaction as provided below (other than payments of interest or dividends) in respect of (a) the assets of the Company, (b) the capital stock of the Company (and any securities convertible into options, warrants, or other rights to acquire such capital stock), or (c) the assumption, directly or indirectly (by operation of law or otherwise), of any indebtedness of the Company for borrowed money, less all cash and cash equivalents held by the Company at closing.

In the event a Transaction is consummated in one or more steps, any additional consideration paid or to be paid in any subsequent step in the Transaction, including without limitation, payments in accordance with promissory notes delivered to the Company in connection with a Transaction or any Contingent Payments in respect of the items set forth in (a)–(c) above, shall be included in the definition of "Transaction Value." "Contingent Payments" means consideration received or receivable by the Company, its employees, former or current equity holders, or any other parties in the form of deferred performance-based payments, "earn-outs", indemnity holdbacks, or other contingent payments based on the future performance of the Company or any of its businesses or assets.

For purposes of valuing consideration included in Transaction Value other than cash payable at closing: (a) the assumption of any indebtedness for borrowed money will be valued at the unpaid principal amount of such assumed liability; (b) Contingent Payments shall be valued at the present value of such Contingent Payments using a discount rate of 5%; (c) the value of any purchase money or other promissory notes shall be deemed to be the face amount thereof; (d) any securities (other than a promissory note) will be valued at the time of the closing of the Transaction (without regard to any restrictions on transferability) as follows: (i) if such securities are traded on a stock exchange, the securities will be valued at the average last sale or closing price for the 10 trading days immediately prior to the closing of the Transaction; (ii) if such securities are traded primarily in over-the-counter transactions, the securities will be valued at the mean of the closing bid and asked quotations similarly averaged over a 10-trading-day period immediately before the closing of the Transaction; and (iii) if such securities have not been traded before the closing of the Sale Transaction, the value of such securities shall be as mutually agreed in good faith by the Company's Board of Directors and Investment Bank; and (e) any assets other than cash or the assets described in the foregoing clauses shall be valued as mutually agreed in good faith by the Company's Board of Directors and Investment Bank.

5. Term.

This Agreement shall have a term of 12 months from the date of this Agreement. The Company may terminate this Agreement at any time, with or without cause, on written notice to Investment Bank. Investment Bank may terminate this Agreement at any time if the Company is in material breach of this Agreement, on written notice to the Company. No expiration or termination of this Agreement shall affect Investment Bank's right to receive, and the Company's obligation to pay, any fees and expenses due, whether or not any Transaction shall be consummated before or after the effective date of termination.

In the event of any termination of this Agreement (other than by the Company for material breach by Investment Bank), Investment Bank shall be entitled to the Success Fee if the Company enters into an agreement prior to the date that is 12 months from the date of termination of this Agreement with an entity first referred to the Company by Investment Bank before the termination of this Agreement, provided that such agreement subsequently results in the consummation of a Transaction. Not more than 10 business days after termination, Investment Bank shall provide to the Company in writing a list of any parties introduced to the Company by Investment Bank, which list shall be binding unless the Company provides a written objection notice within 10 days after receipt. . . .

EXERCISE 5.1

Skip ahead to subsection E. of this chapter and read Item 1.01 describing the basic terms of Avon's acquisition of Silpada. Assume that Investment Bank represented Silpada pursuant to an engagement letter that included the above provisions. Based on the information contained in Item 1.01 only, how much compensation is Investment Bank entitled to from Silpada upon the closing of the deal?

B. CONFIDENTIALITY AGREEMENT

A confidentiality agreement, also called a non-disclosure agreement or NDA, is typically the first agreement entered into by bidder and target with respect to a potential M&A transaction. Bidder's signature on the agreement is a standard condition to target giving bidder access to its files and personnel. Bidder will require this access so it can assess target's business to determine whether it wants to go forward with a deal and, if so, what price it is willing to pay. Target needs the protection of a confidentiality agreement in case the deal falls through so that it has recourse in the event bidder then uses target information to compete with target.

If the parties contemplate the deal consideration will include bidder securities, target will need access to bidder's files and personnel so that it can get comfortable with bidder's securities. In such an event, the confidentiality agreement will be bilateral, meaning it will address both bidder and target confidential information.

Below is a brief description of the key provisions of a confidentiality agreement.

Definition of Evaluation Material. Evaluation Material is often the defined term used in an M&A related confidentiality agreement to delineate the types of information covered by the agreement. Target will want the definition to include all information it furnishes to bidder, regardless of the form of communication, e.g., written, oral, visual. For an M&A transaction, the definition should include the fact that a transaction is being contemplated and the status of negotiations. Below is the sample language.

"**Evaluation Material**" means all information, data, reports, interpretations, forecasts, business plans and records, financial or otherwise, and whether written, oral, electronic, visual or otherwise (whatever the form or storage medium), concerning or related to Target, any of its affiliates, subsidiaries or joint ventures, or any of the businesses, properties, products, intellectual property, product designs and plans, technical know-how, marketing information, services, costs and pricing information, methods of operation, employees, financial condition, operations, assets, liabilities, results of operations and/or prospects of any of the foregoing (whether prepared by Target, any of its Representatives (as defined below) or otherwise) that previously has been or may be furnished to you or any of your Representatives by or on behalf of Target or any of its Representatives (collectively, "**Information**"), as well as all notes, analyses, compilations, summaries, extracts, studies, interpretations or other materials prepared by Recipient or any of your Representatives that contain, reflect or are generated from, in whole or in part, any such Information, and in each case regardless of whether or not specifically marked as confidential. The term "**Evaluation Material**" includes, without limitation, the existence, terms, conditions and other facts with respect to any transaction between you and Target (the "**Transaction**") (including without limitation, the status thereof and any drafts of any term sheet, letters of intent or agreements related to the Transaction). You acknowledge and agree that the Evaluation Material may include Information made available to Target or any of its Representatives pursuant to confidentiality agreements or other obligations of confidentiality between Target and/or one or more of its Representatives and third parties.

Permitted Use of Evaluation Material. This section requires the recipient of Evaluation Material to keep it confidential and specifies how the information can be used and who may have access to it. Below is sample language.

2.   Nondisclosure of Evaluation Material. You hereby agree that you shall, and you shall cause your Representatives to: (i) keep the Evaluation Material strictly confidential in accordance with the terms of this letter agreement, (ii) use the Evaluation Material solely for the purpose of evaluating a possible Transaction with Target, and (iii) without the prior written consent of Target, not disclose any of the Evaluation Material to any person; provided, however, that you may disclose any of the Evaluation Material to your Representatives who need to know such Information for the sole purpose set forth in clause (ii) above and who agree to be bound by the terms hereof to the same extent as if they were parties hereto or by confidentiality restrictions at least as restrictive as those set forth in this letter agreement. You hereby agree to notify Target immediately upon discovery of any unauthorized use or disclosure of Evaluation Material or any other breach of this letter agreement by you or any of your Representatives, and will reasonably cooperate with Target to assist Target to regain possession of the Evaluation Material and prevent its further unauthorized use or disclosure. . . .

As used in this letter agreement, the term "**Representative**" means, with respect to any person, such person's affiliates and joint ventures and any of the foregoing persons' respective partners, members, managers, directors, officers, employees, agents, representatives, advisors (including, without limitation, financial advisors, bankers, information agents, proxy solicitors, consultants, counsel and accountants), controlling persons, equity partners, and financing sources.

Exceptions to Confidentiality. It is standard for a confidentiality agreement to exclude the following types of information from its coverage:

- Information that is or becomes public other than through the recipient's breach of the agreement.

- Information that was available to recipient on a non-confidential basis prior to disclosure.

- Information that was in the recipient's possession prior to disclosure.

- Information that becomes available through a third party not obliged to keep it confidential.

- Information independently developed by the recipient without using the confidential information.

The basic idea is that it is not fair to bar bidder from using information that it obtained or obtains independent of target. Below is the sample language.

The term **"Evaluation Material"** does not include Information that (i) is or becomes generally available to the public (other than as a result of a disclosure by you or any of your Representatives in violation of this agreement or any other obligation of confidentiality), (ii) was within your or your Representatives' possession prior to it being furnished to you by or on behalf of Target or any of its Representatives or thereafter becomes available to you or your Representatives, in either case without knowledge of it being subject to any contractual, legal, fiduciary or other obligation of confidentiality to the Target or any other person with respect to such Information, or (iii) was or is developed by you or any of your Representatives without reference to or use of the Evaluation Material.

Return of Evaluation Material. This provision addresses what bidder is to do with target's Evaluation Material if a deal never materializes. Below is the sample language.

---

3.   **Return and Destruction of Evaluation Material.** If you decide that you do not wish to participate in the Transaction, you will promptly inform the Target of that decision. In that case, or at any time upon the written request of the Target for any reason, you will promptly deliver to the Target or destroy (at your option) all Evaluation Material in your possession without keeping any copies, in whole or part thereof in any medium whatsoever; provided, however, that (x) you and your Representatives shall be entitled to retain the minimum number of copies of the Evaluation Material to the extent necessary to comply with applicable Law which shall be used solely for such purposes and (y) to the extent deleting Evaluation Material stored electronically on your back-up or archiving system is not reasonably practicable, you shall not be required to destroy such Evaluation Material, but all such Evaluation Material that remains stored electronically on your back-up or archiving system shall remain subject to all confidentiality obligations specified in this Agreement. In the event of such a decision or request, you shall cause one of your authorized officers to deliver to the Target a certificate stating that you have complied with all of the requirements of this Section 3. Notwithstanding the return or the destruction of the Evaluation Material or the termination of discussions regarding the Transaction, you and your Representatives will continue to be bound by your and their obligations of confidentiality and other obligations under this Agreement.

Term. A term provision specifies when the parties' obligations under the agreement end. The disclosing party typically will want the recipient obligations to run into perpetuity while recipient will want a specific end date. What the parties ultimately agree on often depends on the nature of the information recipient will be disclosing. Target will be less concerned about disclosing information that will become obsolete or dated within a relatively short period of time but may insist on an indefinite term for a trade secret like the formula for Coca-Cola. Below is sample language:

4. **Term.** The obligations of each party under Section 2 of this Agreement shall terminate and be of no further force or effect on the date that is the earlier of (i) two years from the date of this Agreement or (ii) the date of the consummation of a Definitive Transaction Agreement.

Standstill. Confidentiality agreements for public targets often include standstills. A public target insists on a standstill to, among other things, prevent bidder from terminating discussions and launching a hostile takeover attempt. (We discuss hostile takeover in Chapter 7). Below is sample language.

5. **Standstill.** Unless approved in advance in writing by Target's board of directors, you agree that neither you nor any Representative acting on behalf of or in concert with you will, for a period of two years after the date of this Agreement, directly or indirectly:

(a)   make any statement or proposal to the board of directors of any of Target, any of Target's Representatives or any of Target's stockholders regarding, or make any public announcement, proposal or offer (including any "solicitation" of "proxies" as such terms are defined or used in Regulation 14A of the Securities Exchange Act of 1934, as amended) with respect to, or otherwise solicit, seek or offer to effect: (i) any business combination, merger, tender offer, exchange offer or similar transaction involving Target or any of its subsidiaries, (ii) any restructuring, recapitalization, liquidation or similar transaction involving Target or any of its subsidiaries, (iii) any acquisition of any of Target's loans, debt securities, equity securities or assets, or rights or options to acquire interests in any of Target's loans, debt securities, equity securities or assets, (iv) any proposal to seek representation on the board of directors of Target or otherwise seek to control or influence the management, board of directors or policies of Target, (v) any request or proposal to waive, terminate or amend the provisions of this Agreement or (vi) any proposal, arrangement or other statement that is inconsistent with the terms of this Agreement, including this;

(b)   instigate, encourage or assist any third party to do, or enter into any discussions or agreements with any third party with respect to, any of the actions set forth in clause (a) above;

(c)   take any action which would reasonably be expected to require Target or any of its affiliates to make a public announcement regarding any of the actions set forth in clause (a) above; or

(d)   acquire (or propose or agree to acquire), of record or beneficially, by purchase or otherwise, any loans, debt securities, equity securities or assets of Target or any of its subsidiaries, or rights or options to acquire interests in any of Target's loans, debt securities, equity securities or assets.

The restrictions set forth in this Section 5. shall immediately terminate upon Target entering into a definitive agreement with respect to, or publicly

> announcing that it plans to enter into, a transaction involving all or a controlling portion of Target's equity securities or all or substantially all of Target's assets (whether by merger, consolidation, business combination, tender or exchange offer, recapitalization, restructuring, sale, equity issuance or otherwise).

Non-solicitation. Because bidder will be interacting with target personnel when reviewing the Evaluation Material, confidentiality agreements often have non-solicitation provisions to prevent bidder from poaching target's employees. Below is sample language.

> **6. Non-Solicitation.** In consideration of the Evaluation Material being furnished to you, you hereby agree that, for a period of one year from the date of this Agreement, you will not, and will cause your Representatives who receive Evaluation Material (other than third party advisors taking action on behalf of an unrelated person without breach of any of the other terms of this letter agreement) not to, directly or indirectly, without obtaining the prior written consent of Target, solicit for employment, hire or employ any (i) officers of Target or any of its subsidiaries or (ii) employees of Target or any of its subsidiaries at the regional manager level or above (whether or not such person would commit any breach of such person's contract of service in leaving such employment or service), which officers or employees are officers or employees of Target or such subsidiary as of the date of this Agreement or who become an officer or employee of Target or such subsidiary before the termination of discussions regarding a Transaction; provided, however, that the restriction on solicitation or hire above shall not restrict your ability to conduct generalized searches for employment (including through the use of general or media advertisements, employment agencies and internet postings) not directly targeted towards Target or Target's officers or employees or hire any person that (i) responds thereto, (ii) contacts you on his or her own initiative without your prior solicitation, or (iii) ceases to be employed by Target six months prior to the commencement of employment discussions between yourself and such officer or employee.

EXERCISE 5.2

Assume that Bidder has signed a confidentiality agreement with Target that includes all of the provisions discussed above.

1. Bidder wants to explore financing options for the potential deal. Can it discuss the deal with its investment bankers at Goldman Sachs?

2. While reviewing Target's Evaluation Material, Bidder discovers that Target has a new product in development that is very similar to a product Bidder has in development. Does this create any problems for Bidder?

3. An employee of Target with an impressive resume applies for a job at Bidder. Can Bidder interview her? Can Bidder hire her?

4.   Bidder decides not to pursue a deal with Target. What is it supposed to do with the Evaluation Material it has in its possession? What about Evaluation Material that is on its email server?

5.   Even though Bidder has decided not to pursue a deal with Target, it is considering buying some shares of Target in the open market for its investment portfolio. Can it do so?

C.   LETTER OF INTENT

A letter of intent (also called a term sheet or memorandum of understanding) is a preliminary outline of the proposed transaction. It serves as a starting point for the drafting and negotiation of the "definitive agreement." A letter of intent is not required and therefore not used in all M&A transactions but is common. Advantages of using a letter of intent include ensuring that bidder and target are on the same page regarding ballpark price and structure of the deal before substantial costs are run up, preventing selective memory loss on key points of the deal, facilitating bidder's pursuit of outside financing for the deal (if necessary), creating deal momentum, and enabling the parties to make their HSR filings before the definitive agreement is finalized. A major disadvantage to a letter of intent is that it may give rise to litigation if negotiations toward a definitive agreement breakdown.

Below is a sample letter of intent.

BIDDER INC.

March 8, 2014

Shoe Co.
1201 E. Speedway Blvd.
Tucson, AZ 85721-0176

Re: Proposal to Acquire Shoe Co.

Dear Mr. Sjostrom:

This letter (this "**Letter**") summarizes the principal terms of the proposed acquisition of Shoe Co. ("**Target**") by Bidder Inc. ("**Bidder**").

1.   **Form of Transaction.** Bidder proposes to acquire all of the business, assets, and liabilities of Target through a merger between Target and a wholly-owned subsidiary of Bidder, with Target surviving the merger (the "**Transaction**").

2.   **Purchase Price.** The proposed purchase price for Bidder's acquisition of Target is $100,000,000 (the "**Purchase Price**") in cash, subject to adjustment, and payable as follows: (a) $80,000,000 payable at the closing of the Transaction; and (b) $20,000,000 to be deposited with a mutually agreeable escrow agent, to be held for a period of three years after the

closing, in order to secure the performance of Target's post-closing obligations under the definitive merger agreement.

3. **Proposed Definitive Agreement** As soon as reasonably practicable after the execution of this Letter, the parties shall commence negotiations of a definitive merger agreement (the "**Definitive Agreement**") for the Transaction, to be drafted by Bidder's counsel. The Definitive Agreement shall include, among other things, the following terms and conditions:

(a) Customary representations and warranties made by parties to a merger transaction, including without limitation a representation that Target owns all intellectual property necessary or desirable to develop, manufacture, market and sell its products and services;

(b) Customary conditions to be satisfied before the parties are obligated to close the transaction, including without limitation (i) the approval of the transaction by the boards of directors of both Bidder and Target; (ii) the approval of the transaction by the stockholders of Target as provided by law; (iii) receipt of all approvals, authorizations and clearances needed from any governmental or regulatory authority or any other person required for consummation of the transaction; (iv) completion of a due diligence investigation of Target by Bidder and its advisors to Bidder's sole satisfaction; (v) delivery of appropriate legal opinions from counsel to Target; and (vi) no material adverse change in the business or financial condition of Target after execution of the Stock Purchase Agreement and prior to the closing of the transaction.

(c) Customary covenants by Target regarding the conduct of its business between the execution of the Definitive Agreement and the closing of the Transaction, including without limitation covenants (i) not to pay any bonuses to its employees (other than in the ordinary course) or make any other extraordinary payments to its employees or stockholders, including without limitation, dividends or other distributions with respect to Target's outstanding capital stock; (ii) not to issue additional capital stock (except upon conversion or exercise or outstanding convertible securities); and (iii) to conduct its business in the ordinary course.

4. **Due Diligence.** From and after the date of this Letter, Target will allow Bidder and its advisors full access to Target's facilities, records, key employees, customers, suppliers, and advisors for the purpose of completing Bidder's due diligence review. The due diligence investigation will include, but is not limited to, review of Target's financial, legal, tax, environmental, intellectual property and labor records and agreements, and any other matters as Bidder's accountants, tax and legal counsel, and other advisors deem relevant.

5. **No-Shop Provision.**

(a) In consideration of the willingness of Bidder to pursue the proposed transaction, Target agrees that, through the earlier of (i) June 30, 2014 and (ii) the date on which Bidder notifies Target, in writing, of its intention not to continue to pursue the proposed transaction (the "**No-Shop Period**"), neither Target nor any director, officer, employee, stockholder, representative or agent of Target will, directly or indirectly, solicit, initiate, entertain or encourage any proposals or offers from any third party relating to any merger or consolidation of Target, the dissolution of Target or the acquisition of a material portion of Target's assets, or participate in any discussions regarding, or furnish to any person any information with respect to, any such transaction.

(b) Target will promptly inform Bidder in writing of any third party inquiries or proposals received by Target during the No-Shop Period.

(c) The covenants in this paragraph 5 will apply to any and all discussions in which Target is currently involved with third parties.

6. Confidentiality; Public Announcements. Neither party shall, without the prior written consent of the other party, disclose to any third party the existence of this Letter, the identity of Bidder or Target or the transactions contemplated by this Letter. The Confidentiality Agreement dated March 1, 2014 executed by Bidder and Target remains in full force and effect.

7. Expenses. Each party shall be responsible for its own legal, accounting and other fees and expenses related to the Transaction. Each party shall indemnify and hold harmless the other party from any claim for broker's or finder's fees arising from the transactions contemplated by this Letter by any person claiming to have been engaged by such party.

8. Termination of Letter. In the event the parties fail to enter into a Definitive Agreement on or before June 30, 2014, the understandings contained in this Letter, unless extended by mutual written agreement of the parties, shall terminate and be of no further force or effect, except for paragraphs 6 and 9 which shall survive any termination of this Letter.

9. Governing Law. This Letter shall be governed by and construed in accordance with the laws of the State of Delaware, without reference to the conflicts of laws provisions thereof.

10. No Binding Agreement. This Letter reflects the intention of the parties, but for the avoidance of doubt neither this Letter nor its acceptance shall give rise to any legally binding or enforceable obligation on any party, except with regard to paragraphs 4 through 7 of this Letter.

11. Miscellaneous. This Letter may be executed in counterparts, each of which shall be deemed to be an original, but all of which together shall constitute one agreement. The headings of the various sections of this Letter have been inserted for reference only and shall not be deemed to be a part of this Letter.

Please indicate your acceptance and approval of the foregoing statement of our mutual intentions, which intentions are subject in all respects to the execution and delivery of the Definitive Agreement (except for the provisions of paragraphs 4 through 7 of this Agreement, which shall be binding on both parties).

This Letter shall be null and void if not accepted by delivery of an executed copy to Bidder no later than 5:00 p.m. on March 7, 2014.

Sincerely,

BIDDER INC.

By: _____

Cai Xu
Chief Executive Officer

Accepted and Approved
as of the date first above written:
SHOE CO.

By: _____

      William K. Sjostrom, Jr.
      Chief Executive Officer

The above letter of intent reflects the common practice of including a non-binding outline of the principal terms of the proposed transaction plus some legally binding provisions such as no-shop and confidentiality.

A no-shop is something a bidder routinely insists be included in a letter of intent to protect against losing the deal to a competing bidder. Basically, a no-shop, as the name indicates, prohibits target from reaching out to other potential bidders in an effort to start a bidding war. If target resists a no-shop, bidder will assert that it is not willing to invest the time and money evaluating target and negotiating a deal unless it gets this protection. Bidder is also concerned that a competing bid will weaken its negotiating position because target now has an alternative deal to that offered by bidder. A no-shop provision is typically included in the acquisition agreement too, as the acquisition agreement will supersede the letter of intent.

As I mentioned above, a major downside to using a letter of intent is that it may up the odds of litigation if the deal falls apart, as demonstrated by the next case.

BUDGET MARKETING, INC. v. CENTRONICS CORP.
United States Court of Appeals, Eighth Circuit
927 F.2d 421 (1991)

JOHN R. GIBSON, CIRCUIT JUDGE.

Budget Marketing, Inc. (BMI) and Charles A. Eagle appeal from an order of summary judgment denying their claims against Centronics Corporation for: (1) breach of implied duty to negotiate in good faith; [and] (2) promissory estoppel. . . . This suit arises out of the breakdown in negotiations for the purchase of BMI by Centronics. . . .

The district court decided this case according to Iowa law, and the parties do not argue that it erred in so doing. . . .

BMI is a Des Moines-based firm that markets and services magazine subscription agreements. Eagle is the president and principal shareholder of BMI. Centronics is a Delaware corporation based in New Hampshire.

In April 1987, BMI and Centronics executed a letter of intent outlining the basic terms of a proposed acquisition of BMI by Centronics. The letter stated that: (1) initial consideration would be $10 million; (2) additional consideration of up to $7 million would be contingent upon BMI meeting certain cash flow objectives over a 36-month period; (3) Centronics would provide additional capital during the 36-month "earn out" period, but BMI was responsible for cash needs until closing;

and (4) BMI was responsible for dealing with any outstanding Federal Trade Commission or Federal Reserve complaints. The letter of intent also stated that completion of the merger depended on four express conditions: (1) satisfactory completion of an accounting, legal, and business review of BMI by Centronics; (2) purchase by BMI of "key man" life insurance coverage for Eagle; (3) avoidance by Centronics of a "significant cash outlay" for taxes because of BMI's planned change in accounting methods; and (4) execution of a definitive and legally binding agreement between BMI and Centronics.

The letter of intent provided that the transaction was subject to approval by the boards of directors of both corporations and by the BMI shareholders. It also contained a specific disclaimer: "[T]his letter shall not be construed as a binding agreement on the part of BMI or Centronics." The letter set a target date for a definitive agreement of May 31, 1987.

Between January and May 1987, Centronics' officials carefully evaluated BMI. On May 21, the parties executed an addendum to the letter of intent that included changes favorable to Centronics.[1] The Centronics' board approved the addendum on May 26, 1987. The addendum changed the target date for the definitive documents to June 30, 1987.

Other steps leading to the proposed merger followed: Centronics' public relations firm issued a press release about the letter of intent, the directors of BMI's parent company and the BMI shareholders approved the proposed merger, and Centronics received all documents necessary to complete the legal, business, and accounting review of BMI.

At the same time, Centronics began considering the acquisition of companies larger than BMI, and, in June 1987, made a formal proposal to acquire the assets of Ecko Group, Inc., for $127 million. In August, Centronics sent its draft of the final agreement to BMI.

Meanwhile, BMI and Eagle began taking the steps necessary to meet the conditions imposed by the letter of intent. Eagle borrowed $750,000 for BMI's use that he personally secured. BMI opened additional branch offices and expanded existing branch operations. BMI also purchased "key man" life insurance coverage for Eagle. Throughout the summer and fall of 1987, Eagle kept Centronics informed of BMI's expansion efforts and the other developments.

During this time, Centronics did not disclose that it might not complete the deal. In August, a Centronics representative confirmed a planned closing date no later than September 30 during a conversation with an official of Norwest Bank, BMI's lender. In mid-September, a Centronics executive participated in a meeting with BMI representatives, an investment banker from R.G. Dickinson, and representatives of Norwest Bank regarding post-closing financing for BMI. All of those present at the meeting proceeded on the assumption that the deal would close, and the Centronics representative said nothing to the contrary. In October, a Centronics

---

[1] [n.1] The primary change concerned consideration. Of the $10 million in "initial consideration," Centronics would pay $8 million without condition, but $2 million would be contingent upon BMI meeting certain performance criteria.

representative discussed with a BMI official a necessary SEC filing that would have to be completed after closing. Also in October, Centronics' president and chief executive officer, Robert Stein, told Philip Boesel, an investment banker with R.G. Dickinson who had been involved with the planned merger, that Centronics was ready to move toward closing the deal with BMI.[2]

In November 1987, Centronics abruptly halted preparations for the merger. After evaluating proposed federal tax legislation, Stein sent a letter to Eagle stating that in spite of Centronics' "good faith efforts," conditions beyond its control made the deal "no longer feasible." The letter stated that the merger would lead to a cash outlay for taxes because of BMI's change in accounting methods, thereby triggering one of the negative conditions of the letter of intent.

On appeal, BMI challenges Centronics' stated reason for terminating negotiations as mere "pretext"[3] because the proposed tax legislation did not apply to the proposed merger and the change of accounting methods would not in fact have resulted in Centronics having to make a cash outlay for taxes.

Eagle and BMI brought this action against Centronics, alleging that together they had invested "hundreds of thousands of dollars" to meet the cash flow requirements of the letter of intent. . . .

The district court granted Centronics' motion for summary judgment, concluding that: (1) Centronics breached no agreement to acquire BMI; (2) the letter of intent disclaimed a duty to negotiate in good faith; (3) Centronics made no agreement or promise that was sufficiently definite to support recovery under promissory estoppel . . . .

I.

BMI concedes that the letter of intent did not constitute a binding agreement to merge, but it contends that the letter did establish a duty on the part of both parties to negotiate in good faith. Breach of that duty, it argues, entitles BMI to reliance damages. Specifically, BMI points to language in the letter setting a target date for executing a definitive agreement and stating that the definitive agreement "will contain mutually agreed terms." BMI further points to the extensive efforts devoted by both parties to bring the merger to fruition during the months preceding and following the execution of the letter as confirming the existence of a good faith duty.

Centronics counters by arguing that the specific language in the letter stating that it "shall not be construed as a binding agreement on the part of BMI or Centronics" means that no binding agreement to negotiate in good faith existed between the parties.

The district court found that the language of the letter of intent "plainly

---

[2] [n.2] In a follow-up letter to the telephone conversation, Boesel wrote to Stein on October 23: "I was pleased with our discussion earlier this week regarding your commitment of finally moving ahead toward a closing on Budget Marketing, Inc."

[3] [n.3] BMI alleges that the October 1987 stock market "crash" caused Centronics to be interested in other, more lucrative acquisition opportunities.

disclaimed any such [implied] duty." We conclude that the district court did not err.

BMI relies primarily on three cases, *Teachers Insurance & Annuity Association v. Tribune Company*, 670 F.Supp. 491 (S.D.N.Y. 1987); *Channel Home Centers v. Grossman*, 795 F.2d 291 (3d Cir. 1986); *Itek Corp. v. Chicago Aerial Industries, Inc.*, 248 A.2d 625 (Del. 1968), arguing that the overall language of the letter, coupled with the parties' conduct, gave rise to an implied duty to negotiate in good faith. The facts of these three cases are plainly distinguishable from the facts before us now.

In *Teachers Insurance & Annuity Association*, the parties had signed a financing commitment letter that, far from disclaiming an intent to be bound, stated that the parties had entered a " 'binding agreement.' " 670 F.Supp. at 491. The court concluded that " '[t]he intention to create mutually binding contractual obligations is stated with unmistakable clarity. . . .' " *Id.* at 499.

Such an intent is not present here. The letter of intent between BMI and Centronics clearly stated that it should not be construed as a binding agreement "[e]xcept for the confidentiality obligations set forth in paragraphs 11 and 12." The fact that the parties expressly designated the confidentiality obligations as the sole exception to the general disclaimer lends further support to our conclusion that no binding agreement to negotiate in good faith can be implied from the overall language of the letter. In *Teachers Insurance & Annuity Association*, the court observed that it must determine the intent of the parties "at the time of their entry into the understanding," 670 F.Supp. at 499, and that a party not wanting to be bound by a preliminary letter can "very easily protect itself by not accepting language that indicates a 'firm commitment' or 'binding agreement.' " *Id.* With these observations in mind, we conclude that the parties here evinced no intent to be bound at the time they signed the letter; the letter clearly disclaims that it is a binding agreement.

Similarly, in *Channel Home Centers*, the Third Circuit found that a detailed letter of intent, signed by a property owner and a prospective tenant, gave rise to a duty to negotiate in good faith because the parties intended their promise to be binding. The court concluded that the agreement contained "an unequivocal promise by [the landlord] to withdraw the store from the rental market and to negotiate the proposed leasing transaction with [the prospective tenant] to completion." *Id.* at 299. No such binding promises are contained in the letter signed by BMI and Centronics. Moreover, *Channel Home Centers* does not suggest that such promises can be implied in the presence of express language disclaiming an intent to be bound.

Finally, *Itek* is equally unpersuasive. The *Itek* court, applying Illinois law, concluded that a jury could find that the parties entered a binding agreement to negotiate in good faith. The court relied in part on language in the letter of intent stating that although the parties would have " 'no further obligation' " to each other if they failed to reach ultimate agreement, they would " 'make every reasonable effort' " to agree upon and execute a final contract. *Id.* at 627. The letter signed by BMI and Centronics did not contain similar language. To the contrary, the letter expressly stated that the parties were not bound. . . .

Courts are reluctant to find implied covenants. *Fashion Fabrics, Inc. v. Retail*

Investors Corp., 266 N.W.2d 22, 27 (Iowa 1978); *Pathology Consultants v. Gratton*, 343 N.W.2d 428, 434 (Iowa 1984). They "must arise from the language used or be indispensable to effecting the intention of the parties." *Gratton*, 343 N.W.2d at 434. While the court may find an implied term on a point not covered by the express terms of the agreement, "there can be no implied contract on a point fully covered by an express contract and in direct conflict therewith." *Snater v. Walters*, 250 Iowa 1189, 98 N.W.2d 302, 307 (1959). Because the facts here fail to meet the Iowa test for an implied contract and because finding an implied duty would contradict the express disclaimer of the letter of intent, we conclude that the parties did not bind themselves to an obligation to negotiate in good faith, and that the district court did not err in so holding.

II.

BMI next argues that oral promises made by Centronics after the execution of the letter of intent establish a triable claim based on promissory estoppel. BMI contends that Centronics, on numerous occasions, gave oral assurances that the deal would be consummated.[4] Relying on those promises, BMI spent substantial sums of money to comply with the conditions stated in the letter of intent. The record shows that BMI regularly apprised Centronics of its efforts and achievements.

Centronics argues that a promissory estoppel claim is foreclosed by the letter of intent, again relying on the disclaimer language. The district court did not rely on the disclaimer, but rejected BMI's promissory estoppel claim because the statements by Centronics were "vague" rather than "clear and definite."

Under Iowa law, a party claiming recovery under promissory estoppel must establish: (1) a clear and definite agreement; (2) that it acted to its detriment in reasonable reliance on the agreement; and (3) that the equities support enforcement of the agreement. *National Bank of Waterloo v. Moeller*, 434 N.W.2d 887, 889 (Iowa 1989). *Moeller* further states that while no Iowa case has "squarely defined" the first element of "agreement," that earlier cases of the Iowa Supreme Court demonstrate that agreement can include a "promise" in which the promisor clearly understands that "the promisee was seeking an assurance upon which he could rely and without which he would not act." *Id.* at 889. This approach, *Moeller* states, adheres to the definition of promissory estoppel found in the Restatement (Second) of Contracts, which states:

> A promise which the promisor should reasonably expect to induce action or
> forbearance on the part of the promisee or a third person and which does

---

4 [n.5] BMI specifically points to: (1) an October 1987 telephone conversation between Stein and Boesel, the investment banker from R.G. Dickinson, in which Stein stated that Centronics was ready to move ahead toward closing; (2) an oral confirmation in August of a September 30 closing date during a conversation between a Centronics representative and a Norwest Bank official; (3) a mid-September meeting at Norwest Bank in which all of those present, including the Centronics representative, proceeded on the assumption the deal would close; (4) a statement by Stein in June 1987 that he wanted to defer closing until BMI met July sales projections, which BMI subsequently did; and (5) a statement in October by a Centronics' official to a BMI representative that a certain SEC filing would have to be made after closing, implicitly indicating that the deal would close.

induce such action or forbearance is binding if injustice can be avoided only by enforcement of the promise. The remedy granted for breach may be limited as justice requires.

Restatement (Second) of Contracts § 90(1) (1979).

Our study of the record convinces us that BMI's promissory estoppel claim should be submitted to a jury. Reasonable jurors could find that Centronics provided oral assurances to BMI and others that it would close on the deal. In October 1987, for instance, Stein told the investment banker, Boesel, that Centronics was ready to "mov[e] ahead toward a closing" of the deal. Eagle stated in his deposition and in a November 1987 letter to Stein that he and Boesel relied on Stein's "positive assurance" during that conversation to go ahead with the loan that R.G. Dickinson subsequently made to Eagle.[5]

In alleged reliance on Centronics' oral assurances, Eagle and BMI endeavored to meet all of the conditions imposed by the letter of intent. BMI opened new offices, expanded existing operations, hired more dealers and "independents," arranged for necessary credit, and purchased "key man" life insurance coverage for Eagle. BMI contends that it expended considerable effort and incurred substantial expense in doing so. Centronics was promptly apprised of the developments at BMI. We conclude that the evidence of Centronics' oral assurances, coupled with BMI's alleged reliance and Centronics' awareness of BMI's reliance, is substantial enough to establish a triable claim under Iowa's promissory estoppel doctrine.

We also observe that the facts of this case closely resemble those in the Second Circuit case, *Arcadian Phosphates, Inc. v. Arcadian Corp.*, 884 F.2d 69 (2d Cir. 1989). In *Arcadian*, the parties had negotiated under the terms of a letter of intent which stated that a " 'binding sales agreement' " would be completed at a later date. *Id.* at 70. After both sides took numerous steps to consummate the deal, the seller changed its position on what percentage of ownership it wanted to retain, thereby triggering suit by the buyer. The Second Circuit reversed summary judgment for the defendant on the plaintiffs' promissory estoppel claim, stating that "Appellants' . . . claim is based on evidence that [the defendant] knew and approved of [the plaintiffs'] expenditures and collateral contracts, but . . . suddenly demanded a majority interest in [the plaintiff corporation] when the phosphate fertilizer business became 'dramatically' profitable." *Id.* at 74. The court concluded that triable issues existed as to whether the seller had made a clear and unambiguous promise to bargain in good faith, whether the buyer had reasonably and foreseeably relied on that promise, and whether the buyer had sustained an injury. *Id.* The court observed that prevailing on a promissory estoppel claim might not entitle the buyer to benefit-of-the-bargain damages. *Id.* at 73. Damages under promissory estoppel are often limited by the extent of the promisee's reliance rather than by the terms of the promise. *Id.*

---

[5] [n.7] The conversation between Stein and Boesel and the subsequent loan to Eagle illustrate a necessary element of promissory estoppel, that of detrimental reliance. Logically, the promise must precede the promisee's alleged reliance. *See Moeller*, 434 N.W.2d at 889. In the case before us, BMI alleges a series of assurances, or promises, and a series of actions taken in reliance on those promises. To ultimately prevail on its promissory estoppel claim, BMI will have to establish that it took specific actions in reliance on specific promises.

The key facts here — the nonbinding letter of intent, the substantial steps taken toward consummating the deal, the aggrieved party's reliance on the assurances and actions of the other party — fit squarely within *Arcadian*.

Looking at the facts in the light most favorable to BMI, as we are required to do in determining a motion for summary judgment, we conclude that BMI has established a triable claim of promissory estoppel that would support an award of reliance damages. We therefore reverse the district court's grant of summary judgment on this issue. . . .

QUESTIONS

1. What is the deal involved in the case? Why didn't it close?

2. What legal claims does BMI bring against Centronics?

3. Why does the court reject these claims?

4. What lessons should an M&A lawyer take from this case?

Occasionally, bidder and target will include in a letter of intent or other document a binding obligation to negotiate in good faith towards a definitive agreement. (*See SIGA Technologies, Inc. v. PharmAthene, Inc.*, 67 A.3d 330 (Del. 2013) for a recent case involving such a provision). Doing so, however, greatly increases the litigation risk if the parties are unable to ultimately strike a deal as either party can claim the other party failed to negotiate in good faith. Thus, lawyers typically strongly discourage a client from signing a letter of intent that includes an obligation. In fact, I recommend including a provision along the lines of the following in all letters of intent:

> The parties agree that this letter of intent does not constitute a binding commitment by either party except with respect to [sections —] above. The non-binding provisions of this letter of intent reflect only the parties' current understanding of the contemplated transaction, and a binding contract will not exist between the parties unless and until they sign and deliver one or more definitive agreements, which will contain material terms not set forth in this letter of intent. No obligations of one party to the other (including any obligation to continue negotiations) or liability of any kind shall arise from executing this letter of intent, a party's partial performance of the terms of this letter of intent, its facilitating or conducting due diligence, its taking or refraining from taking any actions relating to the proposed transaction or any other course of conduct by the parties other than breach of [sections —] above. The parties agree that neither party shall have a duty to negotiate in good faith and that either party may discontinue negotiations at any time for any reason or no reason. Any letters, drafts or other communications shall have no legal effect and do not constitute evidence of any oral or implied agreement between the parties.

D.   DUE DILIGENCE

In the M&A context, "due diligence" refers to the in-depth investigation of target and its business. Bidder undertakes due diligence of target to confirm that it makes sense to go forward with the deal, identify factors that impact what bidder is willing to pay, uncover risks associated with owning target's business, and pinpoint obstacles to closing the deal and integrating target's business with bidder's business. Thus, among other things, bidder will pour over target's business records and other documents, interview target's key personnel, and analyze target's competitive position and projected future performance.

A due diligence investigation consists of two components: business and legal, although there is often overlap between the two. Business due diligence is typically done by personnel of bidder, bidder's outside accounting firm, its investment banking firm, and oftentimes consultants retained by bidder. Legal due diligence is done by personnel of the law firm representing bidder in the deal. Our discussion here focuses on legal due diligence given this is an M&A law book.

Legal due diligence typically starts with bidder's counsel sending target's counsel a due diligence request list. This list sets forth various categories of materials target is to provide bidder's counsel, including corporate matters, securities issuances, material contracts, financing documents, financial statements, real estate, labor, employee benefits, litigation, intellectual property, environmental, insurance matters, taxes, and governmental filings. Below is a sample first part of a due diligence request list. As you can see, it is comprised of the specific materials requested in the category of corporate matters. A request will include similar specifics for each of the broad categories of information and will thus typically run 15 to 20 pages long.

Initial Due Diligence Request List

In connection with the potential acquisition of Shoe Co. (the "Company") by our client, Bidder, Inc., please provide us with the following materials for our review. Note that our due diligence investigation is ongoing, and we will submit additional due diligence requests as necessary.

Unless otherwise indicated, please make the materials available for all periods subsequent to December 31, 2008 and include all amendments, supplements and other ancillary documents. Please do not hesitate to contact us at 520-555-1373 with any questions or concerns regarding this request.

1.   **Corporate Matters.**

   (a)   Organizational documents of the Company and each of its subsidiaries (e.g. certificates of incorporation, Bylaws, certificates of formation, limited liability company agreements).

   (b)   Organizational structure chart of the Company and its subsidiaries identifying the legal name, type of entity, ownership and jurisdiction of organization.

   (c)   Minute books of the Company and each of its subsidiaries, including minutes of meetings and actions by written consent of the board of directors (or its equivalent) of the Company and any of its committees and minutes of meetings and actions by written consent of the shareholders of the Company.

(d)   Communications with shareholders, including annual reports, proxy statements and correspondence.

(e)   Agreements relating to the ownership and control of the Company and its subsidiaries, including all shareholder agreements, voting agreements, transfer restriction agreements, stock purchase rights, and warrants.

(f)   Summary of the corporate history of the Company and any predecessors, including any mergers, acquisitions, changes in control and divestitures.

(g)   List of places where the Company is qualified to do business.

(h)   List of places where the Company operates its business or maintains inventory, owns or leases property or has employees, agents or independent contractors. Include the number of employees and a description of operations or services performed at each location.

(i)   List and description of all transactions between the Company and any shareholder, director, officer, employee or affiliate of the Company (or any entity or person formerly having the status thereof), including amounts and names of parties involved, during the past ten years.

(j)   Agreements relating to ownership of or investments in any business or enterprise, including joint ventures and minority equity investments. . . .

Due diligence is typically done by a team of junior associates overseen by a junior partner or senior associate. The size of the team depends on the amount of materials that needs to be reviewed. It is tedious but important work because missing something (like a change of control provision in a significant contract) can end up costing the client a lot of money.

In the old days, physical copies of the various materials would be made available to bidder's counsel in a "data room" at target's headquarters or target counsel's offices. Bidder's due diligence team would then spend days or weeks in the data room reviewing documents. These days, a target typically creates a "virtual data room," or VDR, which allows the due diligence team to access the documents online. A VDR results in cost savings to both bidder and target because it reduces travel and printing costs and related professional fees and speeds up the due diligence process because all parties can access documents simultaneously.

The supervising attorney and team members will typically be part of the firm's M&A group. They will pull in attorneys from other groups to review materials in specialized areas such as intellectual property, employee benefits, real estate, and environmental law.

Generally, the team's job is to check that target's legal house is in order, uncover potential issues or liabilities associated with target, and flag document provisions that will be triggered or implicated by the deal. For example, a review of a material contract of target should include the following:

- Who are the parties to the contract?

- Is the contract assignable? How is assignment defined?

- Is there a change of control provision? If so, does this transaction constitute a change of control?

- When does the contract terminate? Is there an automatic renewal provision? What does the contract say about early termination?

- What are the basic economics of the contract? How is the pricing determined?

- Does the contract include a non-compete, exclusivity, and/or most favored nation provision?[6]

- Has either party breached the contract?

- Has target received or sent any notices concerning the contract?

- Has the contract been amended?

A reviewer normally uses a due diligence checklist to ensure he or she doesn't forget to look for certain things during the review and makes notes on what he or she finds. The notes are then used by the team to produce a due diligence memo summarizing its findings from the review. Typically, a reviewer will promptly report any major issue he or she uncovers so that target's counsel can be made aware of it and it can be factored into negotiations and reflected in the acquisition agreement if necessary.

Target's counsel also performs legal due diligence on target. The primary purpose of this due diligence is so that target's counsel can prepare the disclosure schedules to the acquisition agreement and deliver to bidder a legal opinion at closing. We discuss disclosure schedules and legal opinions below. If the deal consideration consists of bidder stock or other securities, as opposed to all cash, target and its counsel will perform due diligence on bidder given that its shareholders will have a stake in bidder post-deal.

E. ACQUISITION AGREEMENTS

An acquisition agreement is the primary legal document in an M&A transaction. Below we cover three different types of acquisition agreements: an asset purchase agreement, stock purchase agreement, and merger agreement. Since each of these agreements documents the same end — bidder's acquisition of target's business — they are similarly organized and contain many of the same provisions. Thus, to save time and space and avoid redundancies, the focus is on an asset purchase agreement ("APA") but the spotlight is on provisions that differ for a stock purchase agreement or merger agreement. In that regard, below you will find a description of various

---

[6] A most favored nation provision is sometimes included in supply agreements. It contractually obligates a seller to provide a product or service to a buyer at a price no higher than the price it provides to any other buyer, now or during the term of the agreement. Here is sample language:

Most Favored Customer. Seller shall not sell the same Goods to any other buyer at prices below those stated in this Agreement. If Seller charges a different buyer a lower price for Goods, Seller shall immediately apply the lower price for the Goods under this Agreement.

components of an asset purchase agreement, including sample language. Most of the sample language is from the asset purchase agreement pursuant to which Avon Products, Inc., a global manufacturer and marketer of beauty and related products whose stock is traded on the New York Stock Exchange, acquired the private company Silpada Designs, Inc., a direct seller of jewelry products primarily in North America. For background on the deal, here is an excerpt from Item 1.01 from the Form 8-K Avon filed with the SEC in connection with executing the APA.

Item 1.01 Entry into a Material Definitive Agreement.

On July 9, 2010, Avon Products, Inc. (the "Company") entered into an Asset Purchase Agreement with SD Acquisition LLC, a wholly-owned subsidiary of the Company (together with the Company, the "Buyer"), Silpada Designs, Inc. (the "Seller"), the stockholders of the Seller, and Gerald A. Kelly, Jr., solely in his capacity as representative of the Seller and the stockholders of the Seller (the "Agreement").

Pursuant to the Agreement, at closing the Buyer will purchase and assume from the Seller substantially all of the assets and liabilities of the Seller, for aggregate cash consideration of approximately $627 million, subject to adjustments for working capital, debt and cash. The Agreement also provides for an affiliate of the Buyer to simultaneously acquire certain real properties, for aggregate cash consideration of approximately $23 million, pursuant to a real property purchase agreement entered into with an affiliate of the Seller.

Additional consideration pursuant to the Agreement may be payable by the Buyer to the Seller in 2015, in the event the Seller's North American business acquired by the Buyer achieves specific EBITDA targets over the 2012, 2013 and 2014 calendar years. While there is no contractual minimum or maximum to this potential additional payment, we estimate that it could range from $50 to $100 million.

The Agreement contains customary representations, warranties and covenants. The Seller has agreed to indemnify the Buyer from and against losses the Buyer may incur arising out of breaches of the Seller's or Seller's stockholders' representations, warranties and covenants contained in the Agreement, subject to specified time and amount limits and other exceptions.

The transaction contemplated by the Agreement is subject to the satisfaction of customary closing conditions, including the termination or expiration of the waiting period under the Hart-Scott-Rodino Antitrust Improvements Act of 1976. . . .

Note that the convention is for bidder's counsel to draft the acquisition agreement. (This is reflected in Paragraph 3 of the above sample Letter of Intent). This means that bidder's counsel prepares the initial draft of the agreement and all revisions as negotiations progress. Target's counsel does, however, typically draft the disclosure schedules (discussed below).

1. Preamble

The preamble (sometimes called the introductory paragraph) is the first paragraph of an acquisition agreement appearing just under the title. It repeats the title of the contract and then sets forth the date of the contract and the parties to the contract. Below is the preamble from the Avon/Silpada APA.

This Asset Purchase Agreement (as it may be amended or supplemented from time to time in accordance with the terms hereof, this "**Agreement**") is entered into as of July 9, 2010 by and among Avon Products, Inc., a New York corporation (the "**Buyer Parent**"), SD Acquisition LLC, a Delaware limited liability company and a wholly-owned Subsidiary of the Buyer (the "**Buyer Sub**" and collectively with the Buyer Parent, the "**Buyer**"), Silpada Designs, Inc., a Kansas corporation (the "**Seller**"), the Stockholders of the Seller named on the signature pages of this Agreement (each, a "**Seller Stockholder**" and collectively, the "**Seller Stockholders**"), and Gerald A. Kelly, Jr., solely in his capacity as representative of the Seller and the Seller Stockholders (the "**Seller Representative**").

Buyer Sub is a party to the agreement because Avon wants the Silpada business contained in a subsidiary instead of Avon itself. Although not legally required, Silpada's stockholders are parties to the agreement presumably at the insistence of Avon so that it has recourse against them in the event problems arise with Silpada's business post-closing. This is common when target is a private company as is the case here. The agreement includes a "Seller Representative" as a party to facilitate negotiation and administration of the agreement. Basically, the other stockholders empower the Seller Representative to take various actions on their behalves with respect to the deal. Here, the Seller Representative is Silpada's largest shareholder and chief executive officer.

2. Recitals

Recitals (also called background) explain why the parties are entering into the agreement. Their purpose is to provide context for the reader. In acquisition agreements, they also often describe additional transactions that will be occurring in connection with the main transaction. Below are the recitals from the Avon/Silpada APA.

RECITALS

A.   The Seller wishes to sell and assign to the Buyer Sub, and the Buyer Sub wishes to purchase and assume from the Seller, substantially all of the assets and liabilities of the Seller (as more fully described herein), on the terms and subject to the conditions set forth in this Agreement;

B.   In accordance with applicable Law, (i) the board of directors of the Seller has deemed this Agreement and the transactions contemplated by this Agreement to be expedient and in the best interests of the Seller, and

(ii) the Seller Stockholders have unanimously authorized this Agreement and the transactions contemplated by this Agreement; and

C. Contemporaneously with the execution and delivery of this Agreement, Avon Capital Corporation, a Delaware corporation and a wholly-owned Subsidiary of the Buyer Parent (the "**Lenexa Buyer Sub**"), Adaplis, L.L.C., a Kansas limited liability company and an Affiliate of the Seller ("**Adaplis**"), and Gerald A. Kelly, Jr., solely in his capacity as representative of Adaplis, have entered into a purchase and sale agreement (the "**Lenexa Purchase Agreement**"), pursuant to which Adaplis will sell, and the Lenexa Buyer Sub will purchase, the Lenexa Real Properties as of the Closing (as defined below) pursuant to the terms and conditions set forth in the Lenexa Purchase Agreement.

Recital C reflects the fact that Silpada's real estate was held in a separate entity, which is often done for tax and estate planning purposes. Thus, an Avon subsidiary entered into a separate agreement with the entity that owned the Silpada's real estate providing for the sale of the real estate contemporaneously with the closing under the APA.

3. Definitions

A common contract drafting technique is the use of defined terms. A defined term is a contract provision that specifies the meaning of a word or phrase used in the contract. When defining a term, the convention is to capitalize the term and put it in quotes. Many drafters also underline or bold the term (or both as the above preamble and recitals demonstrate) where it is defined to aid the reader in locating the definition. To signify that you are using a previously defined term in the contract, you simply capitalize the word (you do not put it in quotes, underline it, or bold it). A contract can have a separate definition section or define terms in context. (Both the preamble and recitals from above provide examples of terms defined in context). Longer contracts such as acquisition agreements define some terms the in context and some terms in a definition section. Oftentimes, the definition section is the first section of an acquisition agreement, although some lawyers prefer to put it at the end of the agreement. Below is an excerpt from the definitions section of the Avon/Silpada APA.

ARTICLE I
DEFINITIONS . . .

The following terms will have the following meanings in this Agreement: . . .

"**Agreement**" has the meaning provided in the Preamble. . . .

"**Average North American Excess**" means (x) the sum of the North American Excess for calendar years 2012, 2013 and 2014, *divided by* (y) three.
. . .

"**Company Assets**" means all assets, rights and properties of every kind, nature, character and description (whether real, personal or mixed, whether tangible or intangible and wherever situated), including the related goodwill, owned or leased by the Seller or any of its Subsidiaries. . . .

"**Confidentiality Agreement**" means the letter agreement dated January 19, 2010 between the Buyer Parent and the Seller. . . .

"**EBITDA**" means, for purposes of Section 2.9 and for any referenced fiscal period, the consolidated net income of the North American Business during the fiscal period determined in accordance with GAAP, *plus* (i) income taxes, depreciation and amortization during such period (expressed as a positive number), (ii) any overhead, financing charges or other general and administrative expense allocated to the North American Business (including any incremental costs resulting from transferring the Employees to the Buyer Parent's 401(k) employee benefit) (expressed as a positive number) (it being understood and agreed that this addition shall not include charges or other costs and expenses relating to products or services provided by or on behalf of the Buyer or its Affiliates to the Seller at the Seller's request), (iii) any one-time extraordinary or non-recurring items related to the North American Business (which may be positive or negative), (iv) interest income and interest expense during such period (which may be positive or negative), (v) any impact from purchase accounting (which may be positive or negative), and (vi) if recorded, any changes to the value of the potential Earnout Payment. For the avoidance of doubt, the Parties recognize that rent expense related to the Lenexa Real Properties historically recorded as an expense by the Seller will be eliminated to reflect the Lenexa Buyer Sub's purchase of the Lenexa Real Properties for periods after the Closing. . . .

"**North American Business**" means the business of selling Company Products conducted by the Buyer Sub and its Subsidiaries after the Closing in the United States and its territories, Canada and Mexico. For the avoidance of doubt, "North American Business" does not include (i) the business of selling Company Products in the United States and its territories, Canada and Mexico for delivery outside of the United States and its territories, Canada and Mexico, (ii) any sales between the Buyer Sub and its Affiliates and (iii) any costs or expenses (including start-up costs and expenses) for any business outside of the United States and its territories, Canada or Mexico. . . .

"**North American Excess**" means, for any calendar year, the actual EBITDA of the North American Business in such calendar year *minus* the EBITDA Benchmark for such calendar year. . . .

"**Organizational Documents**" means any charter, certificate of incorporation, articles of association, limited liability company agreement, partnership agreement, membership agreement, bylaws, operating agreement, trust agreement or related agreements or similar formation or governing documents and instruments. . . .

Notice that some of the above terms are defined in the definition section (e.g., "Company Assets"), while other terms are defined in context with the location cross referenced in the definition section (e.g. "Agreement"). This is standard practice. Definition sections for acquisition agreements are normally quite long. For example, the one in the Avon/Silpada APA is 15 pages (the body of the agreement is 85 pages in total).

4. Purchase and Sale/Merger

The only sections that vary significantly in an acquisition agreement depending on the structure of the deal are the sections addressing what is being purchased and sold (if the deal is structured as an asset purchase or stock purchase) or what occurs in the merger (if the deal is structured as a merger). Thus, below, there is a separate subsection for each of the three deal structures describing these sections.

a. Asset Purchase

1.   Included and Excluded Assets

An asset purchase agreement will have a section that specifies which target assets bidder is buying and which target assets bidder is not buying. Below is the relevant language from Avon/Silpada APA.

2.1. Purchase and Sale of the Transferred Assets. Upon the terms and subject to the conditions set forth in this Agreement and on the basis of and in reliance upon the representations, warranties, obligations and agreements set forth in this Agreement, upon the occurrence of the Closing as described in Article III and as of the Effective Time, the Seller will sell, transfer, convey, assign and deliver to the Buyer Sub, and the Buyer Sub (or one or more Affiliates of the Buyer Parent as the Buyer Parent may designate) will purchase from the Seller and Silpada International Holdings, all of the Seller's and each Seller Stockholder's right, title and interest in and to all of the assets, properties, rights and claims of the Seller and Silpada International Holdings, whether tangible or intangible (including the Intellectual Property, the IT Assets and the stock of the Transferred Subsidiaries), real, personal or mixed, except for the Excluded Assets (collectively, the "**Transferred Assets**"), free and clear of any Liens, except Permitted Liens.

2.2. Purchase and Sale of the Transferred Assets. Notwithstanding anything to the contrary in Section 2.1, the Buyer Sub shall not purchase, and the Seller and the Seller Stockholders shall retain (and there shall be excluded from the Transferred Assets), the following assets, properties, rights and claims of the Seller (collectively, the "**Excluded Assets**"):

(a) all Cash and Cash Equivalents as of the Effective Time, except Transferred Cash;

(b) the minute books, stock transfer records or other records related to the corporate organization of the Seller;

(c) all personnel records and other records that the Seller is required by law to retain in its possession (provided that the Seller will deliver copies thereof to the Buyer Sub at or prior to the Closing);

(d) all Contracts for investment banking or brokerage services in connection with this Agreement, any Ancillary Agreement and/or the transactions contemplated hereby or thereby; . . .

(f) all Tax assets (including duty and tax refunds and prepayments) of the Seller, any Seller Stockholder or any of their respective Affiliates;

(g) the Seller 401(k) Profit Sharing Plan;

> **(h)**   those Permits that are non-assignable or non-transferable;
>
> **(i)**   the Seller's directors' and officers' insurance policy; and
>
> **(j)**   all rights of the Seller, the Seller Representative and the Seller Stockholders under this Agreement and the Ancillary Agreements.

The above list of Excluded Assets is typical.

Neither a merger agreement nor a stock purchase agreement has an Included and Excluded Assets section because, as you know, with a merger or stock purchase deal structure, it is not possible for bidder to leave target assets behind as part of the merger or stock purchase. Target would have to move assets out of itself prior to the deal.

2.   Assumption of Liabilities

Similar to how an asset purchase agreement handles purchased assets, the agreement typically has a section that specifies which target liabilities bidder is assuming and which target liabilities bidder is not assuming. Below is the relevant language from Avon/Silpada APA.

2.3.   Assumption of Liabilities. Upon the terms and subject to the conditions set forth in this Agreement, upon the occurrence of the Closing as described in Article III and as of the Effective Time, the Buyer Sub shall assume all the Liabilities of the Seller excluding the Excluded Liabilities (the "**Assumed Liabilities**"). The Buyer shall not assume or have any responsibility of any nature with respect to any Liability that is not an Assumed Liability, whether arising out of, relating to, or in connection with the Seller, the Transferred Assets or the Employees.

2.4.   Excluded Liabilities. Notwithstanding anything to the contrary in Section 2.3, the Buyer Sub shall not assume, and the Seller shall retain (and there shall be excluded from the Assumed Liabilities), the following Liabilities of the Seller (collectively, the "**Excluded Liabilities**"):

(a)   any and all Indebtedness as of the Effective Time (including any Company Guaranties), excluding (i) Specified Indebtedness, which shall be an Assumed Liability, and (ii) any Indebtedness the Buyer Sub agrees to assume and that is included in the Estimated Indebtedness Amount and the Actual Indebtedness Amount, which shall be an Assumed Liability;

(b)   any and all Liabilities arising out of, relating to, or in connection with Taxes of the Seller, any Seller Stockholder or any Affiliate or Related Party of the Seller or any Seller Stockholder;

(c)   any and all Liabilities arising out of, relating to, or in connection with any Excluded Asset; and

(d)   any and all Liabilities arising out of, relating to, or in connection with any of the Seller's, the Seller Representative's or any Seller Stockholder's obligations under this Agreement and the Ancillary Agreements.

This language should look familiar because we saw essentially the same thing in Section A.1. of Chapter 4. As we learned in that chapter, keep in mind that bidder may nonetheless be liable on Excluded Liabilities under the common law of successor liability depending on the facts.

As is the case with an Included and Excluded Assets section, neither a merger agreement nor a stock purchase agreement has an Assumption of Liabilities section because with a merger or stock purchase deal structure it is not possible for bidder to leave target liabilities behind as part of the merger or stock purchase. Target would have to move liabilities out of itself prior to the deal.

3.   Purchase Price

The purchase price section specifies how much bidder is paying for target's assets, the form of consideration (cash, stock, debt, or a combination of any of the foregoing), and when bidder is paying the purchase price to target. Below is the relevant language from Avon/Silpada APA.

2.6. Purchase Price. In consideration of the sale to the Buyer Sub of the Transferred Assets and the other transactions contemplated under this Agreement, and provided that all of the conditions precedent to the obligations of the Buyer and the Seller set forth in Article III of this Agreement have been satisfied or waived before or at the Closing as described in Article III, the Buyer will pay or cause to be paid an aggregate purchase price (the "**Purchase Price**") of (x) $627,000,000 in cash at the Closing in accordance with this Section 2.6, *plus* (y) any Earnout Amount to the Seller in accordance with Section 2.9, *plus or minus* (z) any adjustments in accordance with the terms of this Article II.

At the Closing, the Buyer will pay or cause to be paid the following amounts to or on behalf of the Seller and/or the Seller Stockholders:

(a)   an aggregate of $627,000,000 in cash to the Seller, adjusted as follows (as adjusted in accordance with this Section 2.6(a), the "**Closing Cash Payment**"):

(i)   *minus* the amount of the Transaction Fees set forth on the Transaction Fees Statement provided pursuant to Section 3.2(a)(viii),

(ii)   *plus or minus* (as applicable) the amount of the Purchase Price adjustment for Working Capital calculated in accordance with Section 2.7(b)(i),

(iii)   *minus* the amount of the Purchase Price adjustment for any Estimated Indebtedness Amount calculated in Section 2.7(b)(ii),

(iv)   *minus* the Escrow Amount, and

(v)   *minus* the Admin Escrow Amount;

as set forth on the Estimated Closing Schedule (which schedule the Seller will complete and deliver to the Buyer as described in Section 2.7(a));

(b)   the Transaction Fees in cash to the Transaction Advisors on behalf of the Seller Stockholders and/or the Seller, in the amounts set forth on the Transaction Fees Statement provided pursuant to Section 3.2(a)(viii);

(c) $50,755,769 in cash (the "**Escrow Amount**") to the Escrow Agent, which the Escrow Agent will hold in the following interest-bearing subaccounts and release to the Seller, or pay to the Buyer Parent, subject to the terms and conditions of the escrow agreement substantially in the form attached as Exhibit A (the "**Escrow Agreement**"):

> **(i)** $2,525,000 in cash will be held in a subaccount to pay any Post-Closing Purchase Price Adjustment as provided in Section 2.8 (the "**Purchase Price Adjustment Escrow Amount**"); and
>
> **(ii)** $48,230,769 in cash will be held in a subaccount (the "**Indemnity Escrow Account**") to pay any indemnity Claim pursuant to Article VIII or Article IX (the "**Indemnity Escrow Amount**"); and

(d) $3,000,000 in cash (the "**Admin Escrow Amount**") to an account designated by the Seller Representative, which the Seller Representative will hold to fund any actions taken on behalf of the Seller and/or the Seller Stockholders as Seller Representative and the unused portion of which the Seller Representative will release to the Seller and/or the Seller Stockholders at such time(s) as the Seller Representative deems appropriate.

As you can see, the deal consideration consists of cash but only a portion of it was paid by the Buyer at Closing. The Buyer held back funds for, among other things, post-closing adjustments and an indemnity escrow.

Below is a purchase price section from a different asset purchase deal as an example of one involving multiple types of consideration (it is from the Asset Purchase Agreement dated as of September 1, 2011 pursuant to which Liquidity Services, Inc. acquired Jacobs Trading, LLC).

Section 2.06.   *Purchase Price; Allocation of Purchase Price.*

   (a)   The purchase price for the Purchased Assets (the "**Purchase Price**") is:

> **(i)** $80,000,000 in cash (the "**Cash Consideration**");
>
> **(ii)**   900,171 shares of Parent Common Stock (the "**Share Consideration**"); and
>
> **(iii)**   a subordinated, unsecured note of Parent in aggregate principal amount of $40,000,000, in substantially the form of Exhibit B hereto (the "**Note**") (clauses (i) through (iii) collectively referred to as the "**Closing Consideration**"); and
>
> **(iv)**   any Earn-Out Payments made in accordance with Section 2.11.

b.   Stock Purchase

A stock purchase agreement will not have an included and excluded assets section or an assumption of liabilities section because it is not possible for bidder to leave assets or liabilities behind in a deal structured as a stock purchase. Thus, the section addressing what is being purchased and sold and for how much is more straightforward. Below is an example from the Stock Purchase Agreement dated July 15, 2013, pursuant to which Joe's Jeans Inc. agreed to acquire Hudson Clothing Holdings, Inc.

1.1 Purchase and Sale. Subject to the terms and conditions in this Agreement, at the Closing, Buyer shall purchase from Sellers, and Sellers shall sell, assign, transfer and convey to Buyer, all of the Shares, free and clear of any and all Encumbrances, other than restrictions imposed by securities laws applicable to unregistered securities generally and those arising hereunder. In furtherance thereof, at the Closing: (a) Buyer shall (i) pay to Sellers an amount equal to the Estimated Aggregate Closing Consideration, (X) by wire transfer of immediately available funds to the account or accounts specified by Sellers' Representatives to Buyer at least two (2) Business Days prior to the Closing Date and (Y) by a Buyer Note allocated among Sellers in proportion to their respective holdings of Shares as set forth in Schedule 1.1(a) (the "Purchase Price Allocation Schedule"), and (ii) pay, or cause to be paid, on behalf of the Company, the outstanding principal and accrued but unpaid interest on the Hudson Notes as of the Closing, by wire transfer of immediately available funds to the accounts designated by the holders of such promissory notes pursuant to the payoff letters delivered in accordance with Section 1.4(a)(v); and (b) Sellers shall deliver, or cause to be delivered, to Buyer all of the Shares, free and clear of any and all Encumbrances, other than restrictions imposed by securities laws applicable to unregistered securities generally and those arising hereunder.

1.2 Calculation of Closing and Final Consideration.

(a)   For purposes of this Agreement, the following terms shall have the respective meanings assigned to such terms below.

(i)   "Aggregate Closing Consideration" means an amount equal to the result of: (A) $97,595,500, minus (B) the outstanding principal and accrued but unpaid interest on the Hudson Notes as of the Closing, plus (C) the amount, if any, by which Net Working Capital exceeds the Net Working Capital Target, minus (D) the amount, if any, by which Net Working Capital is less than the Net Working Capital Target, minus (E) the Transaction Expenses of the Seller Parties in excess of $2,000,000, minus (F) the amount of any Indebtedness of the Acquired Entities not being repaid as of the Closing Date.

(ii)   "Net Working Capital" means, with respect to the Acquired Entities, the total current assets minus total current liabilities of the Acquired Entities as of the close of business on the Closing Date (including Tax liabilities), in each case excluding the outstanding principal and accrued but unpaid interest on the Hudson Notes as of the Closing, the current portion of Indebtedness, the Transaction Expenses of the Seller Parties up to in the aggregate $2,000,000 and the Transaction Expenses of the Seller Parties in excess of $2,000,000 which are included in the definition of Aggregate Closing Consideration, and determined as set forth on Schedule 1.2(a)(ii).

(b)   At least two (2) Business Days prior to the Closing Date, the Sellers' Representatives shall deliver to Buyer a statement of the Company's estimate of the Aggregate Closing Consideration (such amount, the "Estimated Aggregate Closing Consideration"), including the Company's calculation of each of the components thereof (such statement, the "Estimated Closing Statement"), which estimate shall be prepared by the

> Company in good faith based upon the books and records of the Company and in accordance with Schedule 1.2(a)(ii). . . .

c. Merger

As is the case with a stock purchase agreement, a merger agreement will not have an included and excluded assets section or an assumption of liabilities section because it is not possible for bidder to leave assets or liabilities behind in a deal structured as a merger. Instead, it will have provisions specifying who is merging into whom, the deal consideration, and other mechanics of the merger. Here are sample provisions from the Avis Budget/Zipcar Merger Agreement.

1.1 The Merger.

(a) Upon the terms and subject to the conditions set forth in this Agreement, and in accordance with the General Corporation Law of the State of Delaware (the "DGCL"), at the Effective Time (as defined below) Merger Sub shall be merged with and into the Company. As a result of the Merger, the separate corporate existence of Merger Sub shall cease, and the Company shall continue as the surviving corporation of the Merger (the "Surviving Corporation"). The Merger shall have the effects set forth in the applicable provisions of the DGCL. Without limiting the generality of the foregoing, at the Effective Time, all of the property, rights, privileges, immunities, powers and franchises of the Company and Merger Sub shall vest in the Surviving Corporation, and all of the debts, liabilities and duties of the Company and Merger Sub shall become the debts, liabilities and duties of the Surviving Corporation.

(b) At the Effective Time, the certificate of incorporation of the Company shall, subject to Section 5.12(b), be amended and restated in its entirety to read identically to the certificate of incorporation of Merger Sub as in effect immediately prior to the Effective Time, except that the name of the Surviving Corporation shall be "Zipcar, Inc." (and excluding any provisions with respect to the incorporator or the initial directors) and, as so amended, shall be the certificate of incorporation of the Surviving Corporation until thereafter changed or amended as provided therein or by applicable Law. In addition, at the Effective Time, the bylaws of the Company shall, subject to Section 5.12(b), be amended and restated in their entirety to read identically to the bylaws of Merger Sub as in effect immediately prior to the Effective Time, except that the name of the Surviving Corporation as used therein shall be "Zipcar, Inc." and, as so amended, shall be the bylaws of the Surviving Corporation until thereafter changed or amended as provided therein or by applicable Law. . . .

2.1 Conversion of Securities. At the Effective Time, by virtue of the Merger and without any action on the part of Parent, Merger Sub, the Company or the holders of any of the following securities:

(a) Conversion of Common Stock. Subject to Section 2.2, each share of common stock, par value $0.001 per share (the "Common Stock"), of the Company (a "Share" or collectively, the "Shares") issued and outstanding immediately prior to the Effective Time, other than Shares to be cancelled in accordance with Section 2.1(b) and other than Dissenting Shares (as defined below), shall be converted into the right to receive $12.25 in cash, without interest (the "Per Share Amount").

(b) Cancellation of Treasury Stock and Parent-Owned Stock. All Shares that are held in the treasury of the Company or owned of record by any of the Subsidiaries of the Company (each a "Company Subsidiary" and collectively, the "Company Subsidiaries"), and all Shares owned of record by Parent, Merger Sub or any of their respective wholly-owned Subsidiaries shall be cancelled and shall cease to exist, with no payment being made with respect thereto.

(c) Merger Sub Common Stock. Each share of common stock, par value $0.01 per share, of Merger Sub issued and outstanding immediately prior to the Effective Time shall be converted into and become one newly and validly issued, fully paid and nonassessable share of common stock of the Surviving Corporation.

The cash to be paid upon the conversion of Shares pursuant to Section 2.1(a) is referred to herein as the "Merger Consideration". At the Effective Time, all of the Shares shall cease to be outstanding, shall be cancelled and shall cease to exist, and each certificate (a "Certificate") formerly representing any of the Shares (other than Shares to be cancelled in accordance with Section 2.1(b) and other than Dissenting Shares) shall thereafter represent only the right to receive the Per Share Amount, in each case without interest, subject to compliance with the procedures for surrender of such Shares as set forth in Section 2.2. Notwithstanding anything in this Agreement to the contrary, if, from the date of this Agreement until the Effective Time, the outstanding shares of Common Stock or the securities convertible into or exercisable for shares of Common Stock shall have been changed into a different number of shares or a different class by reason of any reclassification, stock split (including a reverse stock split), recapitalization, split-up, combination, exchange of shares, readjustment, or other similar transaction, or a stock dividend or stock distribution thereon shall be declared with a record date within said period, the Per Share Amount and any other similarly dependent items, as the case may be, shall be appropriately adjusted to provide the holders of Shares the same economic effect as contemplated by this Agreement prior to such event. . . .

5. Exchange Ratios

If the deal is structured as a merger or stock purchase and the deal consideration consists of, or includes, bidder stock, the acquisition agreement will normally specify an "exchange ratio" for determining how many shares will be issued to each target shareholder (an asset purchase agreement does not normally include an exchange ratio because in that deal structure all shares are issued to target as opposed to target's shareholders so there is no need for one). Here is the sample language from the July 21, 2013 merger agreement pursuant to which Spartan Stores agreed to acquire Nash-Finch Company.

> **(c)** **Conversion of Common Stock.** . . . [E]ach share of Nash-Finch Common Stock issued and outstanding immediately prior to the Effective Time (other than Excluded Shares) shall be converted into the right to receive 1.20 (the "**Exchange Ratio**") fully paid and nonassessable shares of Spartan Stores Common Stock (the "**Merger Consideration**"), whereupon such shares of Nash-Finch Common Stock will no longer be outstanding and all rights with respect to each share of Nash-Finch Common Stock will cease to exist, except the right to receive the Merger Consideration, any cash in lieu of fractional shares payable pursuant to Section 3.7, and any dividends or other distributions payable pursuant to Section 3.4, upon surrender of Certificates or Book-Entry Shares, in accordance with Section 3.3. No interest shall be paid or will accrue on any payment to holders of Certificates or Book-Entry Shares pursuant to the provisions of this Article III.

If bidder is public, its stock price will fluctuate in the trading markets during the gap period. To account for these fluctuations, bidder and target may instead agree to use a floating exchange ratio, i.e., a ratio that changes with fluctuations in bidder's stock. Here is the sample language from the November 8, 2012 merger agreement pursuant to which priceline.com Incorporated ("Parent") agreed to acquire KAYAK Software Corporation (the "Company").

> **(a)** **Merger Consideration.** Each share of Class A common stock, par value $0.001 per share (the "**Class A Common Stock**"), and each share of Class B common stock, par value $0.001 per share (the "**Class B Common Stock**"), of the Company (collectively, the "**Shares**") issued and outstanding immediately prior to the Effective Time (other than (i) Shares owned by Parent, Merger Sub or any other direct or indirect wholly-owned subsidiary of Parent and Shares owned by the Company or any direct or indirect wholly-owned subsidiary of the Company, and in each case not held on behalf of third parties, and (ii) Shares that are owned by stockholders that have perfected and not withdrawn a demand for appraisal rights pursuant to § 262 of the DGCL ("**Dissenting Stockholders**") ((i) and (ii), collectively, the "**Excluded Shares**")) shall be converted into the right to receive, at the election of the holder thereof as provided in this Article IV, the following consideration:
>
> **(i)** Subject to Section 4.2, each Share that is a Cash Election Share shall be converted into the right to receive $40.00 in cash (the "**Per Share Cash Consideration**").
>
> **(ii)** Subject to Section 4.2, each Share that is a Stock Election Share shall be converted into a portion of a share (the "**Exchange Ratio**") of common stock, par value $0.008 per share, of Parent (the "**Parent Common Stock**") equal to the quotient (the "**Exchange Ratio**") determined by dividing (A) $40.00 by (B) the Parent Trading Price (the "**Per Share Stock Consideration**"); provided that (x) if the number determined by dividing $40.00 by the Parent Trading Price is less than or equal to 0.05728, then the Exchange Ratio shall be 0.05728, and (y) if the number determined by dividing $40.00 by the Parent Trading Price is greater than

or equal to 0.07001, then the Exchange Ratio shall be 0.07001. . . .

The merger agreement defines "Parent Trading Price" as follows: "[T]he term **"Parent Trading Price"** means the thirty (30) day aggregate volume-weighted average per share price, rounded to two decimal points, of Parent Common Stock on the NASDAQ Global Select Market ("**NASDAQ**") (as reported by The Wall Street Journal) for the period of the thirty (30) consecutive trading days ending on the second-to-last full trading day prior to the Closing Date."

The above provision makes a distinction between "Per Share Cash Consideration" and "Per Share Stock Consideration" because priceline.com and KAYAK agreed to allow KAYAK's shareholders to elect which form of consideration they wanted.

The proviso at the end of (a)(ii) is an example of what M&A attorneys call a "collar." It provides both a floor and a cap on the number of shares that bidder will issue at closing. The basic idea behind including a collar is to protect the parties against an extreme change in bidder's stock price between signing and closing.

EXERCISE 5.3

1.   Assume that you own 1,000 shares of KAYAK Class B Common Stock and have elected to receive priceline.com Common Stock in the deal. How many shares of priceline.com Common Stock will you be issued following closing of the deal if the Parent Trading Price is $620.00? $750.00? $500.00?

2.   Assume that the Closing Date for the priceline.com/KAYAK deal occurred on June 4, 2013. What is the Parent Trading Price?

6.   Post-Closing Purchase Price Adjustment

Bidder often bases what it is willing to pay for target's business in part on target's recent financial performance, including performance right up to the date of closing. Because financial statements take some time to prepare, financial data through closing will not be available until after closing. Thus, acquisition agreements frequently include a post-closing purchase price adjustment section that increases or decreases the purchase price ultimately paid by bidder once target financial statements as of the closing date are available. Below is the relevant section from the Avon/Silpada APA.

2.8.   Post-Closing Purchase Price Adjustment.

   (a)   The Purchase Price will be adjusted after the Closing in accordance with this Section 2.8 dollar for dollar:

   (i)   upward by the amount by which the Estimated Indebtedness Amount exceeds the Actual Indebtedness Amount (as determined in accordance with the provisions set forth below), or

   (ii)   downward by the amount by which the Actual Indebtedness Amount exceeds the Estimated Indebtedness Amount; and

(iii)   upward by the amount by which the Actual Working Capital Amount (as determined in accordance with the provisions set forth below) exceeds the Estimated Working Capital Amount, or

(iv)   downward by the amount by which the Estimated Working Capital Amount exceeds the Actual Working Capital Amount; and

(v)   upward by the amount of the Actual Cash and Cash Equivalents Amount.

The "**Post-Closing Purchase Price Adjustment**" will be the net amount of the sum of the adjustments made pursuant to clauses (i) or (ii) (whichever applies) *plus* clauses (iii) or (iv) (whichever applies) *plus* clause (v).

(b)   If the Post-Closing Purchase Price Adjustment results in the upward adjustment of the Purchase Price, no later than the fifth (5th) Business Day after the earliest of:

(i)   if the Buyer has not received a Seller Objection Notice within the 30-day period after the Buyer gives the Seller Representative the Actual Closing Schedule, the expiration of such 30-day period, and

(ii)   if the Buyer has received a Seller Objection Notice within such period, (A) the resolution by the Buyer and the Seller Representative of all differences regarding the Actual Closing Schedule and the Purchase Price adjustment amount, or (B) the receipt of the Appointed Arbiter determination as set forth in Section 2.8(g),

then, (x) the Buyer will pay to the Seller in cash the amount of the upward adjustment; and (y) the Seller Representative and the Buyer will deliver Joint Written Instructions instructing the Escrow Agent to pay to the Seller the entire Purchase Price Adjustment Escrow Amount in immediately available funds within two (2) Business Days after receipt of the Joint Written Instructions.

(c)   If the Post-Closing Purchase Price Adjustment results in the downward adjustment of the Purchase Price, no later than the fifth (5th) Business Day after the earliest of:

(i)   if the Buyer has not received a Seller Objection Notice within the 30-day period after the Buyer gives the Seller Representative the Actual Closing Schedule, the expiration of such 30-day period, and

(ii)   if the Buyer has received a Seller Objection Notice within such period, (A) the resolution by the Buyer and the Seller Representative of all differences regarding the Actual Closing Schedule and the Purchase Price adjustment amount, or (B) the receipt of the Appointed Arbiter determination as set forth in Section 2.8(g), the Seller Representative and the Buyer will deliver Joint Written Instructions to the Escrow Agent instructing the Escrow Agent to pay, in immediately available funds within two (2) Business Days after receipt of the Joint Written Instructions, from the Purchase Price Adjustment Escrow Amount:

(x)   to the Buyer Parent (A) if the downward adjustment amount equals or is less than the Purchase Price Adjustment Escrow Amount, an amount equal to the downward adjustment in the Purchase Price, and (B) if the downward adjustment amount exceeds the Purchase Price Adjustment Escrow Amount, the Purchase Price Adjustment Escrow Amount; and

(y)   if the downward adjustment amount is less than the Purchase Price Adjustment Escrow Amount, to the Seller from the Purchase Price Adjustment Escrow Amount the balance of the Purchase Price Adjustment Escrow Amount.

In addition, if the downward adjustment amount exceeds the Purchase Price Adjustment Escrow Amount, on the date that the Seller Representative and the Buyer deliver Joint Written Instructions to the Escrow Agent pursuant to the foregoing sentence, the Seller will pay (and if the Seller does not pay, the Seller Stockholders on a joint and several basis will pay) to the Buyer Parent by wire transfer of immediately available funds to the account designated by the Buyer Parent the amount by which the downward adjustment amount exceeds the Purchase Price Adjustment Escrow Amount.

(d)   The Buyer will prepare in good faith and deliver to the Seller Representative within 60 calendar days after the Closing Date a schedule in the form attached as Exhibit C (the "**Actual Closing Schedule**") that sets forth the Buyer's reasonable calculation of the actual total amount of:

(i)   Working Capital as of 11:59 p.m. Central Time on the Closing Date (the "**Actual Working Capital Amount**"); and

(ii)   any Specified Indebtedness and any other Indebtedness as of 11:59 p.m. Central Time on the Closing Date that the Buyer Sub has agreed to assume and that is not included in the Actual Working Capital Amount (the "**Actual Indebtedness Amount**"); and

(iii)   any Transferred Cash as of 11:59 p.m. Central Time on the Closing Date that is not included in the Actual Working Capital Amount (the "**Actual Cash and Cash Equivalents Amount**").

The Buyer will prepare the Actual Indebtedness Amount, the Actual Working Capital Amount and the Actual Cash and Cash Equivalents Amount in accordance with this Section 2.8, Exhibits B and C and the methodologies (including with respect to application of GAAP, classification and estimation) used in the preparation of the Interim Balance Sheet, and deliver the Actual Closing Schedule accompanied by a certification to such effect from an executive officer of the Buyer Sub.

(e)   The Seller Representative must give written notice (the "**Seller Objection Notice**") to the Buyer specifying in reasonable detail the Seller Representative's objections to any amount reflected on the Actual Closing Schedule within 30 calendar days after its receipt of the Actual Closing Schedule. Any item on the Actual Closing Schedule to which the Seller Representative does not timely object in a Seller Objection Notice will be deemed to be accepted by the Seller Representative; and any amounts included within the item will be deemed to be final, binding and conclusive. If the Seller Representative does not give a Seller Objection Notice within the 30-day period, then the Buyer's determinations of the amounts on the Actual Closing Schedule will be final, binding and conclusive on the Parties.

(f)   If the Seller Representative gives the Buyer a Seller Objection

Notice within 30 calendar days after its receipt of the Actual Closing Schedule, then the Buyer and the Seller Representative will negotiate in good faith to resolve any disputed items concerning the Actual Closing Schedule for the 20 calendar days after the Buyer's receipt of the Seller Objection Notice, and any such items (and any amounts included within such items) resolved during such negotiations will be final, binding and conclusive on the Parties.

(g)   If the Buyer and the Seller Representative are unable to resolve all disputed items within the 20-day period set forth in Section 2.8(f), then the Buyer and the Seller Representative will submit only those items remaining in dispute for resolution to the Appointed Arbiter. The Buyer and the Seller Representative will, and will cause their respective accountants to, cooperate fully with the Appointed Arbiter to facilitate its resolution of the dispute, including by providing and explaining as requested the information, data and work papers used by each Party to prepare the Actual Closing Schedule and their interpretation of the dispute. The Appointed Arbiter will determine and report to the Buyer and the Seller Representative its determination on the remaining disputed items submitted for resolution (and only such remaining disputed items submitted for resolution) within 15 Business Days after the dispute is submitted to the Appointed Arbiter, and the Appointed Arbiter's determination will be final, binding and conclusive on the Buyer and the Seller, except to correct manifest clerical or mathematical errors. The Buyer (1/2) and the Seller (1/2) will bear equally the fees, costs and expenses of the Appointed Arbiter.

(h)   After delivery of the Actual Closing Schedule, the Buyer will provide the Seller Representative and its Representatives, and the Seller will provide the Buyer and its Representatives, reasonable access during normal business hours and without significant disruption to the business of the Buyer or the Seller (as applicable) (i) to the books and records in their possession or under their control containing information directly relevant to the Actual Closing Schedule, Estimated Closing Schedule or Seller Objection Notice (as applicable) and (ii) to the employees or other Representatives responsible for preparing the Actual Closing Schedule, Estimated Closing Schedule or Seller Objection Notice (as applicable). However, in no event will any Party be required to provide access to, or be deemed to have waived any privilege with respect to, any books, records or other information that it reasonably believes is privileged.

(i)   No single item will be given duplicative effect when calculating the various adjustments to the Purchase Price under this Section 2.8.

Notice that the section addresses how the purchase price adjustment is calculated, how money changes hands for any adjustment, and how any dispute regarding the calculation is to be resolved.

7.   Earnouts

An earnout is a provision of an acquisition agreement that provides for bidder making an additional purchase price payment (or payments) if target's business meets specified milestones post-closing. Earnouts are used most often when target is insisting on a higher purchase price based on what bidder views as overly optimistic projections of the post-closing performance of target's business. Thus, bidder agrees to pay the extra amount target is demanding but only if target's business hits the post-closing projections. An earnout also incentivizes any former target employee shareholders whom bidder has kept on post-closing to work hard. Additionally, an earnout can allow bidder to, in a sense, partially fund the acquisition through the future earning power of target's business.

Below is the earnout provision from the Avon/Silpada APA.

2.9. Earnout.

(a)   As part of the Purchase Price, the Buyer shall pay or cause to be paid to the Seller the Earnout Amount as determined in accordance with this Section 2.9 (the "**Earnout Payment**"), upon the later to occur of (x) thirty-one (31) days after the delivery by the Buyer Sub of the Earnout Statement pursuant to Section 2.9(d) or (y) ten (10) days following the resolution of all disputed matters properly included in an Earnout Statement Objection Notice in accordance with Section 2.9(e). The Earn-out Payment shall be paid by wire transfer of immediately available funds pursuant to wire transfer instructions provided by the Seller to the Buyer Parent at least two Business Days prior to the date the Earnout Payment is required to be paid.

(b)   The amount of the Earnout Payment (the "**Earnout Amount**") shall be equal to the greater of (1) the product of (x) 2.26 *times* (y) the Average North American Excess, and (2) $0. For example, if the Average North American Excess is $25.0 million, the Earnout Amount would be $56.5 million (2.26 x $25.0 million).

(c)   Within ninety (90) days following each of December 31, 2012 and December 31, 2013, the Buyer Sub shall prepare and deliver to the Buyer Parent and the Seller Representative a statement reflecting its good faith calculations of the EBITDA and the North American Excess for the preceding calendar year. The statement shall be prepared in accordance with this Agreement and GAAP and shall be accompanied by any financial statements of the North American Business used in calculating EBITDA, all of which shall be certified by the Chief Financial Officer (or officer of equivalent or similar position) of the Buyer Sub. The Buyer Parent and the Seller Representative may discuss the calculation of EBITDA and the North American Excess and make any mutually agreed changes, but the failure to do so shall not prejudice the rights of any Party pursuant to this Section 2.9.

(d)   Within ninety (90) days after December 31, 2014, the Buyer Sub shall prepare and deliver to the Buyer Parent and the Seller Representative a statement (the "**Earnout Statement**") setting forth its good faith calcu-lation of the EBITDA and the North American Excess for the 2012, 2013 and 2014 calendar years (which, for the avoidance of doubt, may be different than those provided under Section 2.9(c)), the Average North American Excess and the Earnout Amount. The EBITDA and the North American Excess for the 2012, 2013 and 2014 calendar years shall be prepared in accordance with this Agreement and GAAP and shall be accompanied by any financial statements of the North American Business used in calculating EBITDA, all of which shall be certified by the Chief

Financial Officer (or officer of equivalent or similar position) of the Buyer Sub.

(e)   The Seller Representative must give written notice to the Buyer Parent, and the Buyer Parent must give written notice to the Seller Representative (each, an "**Earnout Statement Objection Notice**"), specifying in reasonable detail the Seller Representative's or the Buyer Parent's objections, as the case may be, to any amount reflected on the Earnout Statement within 30 calendar days after receipt of the Earnout Statement. Any item on the Earnout Statement to which the Seller Representative and the Buyer Parent do not timely object in an Earnout Statement Objection Notice will be deemed to be accepted by the Seller Representative and the Buyer Parent; and any amounts included within such item will be deemed to be final, binding and conclusive. If the Seller Representative and the Buyer Parent do not give an Earnout Statement Objection Notice within the 30-day period, then the Buyer Sub's determinations of the amounts on the Earnout Statement will be final, binding and conclusive on the Parties.

(f)   If the Seller Representative gives the Buyer Parent, or the Buyer Parent gives the Seller Representative, an Earnout Statement Objection Notice within 30 calendar days after receipt of the Earnout Statement, then the Buyer Parent and the Seller Representative will negotiate in good faith to resolve any disputed items concerning the Earnout Statement for the 20 calendar days after receipt of any Earnout Statement Objection Notice, and any such items (and any amounts included within such items) resolved during such negotiations will be final, binding and conclusive on the Parties.

(g)   If the Buyer Parent and the Seller Representative are unable to resolve all disputed items within the 20-day period set forth in Section 2.9(f), then the Buyer Parent and the Seller Representative will submit only those items remaining in dispute for resolution to the Appointed Arbiter. The Buyer Parent and the Seller Representative will, and will cause their respective accountants to, cooperate fully with the Appointed Arbiter to facilitate its resolution of the dispute, including by providing and explaining as requested the information, data and work papers used by such Party to prepare the Earnout Statement, the Earnout Statement Objection Notice and their interpretation of the dispute. The Appointed Arbiter will determine and report to the Buyer Parent and the Seller Representative its determination on the remaining disputed items submitted for resolution (and only such remaining disputed items submitted for resolution) within 15 Business Days after the dispute is submitted to the Appointed Arbiter, and the Appointed Arbiter's determination will be final, binding and conclusive on the Parties, except to correct manifest clerical or mathematical errors. The Buyer Parent and the Seller will bear equally the fees, costs and expenses of the Appointed Arbiter.

(h)   After delivery of the Earnout Statement, the Buyer Sub will provide the Buyer Parent, the Seller Representative and their respective Representatives reasonable access during normal business hours and without significant disruption to the business of the Buyer Sub, the Buyer Parent or the Seller (as applicable) (i) to the books and records in their possession or under their control containing information directly relevant to the Earnout Statement or the Earnout Statement Objection Notice (as applicable) and (ii) to the employees or other Representatives responsible

> for preparing the Earnout Statement or the Earnout Statement Objection Notice (as applicable). However, in no event will any Party be required to provide access to, or be deemed to have waived any privilege with respect to, any books, records or other information that it reasonably believes is privileged.
>
> [See Section E.3. of this chapter for definitions of various terms used in the above provisions.]

Earnout provisions are very deal specific and heavily negotiated. The key part is the milestone that triggers the earnout payment or payments. Common milestones include target's business achieving a specified amount of sales or EBITDA within a certain time period.

QUESTIONS

1. How is the Silpada earnout calculated?

2. What happens if the parties do not agree on the calculation?

3. By when does Avon have to make the earnout payment?

A big and contentious issue in negotiating an earnout is control over target's business during the earnout period. Target's shareholders will want a high level of control over target's business in an effort to ensure that the business meets the earnout milestone. They will also want bidder to provide some level of support to and refrain from taking actions that might cannibalize sales. Conversely, bidder will want the freedom to integrate target's business into its operations as it sees fit. Bidder will also be concerned about decisions that favor the short term goal of hitting the earnout milestone at the expense of the long term health of the business, such as reallocating funds from product development to marketing. Thus, the M&A attorneys negotiating the earnout provision will have to balance these competing objectives in reaching a solution that is amenable to bidder and target and then reduce it to contractual language. This is no easy task and may nonetheless be at the center of post-deal litigation as the next case demonstrates.

O'TOOL v. GENMAR HOLDINGS, INC.
United States Court of Appeals, Tenth Circuit
387 F.3d 1188 (2004)

BRISCOE, Circuit Judge.

Defendants Genmar Holdings, Inc., Genmar Industries, Inc., and Genmar Manufacturing of Kansas, Inc., appeal a jury verdict in favor of plaintiffs Horizon Holdings, LLC (f/k/a Horizon Marine LC) and Geoffrey Pepper on plaintiffs' claim for breach of contract. . . .

I.

Pepper started working in the recreational boat manufacturing industry in 1977 and he held a variety of engineering and management positions with approximately six different manufacturers between 1977 and 1997. In early 1997, Pepper, his wife, and a group of investors purchased an industrial building in Junction City, Kansas, and formed their own recreational boat manufacturing company, Horizon Marine LC (Horizon). Pepper served as president, and as such was responsible for the overall operations of the company. Pepper's wife Phyllis assumed an administrative role in the business. Pepper's daughter and son-in-law, plaintiffs Cassandra and John O'Tool, were initial investors in Horizon. Cassandra served as Horizon's director of human resources, and John oversaw Horizon's manufacturing operations.

Pepper's initial goal was to manufacture and sell aluminum jon boats (a/k/a utility boats) he had designed. He hoped to subsequently expand Horizon's product line to include pontoon and deck boats. Horizon began producing jon boats in October 1997. By early 1998, Horizon had not earned a profit and, in Pepper's words, was "still struggling." Pepper was optimistic, however, that Horizon was making "significant progress" in terms of sales and production, and he believed Horizon would begin earning a profit by the summer of 1998.

In August 1998, defendants Genmar Holdings, Inc., and Genmar Industries, Inc., (collectively "Genmar") approached Pepper about purchasing Horizon. Genmar, the world's largest recreational boat manufacturer, manufactures approximately eighteen different brands of boats in approximately twelve manufacturing plants throughout the United States. At the time it approached Horizon, Genmar primarily produced "deep V" boats typically used by fishermen in the northern part of the United States. Genmar wanted to expand into the southern boat market by producing entry-level, shallow-bottom boats, such as the aluminum jon boats being produced by Horizon. Genmar viewed Horizon as a potential future competitor in the southern boat market and believed that, by purchasing Horizon, it could enter the southern boat market sooner than if it created its own manufacturing facility and boat line.

Negotiations culminated in the sale of Horizon to Genmar in December 1998. Under the terms of the parties' written purchase agreement, Genmar created a new subsidiary, defendant Genmar Manufacturing of Kansas, LLC (GMK), that assumed all of the assets and liabilities of Horizon. GMK also offered written employment agreements to Pepper, who assumed the presidency of GMK, and to Pepper's daughter and son-in-law, both of whom assumed managerial positions with GMK similar to the ones they held with Horizon.

The purchase price paid by Genmar for Horizon was comprised of two components: (1) cash consideration of $2.3 million dollars; and (2) "earn-out consideration." The purchase agreement detailed how the "earn-out consideration" was to be calculated:

> For a period of five (5) years from and after the Closing, Purchaser agrees to remit to Seller as additional consideration and part of the aggregate Purchase Price hereunder an amount equal to a percentage of all annual

gross revenues ("Annual Gross Revenues"), subject to achieving certain gross profit percentages [13% or more in the first year of GMK's operation, and 14% or more thereafter], from the sale of (i) Seller's Horizon (or any direct successor) brand boats, trailers, pre-rigging, parts and accessories (collectively the "Seller Products") and (ii) the manufacture of Purchaser's boats (Genmar Holdings' brands) in Seller's Junction City, Kansas plant facility after the Closing Date, in each case of (i) and (ii) above based upon the annual published dealer list price to a maximum of $5,200,000 (the "Earn-Out Consideration").

At closing, Genmar made an advance payment of $200,000 of earn-out consideration to Horizon, which amount was to be deducted from earn-out consideration payments due to Horizon after the second quarter of 1999.

Pepper's understanding of the earn-out provision was that production of Horizon boats and accessories would afford GMK the most potential for achieving gross revenues and in turn maximizing the earn-out consideration. This was because, in addition to receiving a dealer list price for each Horizon boat sold to a dealer, GMK would receive gross revenues for engines, trailers, and other accessories that were sold with the Horizon boats. Pepper was confident he could achieve the maximum earn-out consideration because, in part, Genmar executives had assured him that Horizon boats would "be the champion of th[e][GMK] facility."

Pepper's expectations and assumptions for GMK's operations were challenged almost immediately after the deal was closed. In early 1999, Pepper was informed by Genmar of a possible trademark conflict with the Horizon brand name and the Horizon brand of boats was renamed "Nova" (one of two trademark names already registered by Genmar). Further, and more problematically for Pepper, it became evident in early 1999 that two of Genmar's own brands of boats, Ranger and Crestliner, would become the priority of the GMK facility. Specifically, Genmar instructed Pepper that, in the event of production conflicts, GMK should give priority to production of Crestliner boats. Genmar also instructed Pepper to focus all of GMK's engineering efforts on developing fifteen new Ranger boat designs.

Genmar's focus on the Crestliner and Ranger brands created dual problems for Pepper and GMK. First, the design of new Ranger models was expensive for GMK (who was expected by Genmar to bear all design and production costs) since the dimensions and materials for the Ranger models were completely different than the existing Nova designs. Second, the Ranger models were significantly harder to build than the relatively simple designs of the Nova and Crestliner boats. That fact, combined with GMK's inexperienced workforce, resulted in longer production times and higher costs for the Ranger boats.

Genmar's focus on the Crestliner and Ranger brands also created a dilemma for Pepper. As noted, the parties' written purchase agreement provided that the earn-out consideration to be paid to Horizon/Pepper by Genmar would be based on GMK's gross revenues meeting or exceeding a certain level. However, because GMK was inefficient at building the new Ranger models, and because it received only a set reimbursement for each Ranger boat (equal to its estimated cost of production), it actually lost money on each Ranger boat produced. With respect to the Crestliner boats, GMK also received only a set reimbursement (again equal to its estimated cost of production), and received no revenues from engines, trailers, or accessories sold with the Crestliner boats.

In May 1999, Pepper wrote a lengthy memo to the president and CEO of Genmar, Grant Oppegaard, expressing his concerns over Genmar's strategy for the GMK facility. In pertinent part, the memo stated: "In order to accomplish our goal [of profitability], we need to get good at something quickly. . . . To infuse 15 totally different Ranger models into our manufacturing operations would spell disaster at this time." Pepper received no response to his memo. Instead, Genmar continued to instruct Pepper and GMK to give priority to producing Crestliner and Ranger boats.

By November 1999, GMK's gross revenues and production were far under budget. Specifically, GMK's gross revenues fell $360,000 short of budget, or $222,000 actual gross revenues versus $582,000 budgeted gross revenues. At the same time, GMK's backlog of orders for Nova boats grew by more than 300,000 units to a total of 616,000 units. The results for December 1999 were similar. GMK's gross revenues fell $209,000 short of budget, or $372,000 versus $581,000. GMK's controller and vice-president of finance attributed these problems to Genmar's continued focus on Crestliner and Ranger boats at the expense of Nova boats.

On December 21, 1999, Pepper was called to a meeting at Genmar's corporate offices in Minneapolis, Minnesota. During the meeting, Oppegaard criticized Pepper's performance as president of GMK and effectively demoted him, offering him an undefined engineering position with Genmar. Oppegaard further instructed GMK to cease production of Nova pontoon and deck boats, and to increase its emphasis on production of Ranger boats.

In February 2000, Pepper asked to meet with Oppegaard to address his concerns about the detrimental effect of Genmar's strategies on Horizon's and Pepper's ability to achieve the earn-out consideration in the purchase agreement. One of Oppegaard's junior executives refused Pepper's request, stating Oppegaard was "not interested in talking about your contracts at all."

On April 5, 2000, Genmar terminated Pepper, his daughter, and his son-in-law from their respective positions at GMK. Under the terms of his employment contract with Genmar, Pepper was prohibited from working in the recreational boat manufacturing industry for a period of two years. Following plaintiffs' terminations, Genmar began converting, or "flipping," GMK's existing Nova dealers to other Genmar brands. Effective July 2001, GMK, at Genmar's direction, completely stopped manufacturing the Nova brand of boats.

Genmar closed the GMK facility in May 2002 and consolidated manufacturing of its aluminum boats into another facility. According to Genmar's estimates, it lost approximately $15 million dollars on the GMK transaction, and GMK never showed a profit. Genmar acknowledged, however, that during the years of GMK's operation, the Ranger and Crestliner subsidiaries were profitable, as was Genmar as a whole. Genmar further acknowledged these profits were attributable, in part, to production of boats at the GMK facility. Genmar also acknowledged its Crestliner manufacturing plant, which prior to the Horizon acquisition produced Ranger aluminum boats, performed better from a financial standpoint after the Ranger production was shifted to the GMK facility. Finally, Genmar acknowledged that it continues to manufacture and sell boats based on designs created by Pepper.

II.

On April 20, 2001, plaintiffs (Horizon, Pepper, his daughter, and son-in-law) filed suit against Genmar. . . . Horizon and Pepper asserted claims for . . . breach of the purchase agreement . . . .

The jury found in favor of Pepper and Horizon on their claim for breach of the purchase agreement and awarded them $2.5 million in damages. . . .

Following the district court's entry of judgment, defendants filed a renewed motion for judgment as a matter of law, or for remittitur or a new trial. . . . The district court denied defendants' motion . . . .

III.

Judgment as a matter of law-breach of contract claim

Defendants contend the district court erred in denying their motion for judgment as a matter of law on the breach of contract claim asserted by plaintiffs Horizon and Pepper. . . .

It is uncontroverted that the parties' written purchase agreement contains a choice-of-law provision stating, in pertinent part, that the agreement "shall be construed, governed by and enforced in accordance with the internal laws of the state of Delaware." Because Kansas generally recognizes such contractual choice-of-law provisions, we are bound to apply Delaware law in interpreting and enforcing the parties' agreement.

During the district court proceedings, Pepper and Horizon asserted alternative theories in support of their breach of contract claim: (1) that defendants breached the express terms of the parties' written purchase agreement; and (2) that defendants breached the implied covenant of good faith and fair dealing associated with the agreement. Defendants challenged both theories in their motion for JMOL. In denying defendants' motion, the district court concluded "there was ample evidence presented at trial to support" the implied covenant theory, and accordingly "decline[d] to address" the breach of express terms theory. On appeal, the parties likewise focus almost exclusively on plaintiffs' implied covenant theory.

"Under Delaware law, an implied covenant of good faith and fair dealing inheres in every contract." *Chamison v. Healthtrust, Inc.*, 735 A.2d 912, 920 (Del. Ch. 1999). "As such, a party to a contract has made an implied covenant to interpret and to act reasonably upon contractual language that is on its face reasonable." *Id.* "This implied covenant is a judicial convention designed to protect the spirit of an agreement when, without violating an express term of the agreement, one side uses oppressive or underhanded tactics to deny the other side the fruits of the parties' bargain." *Id.* "It requires the [finder of fact] to extrapolate the spirit of the agreement from its express terms and based on that 'spirit,' determine the terms that the parties would have bargained for to govern the dispute had they foreseen the circumstances under which their dispute arose." *Id.* at 920-21. The "extrapolated term" is then "implie[d] . . . into the express agreement as an implied covenant," and its breach is treated "as a breach of the contract." *Id.* "The implied covenant cannot contravene the parties' express agreement and cannot be used to forge a new agreement beyond the scope of the written contract." *Id.*

The overarching theme of the breach of implied covenant theory asserted by Pepper and Horizon is "that Genmar's entire course of conduct frustrated and impaired [their] realization of the Earn-Out" provided in the parties' agreement. In particular, Pepper and Horizon point to the following actions taken by Genmar following its acquisition of Horizon: (1) changing the brand name of the boats from Horizon to Nova; (2) immediately shifting GMK's production priority from Horizon/Nova boats to Ranger and Crestliner boats; (3) requiring GMK, rather than Ranger or another subsidiary, to bear the costs of designing and producing the new line of Ranger boats; (4) failing to give Pepper operational control over GMK; (5) reimbursing GMK only at "standard cost" for the manufacture of Ranger and Crestliner boats, thereby impairing realization of the earn-out triggers; (6) discontinuing the Horizon/Nova brand of boats; (7) "flipping" Horizon/Nova dealers to other Genmar brands; and (8) shutting down the GMK facility.

Defendants contend all of these actions were expressly contemplated under the terms of the parties' agreement and thus could not form the basis for a violation of the implied covenant of good faith and fair dealing. For reasons discussed below, we disagree.

Changing name of boats from Horizon to Nova. The earn-out provision of the parties' agreement stated, in pertinent part, that calculation of earn-out consideration would be based on the sale of "Horizon (or any direct successor) brand boats." According to defendants, this language "specifically contemplate[d]" the change from the Horizon brand name to the Nova brand name. Defendants further argue that the brand name change occurred at the same time the agreement was finalized, and thus "was part of the agreement, not a violation of it."

We reject defendants' arguments. Although it is true the agreement was broadly worded to encompass GMK's sales of any successor brands of boats, there is otherwise no discussion in the agreement of when or how this might occur. Further, in light of the evidence presented at trial, we conclude the jury reasonably could have inferred that defendants fully intended, prior to signing the agreement with Pepper and Horizon, to change the brand name of the Horizon boats, yet failed to reveal that fact to Pepper and Horizon in a timely fashion (i.e., in time to allow Pepper and Horizon to consider it as part of the contract negotiations). Thus, we conclude the immediate brand name change was not expressly contemplated by the terms of the agreement and could have been considered under plaintiffs' breach of implied covenant theory.

Giving production priority to non-Horizon boats. The parties' agreement does, as noted by defendants, make reference to GMK producing other Genmar boat brands. For example, the earn-out provision of the agreement indicates that Pepper and Horizon were to receive credit for sales "of Purchaser's boats (Genmar Holdings' brands)." Importantly, however, the agreement is otherwise silent with respect to which brand of boats was to receive production priority from GMK. Thus, we conclude defendants' immediate post-acquisition decision to emphasize the production of Ranger and Crestliner boats over the production of Horizon/Nova boats was not expressly contemplated by the terms of the parties' agreement.

Design and production costs of Ranger boats. The parties' agreement contains no mention of the fact that GMK would be required to bear the costs of designing and producing a new line of Ranger boats, and defendants do not suggest otherwise.

Failure to give Pepper operational control over GMK. Again, the parties' agreement contains no mention of precisely how management decisions at GMK would be made, and defendants do not suggest otherwise. Defendants, however, point to language in Pepper's employment contract specifying that he would be "subject to the general supervision," and would act "pursuant to the orders, advice, and direction," of Genmar. Although this language states the obvious, i.e., that Pepper was required to answer to and follow the directions of Genmar, it does not expressly address the issue raised by plaintiffs, i.e., how much authority Pepper retained to determine production priorities for the GMK facility.

"Flipping" Horizon/Nova dealers to other Genmar brands. Nothing in the parties' agreement addresses defendants' authority to "flip" Horizon/Nova dealers to other Genmar brands, and defendants do not assert otherwise.

Closing GMK facility. Finally, nothing in the parties' agreement directly addresses the possible closing of the GMK facility. Thus, defendants' decision to close the GMK facility was not expressly covered or authorized under the terms of the agreement.

Defendants also argue that plaintiffs' "implied covenant claim . . . fails because there is no evidence the parties would have agreed to the obligations the District Court imposed by implication." For example, defendants contend there is no "basis to find that the parties 'would have agreed' that Pepper would have complete discretion to refuse to manufacture Ranger and Crestliner boats." "Nor," defendants argue, "is there any basis to find that the parties 'would have agreed' to maintain the Horizon name."

Defendants' arguments, in our view, ignore the spirit of the parties' agreement. As noted, the agreement expressly stated the purchase price paid by defendants to Pepper/Horizon would be comprised of two components: (1) cash consideration upon closing; and (2) earn-out consideration, based upon GMK meeting or exceeding certain gross revenue goals, for five years following closing. The obvious spirit of this latter component was that Pepper, as president of GMK, would be given a fair opportunity to operate the company in such a fashion as to maximize the earn-out consideration available under the agreement (approximately $5.2 million dollars over five years).

With that spirit in mind, we conclude a reasonable finder of fact could have concluded the parties (had they actually thought about it) would not have simultaneously included within the agreement provisions expressly allowing Genmar to: (1) immediately change the brand name of the boats designed and produced by GMK; (2) set production schedules or priorities that effectively reduced the maximum earn-out consideration available to Pepper; (3) impose significant design and production costs upon GMK for other Genmar brands of boats, while simultaneously limiting the amount of reimbursement GMK could obtain for actually producing other Genmar brands of boats to the "standard cost" of production; or (4) "flip" Horizon dealers to other brands of Genmar boats. *See generally Katz v. Oak Indus., Inc.*, 508 A.2d 873, 880 (Del. Ch. 1986) (stating the legal test for implying contractual obligations is whether it was "clear from what was expressly agreed upon that the parties who negotiated the express terms of the contract would have agreed to proscribe the act later complained of as a breach of the implied covenant of good faith-had they thought to negotiate with respect to that matter"). . . .

AFFIRMED.

QUESTIONS

1. What is the deal involved in the case?

2. What were the terms of the earn-out provision? According to the plaintiffs, why wasn't GMK able to meet the provision's requirements?

3. How did Genmar breach the purchase agreement?

4. In hindsight, what should Genmar have done differently?

---

8. Closing Mechanics

These provisions specify the closing date, where the closing is to take place, and what each party is to deliver at closing. Below is the closing mechanics provisions from the Avon/Silpada APA.

3.1. The Closing. The closing of the transactions contemplated under this Agreement (the "**Closing**") will take place upon the terms and subject to the conditions of this Agreement, through the electronic transmission of signature pages and other required deliveries through the Buyer's and the Seller's respective counsels at 3:00 p.m. Central Time on the date that is five (5) Business Days after the delivery, satisfaction or waiver of the items and conditions set forth in this Article III (other than those items and conditions that by their nature are to be delivered or satisfied at the Closing, but subject to the delivery, satisfaction or waiver of those items or conditions), or at such other time and place and on such other date as the Buyer Parent and the Seller Representative agree in writing (the "**Closing Date**"). Upon occurrence of the Closing, the effective time of the purchase and sale described in Sections 2.1-2.4 will be 11:59 p.m. Central Time on the Closing Date (the "**Effective Time**").

3.2. Deliveries at Closing.

(a) The Seller will deliver, or cause to be delivered, to the Buyer the following at the Closing (or at such other time as stated below):

(i) each Ancillary Agreement (other than the Lenexa Purchase Agreement) not specifically referred to in Section 3.2(a)(ii)-(xiii) below, duly executed by the Seller, the Seller Representative and/or the Seller Stockholders (as applicable);

(ii) the Payment Schedule, which will be delivered to the Buyer at least three (3) Business Days before the Closing Date;

(iii) a non-foreign affidavit from the Seller dated as of the Closing Date that conforms to the model certification set forth in Treasury Regulations Section 1.1445-2(b)(2)(iv)(B);

(iv) the Escrow Agreement, duly executed by the Seller Representative and the Escrow Agent;

(v) a consent and estoppel certificate substantially in the form attached as Exhibit E from each landlord of the Company's Leased Real Property (other than the Company's Leased Real Property in Thailand, provided that the Company complies with Section 7.3(b) with respect to such property);

(vi) (A) the Assignment of Intellectual Property, executed by the Seller and Silpada International Holdings (and any other Subsidiaries as may be appropriate), and any and all other documents, agreements, certificates and other instruments as may be necessary to register any Intellectual Property in the name of the Buyer Sub or designee thereof, and (B) the Assignment of Trademarks, the Assignment of Copyrights and Assignment of Domain Names, executed by the Seller and Silpada International Holdings (and any other Subsidiaries as may be appropriate), and any and all other documents, agreements, certificates and other instruments as may be necessary to register the Trademarks and Copyrights constituting the Intellectual Property in the name of the Buyer Sub or designee thereof;

(vii) (A) the Consents set forth on Section 3.2(a)(vii) of the Disclosure Schedule, in form and substance reasonably acceptable to the Buyer, and such other material Consents of third Persons necessary for the consummation of the transactions contemplated under this Agreement and the Ancillary Agreements, in form and substance reasonably acceptable to the Buyer (it being understood and agreed that any Consent set forth on Section 4.3 of the Disclosure Schedule but not set forth on Section 3.2(a)(vii) of the Disclosure Schedule shall not be required to be delivered pursuant to this Section 3.2(a)(vii)), and (B) evidence, in form and substance reasonably acceptable to the Buyer, that all Liens (other than Permitted Liens) on the Transferred Assets have been removed;

(viii) a statement of the Transaction Fees (the "**Transaction Fees Statement**"), which statement will be delivered to the Buyer at least two (2) Business Days prior to the Closing, accompanied by letters, which letters will be delivered at the Closing, signed by each Transaction Advisor and substantially in the form attached as Exhibit F;

(ix) a reasonably current certificate of existence or good standing of the Seller issued by the Secretary of State of the State of Kansas;

(x) a copy of the articles of incorporation of the Seller, certified by the Secretary of State of the State of Kansas; a copy of the bylaws of the

Seller, certified by the Seller's Secretary; and a copy of all consents, resolutions or similar actions of (A) the Seller, certified by the Seller's Secretary, and (B) each Seller Stockholder who is not a natural personal, certified by the respective Seller Stockholder, in each case (A) and (B) approving the transactions contemplated by this Agreement and the Ancillary Agreements;

(xi)   payoff letters with respect to any Indebtedness (excluding any Indebtedness the Buyer Sub has agreed to assume) for borrowed money of the Seller or its Subsidiaries in a form reasonably acceptable to the Buyer and its lenders;

(xii)   a certificate executed by an executive officer of the Seller, dated the Closing Date, certifying to the fulfillment of the conditions in Sections 3.3(a) and 3.3(b); and

(xiii)   releases in the form attached as Exhibit G (the "**Seller Releases**"), duly executed by each of the Seller and each Seller Stockholder.

(b)   The Buyer will deliver, or cause to be delivered, to the Seller the following at the Closing:

(i)   the Closing Cash Payment to the Seller in accordance with the wire transfer instructions set forth on the Payment Schedule;

(ii)   the Escrow Amount to the Escrow Agent in accordance with its wire transfer instructions to the Buyer;

(iii)   the Admin Escrow Amount to the Seller Representative in accordance with his wire transfer instructions to the Buyer;

(iv)   the Transaction Fees to the Transaction Advisors on behalf of the Seller and/or the Seller Stockholders in accordance with the wire transfer instructions set forth on the Transaction Fees Statement;

(v)   a certificate executed by the Buyer, dated the Closing Date, certifying to the fulfillment of the conditions in Sections 3.4(a) and 3.4(b);

(vi)   a resale exemption certificate from the Buyer dated as of the Closing Date that conforms to the model certification set forth in Kansas Administration Regulation Section 92-19-25b(c); and

(vii)   the Escrow Agreement and the other Ancillary Agreements (other than the Lenexa Purchase Agreement) executed by the Buyer Parent and/or the Buyer Sub (as applicable).

9. Representations and Warranties

a. Introduction

Representations and warranties, or "reps" for short, are assertions of fact by the contracting parties. In an acquisition agreement, they serve multiple purposes, including:

1. providing a party with recourse for post-closing problems,

2. allocating the risk of an unknown fact to one of the parties,

3. obliging target to disclose information about its business, and

4. providing a basis for a party to walk away from the deal.

The reps article is normally the longest part of the acquisition agreement and is heavily negotiated.

Below is a sample rep made by target regarding the permits and licenses for conducting its business.

Seller represents and warrants to Buyer as follows:

(a) Permits. All Permits held by Seller are set forth on the Disclosure Schedule. Seller holds all Permits necessary for the ownership and lease of its properties and assets and the lawful conduct of its business under and pursuant to all applicable Laws. Seller is duly licensed, to the extent required, to conduct its business in all jurisdictions in which its business is being conducted and is in compliance with all of the terms and conditions of such licenses.

Thus, if post-closing Buyer discovers that Seller did not in fact have a permit necessary for the conduct of its business, Buyer will have a breach of contract claim against seller (purpose #1). Looking at things differently, the rep allocates to Seller the risk of it not having a necessary permit (purpose #2). If the agreement did not contain the above rep, this risk would be on Buyer. In other words, Buyer would have no recourse against Seller under the agreement because Seller made no rep about permits.

Notice that the first sentence of the rep requires Seller to disclose all of its permits on the "Disclosure Schedule." As we discuss below, a disclosure schedule is part of the acquisition agreement that serves a number of purposes. In this situation, Seller will prepare a list of all of its Permits for Seller's counsel to include in the Disclosure Schedule. Thus, this is an example of a rep that obliges target to disclose information about its business (purpose #3), i.e., its business permits.

As for purpose #4, if Buyer discovers during the gap period that a rep made by target is not true, under the closing conditions provisions of the agreement (discussed below) bidder may be able to terminate, or walk away from, the deal instead of closing.

b. Qualifiers

Qualifiers are a heavily negotiated aspect of reps. A qualifier is language that qualifies, or softens, a rep, covenant, condition, or other contractual provision. Common qualifiers in the M&A context are knowledge, materiality, and exceptions. Below is the permits rep from above with each of these three types of qualifiers added (additions are underlined and italicized).

Seller represents and warrants to Buyer, *except as otherwise specified on the Disclosure Schedule*, as follows:

(a)   Permits. All *material* Permits held by Seller are set forth on the Disclosure Schedule. *To Seller's knowledge,* Seller holds all *material* Permits necessary for the ownership and lease of its properties and assets and the lawful conduct of its business under and pursuant to all applicable *material* Laws. *To Seller's knowledge,* Seller is duly licensed, to the extent required, to conduct its business in all jurisdictions in which its business is being conducted and *to its knowledge* is in compliance with all of the *material* terms and conditions of such licenses.

A key issue when it comes to knowledge and materiality qualifiers is the definition of these terms. It is fairly common for an acquisition agreement to define the term knowledge. Here's a sample definition:

For purposes of this Agreement, "knowledge" means the actual knowledge of the Company's executive officers.

Note that this definition favors the maker of the rep because it is limited to actual as opposed to constructive knowledge (things the executive officers did not know but should have known).

Conversely, it is fairly common for the term material not to be defined in the agreement, in part because it is a term that is difficult to define with precision. As a result, on occasion, contracting parties will disagree as to whether something is material and the issue ends up in court. A number of courts have held that something is material if knowledge of it would affect a person's decision-making process. If this is not the definition the parties have in mind, the contract should specify a different definition such as "important enough to merit attention." Acquisition agreements often use the related terms "Material Adverse Effect" (MAE for short) or "Material Adverse Change" (MAC for short) and these terms normally are defined in the agreement. Here's a Seller rep from the Avon/Silpada APA that contains an MAE qualifier (emphasis added).

4.12.   Absence of Certain Changes. Since December 31, 2009: (a) the Seller and its Subsidiaries have been operated in the ordinary course of business consistent with past practice, (b) there has not occurred any event or condition that, individually or in the aggregate, has had or is reasonably likely to have a *Material Adverse Effect* . . . .

And here's the agreement's definition of MAE.

> "**Material Adverse Effect**" means any change, circumstance or event that is materially adverse to the Seller and its Subsidiaries, taken as a whole, or the Company Assets, business, operations or financial condition of the Seller and its Subsidiaries, taken as a whole; except that none of the following, in and of itself or themselves, shall constitute a Material Adverse Effect: (i) any change in the United States or foreign economies or securities or financial markets in general, (ii) any changes after the date of this Agreement in applicable Laws or accounting rules not uniquely relating to the Seller, and (iii) any outbreak of hostilities, acts of war or terrorism or military actions or any escalation or material worsening of any such hostilities, acts of war or terrorism or military actions existing or underway as of the date of this Agreement, provided, in each case (i), (ii) and (iii), that such change, circumstance or event does not disproportionately adversely affect the Seller and its Subsidiaries compared to other companies of similar size operating in the jewelry or direct sales industry.

Notice that the definition includes an undefined materiality qualifier so query how helpful the definition would be in resolving a dispute as to whether something amounted to an MAE or not.

As for an exceptions qualifier, one appears in the lead in to the Permits rep ("except as otherwise specified on the Disclosure Schedule . . . ."). This language allows Seller to exclude, or carve out, from the rep anything it lists on the Disclosure Schedule. Thus, if Seller puts on the Disclosure Schedule that it does not have the permit required to operate its plant, it would not be in breach of the rep even if the permit is material. A bidder will, of course, carefully review a disclosure schedule prior to signing the agreement. If something big shows up, it can derail the deal.

c. Target's Reps

Bidder will require target to make extensive reps about its business given that is what is being sold. Customary types of reps made by target include:

- *Organization and Good Standing*: Target is duly organized and in good standing under the laws of its state of incorporation.

- *Authority*: Target has the legal authority to consummate the deal.

- *Compliance with Law*: Target is in compliance with all applicable laws and regulations.

- *Financial Statements:* Target's financial statements are complete and accurate and fairly present the financial condition of the business.

- *Assets*: Target has good title to its assets free and clear of all liens. The assets are sufficient for the operation of target's business.

- *Third Party Consents*: No third party consents are required to transfer the assets or consummate the deal.

- *Liabilities*: Target has disclosed all liabilities.

- *Litigation*: Target has disclosed all litigation in which it is involved.

- *Taxes*: Target has filed all required tax returns and timely paid all taxes due.

- *Material Contracts*: Target has disclosed all material contracts.

- *Environmental*: Target's business is in compliance with all environmental laws and regulations.

- *Employee Matters; ERISA*: Target has disclosed the names, titles, and salaries of all of its employees and all employee benefit plans. Target is in compliance with ERISA.

- *Intellectual Property*: Target has disclosed all of its intellectual property and has sufficient rights to use it in its business.

The actual language of the reps is much more elaborate than the brief descriptions above and will include various qualifiers. In that regard, here are some sample target reps from the Avon/Silpada APA.

ARTICLE IV
REPRESENTATIONS AND WARRANTIES OF THE SELLER

The Seller represents and warrants to the Buyer as of the date hereof, as of the Closing and as of the Effective Time as follows, except as otherwise disclosed to the Buyer in the corresponding section or subsection of the schedule delivered to the Buyer by the Seller in connection with the execution of this Agreement (with specific reference to the representations and warranties in this Agreement to which the information in the corresponding section or subsection of the schedule relates) (the "**Disclosure Schedule**"):

4.1.   Organization and Good Standing. The Seller and each of its Subsidiaries is duly organized or incorporated, validly existing and in good standing under the Laws of its jurisdiction of organization or incorporation and has all requisite power and authority to own, lease, operate and otherwise hold its properties and assets and to carry on its business as presently conducted. The Seller and each of its Subsidiaries is duly qualified or licensed to do business as a foreign corporation or organization and is in good standing in each jurisdiction in which the nature of the business conducted by it or the assets or properties owned or leased by it requires qualification, except where the failures to be so qualified would not be reasonably likely to have a Material Adverse Effect.

4.2.   Authorization and Effect of Agreement. The Seller and each of its Subsidiaries has all requisite right, power and authority to execute and deliver each Company Agreement and to perform its obligations under each Company Agreement and to consummate the transactions contemplated under each Company Agreement. The execution and delivery of each Company Agreement by the Seller and its Subsidiaries and the performance by the Seller and its Subsidiaries of their obligations under each Company Agreement and the consummation of the transactions contemplated under each Company Agreement have been duly and validly authorized by all requisite action, and no other action (corporate, shareholder or otherwise) is necessary to authorize the execution, delivery and performance by the Seller and its Subsidiaries of each Company Agreement or the consummation of the transactions contemplated under each Company Agreement. In accordance with applicable Law and the Seller's Organizational Documents, the board of directors of the Seller has unanimously deemed this Agreement and the Ancillary Agreements and the transactions contemplated by this Agreement and the Ancillary Agreements to be expedient and in the best interests of the Seller and has unanimously approved this Agreement and the Ancillary Agreements and the transactions contemplated by this Agreement and the Ancillary Agreements, and the Seller Stockholders have unanimously authorized and approved this Agreement and the Ancillary Agreements and the transactions contemplated by this Agreement and the Ancillary Agreements. This Agreement and the Lenexa Purchase Agreement have been, and each other Company Agreement upon execution and delivery thereof will be, duly and validly executed and delivered by the Seller and its Subsidiaries, and this Agreement and the Lenexa Purchase Agreement constitute, and each other Company Agreement upon execution and delivery thereof will constitute, a legal, valid and binding obligation of the Seller and its Subsidiaries, enforceable against the Seller and its Subsidiaries in accordance with its terms, subject to applicable bankruptcy, insolvency, fraudulent conveyance, reorganization, moratorium and similar Laws affecting creditors' rights and remedies generally.

4.3. Consents and Approvals; No Violations. Except as required under the HSR Act, no notice to or filing with, and no Permit or Consent of any Governmental Authority or any other Person is necessary or required to be obtained, made or given by the Seller or any of its Subsidiaries in connection with the execution and delivery of any of the Company Agreements, the performance by the Seller of its obligations under any of the Company Agreements and the consummation of the transactions contemplated by any of the Company Agreements. Neither the execution, delivery or performance of any of the Company Agreements nor the consummation of the transactions contemplated by any of the Company Agreements nor compliance by the Seller or its Subsidiaries with any of the provisions of any of the Company Agreements will (a) conflict with or result in any breach of any provision of any Organizational Documents of the Seller or any of its Subsidiaries, (b) result in a violation or breach of, or constitute (with or without due notice or lapse of time or both) a default (or give rise to any right of termination, modification, cancellation or acceleration or loss of material benefits) under or result in the creation of any Lien on any of the assets or properties of the Seller or any of its Subsidiaries, any of the terms, conditions or provisions of any Contract to which the Seller or any of its Subsidiaries is a party or any of their respective assets or properties may be subject or bound, (c) violate any Permit applicable to the Seller or any of its Subsidiaries or to which the Seller or any of its Subsidiaries or any of their respective assets or properties may be subject or bound or (d) violate any Laws applicable to the Seller or any of its Subsidiaries or any of their respective assets or properties. . . .

4.9. Litigation. As of the date hereof, there is no action, arbitration, hearing, proceeding, claim, demand, dispute, suit, opposition, challenge, grievance, charge, inquiry or investigation (whether civil, criminal, administrative or other, collectively, "**Proceedings**") pending or, to the Company's Knowledge, threatened, that questions the validity of this Agreement or any Ancillary Agreement or any action taken or to be taken in connection with this Agreement or any Ancillary Agreement or that seeks to prevent, enjoin, alter or delay any of the transactions contemplated by this Agreement or any Ancillary Agreement. There are no (i) Proceedings pending or, to the Company's Knowledge, threatened, that relate to the Seller or any of its Subsidiaries or the Company Assets or the Company Products; or (ii) outstanding judgments, writs, injunctions, orders, decrees or settlements that apply, in whole or in part, to the Seller or any of its Subsidiaries or the Company Assets or the Company Products.

4.10.   Assets Necessary to the Seller; Title. The Seller owns, leases or has the legal right to use the Company Assets, which constitute all the properties, assets and Contract rights necessary to the conduct and operation of the business of the Seller as currently conducted. The Seller has marketable title to, or a valid leasehold interest in, all the Company Assets (except Contract rights), in each case, including those assets reflected on the Interim Financial Statements, free and clear of all Liens, except Permitted Liens; upon the occurrence of the Closing and as of the Effective Time, the Seller will transfer such marketable title to, or valid leasehold interest in, the Transferred Assets to the Buyer Sub, free and clear of all Liens, except Permitted Liens. All tangible Company Assets material to the operations of the Seller are operating in the ordinary course of business, subject to normal maintenance and repair. Immediately following the Closing, none of the Seller, any Seller Stockholder nor any Affiliate or Related Party of the Seller or any Seller Stockholder will own, lease or otherwise hold any of the Company Assets.

4.11.   Financial Statements.

(a)   The Seller has delivered to the Buyer complete and accurate copies of the audited consolidated balance sheets, statements of income, statements of changes in stockholders' equity and statements of cash flows for the Seller and its Subsidiaries as of and for each of the years ended December 31, 2009, December 31, 2008, December 31, 2007 and December 31, 2006 (collectively, the "**Financial Statements**"), and the unaudited balance sheet (the "**Interim Balance Sheet**"), statements of income, statements of changes in stockholders' equity and statements of cash flows for the Seller and its Subsidiaries as of and for the five-month period ended May 31, 2010 (collectively, the "**Interim Financial Statements**") and, in the case of the Financial Statements, the related opinions of Marks Nelson Vohland Campbell Radetic LLC, the independent accountants of the Seller.

(b)   The balance sheets (including the related notes) included in the Financial Statements and the Interim Financial Statements fairly present in all material respects the financial position of the Seller and its Subsidiaries as of their respective dates, and the statements of income, statements of changes in stockholders' equity and statements of cash flows (including the related notes) included in the Financial Statements and the Interim Financial Statements fairly present in all material respects the results of operations and cash flows of the Seller and its Subsidiaries as of and for the respective periods then ended. Each of the Financial Statements and Interim Financial Statements (i) has been prepared in accordance with GAAP (subject to, in the case of the Interim Financial Statements, the absence of footnotes and similar presentation items), consistently applied during the periods involved, and (ii) has been prepared in accordance with the books and records of the Seller consistent with past practice.

(c) There are no off balance sheet transactions, arrangements, obligations, or relationships attributable to the business of the Seller or its Subsidiaries or to which the Seller or its Subsidiaries is party that may have a material adverse effect on the financial condition, results of operations, liquidity or capital resources of the Seller and its Subsidiaries. . . .

4.12. <u>Absence of Certain Changes.</u> Since December 31, 2009: (a) the Seller and its Subsidiaries have been operated in the ordinary course of business consistent with past practice, (b) there has not occurred any event or condition that, individually or in the aggregate, has had or is reasonably likely to have a Material Adverse Effect, (c) the Seller and its Subsidiaries have not suffered the loss of service of any directors, Employees, consultants, independent contractors or agents (collectively, **"Personnel"**) who are material, individually or in the aggregate, to the operations or conduct of the Seller and its Subsidiaries, (d) there have been no cancellations or terminations, or threatened cancellations or terminations, by any material supplier, customer or contractor of the Seller or any of its Subsidiaries, and (e) there has been no material damage to or loss or theft of any of the material Company Assets. . . .

4.22. <u>Intellectual Property.</u>

(a) Section 4.22(a) of the <u>Disclosure Schedule</u> sets forth true and complete lists of (i) all Intellectual Property owned or held exclusively by the Seller or its Subsidiaries (**"Owned Intellectual Property"**) that is registered or subject to an application for registration, indicating for each item the registration or application number, the applicable filing jurisdiction and the date of filing or issuance, and (ii) all unregistered Trademarks, material unregistered Copyrights and material Trade Secrets by subject, together with a brief description of the Company Products and services associated therewith. The Seller or its Subsidiaries exclusively owns (beneficially and of record where applicable) all Owned Intellectual Property, free and clear of all Liens, exclusive licenses, and non-exclusive licenses not granted in the ordinary course of business. The Owned Intellectual Property is valid, subsisting and enforceable, and is not subject to any outstanding order, judgment, decree or agreement adversely affecting the Seller's or its Subsidiaries' use of, or its rights to, such Intellectual Property. The Seller and its Subsidiaries have registered the copyrights for, or has submitted an application for the registration of the copyrights for, all copyrightable works in the Company Products.

(b) Section 4.22(b) of the <u>Disclosure Schedule</u> sets forth a true and complete list of (i) all agreements under which the Seller or any of its Subsidiaries is licensed or otherwise permitted by a third party to use any Intellectual Property (other than the Software licenses listed in Section 4.23(c) of the <u>Disclosure Schedule</u>), and (ii) all agreements under which a third party is licensed or otherwise permitted to use any Intellectual Property (collectively the agreements described under foregoing clauses (i) and (ii) and the Software licenses listed in Section 4.23(c) of the Disclosure Schedule are the "**Intellectual Property Contracts**," which include non-assertion agreements, settlement agreements, trademark coexistence agreements and trademark consent agreements). Each Intellectual Property Contract is valid, subsisting and enforceable against the other party, and is in full force and effect, subject to applicable bankruptcy and insolvency laws and general principles of equity, and will continue to be so immediately following the consummation of the transactions contemplated by this Agreement. No Intellectual Property Contract is subject to any outstanding order, judgment, decree or agreement adversely affecting the Seller's or any of its Subsidiaries' use thereof or its rights thereto. No claim has been threatened or asserted in writing that the Seller or any of its Subsidiaries, or to the Company's Knowledge another Person, has breached any Intellectual Property Contract. There exists no event, condition or occurrence that, with the giving of notice or lapse of time, or both, would constitute a breach or default by the Seller or any of its Subsidiaries, or to the Company's Knowledge another Person, under any Intellectual Property Contract. No party to any Intellectual Property Contract has given notice of its intention to cancel, terminate, change the scope of rights under, or fail to renew such Intellectual Property Contract. Neither the Seller, any of its Subsidiaries nor to the Company's Knowledge any other party to any Intellectual Property Contract, has repudiated in writing any material provision thereof. Consummation of the transactions contemplated by this Agreement will not place the Seller or any of its Subsidiaries in breach or default of any Intellectual Property Contract, or trigger any modification, termination or acceleration thereunder, or create any license under or Lien on Intellectual Property owned or held by the Buyer.

(c)   The Seller and each of its Subsidiaries has sufficient rights to use all Intellectual Property used in their respective business as presently conducted and as proposed to be conducted, all of which rights shall survive unchanged the consummation of the transactions contemplated by this Agreement.

(d)   The Seller and its Subsidiaries have filed, in the appropriate offices in the United States and all foreign countries in which it has registered or applied to register Copyrights or Trademarks, statements of ownership and, for exclusive licenses or where otherwise advisable, its license interest, for all registered or applications to register Copyrights and Trademarks in which the Seller or any of its Subsidiaries claims an ownership interest in such jurisdictions.

(e)   The employees who prepare works that are the subject of (i) Copyrights to which the Seller or any of its Subsidiaries claims ownership, (ii) registered claims of Copyrights, or (iii) pending applications for registration of claims of Copyrights, prepared such works within the scope of his or her employment. All past and present employees, consultants and contractors who contributed to the creation of any works subject to Copyrights for or on behalf of the Seller or any of its Subsidiaries (x) did so within the scope of their employment; (y) have executed valid and binding agreements assigning to the Seller or any of its Subsidiaries all rights, title and interest in and to such Intellectual Property; or (z) have licensed the Seller to use such Intellectual Property, copies of which agreements and licenses have been provided to Buyer.

(f)   The Seller and its Subsidiaries have confidentiality agreements with all of its employees, consultants, contractors, manufacturers, independent sales representatives and vendors of goods, which obligate each such Person to maintain the confidentiality of (i) the Trade Secrets owned or used by the Seller or any of its Subsidiaries and (ii) all other information held in confidence by the Seller or any of its Subsidiaries.

(g)   There are no proceedings, Claims or challenges pending, asserted or, to the Company's Knowledge, threatened against the Seller or its Subsidiaries concerning the ownership, validity, registerability, enforceability, infringement or use of, or licensed right to use, any Intellectual Property. To the Company's Knowledge, no valid basis for any such litigation, proceeding, Claim or challenge exists. To the Company's Knowledge, no Person is violating any Owned Intellectual Property right of the Seller or its Subsidiaries. The Seller and each of its Subsidiaries have not infringed or otherwise violated the Intellectual Property rights of any third party in the past six (6) years.

(h)   All registration, maintenance and renewal fees that are due before or within ninety (90) days after the Closing Date in respect of the Intellectual Property, and to the Company's Knowledge in respect of Licensed Intellectual Property, will be paid before the Closing.

(i)   The Seller and its Subsidiaries have taken all reasonable measures to protect the Owned Intellectual Property and to protect the confidentiality of all Trade Secrets that are owned, used or held by the Seller and its Subsidiaries, and to the Company's Knowledge, such Trade Secrets have not been used, disclosed to or discovered by any Person except pursuant to valid and appropriate non-disclosure agreements which have not been breached, nor, to the Company's Knowledge, has any Person misappropriated any of its Trade Secrets.

(j)   Neither the Seller nor any of its Subsidiaries has received any notice or is subject to any actual or threatened proceedings claiming or alleging that its products, services or businesses infringe, misappropriate or violate the Intellectual Property rights of any third party, nor are there any proceedings or Claims pending in which the Seller or any of its Subsidiaries alleges that any Person is infringing, misappropriating or otherwise violating any Intellectual Property or Intellectual Property Contract.

(k)   The consummation of the transactions contemplated by this Agreement will not, to the Company's Knowledge, (i) result in the loss of, or otherwise adversely affect, any rights of the Seller or any of its Subsidiaries in any Intellectual Property or (ii) require the Seller any of its Subsidiaries or any other party to grant to anyone any rights with respect to any Intellectual Property.

(l)   The Seller and its Subsidiaries do not hold any Patents.

(m)   The Seller and each of its Subsidiaries (i) takes reasonable measures, directly or indirectly, to ensure the confidentiality, privacy and security of customer, employee and other confidential information, and (ii) complies and has complied with applicable data protection, privacy and similar Laws, regulations, directives and codes of practice in any jurisdiction relating to any data processed by the Seller or any of its Subsidiaries.

(n) No Trademark registration or application for a Trademark registration of the Seller or any of its Subsidiaries in any jurisdiction worldwide has been denied, rejected, canceled, terminated, abandoned, declared invalid or unenforceable, or been subject to any adverse determination or proceeding, or the institution of any proceeding, affecting the Seller's or any of its Subsidiaries' rights to register, keep, maintain or enforce such Trademark registration or application for such Trademark registration, and neither the Seller nor any of its Subsidiaries has received any notice of the foregoing. . . .

4.27. No Other Representations or Warranties. Notwithstanding anything to the contrary in this Agreement, it is the explicit intent of each Party, and the Parties agree, that none of the Seller, the Seller Representative or any of their respective representatives has made or is making any representation or warranty, express or implied, written or oral, including any implied representation or warranty, as to the condition, merchantability, usage, suitability or fitness for any particular purpose with respect to the Transferred Assets, the Seller or any of its Subsidiaries, the Company Assets, or any part thereof, except those representations and warranties contained in this Agreement and the Ancillary Agreements.

EXERCISE 5.4

Carefully review the above target reps and underline all qualifiers contained in them. Also, identify at least 10 places in which you could insert a qualifier that would benefit Seller.

EXERCISE 5.5

Assume you represented Silpada in its sale to Avon. While performing due diligence on Silpada prior to the parties signing the APA, you become aware of the items below. Refer to the Silpada reps excerpted above and determine which of the below items need to be included in the Disclosure Schedule. Be prepared to explain why. If you need more information to make a determination with respect to a particular item, specify what you need.

1. For the last five years, Silpada has sent an employee to Tucson, Arizona to sell products at the Tucson Gem Show. Silpada is not registered as a foreign corporation in Arizona.

2. Silpada's bank loan requires the consent of the bank in order for Silpada to sell any material amount of its assets.

3. All of Silpada's assets are subject to a security interest in favor of the bank.

4. Silpada recently received a letter from a former employee threatening to sue it for "violating his constitutional rights." You asked Silpada's director of human resources about the person, and she said he is a "whackadoodle."

5.   Silpada recently received a cease and desist letter from a company claiming that some Silpada marketing materials infringe on the company's trademark rights.

6.   Silpada's controller mentioned to you that some minor accounting errors were made in preparing the interim financial statements.

7.   A Silpada storage facility was damaged in a storm last week.

8.   Two Silpada employees recently tendered their resignations.

9.   Silpada holds a patent on a jewelry-making technique it no longer utilizes.

10.   The Silpada employees who write the copy for Silpada's website have not signed copyright assignment agreements or confidentiality agreements.

d.   Bidder's Reps

Bidder's reps are much less extensive than target's. If it's a cash deal, all target generally cares about is that bidder can legally and financially close the deal. Thus, bidder's reps include the following and not much more:

- *Organization and Good Standing*: Bidder is duly organized and in good standing under the laws of its state of incorporation.

- *Authority*: Bidder has the legal authority to consummate the deal.

- *Sufficiency of Funds:* Bidder has sufficient funds to complete the deal.

Here are some sample bidder reps from the Avon/Silpada APA:

ARTICLE VI
REPRESENTATIONS AND WARRANTIES OF THE BUYER

The Buyer represents and warrants to the Seller as of the date hereof, as of the Closing and as of the Effective Time as follows:

6.1.   Organization and Good Standing. The Buyer Parent is duly organized, validly existing and in good standing under the Laws of its jurisdiction of organization and has all requisite power and authority to own, lease, operate and otherwise hold its properties and assets and to carry on its business as presently conducted. The Buyer Sub is duly organized, validly existing and in good standing under the Laws of its jurisdiction of incorporation.

6.2.   Authorization and Effect of Agreement. The Buyer has all requisite right, power and authority to execute and deliver each Buyer Agreement and to perform its obligations under each Buyer Agreement and to consummate the transactions contemplated by each Buyer Agreement. The execution and delivery of each Buyer Agreement by the Buyer Parent and the Buyer Sub and the performance by the Buyer Parent and the Buyer Sub of their obligations under each Buyer Agreement and the consummation of the transactions contemplated by each Buyer Agreement have been duly and validly authorized by all requisite action on the part of the Buyer Parent and the Buyer Sub and no other action (corporate, limited liability company, shareholder or otherwise) on the part of the Buyer Parent or the Buyer Sub is necessary to authorize the execution, delivery and performance by the Buyer Parent and the Buyer Sub of each Buyer Agreement or the consummation of the transactions contemplated by each Buyer Agreement. This Agreement has been, and each other Buyer Agreement upon execution and delivery thereof will be, duly and validly executed and delivered by the Buyer Parent and the Buyer Sub, and this Agreement constitutes, and each other Buyer Agreement upon execution and delivery thereof will constitute, a legal, valid and binding obligation of the Buyer Parent and the Buyer Sub, enforceable against the Buyer Parent and the Buyer Sub in accordance with its terms, subject to applicable bankruptcy, insolvency, fraudulent conveyance, reorganization, moratorium and similar Laws affecting creditors' rights and remedies generally. . . .

6.5. Sufficiency of Funds. On the Closing Date, the Buyer will have sufficient funds to effect the Closing and pay the Purchase Price under this Agreement.

6.6. No Broker. The Buyer Parent is solely responsible for any agent, broker, investment banker, financial advisor or other firm or Person that is or will be entitled to any broker's or finder's fee or any other commission or similar fee in connection with any of the transactions contemplated by this Agreement or any Ancillary Agreement based upon arrangements made by, or on behalf of, the Buyer.

6.7. No Other Representations or Warranties. Notwithstanding anything to the contrary in this Agreement, it is the explicit intent of each Party, and the Parties agree, that neither the Buyer nor any of its representatives has made or is making any representation or warranty, express or implied, written or oral, except those representations and warranties contained in this Agreement.

If the deal consideration includes bidder securities, bidder's reps will be more elaborate because target will require various reps about the condition of bidder's business.

e. Non-Reliance Provisions

Section 4.27 from the above Seller reps and Section 6.7 from the above Buyer reps from the Avon/Silpada APA are examples of non-reliance provisions. These provisions are generally intended to limit a party's ability to make fraud claims based upon representations made outside of the acquisition agreement (for example, in emails or conversations between the parties as part of the due diligence or negotiation process). The next case addresses the scope and effect of a non-reliance provision.

TRANSDIGM INC. v. ALCOA GLOBAL FASTENERS, INC.
Delaware Chancery Court
2013 Del. Ch. LEXIS 137 (May 29, 2013)

PARSONS, Vice Chancellor.

This dispute between parties to a stock purchase agreement relates to the regrettably familiar situation where a buyer claims that the seller engaged in fraud related to the transaction or misrepresented facts in the stock purchase agreement. Involved are, on one side, a Delaware corporation which purchased all issued and outstanding shares of two companies and, on the other side, the prior owner of those companies, including a Delaware corporation and its Delaware and UK subsidiaries, which owned the companies that were sold. . . .

The buyer's main contentions of fraud relate to the facts that: (1) one of the purchased company's key customers had expressed to the sellers that it intended to buy 50% less from the purchased company; and (2) the sellers had offered, and the key customer agreed to, a 5% price discount effective after the closing date. According to the buyer, the sellers' failure to disclose these known facts was fraudulent concealment and the stock purchase agreement's broad anti-reliance language does not bar a claim for such concealment. . . .

TransDigm Inc. is a Delaware corporation. TransDigm Inc. is the parent company of Plaintiffs/Counterclaim Defendants McKechnie Aerospace Investments, Inc. ("McKechnie USA"), a Delaware corporation, and McKechnie Aerospace (Europe) Ltd. ("McKechnie UK"), a company organized under the laws of England and Wales (collectively, the "Sellers" or "TransDigm").

Before the execution of the stock purchase agreement that is the subject of this dispute, McKechnie USA was the sole shareholder of Valley–Todeco, Inc., and McKechnie UK was the sole shareholder of Linread Ltd. ("Linread," and together with Valley–Todeco, Inc., the "Fastener Subsidiaries"). The Fastener Subsidiaries engaged in the design, development, manufacture and distribution of fasteners, fastening systems, and bearings.

. . . Plaintiff, Alcoa Global Fasteners, Inc., is a Delaware corporation (the "Buyer" or "Alcoa"). . . .

Alcoa purchased all issued and outstanding shares of the Fastener Subsidiaries pursuant to a stock purchase agreement executed on January 28, 2011 (the "Purchase Agreement" or "SPA"). The dispute addressed in this Memorandum Opinion relates to Alcoa's purchase of Linread. One of Linread's most important customers, if not *the* most important customer, was Airbus. Under a contract covering the period January 1, 2005 to December 31, 2008, Airbus had agreed to purchase lockbolts from Linread (the "Airbus Contract"). In 2008, Linread and Airbus extended the term of the Airbus Contract until December 31, 2012.

During its due diligence into Linread's business in connection with the SPA, it immediately became clear to Alcoa that Linread's future success depended on its business relationship with Airbus. Alcoa therefore asked questions to understand the scope of Linread's business with Airbus and the strength and potential for future success of the Linread-Airbus business relationship. At a January 6, 2011 meeting between Alcoa and TransDigm representatives, for example, Alcoa inquired as to whether there were any disputes between Linread and any of its customers, including Airbus, with respect to any matter, including pricing. Representatives of TransDigm, which tightly controlled information regarding Airbus during Alcoa's due diligence, responded that there were not. Alcoa also specifically inquired about payment terms governing TransDigm's relationships with its customers, including Airbus, and about whether any agreements with those customers included cost savings, rebate requirements, or price negotiations. Although TransDigm had information at that time that would have been responsive to Alcoa's questions, TransDigm intentionally did not reveal some of that information in its responses.

After the Purchase Agreement was executed and the deal closed on March 8, 2011, Alcoa learned of two important interactions with Airbus. First, on October 26, 2009, Airbus officials expressed dissatisfaction to McKechnie UK and Linread representatives about the prices it was paying for certain lockbolts under the Airbus Contract. In response, McKechnie UK's CEO verbally offered to give Airbus a 5% discount on all lockbolts purchased under the Airbus Contract starting on January 1, 2012. On December 18, 2009, Linread's General Manager memorialized this offer in an email to Airbus. Around September 15, 2010, Airbus accepted this discount. Although McKechnie UK then authorized Linread's general manager to sign the proposed amendment to the Airbus Contract, it was not signed at that time. Second, during an October 6, 2010 meeting, Airbus indicated to McKechnie and Linread that Airbus seriously was considering moving 50%–55% of its lockbolt business to a European competitor.

Alcoa alleges that TransDigm devised a scheme to conceal and suppress this information from Alcoa during its due diligence. For example, Alcoa alleges that McKechnie UK's President emailed Linread's General Manager on January 1, 2011 stating, "I am not sure what Alcoa knows about our Airbus business and their direction on lockbolts with them. I would keep the story consistent and speak to the expiration date only." . . .

TransDign avers that Alcoa has not stated a claim for fraudulent and active concealment of material information because Alcoa's express disclaimer in the Purchase Agreement of reliance on any representations outside of that Agreement preclude it from alleging that it reasonably relied on such extra-contractual representations. . . .

TransDigm . . . argues that [Alcoa's fraud claim] is barred by the Purchase Agreement. Specifically, TransDigm asserts that Alcoa's express representation in Section 5.8 of the Purchase Agreement that it was provided with all material information necessary to make an informed decision before it purchased the Fastener Subsidiaries precludes Alcoa from bringing its [fraud claim]. TransDigm also contends that Alcoa cannot prove reasonable reliance on the alleged fraudulent misrepresentation because Alcoa represented in Section 5.8 that it agreed to purchase the shares "without reliance" on any express or implied representation or warranty not expressly set forth in the Purchase Agreement. Section 5.8 states in relevant part:

Buyer has undertaken such investigation and has been provided with and
has evaluated such documents and information as it has deemed necessary
to enable it to make an informed decision with respect to the execution,
delivery and performance of this Agreement and the transactions contemplated hereby. Buyer agrees to accept the Shares *without reliance upon
any express or implied representations or warranties of any nature,
whether in writing, orally or otherwise,* made by or on behalf of or imputed
to TransDigm or any of its Affiliates, except as expressly set forth in this
Agreement.

Alcoa counters that [its fraud claim] is consistent with this representation and
warranty. In Section 5.8, Alcoa admittedly disclaimed reliance on any extra-
contractual representations. But, Alcoa argues, [its fraud claim] is not based on any
extra-contractual *representation* by TransDigm; rather, it arises from the intentional and affirmative *concealment* of material facts. According to Alcoa, its
representation and warranty in Section 5.8 does not preclude such a claim.

Alcoa alleges that it relied on both pre-closing representations and omissions of
TransDigm. The Counterclaim states: "Alcoa reasonably and justifiably relied upon
the pre-closing representations and material omissions of Counterclaim–Defendants [TransDigm] as to Linread's business relationship with Airbus in determining
whether to purchase Linread shares, in determining how much it was willing to
offer and ultimately pay for the Linread shares, and in negotiating, and ultimately
agreeing upon, the terms of the SPA."

Based on Alcoa's representation in Section 5.8, I hold that it could not reasonably
and justifiably have relied on extra-contractual pre-closing representations of
TransDigm. For the reasons that follow, however, I conclude that [Alcoa has stated]
. . . a claim for fraudulent and active concealment based on TransDigm's alleged
omissions.

TransDigm relies almost exclusively on the Delaware Supreme Court's recent
decision in *RAA Management, LLC v. Savage Sport Holdings, Inc.*[7] to argue that
the Purchase Agreement's language bars Alcoa's claims. That case involved the
following provision in a nondisclosure agreement:

You [the potential acquirer] understand and acknowledge that neither the
Company nor any Company Representative is making any representation
or warranty, express or implied, as to *the accuracy or completeness* of the
Evaluation Material or of any other information concerning the Company
provided or prepared by or for the Company, and none of the Company nor
the Company Representatives, will have any liability to you or any other
person resulting from your use of the Evaluation Material or any such
other information. *Only those representations or warranties that are made
to a purchaser in the Sale Agreement* when, as and if it is executed, and
subject to such limitations and restrictions as may be specified [in] such a
Sale Agreement, *shall have any legal effect.*[8]

---

[7] [n.49] 45 A.3d 107 (Del.2012).

[8] [n.50] *Id.* at 110 (emphasis added).

There, the potential acquirer, RAA, expressly not only agreed that the selling company was making no representation or warranty as to the accuracy or completeness of any information being provided to RAA, but it also agreed that only representations the company might make in a later sale agreement would have any legal effect. Here, the accuracy and completeness of the information TransDigm provided Alcoa is key to Alcoa's claim for active concealment of material information. There is no argument, however, that Alcoa agreed in the Purchase Agreement that TransDigm was making no representation as to the "accuracy and completeness" of the information TransDigm provided to Alcoa. Nor did Alcoa disclaim reliance on extra-contractual *omissions*.

TransDigm makes light of this distinction. It argues that it effectively did secure this disclaimer with language stating that "Buyer has . . . been provided with and has evaluated such documents and information as it has deemed necessary to enable it to make an informed decision with respect to the execution . . . of this Agreement." In this broad representation by Alcoa, Alcoa agrees that TransDigm provided it with information Alcoa deemed sufficient in making its decision to enter into the Purchase Agreement. Consistent with this representation, and absent contrary language elsewhere in the Agreement, however, Alcoa reasonably could have relied on the assumption that TransDigm was not actively concealing information that was responsive to Alcoa's inquiries and that TransDigm was not engaged in a scheme to hide information material to Alcoa's purchase of Limead. In other words, the language in Section 5.8 does not clearly disclaim reliance on the type of concealment and omission that Alcoa alleges here.

TransDigm cites no case holding that a party to an agreement with language similar to that in the Purchase Agreement would be precluded from recovering for fraudulent and active concealment of material information. This contrasts with two cases the Supreme Court discussed in detail in reaching its decision in *RAA Management*. The agreements at issue in those two cases, unlike the agreement at issue here, contained language expressly disclaiming reliance on both the *omission* of information and extra-contractual *representations*.[9] For example, in *In re IBP, Inc. Shareholders Litigation*, an acquiring corporation sought to rescind a contract on the grounds of fraudulent inducement based on misrepresentations and omissions made during the due diligence process.[10] The Court of Chancery rejected the fraud claim based on the following language in the confidentiality agreement that the parties had entered into at the beginning of the due diligence process:

> We [the acquirer] understand and agree that none of the Company, its advisors or any of their . . . representatives (i) have made or make any representation or warranty, express or implied, as to *the accuracy or*

---

[9] [n.52] The two cases are Great Lakes Chemical Corp. v. Pharmacia Corp., 788 A.2d 544 (Del. Ch. 2001) and In re IBP, Inc. Shareholders Litigation, 789 A.2d 14 (Del. Ch. 2001). In *Great Lakes*, the buyer represented that "[n]one of [the sellers] make any express or implied representation or warranty as to the accuracy or completeness of the information contained herein or made available in connection with any further investigation of the Company," and that "[e]ach of [the sellers] expressly disclaims any and all liability that may be based on such information or errors therein or omissions therefrom." Great Lakes Chem. Corp., 788 A.2d at 552.

[10] [n.53] RAA Mgmt., LLC, 45 A.3d at 114.

completeness of the Evaluation Material or (ii) shall have any liability whatsoever to us or our Representatives relating to or resulting from the use of the Evaluation Material or any errors therein *or omissions therefrom*, except in the case of (i) and (ii), to the extent provided in any definitive agreement relating to a Transaction.[11]

The difference in language between the nondisclosure agreement in *RAA Management* and the agreements in the cases that Opinion discussed renders *RAA Management* distinguishable from this case. Thus, based on the terms of the Purchase Agreement here, I conclude that Alcoa conceivably could prevail on its claim for fraudulent and active concealment of material information. I therefore deny TransDigm's motion to dismiss [Alcoa's fraud claim]. . . .

QUESTIONS

1. What is the deal involved in the case?

2. What information did TransDigm allegedly conceal from Alcoa?

3. Why wasn't Alcoa's fraud claim precluded by the non-reliance provision of the SPA?

4. In hindsight, what should have TransDigm included in the SPA?

---

10. Covenants

A covenant is simply a promise to do something (an affirmative covenant) or to not do something (a negative covenant). An acquisition agreement normally includes both pre-closing and post-closing covenants.

a. Pre-Closing Covenants

Pre-closing covenants address issues that may come up during the period from when the parties sign the acquisition agreement to closing (what we referred to earlier as the gap period). This is because as the soon- to- be owner of target's business bidder will be concerned about how target's business is operated during the gap period. Thus, bidder will include in the acquisition agreement what is commonly called an interim operating covenant. Here is the one from the Avon/Silpada APA:

---

[11] [n.54] *Id.* The Court of Chancery explained: "[A] contextually-specific factor — the Confidentiality Agreement — contributes to the caution with which Tyson [the acquirer] should have taken any oral assurances or representations from IBP during the Merger negotiation process. Tyson had agreed that it could not use any oral or written due diligence information (*or omissions therefrom*) as a basis for a lawsuit unless that issue was covered by a specific provision of a subsequent, written contract." In re IBP, Inc. S'holders Litig., 789 A.2d 14, 73 (Del. Ch. June 18, 2001).

7.4. **Conduct of Business.** Except as required by this Agreement or with the prior written consent of the Buyer (which consent will be granted or denied within 3 Business Days after the receipt of a request), from the date of this Agreement until the Effective Time, the Seller Stockholders and the Seller will (i) operate its business in the ordinary course, (ii) preserve intact its business and maintain its business relationships and goodwill with its employees, sales representatives, independent contractors, suppliers and service providers of and to its business, (iii) not take any action that would be required to be disclosed pursuant to Section 4.12, and (iv) not do any of the following:

(a)   effect any change in the capitalization or issued or outstanding stock or other equity interests of the Seller or make any amendment to the Organizational Documents of the Seller;

(b)   merge or consolidate the Seller with any other Person, or restructure, reorganize or completely or partially liquidate the Seller or otherwise enter into any agreements or arrangements imposing material changes or restrictions on the Company Assets;

(c)   purchase, sell, lease, let lapse, exchange or otherwise dispose of or acquire any material property or assets (other than transactions occurring in the ordinary course of business) or make any material capital expenditures;

(d)   enter into, amend, modify or terminate, or cancel, modify or waive any provision of, any Material Contract or Real Property Lease (provided that, at the Buyer's request, the Company shall terminate, with no cost or other Liability to the Company, its Real Property Leases with Adaplis as of the Closing), or modify or waive any material Claims or rights of the Seller;

(e)   create, incur or forgive any material Indebtedness (except that the Seller may incur or create Special Indebtedness in the ordinary course of business) or otherwise make or forgive any material loans, advances, guarantees or capital contributions to or investments in any Person, create or incur any Lien on the Shares or other capital stock of the Seller or create or incur any material Liens on the Company Assets;

(f)   settle or compromise any Proceeding, pending or threatened (in each case, except for claims under Insurance Policies within applicable policy limits);

(g)   (i) make any changes with respect to accounting policies or procedures, except as required by changes in GAAP, (ii) make any material Tax election (including an election to treat any disregarded entity as an association taxable as a corporation), or (iii) terminate or revoke any election to be treated as an "S" corporation for federal income Tax purposes under § 1362 of the Code or under any analogous or similar provision of state or local law in any jurisdiction where the Seller is required to file a Tax Return;

(h)   (i) grant, extend, amend, waive or modify any material rights in or to, nor sell, assign, lease, transfer, license, let lapse, abandon, cancel, or otherwise dispose of, or extend or exercise any option to sell, assign, lease, transfer, license, or otherwise dispose of, any Intellectual Property, or (ii) fail to exercise a right of renewal or extension under any Intellectual Property Contract, in each case other than in the ordinary course of business;

(i) except as required by a Law and except for the Closing Employee Bonuses listed on Section 4.20(h) of the Disclosure Schedule, (i) increase the compensation (including, among other things, base compensation or commissions) or benefits of any Personnel (including severance benefits), except for base salary increases of up to 5% per Employee in the Ordinary Course of Business consistent with past practice, (ii) grant any bonus, retention bonus or incentive compensation award to any Personnel, except for special bonuses awarded to certain Employees following the successful completion of the National Conference in the Ordinary Course of Business consistent with past practice, (iii) enter into any Contract with any Personnel regarding his or her employment, compensation, severance or benefits which increases or otherwise enhances such Personnel's compensation, severance or benefits or (iv) adopt, amend or terminate any Benefit Plan other than the Seller 401(k) Profit Sharing Plan;

(j) issue, sell, pledge, dispose of, grant, transfer, encumber or authorize the issuance, sale, pledge, disposition, grant, transfer, lease, license, guarantee or encumbrance of, any shares of capital stock or other securities of the Seller or securities convertible or exchangeable into or exercisable for any shares of such capital stock or other securities of the Seller, or any options, warrants or other rights of any kind to acquire any shares of such capital stock or other securities of the Seller or such convertible or exchangeable securities;

(k) repurchase, redeem, repay or otherwise acquire any outstanding shares of capital stock or other securities of the Seller;

(l) declare, set aside, make or pay any dividend or other distribution, payable in cash, stock, property or otherwise, with respect to the capital stock or other securities of the Seller (except for dividends and distributions paid by any Subsidiary to any other Subsidiary or the Seller and dividends of Cash and Cash Equivalents to the Seller Stockholders prior to the Closing);

(m) (i) accelerate the delivery or sale of any Company Products or, other than in the ordinary course of business, offer discounts on the sale of any Company Products, (ii) defer any actions, expenditures or investments appropriate (other than in the ordinary course of business) or necessary to operate and conduct the Seller's business, (iii) make any material change in the levels of materials or supplies used in the conduct of the Seller's business or (iv) engage in any practice to accelerate the collection of any accounts receivable or delay payment of any accounts payable or other liabilities beyond their scheduled due dates or otherwise manage cash in a manner similar to any of the foregoing;

(n) take any action or omit to take any action that is reasonably likely to result in any of the conditions set forth in Sections 3.3 through 3.5 not being satisfied; or

(o) enter into any legally binding commitment with respect to any of the foregoing.

Other standard pre-closing covenants go to completing the deal. In other words, they require bidder, target, or both to take various actions that facilitate the closing of the transaction. These sorts of covenants include:

- The parties promising to use their best efforts to consummate the transaction.

- Target promising to provide bidder and its representatives access to target's employees and premises to facilitate bidder's due diligence investigation.

Here's an example of the latter from the Avon/Silpada APA.

7.2. Access and Investigation.

(a)   Between the date of this Agreement and the Effective Time, the Seller and the Seller Stockholders will (i) afford the Buyer and its Representatives reasonable access during normal business hours to the Seller's Employees, consultants, suppliers, properties, Contracts, books and records, and other documents and data, and (ii) make available to the Buyer and its Representatives copies of all such Contracts, books and records, and other existing documents and data as the Buyer may reasonably request, subject in each case to the terms of any confidentiality agreements and processes entered into between the Seller and the Buyer and its Representatives with respect to all or any part of such access and information.

(b)   The Seller will provide the Buyer and its Representatives with reasonable access to all properties and facilities owned or occupied by the Seller, together with all documents relevant to any environmental condition or compliance of the Seller and/or properties owned or occupied by the Seller and Persons knowledgeable with the Seller's operations, to permit the Buyer and its Representatives to conduct, at its own cost, whatever environmental investigations and assessments it, in its sole discretion, deems necessary or appropriate during normal business hours and with at least three (3) Business Days prior notice; provided, however, that if the Buyer and its Representatives desire to conduct such environmental investigations and assessments, the Seller may condition any access by any such Representatives upon evidence of appropriate levels of insurance and an undertaking to repair any damage caused by such investigations or assessments.

---

b. Post-Closing Covenants

As the name indicates, post-closing covenants are covenants that apply after the deal closes. Examples include a mutual covenant to keep certain business and tax records relating to the deal for a specified period of time, covenants by target not to compete with bidder or to solicit former target employees that bidder has hired, and a covenant by bidder to employ specified former target employees. Here's the sample language from the Avon/Silpada APA:

7.7. Restrictive Covenants.

(a) For a period of three (3) years after the Closing Date, the Seller and each Seller Stockholder will not, and the Seller and each Seller Stockholder will cause its Affiliates not to, directly or indirectly, without the prior written consent of the Buyer Parent, employ or solicit for employment any director, officer or employee of the Buyer Sub or any of its Subsidiaries or encourage any of the foregoing persons to terminate his or her relationship with the Buyer Sub or any of its Subsidiaries.

(b) For a period of three (3) years after the Closing Date, the Seller and each Seller Stockholder will not, and the Seller and each Seller Stockholder will cause its Affiliates not to, directly or indirectly, engage in, hold an interest in, own, manage, operate, control, direct, be connected with as a stockholder (other than as a holder of less than two percent (2%) of a publicly-traded security), joint venturer, partner, consultant or employee with any Person that competes with the Buyer or its Affiliates in the United States and its territories, Canada and/or Mexico in the jewelry industry and/or direct-selling industry.

11. Closing Conditions

Closing conditions specify conditions that must be fulfilled or waived before a party is obligated to close on the transaction. Here are the bulk of the closing conditions sections from the Avon/Silpada APA.

3.3. Conditions to the Buyer's Obligation to Close. The Buyer's obligation to purchase the Transferred Assets and to take the other actions required to be taken by the Buyer at the Closing is subject to the satisfaction, at or prior to the Closing, of each of the following conditions (any of which may be waived by the Buyer, in whole or in part):

(a) Each of the representations and warranties of the Seller contained in Article IV and of the Seller Stockholders contained in Article V: (i) that is a Fundamental Representation of the Seller or the Seller Stockholders shall be true and correct in all respects as of the date hereof and as of the Closing as if made on and as of the Closing (except for such representations and warranties that are made as of a specific date which shall speak only as of such date), and (ii) that is not a Fundamental Representation of the Seller or the Seller Stockholders shall be true and correct (in each case without giving effect to any limitations as to materiality or Material Adverse Effect set forth therein) as of the date hereof and as of the Closing as if made on and as of the Closing (except for such representations and warranties that are made as of a specific date which shall speak only as of such date), with only such exceptions as have not had or would not reasonably be expected to have, individually or in the aggregate, a Material Adverse Effect or materially impede or delay the ability of any Party to consummate the transactions under this Agreement.

(b) The Seller, the Seller Representative and the Seller Stockholders have performed or complied with, in all material respects, all agreements and covenants required to be performed or complied with by any Seller Stockholder, the Seller Representative or the Seller under this Agreement at or prior to the Closing Date, and the Seller has delivered all items required to be delivered at the Closing pursuant to Section 3.2(a).

(c)   Since the date of this Agreement, there has not occurred any change, event, circumstances or development that has had, or is reasonably likely to have, a Material Adverse Effect. . . .

3.4. Conditions to the Seller's Obligation to Close. The Seller's and the Seller Stockholders' obligation to sell the Transferred Assets and to take the other actions required to be taken by the Seller and the Seller Stockholders at the Closing is subject to the satisfaction, at or prior to the Closing, of each of the following conditions (any of which may be waived by the Seller Representative, in whole or in part):

(a)   Each of the representations and warranties of the Buyer contained in Article VI of this Agreement: (i) that is a Fundamental Representation of the Buyer shall be true and correct in all respects as of the date hereof and as of the Closing as if made on and as of the Closing (except for such representations and warranties that are made as of a specific date which shall speak only as of such date), and (ii) that is not a Fundamental Representation of the Buyer shall be true and correct (in each case without giving effect to any limitations as to materiality or Material Adverse Effect set forth therein) as of the date hereof and as of the Closing as if made on and as of the Closing (except for such representations and warranties that are made as of a specific date which shall speak only as of such date), with only such exceptions as would not reasonably be expected to materially impede or delay the ability of the Buyer to consummate the transactions under this Agreement.

(b)   The Buyer has performed or complied with, in all material respects, all agreements and covenants required to be performed or complied with by the Buyer under this Agreement on or prior to the Closing Date, and the Buyer has delivered all items required to be delivered at the Closing pursuant to Section 3.2(b). . . .

3.5. Conditions to All Parties' Obligations to Close. The Parties' obligations to purchase and sell the Transferred Assets and to take the actions required to be taken by the Parties at the Closing are subject to the satisfaction, at or prior to the Closing, of each of the following conditions (any of which (to the extent legally permitted) may be waived by the Parties, in whole or in part):

(a)   The waiting period under the HSR Act shall have expired or been terminated.

(b)   No court or other Governmental Authority of competent jurisdiction shall have enacted, issued, promulgated, enforced or entered any Law (whether temporary, preliminary or permanent) that is in effect and restrains, enjoins or otherwise prohibits the consummation of the transactions contemplated by this Agreement.

(c)   There is no Proceeding pending by any Governmental Authority challenging or seeking to restrain or prohibit the transactions contemplated by this Agreement.

(d)   There is no Proceeding pending by any Governmental Authority

> relating to the compliance by any Seller Stockholder, the Seller or any of its Subsidiaries or any supplier or Intermediary of the Seller or any of its Subsidiaries, with any Anti-Corruption Laws.

Notice that the obligation of Buyer to close is tied to the reps and pre-closing covenants of Seller contained elsewhere in the agreement (Seller's obligation to close is likewise tied to bidder's reps and pre-closing covenants). In other words, if a Seller rep turns out to be false (even if true when the agreement was signed) or if Seller fails to comply with one of its pre-closing covenants, bidder does not have to close, subject to any materiality or similar qualifier contained in the closing condition.

In that regard, target will be concerned about bidder being able to refuse to close based on what could be characterized as a technicality, e.g., a breach of an unimportant target rep, because buyer could use this as leverage to renegotiate the price or as a means for it to walk away from the deal entirely. Conversely, bidder would like the flexibility potentially afforded it by tight closing conditions. Thus, the extent to which closing conditions are qualified is often heavily negotiated.

The next case addresses considerations for determining whether negative developments at target amount to a material adverse effect ("MAE") and thereby excuse bidder from having to close.

HEXION SPECIALTY CHEMICALS, INC. v. HUNTSMAN CORP.
Delaware Chancery Court
965 A.2d 715 (2008)

LAMB, VICE CHANCELLOR

In July 2007, just before the onset of the ongoing crisis affecting the national and international credit markets, two large chemical companies entered into a merger agreement contemplating a leveraged cash acquisition of one by the other. The buyer is a privately held corporation, 92% owned by a large private equity group. . . .

While the parties were engaged in obtaining the necessary regulatory approvals, the seller reported several disappointing quarterly results, missing the numbers it projected at the time the deal was signed. After receiving the seller's first quarter 2008 results, the buyer and its parent, through their counsel, began exploring options for extricating the seller from the transaction. . . . [T]his process focused on whether the seller had suffered a material adverse effect. . . .

The complaint . . . seeks a declaration that the seller suffered a material adverse effect, thus excusing the buyer's obligation to close. The seller answered and filed counterclaims seeking, among other things, an order directing the buyer to specifically perform its obligations under the merger agreement. . . .

I.

A. *The Parties*

The plaintiffs and counterclaim defendants in this action are Hexion Specialty Chemicals, Inc., Apollo Global Management, LLC, and various entities through which Apollo Global Management conducts its business (Apollo Global Management and its related entities are collectively referred to as "Apollo"). Hexion, a New Jersey corporation, is the world's largest producer of binder, adhesive, and ink resins for industrial applications. Apollo Global Management, a Delaware limited liability company, is an asset manager focusing on private equity transactions. Through its ownership in Hexion's holding company, Apollo owns approximately 92% of Hexion.

The defendant and counterclaim plaintiff in this action is Huntsman Corporation, a Delaware corporation. Huntsman, a global manufacturer and marketer [of] chemical products, operates five primary lines of business: Polyurethanes, Advanced Materials, Textile Effects, Performance Products and Pigments.

B. *Procedural History*

On July 12, 2007, Hexion and Huntsman signed a merger agreement whereby Hexion agreed to pay $28 per share in cash for 100% of Huntsman's stock. The total transaction value of the deal was approximately $10.6 billion, including assumed debt. The plaintiffs filed suit in this court on June 18, 2008 seeking declaratory judgment on three claims: (1) Hexion is not obligated to close if the combined company would be insolvent and its liability to Huntsman for failing to close is limited to no more than $325 million; (2) Huntsman has suffered a Company Material Adverse Effect ("MAE"); and (3) Apollo has no liability to Huntsman in connection with the merger agreement. On July 2, 2008, Huntsman filed its answer and counterclaims requesting declaratory judgment that: (1) Hexion knowingly and intentionally breached the merger agreement; (2) Huntsman has not suffered an MAE; and (3) Hexion has no right to terminate the merger agreement. Also, Huntsman's counterclaims seek an order that Hexion specifically perform its obligations under various sections of the merger agreement, or, alternatively, and in the event Hexion fails to perform, the award of full contract damages. . . .

II.

Hexion argues that its obligation to close is excused as a result of a Company Material Adverse Effect in the business of Huntsman. For the reasons detailed below, Hexion's argument fails.

A. *The "Chemical Industry" Carve-Outs are Inapplicable*

Section 6.2(e) of the merger agreement states that Hexion's obligation to close is conditioned on the absence of "any event, change, effect or development that has had or is reasonably expected to have, individually or in the aggregate," an MAE.

MAE is defined in section 3.1(a)(ii) as:

> any occurrence, condition, change, event or effect that is materially adverse to the financial condition, business, or results of operations of the Company and its Subsidiaries, taken as a whole; *provided, however*, that in no event shall any of the following constitute a Company Material Adverse Effect: (A) any occurrence, condition, change, event or effect resulting from or relating to changes in general economic or financial market conditions, except in the event, and only to the extent, that such occurrence, condition, change, event or effect has had a disproportionate effect on the Company and its Subsidiaries, taken as a whole, as compared to other Persons engaged in the chemical industry; (B) any occurrence, condition, change, event or effect that affects the chemical industry generally (including changes in commodity prices, general market prices and regulatory changes affecting the chemical industry generally) except in the event, and only to the extent, that such occurrence, condition, change, event or effect has had a disproportionate effect on the Company and its Subsidiaries, taken as a whole, as compared to other Persons engaged in the chemical industry. . . .

The parties disagree as to the proper reading of this definition. Hexion argues that the relevant standard to apply in judging whether an MAE has occurred is to compare Huntsman's performance since the signing of the merger agreement and its expected future performance to the rest of the chemical industry. Huntsman, for its part, argues that in determining whether an MAE has occurred the court need reach the issue of comparing Huntsman to its peers if and only if it has first determined that there has been an "occurrence, condition, change, event or effect that is materially adverse to the financial condition, business, or results of operations of the Company and its Subsidiaries, taken as a whole. . . ." Huntsman here has the better argument. The plain meaning of the carve-outs found in the proviso is to prevent certain occurrences which would *otherwise* be MAE's being found to be so. If a catastrophe were to befall the chemical industry and cause a material adverse effect in Huntsman's business, the carve-outs would prevent this from qualifying as an MAE under the Agreement. But the converse is not true-Huntsman's performance being disproportionately worse than the chemical industry in general does not, in itself, constitute an MAE. Thus, unless the court concludes that the company has suffered an MAE as defined in the language coming before the proviso, the court need not consider the application of the chemical industry carve-outs.

Hexion bases its argument that Huntsman has suffered an MAE principally on a comparison between Huntsman and other chemical industry firms. Hexion's expert witness, Telly Zachariades of The Valence Group, largely focused on this at trial. Zachariades testified regarding a comparison of the performance of Huntsman during the second half of 2007 and first half of 2008, relative to two sets of benchmark companies which he chose as representative of the industry-the Bloomberg World Chemical Index and the Chemical Week 75 Index. Zachariades compared Huntsman to these two benchmarks in a variety of different areas, both backward and forward-looking, and, in each, found Huntsman significantly worse than the mean, and, in most, in the bottom decile. This potentially would be compelling evidence if it was necessary to reach the carve-outs, although Huntsman's expert, Mark Zmijewski, managed to cast doubt on Zachariades's analysis. However, because, as discussed below, Huntsman has not suffered an MAE, the court need not reach the question of whether Huntsman's performance has been disproportionately worse than the chemical industry taken as a whole.

B. *Huntsman Has Not Suffered An MAE*

For the purpose of determining whether an MAE has occurred, changes in corporate fortune must be examined in the context in which the parties were transacting. In the absence of evidence to the contrary, a corporate acquirer may be assumed to be purchasing the target as part of a long-term strategy. The important consideration therefore is whether there has been an adverse change in the target's business that is consequential to the company's long-term earnings power over a commercially reasonable period, which one would expect to be measured in years rather than months. A buyer faces a heavy burden when it attempts to invoke a material adverse effect clause in order to avoid its obligation to close. Many commentators have noted that Delaware courts have never found a material adverse effect to have occurred in the context of a merger agreement. This is not a coincidence. The ubiquitous material adverse effect clause should be seen as providing a "backstop protecting the acquirer from the occurrence of unknown events that substantially threaten the overall earnings potential of the target in a durationally-significant manner. A short-term hiccup in earnings should not suffice; rather [an adverse change] should be material when viewed from the longer-term perspective of a reasonable acquirer." This, of course, is not to say that evidence of a significant decline in earnings by the target corporation during the period after signing but prior to the time appointed for closing is irrelevant. Rather, it means that for such a decline to constitute a material adverse effect, poor earnings results must be expected to persist significantly into the future.

Hexion protests being shouldered with the burden of proof here, urging the court that Huntsman bears the burden of showing the absence of an MAE, because that is a condition precedent to closing. In support of this proposition Hexion cites no cases directly related to material adverse effect clauses. Instead, Hexion cites two cases for the general proposition that "a party who seeks to recover upon a contract must prove such facts as are necessary to establish a compliance with conditions precedent thereto cannot be denied." This is undoubtedly true, so far as it goes. Hexion argues that [*In re*] *IBP*, [*Inc. S'holders Litig*, 789 A.2d 14 (Del. Ch. 2001)] in placing the burden to prove a material adverse effect on the buyer, is distinguishable because in *IBP* the material adverse effect clause was drafted in the form of a representation and warranty that no material adverse effect had occurred.[12] But material adverse effect clauses are strange animals, *sui generis*

---

[12] [n.59] *IBP*, 789 A.2d at 65. Hexion's entire argument on the subject is restricted to two sentences in footnote 35 of its post-trial brief. Given the extraordinary effect a difference in which party carries the burden could have on the outcome of this litigation, the fact that it spends but two sentences attempting to distinguish the leading case in this jurisdiction on the subject of material adverse effect clauses leaves the court suspicious that Hexion simply could not muster from the case law any stronger argument on the subject.

among their contract clause brethren. It is by no means clear to this court that the form in which a material adverse effect clause is drafted (i.e., as a representation, or warranty, or a condition to closing), absent more specific evidence regarding the intention of the parties, should be dispositive on the allocation of the burden of proof. Typically, conditions precedent are easily ascertainable objective facts, generally that a party performed some particular act or that some independent event has occurred. A material adverse effect clause does not easily fit into such a mold, and it is not at all clear that it ought to be treated the same for this purpose. Rather, for the same practical reasons that the court in *IBP* cites, it seems the preferable view, and the one the court adopts, that absent clear language to the contrary, the burden of proof with respect to a material adverse effect rests on the party seeking to excuse its performance under the contract. This outcome is also in accord with this court's holding that in determining the allocation of the burden of proof in suits for declaratory judgment, "the better view is that a plaintiff in a declaratory judgment action should always have the burden of going forward."[13] This rule would also place the burden of proof that an MAE has occurred on Hexion, as the initial seeker of a declaratory judgment that an MAE has occurred. Furthermore, as the parties jointly stipulate, the question is "[w]hether Hexion has established that a 'Company Material Adverse Effect,' as defined in the Merger Agreement, has occurred."[14] This again places the burden to show the existence of an MAE squarely on Hexion.

The issue then becomes what benchmark to use in examining changes in the results of business operations post-signing of the merger agreement-EBITDA or earnings per share. In the context of a cash acquisition, the use of earnings per share is problematic. Earnings per share is very much a function of the capital structure of a company, reflecting the effects of leverage. An acquirer for cash is replacing the capital structure of the target company with one of its own choosing. While possible capital structures will be constrained by the nature of the acquired business, where, as here, both the debt and equity of the target company must be acquired, the capital structure of the target prior to the merger is largely irrelevant. What matters is the results of operation of the business. Because EBITDA is independent of capital structure, it is a better measure of the operational results of the business. Changes in Huntsman's fortunes will thus be examined through the lens of changes in EBITDA. This is, in any event, the metric the parties relied on most heavily in negotiating and modeling the transaction.

---

[13] [n.63] Those Certain Underwriters at Lloyd's, London v. Nat'l Installment Ins. Servs., Inc., 2007 WL 4554453 (Del. Ch.) (quoting Rhone-Poulenc v. GAF Chem. Corp., 1993 Del. Ch. LEXIS 59, at *7 (Apr. 6, 1993)).

[14] [n.64] Joint Pretrial Stipulation and Order at 9. This is the framing of the question under the Defendant-Counterclaim Plaintiff's heading. The Plaintiff-Counterclaim Defendant's frame the same question as "Whether under Section 6.2(e) of the Merger Agreement, Huntsman has, since execution of the Merger Agreement, experienced events, changes, effects or developments that have had or are reasonably expected to have, in the aggregate, a Company Material Adverse Effect on Huntsman such that if the conditions to the closing of the Merger were measured now, Hexion would have no obligation to effect the Merger and would bear no liability and no obligation to pay any termination or other fee to Huntsman as a result of the failure of the Merger to be consummated." *Id.* at 7. Thus while Huntsman framed the question in terms of the burden being placed on Hexion, Hexion framed the question in the pretrial order in burden-neutral terms.

Hexion focuses its argument that Huntsman has suffered an MAE along several lines: (1) disappointing results in Huntsman's earnings performance over the period from July 2007 through the present; (2) Huntsman's increase in net debt since signing, contrary to the expectations of the parties; and (3) underperformance in Huntsman's Textile Effects and Pigments lines of business.

1. *Huntsman Has A Difficult Year After The Signing Of The Merger Agreement*

There is no question that Huntsman's results from the time of signing in July 2007 until the end of the first half of 2008 have been disappointing. Huntsman's first-half 2008 EBITDA was down 19.9% year-over-year from its first-half 2007 EBITDA. And its second-half 2007 EBITDA was 22% below the projections Huntsman presented to bidders in June 2007 for the rest of the year.

Realizing, however, that these results, while disappointing, were not compelling as a basis to claim an MAE, Hexion focused its arguments on Huntsman's repeated misses from its forecasts. In its "Project Nimbus" forecasts, Huntsman management projected 2008 consolidated EBITDA of $1.289 billion. As of August 1, 2008, Huntsman management['s] projected EBITDA for 2008 was $879 million, a 32% decrease from the forecast the year before. Hexion points to these shortfalls from the 2007 projections and claims that Huntsman's failure to live up to its projections are key to the MAE analysis.

But this cannot be so. Section 5.11(b) of the merger agreement explicitly disclaims any representation or warranty by Huntsman with respect to "any projections, forecasts or other estimates, plans or budgets of future revenues, expenses or expenditures, future results of operations . . . , future cash flows . . . or future financial condition . . . of [Huntsman] or any of its Subsidiaries . . . heretofore or hereafter delivered to or made available to [Hexion or its affiliates] . . . ." The parties specifically allocated the risk to Hexion that Huntsman's performance would not live up to management's expectations at the time. If Hexion wanted the short-term forecasts of Huntsman warranted by Huntsman, it could have negotiated for that. It could have tried to negotiate a lower base price and something akin to an earn-out, based not on Huntsman's post-closing performance but on its performance between signing and closing. Creative investment bankers and deal lawyers could have structured, at the agreement of the parties, any number of potential terms to shift to Huntsman some or all of the risk that Huntsman would fail to hit its forecast targets. But none of those things happened. Instead, Hexion agreed that the contract contained no representation or warranty with respect to Huntsman's forecasts. To now allow the MAE analysis to hinge on Huntsman's failure to hit its forecast targets during the period leading up to closing would eviscerate, if not render altogether void, the meaning of section 5.11(b). It is a maxim of contract law that, given ambiguity between potentially conflicting terms, a contract should be read so as not to render any term meaningless. Thus, the correct interpretation cannot be that section 6.2(e) voids section 5.11(b), making it a condition precedent to Hexion's obligation to consummate the merger that Huntsman substantially meet its forecast targets. Rather, the correct analysis is that Huntsman's failure to hit its forecasts cannot be a predicate to the determination of an MAE in Huntsman's business. Moreover, at trial Jordan Zaken, one of the Apollo partners involved in negotiating the Huntsman deal on behalf of Hexion, admitted on cross-examination that Hexion and Apollo never fully believed Huntsman's forecasts. Those forecasts, therefore, cannot be the basis of a claim of an MAE, since they never formed part of the expectations of the parties (in a strict contractual sense) to begin with.

Rather, as Huntsman's expert Zmijewski testified at trial, the terms "financial condition, business, or results of operations" are terms of art, to be understood with reference to their meaning in Regulation S-K and Item 7, the "Management's Discussion and Analysis of Financial Condition and Results of Operations" section of the financial statements public companies are required to file with the SEC. In this section, a company is required to disclose its financial result for the period being reported, along with its pro forma financial results for the same time period for each of the previous two years. Zmijewski testified at trial that these results are analyzed by comparing the results in each period with the results in the same period for the prior year (i.e., year-end 2007 results to year-end 2006 results, first-quarter 2005 results to first-quarter 2004 results, and so forth). The proper benchmark then for analyzing these changes with respect to an MAE, according to Zmijewski (and the analysis the court adopts here), is to examine each year and quarter and compare it to the prior year's equivalent period. Through this lens, it becomes clear that no MAE has occurred. Huntsman's 2007 EBITDA was only 3% below its 2006 EBITDA, and, according to Huntsman management forecasts, 2008 EBITDA will only be 7% below 2007 EBITDA. Even using Hexion's much lower estimate of Huntsman's 2008 EBITDA, Huntsman's 2008 EBITDA would still be only 11% below its 2007 EBITDA. And although Huntsman's fourth quarter 2007 EBITDA was 19% below its third quarter 2007 results, which were in turn 3% below its second quarter 2007 results, Huntsman has historically been down on a quarter-over-quarter basis in each of the third and fourth quarters of the year.[15] Moreover, comparing the trailing-twelve-months EBITDA for second quarter 2007 to second quarter 2008, the 2008 result is only down 6% from 2007.

Of course, the expected future performance of the target company is also relevant to a material adverse effect analysis. Hexion, on the basis of its estimates of Huntsman's future profitability, urges that Huntsman has or is expected to suffer an MAE. Hexion estimates that Huntsman will earn only $817 million in 2008, and that its earnings will contract further in 2009, to $809 million.

Huntsman responds with its own projections, that it will generate $878 million of EBITDA in 2008, and $1.12 billion of EBITDA in 2009. To support its projections, Huntsman offered testimony at trial by Peter Huntsman, its CEO, Kimo Esplin, its CFO, Tony Hankins, the President of its Polyurethanes division, Paul Hulme, President of its Materials and Effects Division, and Simon Turner, Senior Vice President of its Pigments division. Each of the division managers described in detail how he expected to reach his target earnings for the following year, and described

---

[15] [n.74] Indeed, Huntsman's Q3 2006 EBITDA was down 26% from Q2 2006, and Q4 2006 was down 21% from Q3. In 2005, a similar pattern appeared as well, with Q3 2005 down 12% from Q2, and Q4 2005 down 43% from Q3. *Id.* Thus, Hexion should have been well aware at signing that the second-half of 2007 was likely to be less lucrative for Huntsman than the first.

both how macroeconomic effects such as sharp increases in the prices of crude oil and natural gas, and the weakening of the dollar relative to the euro, contributed to a reduction in Huntsman's 2008 earnings and how the recent reversal of the trend in several of those macroeconomic effects could be expected to positively change future EBITDA results. While the court recognizes that management's expectations for a company's business often skew towards the overly optimistic, especially in the presence of litigation, the court ultimately concludes that Hexion's projections reflect an overly pessimistic view of Huntsman's future earnings.

The fact that Hexion offered little detail as to how it arrived at its projections for Huntsman's business also diminishes the weight its projections deserve. Ultimately, the likely outcome for Huntsman's 2009 EBITDA is somewhere in the middle. This proposition is confirmed by current analyst estimates for Huntsman 2009 EBITDA, which average around $924 million. This would represent a mere 3.6% decrease in EBITDA from 2006 to 2009, and a result essentially flat from 2007 to 2009. The court also notes that in two of the four original deal models Apollo produced in June of 2007 to justify its $28 per share offer, Huntsman's projected 2009 EBITDA was significantly below this estimate, at $833 million in the "Hexion Management Flat Case," and at a mere $364 million in its recession case. The other two models ("Hexion Management Case" and "Hexion Management Case with Interest Rates Run at Caps") are essentially the same as each other except with respect to the expected interest rates on the debt facilities. Thus in only one of Hexion's three views of future operating performance of Huntsman at the time of signing did Huntsman perform better in 2009 than it is presently expected to by analysts.

These results do not add up to an MAE, particularly in the face of the macroeconomic challenges Huntsman has faced since the middle of 2007 as a result of rapidly increased crude oil and natural gas prices and unfavorable foreign exchange rate changes. Ultimately, the burden is on Hexion to demonstrate the existence of an MAE in order to negate its obligation to close, and that is a burden it cannot meet here.

2. *Huntsman's Net Debt Expands During The Same Period*

Hexion urges that Huntsman's results of operations cannot be viewed in isolation, but should be examined in conjunction with Huntsman's increase in net debt. As of the end of June 2007, Huntsman forecast that its net debt at the end of 2008 would be $2.953 billion. At the time, its net debt stood at $4.116 billion. It expected that this reduction in debt would be financed by the divestiture of three of its divisions (which was accomplished by the end of 2007) and by its operating cash flows. Things did not go according to plan. Driven largely by dramatic increases in the prices of inputs and growth in accounts receivables, working capital expanded during this time by $265 million, while foreign exchange effects on the outstanding debt balances resulted in a dollar-denominated increase in the notional value of Huntsman's debt of an additional $178 million. All told, rather than shrinking by a billion dollars, Huntsman's net debt since signing has expanded by over a quarter of a billion dollars.

Hexion points to this debt expansion as further evidence (when combined with the results of operations discussed above) of an MAE based on changes in the financial condition of Huntsman. Huntsman, of course, points out that this increase in net debt from signing until the present is only on the order of 5% or 6% (depending upon which date one chooses to measure Huntsman's debt, since weekly changes in the total debt as a result of working capital fluctuations can be as much as plus or minus $100 million), a far cry from an MAE based on financial condition. Hexion responds that this view ignores the fact that "post-signing Huntsman received $794 million in cash proceeds from divestitures that were to have been used to repay debt. The assets were sold along with their revenue generating capacity. An apples-to-apples comparison (adjusting to eliminate the divestiture proceeds) would show an increase in net debt of 32%." This argument initially appears attractive, but examination of Apollo's initial deal-model negates any persuasive power it might have initially held. In all four of the cases which Apollo modeled, Huntsman's net debt at closing is assumed to be $4.1 billion. All of Hexion's assumptions about the value of the deal were predicated on Huntsman net debt levels on that order-the projected decrease in Huntsman's net debt of a billion dollars was simply an added attraction. Hexion cannot now claim that a 5% increase in net debt from its expectations in valuing the deal, even combined with the reduced earnings, should excuse it from its obligation to perform on the merger agreement.

3. Challenging Times At Textile Effects And Pigments

Both in its pretrial brief and at trial, Hexion focused most of its attention on two Huntsman divisions which have been particularly troubled since the signing of the merger agreement-Pigments and Textile Effects. These two divisions were expected to compose only 25% of Huntsman's adjusted EBITDA in 2008-14% coming from Pigments, and 11% coming from Textile Effects. Little space need be spent on this argument as it falls under its own weight.

First, as already discussed, under the terms of the merger agreement, an MAE is to be determined based on an examination of Huntsman taken as a whole. A close examination of two divisions anticipated to generate at most a fourth of Huntsman's EBITDA is therefore only tangentially related to the issue. Although the results in each of these two divisions, if standing alone, might be materially impaired, as already illustrated above, Huntsman as a whole is not materially impaired by their results. If it is unconvincing to say Huntsman's business as a whole has been materially changed for the worse, it is even more unconvincing to claim that 75% of Huntsman's business is fine, but that troubles in the other 25% materially changes the business as a whole.

Additionally, there is reason to believe that much of Huntsman's troubles in each of these divisions are short-term in nature. Paul Hulme, the President of Huntsman's Advanced Materials and Textile Effects business, testified at trial regarding the headwinds Textile Effects has faced over the last year. Huntsman first acquired the Textile Effects business from CIBA in June 2006, just over two years ago, for $158 million. At that time, Textile Effects was burdened with an inflated cost structure, which Hulme set about to change as part of Huntsman's Project Columbus (which is still ongoing). Included in this restructuring is the closing of certain plants in Europe and the construction and expansion of Huntsman's Textile

Effects presence in Asia, allowing Huntsman to follow the shift in the textile manufacturing market there and minimize its manufacturing costs and foreign exchange rate change exposures. Moreover, the Textile Effects business faced a so-called "perfect storm" of macroeconomic challenges in the first-half of 2008: its costs for inputs were inflated by the dramatic weakening of the dollar against the euro, and the strengthening of the Swiss franc, Indian rupee, and Chinese ren minh bi. Additionally, petroleum derivatives form a large portion of the inputs to the Textile Effects manufacturing processes, and the dramatic increase in the price of crude oil over the same period caused input costs to balloon further. Notably, most of these macroeconomic changes have been reversing over the period since the end of the second quarter of 2008. In addition, Huntsman has been able to develop some traction in passing price increases into the market since July 2008.

As for Pigments, titanium dioxide is a notoriously cyclical business, which Apollo well knew at the time of bidding. During an initial presentation meeting with the management of Huntsman, Josh Harris of Apollo expressed to Peter Huntsman that Apollo knew as much about the titanium dioxide business as Huntsman did. Apollo had over the year prior to negotiating the Huntsman deal been in negotiations with Kerr McGee, one of Huntsman's competitors in the titanium dioxide business, to acquire Kerr McGee's pigments business. Apollo was therefore well familiar with the cyclicality that business is known to face. Hexion focuses its argument on Huntsman's use predominantly of the sulfate process, while the majority of its competitors use the chlorine process for manufacturing titanium dioxide. As a result of a recent run-up in the price of sulfuric acid, a key input to the sulfate process, Huntsman has thus faced increased input costs that its competitors have not shared. Nevertheless, Tronox, one of Huntsman's major competitors in the pigments business and a user of the chlorine process, is itself facing financial distress, partly as a result of its own cost increases, illustrating that the present pain in the pigments business is not restricted to those manufacturers using the sulfate process. . . .

For all the foregoing reasons, the court has today entered an Order and Final Judgment granting Huntsman Corporation relief in accordance with the findings of fact and conclusions of law set forth in this Opinion.

QUESTIONS

1. What is the deal involved in the case?

2. What negative developments occurred concerning Huntsman's business after the deal was signed? Why is Hexion arguing these developments constituted an MAE?

3. Why does the court conclude that Huntsman has not suffered an MAE? What are the "Chemical Industry" carve-outs and how do they fit into the analysis?

4. In hindsight, what could Hexion have done differently?

---

12. Termination

A termination provision specifies the circumstances under which a party can terminate an acquisition agreement after signing but prior to closing. Below is the termination provision from the Avon/Silpada APA.

11.1. Termination Events. This Agreement may, by notice given prior to or at the Closing, be terminated:

    (a)   by either the Buyer Parent or the Seller if (i) the Closing has not occurred (other than through the failure of any Party seeking to terminate this Agreement to comply in all material respects with its obligations under this Agreement) on or before the date that is 75 days after the date of this Agreement, or such later date as the Parties may agree upon (the "**Outside Date**"); provided, however, that if the sole reason that the Closing has not occurred is that the condition set forth in Section 3.5(a) has not been fulfilled on or prior to the date that is 75 days after the date of this Agreement, such date shall automatically be extended to the date that is 90 days after the date of this Agreement, which date shall be the "Outside Date" for all purposes of this Article XI, or (ii) any condition set forth in Section 3.5 is incapable of being satisfied prior to the Outside Date;

    (b)   by the Buyer Parent (but only so long as the Buyer is not in material breach of its obligations under this Agreement) if there has been a material breach of any representation, warranty, covenant or agreement of the Seller or the Seller Stockholders such that one or more of the conditions to Closing set forth in Section 3.3 and Section 3.5 are not capable of being fulfilled as of the Outside Date;

    (c)   by the Seller Representative (but only so long as the Seller and the Seller Stockholders are not in material breach of their respective obligations under this Agreement) if there has been a material breach of any representation, warranty, covenant or agreement of the Buyer such that one or more of the conditions to Closing set forth in Section 3.4 and Section 3.5 are not capable of being fulfilled as of the Outside Date; or

    (d)   by mutual consent of the Buyer Parent and the Seller.

---

13. Indemnification

An indemnification provision obligates a party to cover specified costs and expenses incurred by another party. Here is sample language from the Avon/Silpada APA.

9.2. Indemnification Obligations of the Seller. From and after the Closing . . . the Seller will indemnify, defend and hold harmless the Buyer Parent and the Buyer Sub, any parent, Subsidiary, associate, Affiliate, shareholder or Representative of any of the foregoing Persons, and their respective representatives, successors and permitted assigns (in each case other than the Seller, any Seller Stockholder or any beneficiary of any Seller Stockholder that is a trust, solely in their capacity as such) (all referred to individually as a "**<u>Buyer Indemnified Party</u>**" and collectively as the "**<u>Buyer Indemnified Parties</u>**") from and against and pay on behalf of or reimburse such party in respect of, all losses, liabilities, demands, claims, actions or causes of action, costs, damages, judgments, debts, settlements, assessments, deficiencies, penalties, fines or expenses, whether or not arising out of any claims by or on behalf of a third party, including interest, penalties, reasonable attorneys' fees and expenses and all amounts paid in investigation, defense or settlement (collectively, "**<u>Losses</u>**") that any Buyer Indemnified Party may suffer, sustain or become subject to, as a result of, in connection with, or relating to or by virtue of:

(a)   any inaccuracy in or breach of any representation or warranty made by the Seller or any Seller Stockholders under this Agreement or in any certificate delivered by the Seller or any Seller Stockholders pursuant to this Agreement;

(b)   any breach or non-fulfillment of any covenant or agreement on the part of the Seller, the Seller Representative or any Seller Stockholders under this Agreement or in any certificate delivered by the Seller, the Seller Representative or any Seller Stockholders pursuant to this Agreement;

(c)   any Excluded Liability . . . .

As you can see, under the above provision, Silpada is obligated to indemnify, or reimburse, Avon and its affiliates for losses relating to a breach of a Silpada rep or covenant. Thus, if post-closing Avon discovers a Silpada rep was false, Avon can seek recovery from Silpada under the APA.

As you probably realize, an indemnification obligation overlaps with the basic principle of contract law that if a party breaches a contract the other party can sue. In other words, if the APA did not contain the above indemnification provision, Avon would still have recourse against Silpada — it could bring a breach of contract claim. Indemnification provisions, however, allow bidder and target to essentially tailor the remedy for breach of contract to the particular deal. This tailoring typically does the following:

- Broadens the remedy for breach to include attorney fees and expenses;
- Narrows the remedy for breach through caps, baskets, and time limitations;
- Specifies the procedure for making an indemnification claim; and
- Provides for escrow or hold-back of deal consideration to serve as a pool of funds bidder can draw down for indemnification claims.

Below is some sample language from the Avon/Silpada APA.

9.4 Indemnification Procedure.

(a) The Buyer Indemnified Party or the Seller Indemnified Party (as applicable, the "**Indemnified Party**") will promptly give the Party or Parties obligated to indemnify the Indemnified Party under this Article IX (the "**Indemnifying Party**") written notice of any Claim (including any pending or threatened Claim by a third party that the Indemnified Party has determined has given or could reasonably give rise to a right of indemnification under this Agreement) to indemnification under this Article IX. The failure to provide notice will not affect any rights under this Agreement, except to the extent the failure actually prejudices the Indemnifying Party. Any notices and communications to the Seller under this Article IX will be given to or made with the Seller Representative. The Parties agree that (i) in this Article IX they intend to shorten the applicable statute of limitations period with respect to certain Claims; (ii) notices for Claims in respect of a breach of a representation, warranty, covenant or agreement must be delivered prior to the expiration of any applicable survival period specified in Section 9.1 for such representation, warranty, covenant or agreement; provided, that if, prior to such applicable date, an Indemnified Party shall have notified the Indemnifying Party in accordance with this Section 9.4 of a Claim for indemnification under this Article IX (whether or not formal legal action shall have been commenced based upon such claim), such Claim shall continue to be subject to indemnification in accordance with this Article IX notwithstanding the passing of such applicable date.

(b) If the indemnity Claim involves a Claim by a third party against any Indemnified Party (a "**Third Party Claim**"), the Indemnifying Party may, within 10 Business Days after receipt of notice and upon written notice to the Indemnified Party, assume on behalf of the Indemnified Party, through counsel of its choosing and at its expense, the settlement or defense of the Third Party Claim so long as:

(i) the Indemnifying Party notifies the Indemnified Party in writing within the 10 Business Day period that the Indemnifying Party will indemnify the Indemnified Party from and against any Losses the Indemnified Party may suffer resulting from, arising out of, relating to, in the nature of, or caused by the Third Party Claim,

(ii) the Third Party Claim involves only money damages and does not seek an injunction or other equitable relief,

(iii) the Indemnifying Party provides the Indemnified Party with evidence reasonably acceptable to the Indemnified Party that the Indemnifying Party will have the financial resources to defend against the Third Party Claim and fulfill the Indemnifying Party's indemnification obligations under this Agreement,

(iv) settlement of, or an adverse judgment with respect to, the Third Party Claim is not, in the good faith judgment of the Indemnified Party, likely to establish a precedential custom or practice adverse to the continuing business interests of the Indemnified Party or the Buyer, and

(v)   the Indemnifying Party conducts the defense of the Third Party Claim actively and diligently;

except that the Indemnified Party may participate in the settlement or defense of the Third Party Claim through counsel chosen by it at its expense; and except that, if the Indemnified Party reasonably determines that representation by the Indemnifying Party's counsel of the Indemnifying Party and the Indemnified Party may present such counsel with a conflict of interests, then the Indemnifying Party will pay the reasonable fees and expenses of the Indemnified Party's counsel. The Indemnified Party and the Indemnifying Party will reasonably cooperate with each other in connection with the Third Party Claim. For the avoidance of doubt, the Indemnified Party may take any actions reasonably necessary to defend such Third Party Claim prior to the time that it receives a notice from the Indemnifying Party in accordance with Section 9.4(b)(i) assuming the settlement or defense of the Third Party Claim. Notwithstanding anything to the contrary in this Section 9.4, the Indemnifying Party may not, without the prior written consent of the Indemnified Party, settle or compromise any action or consent to the entry of any judgment in respect of any Third Party Claim, other than a solely monetary settlement including (i) full payment by the Indemnifying Party, (ii) a full release of the Indemnified Party and (iii) no finding or admission of any wrongdoing or violation of Law. If the Indemnifying Party is not contesting the Third Party Claim in good faith, then the Indemnified Party may conduct and control, through counsel of its own choosing and at the expense of the Indemnifying Party, the settlement or defense of the Third Party Claim, and the Indemnifying Party will cooperate with the Indemnified Party and its counsel in connection with such settlement or defense. Notwithstanding the foregoing, the Indemnified Party may not settle, compromise or consent to the entry of any judgment with respect to any Claim which it is seeking indemnification from the Indemnifying Party or admit to any liability with respect to such Claim without the prior written consent of the Indemnifying Party. The failure of the Indemnified Party to participate in, conduct or control the defense will not relieve the Indemnifying Party of any obligation they may have under this Agreement or otherwise under the Laws.

(c)   The Indemnified Party and Indemnifying Parties will reasonably cooperate with each other to implement the provisions of this Section 9.4.

9.5. Calculation of Indemnity Payments. In connection with any indemnity Claim, the amount of any Losses for which indemnification is provided under Article VIII or this Article IX in connection with such indemnity Claim will be (a) calculated on an After-Tax Basis, with the Indemnified Party reimbursing the Indemnifying Party for any Tax Benefit actually realized from the payment of the indemnity Claim within 10 days after the filing of the Tax Return reporting such Tax Benefit, and (b) (i) reduced by the amount of any insurance proceeds actually received by the Indemnified Party in connection with such indemnity Claim or such Losses and (ii) increased by the amount of any costs of collection in connection with such indemnity Claim or such Losses; provided that if the Indemnified Party actually receives any insurance proceeds in connection with such indemnity Claim or such Losses after the Indemnifying Parties indemnifies the Indemnified Party for such Losses, the Indemnified Party will remit to the Indemnifying Party any such insurance proceeds actually received, but only up to the amount of indemnification proceeds actually received from the Indemnifying Party.

9.6. Tax Matters. The rights and obligations of the Parties with respect to indemnification for any Tax matters (except as specifically provided elsewhere in this Article IX or in this Agreement) will be governed solely by Article VIII.

9.7. Relation of Indemnity to Indemnity Escrow Amount. Other than with respect to Taxes (which are governed by Article VIII):

(a)   If a Buyer Indemnified Party is entitled to indemnification from the Seller under Article IX, the Buyer will collect the amount due for indemnification (subject to the procedures and limitations set forth in this Agreement) solely from the funds then held in the Indemnity Escrow Account under the Escrow Agreement, except in the case of a breach of Section 2.8, for which any other recourse is expressly permitted.

(b)   From and after the Closing, the right to indemnification of the Indemnified Parties pursuant to Article IX will be (i) the sole and exclusive remedy for any breach of any representation or warranty of an Indemnifying Party, and (ii) the sole and exclusive monetary remedy for any breach of any covenant or agreement of an Indemnifying Party (it being understood that the Parties have the right to seek equitable relief, including specific performance), in either case (i) or (ii), whether a contract claim, a tort claim, a statutory claim or otherwise (other than with respect to any Losses arising out of fraud or criminal misconduct or bad faith), (A) under this Agreement or the Disclosure Schedule, (B) in any certificate or other document delivered by or on behalf of any Party under this Agreement or (C) otherwise arising from or in connection with the transactions contemplated under this Agreement.

9.8. Indemnification Amounts; Limitations. Except with respect to an indemnification Claim under Article VIII, notwithstanding anything to the contrary in this Agreement:

(a)   the Seller will not be liable for any indemnification Claim pursuant to Section 9.2(a) (other than with regard to a breach of any Fundamental Representations or Extended Representations made by the Seller or the Seller Stockholders) unless and until the Dollar amount of all indemnifiable Losses under this Agreement in the aggregate exceeds $6,270,000, in which case the Seller will be obligated to indemnify the Indemnified Party for the total amount of all indemnifiable Losses. For the avoidance of doubt, any indemnifiable Losses in connection with a breach of any Fundamental Representation or Extended Representation shall be subject to indemnification under Section 9.2(a) without regard to the foregoing threshold.

(b)   in no event will the aggregate indemnification obligations of the Seller pursuant to Section 9.2 exceed the Indemnity Escrow Amount, except that an Indemnified Party's right to seek indemnification under this Agreement for any Losses arising out of fraud or criminal misconduct or bad faith will not be subject to or limited by the limits contained in this Section 9.8.

(c)   the Seller will not be liable for any Losses that have been expressly included in the calculation of the Post-Closing Purchase Price Adjustment Amount pursuant to Section 2.8.

(d)   the Seller will not be liable for any incidental, consequential or punitive damages from a breach of the representations and warranties or covenants contained in this Agreement unless (i) the Seller or any Seller Stockholder (or in the case of a Seller Stockholder that is a trust, the trustee and/or any beneficiary of such trust) had actual knowledge of the breach and did not disclose it on the <u>Disclosure Schedule</u> or (ii) such damages are awarded in connection with a Third Party Claim.

(e)   The Indemnified Parties and Tax Indemnitees are required to take commercially reasonable action to mitigate their Losses.

14.   Disclosure Schedules

Disclosure schedules provide fact-specific disclosures relating to reps or, as mentioned above, exceptions to specific statements in the reps. Here is an example of a rep requiring fact-specific disclosure.

4.25.   Bank Accounts. Section 4.25 of the <u>Disclosure Schedule</u> sets forth a complete and accurate list of (a) the names and locations of all banks, trust companies, securities brokers and other financial institutions at which the Seller or any of its Subsidiaries has an account or safe deposit box or maintains a banking, custodial, trading or other similar relationship, (b) a complete and accurate list and description of each such account, box and relationship and (c) the name of every Person authorized to draw on each such account or box or having access to each such account or box.

Normally, the items necessary to prepare the affirmative disclosure schedule are included in the deal's due diligence materials. Thus, target's counsel (likely a lower level associate on the deal) would review the relevant materials and produce the list. Below is an example of what the list might look like:[16]

DISCLOSURE SCHEDULE

This Disclosure Schedule is delivered by Silpada Designs, Inc., to Avon Products, Inc. pursuant to the Asset Purchase Agreement dated as of July 9, 2010 (the "Agreement") by and among Avon Products, Inc., SD Acquisition LLC, the Silpada Designs, Inc., the stockholder of Silpada Designs, Inc., and Gerald A. Kelly, Jr. Capitalized terms not otherwise defined herein shall have the same meanings ascribed to them in the Agreement.

The inadvertent omission of an item from a section of the Disclosure Schedule shall not be a breach of the Agreement if such item is disclosed in

---

[16] I say "might look like" because unlike most other examples, this one is not an excerpt from the actual document because companies are not generally required to file the disclosure schedule of an acquisition agreement with the SEC. Thus, I was unable to get a copy of the Avon/Silpada APA disclosure schedule.

another section of the Disclosure Schedule in a manner which makes the item understandably applicable to the section from which omitted. The inclusion of any item in any section of the Disclosure Schedule shall not constitute evidence of the materiality of such item, evidence that such item is required to be disclosed in the Disclosure Schedule or an admission of any pending or threatened charge, claim or proceeding or any breach of or event of default under any contract. The fact that any item is disclosed in any section of the Disclosure Schedule shall not give rise to any implication that the failure to disclose it would result in any breach of any representation or warranty contained in the Agreement. The attachments to any section of this Disclosure Schedule form an integral part of the Disclosure Schedule and are incorporated by reference for all purposes as if set forth fully herein.
. . .

SECTION 4.25

Bank Accounts

1. Working capital account
    Commerce Bank
    Account Number: 00112389234
    Signatories: Gerald A. Kelly, Jr., Jennifer F. Bach, Rodrigo K. Velenzuela

2. Payroll account
    Commerce Bank
    Account Number: 00112389958
    Signatories: Gerald A. Kelly, Jr., Jennifer F. Bach, Rodrigo K. Velenzuela

Here is an example of a rep from the Avon/Silpada APA and related exception disclosure.[17] The lead-in to the reps has been included because it contains the language that allows exceptions to be set forth on the Disclosure Schedule.

ARTICLE IV
REPRESENTATIONS AND WARRANTIES OF THE SELLER

The Seller represents and warrants to the Buyer as of the date hereof, as of the Closing and as of the Effective Time as follows, except as otherwise disclosed to the Buyer in the corresponding section or subsection of the schedule delivered to the Buyer by the Seller in connection with the execution of this Agreement (with specific reference to the representations and warranties in this Agreement to which the information in the corresponding section or subsection of the schedule relates) (the "**Disclosure Schedule**"): . . .

---

[17] I made up this disclosure because, as mentioned in the preceding footnote, I do not have a copy of the actual Disclosure Schedule.

4.18. Environmental.

(a) The Seller and each of its Subsidiaries is and has been in material compliance with all Environmental Laws applicable to the operations of the Seller and its Subsidiaries . . . .

SECTION 4.18
Environmental

A diesel fuel spill occurred on the grounds of the Company's headquarters in Lenexa, Kansas. Samples have shown the presence of hydrocarbon at levels requiring remediation. The state of Kansas has been notified.

F. CLOSING DOCUMENTS

This section discusses the principal documents that an acquisition agreement typically requires the parties to deliver (or cause to be delivered) at the closing. A closing is when bidder pays (and/or issues) the deal consideration and target (or target's shareholders) transfers ownership of target's business to bidder. The closing documents each party is required to deliver at closing will be listed in the acquisition agreement under the heading "Closing Deliveries" or something similar. Common closing documents include closing certificates, secretary's certificates, and opinion letters.

1. Closing Certificates

A closing certificate (sometimes called an officer's certificate) is normally delivered by both bidder and target at closing. It is a document signed by an officer of the respective company specifying that as of the date of the certificate, i.e., the closing date, (1) the representations and warranties made by the company in the acquisition agreement are true and correct, (2) the company has performed all covenants it was required to perform during the gap period by the acquisition agreement, and (3) all applicable closing conditions specified in the acquisition agreement have been satisfied.

Here is my educated guess of what the closing certificate delivered by Silpada to Avon for that deal looked like.

CLOSING CERTIFICATE
SILPADA DESIGNS, INC.

The undersigned, Gerald A. Kelly, Jr., Chairman and Chief Executive Officer of Silpada Designs, Inc., a Kansas Corporation, (the **"Seller"**), hereby certifies on behalf of the Seller, pursuant to Section 3.2(a)(xii) of the Asset Purchase Agreement dated as of July 9, 2010 (the **"Agreement"**), by and among Avon Products, Inc., SD Acquisition LLC, Seller, Seller's stockholders, and Gerald A. Kelly, Jr., that:

1.   Each of the representations and warranties of the Seller contained in Article IV of the Agreement: (i) that is a Fundamental Representation of the Seller is true and correct in all respects as of the date hereof as if made on and as of the date hereof (except for such representations and warranties that are made as of a specific date which shall speak only as of such date), and (ii) that is not a Fundamental Representation of the Seller is true and correct (without giving effect to any limitations as to materiality or Material Adverse Effect set forth therein) as of the date hereof as if made on and as of the date hereof (except for such representations and warranties that are made as of a specific date which shall speak only as of such date), with only such exceptions as have not had or would not reasonably be expected to have, individually or in the aggregate, a Material Adverse Effect or materially impede or delay the ability of any Party to consummate the transactions under this Agreement.

2.   The Seller has performed or complied with, in all material respects, all agreements and covenants required to be performed or complied with by the Seller under this Agreement at or prior to the date hereof, and the Seller has delivered all items required to be delivered at the Closing pursuant to Section 3.2(a) of the Agreement.

Capitalized terms used and not otherwise defined herein shall have the meanings ascribed to them in the Agreement.

IN WITNESS WHEREOF, the undersigned has executed this Officer's Certificate on behalf of the Company as of this 28th day of July, 2010.

SILPADA DESIGNS, INC.

By *Gerald A. Kelly, Jr.*
Name: Gerald A. Kelly, Jr.
Title: Chairman and Chief Executive
Officer

2. Secretary's Certificates

A secretary's certificate is normally delivered by both bidder and target at closing. It is a document signed by the secretary of the respective company certifying various corporate documents. In this context, a secretary is the company officer responsible for maintaining the company's books and records. Here is my educated guess of what the secretary's certificate delivered by Silpada to Avon for that deal looked like.

Secretary's Certificate

The undersigned, Aaron K. Jones, hereby certifies that he is the duly elected and acting Secretary of Silpada Designs, Inc., a Kansas corporation (the "**Company**"), and that, as such, he is duly authorized to execute and deliver this Secretary's Certificate on behalf of the Company. He hereby further certifies on behalf of the Company that:

1.   Attached hereto as Exhibit A is a true, correct and complete copy of the Articles of Incorporation of the Company, together with all amendments thereto (the "**Articles**"), which Articles are in full force and effect as of the date hereof.

2.   Attached hereto as Exhibit B is a true, correct and complete copy of the Bylaws of the Company, together with all amendments thereto (the "**Bylaws**"), which Bylaws are in full force and effect on the date hereof.

3.   Attached hereto as Exhibit C is a true, correct and complete copy of resolutions of the board of directors of the Company (the "**Resolutions**"). The Resolutions are the only resolutions adopted by the board of directors of the Company in relation to the subject matter thereof and were duly adopted in accordance with the provisions of the Articles and Bylaws. The Resolutions have not been rescinded, amended or otherwise modified since the date of their adoption and are in full force and effect on the date hereof.

4.   Attached hereto as Exhibit D is a Certificate of Good Standing for the Company certified by the Secretary of State of the State of Kansas.

5.   Each of the persons named below is a duly elected, qualified and acting officer of the Company holding the office or offices set forth opposite his or her name, the signature appearing opposite each name below is the true and genuine signature of that person, and each of the persons named below is authorized to execute and deliver on behalf of the Company, each document to which it is a party and all other agreements, documents and certificates to be delivered by the Company pursuant thereto.

Name	Office	Signature
Gerald A. Kelly, Jr.	Chairman and Chief Executive Officer	*Gerald A. Kelly, Jr.*
Nancy G. Beckman	Chief Financial Officer	*Nancy G. Beckman*

Capitalized terms used and not otherwise defined herein shall have the meanings ascribed to them in the Asset Purchase Agreement dated as of July 9, 2010, by and among Avon Products, Inc., SD Acquisition LLC, the Company, the Company's stockholders, and Gerald A. Kelly, Jr.

IN WITNESS WHEREOF, the undersigned has executed this Secretary's Certificate on behalf of the Company as of this as of this 28th day of July, 2010.

SILPADA DESIGNS, INC.

By *Aaron K. Jones*

Name: Aaron K. Jones

Title: Secretary

The undersigned hereby certifies that the person named above is the duly elected, qualified and acting Secretary of the Company, and that the signature appearing above is his true and genuine signature.

IN WITNESS WHEREOF, the undersigned has executed this Secretary's Certificate on behalf of the Company as of the date set forth above.

SILPADA DESIGNS, INC.

By *Nancy G. Beckman*

Name: Nancy G. Beckman
Title: Chief Financial Officer

3. Legal Opinions

In the M&A context, a legal opinion is a letter from the attorney or law firm of one party to the deal to the other party to the deal that addresses various legal issues with respect to the deal. Thus, at closing bidder's law firm will deliver an opinion letter to target and target's legal counsel will deliver an opinion letter to bidder (this requirement would be reflected in the acquisition agreement). The parties' attorneys will normally negotiate (sometimes heavily) the contents of these letters during the gap period.

The Avon/Silpada deal did not require any parties to deliver legal opinions (not requiring a legal opinion has become more common recently). Thus, the below sample opinion letter from target to bidder is not from that deal.

Payne & Fear LLP

April 25, 2013

Wildcat Corp.
1721 E. Enke Drive
Tucson, AZ, 85721

Ladies/Gentlemen:

We represent Sjostrom Brothers, Inc. ("Seller") in connection with the transactions contemplated by that certain Stock Purchase Agreement (the "Purchase Agreement") dated as of October 23, 2013 by and among Seller and Wildcat Corp., an Arizona corporation ("Buyer"). This opinion letter is delivered to you pursuant to Section 4.2(e) of the Purchase Agreement. Capitalized terms not otherwise defined herein shall have the meaning given to them in the Purchase Agreement.

In rendering the opinions set forth herein, we have examined originals or copies, certified or otherwise identified to our satisfaction, of such (1) records of Seller and the Company; (2) certificates of officers of Seller and the Company; (3) certificates of public officials; and (4) other documents, records, and papers as we have deemed relevant or necessary as the basis for such opinions, and we have made such inquiries of law and fact as we have deemed relevant or necessary as the basis for such opinions, including any of the foregoing delivered at the Closing. As to various factual matters material to the opinions set forth herein, we have, without any investigation or independent verification, relied upon the response of officers of Seller and the Company to such inquiries and such certificates and other statements, documents, records, and papers with respect to the facts set forth therein.

Based upon the foregoing, and subject to the qualifications set forth below, we are of the opinion that:

1. Each of Seller and the Company is a corporation duly incorporated, validly existing and in good standing under the laws of the State of Delaware. The Company is duly qualified or registered as a foreign corporation to transact business, and is in good standing, under the Laws of all jurisdictions where the nature of its business or the nature and location of its assets requires such qualification or registration.

2. The Company has all requisite corporate power and authority to own, lease and operate its properties and to carry on the Business as presently conducted.

3. Seller has full corporate power and authority, and has been duly authorized by all necessary corporate action, to enter into and perform its obligations under the Purchase Agreement and Seller's Ancillary Documents, and to consummate the transactions contemplated by the Purchase Agreement.

4. The Purchase Agreement and each of Seller's Ancillary Documents have been duly executed and delivered by duly authorized officers of Seller. The Purchase Agreement and each of Seller's Ancillary Documents constitute legal, valid and binding obligations of Seller, enforceable against Seller in accordance with their respective terms (except to the extent that enforcement may be affected by Laws relating to bankruptcy, reorganization, insolvency or similar Laws in effect that affect the enforcement of creditors' rights generally and by the availability of injunctive relief, specific performance and other equitable remedies).

5. The execution, delivery and performance by Seller of the Purchase Agreement and Seller's Ancillary Documents, and the consummation by Seller of the transactions contemplated thereby, do not and will not (with the passing of time and the giving of notice or both) violate or conflict with or result in a breach of, or constitute a default under, or result in the termination, cancellation or acceleration of any right or obligation under: (i) Seller's or the Company's certificate of incorporation or Bylaws; (ii) any Company Contract (except as set forth in Section 2.3(d) of the Disclosure Schedule); (iii) any Law applicable to the Company or to Seller; or (iv) any Judgment or any arbitration award to which the Company or Seller is a party or by which the Company or Seller or their respective properties and assets are bound.

The opinions set forth above are subject to the following qualifications:

A. We have assumed the genuineness of all signatures, the authenticity of all documents submitted to me as originals, the conformity to the originals of all documents submitted to me as copies and the authenticity of the originals of all such latter documents. We have also assumed the accuracy of the factual matters contained in the documents I have examined.

B. We have assumed that each of the parties to the Purchase Agreement and Seller's Ancillary Documents (other than Seller and the Company) have all requisite power and authority, and have taken all necessary actions, (i) to execute and deliver the Purchase Agreement and Seller's Ancillary

Documents; and (ii) to effect the transactions contemplated thereby. We have assumed that each of the parties to Seller's Ancillary Documents who is a natural individual has the legal capacity (a) to execute and deliver such documents; and (b) to effect the transactions contemplated thereby. We have assumed that the execution, delivery and performance of the Purchase Agreement and Seller's Ancillary Documents by each party thereto (other than Seller and the Company) will not violate (x) applicable Law or (y) any order, writ, judgment, injunction, decree, determination or award which binds such party or any of its properties. We have assumed the due execution and delivery for value of the Purchase Agreement and Seller's Ancillary Documents by each of the parties thereto (other than Seller and the Company). We have assumed that (1) each of the Purchase Agreement and Seller's Ancillary Documents is the legal, valid and binding obligation of the parties thereto (other than Seller, and the Company), enforceable against each of such parties in accordance with the terms, and (2) that no consent, approval, authorization, declaration or filing by or with any governmental commission, board or agency is required for the valid execution and delivery of the Purchase Agreement or Seller's Ancillary Documents by the parties thereto (other than Seller and the Company).

C.   We express no opinion as to the Laws of, or the effect or applicability of the Laws of, or as to any matter subject to any laws other than: (i) the Laws of the State of Minnesota, (ii) the Federal laws of the United States of America, and (iii) the General Corporation Law of the State of Delaware.

D.   We do not render any opinion as to the enforceability of Sections 6.8, 11.11, 11.15 or 11.18 of the Purchase Agreement. We do not render any opinion as to the enforceability of any provision of the Purchase Agreement to the extent that it provides for indemnification in violation of public policy.

E.   We express no opinion as to the applicability or effect of any securities or anti-trust laws.

The opinions set forth above are limited to the matters expressly set forth herein and to laws and facts existing on the date hereof and no opinion is to be implied or inferred beyond the matters expressly so stated. We do not undertake to advise you of any changes in such Laws or facts which may occur after the date hereof. This opinion letter is rendered solely for your benefit in connection with the transactions contemplated by the Purchase Agreement and may not be relied upon by any other person or used for any other purpose without my written consent.

Very truly yours,

Payne & Fear LLP

4.   Other Closing Documents

Pursuant to a state's merger statute, a merger is not effective until a document called a certificate or articles of merger is filed by the surviving corporation with the secretary of state in its state of incorporation.[18] This document will be signed

---

[18] *See, e.g.*, MBCA § 11.06; DGCL § 251(c). Under the DGCL, the surviving corporation can file the

by an agent of the surviving corporation as part of the closing and is normally filed the same day as closing. Here is my educated guess of what the certificate of merger for the Avis Budget/Zipcar deal looked like.

CERTIFICATE OF MERGER
OF
MILLENNIUM ACQUISITION SUB, INC.
INTO
ZIPCAR, INC.

Pursuant to Title 8, § 251(c) of the Delaware General Corporation Law, the undersigned corporation executed the following Certificate of Merger:

FIRST: The name and state of incorporation of each of the constituent corporations of the merger is as follows:

Name	State of Incorporation
Millennium Acquisition Sub, Inc.	Delaware
Zipcar, Inc.	Delaware

SECOND: An Agreement and Plan of Merger has been approved, adopted, certified, executed and acknowledged by each of the constituent corporations in accordance with § 251(c) of the Delaware General Corporate Law.

THIRD: The name of the surviving corporation is Zipcar, Inc.

FOURTH: The Certificate of Incorporation of the surviving corporation shall be its Certificate of Incorporation.

FIFTH: The executed Agreement and Plan of Merger is on file at an office of the surviving corporation. The address of such office is 25 First Street, 4th Floor, Cambridge, MA 02141.

SIXTH: A copy of the Agreement and Plan of Merger will be furnished by the surviving corporation, on request and without cost, to any stockholder of any constituent corporation.

IN WITNESS WHEREOF, said surviving corporation has caused this certificate to be signed by an authorized officer on March 14, 2013.

By:　　__/s/ Scott W. Griffith__
Authorized Officer
Name: Scott W. Griffith
Title: Chief Executive Officer

Note that there is a similar filing requirement for a deal structured as a share exchange but not for a deal structured as an asset purchase or stock purchase.

---

entire agreement and plan of merger instead of a certificate of merger but the standard practice is to go with a certificate of merger.

For an asset purchase, closing documents also include various transfer documents because the transfer does not occur by operation of the law (as is the case with a merger). These documents include a bill of sale for tangible personal property, an assignment and assumption agreement for the transfer of contracts and intellectual property rights, and deeds for the transfer of real property.

For a stock purchase, target's shareholders will need to sign over and deliver their stock certificates to bidder at closing.

G. PUBLIC TARGET DEALS

With a few exceptions, deal documentation is the same regardless if target is a public company. We discuss the principle differences below.

1. Fewer Target Representations and Warranties

An acquisition agreement for a public target will have fewer representations and warranties than one for a private target. This is because a public target is subject to extensive disclosure obligations under federal securities laws. Thus many of the reps that would be included for a private target deal can be left out because the substance of them is captured by a broad rep by target with respect to its SEC filings. Here is an example of such a rep from the Agreement and Plan of Merger dated July 28, 2013 between Hudson's Bay Company, Harry Acquisition Inc. and Saks Incorporated pursuant to which Hudson's agreed to acquire Saks through a reverse triangular merger. At the time, Saks' common stock was traded on the NYSE under the symbol SKS.

Section 4.4 **Reports and Financial Statements**.

(a) The Company [Saks] has filed or furnished all forms, statements, certifications, documents and reports required to be filed or furnished prior to the date hereof by it with the SEC since January 28, 2012 (as amended and supplemented from time to time, the "Company SEC Documents"), each of which, in each case as of its date, or, if amended, as finally amended prior to the date of this Agreement, complied as to form in all material respects with the applicable requirements of the Securities Act, the Exchange Act and the Sarbanes-Oxley Act, as the case may be, and the applicable rules and regulations promulgated thereunder, as of the date filed with the SEC, and none of the Company SEC Documents contained any untrue statement of a material fact or omitted to state any material fact required to be stated therein or necessary to make the statements therein, in light of the circumstances under which they were made, not misleading. As of the date hereof, there are no outstanding or unresolved comments received from the SEC with respect to any of the Company SEC Documents, and, to the Knowledge of the Company, none of the Company SEC Documents is the subject of outstanding SEC comment or outstanding SEC investigation.

---

2. No Indemnification for Bidder

An acquisition agreement for a public target does not typically include indemnification provisions or a related holdback or escrow. This is because most public targets are owned by a diverse, large, and dispersed group of shareholders and therefore have no identifiable party to stand behind an indemnification obligation.

3. Deal Protection Devices

Deal protection devices are provisions of an acquisition agreement designed to protect bidder from losing the deal to a competing bidder. While some of these devices are included in private target deals, they are much more common and elaborate in public target deals. This is because SEC disclosure obligations applicable to public targets increase bidder's risk of being out bid, or jumped. Specifically, potential competing bidders will learn of the deal shortly after the acquisition agreement is signed and will be able to get their hands on the acquisition agreement as soon as target files its Item 1. Form 8-K for the deal. Thus, they will know the exact terms under which bidder has agreed to buy target and therefore what they have to beat.

Even though target will have already signed the acquisition agreement at this point, for reasons we discuss in the next chapter, the agreement will likely include a "fiduciary out" — a provision allowing target to get out of the deal if, among other things, a competing bidder makes a topping, or superior, bid. Hence, deal protection devices are designed in large part to decrease the likelihood of competing bids.

Deal protection devices include no-shops, force-the-vote provisions, matching rights, breakup fees, and voting agreements, each of which is described briefly below.

As discussed in Section B above, a *no-shop* prohibits target from reaching out to other potential bidders in an effort to start a bidding war. It is sometimes coupled with a *go-shop* to assuage target board fiduciary duty concerns (see next chapter). A go-shop is basically an exception to a no-shop that allowing target to solicit, discuss, and negotiate an alternative transaction with a third party for a specified period of time, usually 30–60 days, after the parties have signed the acquisition agreement.

A *force the vote provision* is sometimes included in an acquisition agreement for a deal that requires target shareholder approval (e.g., merger, asset purchase). Specifically, it obligates target's board of directors to submit the proposed deal to a target shareholder vote even if the board no longer recommends the deal. Such provisions are explicitly allowed under some state's corporate codes.[19] Bidder hopes the provision will deter a third party from making a competing bid because the third party will know that action on its bid will be delayed until after the shareholder vote on bidder's bid is completed. This delay may be several months as

---

[19] *See, e.g.,* DGCL § 146; MBCA § 8.26.

target will have to prepare, file, and distribute a proxy materials for the vote. Further, target's shareholders may end up voting in favor of bidder's bid not wanting to pass on the bird in the hand.

Matching rights give a bidder the right to increase its offer before target's board of directors decides to go with a competing bid.

A *break-up fee*, also called a termination fee, is a fee payable by target to bidder if the deal does not ultimately close because, for example, target's board exercises its fiduciary out. A break-up fee is specified in the acquisition agreement, normally as a flat dollar amount. Break-up fees are typically in the range of 3 percent to 4 percent of the total deal consideration. Thus, for a $1 billion deal, the break-up fee will be $30,000,000 to $40,000,000. Among other things, break-up fees alleviate to some extent the pain felt by bidder in losing the deal because at least it gets a sizable cash payment that will likely more than cover the expenses it incurred in pursuing target. Deals also sometimes include a so called reverse break-up fee. This is a fee payable by bidder to target if the deal does not ultimately close because, for example, bidder failed to obtain financing for the deal.

Voting agreements, also called lock-ups, are often implemented in deals that require target shareholder approval (e.g., merger, asset purchase). They are entered into between bidder and significant target shareholders concurrently with the acquisition agreement. A voting agreement obligates the shareholder signatory to vote his or her shares in favor of the deal and against any competing transaction.

EXERCISE 5.6

Review the priceline.com/KAYAK merger agreement (available for download at www.sjobiz.org/mna) and identify the deal protection devices included in the agreement.

Chapter 6

HOSTILE DEALS

A hostile deal, or takeover, is the label given to an acquisition where target's board of directors is (at least initially) against target being acquired by bidder. In this chapter we discuss deal structure options for a hostile takeover, defensive tactics target can implement to thwart a hostile takeover attempt, and state anti-takeover statutes. The chapter closes with a case study of the protracted, but ultimately successful, takeover of PeopleSoft, Inc. by Oracle Corporation, which closed in 2005. We cover fiduciary duty implications of defensive tactics in the next chapter. Generally only a public company can be acquired against the will of its board of directors, so in this chapter assume that target is public.

A. COMMENCING A HOSTILE TAKEOVER

A hostile takeover attempt often begins with bidder sending target's board a so-called "bear hug" letter outlining a preliminary offer for target and inviting target's board to negotiate with bidder towards a friendly deal. Typically, bidder publicly discloses the letter to turn up the heat on target's board.[1] Below is a bear hug letter sent by Microsoft to Yahoo! in 2008.

Board of Directors
Yahoo! Inc.
701 First Avenue
Sunnyvale, CA 94089
Attention: Roy Bostock, Chairman
Attention: Jerry Yang, Chief Executive Officer

Dear Members of the Board:

I am writing on behalf of the Board of Directors of Microsoft to make a proposal for a business combination of Microsoft and Yahoo!. Under our proposal, Microsoft would acquire all of the outstanding shares of Yahoo! common stock for per share consideration of $31 based on Microsoft's closing share price on January 31, 2008, payable in the form of $31 in cash or 0.9509 of a share of Microsoft common stock. Microsoft would provide each Yahoo! shareholder with the ability to choose whether to receive the consideration in cash or Microsoft common stock, subject to pro-ration so that in the aggregate one-half of the Yahoo! common shares will be exchanged for shares of Microsoft common stock and one-half of the Yahoo! common shares will be converted into the right to receive cash. Our proposal is not subject to any financing condition.

---

[1] A publicly disclosed letter is called a "grizzly bear hug." If bidder keeps the letter private, it's called a "teddy bear hug."

Our proposal represents a 62% premium above the closing price of Yahoo! common stock of $19.18 on January 31, 2008. The implied premium for the operating assets of the company clearly is considerably greater when adjusted for the minority, non-controlled assets and cash. By whatever financial measure you use — EBITDA, free cash flow, operating cash flow, net income, or analyst target prices — this proposal represents a compelling value realization event for your shareholders.

We believe that Microsoft common stock represents a very attractive investment opportunity for Yahoo!'s shareholders. Microsoft has generated revenue growth of 15%, earnings growth of 26%, and a return on equity of 35% on average for the last three years. Microsoft's share price has generated shareholder returns of 8% during the last one year period and 28% during the last three year period, significantly outperforming the S&P 500. It is our view that Microsoft has significant potential upside given the continued solid growth in our core businesses, the recent launch of Windows Vista, and other strategic initiatives.

Microsoft's consistent belief has been that the combination of Microsoft and Yahoo! clearly represents the best way to deliver maximum value to our respective shareholders, as well as create a more efficient and competitive company that would provide greater value and service to our customers. In late 2006 and early 2007, we jointly explored a broad range of ways in which our two companies might work together. These discussions were based on a vision that the online businesses of Microsoft and Yahoo! should be aligned in some way to create a more effective competitor in the online marketplace. We discussed a number of alternatives ranging from commercial partnerships to a merger proposal, which you rejected. While a commercial partnership may have made sense at one time, Microsoft believes that the only alternative now is the combination of Microsoft and Yahoo! that we are proposing. . . .

We would value the opportunity to further discuss with you how to optimize the integration of our respective businesses to create a leading global technology company with exceptional display and search advertising capabilities. You should also be aware that we intend to offer significant retention packages to your engineers, key leaders and employees across all disciplines.

We have dedicated considerable time and resources to an analysis of a potential transaction and are confident that the combination will receive all necessary regulatory approvals. We look forward to discussing this with you, and both our internal legal team and outside counsel are available to meet with your counsel at their earliest convenience.

Our proposal is subject to the negotiation of a definitive merger agreement and our having the opportunity to conduct certain limited and confirmatory due diligence. In addition, because a portion of the aggregate merger consideration would consist of Microsoft common stock, we would provide Yahoo! the opportunity to conduct appropriate limited due diligence with respect to Microsoft. We are prepared to deliver a draft merger agreement to you and begin discussions immediately.

In light of the significance of this proposal to your shareholders and ours, as well as the potential for selective disclosures, our intention is to publicly release the text of this letter tomorrow morning.

Due to the importance of these discussions and the value represented by our proposal, we expect the Yahoo! Board to engage in a full review of our proposal. My leadership team and I would be happy to make ourselves available to meet with you and your Board at your earliest convenience. Depending on the nature of your response, Microsoft reserves the right to pursue all necessary steps to ensure that Yahoo!'s shareholders are provided with the opportunity to realize the value inherent in our proposal.

We believe this proposal represents a unique opportunity to create significant value for Yahoo!'s shareholders and employees, and the combined company will be better positioned to provide an enhanced value proposition to users and advertisers. We hope that you and your Board share our enthusiasm, and we look forward to a prompt and favorable reply.

Sincerely yours,
/s/ Steven A. Ballmer
Steven A. Ballmer
Chief Executive Officer
Microsoft Corporation

It is possible that target's board will decide to pursue a friendly deal with bidder. Frequently, however, target's board rebuffs bidder's overtures. Such a rebuff will be followed by some bidder saber-rattling about launching a hostile takeover. If saber-rattling does not get target to the negotiating table and bidder is truly committed to acquiring target, bidder will then file paperwork with the SEC for a tender offer and/or proxy contest (discussed below) and the hostile takeover attempt will be on. (Microsoft did some saber-rattling which failed to have the desired effect on Yahoo! and ultimately decided to abandon its pursuit).

Before sending a bear hug letter, it is common for bidder to buy some of target's stock in the open market. Given a large purchase of a public company's shares may be a precursor to a hostile takeover attempt, § 13(d) of the Exchange Act[2] and SEC rules promulgated thereunder generally require a person (i.e., bidder) to make a public filing on Schedule 13D with the SEC within 10 days of directly or indirectly acquiring more than 5% of a public company's shares. In the filing, the person must disclose, among other things, the number of shares acquired and the intent behind acquiring the shares. The filing is often the first indication to target that bidder is considering pursuing a takeover.

SEC rules require the filer to amend its Schedule 13D if it materially increases or decreases its percentage ownership of shares. A change of 1% or more is deemed material. A change of less than 1% may be material depending on the facts and circumstances.

B.   DEAL STRUCTURE OPTIONS

As alluded to above, bidder has two choices when it comes to a hostile takeover attempt, it can either launch a tender offer or a proxy contest.

---

[2] Congress added § 13(d) to the Exchange Act in 1968 as part of the Williams Act.

1.   Tender Offer

As we learned in Chapter 3, a tender offer in the M&A context is basically when bidder acquires a public target through a stock purchase. If the deal is friendly, bidder and target negotiate an acquisition agreement that specifies the terms of the tender offer and mechanics of the deal. The boards of both bidder and target then formally approve the agreement, and it is signed. Bidder then prepares and files with the SEC a Schedule TO and related documents for the deal.

In the hostile context, bidder bypasses target's board and goes directly to target's shareholders with an offer to buy at least a majority of target's shares. Remember, a stock purchase is the only deal structure that does not require target board approval or a shareholder vote. Instead, each target shareholder decides individually whether or not to tender his or her shares in the deal; target's board has no say in this decision. If enough shareholders tender, bidder closes on the tender offer, becomes the majority shareholder of target, removes target's directors and replaces them with bidder's people. Target's new board then approves a second-step merger between target and a subsidiary of bidder to squeeze out any target shareholders that did not tender their shares to bidder. When the dust settles, target's business ends up in a wholly-owned subsidiary of bidder.

As we discussed in Chapter 3, SEC tender offer rules (1) impose on bidder various requirements regarding its offer to target's shareholders, (2) require bidder to file certain documents with the SEC; and (3) require bidder to disseminate specified information to target shareholders. One of the things we did not discuss in Chapter 3 because it is of little significance in the friendly tender offer context is target's obligation to file Schedule 14D-9. This Schedule, among other things, requires target's board to indicate whether it recommends, opposes, is unable to take a position on, or is neutral regarding the tender offer. Target must make this filing within ten business days of commencement of bidder's tender offer. Sometimes target will disseminate a so-called "stop-look-and-listen communication" before filing its Schedule 14D-9 requesting its shareholders to defer deciding whether to tender until target's board has indicated its position on the deal.

2.   Proxy Contest

In a proxy contest, or fight, bidder seeks to take over target's board of directors by getting its people elected to fill a majority of board seats. Taking over target's board makes all deal structure options available because the board will no longer be opposed to the takeover. In other words, the deal will transition from hostile to friendly upon completion of a successful proxy contest.

This option is called a proxy contest because, as discussed in Chapter 3, for public companies the overwhelming majority of shareholder voting occurs via proxy. Thus, in advance of the target's next board of directors' election, bidder will send target's shareholders proxy materials soliciting their proxies to vote in favor of bidder's slate of directors. This means that target's shareholders will receive two sets of proxy materials — one set from target soliciting proxies for the slate of directors selected by target and bidder's set putting forth an alternative slate. Bidder and target will then engage in essentially a political campaign trying to convince target shareholders to use its respective proxy card to vote for its slate.

If bidder does not want to wait for target's next annual election of directors, it could perhaps launch a proxy contest to remove target's board of directors and immediately elect bidder's replacements. Alternatively, bidder could perhaps seek written consents from shareholders for the same purposes. I say "perhaps" because whether these options are available depends on target's state of incorporation and organizational documents, as discussed below.

As we discussed in Chapter 3, proxy solicitation is regulated by SEC rules. For the most part, the same rules that apply to a public target when soliciting its own shareholders apply to a hostile bidder soliciting a public target's shareholders. Thus, for example, bidder must prepare and file with the SEC a preliminary proxy statement that includes the same basic information as target's proxy statement (bidder gets this information from target's public filings) plus a discussion of why target shareholders should go with bidder's slate of directors, and the slate's plans for target if successful. It then must respond to any SEC comments and file a definitive proxy statement. Normally, bidder and target also send out so-called "fight letters" to target's shareholders making more elaborate cases for their slates than they included in their respective proxy statements.

Bidder will obviously need some sort of access to target's shareholder list so that it can communicate directly with target's shareholders. This issue is addressed by Exchange Act Rule 14a-7 which is known as the "divulge or mail" rule. The rule generally requires target to either (1) provide bidder with a list of its shareholders or, at target's option, (2) mail bidder's materials to target's shareholders for bidder. Target will almost always go with option (2) so that it has advance notice of what bidder is sending out to target's shareholders and when.

State law also comes into play concerning bidder's access to target's shareholder list. Most state corporate law statutes afford shareholders the right to inspect a corporation's books and records (bidder will be a target shareholder because it will have acquired shares of target in the open market before commencing the proxy fight). Among the items a shareholder is entitled to inspect and copy under these provisions is a shareholder list. For example DGCL § 220 provides:

> (b) Any stockholder, in person or by attorney or other agent, shall, upon written demand under oath stating the purpose thereof, have the right during the usual hours for business to inspect for any proper purpose, and to make copies and extracts from:
>
> > (1) The corporation's stock ledger, a list of its stockholders, and its other books and records . . . .[3]

Notice that a shareholder has to specify a "proper purpose" for examining records. Section 220(b) defines "proper purpose" as "a purpose reasonably related to such person's interest as a stockholder." Using the list in connection with a proxy

---

[3] § 16.02 is the analogous MBCA provision.

contest is generally considered to fall within this language, as the next case indicates.

HATLEIGH CORP. v. LANE BRYANT, INC.
Delaware Chancery Court
428 A.2d 350 (1981)

HARTNETT, Vice Chancellor.

Plaintiff Hatleigh Corporation ("Hatleigh") filed a demand, pursuant to 8 Del. C. s 220, to inspect and copy a list of the stockholders of defendant Lane Bryant, Inc. a Delaware corporation. Lane Bryant resisted the demand and this is my decision after trial in favor of Hatleigh.

I

Hatleigh is the record holder of 1,000 shares of common stock of Lane Bryant, Inc. and owns beneficially an additional 697,300 shares or 15.3% of the outstanding shares. On November 5, 1980, acting on behalf of Hatleigh, Mr. Marshall Jacobs requested Lane Bryant, Inc. to provide Hatleigh with a stockholder list. The demand stated that it was made:

"For the purpose of communicating with Lane's stockholders on matters relating to mutual interest as stockholders, to communicate with Lane's stockholders in order to influence the policy of Lane's management, to inquire of the stockholders as to their opinions of the management of Lane and whether they would support Hatleigh's efforts to seek representation on Lane's Board of Directors, to solicit the proxies of other stockholders in connection with the next annual meeting of stockholders, and more specifically to obtain the list to enable solicitation of proxies in connection with the election of members to the Board of Directors of Lane."

8 Del. C. s 220 provides in part:

(b) Any stockholder, in person or by attorney or other agent, shall, upon written demand under oath stating the purpose thereof, have the right during the usual hours for business to inspect for any proper purpose the corporation's stock ledger, a list of its stockholders . . . . and to make copies or extracts therefrom. A proper purpose shall mean a purpose reasonably related to such person's interest as a stockholder . . . .

(c) . . . The Court of Chancery is hereby vested with the exclusive jurisdiction to determine whether or not the person seeking inspection is entitled to the inspection sought . . . . Where the stockholder seeks to inspect the corporation's stock ledger or list of stockholders and he has complied with the provisions of this section respecting the form and manner of making demand for inspection of such documents, the burden of proof shall be upon the corporation to establish that the inspection he seeks is for an improper purpose . . . .

It is conceded by Lane Bryant that Hatleigh's demand technically complies with the requirements of 8 Del. C. s 220 and that one of the stated purposes the solicitation of stockholder proxies is a proper purpose under the statute. Lane Bryant contends, however, that the demand was not bona fide because Hatleigh had not on November 5, 1980 formed an intention to actually solicit proxies but was seeking the list of stockholders for a different purpose. Lane Bryant points out that a previous demand of Hatleigh on August 7, 1980 for the same stockholder list was denied by me on October 20, 1980. At that time I found, after trial, that the August demand did not state that Hatleigh had an intention to seek proxies, that Hatleigh had not, in August, formed an intention to seek proxies, and that its stated purposes were inadequate. I held, therefore, that the August demand did not set forth a proper purpose to justify access to the stockholder list. And I further held that Hatleigh, at trial, had not corrected the defect by showing that a proper purpose existed.

At the most recent trial Hatleigh showed that its Board of Directors decided on November 5, 1980, to seek stockholder proxies for use at the next annual stockholders meeting of Lane Bryant. Testimony was also adduced which showed that on October 8, 1980, a final effort was made to compromise Hatleigh's differences with Lane Bryant but was a failure. This failure, it is contended, acted as the final catalyst which caused the directors of Hatleigh to form an intention to seek the proxies.

Lane Bryant, however, points out that the decision of the Board of Directors of Hatleigh to seek proxies occurred only sixteen days after my October 20, 1980, opinion and the action was taken only after the Board was advised that it would be necessary to undertake a proxy solicitation in order to secure the desired stockholder list. It was also shown that a proxy soliciting firm was retained by Hatleigh only two days before the date originally scheduled for this trial.

After reviewing all the evidence, however, I am convinced that Hatleigh's November 5, 1980, decision to solicit proxies was bona fide and the fact that my October opinion may have contributed to that decision is of little relevance. I also find that Hatleigh's failure to retain a proxy soliciting firm until two days before trial does not show that it had not formed a bona fide intention to solicit proxies at the time of its demand for a stockholder list.

II

Lane Bryant also claims that the most recent demand for a stockholder list was invalid because it was premature. It was made on November 5, 1980, and the next annual meeting is not scheduled until May of 1981. The lack of imminence of a stockholders meeting is, however, irrelevant to the issue of whether a stockholder has a right to inspect and copy a stockholder list if a proper purpose for the inspection exists. If a demand for the inspection of a stockholder list is made for the purpose of soliciting proxies and there is a bona fide intent to solicit proxies at the time of the demand, there is no reason why the demand must be made within a certain number of days of the next scheduled stockholders meeting. The statute imposes no such requirement and it is difficult to perceive how prejudice can result from the list being made available at an early date instead of on the eve of an annual meeting. If the time of the demand has any relevance it is only to show the lack of a bona fide intent to solicit proxies but I am convinced that Hatleigh had a bona fide intent to solicit stockholder proxies for the next annual meeting at the time it made its November 5, 1980, demand.

In my October 20, 1980, opinion denying the earlier request of Hatleigh for the stockholder list of Lane Bryant, I did state that the August demand was premature. In that opinion I cited *AAR Corp. v. Brooks & Perkins, Inc.*, Del. Ch., unreported, (C.A. # 6222-NC, Oct. 22, 1980). Neither of these opinions, however, holds that an otherwise proper demand for a stock list is premature merely because it was made several months prior to the next annual meeting. In both of those cases the demand was premature only because the stockholder had not formed a bona fide intent to seek the stockholder list at the time of the demand.

The claim of Lane Bryant that the proxy solicitation has not yet received clearance from the Securities and Exchange Commission is irrelevant. . . .

IV

Having decided that Hatleigh is entitled to a reasonable inspection of the list of stockholders of Lane Bryant, a question arises as to the scope of the inspection. A number of shares of Lane Bryant are listed on the books of the corporation as being held by "CEDE & CO." This denotes a recognized central certificate depository system whereby various brokerage firms hold stock that is actually owned by their customers in the name of CEDE & CO. or in the name of other similar firms organized to hold shares of stock for others. Lane Bryant claims that it has no obligation to furnish Hatleigh with a breakdown of the CEDE & CO. listings to show the names of the various brokerage firms holding Lane Bryant stock for clients in that name. Vice Chancellor Brown recently addressed this issue in the unreported case of *Giovanini v. Horizon Corp.*, Del. Ch., (C.A. # 5961-NC, Sept. 12, 1979). He stated:

> Evidence was offered as to the workings of CEDE & CO. which is the name utilized by Depository Trust Company to hold shares held by it for others. Depository Trust Company is an association of more than 200 brokerage houses and financial institutions which was formed for the purpose of holding shares held in street name for the beneficial interest of customers of the brokerage firms and financial institutions. In other words, the name "CEDE & Co." appearing on the corporate stock ledger is thrice removed from the true beneficial owner. The brokerage house holds the stock for the benefit of its customer, but it holds title through the Depository Trust Company which in turn uses the name CEDE & Co. for this purpose. This is done, as I understand it, for the benefit of those firms participating in the Depository Trust Company so as to simplify their stock transfer transactions on behalf of their customers.

> This mechanism of convenience for the brokerage firms, however, prevents the stock ledger from revealing to one examining it just which brokerage firms hold shares and the number of shares held by each. This information, or "breakdown", of shares can be provided to the corporation at its request. Again, through the wonders of modern computer technology,

this can apparently be accomplished in a matter of minutes. When the breakdown is disclosed the identity of the brokerage firms holding stock under the name of "CEDE & Co.", can be learned and contact can then be made with them in order to ascertain the number of beneficial owners on whose behalf they hold stock in street name so that a proper amount of informational materials may then be forwarded to the brokerage firms for distribution to the beneficial owners. Plaintiff seeks this "breakdown" list as to CEDE in order that he too may get his proxy solicitation materials into the hands of the beneficial owners in ample time for the annual meeting.

The question was addressed to some extent in *Bear, Stearns & Co. v. Pabst Brewing Company*, Del. Ch., unreported, C.A.No.5456, N.C. (November 25, 1977). There the request for the CEDE breakdown was refused. However, it was expressly so held because of a lack of evidence. It was also observed there that if the list of stockholders maintained by the corporation as of a specified date included such a breakdown of broker-holders, then it should be furnished to a stockholder seeking a list for a proper purpose under s 220 so as to place him on a par with the corporation. Also in that case, the list was being sought for the purpose of making a tender offer; it was not being sought in the context of a race to meet an established deadline for a meeting of shareholders as is the situation here. Thus, I do not feel that the ruling in Bear, Stearns mandates a denial of the CEDE breakdowns. Since the evidence here shows that such a breakdown is readily available to the corporation for the purpose of making its contact with its shareholders, then I feel that such information should be made available to the plaintiff forthwith so that his list of stockholders for his proper purpose of soliciting their proxies is at least equivalent, in this aspect, with the list available to the corporation for the same purpose.

As to the magnetic computer tape available from the transfer agent, it appears that there is precedent for requiring the corporation to authorize its delivery to a s 220 plaintiff. It was done in *Tannetics, Inc. v. A. J. Industries, Inc.*, 2 Del. Corp. Law Journal 348 (1974).

It is therefore clear that the listing of CEDE & CO. as the holder of stock of Lane Bryant is merely a method utilized by brokerage firms to hold stock for their customers and is done solely for the convenience of the brokers. A CEDE breakdown showing the names of the brokerage firms and the number of shares they hold is readily available to Lane Bryant and without it there would be no practical way for Hatleigh to learn how many copies of its proposed communication it should send to CEDE & CO. for distribution to the brokerage firms and thence to the true owners of Lane Bryant stock.

I therefore find that Hatleigh is entitled to a breakdown of the CEDE & CO. listings and other similar listings generally recognized as indicating the shares of stock are being held for brokerage firms and similar financial institutions. . . .

VI

Because I have held that Hatleigh is entitled to an inspection of the stock list pursuant to 8 Del. C. s 220, it is not necessary to consider Hatleigh's argument that it is also entitled to an inspection pursuant to the By-laws of Lane Bryant. . . .

QUESTIONS

1. What was Hatleigh's stated purpose for its demand to inspect and copy Lane Bryant's list of stockholders?

2. Why do you think Lane Bryant resisted the demand?

3. Who is CEDE & CO.? What does it have to do with this case?

4. Why did Hatleigh want the breakdown of CEDE & CO. listings?

C. DEFENSIVE TACTICS

A company can implement a number of different measures to make it more difficult for a hostile bidder to succeed in a takeover (and less likely that one will even be launched). This section first discusses the two most prominent defenses: the poison pill and the staggered board. It then describes various other measures that companies implement to reinforce these defenses.

1. Poison Pill

A poison pill is the colloquial name for a shareholders' rights plan that is adopted by a corporation's board of directors to make a hostile tender offer for a corporation's shares prohibitively expensive. A typical poison pill provides target's shareholders, other than a hostile bidder, the right to buy target stock at a substantial discount. To give you a sense for the specifics of a poison pill, below is an excerpt from a Form 8-K of Health Management Associates, Inc. regarding the shareholder rights plan it adopted on in May 2013:

Item 1.01 Entry into a Material Definitive Agreement.

On May 24, 2013, the Board of Directors (the "Board of Directors") of Health Management Associates, Inc., a Delaware corporation (the "Corporation"), adopted a shareholder rights plan (the "Rights Plan"). The Board of Directors believes that adopting the Rights Plan at this time is prudent and in the best interests of the Corporation and its stockholders.

On May 6, 2013, Glenview Capital Management, LLC ("Glenview") filed a Schedule 13D with respect to its approximately 14.56% interest in the Corporation's outstanding shares of common stock. Glenview previously disclosed its position on a Schedule 13G, which reflected a passive investment intent. By converting to a Schedule 13D at this time, Glenview has disclosed that it may, among other things, increase its ownership stake in the Corporation, influence control of the Corporation, and seek to have the Corporation undertake a change in control or other extraordinary transaction. In addition, on May 22, 2013, affiliates of Glenview provided the Corporation with notice that it made a filing under the Hart-Scott-Rodino Antitrust Improvements Act of 1976, as amended ("HSR Act"), which notice indicates that these affiliates presently intend to acquire, collectively, up to approximately $2.2 billion of the Corporation's outstanding common stock.

In light of Glenview's Schedule 13D filing, as well as its filing under the HSR Act, the Board of Directors determined to implement the Rights Plan. The Board of Directors believes that the Rights Plan will help promote the fair and equal treatment of all stockholders of the Corporation (not just Glenview) and ensures that the Board of Directors remains in the best position to discharge its fiduciary duties to the Corporation and its stockholders. The Rights Plan adopted by the Board of Directors, which has a short one-year term and a 15% threshold, reflects the Board of Directors' effort to balance these concerns with best corporate governance practices.

The Board of Directors and the Corporation's management remain committed to taking such actions that are in the best interest of the Corporation and all of its stockholders and enhancing shareholder value.

In adopting the Rights Plan, the Board authorized the issuance of one right (a "Right") for each outstanding share of common stock, par value $0.01 per share, of the Corporation (the "Common Stock"). The issuance is effective as of June 3, 2013 to stockholders of record on that date (the "Record Date"). Each Right, once exercisable, entitles the registered holder to purchase from the Corporation one one-thousandth (1/1000) of a share of preferred stock of the Corporation, designated as Series A Junior Participating Preferred Stock, par value $0.01 per share (the "Preferred Stock"), at a price of $45.00 per one one-thousandth (1/1000) of a share (the "Exercise Price"), subject to certain adjustments. The description and terms of the Rights are set forth in a Rights Agreement (as it may be supplemented or amended from time to time, the "Rights Agreement"), dated as of May 24, 2013, by and between the Corporation and American Stock Transfer & Trust Company, LLC, as Rights Agent (the "Rights Agent").

The Rights Agreement is intended to protect the Company and its stockholders from efforts to obtain control of the Company that the Board of Directors determines are not in the best interests of the Company and its stockholders, and to enable all stockholders to realize the long-term value of their investment in the Company. The Rights Agreement is not intended to interfere with any merger, tender or exchange offer or other business combination approved by the Board of Directors.

As discussed below, initially the Rights will not be exercisable, certificates will not be sent to stockholders and the Rights will automatically trade with the Common Stock.

The Rights, unless earlier redeemed or exchanged by the Board of Directors, become exercisable upon the close of business on the day (the "Distribution Date") which is the earlier of (a) the tenth (10th) business day following a public announcement that a person or group of affiliated or associated persons, with certain exceptions set forth below, has acquired beneficial ownership of fifteen percent (15%) or more of the outstanding voting shares of the Corporation (an "Acquiring Person") and (b) the tenth (10th) business day (or such later date as may be determined by the Board of Directors prior to such time as any person or group of affiliated or associated persons becomes an Acquiring Person) after the date of the commencement by any person (other than an Exempt Person, as defined in the Rights Agreement) of a tender or exchange offer, the consummation of which would result in such person or group of affiliated or associated persons becoming an Acquiring Person.

An Acquiring Person does not include (a) the Corporation, (b) any subsidiary of the Corporation, (c) any employee benefit plan or employee stock plan of the Corporation or of any subsidiary of the Corporation, or any trust or other entity organized, appointed, established or holding voting shares for or pursuant to the terms of any such plan, (d) any person who the Board of Directors determines in good faith becomes the owner of fifteen percent (15%) or more of the shares of voting stock of the Corporation then outstanding inadvertently and without any intention of changing or influencing control of the Corporation (unless and until such person fails to divest itself, as soon as practicable, of beneficial ownership of a sufficient number of shares of voting stock of the Corporation so that such person would no longer otherwise qualify as an Acquiring Person), (e) any person who, as of 5:00 p.m. New York City time on May 24, 2013, is the beneficial owner of fifteen percent (15%) or more of the shares of voting stock of the Corporation then outstanding; provided, however, that if any such person thereafter becomes the beneficial owner of additional shares of voting stock of the Corporation representing one-quarter of one percent (0.25%) of the then-outstanding voting stock of the Corporation (subject to certain exceptions), then such person will be deemed to be an Acquiring Person unless upon becoming the beneficial owner of such additional shares of voting stock of the Corporation such person does not beneficially own fifteen percent (15%) or more of the shares of voting stock of the Corporation then outstanding, or (f) any person who becomes the owner of fifteen percent (15%) of the voting stock of the Corporation then outstanding as the result of an acquisition of shares of voting stock of the Corporation by the Corporation which, by reducing the number of shares outstanding, increases the proportionate number of shares of voting stock of the Corporation beneficially owned by such person so that such person would otherwise become an Acquiring Person; provided, however, that if any such person thereafter becomes the beneficial owner of additional shares of voting stock of the Corporation representing one-quarter of one percent (0.25%) of the then-outstanding voting stock of the Corporation (subject to certain exceptions), then such person will be deemed to be an Acquiring Person unless upon becoming the beneficial owner of such additional shares of voting stock of the Corporation such person does not beneficially own fifteen percent (15%) or more of the shares of voting stock of the Corporation then outstanding.

Prior to the Distribution Date, the Rights will not be exercisable, will not be represented by a separate certificate, and will not be transferable apart from the Common Stock, but will instead be evidenced, with respect to any of the Common Stock certificates outstanding as of the Record Date, by such Common Stock certificate with a copy of the Summary of Rights to Purchase Series A Junior Participating Preferred Stock attached thereto (or in the case of uncertificated shares of Common Stock, by book-entry account that evidences record ownership for such shares). Until the Distribution Date (or earlier redemption, exchange or expiration of the Rights), new Common Stock certificates issued after the Record Date will contain a legend incorporating the Rights Agreement by reference, or, in the case of uncertificated shares of Common Stock, such legend shall be included in a notice to the record holder of such shares. Until the Distribution Date (or earlier redemption, exchange or expiration of the Rights), the surrender for transfer of any of the Common Stock certificates outstanding as of the Record Date (or the effectuation of a book-entry transfer of shares of Common Stock), with or without a copy of the Summary of Rights attached thereto, will also constitute the transfer of the Rights associated with the Common Stock represented by such certificate. As soon as practicable following the Distribution Date, separate certificates evidencing the Rights ("Right Certificates") will be mailed to holders of record of the Common Stock as of the close of business on the Distribution Date, and such separate certificates alone will evidence the Rights from and after the Distribution Date.

The Rights are not exercisable until the Distribution Date. The Rights will expire upon the close of business on the earliest to occur of: (i) May 24, 2014, (ii) the date on which the rights are redeemed or exchanged by the Corporation in accordance with the Rights Agreement and (iii) the date of the Corporation's 2014 annual meeting of stockholders if requisite stockholder approval of the Rights Agreement is not obtained at such meeting.

Shares of Preferred Stock purchasable upon exercise of the Rights will be non-redeemable and, unless otherwise provided in connection with the creation of a subsequent series of preferred shares, will be subordinate to any other series of the Corporation's preferred shares. The Preferred Stock may not be issued except upon exercise of Rights or in connection with a redemption or exchange of Rights. Each share of Preferred Stock will be entitled to receive when, as and if declared by the Board of Directors, a quarterly dividend in an amount equal to the greater of $1.00 per share or one thousand (1,000) times the cash dividends declared on the Common Stock. In addition, the holders of the Preferred Stock are entitled to receive one thousand (1,000) times any non-cash dividends (other than dividends payable in equity securities) declared on the Common Stock, in like kind. In the event of the liquidation of the Corporation, the holders of Preferred Stock will be entitled to receive, for each share of Preferred Stock, a payment in an amount equal to the greater of $1,000 or one thousand (1,000) times the payment made per share of Common Stock. Each share of Preferred Stock will have one thousand (1,000) votes, voting together with the Common Stock. In the event of any merger, consolidation or other transaction in which Common Stock is exchanged, each share of Preferred Stock will be entitled to receive one thousand (1,000) times the amount received per share of Common Stock. The rights of Preferred Stock as to dividends, liquidation and voting are protected by anti-dilution provisions.

The Exercise Price and the number of shares of Preferred Stock issuable upon exercise of the Rights are subject to certain adjustments from time to time in the event of a stock dividend on, or a subdivision or combination of, the Common Stock. The Exercise Price also is subject to adjustment in the event of extraordinary distributions of cash or other property to holders of Common Stock.

Unless the Rights are earlier redeemed or exchanged, in the event that a person or group becomes an Acquiring Person, the Rights Agreement provides that proper provisions will be made so that each holder of record of a Right (other than Rights beneficially owned by an Acquiring Person and certain affiliates, associates and transferees thereof, whose Rights will thereupon become null and void), will thereafter have the right to receive, upon the exercise of each outstanding Right and payment of the Exercise Price, that number of shares of Preferred

Stock having a fair market value determined in accordance with the Rights Agreement at the time of the transaction equal to approximately two (2) times the Exercise Price (such value to be determined with reference to the fair market value of the Common Stock as provided in the Rights Agreement).

In addition, unless the Rights are earlier redeemed or exchanged, in the event that, after the time that a person or group becomes an Acquiring Person, the Corporation were to be acquired in a merger or other business combination (in which any shares of Common Stock are changed into or exchanged for other securities or assets) or more than fifty percent (50%) of the assets or earning power of the Corporation and its subsidiaries (taken as a whole) were to be sold or transferred in one or a series of related transactions, the Rights Agreement provides that proper provision will be made so that each holder of record of a Right (other than Rights beneficially owned by an Acquiring Person and certain affiliates, associates and transferees thereof, whose Rights will thereupon become null and void) will from and after such date have the right to receive, upon payment of the Exercise Price, that number of shares of common stock of the acquiring company having a fair market value at the time of such transaction determined in accordance with the Rights Agreement equal to approximately two (2) times the Exercise Price.

At any time after any person or group becomes an Acquiring Person and prior to the acquisition by such person or group of fifty percent (50%) or more of the outstanding voting shares, the Board of Directors of the Corporation may exchange the Rights (other than Rights owned by such person or group which will have become null and void), in whole or in part, for shares of Common Stock in accordance with the Rights Agreement.

Fractions of shares of Preferred Stock (other than fractions which are integral multiples of one one-thousandth (1/1000) of a share) may, at the election of the Corporation, be evidenced by depositary receipts. The Corporation may also issue cash in lieu of fractional shares which are not integral multiples of one one-thousandth (1/1000) of a share.

At any time prior to such time as any person or group becomes an Acquiring Person, the Board of Directors may redeem the Rights in whole, but not in part, at a price of $0.01 per Right, subject to adjustment (the "Redemption Price"). The determination of the Board of Directors to redeem the Rights may be made on such basis and be subject to such conditions as the Board of Directors, in its sole and absolute discretion, may establish. Immediately upon the effective time of the redemption of the Rights, and without any further action and notice, the right to exercise the Rights will terminate and the only right of the holders of Rights will be to receive the Redemption Price. At the option of the Board of Directors, the Redemption Price may be paid in cash to each Rights holder or by the issuance of shares of Preferred Stock or Common Stock having a fair market value, determined in accordance with the Rights Agreement, equal to such cash payment.

For as long as the Rights are then redeemable, the Corporation (at the direction of the Board of Directors in its sole and absolute discretion) may amend the Rights Agreement in any manner without the approval of any holders of the Rights. At any time when the Rights are not then redeemable, the Corporation (at the direction of the Board of Directors) may amend the Rights Agreement without the approval of any holders of the Rights (i) to cure any ambiguity, (ii) to correct or supplement any provision contained in the Rights Agreement that may be inconsistent with any other provisions in the Rights Agreement or otherwise defective, (iii) to shorten or lengthen any time period in the Rights Agreement or (iv) in any way that will not materially adversely affect the interests of the holders of Rights (other than an Acquiring Person or any other person in whose hands Rights are null and void under the provisions of Section 7(e) of the Rights Agreement). No supplement or amendment shall be made which (a) changes the Redemption Price, (b) causes the Rights Agreement to again become amendable other than in accordance with the Rights Agreement or (c) causes the Rights again to become redeemable.

Until a Right is exercised, the holder, as such, will have no rights as a stockholder of the Corporation, including, without limitation, the right to vote or to receive dividends.

The Rights will have certain anti-takeover effects. The Rights will cause substantial dilution to any person or group that attempts to acquire the Corporation without the approval of the Board of Directors. As a result, the overall effect of the Rights may be to render more difficult or discourage any attempt to acquire the Corporation even if such acquisition may be favorable to the interests of the Corporation's stockholders. Because the Board of Directors can redeem the Rights, however, the Rights should not interfere with a merger or other business combination approved by the Board of Directors.

The Certificate of Designations of Series A Junior Participating Preferred Stock and the Rights Agreement (which includes the form of Certificate of Designations of Series A Junior Participating Preferred Stock as Exhibit A to the Rights Agreement, the Summary of Rights to Purchase Series A Junior Participating Preferred Stock as Exhibit B to the Rights Agreement and the form of Right Certificate as Exhibit C to the Rights Agreement), are included as Exhibit 3.1 and Exhibit 4.1, respectively hereto and are incorporated herein by reference. For a full description of the terms of the Rights, investors are encouraged to carefully review the Rights Agreement and its Exhibits.

QUESTIONS

1. Under what situations is Health Management's poison pill triggered?

2. What happens upon triggering of the pill?

3. If you were a Health Management shareholder, would you be in favor or opposed to its board implementing a poison pill? Why?

A board of directors can adopt a shareholders' rights plan without shareholder approval because corporate law statutes empower the board to issue rights.[4] Health Management's certificate includes blank-check preferred stock, and thus its board was able to have the rights exercisable for a new class of preferred stock it created in connection with the rights plan. If Health Management did not have blank-check preferred, the board of directors could still adopt a poison pill, but the rights would have to be exercisable for common stock.

A poison pill greatly reduces the chances of target being taken over through a hostile tender offer because it greatly increases the cost of the tender offer. Thus, most would be hostile acquirers will determine that after taking these costs into account, the deal does not make economic sense and therefore will not pursue it. There have, however, been a few reported instances of a pursuer intentionally triggering a poison pill.[5]

Note that poison pills are redeemable at the option of the company (as is the case with the Health Management pill described above). This allows a company to remove the pill for a friendly deal. It also means that a bidder can remove the pill through a successful electoral proxy fight to take over the board (that is where a staggered board comes into play, as I discuss in the next subsection). In other words, a poison pill does not protect target from a bidder launching a proxy fight. Target lawyers tried to close this gap by including dead-hand and slow-hand provisions in shareholders' rights plans. A dead-hand provision allowed a pill to be redeemed only by directors in office at the time the poison pill was adopted. A slow-hand provision restricted a newly-elected board from redeeming the pill for a specified period of time (typically six months). The Delaware Supreme Court has invalidated both dead-hand and slow-hand provisions as impermissibly impinging on the authority of a newly elected board to manage the business and affairs of the corporation. Dead-hand provisions have been upheld in Pennsylvania and Georgia so there is variation among jurisdictions on these types of poison pill provisions.

2. Staggered Board

The default rule under corporate law statutes is that a director's term is generally one year.[6] A corporation can, however, choose to stagger, or classify, its board so that terms of only a portion of its directors expire in a particular year. For example, DGCL § 141(d) provides:

> The directors of any corporation organized under this chapter may, by the certificate of incorporation or by an initial bylaw, or by a bylaw adopted by a vote of the stockholders, be divided into 1, 2 or 3 classes; the term of office of those of the first class to expire at the first annual meeting held after such classification becomes effective; of the second class 1 year thereafter;

---

[4] *See* DGCL § 157(a); MBCA § 6.24(a).

[5] *See, e.g.*, Versata Enterprises, Inc. v. Selectica, Inc., 5 A.3d 586 (Del. 2010) (discusses Versata's intentional triggering of Selectica's poison pill; the case is included in Chapter 7).

[6] *See, e.g.*, MBCA § 8.05(b); DGCL § 141(b). I say "generally" because a director's term technically lasts until the next election, which is normally a year later, but could be sooner or later than that. *See id.*

of the third class 2 years thereafter; and at each annual election held after such classification becomes effective, directors shall be chosen for a full term, as the case may be, to succeed those whose terms expire. The certificate of incorporation or bylaw provision dividing the directors into classes may authorize the board of directors to assign members of the board already in office to such classes at the time such classification becomes effective.[7]

A staggered board serves as a powerful defense against a bidder launching an electoral proxy contest. Specifically, a corporation will stagger its directors into three groups (the maximum allowed), and thus only one-third of its board seats will come up for election each year. Therefore, to win a majority of board seats through a proxy fight, a bidder would have to mount and win two electoral proxy contests in three years. This increases the cost of the proxy fight because it doubles the number of required solicitations and stretches the bidder's campaign over more than one year. It also decreases the odds of the bidder ultimately succeeding because even shareholders who are in favor of bidder acquiring target may be reluctant to vote for bidder's slate because of the required two rounds of elections. Voting in the bidder's slate in the first round puts the board in limbo for a year. During this year, the incumbents retain control but they are aware that they will soon lose their positions. The entire board will have to deal with the internal divisions and friction caused by having one-third of the board composed of a competing faction. Given these factors, many bidders will conclude it does not make sense to pursue a proxy fight. Hence, the odds of one being launched against a target with a staggered board are greatly reduced. Put differently, a staggered board does not make it impossible for a bidder to launch and win an electoral proxy fight. It just makes the fight more expensive and time consuming, and therefore less likely to occur.

Here is a sample provision staggering a board into three classes:

The Board of Directors shall be divided into three classes. Initially, the Board of Directors shall designate by resolution, from among its members, directors to serve as class I directors, class II directors, and class III directors. To the extent possible, the classes shall have the same number of directors. The term of office of the class I directors shall continue until the first annual meeting of stockholders after the date on which the corporation establishes the classified board and until their successors are elected and qualify. The term of office of the class II directors shall continue until the second annual meeting of stockholders after the date on which the corporation establishes the classified board and until their successors are elected and qualify. The term of office of the class III directors shall continue until the third annual meeting of stockholders following the date on which the corporation establishes the classified board and until their successors are elected and qualify. At each annual meeting of the stockholders of a corporation, the successors to the class of directors whose term expires at that meeting shall be elected to hold office for a term continuing until: (i) the annual meeting of stockholders held in the

---

[7] The analogous MBCA provision is § 8.06.

> third year following the year of their election; and (ii) their successors are elected and qualified.

3. Other Defensive Mechanisms

For Cause Requirement. The default rule under corporate law statutes is that a company's shareholders can remove directors at any time with or without cause.[8] For example, MBCA § 8.08(a) provides: "The shareholders may remove one or more directors with or without cause unless the articles of incorporation provide that directors may be removed only for cause." A company who is concerned about being hostilely acquired should override this default rule by including a "for cause" requirement in its charter. Here is sample charter language to that effect:

> Any director or the entire Board of Directors may be removed by the shareholders only for cause.

"Cause" generally includes fraudulent or criminal conduct and gross abuse of office amounting to a breach of trust. Note that Delaware flips the default rule for corporations with staggered boards. Specifically, under the DGCL, a director on a staggered board may only be removed for cause unless the corporation's charter otherwise provides.

Imposing a "for cause" requirement essentially prevents a hostile bidder from removing a target's board and replacing it with its own directors because presumably it will not be able to demonstrate the requisite cause with respect to a majority of directors. In other words, the provision limits a hostile bidder's ability to replace target directors to prevailing at an annual election as opposed to through a special meeting or written consent solicitation seeking removal and replacement.

No Shareholder Action by Written Consent. The default rule under corporate law statutes is that shareholders can take action by written consistent in lieu of a formal shareholders' meeting.[9] For example, DGCL § 228(a) provides:

> (a) Unless otherwise provided in the certificate of incorporation, any action required by this chapter to be taken at any annual or special meeting of stockholders of a corporation, or any action which may be taken at any annual or special meeting of such stockholders, may be taken without a meeting, without prior notice and without a vote, if a consent or consents in writing, setting forth the action so taken, shall be signed by the holders of outstanding stock having not less than the minimum number of votes that would be necessary to authorize or take such action at a meeting at which all shares entitled to vote thereon were present and voted and shall be delivered to the corporation by delivery to its registered office in this State, its principal place of business or an officer or agent of the corporation

---

[8] *See* MBCA § 8.08(a); DGCL § 141(k).

[9] *See* MBCA § 7.04; DGCL § 228.

having custody of the book in which proceedings of meetings of stockholders are recorded. Delivery made to a corporation's registered office shall be by hand or by certified or registered mail, return receipt requested.

Hence, under the above default rule, a hostile bidder could seek to remove target's board by simply convincing target shareholders who own the requisite number shares to sign a piece of paper consenting to removal. In other words, bidder would not have to call a special shareholders' meeting which means target will likely have less time and opportunity to counter bidder's attempt to replace the board.

As you probably noticed when reading the above statutory language, a Delaware company can eliminate the possibility of having its board removed by written consent by including a provision in its charter. Below is sample language:

Any action required or permitted to be taken by the stockholders of the Corporation must be effected at a duly called annual or special meeting of such holders. Any such action may not be effected by consent in writing.

Note that the default rule under the MBCA is that shareholder action by written consent requires *all* shareholders to sign. Thus, a company in an MBCA state that has adopted this rule will not need to include a "no shareholder action by written consent" provision in its charter because it will be essentially impossible for a hostile bidder to get all target shareholders to sign. (Presumably some of target's shares will be owned by target's board members and management who are against the deal and therefore won't sign).

No Board Expansion. Typically, a corporation's bylaws either specify the size of a corporation's board of directors or that the size is to be determined from time to time by the existing board. In this scenario, a possible way around a staggered board is for a hostile bidder to get sufficient target shareholder support at a shareholders' meeting or through written consent to amend target's bylaws to expand the size of the board to create vacancies that are then filled by bidder's people. For example, if the size of target's board is increased from five to eleven and the new six slots are filled with bidder candidates, bidder's people would then represent a majority of target's board. This is a possibility because under state corporate law shareholders have the power to unilaterally amend a corporation's bylaws. By unilaterally, I mean shareholders can themselves initiate and adopt a bylaw change with no involvement of the board. Most everything else shareholders get to vote on (charter amendments, mergers, dissolution, etc.) requires board approval followed by shareholder approval.

A company can eliminate the possibility of shareholders unilaterally amending the company's bylaws to expand the board by specifying in its charter that only the existing board can change the board's size. Below is sample language:

The number of Directors of the Corporation shall be fixed from time to time by affirmative vote of a majority of the Directors then in office.

Including the provision in the charter works because shareholders cannot unilaterally amend a company's charter; a charter amendment always requires board approval.

Limits on Calling a Special Meeting. The MBCA, and thus many states, allow shareholders holding at least 10% of the corporation's voting power to call a special meeting.[10] Thus, depending on a corporation's state of incorporation, a hostile bidder may be able to acquire 10% of a corporation's shares in the open market and as a result have the power to call a special shareholders' meeting to, for example, remove the corporation's board of directors and elect the hostile bidder's slate. A corporation can eliminate this possibility by providing in its charter that only the board can call a special meeting (if allowed under the applicable corporate statute; it's not allowed under the MBCA) or make the possibility less likely to occur by raising the percentage voting power threshold that a shareholder must have to call a special meeting (the MBCA allows the percentage to be raised to 25%). Below is sample language.

> Special meetings of stockholders for the transaction of such business as may properly come before the meeting may be called (i) by order of the Board of Directors or, (ii) by stockholders holding together at least a majority of all the shares of the Corporation entitled to vote at the meeting.

Note that the rule under the DGCL is that a special shareholders' meeting "may be called by the board of directors or by such person or persons as may be authorized by the certificate of incorporation or by the bylaws."[11] Thus, if the charter or bylaws of a Delaware corporation does not provide that someone other than the board of directors can call a special meeting, only the board of directors can call one.

Advance Notice Requirement. A shareholder generally has the right to put forth a proposal for voting on by his or her fellow shareholders at a corporation's annual meeting. Thus, a hostile bidder could, for example, introduce a proposal to remove the board, elect an alternative slate, expand the board, etc. (depending on what defenses the corporation has in place). A corporation can avoid being caught off guard by a surprise last minute shareholder proposal by including an advance notice provision in its bylaws. This sort of provision requires a shareholder to notify the corporation a specified period in advance of the proposal it will be putting forth at the annual meeting. If the shareholder does not comply with the provision, the corporation can refuse to allow the proposal to be voted upon at the meeting. Requiring advance notice gives a corporation time to figure how best to respond in advance of the shareholder vote. Below is sample advance notice bylaw language.

---

[10] *See* MBCA § 7.02(a)(2).

[11] DGCL § 211(d).

(B) For nominations or other business to be properly brought before an annual meeting by a stockholder, the stockholder must have given timely notice thereof in writing to the Secretary of the Corporation and such other business must otherwise be a proper matter for stockholder action. To be timely, a stockholder's notice shall be delivered to the Secretary at the principal executive offices of the Corporation not later than the close of business on the 60th day nor earlier than the close of business on the 90th day prior to the first anniversary of the preceding year's annual meeting, provided, however, that in the event that the date of the annual meeting is more than 30 days before or more than 60 days after such anniversary date, notice by the stockholder to be timely must be so delivered not earlier than the close of business on the 90th day prior to such annual meeting and not later than the close of business on the later of (a) the 60th day prior to such annual meeting, or (b) the 10th day following the day on which public announcement of the date of such meeting is first made by the Corporation. In no event shall the public announcement of an adjournment of an annual meeting commence a new time period for the giving of a stockholder's notice as described above. Such stockholder's notice shall set forth (A) as to each person whom the stockholder proposes to nominate for election or re-election as a director all information relating to such person that is required to be disclosed in solicitations of proxies for election of directors in an election contest, or is otherwise required, in each case pursuant to Regulation 14A under the Securities Exchange Act of 1934, as amended (the "Exchange Act") and Rule 14a-11 thereunder (including such person's written consent to being named in the proxy statement as a nominee and to serving as a director if elected); (B) as to any other business that the stockholder proposes to bring before the meeting, a brief description of the business desired to be brought before the meeting, the reasons for conducting such business at the meeting and any material interest in such business of such stockholder and the beneficial owner, if any, on whose behalf the proposal is made; and (C) as to the stockholder giving the notice and the beneficial owner, if any, on whose behalf the nomination or proposal is made (1) the name and address of such stockholder, as they appear on the Corporation's books, and of such beneficial owner and (2) the class and number of shares of the Corporation which are owned beneficially and of record by such stockholder and such beneficial owner.

Supermajority Voting Requirement. A supermajority voting requirement refers to a corporation including a provision in its charter to increase the number of affirmative votes required for shareholder approval of specified actions, e.g., amending the corporation's charter, amending the corporation's bylaws, or approving a merger. As you know from Chapter 2, default voting standards vary by state and matter up for a vote from more votes for than against to a majority of outstanding shares. A corporation may decide to raise the standard to make it more difficult for a hostile bidder to secure the necessary votes to (1) dismantle antitakeover defenses in a corporation's charter and bylaws, and (2) secure enough shares in a tender offer to ensure approval of a second-step merger. Below is sample charter language:

(B) The Board is expressly empowered to adopt, amend or repeal the Bylaws of the Company. Any adoption, amendment or repeal of the Bylaws of the Company by the Board shall require the approval of a majority of the authorized number of directors. The stockholders shall also have power to adopt, amend or repeal the Bylaws of the Company; provided, however, that, in addition to any vote of the holders of any class or series of stock of the Company required by law or by this Amended and Restated Certificate of Incorporation, such action by stockholders shall require the affirmative vote of the holders of at least sixty-six and two-thirds percent (66 2/3%) of the voting power of all of the then-outstanding shares of the capital stock of the Company entitled to vote generally in the election of directors, voting together as a single class. . . .

(F) Notwithstanding any other provisions of this Certificate of Incorporation or any provision of law which might otherwise permit a lesser vote or no vote, but in addition to any affirmative vote of the holders of any particular class or series of the Corporation required by law or by this Certificate of Incorporation or any certificate of designation filed with respect to a series of Preferred Stock that may be designated from time to time, the affirmative vote of the holders of at least sixty-six and two-thirds percent (66 2/3%) of the voting power of all of the then-outstanding shares of capital stock of the Corporation entitled to vote generally in the election of directors, voting together as a single class, shall be required to alter, amend or repeal Articles V, VI, VII and VIII [these are the Articles that include takeover defenses].

EXERCISE 6.1

Review the certificate of incorporation and bylaws of Zipcar available at www.sjobiz.org/mna. List the defensive mechanisms included in those documents.

D. STATE ANTI-TAKEOVER STATUTES

Many state corporate codes include provisions designed to impede hostile takeovers. State legislatures adopted these provisions normally following lobbying by local companies worried about, or in the midst of battling, hostile takeover attempts. Legislatures were particularly concerned that a successful bidder would close operations in the state, resulting in mass employee terminations. Below is a brief description of various state anti-takeover provisions. The specific details of these provisions vary by state. Thus, a particular state's provision may have different features than what I describe below.

Control shares acquisition provisions. These provisions require a bidder to obtain approval of a majority of target's outstanding shares before acquiring a large block (e.g., 20 percent) of target stock in order to have the right to vote the shares. As a result, a bidder contemplating a hostile tender offer is essentially required to get shareholder approval before proceeding with it. The corporate law statutes of 27 states include this type of provision. The DGCL is not among them. Below as an example is the provision from the Wisconsin Business Corporation Law.

180.1150 Control share voting restrictions.

(1)   In this section: . . .

   (b)   "Person" includes 2 or more individuals or persons acting as a group for the purpose of acquiring or holding securities of a resident domestic corporation, but does not include a bank, broker, nominee, trustee or other person that acquires or holds shares in the ordinary course of business for others in good faith and not for the purpose of avoiding this section unless the person may exercise or direct the exercise of votes with respect to the shares at a meeting of shareholders without further instruction from another.

   (c)   "Resident domestic corporation" has the meaning given in s. 180.1130 (10m).[12]

(2)   Unless otherwise provided in the articles of incorporation of a resident domestic corporation or otherwise specified by the board of directors of the resident domestic corporation in accordance with s. 180.0824 (3), and except as provided in sub. (3) or as restored under sub. (5), the voting power of shares of a resident domestic corporation held by any person, including shares issuable upon conversion of convertible securities or upon exercise of options or warrants, in excess of 20% of the voting power in the election of directors shall be limited to 10% of the full voting power of those shares.

(3)   Shares of a resident domestic corporation held, acquired or to be acquired in any of the following circumstances are excluded from the application of this section: . . .

   (e)   Shares acquired under s. 180.1101 [merger], 180.1102 [share exchange], or 180.1104 [short form merger] if the resident domestic corporation is a party to the merger or share exchange.

   (f)   Shares acquired from the resident domestic corporation. . . .

---

[12] S.189.1130(10m) provides: " 'Resident domestic corporation' " means a resident domestic corporation, as defined in s. 180.1140 (9), if that corporation has a class of voting stock that is registered or traded on a national securities exchange or that is registered under § 12 (g) of the Securities Exchange Act." S. 180.1140(9) provides as follows:

(a) "Resident domestic corporation" means a domestic corporation that, as of the stock acquisition date in question, satisfies any of the following:

   1. Its principal offices are located in this state.

   2. It has significant business operations located in this state.

   3. More than 10% of the holders of record of its shares are residents of this state.

   4. More than 10% of its shares are held of record by residents of this state.

(b) For purposes of par. (a) 3. and 4., the record date for determining the percentages and numbers of shareholders and shares is the most recent record date established before the stock acquisition date in question, and the residence of each shareholder is the address of the shareholder which appears on the records of the resident domestic corporation.

(i)   Shares acquired in a transaction incident to which the shareholders of the resident domestic corporation have voted under sub. (5) to approve the person's resolution delivered under sub. (4) to restore the full voting power of all of that person's shares.

(4)   A person desiring a shareholder vote under sub. (5) shall deliver to the resident domestic corporation at its principal office a form of shareholder resolution with an accompanying notice containing all of the following:

(a)   The identity of the person.

(b)   A statement that the resolution and notice are submitted under this section.

(c)   The number of shares of the resident domestic corporation owned by the person of record and beneficially under the meaning prescribed in rule 13d-3 under the securities exchange act of 1934.

(d)   A specification of the voting power the person has acquired or proposes to acquire for which shareholder approval is sought.

(e)   The circumstances, terms and conditions under which shares representing in excess of 20% of the voting power were acquired or are proposed to be acquired, set forth in reasonable detail, including the source of funds or other consideration and other details of the financial arrangements of the transactions.

(f)   If shares representing in excess of 20% of the voting power were acquired or are proposed to be acquired for the purpose of gaining control of the resident domestic corporation, the terms of the proposed acquisition, including but not limited to the source of funds or other consideration and the material terms of the financial arrangements for the acquisition, any plans or proposals of the person to liquidate the resident domestic corporation, to sell all or substantially all of its assets, or merge it or exchange its shares with any other person, to change the location of its principal office or of a material portion of its business activities, to change materially its management or policies of employment, to alter materially its relationship with suppliers or customers or the communities in which it operates, or make any other material change in its business, corporate structure, management or personnel, and such other material information as would affect the decision of a shareholder with respect to voting on the resolution.

(5)

(a)   Within 10 days after receipt of a resolution and notice under sub. (4), the directors of the resident domestic corporation shall fix a date for a special meeting of the shareholders to vote on the resolution. The meeting shall be held no later than 50 days after receipt of the resolution and notice under sub. (4), unless the person agrees to a later date, and no sooner than 30 days after receipt of the resolution and notice, if the person so requests in writing when delivering the resolution and notice.

(b)   The notice of the meeting shall include a copy of the resolution and notice delivered under sub. (4) and a statement by the directors of their position or lack of position on the resolution.

(c)   Regular voting power is restored if at the meeting called under par. (a) at which a quorum is present a majority of the voting power of shares represented at the meeting and entitled to vote on the subject matter approve the resolution.

(d)   A resident domestic corporation is not required to hold more than 2 meetings under par. (a) in any 12-month period with respect to resolutions and notices presented by the same person unless the person pays to the corporation, in advance of the 3rd or subsequent such meeting the reasonable expenses of the meeting including, without limitation, fees and expenses of counsel, as estimated in good faith by the board of directors of the resident domestic corporation and communicated in writing to the person within 10 days after receipt of a 3rd or subsequent resolution and notice from the person. In such event, notwithstanding par. (a), the directors may fix a date for the meeting within 10 days after receipt of payment in full of such estimated expenses rather than within 10 days after receipt of the resolution and notice.

(6)   Any sale or other disposition of shares by a person holding both shares having full voting power and shares having voting power limited under sub. (2) shall be deemed to reduce the number of shares having limited voting power until such shares are exhausted.

(7)   A corporation that is not a resident domestic corporation may elect, by express provision in its articles of incorporation, to be subject to this section as if it were a resident domestic corporation unless its articles of incorporation contain a provision stating that the corporation is a close corporation under ss. 180.1801 to 180.1837.

EXERCISE 6.2

Bidder is considering launching a hostile tender offer to acquire target. Target is a Wisconsin corporation. Make a list of questions you need answered to determine whether the Wisconsin control share acquisition statute will apply to the deal. Also, advise bidder as to the effect if the statute does apply.

Business combination provisions. These provisions generally prohibit a target shareholder (or affiliate of such shareholder) from engaging in a business combination (merger, asset purchase, stock purchase, etc.) with target for a specified period of years following the date that the shareholder's percentage ownership of target's outstanding shares crosses a specified threshold. For example, DGCL § 203(a) provides as follows:

(a) Notwithstanding any other provisions of this chapter, a corporation shall not engage in any business combination with any interested stockholder for a period of 3 years following the time that such stockholder became an interested stockholder, unless:

   (1) Prior to such time the board of directors of the corporation approved either the business combination or the transaction which resulted in the stockholder becoming an interested stockholder;

   (2) Upon consummation of the transaction which resulted in the stockholder becoming an interested stockholder, the interested stockholder owned at least 85% of the voting stock of the corporation outstanding at the time the transaction commenced, excluding for purposes of determining the voting stock outstanding (but not the outstanding voting stock owned by the interested stockholder) those shares owned (i) by persons who are directors and also officers and (ii) employee stock plans in which employee participants do not have the right to determine confidentially whether shares held subject to the plan will be tendered in a tender or exchange offer; or

   (3) At or subsequent to such time the business combination is approved by the board of directors and authorized at an annual or special meeting of stockholders, and not by written consent, by the affirmative vote of at least 66 2/3% of the outstanding voting stock which is not owned by the interested stockholder.

See DGCL § 203(c) for definitions of various terms used in the above provision.

The effect of this type of provision is to force a bidder who has successfully completed a hostile tender offer for a majority of target's stock to wait the specified number of years to effect a merger or other transaction to squeeze out target shareholders that did not tender unless it gets the specified shareholder approval of the transaction. The corporate law statutes of 33 states contain this type of provision.

EXERCISE 6.3

Bidder owns 15% of Target's outstanding common stock. Bidder acquired the stock two years ago when it made a strategic investment in Target. Target is a Delaware corporation and its board has agreed to be acquired by Bidder in a deal structured as a reverse triangular merger. Will DGCL § 203 apply to the deal? If so, what needs to happen so the deal complies with the provision?

Directors' duties provisions. These provisions, also known as "other constituency" statutes, explicitly authorize directors to consider factors other than maximizing shareholder value when deciding whether rejecting a takeover bid or fighting a hostile takeover attempt is in the best interests of the corporation. The corporate law statutes of 32 states contain this type of provision. The DGCL does not.

The application of and list of factors in these provisions vary by state. For example, Ohio's provision states as follows:

> [A] director, in determining what the director reasonably believes to be in the best interests of the corporation, shall consider the interests of the corporation's shareholders and, in the director's discretion, may consider any of the following:
>
> (1) The interests of the corporation's employees, suppliers, creditors, and customers;
>
> (2) The economy of the state and nation;
>
> (3) Community and societal considerations;
>
> (4) The long-term as well as short-term interests of the corporation and its shareholders, including the possibility that these interests may be best served by the continued independence of the corporation.[13]

In contrast, Arizona's provision states as follows:

> In discharging the duties of the position of director under this chapter, a director of an issuing public corporation, in considering the best interests of the corporation, shall consider the long-term as well as the short-term interests of the corporation and its shareholders including the possibility that these interests may be best served by the continued independence of the corporation. This section shall not modify the duties of the position of director in any matter outside the scope of this chapter.[14]

The above provision appears in the Arizona corporate law statute chapter that addresses corporate takeovers. In other words, the Arizona provision is limited to the takeover context. Conversely, the Ohio provision appears in the Ohio corporate law statute that specifies the duties of directors generally and thus applies to all director decisions, not just those related to takeovers.

Fair price provisions. These provisions require a bidder who has successfully completed a hostile tender offer for a majority of target's stock to pay the non-tendering shareholders a fair price in any follow up squeeze out transaction unless the transaction receives approval of a supermajority (generally, two-thirds) of such non-tendering shares. The definition of fair price as used in these provisions is based on a typically complex formula that varies by state. For example, a number of states define fair price as the greater of (1) the highest price paid by bidder for target's shares in a specified period (e.g., five years) before the proposed squeeze out transaction is announced, and (2) the market value per share of target's stock on the date the proposed squeeze out transaction is announced.

---

[13] Ohio Rev. Code § 1701.59(E).

[14] Ariz. Rev. Stat. § 10-2702.

The provisions are designed to prevent a bidder from using the threat of a second-step squeeze out at a low price or for undesirable consideration as a mechanism for pressuring target shareholders into tendering. The corporate law statutes of 27 states contain this type of provision. Below as an example is the provision from the Minnesota Business Corporations Act:

302A.675 TAKEOVER OFFER; FAIR PRICE.

Subdivision 1.   **Fair price requirement.** An offeror may not acquire shares of a publicly held corporation within two years following the last purchase of shares pursuant to a takeover offer with respect to that class, including, but not limited to, acquisitions made by purchase, exchange, merger, consolidation, partial or complete liquidation, redemption, reverse stock split, recapitalization, reorganization, or any other similar transaction, unless the shareholder is afforded, at the time of the proposed acquisition, a reasonable opportunity to dispose of the shares to the offeror upon substantially equivalent terms as those provided in the earlier takeover offer.

Subdivision 2.   **Exception.** Subdivision 1 does not apply if the proposed acquisition of shares is approved, before the purchase of any shares by the offeror pursuant to the earlier takeover offer, by a committee of the board, comprised solely of directors who:

(1)   neither are officers or employees of, nor were during the five years preceding the formation of the committee officers or employees of, the corporation or a related organization;

(2)   are neither the offerors nor affiliates or associates of the offeror;

(3)   were not nominated for election as directors by the offeror or an affiliate or associate of the offeror; and

(4)   were directors at the time of the first public announcement of the takeover offer or were nominated, elected, or recommended for election as directors by a majority of the directors.

See Minn. Stat. § 302A.011 for definitions of various terms used in the above provision.

EXERCISE 6.4

Bidder has acquired 70% of Target's outstanding common stock through a tender offer. Target is a Minnesota corporation whose stock is traded on the NASDAQ Capital Market. Bidder now wants to complete a back-end merger to squeeze out the Target shareholders who did not tender. How should it proceed in light of the above provision?

Poison pill endorsement provisions. These provisions explicitly authorize the board of directors to adopt a shareholders' rights plan. Here's an example from Illinois's corporate statute:

> [A] corporation may create and issue, whether or not in connection with the issue and sale of its shares or bonds, rights or options entitling the holders thereof to purchase from the corporation, upon such consideration, terms and conditions as may be fixed by the board, shares of any class or series, whether authorized but unissued shares, treasury shares or shares to be purchased or acquired, notes of the corporation or assets of the corporation. The terms and conditions of such rights or options may include, without limitation, restrictions or conditions that preclude or limit the exercise, transfer or receipt of such rights or options by any person or persons owning or offering to acquire a specified number or percentage of the outstanding common shares or other securities of the corporation, or any transferee or transferees of any such person or persons, or that invalidate or void such rights or options held by any such person or persons or any such transferee or transferees. . . .[15]

The Delaware Supreme Court has sanctioned poison pills, so there is no need for the DGCL to contain such a provision. Other states enacted them either because of an absence of case law on the issue, or, in a few states, because of case law prohibiting the use of poison pills. The corporate statutes of 25 states include this type of provision.

QUESTIONS

1. Which anti-takeover provisions are included in Nevada's corporate law statute?

2. Which anti-takeover provisions are included in New York's corporate law statute?

3. Which anti-takeover provisions are included in Delaware's corporate law statute?

4. Which anti-takeover provisions are included in California's corporate law statute?

Various state anti-takeover statutes have been challenged in court over the years, with some cases reaching the U.S. Supreme Court. The next case involves a challenge to three Virginia anti-takeover provisions plus a fourth more general provision.

---

[15] Ill. Rev. Stat. ch. 32 para 6.05.

WLR FOODS, INC. v. TYSON FOODS, INC.
United States District Court, Western District of Virginia
861 F. Supp. 1277 (1994)

MICHAEL, District Judge.

Tyson Foods, Inc. (Tyson) has commenced a hostile attempt to take over WLR Foods, Inc. (WLR). In doing so, it has made a tender offer to WLR shareholders of $30 per share. WLR has filed suit seeking a declaratory judgment affirming various measures undertaken by WLR to defend against Tyson's takeover attempt. Tyson has counterclaimed, asserting that such measures are illegal, that WLR's Board of Directors has breached its fiduciary duty, and that Virginia's statutory scheme affecting hostile takeover attempts is unconstitutional.

Presently before the court is Tyson's motion for a preliminary injunction challenging the constitutionality of four Virginia statutes that affect its attempt to take over WLR. The issues before the court are (1) whether the Virginia statutes are preempted by the Williams Act, 15 U.S.C. §§ 78m(d)-(e), 78n(d)-(f); and (2) whether the Virginia statutes violate the Commerce Clause, U.S. Const. art. I, § 8, cl. 3. Tyson's motion for a preliminary injunction is denied.

I.

Tyson's constitutional challenge implicates four separate Virginia statutes ("the Virginia statutes"). The first is the Control Share Acquisitions Act ("Control Share Act"), Va.Code Ann. §§ 13.1–728.1 to –728.9 (Michie 1993). Generally, the Control Share Act denies voting rights to any shares held by an acquiror not approved by a Virginia corporation's Board of Directors, unless a majority of disinterested shares votes to grant such rights in a shareholder referendum. *Id.* § 13.1–728.3. "Interested" shares may not vote, and they are defined to include shares held by (1) the acquiror; (2) any officer of the target corporation; and (3) any employee of the target corporation who is also a director. *Id.* § 13.1–728.1. The Control Share Act's provisions apply upon a person's acquisition of at least one-fifth of the total votes entitled to be cast in an election of directors. *Id.* . . . .

The second statute at issue is the Affiliated Transactions Act, Va.Code Ann. §§ 13.1-725 to -727.1 (Michie 1993). As applied to this case, this statute makes it very difficult to merge with or otherwise absorb a Virginia corporation acquired in a tender offer for three years after the acquisition. Pursuant to this statute, Tyson would not be permitted to engage in an "affiliated transaction"[16] with WLR for three years unless the transaction was approved by (1) a majority, but not less than

---

[16] [n.1] An affiliated transaction includes (1) a merger involving WLR and Tyson; (2) a share exchange in which Tyson acquires a class or series of voting shares of WLR; (3) disposition to Tyson of WLR's assets in excess of five percent of WLR's net worth, or any guaranty by WLR of Tyson's indebtedness in excess of five percent of WLR's net worth; (4) disposition to Tyson of more than five percent of the fair market value of voting shares in WLR; (5) dissolution of WLR if proposed by Tyson; and (6) any transaction which has the effect of increasing by more than five percent the percentage of voting shares in WLR owned by Tyson. Va.Code Ann. § 13.1–725 (Michie 1993).

two, of WLR's "disinterested directors";[17] *and* (2) two-thirds of voting shares in WLR, other than shares beneficially held by Tyson. *Id.* § 13.1-725.1. After three years, WLR may engage in an affiliated transaction with Tyson if (1) approved by two-thirds of voting shares in WLR, other than shares beneficially held by Tyson; *or* (2) approved by a majority of disinterested directors; *or* (3) Tyson pays a statutorily defined value to each class of WLR's voting securities. *Id.* §§ 13.1-726, -727.

The third statute affecting Tyson's tender takeover attempt is Va.Code Ann. § 13.1-646 (Michie 1993) ("Poison Pill Statute"). This statute authorizes a corporation's directors to issue discriminatory rights in favor of specific persons or classes, limited only by Va.Code § 13.1-690, governing directors' business judgment. *Id.* § 13.1-646(B). WLR has used this statute to enact a "flip-in" poison pill, which triggers upon the accumulation of fifteen percent or more of WLR stock by any shareholder. When triggered, WLR's poison pill allows all shareholders, except the shareholder who has accumulated at least fifteen percent of the shares, to purchase $136 worth of WLR stock for only $68. When exercised, this will substantially reduce the percentage of total shares held by Tyson, while simultaneously diminishing the value of each share. As an example, if Tyson accumulated sixty percent of 10,000,000 WLR shares outstanding through its $30 per share tender offer, the poison pill would trigger and could reduce Tyson's stake to only 21.3 percent, and the value of each share could drop from $30 to $20.33.

The final statute at issue is Va.Code Ann. § 13.1-690 (Michie 1993) ("Business Judgment Statute"). This court previously has ruled that § 690 focuses on the procedural indicia of good faith business judgment as measured by resort to an informed decisionmaking process, thus making irrelevant the substantive advice received by directors. *WLR Foods, Inc. v. Tyson Foods, Inc.*, 857 F.Supp. 492 (W.D.Va.1994). In short, the statute focuses on whether directors relied upon information and advice which they believed in good faith to be competent and reliable. *See id.* at 497. Tyson alleges that this prevents it from discovering whether WLR's directors acted in the best interests of the corporation in utilizing the other three statutes to defend against Tyson's takeover attempt.

II.

In deciding whether to issue a preliminary injunction, the court must consider four factors: (1) the likelihood of irreparable harm to Tyson without the injunction; (2) the likelihood of harm to WLR with the injunction; (3) Tyson's likelihood of success on the merits; and (4) the public interest. These four factors are to be weighed flexibly based on a sliding-scale approach; a strong showing by a party with regard to one factor reduces the need for that party to make a strong showing concerning other factors. The balance of hardships created by the likelihood of irreparable harm to each side is the most important consideration, and because of the extraordinary nature of a preliminary injunction the harm to the movant truly

---

[17] [n.2] "Disinterested directors" essentially is defined to consist of WLR directors who were directors before Tyson acquired WLR. *Id.*

must be irreparable, rather than merely substantial, for a preliminary injunction to be granted.

In this case, the balance of hardships and the public interest are tied to the likelihood of success on the merits. Several cases recognize the harm caused to tender offerors by delay or defeat of its offer caused by improper or illegal tactics undertaken by management. *See, e.g., Dan River*, 701 F.2d at 283–84; *Kennecott Corp. v. Smith*, 637 F.2d 181, 190 (3d Cir. 1980); *Bendix Corp. v. Martin Marietta Corp.*, 547 F.Supp. 522, 532 (D.Md. 1982). In this case, Tyson alleges that the acquisition of WLR presents a unique business opportunity and that allowing WLR's management to improperly block the takeover would cause irreparable harm. Any potential harm to Tyson, however, is predicated on the invalidity of the statutes. If the statutes are constitutional, then WLR's use of them is not improper. Likewise, if the statutes are unconstitutional, then the delay in Tyson's takeover caused by WLR's use of the statutes potentially could cause great harm to Tyson. The court notes, however, that Tyson has presented no evidence that WLR's directors are preventing dissemination of information to shareholders or that they have taken any actions to entrench themselves further subsequent to Tyson's filing of the preliminary injunction motion. The possibility exists, of course, that before final judgment is entered in this matter WLR's directors could take such action or that the poison pill could trigger, but the extent of harm caused to Tyson would depend upon the constitutionality of the statutes pursuant to which the directors acted.

Similarly, the extent of harm caused to WLR by a preliminary injunction would depend upon the likelihood of success on the merits. If the court eventually declares the Virginia statutes constitutional but grants the preliminary injunction, WLR is robbed of its opportunity to take legitimate defensive measures presumably designed to ensure the adequacy of Tyson's tender offer. Conversely, if the statutes are unconstitutional WLR would suffer no harm because its actions pursuant to the statutes would have been invalid.

Furthermore, the public interest is directly tied to the likelihood of success on the merits when the issue is the validity of statutes. If the statutes are valid, then the public interest is served by their enforcement. If they are unconstitutional, then the public interest is served by their invalidation. Because in this case the other three *Blackwelder* factors flow from it, the likelihood of success on the merits will determine whether the court will grant a preliminary injunction. . . .

IV.

The first question in this case is whether the Williams Act, 15 U.S.C. §§ 78m(d)-(e), 78n(d)-(f), preempts the Virginia statutes. Pursuant to the Supremacy Clause of the United States Constitution, federal law is the "supreme law of the Land . . . , any Thing in the Constitution or Laws of a State to the Contrary notwithstanding." U.S. Const. art. VI, cl. 2. In addition to an explicit indication by Congress of its intent to preempt state law, state statutes are preempted when it is physically impossible to comply with both federal and state laws or when "the state 'law stands as an obstacle to the accomplishment and execution of the full purposes and objectives of Congress.'" *CTS Corp. v. Dynamics Corp. of America*, 481 U.S. 69,

78-79, 107 S.Ct. 1637, 1644, 95 L.Ed.2d 67 (1987) (quoting *Hines v. Davidowitz*, 312 U.S. 52, 67, 61 S.Ct. 399, 404, 85 L.Ed. 581 (1941)). Tyson contends that federal law preempts the Virginia statutes because they stand as an obstacle to the purposes and objectives of the Williams Act.

The Williams Act regulates disclosure to shareholders and procedures required in tender offers. . . .

The primary purpose of the Williams Act is to protect shareholders from the coercive aspects of tender offers by "plac[ing] investors on an equal footing with the takeover bidder." *CTS*, 481 U.S. at 82, 107 S.Ct. at 1645-46 (quoting *Piper v. Chris-Craft Indus., Inc.*, 430 U.S. 1, 30, 97 S.Ct. 926, 943, 51 L.Ed.2d 124 (1977)). The Williams Act protects investors in part by attempting to maintain a balance between management and the offeror to create a fairly level playing field in the contest for shares. *See Edgar v. MITE Corp.*, 457 U.S. 624, 633, 102 S.Ct. 2629, 2636, 73 L.Ed.2d 269 (1982) (plurality opinion) ("[I]t is also crystal clear that a major aspect of the effort to protect the investor was to avoid favoring either management or the takeover bidder."). This has led to the view endorsed by Tyson that balance between management and the offeror is an independent purpose of the Williams Act. As a result, Tyson asserts that the Williams Act preempts the Virginia statutes if they deprive a tender offer of a "meaningful opportunity for success."[18]

This court rejects the meaningful opportunity for success test for determining whether the Williams Act preempts the Virginia statutes. Creating neutrality between management and the offeror simply is not an independent purpose of the Williams Act. "Neutrality is, rather, but one characteristic of legislation directed toward a different purpose — the protection of investors." *Piper*, 430 U.S. at 29, 97 S.Ct. at 943.[19] Even the three justice plurality in *MITE*, which Tyson reads as supporting its view, makes that distinction. "Congress sought to protect the investor not only by furnishing him with the necessary information but also by withholding from management or the bidder any undue advantage *that could frustrate the exercise of an informed choice*." *MITE*, 457 U.S. 624, 634, 102 S.Ct. 2629, 2636 (emphasis added). In *CTS*,[20] the Court clarified that "the overriding concern of the MITE plurality was that the . . . statute considered in that case operated to favor management against offerors, *to the detriment of shareholders*." *CTS*, 481 U.S. at 81-82, 107 S.Ct. at 1645 (emphasis added). Management must not be permitted to gain an undue advantage *over the investors*, but the Williams Act simply does not

---

[18] [n.3] The "meaningful opportunity for success" test also has been used by a few district courts in deciding whether the Williams Act preempts state statutes. *See, e.g.*, Topper Acquisition Corp. v. Emhart Corp., No. 89–00110–R, 1989 U.S.Dist. LEXIS 9910, at *12 (E.D.Va. Mar. 23, 1989) ("[T]he Williams Act preempts state anti-takeover statutes which deprive a hostile bidder of a 'meaningful opportunity for success.' "); West Point–Pepperell, Inc. v. Farley, Inc., 711 F.Supp. 1096, 1103 (N.D.Ga. 1989) (finding preemption if a statute leaves a hostile offeror with no meaningful opportunity for success absent approval from the board that it seeks to replace); BNS, Inc. v. Koppers Co., Inc., 683 F.Supp. 458, 469 (D.Del. 1988) (creating the meaningful opportunity for success test).

[19] [n.4] Neither the plurality in *MITE* nor the Court in *CTS* questioned any part of *Piper*.

[20] [n.5] The Court in *CTS* noted that it was not bound by the reasoning in *MITE* because it was not a majority opinion. It stated that "[w]e need not question that reasoning, however, because we believe the [statute] passes muster even under the broad interpretation of the Williams Act articulated by Justice White in *MITE*." *CTS*, 481 U.S. at 81, 107 S.Ct. at 1645.

mandate that management have no advantage over the offeror, as long as such advantage does not harm the investors. The crucial relationships are those between the investors and management and between the investors and the offeror, not the relationship between management and the offeror. The purpose of the Williams Act is to protect investors by ensuring an informed choice; therefore, the Virginia statutes are preempted if they favor either management or the tender offeror over the investors.

The Virginia statutes clearly give power to management and remove it from tender offerors, but they are preempted only if they do so to the detriment of shareholders. Viewing all of the statutes collectively, the statutory "scheme" puts several obstacles in the way of Tyson's tender offer. First, if Tyson acquires more than fifteen percent of WLR's shares a poison pill will trigger, substantially reducing Tyson's percentage of ownership and the value of each share.[21] Then, pursuant to the Control Share Act, unless the directors opt out of its provisions, disinterested shareholders could vote to take away voting rights from any shares that Tyson owns. If Tyson nonetheless managed to take over WLR, it effectively would be precluded from merging it into Tyson for at least three years pursuant to the Affiliated Transactions Act. Furthermore, pursuant to the Business Judgment Statute the decisions of WLR's directors in enacting defensive measures could be reviewed only for good faith business judgment, with no discovery of the substantive advice that the directors received in reaching their decisions.

The Virginia statutes do not stand as an obstacle to the purposes and objectives of the Williams Act. In *CTS*, the Supreme Court reviewed an Indiana statute virtually identical to the Control Share Act and held that it was not preempted by the Williams Act. *CTS*, 481 U.S. at 81-84, 107 S.Ct. at 1645-46. The Control Share Act furthers the policy of investor protection by allowing disinterested shareholders to vote as a group and avoid the coercive nature of two-tiered tender offers, in which shareholders are virtually forced to tender out of fear that a successful offeror will seize control and buy non-tendered shares at a depressed price. *Id.* at 83, 107 S.Ct. at 1646. The Control Share Act excludes management and the tender offeror and allows disinterested shareholders collectively to evaluate the fairness of the offer. *Id.* at 83-84, 107 S.Ct. at 1646. Furthermore, by requiring offerors to furnish target corporations with a control share acquisition statement,[22] which then must be mailed by the target corporation to shareholders, *see* Va.Code Ann. § 13.1-728.6(B)(1) (Michie 1993), the Control Share Act facilitates the free exercise of informed choices by independent investors.[23]

---

[21] [n.6] Assuming 10,000,000 shares in WLR outstanding with a value of $30 per share, Tyson would need to hold approximately eighty-five percent of WLR shares after the tender offer in order to retain a majority after the poison pill triggered.

[22] [n.7] The control share acquisition statement provides shareholders with even more information than is required by the Williams Act. *Compare* Va.Code § 13.1–728.4 *with* 15 U.S.C. § 78n(d)(1) and 17 C.F.R. §§ 240.13d–1, 240.14d–3.

[23] [n.8] Tyson also asserts that the Control Share Act is preempted by § 14(a) of the Securities Exchange Act of 1934, 15 U.S.C. § 78n, because § 14(a) occupies the field of the regulation of proxy solicitation. The court finds no evidence in § 14(a) that Congress intended to do so. Moreover, the Control Share Act does not seek to regulate the process of proxy solicitation, which is the focus of § 14(a); rather, it merely affects the timing of when solicitation may begin. *See* Va.Code Ann. § 13.1–728.5(E) (Michie

Likewise, the Affiliated Transactions Act does not stand as an obstacle to the purposes and objectives of the Williams Act. Although it makes tender offers less attractive by effectively delaying a merger for at least three years, it does not regulate the procedures or disclosures required in a tender offer. It applies whether an acquisition was made by tender offer or any other means of gaining control. As the Seventh Circuit recognized in *Amanda Acquisition Corp. v. Universal Foods Corp.*, 877 F.2d 496 (7th Cir. 1989) where it held that the Williams Act does not preempt a statute very similar to the Affiliated Transactions Act, "[d]elay in completing a second-stage merger may make the target less attractive, and thus depress the price offered or even lead to an absence of bids; it does not, however, alter any of the procedures governed by federal regulation." *Id.* at 504.

To the extent that it does affect Tyson's tender offer, however, the Virginia legislature apparently intended the Affiliated Transactions Act to protect minority shareholders from self-dealing by the majority and to discourage corporate raiders from using a target corporation's assets for the raider's own devices or from extracting greenmail from the target. Revised Joint Bar Comm. Commentary to § 13.1-725 of the Virginia Stock Corporation Act, *Virginia Corporation Law* 239 (Michie 1992). Like the Control Share Act, the Affiliated Transactions Act gives independent shareholders a tool to prevent abuses by an acquiror. It interferes neither with the procedures set up by the Williams Act nor with the ability of shareholders to make an informed choice about a tender offer.

The Poison Pill Statute also does not stand as an obstacle to the purposes and objectives of the Williams Act. It gives management a very strong tool to use to block a tender offer, but directors may not do so to the detriment of the shareholders. Any action by directors regarding poison pills is explicitly subject to the provisions of the Business Judgment Statute. *See* Va. Code Ann. § 13.1-646(B) (Michie 1993). Directors are precluded from adopting or refusing to redeem a poison pill if to do so does not comport with the directors' "good faith business judgment of the best interests of the corporation." *Id.* § 13.1-690. The Poison Pill Statute creates the potential for management to entrench itself at the expense of the shareholders, but the possibility of incurring personal liability for breach of fiduciary duty provides a strong incentive for directors to use poison pills only to defeat inadequate offers. In fact, a 1988 study conducted by Georgeson & Company, Inc., a leading proxy solicitation firm, found that target corporations with poison pills received an average final offer 78.5% greater than the price of its stock six months before the commencement of the tender offer, while corporations without poison pills gained only 57%. *See* Fogg & Sterling, *Poison Pill Update, in* M. Katz & R. Loeb, *Acquisitions and Mergers 1988* 817, 844 (1988). Furthermore, the study revealed that target corporations with poison pills outperformed the S & P 500 Index by 53%, while corporations with no poison pills performed only 31% better than the Index. *Id.* at 845. Provided that directors utilize poison pills in the best interests of the corporation, as Virginia's Poison Pill Statute requires, poison pills may be an effective method for increasing the bid in tender offers.

1993). Tyson further contends that the Control Share Act is preempted because § 13.1–728.4(6) requires more information to be sent to shareholders than the SEC mandates. In light of the above discussion concerning the fundamental purpose of the Williams Act, such a contention is without support.

Reviewing director conduct pursuant to the above three statutes, using the Business Judgment Statute, also does not cause the Virginia statutory "scheme" to be preempted. Directors must act based on their good faith business judgment of the best interests of the corporation. *See* Va.Code § 13.1-690. Tyson asserts that directors wishing to defeat a hostile tender offer need only hear advice from competent sources and their decisions become insulated from judicial scrutiny. The court disagrees. Courts must look to procedural indicia of good faith business judgment; resort to an informed decisionmaking process must be undertaken in good faith. Directors are entitled to *rely* on competent advice, not to hear and disregard it just to go through the motions of satisfying § 690. This prevents directors from attempting to defeat a tender offer unless they rely in good faith on competent advice and information stating that the offer is not in the best interests of the corporation. Although the court expresses no opinion concerning whether WLR's directors complied with § 690 in attempting to defeat Tyson's tender offer, the statute itself does not stand as an obstacle to the purposes and objectives of the Williams Act, even when used in conjunction with the other three statutes at issue.[24] Management still is unable to interfere with investors' free exercise of an informed choice in responding to a tender offer.[25]

The Virginia statutory "scheme" makes tender offers for Virginia corporations more difficult than they would be absent the statutes. Although the statutes seem to give power to management with the same hand that takes it away from offerors, they do not do so to the detriment of investors. The Williams Act does not grant investors a right to tender their shares at a premium; it merely provides that certain information must be provided and certain procedures must be followed to ensure that investors are permitted to make an informed choice. The cumulative effect of the Virginia statutes does not interfere with those objectives in any way. As a result, the Williams Act does not preempt the Virginia statutes, either separately or together.

V.

The court next must decide whether the Virginia statutes violate the Commerce Clause of the United States Constitution, U.S. Const. art. 1, § 8, cl. 3. Although on its face the Commerce Clause merely gives Congress the power to regulate

---

[24] [n.9] Management's compliance with its fiduciary duties does not affect the constitutional issues presented.

In the unlikely event that management were to take actions designed to diminish the value of the corporation's shares, it may incur liability under state law. But this problem does not control our pre-emption analysis. Neither the [Williams] Act nor any other federal statute can assure that shareholders do not suffer from the mismanagement of corporate officers and directors. *CTS*, 481 U.S. at 85 n. 9, 107 S.Ct. at 1647 n. 9.

[25] [n.10] Because the Business Judgment Statute requires directors to act in the best interests of the corporation, it also ensures that Virginia's statutory "scheme" passes Tyson's broad "meaningful opportunity for success" test. All that an offeror must do in order to have a meaningful opportunity for success is present a high enough offer, acceptance of which is in the best interests of the corporation. Directors then could opt out of the Control Share Act and redeem the poison pill. Furthermore, if they believed that an immediate merger was in the best interests of the corporation, they could vote to override the restrictions of the Affiliated Transactions Act and encourage shareholders to do the same.

commerce among the states, "it has been settled for more than a century that the Clause prohibits States from taking certain actions respecting interstate commerce even absent congressional action." *CTS Corp. v. Dynamics Corp. of America*, 481 U.S. 69, 87, 107 S.Ct. 1637, 1648, 95 L.Ed.2d 67 (1987). Tyson asserts that the Virginia statutes violate the dormant Commerce Clause in two ways. First, Tyson argues that the statutes clearly discriminate against interstate commerce and are not justified by a valid purpose unrelated to economic protectionism. Secondly, Tyson contends that the statutes impose a burden on interstate commerce that exceeds the statutes' putative local benefits.

As an initial matter, there can be no doubt that the Virginia statutes affect interstate commerce. "It is well settled that actions are within the domain of the Commerce Clause if they burden interstate commerce or impede its free flow." *Carbone*, 511 U.S. at ___, 114 S.Ct. at 1682 (citing *NLRB v. Jones & Laughlin Steel Corp.*, 301 U.S. 1, 31, 57 S.Ct. 615, 621, 81 L.Ed. 893 (1937)). The Virginia statutes clearly do so by affecting the interstate market for corporate control. In fact, this principle was so obvious to the Supreme Court in *CTS* that it did not bother to say so; it simply considered whether the statute at issue violated the Commerce Clause.

A.

The first way in which Tyson contends that the Virginia statutes violate the Commerce Clause is by discriminating against interstate commerce. There is no dispute that the Virginia statutes treat in-state and out of state tender offerors the same way; the statutes apply regardless of who tries to take over a Virginia corporation. Statutes may discriminate, however, even if they treat in-state and out of state offerors equally. Tyson asserts that the statutes discriminate against interstate commerce because they impose an effective ban on interstate commerce in corporate control of Virginia corporations. To prevail on this issue, Tyson attempts to position this case within the line of cases culminating in *Carbone*.

In *Carbone*, the Supreme Court analyzed a local ordinance that required all nonhazardous solid waste in Clarkstown, New York to be taken to a transfer station for separation of recyclable from non-recyclable items. *Id.* at ___, 114 S.Ct. at 1680. All waste processors, whether in-state or out of state, were prohibited from processing solid waste anywhere other than at the designated transfer station, where they were required to pay a tipping fee even if the waste had already been sorted before arriving at the station. *Id.* at ___, 114 S.Ct. at 1681. The Court held that the ordinance violated the Commerce Clause because it hoarded a local resource and squelched all competition for separating recyclable from non-recyclable waste. *Id.* at ___, 114 S.Ct. at 1683. *See also Fort Gratiot Sanitary Landfill, Inc. v. Michigan Dept. of Natural Resources*, 504 U.S. 353, 112 S.Ct. 2019, 119 L.Ed.2d 139 (1992) (invalidating a statute prohibiting landfill operators from accepting solid waste generated outside of the county because of the statute's protectionist nature); *Dean Milk Co. v. Madison*, 340 U.S. 349, 354, 71 S.Ct. 295, 297, 95 L.Ed. 329 (1951) (invalidating an ordinance that made it unlawful to sell milk as pasteurized unless it was processed within five miles of the city because the ordinance protected a local industry from any competition from out of state); *Brimmer v. Rebman*, 138 U.S. 78, 82-83, 11 S.Ct. 213, 214, 34 L.Ed. 862 (1891) (invalidating a Virginia statute imposing special inspection fees on meat from animals slaughtered more than 100 miles from the place of sale because the statute effectively prevented the sale of meat from animals slaughtered in distant states).

The Virginia statutes do not have the same effect as the statutes struck down in the *Carbone* line of cases. By Tyson's own admission, these case stand for the proposition that a statute clearly discriminates against interstate commerce if it completely eliminates the flow of interstate commerce in an article of commerce. Tyson's Supp. Mem. on Constit. Issues at 30. The Virginia statutes do not completely eliminate the flow of interstate commerce in hostile takeover attempts of Virginia corporations. More to the point, they do not remove competition for corporate control or hoard a local resource. Any potential acquiror that makes an adequate offer may gain control of a Virginia corporation; the Virginia statutes make it more expensive to do so.

In the *Carbone* line of cases, similarly situated entities were treated differently. In *Carbone*, 511 U.S. 383, 114 S.Ct. 1677, one transfer station could separate waste, but others could not do so. In *Fort Gratiot*, 504 U.S. 353, 112 S.Ct. 2019, some solid waste producers could dump their waste, but others could not do so. In *Dean Milk*, 340 U.S. 349, 71 S.Ct. 295, some producers could sell their milk as pasteurized, but others could not do so. In *Brimmer*, 138 U.S. 78, 11 S.Ct. 213, some dealers could sell their meat without a special fee, but others could not do so. In this case, however, everyone stands on equal footing in making tender offers to shareholders of Virginia corporations. As the Supreme Court stated, "[b]ecause nothing in the [statutes] imposes a greater burden on out-of-state offerors than it does on similarly situated [in-state] offerors, we reject the contention that the [statutes] discriminate[ ] against interstate commerce." *CTS*, 481 U.S. at 88, 107 S.Ct. at 1649.[26]

B.

The second way in which Tyson contends that the Virginia statutes violate the Commerce Clause is pursuant to the balancing test enunciated in *Pike v. Bruce Church, Inc.*, 397 U.S. 137, 90 S.Ct. 844, 25 L.Ed.2d 174 (1970). Pursuant to the *Pike* test, the Virginia statutes violate the Commerce Clause if they impose a burden on interstate commerce that clearly exceeds their putative local benefits. *See id.* at 142, 90 S.Ct. at 847. WLR asserts, however, that the *Pike* test no longer applies to Commerce Clause challenges to state laws regulating intrastate corporate governance, based on the Supreme Court's treatment of the issue in *CTS*. In that case, the Court rejected the argument that Indiana's Control Share Act violates the Commerce Clause because of its potential to hinder tender offers, but it did so without ever mentioning the *Pike* test. This has caused some courts to conclude that the *Pike* test no longer applies in this area. Although the Court did not mention *Pike* by name, it examined tender offers' effect on interstate commerce and the local interests that Indiana sought to advance through the Control Share Act. Without explicitly referring to *Pike*, the Court implicitly found that a state's interests in

---

[26] [n.11] In *CTS*, the Court did not even address the *Carbone* line of cases, amplifying the distinction between the regulations struck down in those cases and statutes that evenhandedly regulate tender offers.

defining the attributes of corporations organized pursuant to its laws were sufficient to justify any burdens on interstate commerce associated with the Control Share Act. Although the *Pike* test may not have been used in name, its logic was used in principle.

In examining the Virginia statutes' effect on interstate commerce, Tyson asserts that they violate the Commerce Clause by effectively foreclosing the opportunity to gain control of a Virginia corporation absent consent of the management. In this area, however, "state regulation of corporate governance is regulation of entities whose very existence and attributes are a product of state law." *CTS*, 481 U.S. at 89, 107 S.Ct. at 1649. By enacting these and other statutes, Virginia has defined the attributes of its corporations. Based upon the four Virginia statutes, a Virginia corporation is an entity (1) in which shareholders holding over one-fifth of the shares have no voting rights absent consent of the directors or the disinterested shareholders (Control Share Act); (2) that cannot be merged into another entity for three years without consent of its directors (Affiliated Transactions Act); (3) that can issue discriminatory rights to the detriment of some of its shareholders, provided that such discrimination is in the best interests of the corporation (Poison Pill Statute); and (4) whose directors must conduct themselves based upon their good faith business judgment of the best interests of the corporation, and who may satisfy this standard by relying in good faith on competent advice received pursuant to an informational process undertaken in good faith (Business Judgment Statute).

"By prohibiting certain transactions, and regulating others, such laws necessarily affect certain aspects of interstate commerce." *Id.* at 90, 107 S.Ct. at 1650. The Virginia statutes make it more difficult and more expensive to gain control of a Virginia corporation, but so do supermajority voting requirements, dissenters' rights, and staggered directors' terms. In fact, states could ban mergers completely without violating the Commerce Clause.

In defining the attributes of its corporations, Virginia "has an interest in promoting stable relationships among parties involved in the corporations it charters, as well as in ensuring that investors in such corporations have an effective voice in corporate affairs." *CTS*, 481 U.S. at 91, 107 S.Ct. at 165. Through the four statutes at issue, Virginia has given certain tools to shareholders and management, acting in the best interests of the corporation, to ensure that tender offers succeed only if they are consistent with the long-term interests of the corporation. Shareholders of Virginia corporations need not fear the coercive pressures of two-tiered tender offers or the prospect of corporate raiders seeking to extract greenmail by threatening to immediately dismantle and sell a corporation's assets.

Virginia need not define its corporations as other states do; it must only provide residents and nonresidents with equal access to them. *Id.* at 94, 107 S.Ct. at 1652. If Virginia believes that hostile tender offers have the potential to be harmful to the corporations that it creates and whose attributes it defines, then it is permitted to enact regulations designed to neutralize that harm. Tyson's argument that such a policy can lead to inefficient management would be better addressed to the Virginia legislature rather than this court. Whether these statutes may limit the number of successful tender offers does not substantially affect the Commerce Clause analysis. *Id.* at 93–94, 107 S.Ct. at 1651–52.

The Commerce Clause does not give Tyson a right to purchase WLR for $30 per share. It merely ensures that Tyson have a chance to do so equal to that of a Virginia resident offering $30 per share. The Virginia statutes do nothing to upset that equality. They make it more difficult for tender offerors, resident and nonresident alike, to gain control of a Virginia corporation. As a result, Tyson is unlikely to succeed on the merits of its Commerce Clause challenge.

VI.

The Virginia statutes, even when viewed as a scheme, are not preempted by the Williams Act and do not violate the Commerce Clause. Whatever the merits or demerits of discouraging tender offers, the Constitution is not concerned with the wisdom of economic policy. "The Constitution does not require the States to subscribe to any particular economic theory." *Id.* at 92, 107 S.Ct. at 1651. . . . Tyson's motion for a preliminary injunction is denied.

An appropriate Order shall this day issue.

————

QUESTIONS

1. What is the deal involved in the case?

2. What are the four statutes at issue? What is the policy behind each of them?

3. On what grounds is Tyson challenging the statutes?

4. What does the court decide? Why?

————

To give you a flavor for the various maneuvers involved in a hostile takeover, below is a case study of Oracle's takeover of PeopleSoft.

David Millstone & Guhan Subramanian, Oracle v. Peoplesoft: *A Case Study*
12 Harv. Negot. L. Rev. 1 (2007)[27]

"There is no possibility of any condition, at any price that PeopleSoft will be sold to anyone. No possibility."

— Craig Conway, CEO and Director, PeopleSoft

"We've got this war game in a box. This has all been pre-scripted. If they launched on J.D. Edwards, we were going to launch on them."

— Larry Ellison, CEO and Director, Oracle

It was 7:30 in the morning, Pacific Standard Time, on Monday, June 2, 2003. Oracle Co-President Safra Catz was on her home exercise bike when the news came

————

across CNBC: two of her major competitors, PeopleSoft and J.D. Edwards (JDEC), had agreed to merge. Catz stared at the screen for just a moment, then leapt off her bike and headed upstairs to her computer. It was true; a deal had been signed over the weekend. Catz's inbox began to fill with a flurry of reaction. A BlackBerried message from Joe Reece, Oracle's banker at Credit Suisse First Boston (CSFB), suggested they discuss "whether it makes sense to stir the pot on this." A junior banker weighed in with a more lengthy analysis. Summaries, statistics, trading multiples, market color. The financial surgeons of Wall Street's most powerful shops were dissecting the deal, probing it for weaknesses, and laying its pathology out for their eminent client. But Catz was cautious. There was one person she needed to talk to before she let slip the dogs of war.

Unsure whether Larry was up yet, she emailed.

Subject: PeopleSoft/J.D. Edwards.

Body: Now would be the time to launch on PeopleSoft.

Thirteen minutes later, at 7:47 am, came Larry's reply:

Subject: RE: PeopleSoft/J.D. Edwards.

Body: Just what I was thinking. Where are you?

It was going to be a long week.

Background

Oracle and PeopleSoft competed in the enterprise application software business: it accounted for approximately 20% of Oracle's revenues (the remainder was database) and 100% of PeopleSoft's. Enterprise application software automates business processes, such as purchasing and selling, accounting, and payroll. The software is a big-ticket item for most companies, with purchase prices often in six or even seven figures. And after paying the large price tag, a company will spend as much as ten times the purchase price to install and integrate the software into its operations: hiring consultants to tailor and install the software; training employees in its use; and even changing the way the company does business in order to make the most of the software's capabilities. Unsuccessful installations have brought havoc to companies, ruined quarters, and ended careers of IT heads. As a result the decision to buy is not taken lightly, and once bought the commitment on both sides is long term.

In addition to paying the purchase price and related installation costs, companies that buy enterprise application software pay two ongoing maintenance fees to the vendor. The first fee gives a buyer access to personalized support: the right to call and ask questions, submit problem reports, etc. The second and larger fee is for software update rights. This second fee gives a buyer access to the latest versions of the software, including bug fixes, product enhancements, and updates.

A company's software can quickly become obsolete if not assiduously updated. Consider, for example, a company that uses software to manage its payroll. If withholding tax laws change and the software is not updated to incorporate the change, the software becomes useless, and the company has no way to pay its employees. For this reason virtually all enterprise application customers pay the update fee. Enterprise software vendors are not contractually obligated to provide updates or even bug fixes to customers who sign up for update rights. Instead, the market runs on trust and reputation. Customers depend vitally on an "implicit contract" with their software vendor to support their mission-critical purchase.

The Predator: Oracle Corp.

Oracle was founded in 1976 by Larry Ellison, the brilliant and fiercely competitive college dropout who still ran the company in 2003. Most of Ellison's $15 billion net worth was tied up in his 26% ownership interest in Oracle. Ellison flew fighter aircraft, raced sailboats, and collected Japanese art. He was known to be a ruthless competitor and once famously paraphrased the Mongol warlord Genghis Khan in a New York Times article: "It is not sufficient that I succeed; all others must fail."[28] In 2003 he was featured in a 60 Minutes II episode entitled "The Most Competitive Man In the World." Fueled by Ellison's unique combination of success and showmanship, many books had been written about him over the years, with titles such as Everyone Else Must Fail: The Unvarnished Truth About Oracle and Larry Ellison; The Oracle of Oracle: The Story of Volatile CEO Larry Ellison and the Strategies Behind His Company's Phenomenal Success; and The Difference Between God and Larry Ellison: God Doesn't Think He's Larry Ellison.

More generously, Ellison had also built a company worth more than $60 billion that provided the technology to manage much of the world's information. By 2003, Oracle had over 41,000 employees and sold products in over 120 countries. It was the largest employer in the world of CalTech and MIT engineers as well as the world's largest employer of Harvard mathematicians. Oracle also had a highly regarded sales culture that produced, among others, Tom Siebel, the founder and CEO of Siebel Systems, and Craig Conway, the CEO of PeopleSoft. The company's competitiveness and success in gaining market share earned it a reputation as a bruising competitor.

Historically, Oracle did not grow through acquisition. The company's biggest deal before PeopleSoft was only $150 million. Most others were barely material. Over its first two decades the company had so much organic growth — doubling in size in some years — that acquisitions were at best an afterthought. Within Oracle the conventional wisdom was that integrations required too much management attention when so much growth could be achieved just by executing well.

All that changed in 2002. Ellison confounded the tech community when he announced that the heady days of 100% growth were over. The bubble had burst. The window of opportunity that had made Ellison and his contemporaries the richest men in the world was closing. Ellison offered the ultimate Silicon Valley heresy: the information technology industry was now mature.

To Ellison, growth and competitiveness would have to come from consolidation, and Ellison wanted to be the consolidator, not the consolidated. That task fell to

---

[28] [n.4] Andrew Pollack, Fast-Growth Oracle Systems Confronts First Downturn, N.Y. Times, Sept. 10, 1990, at D1.

Ellison's right-hand woman, Oracle's Co-President Safra Catz. Catz graduated from the Wharton School and then began law school at the University of Pennsylvania. She moved to Harvard Law School where she was recruited by the investment banking firm of Donaldson Lufkin & Jenrette (DLJ). After working for 12 years as a banker at DLJ, where she rose quickly to the level of managing director, she was recruited by Oracle, her client, in April 1999. By 2004, Catz shared overall operating responsibility for the company with Ellison; she also managed its M&A strategy. She was named by the Wall Street Journal as one of "50 Women to Watch" in American business. She was also widely rumored to be Ellison's likely successor, though she publicly disclaimed any interest in the top job at Oracle.

The Prey: PeopleSoft

PeopleSoft was founded in 1987 by David Duffield, a billionaire in his own right, who still owned 8% of the company when Oracle launched its bid. Duffield was the anti-Ellison: a warm, grandfatherly character who kept three dogs and four birds at home and had donated a substantial amount of his fortune to animal rights organizations. Often appearing in his trademark Hawaiian shirts, Duffield was famous for encouraging a supportive, familial culture among "People people," the 8,300 employees at his firm where he was known to sign emails with his initials "D.A.D." PeopleSoft's first product was a human resources offering, and by 2004 it continued to enjoy widespread customer acceptance for its HR products. In addition, PeopleSoft sold financial management systems, customer relations management software, supply chain management products, and related consulting services.

In 1999, at the age of 59, Duffield retired as CEO (retaining the Chairman title) and brought in Craig Conway as his successor. Conway had been Vice President of Sales & Marketing at Oracle from 1985 to 1992. Ellison claimed that Conway was fired by his direct boss at Oracle, Ray Lane, because Conway was a "bad apple and had to go." Conway had a more benign interpretation of events: "Ray and I looked at each other and concluded that one of us was probably redundant to the cause."

Conway bounced back to become the "Clint Eastwood of software," leading turnaround efforts at TGV and OneTouch before accepting the top job at People-Soft. PeopleSoft's dramatic growth over its first ten years had slowed, and Conway was viewed by many as the person capable of taking the company to the next level. One year after Conway joined the company, PeopleSoft unveiled the newest version of its signature software, PeopleSoft 8, to strong reviews from customers and analysts.

Contact

In June 2002, one year before the takeover contest unfolded, Conway was thinking about how to build critical mass in application software. With his board's approval, Conway approached Ellison, whom he had not spoken to since he left Oracle in 1992. Conway proposed a merger between PeopleSoft and Oracle's enterprise software business. Oracle would be the new company's majority shareholder and Conway would be its CEO. Ellison was enthusiastic about the combination:

> Increasing the size of the business gives us tremendous economies of scale and efficiencies, and makes us more profitable and more competitive. We can put more engineers on product development because we have more customers. That makes the products better, which in turns gets us additional customers. We amortize our engineering costs over a larger customer base. That makes us more profitable.

Ellison instructed Catz to put a team together. Within days, senior managers from each company converged at the Lafayette Park Hotel on the East Bay in San Francisco to sift through the particulars of Conway's proposal. The mood was optimistic at the meeting, which lasted most of the day. While there were some technical complications, both sides thought that the deal made sense overall. They agreed to meet again with larger teams. It was the last thing that the two companies would ever agree on.

The second meeting never happened. Two stories later emerged as to why. According to Catz:

> It was really, really simple. And it's interesting because Craig Conway also testified under oath and came up with something different, which was really magical. But the reality is that Craig and Larry got back on the phone [after the Lafayette Park Hotel meeting] and they both indicated that their teams wanted to go forward. Larry says "We're interested in acquiring PeopleSoft." And Craig says, "Well, I want to merge the two applications businesses, but I want to run it. Oracle can be our largest shareholder, but I need to be in charge." And Larry didn't go along with that concept. He thought that we could run it better as part of Oracle and run it better, period, than Craig could. And since Craig was very interested in his own job, he just said, "That's not going to work," and got off the phone.

PeopleSoft thought the holdup was Oracle's insistence on using its own product going forward. Unlike Oracle's enterprise application product, which could run only on Oracle's database, PeopleSoft's software worked across platforms. George "Skip" Battle, a PeopleSoft director, explained:

> What we wanted was a company that was separate from the database business. So the only way we were interested in doing it is if it were a standalone company. We wouldn't be interested in having our applications software straitjacketed into any single database manufacturer. And I think Oracle really was looking at the apps business as a way of enhancing their position on the database side.

In any case, there was no meeting of the minds and no more meetings between Oracle and PeopleSoft. By September 2002, Conway, speaking about Ellison, stated, "When you alienate everybody, you become someone no one wants to play with." It was clear that after a decade-long détente, the bad blood between Ellison and Conway had resurfaced.

The Initial Attack

On June 6, 2003, D-Day, Oracle launched its "war game in a box."[29] Oracle's attack was surprising, but unlike its storied predecessor, it was not overwhelming.

Oracle's announced tender for PeopleSoft at $16 per share offered almost no premium to the market price at the time. In fact, the offer price was 3.6% below the 30-day average trading price and 12.1% below the 180-day average trading price prior to the offer. Exhibit 1A provides information on PeopleSoft's share price during the ten years before the bid, relative to the Dow Jones Computer Software Index. Exhibit 1B provides information on PeopleSoft's share price from January 2002 through October 2004.

Although CSFB, Oracle's bankers on the deal, had opined that $16 was too low and would be a tactical mistake,[30] Catz explained the decision to go with the $16 offer:

> When, all of a sudden PeopleSoft moved to buy JDEC, it was absolutely obvious that they had come to a conclusion that they couldn't possibly stay independent. Their shareholders were now presented with the question: what do we do? So this was the perfect time to give those shareholders another option. And we thought, "Gee, maybe we can get it at this price because to anybody but Oracle, and maybe SAP, this company was not worth a cent over $16."

The offer was not well-received. Investors considered it suspicious and almost comically below market. "It was not credible," recalled a large PeopleSoft investor. "I was on the conference call when they announced it. Oracle did nothing on the call to foster credibility. They sounded as if they had some Machiavellian strategy to destroy a competitor. Pretty heavyweight investment bankers opined privately that Oracle had made a terrible mistake."

While the Street was skeptical, Conway was incensed. The PeopleSoft CEO heard about the offer in Amsterdam, on his way to visit with customers. Without consulting his board, he called the bid "atrociously bad behavior from an atrociously bad company." He likened the offer to a wedding with Oracle's CEO, Larry Ellison, "showing up with a shotgun trying to get someone to marry him." And he sent out a company-wide voicemail telling employees that "it should go without saying that there is no possibility that PeopleSoft would consider selling the company to Oracle."

The PeopleSoft board convened to assess the offer on Sunday, June 8, with Conway, still in Amsterdam, participating via speakerphone. Exhibit 2 provides a list of the eight PeopleSoft board members (including Michael Maples, who joined

---

[29] [n.9] Catz took issue with this characterization, suggesting it may have been the product of some errant language. "The concept of going hostile on PeopleSoft was not part of a 'war game in a box.' There was no war game in a box. There was no box. The Department of Justice subpoenaed 'the box' and subpoenaed the documents, none of which exist. It was just in our own hypotheticals: 'Gee, if this happens, we should do this. If PeopleSoft turns this deal, the JDEC deal, into a cash deal, we should bid for JDEC.' It was that kind of a discussion."

[30] [n.10] As Catz candidly related, "The truth is that we're not very good advice takers at Oracle."

the board from J.D. Edwards just after the bid was launched) along with brief biographies of each. Other than Duffield (who owned 7.6% of PeopleSoft) and Conway (who owned 1.4%), the remaining six directors collectively owned 1.5% of the stock — typical for a company of PeopleSoft's size.

Conway quickly turned the meeting over to Andrew Bogen of Gibson Dunn & Crutcher, PeopleSoft's outside legal counsel. Bogen, a highly experienced M&A lawyer, briefed the board on its responsibilities under Delaware law in the face of a hostile offer. Delaware law requires board members, as fiduciaries of the company, to dispassionately and carefully evaluate any bona fide offer. According to Bogen, Conway's immediate dismissal of the offer, and his stated unwillingness to consider any offer, could be construed as violations of the board's fiduciary duties. In order to distance the company from those comments, Bogen recommended that the board establish a "Transaction Committee," comprised solely of independent directors, to evaluate and respond to Oracle's offer.

The majority view was that Conway's rhetoric was troubling and needed to be toned down. The board adopted Bogen's recommendation to form a Transaction Committee, with Skip Battle as the chair. Battle was an independent director at PeopleSoft who had considerable experience in difficult business situations: when the dot-com start-up venture AskJeeves nearly went bust in 2000, Battle, an early-stage investor, stepped in and engineered a turn-around that eventually led to the sale of AskJeeves to Barry Diller's IAC in 2005. The other members of the Transaction Committee were the other independent directors: Frank Fanzilli, Steven Goldby, Cyril Yansouni, and (shortly thereafter) Michael Maples. According to PeopleSoft's SEC filings:

> The Transaction Committee is responsible for evaluating the Oracle tender offer, including any amendments thereto, and any related activities of Oracle in connection with its announced intent to acquire PeopleSoft. The Transaction Committee is also responsible for advising the Board on making recommendations to stockholders and any other actions the Board make [sic] take in response to Oracle's offer.[31]

The Transaction Committee was the easy call. More difficult was deciding how to deal with Oracle. The problem the board faced was that, as they saw it, Oracle's actions made no sense. If Oracle was interested in a transaction, why didn't it first approach the board privately? And if it actually wanted to buy PeopleSoft, why did it offer such a pathetic premium? As Battle explained:

> I thought that this was a tremendously disruptive thing to do that was clearly an advantage to Oracle in the competitive environment. I didn't know if they wanted to buy or not. What they say about hostiles is that you come in hard, you come in high, and you come in once. They were low, they were lame, and they looked like they were trying to screw up the asset.

Hostile bids are always disruptive, but for industry-specific reasons that both PeopleSoft and Oracle understood, Oracle's bid was a particularly serious threat to

---

[31] [n.14] PeopleSoft Inc., Proxy Statement for the 2004 Annual Meeting of Stockholders (Form PRER14A) 7 (Feb. 23, 2004).

PeopleSoft. PeopleSoft's customers, like Oracle's, do not simply purchase software the way one might purchase a word processor or a video game. They are purchasing a relationship with the vendor. Anything that is perceived to threaten that relationship in the long term will impair business in the short term. This feature of the enterprise application software business derives from the longevity of the software (typically five years or more) and the enormous costs of adopting and implementing the software. If PeopleSoft's customers believed a victorious Oracle would discontinue support for the products at some point in the future, they would stop purchasing products right now. Battle described the dilemma that would consume the PeopleSoft board for the next 18 months:

> When people buy these large-ticket enterprise software licenses, they buy it on the basis of features, they buy it on the basis of support, and they buy it on the basis of company viability. By the time we had gotten together on Sunday, Oracle had already made some statements that said "We're not going to actively market PeopleSoft software." And the analysts,[32] Gartner and others, had come out with some statements that said, "Don't buy until you see where this is going to go." So anything that we do to get in the way of license sales is going to hurt shareholder value. That drove us for 18 months. The Delaware courts hate comments like the one that Conway made about "We'll never sell to those guys." But our customers and prospects don't hate it. We had something like twenty-three or twenty-four days to the end of the quarter. Seventy percent of license deals come in the last three days. So the first thing we're saying is: "How are we going to keep this company together?" The headline is "Oracle Launches Hostile Takeover." If the headline on the 2nd of July is "PeopleSoft Announces a Serious Miss in Software Licenses," our shareholder value is toast.

As a source close to the situation remarked, Oracle's initial strategy was "either incredibly evil or incredibly stupid." The evil interpretation — held by many at PeopleSoft and on the Street — was that Oracle's bid was not serious and was calculated to wound PeopleSoft. The pending bid would create a cloud of "fear, uncertainty, and doubt" over PeopleSoft, impairing its ability to sell software to new customers who would be relying on PeopleSoft to be there for updates and support. Thus a low-ball bid could be a self-fulfilling prophecy, reducing value until $16 was actually a good price. Alternatively, the bid could deliver a blow sufficient to cripple PeopleSoft as a competitor. The Darwinian realities of the market would do the rest.

Oracle was looking to acquire PeopleSoft "for the sole purpose of killing it," Conway insisted. PeopleSoft formalized this accusation in a suit filed against Oracle on June 13, 2003, just one week after Oracle's announcement. The complaint alleged deceptive business practices, tortious interference, and a litany of other misdeeds. The suit was filed in Alameda County, California, PeopleSoft's hometown. Specifically, PeopleSoft alleged:

> A concerted scheme by Oracle and its agents to: (i) interfere with PeopleSoft's plan to merge with J.D. Edwards & Co. ("J.D. Edwards"); (ii)

---

[32] [n.15] Due to the complexity of the software and the importance of the purchasing decisions, companies rely heavily on independent analysts such as Gartner for purchasing recommendations.

undermine PeopleSoft's viability by creating uncertainty and doubt in the minds of PeopleSoft's customers and prospective customers; and (iii) undercut PeopleSoft's business operations by disparaging PeopleSoft's products, services and future prospects, all under the guise of a disingenuous tender offer.

PeopleSoft's story gained traction from outside commentators on the deal. A Barron's article dated June 9 stated that analysts and investment bankers "seem to agree that Ellison is not terribly serious about buying PeopleSoft," but "by making a run at the company through an offer that was market value in cash, Ellison at the very least can create confusion, uncertainty and chaos among the customers and employees of both PeopleSoft and J.D. Edwards." A hedge fund partner was quoted as saying: "This isn't a takeover; it's a hostage-taking."

The sinister interpretation also found support in some internal Oracle documents. An email from CSFB's Joe Reece entitled "twist in the wind" advised Catz to keep the bid low "to create doubts in the minds of the market" and thereby produce "a decline in the price [of PeopleSoft]." Although this email became "Exhibit A" in PeopleSoft's case, it was technically from CSFB, not Oracle. Careful analysis of Oracle's statements in the first few weeks demonstrates that Ellison and his team hewed closely to their talking points. Oracle would support PeopleSoft's products but not produce a new version.[33] Oracle would offer customers trouble-free migration onto Oracle's platform. Otherwise, customers would be supported with what they had. The deal only made sense, Catz and Ellison insisted, if Oracle could cultivate PeopleSoft's customer base.

Even PeopleSoft noticed Oracle's message discipline. An internal report to Conway from a team sent to comb through the public record for Ellison's misstatements concluded:

> [We] have gone through the scripts and found nothing condemning. Ever since his initial interview June 6, [Ellison] has managed to stay on point. The interviewers try to pin him on his intention not to enhance/support our products/customers, but he continually sticks to the "we will support but not actively market" story line. This is the same issue we had this summer in trying to find quotes and couldn't. I think everyone (from us to the press) picked up on Larry/Oracle's initial misstep and took full advantage to the point where it was widely believed Larry said more than he actually did.

Oracle may have been pledging support, but no one heard them in the din of accusations. Catz noted:

> We're saying "the sky is blue" and they are claiming that we said the sky is black. And I have it written in transcripts — in transcripts — that we said that the sky was blue. And we could not get the message out. We were extremely frustrated because we could not get the truth out. And it was just

---

[33] [n.21] New versions, denominated with integers — e.g. PeopleSoft 7 or PeopleSoft 8 — are wholesale overhauls of the software. Updates, which are fixes and improvements to an existing version, were the primary source of contention.

the most frustrating experience when you're telling the truth and the truth does not come out.

"This is the most heavily PR'ed case that I have ever been involved in," said one experienced dealmaker close to Oracle. He added, "If you look at Oracle's results through all of this, I think the PR people were a disaster." As one person close to Oracle admitted, "Conway very artfully depicted PeopleSoft as the little guy getting picked on."

Upbraided by the financial community and losing ground in the press, Oracle quickly changed course. On June 18, just seven trading days after its initial $16 offer, Oracle raised its bid 20% to $19.50, for a total offer value of $6.3 billion. Catz explained the reasoning:

> As [Oracle CFO and later Chairman] Jeff Henley and [Oracle Co-President] Charles Phillips talked to the owners of the stock, they were told that $16 was not enough. It made us look like we weren't serious and that we were just trying to muck up their deal with JDEC. Now of course, if you're a seller you're going to say whatever you can to get the buyer to raise the price. But we decided that at $19.50 the deal still worked for us — and only us — and we could afford it. We spoke to the holders of a majority of the shares and $19.50 was above where every one of them indicated they would sell their shares to us. In fact many were saying, "Give us $18 and it's over." At $19.50 we were comfortably above the clearing price.

But it was too late. PeopleSoft's board took only a day to reject this offer, saying it undervalued the company and citing additional risks to the deal such as regulatory review.

PeopleSoft Raises the Drawbridge

Before 1983, a target board's determination of inadequacy would not have prevented a hostile takeover bid if a majority of the shareholders wanted to accept the offer. But the world changed in 1983 with the invention of the "shareholder rights plan," better known as a "poison pill." The pill that PeopleSoft had in place was typical: if any individual or entity acquired more than 20% of PeopleSoft's shares without the approval of PeopleSoft's board, all other shareholders would have the right to buy shares at 50% of the prevailing market price. The exercise of these deep-in-the-money options would severely dilute the hostile bidder from 20% to 1.4%. In our two decades of experience, no hostile bidder has ever "broken through" (triggered) a poison pill. As a result most practitioners and academic commentators today consider the pill to be a "show stopper" against a hostile bidder. The consequence is that a target board can unilaterally veto a hostile takeover bid through the use of a pill.

The Delaware Supreme Court upheld the validity of the poison pill in its seminal 1985 decision *Moran v. Household International*,[34] and further solidified the pill in

---

[34] [n.23] 500 A.2d 1346 (Del. 1985).

its 1989 decision *Paramount Communications v. Time*.[35] In *Time*, the Court held that "[d]irectors are not obligated to abandon a deliberately conceived plan for a short-term shareholder profit unless there is clearly no basis to sustain the corporate strategy."[36] Notwithstanding the sweeping language in *Time*, the Delaware courts have repeatedly noted that the ability to maintain a pill is not unlimited; rather, courts will scrutinize the decision to keep a pill under the "intermediate" standard of review set out in *Unocal v. Mesa Petroleum*.[37] The *Unocal* test has two parts: first, the target board must demonstrate that the hostile bid presents a "threat" to the corporation; and second, the target board must demonstrate that its defensive response was "reasonable in relation to the threat posed."[38] Although the *Unocal* test has been characterized as "enhanced" judicial scrutiny (in contrast to the extremely deferential "business judgment review"), no Delaware court since Time has required a target board to eliminate ("redeem") its poison pill under *Unocal's* two-part test.

In addition to its poison pill, which was already in place when Oracle launched its bid, PeopleSoft rapidly erected four other defenses over the next two months:

Bulking Up: The JDEC Deal Re-Cut and Re-Spun

The Oracle offer had immediate consequences for PeopleSoft's pending acquisition of J.D. Edwards. Because PeopleSoft would be required to issue a significant number of new shares to acquire JDEC, a shareholder vote was required by stock exchange listing rules. Oracle wanted PeopleSoft shareholders to vote no in order to signal that they preferred the $16 cash offer. For PeopleSoft, closing the JDEC deal would increase the size of the prospective deal for Oracle by almost 30%, and would force Oracle to acquire an additional company it might not be interested in (at least at the price it was prepared to pay for PeopleSoft).

On June 16, PeopleSoft amended the terms of its merger agreement to include significant cash consideration, thereby avoiding the shareholder vote. Although it thwarted shareholders who might have opposed the deal, this move was part of the standard defense playbook and legally unremarkable. What raised eyebrows was PeopleSoft's second announcement that day: expected synergies from the deal had been revised upward, from $85 million on May 31st, to $167 million just two weeks later (and one week after the Oracle bid), on June 11th. According to a banker present at the June 11th meeting, no board member questioned the revisions. PeopleSoft directors later testified that management had always expected $150-$200 million in synergies, but a lower number had been used initially in order to be conservative.

---

[35] [n.24] 571 A.2d 1140 (Del. 1989).

[36] [n.25] *Id.* at 1154 (emphasis added).

[37] [n.26] 493 A.2d 946 (Del. 1985).

[38] [n.27] *Id.* at 954-56, 958.

Golden and Tin Parachutes

In August 2003, two months after the initial offer, PeopleSoft's board approved amendments to its severance policies to provide large cash payments to senior executives (so called "golden parachutes") in the event of a change of control. Consistent with PeopleSoft's egalitarian spirit, the program was expanded to cover all employees (the somewhat sarcastically named "tin parachutes"). In view of Oracle's announced expectations regarding staff reductions, the cost of the new severance packages was estimated at $200 million.

Antitrust

In any proposed merger or acquisition larger than $50 million, the Department of Justice (DOJ) (or in some cases the Federal Trade Commission) must determine whether the deal is anticompetitive. Under the Hart-Scott-Rodino Antitrust Improvements Act of 1976, the first review is perfunctory, while the "second request," if it is demanded, is long, data-intensive, and thorough.[39] If the DOJ concludes that the deal is anticompetitive, it can sue to block the transaction or negotiate with the parties to obtain divestment of certain assets after the consummation of the deal.

During the review process, private parties can lobby the DOJ to try to influence its decision. In the days immediately following the Oracle bid, PeopleSoft launched a massive campaign to encourage the DOJ to block. According to Skip Battle, pushing for antitrust review was "the biggest decision we made in the whole process." The difficulty stemmed from the one-way nature of the decision: once PeopleSoft claimed that the deal was anticompetitive, it lost any ability to reverse itself and later support the deal. In contrast, the poison pill, though potent, could always be revoked by a target board.

Antitrust dominated PeopleSoft's second board meeting after the Oracle bid, on Tuesday, June 10th. Gibson Dunn cautioned against too public an antitrust campaign, arguing that it could backfire and give Oracle an argument in the Delaware courts that PeopleSoft was not open to a deal. Conway saw antitrust as a silver bullet. At one point he told the board: "We will keep or lose the company immediately following the Justice Department decision . . . the rest is completely and only a matter of money, which we do not control." Battle felt it was a close call, but ultimately came to support an antitrust campaign:

> We believed that there was no way this thing would be approved without a second request. You go from three to two [competitors in the enterprise applications market], it seems pretty obvious. And so we knew that this deal was going to be hung up in multiple levels of antitrust review. Our lawyers were completely convinced that this would require a second request, and

---

[39] [n.28] As Battle put it, "There's a first review and a second review, if necessary. And I've been involved in a second review before. And in terms of time and effort, in a first review, you can probably put the documents in my station wagon. In a second review, you're going to be backing up Safeway trucks."

they believed that there was a substantial likelihood that the government would move to block.

So our decision was, do we throw ourselves on the side of the government in that assessment or not? And we decided to put ourselves on the side of that government assessment, because it would be a tonic to our customers and our prospects, and would likely maximize license sales. So if we were wrong, we'd have a better share price to negotiate from.

Without consulting Gibson Dunn, PeopleSoft hired Gary Reback as its lead antitrust counsel. Reback, best known for his crusade against Microsoft on behalf of Netscape, was described by the American Lawyer as "brilliant and exceptionally intense" and by Wired magazine as "the only man Bill Gates fears." Reback and Conway set off on an antitrust roadshow, which had immediate payoffs: in the first week after Oracle's bid, Richard Blumenthal, State Attorney General for Connecticut (one of PeopleSoft's biggest customers), sued to block the merger. And shortly thereafter, just as Battle had predicted, the Department of Justice issued a second request.

The Customer Assurance Program (CAP)

On June 9, 2003, three days after Oracle announced its bid, Kyle Bowker, a senior sales executive at PeopleSoft, sent an email to his staff announcing a new program. PeopleSoft would offer customers rebates of two times their money in the event an acquirer discontinued new sales of the PeopleSoft product line or "materially reduce[d] support services" for PeopleSoft products within two years from the customer contract date. The program was initiated without formal board approval and without public disclosure, though it was later ratified by the board and disclosed in general terms in SEC filings.

Although the CAP received attention in the press as "a new kind of poison pill," Oracle initially did not worry about the CAP. Catz explained:

> The moment we saw the CAP, my initial reaction was, "No problem." We're going to support the products. Why would we not support the products? I was not concerned about it. And Larry wasn't concerned about it, because it would only be triggered in the event that we did something against our own interest. So why would we do that? So I was not worried about the first version.

Over the next 18 months, the program evolved through five different versions, most notably increasing the payment multiples to a sliding scale between two and five times the purchase price (with the multiple increasing as the size of the contract increased), and doubling the length of the protection period to four years. Exhibit 3 provides the details on these refinements. By November 2004, the CAP mandated $2.0 billion in payments to PeopleSoft customers if Oracle acquired PeopleSoft and then reduced support for its products.

As the CAP liability continued to accrue at a ferocious pace, Ellison and Catz became worried about the sheer magnitude of the potential liability (amounting to more than one-third of PeopleSoft's pre-bid market capitalization) and the vagueness of the support trigger. As Ellison described in October 2004:

> The biggest concern I have right now is something I learned very recently,
> which is the ambiguity in some of the [CAP] contracts. The trouble is we
> live in a litigious world. And some customers might decide to take
> advantage of the insurance, just see what happens in court — or, at the very
> least, use that as a negotiating technique against us. . . . Someone will say,
> "All right, I have this offer of five times my money back, but why don't you
> just cut my maintenance fees in half instead and forget the whole thing."
> And we end up having to do that with hundreds and hundreds of customers,
> which will be very expensive.

Two features of the CAP were particularly noteworthy. First, like PeopleSoft's
antitrust defense (and unlike the poison pill), the CAP could not be pulled back by
PeopleSoft because it was a contractual term embedded in customer contracts.
Therefore, the CAP could not be used as a bargaining chip against Oracle, to be
eliminated in exchange for a higher price. Second, the magnitude of the CAP
payments was not the product of arms-length bargaining: customers clearly liked
higher CAP payments, and PeopleSoft liked higher CAP payments too because
larger contingent payments would yield a larger deterrent effect, and only Oracle
— not PeopleSoft — would suffer the negative consequences of the accrued liability.
PeopleSoft recognized this benefit in its SEC filings: "The terms of the customer
assurance program require an acquisition by an entity other than PeopleSoft;
therefore no action taken unilaterally by PeopleSoft would, by itself, result in the
recognition of a contingent liability."

In short, the CAP was the perfect defense, a win-win for both PeopleSoft and its
customers. At a conference held at Tulane Law School while the CAP was being
litigated, Steven Koch, head of global M&A at CSFB, told Vice Chancellor Leo
Strine who would eventually hear the case: "If this [the CAP] is legitimate, I'm
going to start running around pitching these contracts to all my clients."

Oracle Turns to Shareholders

All of these defenses were arrayed against Oracle by the end of the summer
2003. Oracle could not buy the company directly through a tender offer. And, as
Catz recalls, PeopleSoft was steadfast in its unwillingness to negotiate:

> There was just absolutely no interest [in negotiating]. There was no one on
> their side to talk to. We were always open to talking. We had an offer on the
> table. And they just absolutely wouldn't talk to us about anything. And they
> weren't interested in any information from us. Literally, there was no one
> to talk to on their side. . . . They were absolutely resolute it would happen
> over their dead bodies.

PeopleSoft's directors felt they had reasons for not coming to the table. They
were unconvinced that Oracle actually wanted a deal. If this were a scheme to
damage their business, then negotiating would play right into Oracle's hand:
PeopleSoft and Oracle would have a duty to amend their Schedules TO and 14D-9
indicating that negotiations were underway, but Oracle could then take an
unreasonable position in the negotiations. Or PeopleSoft might make progress with

Oracle, then be blocked by the Department of Justice. PeopleSoft's customers would fear for the company's long-term viability and abandon purchases. There were just too many scenarios in which PeopleSoft got jilted at the altar.

Also diminishing the chances of a negotiated solution was the growing level of distrust and animosity. PeopleSoft was convinced that it was fighting for its life. For its employees, the prospect of mass layoffs loomed large. If PeopleSoft faltered in one quarter, there might not be another to make it up. PeopleSoft and Oracle salespeople sparred every day over prospective accounts. Battle remembers it as a streetfight: "Oracle salespeople were saying in pitches that you can't buy People-Soft software; 'They're going to be dead. They're gone. They're history. You shouldn't be buying it. Don't be a chump. You'll get fired.' That sort of stuff."

Oracle, for its part, was infuriated at what it felt was the incredible disinformation emanating from PeopleSoft. It was as if the tender offer had given PeopleSoft license to say whatever it wanted, no matter how strained or factually inaccurate.

In one famous exchange that reflected the tenor of the time, Conway, pressed by a reporter on why he would not consider an offer at any price, declared, "It's like me asking if I could buy your dog so I can go out back and shoot it." At an Oracle analyst conference Ellison responded, "I think at one point Craigy thought I was going to shoot his dog. If Craigy and his dog were standing next to each other, trust me, if I had one bullet, it wouldn't be for the dog." Conway and his dog both showed up to PeopleSoft's next analyst conference clad in bullet proof vests.[40]

Having no one at PeopleSoft to negotiate with, Oracle turned to shareholders. In November 2003, Oracle nominated five candidates to stand for election to the PeopleSoft board of directors, and proposed a bylaw change that would expand the board by one seat from eight to nine. Because shareholders could effectively pass the bylaw amendment and fill the seat in one meeting, the contest offered Oracle the opportunity to take control of PeopleSoft by electing a majority of its directors at its annual meeting on March 25, 2004.

To rally support for its nominees, Oracle raised its offer to $26.00 per share in cash on February 4, a 63% increase over the initial bid and $9.4 billion in total value. Oracle declared in its press release, "This is our final price. We urge PeopleSoft's directors to seriously consider our offer and put the interests of their stockholders first." But Oracle did not yet have a clean shot. The Department of Justice would shortly announce whether it intended to block the transaction on antitrust grounds. Catz explained:

> We had thought that at the antitrust division . . . cooler heads would prevail, and that [PeopleSoft] itself would be impacted by an extremely generous offer for their shares, and this showed our seriousness about it. We just did not think the Department of Justice was going to block us. Because I knew the market very, very well, and I knew it was painfully

---

[40] [n.37] Cross-examined on his comment in the Delaware litigation, Ellison noted tongue-in-cheek that the "dog never said anything about me." To which Vice Chancellor Strine added: "That you could understand."

competitive. And the concept that PeopleSoft was actually a price leader, meaning the lowest price, was just absurd.

So we didn't think [the DOJ] would block. We thought maybe the higher price would energize the "let's get this deal done" group [at PeopleSoft]. And that was really a mistake because what we didn't know was that PeopleSoft had basically put in their own unstoppable poison pill, which is to get the Justice Department involved. . . . The fact that they did that and that it was really out of their hands — and then they hid behind the Justice Department when they rejected $26 ultimately. They hid behind what they had set in motion.

PeopleSoft cited regulatory concerns in dismissing Oracle's revised bid, but its recommendation to shareholders focused on the inadequacy of the $26.00 per share offer. The first bullet read:

The revised offer price is inadequate and does not reflect PeopleSoft's real value.

In case the point was missed, Conway added, "Oracle's offer does not begin to reflect the company's real value." These statements raised obvious questions about what PeopleSoft believed the company's real value to be. Lee Geishecker of the Gartner Group commented that Oracle's offer was considered so generous in some circles that investors must be wondering whose interests the PeopleSoft board is looking after.

But these questions were quickly overshadowed. On February 10, 2004, People-Soft got word that the DOJ intended to sue. An ecstatic Duffield emailed Conway saying, "Obviously this is huge. You and your team have performed heroically throughout this ordeal. Let's just hope the formal announcement by the Justice Department is zealous and unwavering." It was. On February 26, 2004, the Department of Justice, joined by seven states, filed suit to block the transaction on antitrust grounds. Knowing that it could not win shareholder support in the face of this litigation, Oracle withdrew its nominees and dropped its proxy contest the same day.

Duffield took a victory lap in an email to Battle. "Hopefully no one else reads your email," he began. "I'd personally like to do something special for the independent directors. . . . It could be lavish like a really good watch (better than Rolex) or a trip to a resort, or maybe even a few more hours with our attorneys."

A Long, Hard Slog

Following the decision to abandon its proxy contest, Oracle retrenched. Catz set about the grueling task of finding a path through PeopleSoft's defenses. The first goal was to take away Conway's silver bullet — antitrust. Preparing for the summer's trial against the government consumed a significant amount of Catz's time. To those who had initially doubted Oracle's sincerity, the company's willingness to go toe-to-toe with the Department of Justice was surprising. In most takeover contests, the government's decision to block a bid causes the bidder to withdraw. But for Catz, this case was not just about PeopleSoft; the future of her industry was at stake:

> It's an extremely tough decision when you are facing the front-page of a complaint that says "United States of America versus you." Most management teams and most boards will not subject their company to that. And the fact that we went ahead and decided that not only would we fight it, but we felt we had to fight it, was based on two things. First, we felt we would win. Second, we felt we had to win because consolidation was very, very important to us. Our business has zero marginal costs for a new license. There are very high fixed costs, very low marginal costs. As a result, scale matters. In a business where scale matters, you have to get scale. There are only two ways to do this: you can sell a lot more somehow; or you can acquire something. And so we had to win in order to defend this principle.

Oracle also took advantage of the lull to reevaluate its strategic posture. On May 14, 2003, Oracle lowered its bid to $21.00 per share citing "changes in market conditions and in PeopleSoft's market valuation." While reducing a bid was a highly unusual step in a takeover contest, PeopleSoft's stock had been declining since the DOJ announcement in February. As Catz recalled:

> By then, the market was really figuring that Oracle was never going to prevail in their case with the government, so it should value PeopleSoft as a stand-alone company. People were starting to catch hold of the fact that two struggling companies together [PeopleSoft and JDEC] does not make a strong company. And so the stock price was starting to reflect the fact that this is really all it's worth.

Conway Falls

On Sept. 9, 2004, one year and three months after Oracle's initial offer, Judge Vaughn R. Walker of the United States District Court for the Northern District of California handed the Department of Justice an embarrassing defeat. In a strongly-worded 164-page opinion, Judge Walker held that the DOJ had failed to prove that a merger between Oracle and PeopleSoft would be likely "substantially to lessen competition" in the business applications software market. Conway announced in an email to employees, "[A]ntitrust concerns were never the centerpiece, only one of many issues." The court's ruling does not mean Oracle will acquire PeopleSoft. However, PeopleSoft's situation was growing desperate and Conway's even more so.

Conway's take-no-prisoners style had been encouraging to customers, but it had also frayed his relationship with his board. Conway often acted without consulting them and sought to control the flow of information. He had also bristled under Bogen's warnings about fiduciary duties, and eventually fired the experienced Gibson Dunn attorney. He was especially incensed by Bogen's decision to take concerns regarding the CAP directly to the board. In notes Conway prepared about the "significant degradation in the relationship" with Gibson Dunn, he cited "No escalation to CFO or CEO — straight to BOD closed session." To replace Bogen, the board hired Victor Lewkow of Cleary Gottlieb in New York City.

As Conway grew increasingly "out of control" (in the words of one person close to the deal), PeopleSoft's board faced a dilemma. Conway was still the public face of PeopleSoft, its cheerleader and lead salesman. What kind of message would it send to dismiss him in the middle of a takeover contest? For better or worse, Conway and PeopleSoft were married. Every way out was messy. Finally, however, Conway went too far. At an analyst day in September 2003, Conway said:

> I don't think the Oracle bid is a current issue. It's a movie that's been playing for a long time. I think people have lost interest in it. The last remaining customers whose business decisions were being delayed have actually completed their sales and completed their orders. So I don't see it as a disruptive factor . . . .

The board and PeopleSoft managers knew this was not true, but the company did not formally retract the statement. Instead, when PeopleSoft released a transcript of the event, the last two sentences of the above text were replaced with substitute, corrected language: "Oracle's tactics have created concern among many users, and that's a problem for us. Fortunately, we've been able to overcome much of it and we expect that we will continue to be able to do so. So I don't see it as a disruptive factor . . . ."

Despite the Orwellian effort to correct the record (as described later by Vice Chancellor Strine), the original statements eventually came back to haunt Conway and the board. In a deposition Conway was grilled about the incident by David Balabanian of Bingham McCutchen and Michael Carroll of Davis Polk & Wardwell, both senior members of Oracle's legal team.

"Did you make those statements?" asked Balabanian.

"Yes," Conway answered.

"Were they true?"

"No, they weren't true. . . . I was promoting, promoting, promoting." Conway said.

"The statements were not true?"

"The statements were promotional. I was selling." Conway said.

"True? False?"

"Absolutely not true."

While Max Gitter from Cleary Gottlieb represented PeopleSoft at the deposition, Carroll intervened at this point to ask Conway whether he was represented individually as well. Conway said that he was not. Carroll then asked whether Conway had thought about consulting with lawyers about the significance of a CEO making false statements to the public markets. Conway said that he had not.

A transcript of the deposition gradually made its way to the PeopleSoft board. Four weeks after the deposition, on September 30, the other board members voted unanimously to remove Conway as CEO. Conway agreed to resign from the board and received a $13.7 million severance package because he was fired without cause.

Battle ran the conference call the next day announcing Conway's dismissal, doing his best to mitigate the obvious damage. "There's no smoking gun, there are no accounting irregularities," Battle assured investors. "[I]t's a matter of the board losing confidence in Craig." David Duffield would reassume his duties as CEO. Later that day, the Department of Justice, chastened or perhaps just afraid of creating any more precedent, elected not to appeal the antitrust verdict. Sixteen months after announcing its bid, Oracle had finally regained the initiative.

Delaware: "Will Leo Roar?"

With the antitrust case now resolved, and Oracle gaining momentum, all eyes turned to Delaware. Oracle had brought suit in the Delaware Court of Chancery seeking the removal of PeopleSoft's poison pill and an injunction to stop the CAP program. Hearing the case would be Vice Chancellor Leo Strine, one of the five judges on the court. Strine was the "wunderkind of U.S. corporate law," recognized among academics, practitioners, and other judges to be the intellectual leader of the court. Strine spoke frequently at practitioner and academic conferences and taught courses at Harvard, the University of Pennsylvania, and Vanderbilt law schools. He had also written provocative articles in academic journals suggesting his receptivity to arguments that target boards of directors should not have unfettered discretion to maintain takeover defenses. The Economist speculated that the Vice Chancellor might want to use the case to do something that no Delaware judge had done in 15 years: "Mr. Strine may yearn to scrap PeopleSoft's poison pill and send a clear message that American boards cannot just say no." If correct, the Vice Chancellor would finally give Oracle a clean shot at attracting a majority of PeopleSoft's shares. As the Economist put it, the 16-month controversy had come down to a single question: "Will Leo roar?"

Strine would evaluate PeopleSoft's use of the poison pill under the two-part Unocal test. Most public commentary focused on the second prong — the "reasonableness" requirement — and predicted that Strine would be unlikely to invalidate the pill in view of the long line of Delaware cases finding pills to be "reasonable." But some focused on Unocal's first prong — the "threat" requirement — and argued that the usual threats that the Delaware courts had endorsed, such as "structural coercion" of shareholders (through two-tier, junk-bond-financed offers) or "substantive coercion"[41] (that shareholders would tender out of ignorance), did not apply here: Oracle had made a fully financed, all-cash offer for 100% of the shares to sophisticated shareholders who had had 16 months to consider the offer. One legal advisor to a major PeopleSoft shareholder estimated a 70% chance that Strine would force PeopleSoft to redeem its pill.

PeopleSoft's CAP presented even more interesting and novel questions of corporate law. The first question was whether the CAP represented a takeover defense at all: Oracle argued that the CAP was intended to operate just like a poison pill (and therefore was subject to Unocal analysis), while PeopleSoft argued that the

---

[41] [n.53] A term coined by Ronald Gilson and Reinier Kraakman in an influential article published in 1989. *See* Ronald Gibson & Reinier Kraakman, Delaware's Intermediate Standard for Defensive Tactics: Is There Substance to Proportionality Review?, 44 Bus. Law. 247 (1989).

CAP was intended solely to assure customers and protect the business (and therefore was subject only to business judgment review). If the CAP was in fact a takeover defense, no one had previously used a threat to customers to satisfy Unocal's first prong, though the language of Unocal indicated that such a threat would be permissible. If the CAP survived the first prong of Unocal analysis, was a $2.0 billion potential liability "reasonable in relation to the threat posed" ? No one could predict with confidence how Strine would answer these questions.[42] Indeed, Strine himself did not seem to know: in a conference with Allen Terrell of Richards, Layton & Finger and Don Wolfe of Potter, Anderson & Corroon, lead Delaware counsel for Oracle and PeopleSoft respectively, Strine admitted, "This is not an easy case."

California Looms

While the combatants faced off in Vice Chancellor Strine's courtroom in Delaware, a parallel skirmish was gaining steam on the west coast. PeopleSoft's California lawsuit, which had originally been dismissed by Oracle as a nuisance at best, was slowly becoming a genuine threat. When it started in June 2003, Oracle was sending two lawyers to court. By October 2004, Oracle was fielding twelve. PeopleSoft was asking for compensatory damages of $1 billion and punitive damages beyond that. Battle thought it was their best weapon:

> It was very critical that this lawsuit was in Oakland, California. The Delaware courts say "We don't care about 3,000 layoffs or 6,000 layoffs. We're tired of this management entrenchment. You've got to be dealing with the shareholders, and there's very little wiggle room you have in your loyalty to shareholder value." So what's going to happen now is instead of a Delaware court with Judge Strine, Larry Ellison's going to be sitting in front of a jury in Oakland. And you know people who get on two or three months of jury trial tend to be folks of very modest incomes. They are scared to death about 6,000 job losses in this area. And the fact that Larry Ellison is one of the richest men in the world and acts flamboyantly puts him right in the crosshairs of why a lot of people think the capitalist system is bad.

---

[42] [n.54] There was a second line of argument as well. In an affidavit filed in the Delaware litigation, one of the authors of this case noted the potential application of an evolving doctrine under § 141(a) of the Delaware corporate code, which mandates that the corporation "shall be managed by or under the direction of a board of directors." In its 1998 decision Quickturn v. Mentor Graphics, the Delaware Supreme Court interpreted this provision to mean that a board cannot tie the hands of a future board: "[T]o the extent that a contract, or a provision thereof, purports to require a board to act or not act in such a fashion as to limit the exercise of fiduciary duties, it is invalid and unenforceable," Quickturn Design Sys. v. Mentor Graphics Corp., 721 A.2d 1281, 1292 (Del. Super. Ct. 1998) (quoting Paramount Commc'n v. QVC Network, 637 A.2d 34, 51 (Del. Super. Ct. 1993)). The CAP seemed to do precisely this. In fact, PeopleSoft acknowledged in SEC filings that because of the CAP "it is possible that the newly elected [Oracle] board might refrain from taking certain actions it might otherwise decide to take relating to products and services." Of course, the Quickturn language read literally would seem to prohibit any contract that did not involve a spot transaction — say, a ten-year lease. One way to narrow the scope of the language in Quickturn would be to distinguish between contracts that tied the hands of both the current board and the future board (such as a ten-year lease) and contracts that only tied the hands of a future board (such as the CAP).

So Ellison's not going to have Strine watching out for him. He's going to have a bunch of people that think he's pond scum. And there's a possibility for a pretty big judgment. And everything is going our way.

The Delaware Trial

The Delaware trial began on October 4, 2004 in downtown Wilmington, Delaware. Strine's courtroom overflowed with reporters, arbitrageurs, and lawyers. The proceedings were simulcast into adjoining rooms so arbs could use their cell phones without disrupting the proceedings. When Ellison declared on the stand that "there are more discussions about lowering the [offer] price than raising the price," and Catz similarly announced that Oracle might reduce its bid "somewhere between a third and a quarter," arbs scrambled to sell shares. Anyone getting service on a PDA could watch the stock prices jump in response to every turn in the testimony. The trial was a study in market efficiency.

Oracle's alleged efforts to "talk down" the PeopleSoft stock infuriated People-Soft's board and bolstered the conclusion that Oracle was not serious. Oracle would move close enough to sow "fear, uncertainty and doubt," then pull back, leaving PeopleSoft "twisting in the wind." For a company that wanted a transaction, PeopleSoft reasoned, Oracle was surprisingly good at never being ready to transact.

Whatever problems Oracle faced, PeopleSoft's were worse. Oracle's lawyers hounded PeopleSoft's directors and officers to explain the tensions in their positions: support for Conway for a year, but abrupt and unceremonious dismissal; willingness to do a deal, but an unprecedented array of defenses; careful oversight of management, but approval of substantially revised projections; belated approval of the CAP, but little understanding of the details.

At the end of the two-week trial, Vice Chancellor Strine requested two more days of testimony on specific aspects of the CAP and PeopleSoft's use of the poison pill. But before the court would reconvene, Strine told Oracle, he needed to have a final, unconditional offer on the table.

Bump and Rush

Catz decided to give Strine more than that. On November 1, 2004, Oracle launched Operation "Bump and Rush." Oracle increased its cash offer from $21.00 to $24.00 per share and declared that $24.00 was its "best and final offer." However, Oracle added a condition: "We will withdraw our offer unless a majority of PeopleSoft shares are tendered into our offer by Nov. 19, 2004." Catz explained:

> We bumped the stock and then we told stockholders they had until the 19th to get in the box or we were leaving. So we didn't give them, "oh, you've got four weeks, you've got a month." It was a bump. We're giving you the price right now and you better get in here or we're leaving.

Catz was tired of holding up PeopleSoft's stock price with her bid and then being told that her bid was insufficient because of where the stock price was. She had put her best and final offer on the table. It was finally time for everyone to choose sides:

It was like chasing your tail: every time you raise your offer, the stock price moves up. I knew that shareholders were interested in our offer, but there was no reason for them to indicate their interest in the offer because there was a poison pill that prevented them from accepting it. There was no point in being in the box. So I had to create a situation where there was a point in being in the box. And the only way was to make sure they understood that we were done. We were leaving and we weren't kidding.

PeopleSoft declared the $24.00 offer to be inadequate and recommended that shareholders not tender. Teams from both companies set off around the country to lobby major shareholders. Battle and Duffield, along with PeopleSoft Vice Chairman and director Aneel Bhusri, conducted marathon meetings with shareholders. To those who met with them, it was clear that Battle and Duffield were not on the same page.

Duffield did not want to sell, focusing on the human costs of a takeover. Any transaction would be followed by a bloodletting at PeopleSoft and, to some extent, at Oracle. Employees would be fired en masse. The businesses in PeopleSoft's hometown that depend on its continued viability would be ruined. Duffield felt he owed a duty to his "People people," the employees who had made him a billionaire and had built his company into a formidable competitor. "Think how many divorces are going to happen because of this," mused one person involved in the deal.

The human costs tore at Battle too, but he was more attuned to the ways of Wall Street. Battle felt that this was not the context in which to open a debate about the free market system. He had assumed a duty to look out for shareholders, and he intended to do just that.

The meetings were punishing. Battle remembers an especially bad day:

We met with three groups of arbs one morning, eight at a shot for an hour from 7:00 to 8:00 to 9:00. That's like being raw meat in a lion's den. Those guys are intemperate and pretty obnoxious. And then at the end of the hour, they'd say, "Well, thank you very much, we appreciate everything you're trying to do for shareholder value," and walk out like we just had a nice cup of coffee together.

Instead of providing a straightforward endorsement of the offer as Catz demanded, the arbs were playing a more nuanced game in the days leading up to November 19. Federal securities rules prevented the PeopleSoft shareholders from talking directly to each other, but investors coordinated their actions through back channels such as PeopleSoft's proxy solicitors. Battle recalled:

One large investor pulled his shares back because we said we know this is going to go above 50%. If it goes to 65%, 68%, 70%, Oracle has no motivation to raise the price. It'll look completely dispositive. If it comes in at 55%, 58%, 60%, then Oracle can't walk away, because they've said they'd stay in the deal. There were two or three shareholders that actually voted some yes and some no to get to a middle-ground result.

It's the only time I've ever seen anybody trust in this process. Some guys trusted our proxy solicitor Alan Miller, that the count was high enough so that they could pull some shares off the table to not make this look like such a mandate. Without that trust there would have been no way of negotiating above $24.

While the vote got as high as 70% in the days leading up to November 19, the final count was 61% of PeopleSoft's shares tendered after certain arbs pulled back shares at the last minute. Oracle achieved the majority that it had demanded in order to stay in the game.

The Deal

During the Delaware trial, a large PeopleSoft shareholder had approached Skip Battle with the strong sense that Oracle would be willing to offer $26.50 in cash, or $27.00 with $24 in cash and $3 in Oracle stock. Battle was cautiously intrigued: "We were getting a lot of pressure from Judge Strine to do something, but there was a lot of fear and suspicion, because if we got to the table and then it blew up, our salespeople said it was going to be really tough to make the fourth quarter." Battle sent his shareholder back to Oracle to make sure the deal was available. On November 29, the shareholder came back with his report: no deal. As Battle described, "Apparently the [Oracle] executives said, 'Are you kidding me? We just won the tender offer. No way.'"

A few days later, Battle was deposed by Oracle's lawyers. Under oath he described his backdoor foray to Oracle and expressed his willingness to take a $26.50 offer back to the PeopleSoft board if it, in fact, was available. It was the first counteroffer, albeit oblique, from PeopleSoft during the 17-month contest. But there was a problem: the deposition had been designated attorneys-eyes-only, and therefore not available to the Oracle board and management.

In order to preserve the confidentiality of Battle's deposition during the resumed Delaware trial, PeopleSoft's lead Delaware counsel Don Wolfe of Potter, Anderson & Corroon requested that the courtroom be "sealed" from the public. Oracle's lead Delaware counsel Allen Terrell of Richards, Layton & Finger conversely requested that the "attorneys-eyes-only" designation be lifted so that the $26.50 counteroffer could be disclosed to the Oracle board. On Thursday, December 9, four days before the trial would begin, Vice Chancellor Strine held a telephone meeting with Wolfe and Terrell. Exhibit 4 provides excerpts from the call. In the call Vice Chancellor Strine removed the attorneys-eyes-only designation so that Battle's deposition transcript could be delivered to Joe Grundfest, head of Oracle's transaction committee and a law professor at Stanford Law School.

The move had its intended effect. Over the weekend of December 11 and 12, the PeopleSoft board authorized their lead transactional lawyers — Doug Smith of Gibson, Dunn & Crutcher and Victor Lewkow of Cleary Gottlieb — to call their counterpart Bill Kelly at Davis Polk, to indicate their willingness to accept $26.50 per share in cash, or $10.3 billion in total consideration. This time, Oracle agreed. On Sunday, December 12, one day before the Delaware trial was scheduled to resume, the PeopleSoft board formally voted to accept the offer, with Duffield and former executive Aneel Bhusri abstaining. The merger was completed on January 7, 2005.

EXHIBIT 1A   PEOPLESOFT SHARE PRICE RELATIVE TO DOW JONES
COMPUTER SOFTWARE INDEX, 1994 TO 2003
(AUGUST 1994 = 100)

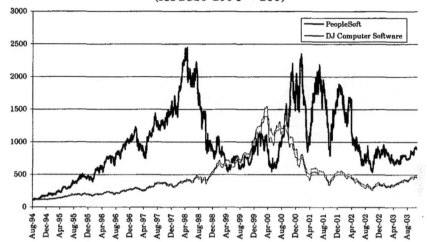

EXHIBIT 1B   PEOPLESOFT SHARE PRICE, JAN. 2002 TO OCT. 2004

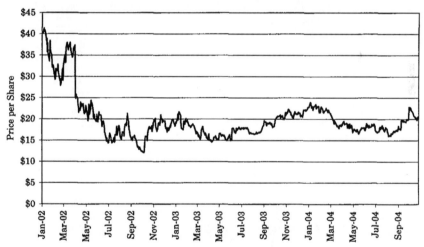

QUESTIONS

1.   Why did Oracle want to acquire PeopleSoft?

2.   Why was PeopleSoft initially against being acquired by Oracle?

3.   What defensive measures did PeopleSoft implement in response to Oracle's overtures? How did Oracle try to get around these defenses?

4.   What were the dollar amounts of the various bids made by Oracle? What prompted the changes in bids? What did Oracle ultimately pay for PeopleSoft?

5.   How much time elapsed between Oracle launching its takeover attempt and closing the deal?

————

Chapter 7

DIRECTOR AND CONTROLLING SHAREHOLDER FIDUCIARY DUTIES

M&A deals involve high stakes decisions by both bidder's and target's boards, decisions that implicate director fiduciary duties. We discuss these duties in detail below as applied to various aspects of an M&A deal. We then look at fiduciary duties of controlling shareholders in the M&A context, an issue that comes up, for example in any deal that involves a second-step merger. Our focus is on Delaware corporate law because it is the most developed and influential in the area.

A. DIRECTOR FIDUCIARY DUTIES

1. Overview

Corporate law imposes two broad fiduciary duties on directors: the duty of care and the duty of loyalty. Generally speaking, the duty of care requires a board to be adequately informed when making a business decision. The duty of loyalty requires a director to act in good faith and the best interests of the corporation.

As described by Vice Chancellor Laster in a 2013 opinion:

> When determining whether directors have breached their fiduciary duties, Delaware corporate law distinguishes between the standard of conduct and the standard of review. The standard of conduct describes what directors are expected to do and is defined by the content of the duties of loyalty and care. The standard of review is the test that a court applies when evaluating whether directors have met the standard of conduct. It describes what a plaintiff must first plead and later prove to prevail.

> Under Delaware law, the standard of review depends initially on whether the board members (i) were disinterested and independent (the business judgment rule), (ii) faced potential conflicts of interest because of the decisional dynamics present in particular recurring and recognizable situations (enhanced scrutiny), or (iii) confronted actual conflicts of interest such that the directors making the decision did not comprise a disinterested and independent board majority (entire fairness). The standard of review may change further depending on whether the directors took steps to address the potential or actual conflict, such as by creating an independent committee, conditioning the transaction on approval by disinterested stockholders, or both. Regardless, in every situation, the standard of review is more forgiving of directors and more onerous for stockholder plaintiffs than the standard of conduct. This divergence is warranted for diverse

policy reasons typically cited as justifications for the business judgment rule.

In re Trados Inc. S'holder Litig., 73 A.3d 17, 35-36 (Del. Ch. 2013) (citations omitted).

We examine each of these standards of review below.

2. The Business Judgment Rule

Under Delaware law, the business judgment rule is a "presumption that in making a business decision the directors of a corporation acted on an informed basis, in good faith and in the honest belief that the action taken was in the best interests of the company."[1] The rule generally prevents a plaintiff from prevailing on a breach of fiduciary duty claim against a board of directors for a bad business decision (such as a decision to sell the company) unless the plaintiff can prove that the board's decision-making process was inadequate or tainted. In other words, a plaintiff needs to prove more than just a board decision turned out poorly for the corporation. Specifically, a plaintiff needs to rebut the presumption by pleading and proving that a majority of directors (1) were interested, (2) lacked independence, (3) were inadequately informed, or (4) acted in bad faith.

If the plaintiff fails to rebut the presumption, the decision will be upheld unless it cannot be attributed to any rational business purpose. Courts apply the waste standard to determine whether a decision was irrational. To meet this standard, a plaintiff "must shoulder the burden of proving that the [decision] was 'so one sided that no business person of ordinary, sound judgment could conclude that the corporation has received adequate consideration.' A claim of waste will arise only in the rare, 'unconscionable case where directors irrationally squander or give away corporate assets.' "[2]

If a plaintiff successfully rebuts the business judgment rule, the burden shifts to the defendant directors to prove that the challenged decision was fair to the corporation.

The next case discusses the Delaware law standard for determining whether a board was adequately informed. Luckily for us, it involves an M&A transaction.

SMITH v. VAN GORKOM
Delaware Supreme Court
488 A.2d 858 (1985)

HORSEY, Justice (for the majority):

This appeal from the Court of Chancery involves a class action brought by shareholders of the defendant Trans Union Corporation ("Trans Union" or "the Company"), originally seeking rescission of a cash-out merger of Trans Union into

---

[1] Aronson v. Lewis, 473 A.2d 805, 812 (Del. 1984).

[2] In re Walt Disney Co. Derivative Litigation, 906 A.2d 27, 73 (Del. 2006) (citations omitted).

the defendant New T Company ("New T"), a wholly-owned subsidiary of the defendant, Marmon Group, Inc. ("Marmon"). Alternate relief in the form of damages is sought against the defendant members of the Board of Directors of Trans Union, New T, and Jay A. Pritzker and Robert A. Pritzker, owners of Marmon.

Following trial, the former Chancellor granted judgment for the defendant directors by unreported letter opinion dated July 6, 1982. . . . Judgment was based on [the finding] that the Board of Directors had acted in an informed manner so as to be entitled to protection of the business judgment rule in approving the cash-out merger. . . . The plaintiffs appeal. . . .

I.

The nature of this case requires a detailed factual statement. The following facts are essentially uncontradicted:

A

Trans Union was a publicly-traded, diversified holding company, the principal earnings of which were generated by its railcar leasing business. During the period here involved, the Company had a cash flow of hundreds of millions of dollars annually. However, the Company had difficulty in generating sufficient taxable income to offset increasingly large investment tax credits (ITCs). Accelerated depreciation deductions had decreased available taxable income against which to offset accumulating ITCs. The Company took these deductions, despite their effect on usable ITCs, because the rental price in the railcar leasing market had already impounded the purported tax savings.

In the late 1970's, together with other capital-intensive firms, Trans Union lobbied in Congress to have ITCs refundable in cash to firms which could not fully utilize the credit. During the summer of 1980, defendant Jerome W. Van Gorkom, Trans Union's Chairman and Chief Executive Officer, testified and lobbied in Congress for refundability of ITCs and against further accelerated depreciation. By the end of August, Van Gorkom was convinced that Congress would neither accept the refundability concept nor curtail further accelerated depreciation.

Beginning in the late 1960's, and continuing through the 1970's, Trans Union pursued a program of acquiring small companies in order to increase available taxable income. In July 1980, Trans Union Management prepared the annual revision of the Company's Five Year Forecast. This report was presented to the Board of Directors at its July, 1980 meeting. The report projected an annual income growth of about 20%. The report also concluded that Trans Union would have about $195 million in spare cash between 1980 and 1985, "with the surplus growing rapidly from 1982 onward." The report referred to the ITC situation as a "nagging problem" and, given that problem, the leasing company "would still appear to be constrained to a tax breakeven." The report then listed four alternative uses of the projected 1982-1985 equity surplus: (1) stock repurchase; (2) dividend increases; (3) a major acquisition program; and (4) combinations of the above. The sale of Trans Union was not among the alternatives. The report emphasized that, despite the overall surplus, the operation of the Company would consume all available equity for the next several years, and concluded: "As a result, we have sufficient time to fully develop our course of action."

B

On August 27, 1980, Van Gorkom met with Senior Management of Trans Union. Van Gorkom reported on his lobbying efforts in Washington and his desire to find a solution to the tax credit problem more permanent than a continued program of acquisitions. Various alternatives were suggested and discussed preliminarily, including the sale of Trans Union to a company with a large amount of taxable income.

Donald Romans, Chief Financial Officer of Trans Union, stated that his department had done a "very brief bit of work on the possibility of a leveraged buy-out." This work had been prompted by a media article which Romans had seen regarding a leveraged buy-out by management. The work consisted of a "preliminary study" of the cash which could be generated by the Company if it participated in a leveraged buy-out. As Romans stated, this analysis "was very first and rough cut at seeing whether a cash flow would support what might be considered a high price for this type of transaction."

On September 5, at another Senior Management meeting which Van Gorkom attended, Romans again brought up the idea of a leveraged buy-out as a "possible strategic alternative" to the Company's acquisition program. Romans and Bruce S. Chelberg, President and Chief Operating Officer of Trans Union, had been working on the matter in preparation for the meeting. According to Romans: They did not "come up" with a price for the Company. They merely "ran the numbers" at $50 a share and at $60 a share with the "rough form" of their cash figures at the time. Their "figures indicated that $50 would be very easy to do but $60 would be very difficult to do under those figures." This work did not purport to establish a fair price for either the Company or 100% of the stock. It was intended to determine the cash flow needed to service the debt that would "probably" be incurred in a leveraged buy-out, based on "rough calculations" without "any benefit of experts to identify what the limits were to that, and so forth." These computations were not considered extensive and no conclusion was reached.

At this meeting, Van Gorkom stated that he would be willing to take $55 per share for his own 75,000 shares. He vetoed the suggestion of a leveraged buy-out by Management, however, as involving a potential conflict of interest for Management. Van Gorkom, a certified public accountant and lawyer, had been an officer of Trans Union for 24 years, its Chief Executive Officer for more than 17 years, and Chairman of its Board for 2 years. It is noteworthy in this connection that he was then approaching 65 years of age and mandatory retirement.

For several days following the September 5 meeting, Van Gorkom pondered the idea of a sale. He had participated in many acquisitions as a manager and director of Trans Union and as a director of other companies. He was familiar with acquisition procedures, valuation methods, and negotiations; and he privately considered the pros and cons of whether Trans Union should seek a privately or publicly-held purchaser.

Van Gorkom decided to meet with Jay A. Pritzker, a well-known corporate takeover specialist and a social acquaintance. However, rather than approaching Pritzker simply to determine his interest in acquiring Trans Union, Van Gorkom assembled a proposed per share price for sale of the Company and a financing structure by which to accomplish the sale. Van Gorkom did so without consulting either his Board or any members of Senior Management except one: Carl Peterson, Trans Union's Controller. Telling Peterson that he wanted no other person on his staff to know what he was doing, but without telling him why, Van Gorkom directed Peterson to calculate the feasibility of a leveraged buy-out at an assumed price per share of $55. Apart from the Company's historic stock market price,[3] and Van Gorkom's long association with Trans Union, the record is devoid of any competent evidence that $55 represented the per share intrinsic value of the Company.

Having thus chosen the $55 figure, based solely on the availability of a leveraged buy-out, Van Gorkom multiplied the price per share by the number of shares outstanding to reach a total value of the Company of $690 million. Van Gorkom told Peterson to use this $690 million figure and to assume a $200 million equity contribution by the buyer. Based on these assumptions, Van Gorkom directed Peterson to determine whether the debt portion of the purchase price could be paid off in five years or less if financed by Trans Union's cash flow as projected in the Five Year Forecast, and by the sale of certain weaker divisions identified in a study done for Trans Union by the Boston Consulting Group ("BCG study"). Peterson reported that, of the purchase price, approximately $50-80 million would remain outstanding after five years. Van Gorkom was disappointed, but decided to meet with Pritzker nevertheless.

Van Gorkom arranged a meeting with Pritzker at the latter's home on Saturday, September 13, 1980. Van Gorkom prefaced his presentation by stating to Pritzker: "Now as far as you are concerned, I can, I think, show how you can pay a substantial premium over the present stock price and pay off most of the loan in the first five years. . . . If you could pay $55 for this Company, here is a way in which I think it can be financed."

Van Gorkom then reviewed with Pritzker his calculations based upon his proposed price of $55 per share. Although Pritzker mentioned $50 as a more attractive figure, no other price was mentioned. However, Van Gorkom stated that to be sure that $55 was the best price obtainable, Trans Union should be free to accept any better offer. Pritzker demurred, stating that his organization would serve as a "stalking horse" for an "auction contest" only if Trans Union would permit Pritzker to buy 1,750,000 shares of Trans Union stock at market price which Pritzker could then sell to any higher bidder. After further discussion on this point, Pritzker told Van Gorkom that he would give him a more definite reaction soon.

---

[3] [n.5] The common stock of Trans Union was traded on the New York Stock Exchange. Over the five year period from 1975 through 1979, Trans Union's stock had traded within a range of a high of $39-1/2 and a low of $24-1/4. Its high and low range for 1980 through September 19 (the last trading day before announcement of the merger) was $38-1/4 –$29-1/2.

On Monday, September 15, Pritzker advised Van Gorkom that he was interested in the $55 cash-out merger proposal and requested more information on Trans Union. Van Gorkom agreed to meet privately with Pritzker, accompanied by Peterson, Chelberg, and Michael Carpenter, Trans Union's consultant from the Boston Consulting Group. The meetings took place on September 16 and 17. Van Gorkom was "astounded that events were moving with such amazing rapidity."

On Thursday, September 18, Van Gorkom met again with Pritzker. At that time, Van Gorkom knew that Pritzker intended to make a cash-out merger offer at Van Gorkom's proposed $55 per share. Pritzker instructed his attorney, a merger and acquisition specialist, to begin drafting merger documents. There was no further discussion of the $55 price. However, the number of shares of Trans Union's treasury stock to be offered to Pritzker was negotiated down to one million shares; the price was set at $38 — 75 cents above the per share price at the close of the market on September 19. At this point, Pritzker insisted that the Trans Union Board act on his merger proposal within the next three days, stating to Van Gorkom: "We have to have a decision by no later than Sunday [evening, September 21] before the opening of the English stock exchange on Monday morning." Pritzker's lawyer was then instructed to draft the merger documents, to be reviewed by Van Gorkom's lawyer, "sometimes with discussion and sometimes not, in the haste to get it finished."

On Friday, September 19, Van Gorkom, Chelberg, and Pritzker consulted with Trans Union's lead bank regarding the financing of Pritzker's purchase of Trans Union. The bank indicated that it could form a syndicate of banks that would finance the transaction. On the same day, Van Gorkom retained James Brennan, Esquire, to advise Trans Union on the legal aspects of the merger. Van Gorkom did not consult with William Browder, a Vice-President and director of Trans Union and former head of its legal department, or with William Moore, then the head of Trans Union's legal staff.

On Friday, September 19, Van Gorkom called a special meeting of the Trans Union Board for noon the following day. He also called a meeting of the Company's Senior Management to convene at 11:00 A.M., prior to the meeting of the Board. No one, except Chelberg and Peterson, was told the purpose of the meetings. Van Gorkom did not invite Trans Union's investment banker, Salomon Brothers or its Chicago-based partner, to attend.

Of those present at the Senior Management meeting on September 20, only Chelberg and Peterson had prior knowledge of Pritzker's offer. Van Gorkom disclosed the offer and described its terms, but he furnished no copies of the proposed Merger Agreement. Romans announced that his department had done a second study which showed that, for a leveraged buy-out, the price range for Trans Union stock was between $55 and $65 per share. Van Gorkom neither saw the study nor asked Romans to make it available for the Board meeting.

Senior Management's reaction to the Pritzker proposal was completely negative. No member of Management, except Chelberg and Peterson, supported the proposal. Romans objected to the price as being too low;[4] he was critical of the timing and suggested that consideration should be given to the adverse tax consequences of an all-cash deal for low-basis shareholders; and he took the position that the agreement to sell Pritzker one million newly-issued shares at market price would inhibit other offers, as would the prohibitions against soliciting bids and furnishing inside information to other bidders. Romans argued that the Pritzker proposal was a "lock up" and amounted to "an agreed merger as opposed to an offer." Nevertheless, Van Gorkom proceeded to the Board meeting as scheduled without further delay.

Ten directors served on the Trans Union Board, five inside (defendants Bonser, O'Boyle, Browder, Chelberg, and Van Gorkom) and five outside (defendants Wallis, Johnson, Lanterman, Morgan and Reneker). All directors were present at the meeting, except O'Boyle who was ill. Of the outside directors, four were corporate chief executive officers and one was the former Dean of the University of Chicago Business School. None was an investment banker or trained financial analyst. All members of the Board were well informed about the Company and its operations as a going concern. They were familiar with the current financial condition of the Company, as well as operating and earnings projections reported in the recent Five Year Forecast. The Board generally received regular and detailed reports and was kept abreast of the accumulated investment tax credit and accelerated depreciation problem.

Van Gorkom began the Special Meeting of the Board with a twenty-minute oral presentation. Copies of the proposed Merger Agreement were delivered too late for study before or during the meeting. He reviewed the Company's ITC and depreciation problems and the efforts theretofore made to solve them. He discussed his initial meeting with Pritzker and his motivation in arranging that meeting. Van Gorkom did not disclose to the Board, however, the methodology by which he alone had arrived at the $55 figure, or the fact that he first proposed the $55 price in his negotiations with Pritzker.

Van Gorkom outlined the terms of the Pritzker offer as follows: Pritzker would pay $55 in cash for all outstanding shares of Trans Union stock upon completion of which Trans Union would be merged into New T Company, a subsidiary wholly-owned by Pritzker and formed to implement the merger; for a period of 90 days, Trans Union could receive, but could not actively solicit, competing offers; the offer had to be acted on by the next evening, Sunday, September 21; Trans Union could only furnish to competing bidders published information, and not proprietary information; the offer was subject to Pritzker obtaining the necessary financing by October 10, 1980; if the financing contingency were met or waived by Pritzker, Trans Union was required to sell to Pritzker one million newly-issued shares of Trans Union at $38 per share.

Van Gorkom took the position that putting Trans Union "up for auction" through a 90-day market test would validate a decision by the Board that $55 was a fair

---

[4] [n.6] Van Gorkom asked Romans to express his opinion as to the $55 price. Romans stated that he "thought the price was too low in relation to what he could derive for the company in a cash sale, particularly one which enabled us to realize the values of certain subsidiaries and independent entities."

price. He told the Board that the "free market will have an opportunity to judge whether $55 is a fair price." Van Gorkom framed the decision before the Board not as whether $55 per share was the highest price that could be obtained, but as whether the $55 price was a fair price that the stockholders should be given the opportunity to accept or reject.

Attorney Brennan advised the members of the Board that they might be sued if they failed to accept the offer and that a fairness opinion was not required as a matter of law.

Romans attended the meeting as chief financial officer of the Company. He told the Board that he had not been involved in the negotiations with Pritzker and knew nothing about the merger proposal until the morning of the meeting; that his studies did not indicate either a fair price for the stock or a valuation of the Company; that he did not see his role as directly addressing the fairness issue; and that he and his people "were trying to search for ways to justify a price in connection with such a [leveraged buy-out] transaction, rather than to say what the shares are worth." Romans testified:

> I told the Board that the study ran the numbers at 50 and 60, and then the subsequent study at 55 and 65, and that was not the same thing as saying that I have a valuation of the company at X dollars. But it was a way — a first step towards reaching that conclusion.

Romans told the Board that, in his opinion, $55 was "in the range of a fair price," but "at the beginning of the range."

Chelberg, Trans Union's President, supported Van Gorkom's presentation and representations. He testified that he "participated to make sure that the Board members collectively were clear on the details of the agreement or offer from Pritzker"; that he "participated in the discussion with Mr. Brennan, inquiring of him about the necessity for valuation opinions in spite of the way in which this particular offer was couched"; and that he was otherwise actively involved in supporting the positions being taken by Van Gorkom before the Board about "the necessity to act immediately on this offer," and about "the adequacy of the $55 and the question of how that would be tested."

The Board meeting of September 20 lasted about two hours. Based solely upon Van Gorkom's oral presentation, Chelberg's supporting representations, Romans' oral statement, Brennan's legal advice, and their knowledge of the market history of the Company's stock,[5] the directors approved the proposed Merger Agreement. . . .

The Merger Agreement was executed by Van Gorkom during the evening of September 20 at a formal social event that he hosted for the opening of the Chicago

---

[5] [n.9] The Trial Court stated the premium relationship of the $55 price to the market history of the Company's stock as follows:

> . . . the merger price offered to the stockholders of Trans Union represented a premium of 62% over the average of the high and low prices at which Trans Union stock had traded in 1980, a premium of 48% over the last closing price, and a premium of 39% over the highest price at which the stock of Trans Union had traded any time during the prior six years.

Lyric Opera. Neither he nor any other director read the agreement prior to its signing and delivery to Pritzker. . . .

On December 19, this litigation was commenced. . . . On January 21, Management's Proxy Statement for the February 10 shareholder meeting was mailed to Trans Union's stockholders. On January 26, Trans Union's Board met and, after a lengthy meeting, voted to proceed with the Pritzker merger. The Board also approved for mailing, "on or about January 27," a Supplement to its Proxy Statement. The Supplement purportedly set forth all information relevant to the Pritzker Merger Agreement, which had not been divulged in the first Proxy Statement.

On February 10, the stockholders of Trans Union approved the Pritzker merger proposal. Of the outstanding shares, 69.9 percent were voted in favor of the merger; 7.25 percent were voted against the merger; and 22.85 percent were not voted.

II.

We turn to the issue of the application of the business judgment rule to the September 20 meeting of the Board.

The Court of Chancery concluded from the evidence that the Board of Directors' approval of the Pritzker merger proposal fell within the protection of the business judgment rule. The Court found that the Board had given sufficient time and attention to the transaction, since the directors had considered the Pritzker proposal on three different occasions, on September 20, and on October 8, 1980 and finally on January 26, 1981. On that basis, the Court reasoned that the Board had acquired, over the four-month period, sufficient information to reach an informed business judgment on the cash-out merger proposal. The Court ruled:

> . . . that given the market value of Trans Union's stock, the business acumen of the members of the board of Trans Union, the substantial premium over market offered by the Pritzkers and the ultimate effect on the merger price provided by the prospect of other bids for the stock in question, that the board of directors of Trans Union did not act recklessly or improvidently in determining on a course of action which they believed to be in the best interest of the stockholders of Trans Union.

The Court of Chancery made but one finding; i.e., that the Board's conduct over the entire period from September 20 through January 26, 1981 was not reckless or improvident, but informed. . . .

Under Delaware law, the business judgment rule is the offspring of the fundamental principle, codified in 8 Del. C. § 141(a), that the business and affairs of a Delaware corporation are managed by or under its board of directors. In carrying out their managerial roles, directors are charged with an unyielding fiduciary duty to the corporation and its shareholders. The business judgment rule exists to protect and promote the full and free exercise of the managerial power granted to Delaware directors. The rule itself "is a presumption that in making a business decision, the directors of a corporation acted on an informed basis, in good faith and in the honest belief that the action taken was in the best interests of the company."

Aronson [*v. Lewis*, 473 A.2d 805 (Del. 1984)] at 812. Thus, the party attacking a board decision as uninformed must rebut the presumption that its business judgment was an informed one.

The determination of whether a business judgment is an informed one turns on whether the directors have informed themselves "prior to making a business decision, of all material information reasonably available to them." *Id.*

Under the business judgment rule there is no protection for directors who have made "an unintelligent or unadvised judgment." *Mitchell v. Highland-Western Glass*, 167 A. 831, 833 (Del. Ch. 1933). A director's duty to inform himself in preparation for a decision derives from the fiduciary capacity in which he serves the corporation and its stockholders. Since a director is vested with the responsibility for the management of the affairs of the corporation, he must execute that duty with the recognition that he acts on behalf of others. Such obligation does not tolerate faithlessness or self-dealing. But fulfillment of the fiduciary function requires more than the mere absence of bad faith or fraud. Representation of the financial interests of others imposes on a director an affirmative duty to protect those interests and to proceed with a critical eye in assessing information of the type and under the circumstances present here.

Thus, a director's duty to exercise an informed business judgment is in the nature of a duty of care, as distinguished from a duty of loyalty. Here, there were no allegations of fraud, bad faith, or self-dealing, or proof thereof. Hence, it is presumed that the directors reached their business judgment in good faith, and considerations of motive are irrelevant to the issue before us.

The standard of care applicable to a director's duty of care has also been recently restated by this Court. In *Aronson, supra*, we stated:

> While the Delaware cases use a variety of terms to describe the applicable standard of care, our analysis satisfies us that under the business judgment rule director liability is predicated upon concepts of gross negligence. (footnote omitted)

473 A.2d at 812.

We again confirm that view. We think the concept of gross negligence is also the proper standard for determining whether a business judgment reached by a board of directors was an informed one. . . .

In the specific context of a proposed merger of domestic corporations, a director has a duty under 8 Del. C. § 251(b), along with his fellow directors, to act in an informed and deliberate manner in determining whether to approve an agreement of merger before submitting the proposal to the stockholders. Certainly in the merger context, a director may not abdicate that duty by leaving to the shareholders alone the decision to approve or disapprove the agreement. . . .

It is against those standards that the conduct of the directors of Trans Union must be tested, as a matter of law and as a matter of fact, regarding their exercise of an informed business judgment in voting to approve the Pritzker merger proposal.

III. . . .

A

. . . On the record before us, we must conclude that the Board of Directors did not reach an informed business judgment on September 20, 1980 in voting to "sell" the Company for $55 per share pursuant to the Pritzker cash-out merger proposal. Our reasons, in summary, are as follows:

The directors (1) did not adequately inform themselves as to Van Gorkom's role in forcing the "sale" of the Company and in establishing the per share purchase price; (2) were uninformed as to the intrinsic value of the Company; and (3) given these circumstances, at a minimum, were grossly negligent in approving the "sale" of the Company upon two hours' consideration, without prior notice, and without the exigency of a crisis or emergency.

As has been noted, the Board based its September 20 decision to approve the cash-out merger primarily on Van Gorkom's representations. None of the directors, other than Van Gorkom and Chelberg, had any prior knowledge that the purpose of the meeting was to propose a cash-out merger of Trans Union. No members of Senior Management were present, other than Chelberg, Romans and Peterson; and the latter two had only learned of the proposed sale an hour earlier. Both general counsel Moore and former general counsel Browder attended the meeting, but were equally uninformed as to the purpose of the meeting and the documents to be acted upon.

Without any documents before them concerning the proposed transaction, the members of the Board were required to rely entirely upon Van Gorkom's 20-minute oral presentation of the proposal. No written summary of the terms of the merger was presented; the directors were given no documentation to support the adequacy of $55 price per share for sale of the Company; and the Board had before it nothing more than Van Gorkom's statement of his understanding of the substance of an agreement which he admittedly had never read, nor which any member of the Board had ever seen.

Under 8 Del. C. § 141(e), "directors are fully protected in relying in good faith on reports made by officers." *Michelson v. Duncan*, Del. Ch., 386 A.2d 1144, 1156 (1978). The term "report" has been liberally construed to include reports of informal personal investigations by corporate officers. However, there is no evidence that any "report," as defined under § 141(e), concerning the Pritzker proposal, was presented to the Board on September 20.[6] Van Gorkom's oral presentation of his understanding of the terms of the proposed Merger Agreement, which he had not seen, and Romans' brief oral statement of his preliminary study regarding the feasibility of a leveraged buy-out of Trans Union do not qualify as § 141(e) "reports" for these

---

[6] [n.16] In support of the defendants' argument that their judgment as to the adequacy of $55 per share was an informed one, the directors rely on the BCG study and the Five Year Forecast. However, no one even referred to either of these studies at the September 20 meeting; and it is conceded that these materials do not represent valuation studies. Hence, these documents do not constitute evidence as to whether the directors reached an informed judgment on September 20 that $55 per share was a fair value for sale of the Company.

reasons: The former lacked substance because Van Gorkom was basically unin-formed as to the essential provisions of the very document about which he was talking. Romans' statement was irrelevant to the issues before the Board since it did not purport to be a valuation study. At a minimum for a report to enjoy the status conferred by § 141(e), it must be pertinent to the subject matter upon which a board is called to act, and otherwise be entitled to good faith, not blind, reliance. Considering all of the surrounding circumstances — hastily calling the meeting without prior notice of its subject matter, the proposed sale of the Company without any prior consideration of the issue or necessity therefor, the urgent time constraints imposed by Pritzker, and the total absence of any documentation whatsoever — the directors were duty bound to make reasonable inquiry of Van Gorkom and Romans, and if they had done so, the inadequacy of that upon which they now claim to have relied would have been apparent.

In support of the defendants' argument that their judgment as to the adequacy of $55 per share was an informed one, the directors rely on the BCG study and the Five Year Forecast. However, no one even referred to either of these studies at the September 20 meeting; and it is conceded that these materials do not represent valuation studies. Hence, these documents do not constitute evidence as to whether the directors reached an informed judgment on September 20 that $55 per share was a fair value for sale of the Company.

The defendants rely on the following factors to sustain the Trial Court's finding that the Board's decision was an informed one: (1) the magnitude of the premium or spread between the $55 Pritzker offering price and Trans Union's current market price of $38 per share; . . . ; and (4) their reliance on Brennan's legal advice that the directors might be sued if they rejected the Pritzker proposal. . . .

(1)

A substantial premium may provide one reason to recommend a merger, but in the absence of other sound valuation information, the fact of a premium alone does not provide an adequate basis upon which to assess the fairness of an offering price. Here, the judgment reached as to the adequacy of the premium was based on a comparison between the historically depressed Trans Union market price and the amount of the Pritzker offer. Using market price as a basis for concluding that the premium adequately reflected the true value of the Company was a clearly faulty, indeed fallacious, premise, as the defendants' own evidence demonstrates.

The record is clear that before September 20, Van Gorkom and other members of Trans Union's Board knew that the market had consistently undervalued the worth of Trans Union's stock, despite steady increases in the Company's operating income in the seven years preceding the merger. The Board related this occurrence in large part to Trans Union's inability to use its ITCs as previously noted. Van Gorkom testified that he did not believe the market price accurately reflected Trans Union's true worth; and several of the directors testified that, as a general rule, most chief executives think that the market undervalues their companies' stock. Yet, on September 20, Trans Union's Board apparently believed that the market stock price accurately reflected the value of the Company for the purpose of determining the adequacy of the premium for its sale.

In the Proxy Statement, however, the directors reversed their position. There, they stated that, although the earnings prospects for Trans Union were "excellent," they found no basis for believing that this would be reflected in future stock prices. With regard to past trading, the Board stated that the prices at which the Company's common stock had traded in recent years did not reflect the "inherent" value of the Company. But having referred to the "inherent" value of Trans Union, the directors ascribed no number to it. Moreover, nowhere did they disclose that they had no basis on which to fix "inherent" worth beyond an impressionistic reaction to the premium over market and an unsubstantiated belief that the value of the assets was "significantly greater" than book value. By their own admission they could not rely on the stock price as an accurate measure of value. Yet, also by their own admission, the Board members assumed that Trans Union's market price was adequate to serve as a basis upon which to assess the adequacy of the premium for purposes of the September 20 meeting.

The parties do not dispute that a publicly-traded stock price is solely a measure of the value of a minority position and, thus, market price represents only the value of a single share. Nevertheless, on September 20, the Board assessed the adequacy of the premium over market, offered by Pritzker, solely by comparing it with Trans Union's current and historical stock price.

Indeed, as of September 20, the Board had no other information on which to base a determination of the intrinsic value of Trans Union as a going concern. As of September 20, the Board had made no evaluation of the Company designed to value the entire enterprise, nor had the Board ever previously considered selling the Company or consenting to a buy-out merger. Thus, the adequacy of a premium is indeterminate unless it is assessed in terms of other competent and sound valuation information that reflects the value of the particular business.

Despite the foregoing facts and circumstances, there was no call by the Board, either on September 20 or thereafter, for any valuation study or documentation of the $55 price per share as a measure of the fair value of the Company in a cash-out context. It is undisputed that the major asset of Trans Union was its cash flow. Yet, at no time did the Board call for a valuation study taking into account that highly significant element of the Company's assets.

We do not imply that an outside valuation study is essential to support an informed business judgment; nor do we state that fairness opinions by independent investment bankers are required as a matter of law. Often insiders familiar with the business of a going concern are in a better position than are outsiders to gather relevant information; and under appropriate circumstances, such directors may be fully protected in relying in good faith upon the valuation reports of their management.

Here, the record establishes that the Board did not request its Chief Financial Officer, Romans, to make any valuation study or review of the proposal to determine the adequacy of $55 per share for sale of the Company. On the record before us: The Board rested on Romans' elicited response that the $55 figure was within a "fair price range" within the context of a leveraged buy-out. No director sought any further information from Romans. No director asked him why he put $55 at the bottom of his range. No director asked Romans for any details as to his study, the reason why it had been undertaken or its depth. No director asked to see the study; and no director asked Romans whether Trans Union's finance department could do a fairness study within the remaining 36-hour period available under the Pritzker offer.

Had the Board, or any member, made an inquiry of Romans, he presumably would have responded as he testified: that his calculations were rough and preliminary; and, that the study was not designed to determine the fair value of the Company, but rather to assess the feasibility of a leveraged buy-out financed by the Company's projected cash flow, making certain assumptions as to the purchaser's borrowing needs. Romans would have presumably also informed the Board of his view, and the widespread view of Senior Management, that the timing of the offer was wrong and the offer inadequate.

The record also establishes that the Board accepted without scrutiny Van Gorkom's representation as to the fairness of the $55 price per share for sale of the Company — a subject that the Board had never previously considered. The Board thereby failed to discover that Van Gorkom had suggested the $55 price to Pritzker and, most crucially, that Van Gorkom had arrived at the $55 figure based on calculations designed solely to determine the feasibility of a leveraged buy-out.[7] No questions were raised either as to the tax implications of a cash-out merger or how the price for the one million share option granted Pritzker was calculated.

We do not say that the Board of Directors was not entitled to give some credence to Van Gorkom's representation that $55 was an adequate or fair price. Under § 141(e), the directors were entitled to rely upon their chairman's opinion of value and adequacy, provided that such opinion was reached on a sound basis. Here, the issue is whether the directors informed themselves as to all information that was reasonably available to them. Had they done so, they would have learned of the source and derivation of the $55 price and could not reasonably have relied thereupon in good faith.

None of the directors, Management or outside, were investment bankers or financial analysts. Yet the Board did not consider recessing the meeting until a later hour that day (or requesting an extension of Pritzker's Sunday evening deadline) to give it time to elicit more information as to the sufficiency of the offer, either from inside Management (in particular Romans) or from Trans Union's own investment banker, Salomon Brothers, whose Chicago specialist in merger and acquisitions was known to the Board and familiar with Trans Union's affairs.

Thus, the record compels the conclusion that on September 20 the Board lacked valuation information adequate to reach an informed business judgment as to the

---

[7] [n.19] As of September 20 the directors did not know: that Van Gorkom had arrived at the $55 figure alone, and subjectively, as the figure to be used by Controller Peterson in creating a feasible structure for a leveraged buy-out by a prospective purchaser; that Van Gorkom had not sought advice, information or assistance from either inside or outside Trans Union directors as to the value of the Company as an entity or the fair price per share for 100 percent of its stock; that Van Gorkom had not consulted with the Company's investment bankers or other financial analysts; that Van Gorkom had not consulted with or confided in any officer or director of the Company except Chelberg; and that Van Gorkom had deliberately chosen to ignore the advice and opinion of the members of his Senior Management group regarding the adequacy of the $55 price.

fairness of $55 per share for sale of the Company. . . .

We conclude that Trans Union's Board was grossly negligent in that it failed to act with informed reasonable deliberation in agreeing to the Pritzker merger proposal on September 20. . . .

We hold, therefore, that the Trial Court committed reversible error in applying the business judgment rule in favor of the director defendants in this case.

On remand, the Court of Chancery shall conduct an evidentiary hearing to determine the fair value of the shares represented by the plaintiffs' class, based on the intrinsic value of Trans Union on September 20, 1980. . . . Thereafter, an award of damages may be entered to the extent that the fair value of Trans Union exceeds $55 per share.

REVERSED and REMANDED for proceedings consistent herewith.

———————

Exculpation Provisions. *Smith v. Van Gorkom* sent shockwaves through the boardrooms of corporate America. It was the first time in memory that the directors of a public company were held personally liable for breach of the duty of care. This gave rise to concerns that quality individuals would be less willing to serve as directors or would "be deterred from making entrepreneurial decisions."[8] Thus, in June 1986, Delaware's governor signed into law a bill that, among other things, amended DGCL § 102 to add subsection (b)(7). This subsection provides as follows:

(b) In addition to the matters required to be set forth in the certificate of incorporation by subsection (a) of this section, the certificate of incorporation may also contain any or all of the following matters: . . .

(7) A provision eliminating or limiting the personal liability of a director to the corporation or its stockholders for monetary damages for breach of fiduciary duty as a director, provided that such provision shall not eliminate or limit the liability of a director: (i) For any breach of the director's duty of loyalty to the corporation or its stockholders; (ii) for acts or omissions not in good faith or which involve intentional misconduct or a knowing violation of law; (iii) under § 174 of this title [director liability for unlawful payment of dividends]; or (iv) for any transaction from which the director derived an improper personal benefit. No such provision shall eliminate or limit the liability of a director for any act or omission occurring prior to the date when such provision becomes effective. All references in this paragraph to a director shall also be deemed to refer to such other person or persons, if any, who, pursuant to a provision of the certificate of incorporation in accordance with § 141(a) of this title, exercise or perform any of the powers or duties otherwise conferred or imposed upon the board of directors by this title.

———————

[8] Legislative Synopsis to S. 533, 133d Del. Gen. Assembly (1986).

The subsection essentially allows a corporation to opt out of having its directors be personally liable for monetary damages for breach of the duty of care. An analogous provision was added to the MBCA in 1990.[9]

A corporation opts out by including a provision, commonly called an exculpation provision, in its charter, and corporations do so as a matter of course. Here is the exculpation provision from Zipcar's charter:

EIGHTH. A director of the Corporation shall not be liable to the Corporation or its stockholders for monetary damages for breach of fiduciary duty as a director, except to the extent that exculpation from liability is not permitted under the General Corporation Law of the State of Delaware as in effect when such breach occurred. No amendment or repeal of this Article EIGHTH shall apply to or have any effect on the liability or alleged liability of any director of the Corporation for or with respect to any acts or omissions of such director occurring prior to such amendment or repeal.

Note that an exculpation provision forecloses a claim against directors for monetary damages for breach of the duty of care. However, it does not foreclose a claim seeking equitable relief. Thus, for example, a plaintiff may be able to get a court to enjoin a merger if the plaintiff can successfully argue, before the merger is closed, that the board was inadequately informed when it decided to approve the deal.

Fairness Opinions. As part of its decision-making process, a target board of directors typically retains an outside advisor, normally an investment banking firm, to render a "fairness opinion" on the deal. Specifically, the advisor will evaluate the deal, do some financial analysis on target, and then conclude that the deal consideration agreed to by target's board is fair, from a financial point of view, to target shareholders.[10] The advisor will normally orally deliver the opinion at the board meeting at which the board approves the deal and then follow up with a written fairness opinion letter addressed to target's board. The letter typically does not define the term "fair" but it is understood to mean that the deal price falls within a range of values that the advisor views as fair. If target is public, it is required to describe in its proxy statement for the deal the fairness opinion relied on by its board and to include a copy of the fairness opinion letter as an attachment to the proxy statement. Here is an excerpt from the Zipcar Proxy Statement for the Avis Budget/Zipcar deal describing the fairness opinion Morgan Stanley rendered to Zipcar's board for the deal:

---

[9] *See* MBCA § 2.02(b)(4).

[10] Theoretically, an outside advisor could conclude that the deal consideration is not fair to target's shareholders, but this rarely, if ever, happens.

> Morgan Stanley was retained by the board of directors to provide it with financial advisory services and a financial opinion in connection with a potential sale of Zipcar. Zipcar selected Morgan Stanley to act as its financial advisor based on Morgan Stanley's qualifications, expertise and reputation and its knowledge of the business and affairs of the company. At the meeting of the Zipcar board of directors on December 31, 2012, Morgan Stanley rendered its oral opinion to the board of directors, which opinion was subsequently confirmed in writing that, as of that date, based upon and subject to the assumptions made, matters considered and qualifications and limitations on the scope of review undertaken by Morgan Stanley, as set forth in its opinion, the $12.25 in cash per share of Zipcar common stock to be received by the holders of shares of Zipcar common stock pursuant to the merger agreement was fair, from a financial point of view, to such holders.

Fairness opinions were routinely used prior to *Smith v. Van Gorkom* but their significance was underscored by that opinion. Specifically, in finding the Trans Union board liable for breach of the duty of care, the court noted that "there was no call by the Board . . . for any valuation study or documentation of the $55 price per share as a measure of the fair value of the Company in a cash-out context." In other words, perhaps the defendants would have prevailed had they obtained a fairness opinion. The court did, however, stop short of requiring a fairness opinion as a matter of law noting that "[o]ften insiders familiar with the business of a going concern are in a better position than are outsiders to gather relevant information; and under appropriate circumstances, such directors may be fully protected in relying in good faith upon the valuation reports of their management."

3.   Enhanced Scrutiny

As indicated above, enhanced scrutiny review applies when directors "faced potential conflicts of interest because of the decisional dynamics present in particular recurring and recognizable situations."[11] In the M&A context, these situations include a board's decision to implement defensive measures in response to a takeover attempt, target board's handling of the sales process if the board is contemplating a "break-up" or "change of control" of target, and target board's sign-off on deal protection measures. We discuss each of these situations below.

a.   Takeover Defenses

We start with the takeover defense area because it is the area in which the courts first developed the concept of enhanced scrutiny. The next case is the foundational case for the concept.

---

[11] *Trados Inc. S'holder Litig.*, 73 A.3d at 36.

UNOCAL CORP. v. MESA PETROLEUM
Delaware Supreme Court
493 A.2d 946 (1985)

MOORE, JUSTICE.

We confront an issue of first impression in Delaware — the validity of a corporation's self-tender for its own shares which excludes from participation a stockholder making a hostile tender offer for the company's stock.

The Court of Chancery granted a preliminary injunction to the plaintiffs, Mesa Petroleum Co., Mesa Asset Co., Mesa Partners II, and Mesa Eastern, Inc. (collectively "Mesa"),[12] enjoining an exchange offer of the defendant, Unocal Corporation (Unocal) for its own stock. The trial court concluded that a selective exchange offer, excluding Mesa, was legally impermissible. We cannot agree with such a blanket rule. The factual findings of the Vice Chancellor, fully supported by the record, establish that Unocal's board, consisting of a majority of independent directors, acted in good faith, and after reasonable investigation found that Mesa's tender offer was both inadequate and coercive. Under the circumstances the board had both the power and duty to oppose a bid it perceived to be harmful to the corporate enterprise. On this record we are satisfied that the device Unocal adopted is reasonable in relation to the threat posed, and that the board acted in the proper exercise of sound business judgment. We will not substitute our views for those of the board if the latter's decision can be "attributed to any rational business purpose." *Sinclair Oil Corp. v. Levien*, Del. Supr., 280 A.2d 717, 720 (1971). Accordingly, we reverse the decision of the Court of Chancery and order the preliminary injunction vacated.

I.

The factual background of this matter bears a significant relationship to its ultimate outcome.

On April 8, 1985, Mesa, the owner of approximately 13% of Unocal's stock, commenced a two-tier "front loaded" cash tender offer for 64 million shares, or approximately 37%, of Unocal's outstanding stock at a price of $54 per share. The "back-end" was designed to eliminate the remaining publicly held shares by an exchange of securities purportedly worth $54 per share. However, pursuant to an order entered by the United States District Court for the Central District of California on April 26, 1985, Mesa issued a supplemental proxy statement to Unocal's stockholders disclosing that the securities offered in the second-step merger would be highly subordinated, and that Unocal's capitalization would differ significantly from its present structure. Unocal has rather aptly termed such securities "junk bonds."[13]

---

[12] [n.1] T. Boone Pickens, Jr., is President and Chairman of the Board of Mesa Petroleum and President of Mesa Asset and controls the related Mesa entities.

[13] [n.3] Mesa's May 3, 1985 supplement to its proxy statement states:

Unocal's board consists of eight independent outside directors and six insiders. It met on April 13, 1985, to consider the Mesa tender offer. Thirteen directors were present, and the meeting lasted nine and one-half hours. The directors were given no agenda or written materials prior to the session. However, detailed presentations were made by legal counsel regarding the board's obligations under both Delaware corporate law and the federal securities laws. The board then received a presentation from Peter Sachs on behalf of Goldman Sachs & Co. (Goldman Sachs) and Dillon, Read & Co. (Dillon Read) discussing the bases for their opinions that the Mesa proposal was wholly inadequate. Mr. Sachs opined that the minimum cash value that could be expected from a sale or orderly liquidation for 100% of Unocal's stock was in excess of $60 per share. In making his presentation, Mr. Sachs showed slides outlining the valuation techniques used by the financial advisors, and others, depicting recent business combinations in the oil and gas industry. The Court of Chancery found that the Sachs presentation was designed to apprise the directors of the scope of the analyses performed rather than the facts and numbers used in reaching the conclusion that Mesa's tender offer price was inadequate.

Mr. Sachs also presented various defensive strategies available to the board if it concluded that Mesa's two-step tender offer was inadequate and should be opposed. One of the devices outlined was a self-tender by Unocal for its own stock with a reasonable price range of $70 to $75 per share. The cost of such a proposal would cause the company to incur $6.1-6.5 billion of additional debt, and a presentation was made informing the board of Unocal's ability to handle it. The directors were told that the primary effect of this obligation would be to reduce exploratory drilling, but that the company would nonetheless remain a viable entity.

The eight outside directors, comprising a clear majority of the thirteen members present, then met separately with Unocal's financial advisors and attorneys. Thereafter, they unanimously agreed to advise the board that it should reject Mesa's tender offer as inadequate, and that Unocal should pursue a self-tender to provide the stockholders with a fairly priced alternative to the Mesa proposal. The board then reconvened and unanimously adopted a resolution rejecting as grossly inadequate Mesa's tender offer. Despite the nine and one-half hour length of the meeting, no formal decision was made on the proposed defensive self-tender.

(i) following the Offer, the Purchasers would seek to effect a merger of Unocal and Mesa Eastern or an affiliate of Mesa Eastern (the "Merger") in which the remaining Shares would be acquired for a combination of subordinated debt securities and preferred stock; (ii) the securities to be received by Unocal shareholders in the Merger would be subordinated to $2,400 million of debt securities of Mesa Eastern, indebtedness incurred to refinance up to $1,000 million of bank debt which was incurred by affiliates of Mesa Partners II to purchase Shares and to pay related interest and expenses and all then-existing debt of Unocal; (iii) the corporation surviving the Merger would be responsible for the payment of all securities of Mesa Eastern (including any such securities issued pursuant to the Merger) and the indebtedness referred to in item (ii) above, and such securities and indebtedness would be repaid out of funds generated by the operations of Unocal; (iv) the indebtedness incurred in the Offer and the Merger would result in Unocal being much more highly leveraged, and the capitalization of the corporation surviving the Merger would differ significantly from that of Unocal at present; and (v) in their analyses of cash flows provided by operations of Unocal which would be available to service and repay securities and other obligations of the corporation surviving the Merger, the Purchasers assumed that the capital expenditures and expenditures for exploration of such corporation would be significantly reduced.

On April 15, the board met again with four of the directors present by telephone and one member still absent. This session lasted two hours. Unocal's Vice President of Finance and its Assistant General Counsel made a detailed presentation of the proposed terms of the exchange offer. A price range between $70 and $80 per share was considered, and ultimately the directors agreed upon $72. The board was also advised about the debt securities that would be issued, and the necessity of placing restrictive covenants upon certain corporate activities until the obligations were paid. The board's decisions were made in reliance on the advice of its investment bankers, including the terms and conditions upon which the securities were to be issued. Based upon this advice, and the board's own deliberations, the directors unanimously approved the exchange offer. Their resolution provided that if Mesa acquired 64 million shares of Unocal stock through its own offer (the Mesa Purchase Condition), Unocal would buy the remaining 49% outstanding for an exchange of debt securities having an aggregate par value of $72 per share. The board resolution also stated that the offer would be subject to other conditions that had been described to the board at the meeting, or which were deemed necessary by Unocal's officers, including the exclusion of Mesa from the proposal (the Mesa exclusion). Any such conditions were required to be in accordance with the "purport and intent" of the offer.

Unocal's exchange offer was commenced on April 17, 1985, and Mesa promptly challenged it by filing this suit in the Court of Chancery. On April 22, the Unocal board met again and was advised by Goldman Sachs and Dillon Read to waive the Mesa Purchase Condition as to 50 million shares. This recommendation was in response to a perceived concern of the shareholders that, if shares were tendered to Unocal, no shares would be purchased by either offeror. The directors were also advised that they should tender their own Unocal stock into the exchange offer as a mark of their confidence in it.

Another focus of the board was the Mesa exclusion. Legal counsel advised that under Delaware law Mesa could only be excluded for what the directors reasonably believed to be a valid corporate purpose. The directors' discussion centered on the objective of adequately compensating shareholders at the "back-end" of Mesa's proposal, which the latter would finance with "junk bonds." To include Mesa would defeat that goal, because under the proration aspect of the exchange offer (49%) every Mesa share accepted by Unocal would displace one held by another stockholder. Further, if Mesa were permitted to tender to Unocal, the latter would in effect be financing Mesa's own inadequate proposal. . . .

[O]n April 22, 1985, Mesa amended its complaint in this action to challenge the Mesa exclusion. . . .

After the May 8 hearing the Vice Chancellor issued an unreported opinion on May 13, 1985 granting Mesa a preliminary injunction. Specifically, the trial court noted that "[t]he parties basically agree that the directors' duty of care extends to protecting the corporation from perceived harm whether it be from third parties or shareholders." The trial court also concluded in response to the second inquiry in the Supreme Court's May 2 order, that "[a]lthough the facts, . . . do not appear to be sufficient to prove that Mesa's principle objective is to be bought off at a substantial premium, they do justify a reasonable inference to the same effect."

As to the third and fourth questions posed by this Court, the Vice Chancellor stated that they "appear to raise the more fundamental issue of whether directors owe fiduciary duties to shareholders who they perceive to be acting contrary to the best interests of the corporation as a whole." While determining that the directors' decision to oppose Mesa's tender offer was made in a good faith belief that the Mesa proposal was inadequate, the court stated that the business judgment rule does not apply to a selective exchange offer such as this.

On May 13, 1985 the Court of Chancery certified this interlocutory appeal to us as a question of first impression, and we accepted it on May 14. The entire matter was scheduled on an expedited basis.

II.

The issues we address involve these fundamental questions: Did the Unocal board have the power and duty to oppose a takeover threat it reasonably perceived to be harmful to the corporate enterprise, and if so, is its action here entitled to the protection of the business judgment rule?

Mesa contends that the discriminatory exchange offer violates the fiduciary duties Unocal owes it. Mesa argues that because of the Mesa exclusion the business judgment rule is inapplicable, because the directors by tendering their own shares will derive a financial benefit that is not available to all Unocal stockholders. Thus, it is Mesa's ultimate contention that Unocal cannot establish that the exchange offer is fair to all shareholders, and argues that the Court of Chancery was correct in concluding that Unocal was unable to meet this burden.

Unocal answers that it does not owe a duty of "fairness" to Mesa, given the facts here. Specifically, Unocal contends that its board of directors reasonably and in good faith concluded that Mesa's $54 two-tier tender offer was coercive and inadequate, and that Mesa sought selective treatment for itself. Furthermore, Unocal argues that the board's approval of the exchange offer was made in good faith, on an informed basis, and in the exercise of due care. Under these circumstances, Unocal contends that its directors properly employed this device to protect the company and its stockholders from Mesa's harmful tactics.

III.

We begin with the basic issue of the power of a board of directors of a Delaware corporation to adopt a defensive measure of this type. Absent such authority, all other questions are moot. Neither issues of fairness nor business judgment are pertinent without the basic underpinning of a board's legal power to act.

The board has a large reservoir of authority upon which to draw. Its duties and responsibilities proceed from the inherent powers conferred by 8 Del. C. § 141(a), respecting management of the corporation's "business and affairs." Additionally, the powers here being exercised derive from 8 Del. C. § 160(a), conferring broad authority upon a corporation to deal in its own stock. From this it is now well established that in the acquisition of its shares a Delaware corporation may deal selectively with its stockholders, provided the directors have not acted out of a sole or primary purpose to entrench themselves in office.

Finally, the board's power to act derives from its fundamental duty and obligation to protect the corporate enterprise, which includes stockholders, from harm reasonably perceived, irrespective of its source. Thus, we are satisfied that in the broad context of corporate governance, including issues of fundamental corporate change, a board of directors is not a passive instrumentality.

Given the foregoing principles, we turn to the standards by which director action is to be measured. In *Pogostin v. Rice*, Del. Supr., 480 A.2d 619 (1984), we held that the business judgment rule, including the standards by which director conduct is judged, is applicable in the context of a takeover. *Id.* at 627. The business judgment rule is a "presumption that in making a business decision the directors of a corporation acted on an informed basis, in good faith and in the honest belief that the action taken was in the best interests of the company." *Aronson v. Lewis*, Del. Supr., 473 A.2d 805, 812 (1984) (citations omitted). A hallmark of the business judgment rule is that a court will not substitute its judgment for that of the board if the latter's decision can be "attributed to any rational business purpose." *Sinclair Oil Corp. v. Levien*, Del. Supr., 280 A.2d 717, 720 (1971).

When a board addresses a pending takeover bid it has an obligation to determine whether the offer is in the best interests of the corporation and its shareholders. In that respect a board's duty is no different from any other responsibility it shoulders, and its decisions should be no less entitled to the respect they otherwise would be accorded in the realm of business judgment. There are, however, certain caveats to a proper exercise of this function. Because of the omnipresent specter that a board may be acting primarily in its own interests, rather than those of the corporation and its shareholders, there is an enhanced duty which calls for judicial examination at the threshold before the protections of the business judgment rule may be conferred.

This Court has long recognized that:

> We must bear in mind the inherent danger in the purchase of shares with corporate funds to remove a threat to corporate policy when a threat to control is involved. The directors are of necessity confronted with a conflict of interest, and an objective decision is difficult.

Bennett v. Propp, Del. Supr., 187 A.2d 405, 409 (1962). In the face of this inherent conflict directors must show that they had reasonable grounds for believing that a danger to corporate policy and effectiveness existed because of another person's stock ownership. *Cheff v. Mathes*, 199 A.2d at 554-55. However, they satisfy that burden "by showing good faith and reasonable investigation. . . ." *Id.* at 555. Furthermore, such proof is materially enhanced, as here, by the approval of a board comprised of a majority of outside independent directors who have acted in accordance with the foregoing standards.

IV.

A.

In the board's exercise of corporate power to forestall a takeover bid our analysis begins with the basic principle that corporate directors have a fiduciary duty to act in the best interests of the corporation's stockholders. *Guth v. Loft, Inc.*, Del. Supr., 5 A.2d 503, 510 (1939). As we have noted, their duty of care extends to protecting the corporation and its owners from perceived harm whether a threat originates from third parties or other shareholders. But such powers are not absolute. A corporation does not have unbridled discretion to defeat any perceived threat by any Draconian means available.

The restriction placed upon a selective stock repurchase is that the directors may not have acted solely or primarily out of a desire to perpetuate themselves in office. *See Cheff v. Mathes*, 199 A.2d at 556; *Kors v. Carey*, 158 A.2d at 140. Of course, to this is added the further caveat that inequitable action may not be taken under the guise of law. *Schnell v. Chris-Craft Industries, Inc.*, Del. Supr., 285 A.2d 437, 439 (1971). The standard of proof established in *Cheff v. Mathes* . . . is designed to ensure that a defensive measure to thwart or impede a takeover is indeed motivated by a good faith concern for the welfare of the corporation and its stockholders, which in all circumstances must be free of any fraud or other misconduct. *Cheff v. Mathes*, 199 A.2d at 554-55. However, this does not end the inquiry.

B.

A further aspect is the element of balance. If a defensive measure is to come within the ambit of the business judgment rule, it must be reasonable in relation to the threat posed. This entails an analysis by the directors of the nature of the takeover bid and its effect on the corporate enterprise. Examples of such concerns may include: inadequacy of the price offered, nature and timing of the offer, questions of illegality, the impact on "constituencies" other than shareholders (i.e., creditors, customers, employees, and perhaps even the community generally), the risk of nonconsummation, and the quality of securities being offered in the exchange. While not a controlling factor, it also seems to us that a board may reasonably consider the basic stockholder interests at stake, including those of short term speculators, whose actions may have fueled the coercive aspect of the offer at the expense of the long term investor.[14] Here, the threat posed was viewed

---

14 [n.11] There has been much debate respecting such stockholder interests. One rather impressive study indicates that the stock of over 50 percent of target companies, who resisted hostile takeovers, later traded at higher market prices than the rejected offer price, or were acquired after the tender offer was defeated by another company at a price higher than the offer price. Moreover, an update by Kidder Peabody & Company of this study, involving the stock prices of target companies that have defeated hostile tender offers during the period from 1973 to 1982 demonstrates that in a majority of cases the target's shareholders benefited from the defeat. The stock of 81% of the targets studied has, since the tender offer, sold at prices higher than the tender offer price. When adjusted for the time value of money, the figure is 64%. The thesis being that this strongly supports application of the business judgment rule in response to takeover threats. . . .

by the Unocal board as a grossly inadequate two-tier coercive tender offer coupled with the threat of greenmail.

Specifically, the Unocal directors had concluded that the value of Unocal was substantially above the $54 per share offered in cash at the front end. Furthermore, they determined that the subordinated securities to be exchanged in Mesa's announced squeeze out of the remaining shareholders in the "back-end" merger were "junk bonds" worth far less than $54. It is now well recognized that such offers are a classic coercive measure designed to stampede shareholders into tendering at the first tier, even if the price is inadequate, out of fear of what they will receive at the back end of the transaction. Wholly beyond the coercive aspect of an inadequate two-tier tender offer, the threat was posed by a corporate raider with a national reputation as a "greenmailer."[15]

In adopting the selective exchange offer, the board stated that its objective was either to defeat the inadequate Mesa offer or, should the offer still succeed, provide the 49% of its stockholders, who would otherwise be forced to accept "junk bonds," with $72 worth of senior debt. We find that both purposes are valid.

However, such efforts would have been thwarted by Mesa's participation in the exchange offer. First, if Mesa could tender its shares, Unocal would effectively be subsidizing the former's continuing effort to buy Unocal stock at $54 per share. Second, Mesa could not, by definition, fit within the class of shareholders being protected from its own coercive and inadequate tender offer.

Thus, we are satisfied that the selective exchange offer is reasonably related to the threats posed. It is consistent with the principle that "the minority stockholder shall receive the substantial equivalent in value of what he had before." *Sterling v. Mayflower Hotel Corp.*, Del. Supr., 93 A.2d 107, 114 (1952). This concept of fairness, while stated in the merger context, is also relevant in the area of tender offer law. Thus, the board's decision to offer what it determined to be the fair value of the corporation to the 49% of its shareholders, who would otherwise be forced to accept highly subordinated "junk bonds," is reasonable and consistent with the directors' duty to ensure that the minority stockholders receive equal value for their shares.

V.

Mesa contends that it is unlawful, and the trial court agreed, for a corporation to discriminate in this fashion against one shareholder. It argues correctly that no case has ever sanctioned a device that precludes a raider from sharing in a benefit available to all other stockholders. However, as we have noted earlier, the principle of selective stock repurchases by a Delaware corporation is neither unknown nor unauthorized. The only difference is that heretofore the approved transaction was the payment of "greenmail" to a raider or dissident posing a threat to the corporate

---

[15] [n.13] The term "greenmail" refers to the practice of buying out a takeover bidder's stock at a premium that is not available to other shareholders in order to prevent the takeover. The Chancery Court noted that "Mesa has made tremendous profits from its takeover activities although in the past few years it has not been successful in acquiring any of the target companies on an unfriendly basis." Moreover, the trial court specifically found that the actions of the Unocal board were taken in good faith to eliminate both the inadequacies of the tender offer and to forestall the payment of "greenmail."

enterprise. All other stockholders were denied such favored treatment, and given Mesa's past history of greenmail, its claims here are rather ironic.

However, our corporate law is not static. It must grow and develop in response to, indeed in anticipation of, evolving concepts and needs. Merely because the General Corporation Law is silent as to a specific matter does not mean that it is prohibited. See *Providence and Worcester Co. v. Baker*, Del. Supr., 378 A.2d 121, 123-124 (1977). In the days when *Cheff, Bennett, Martin* and *Kors* were decided, the tender offer, while not an unknown device, was virtually unused, and little was known of such methods as two-tier "front-end" loaded offers with their coercive effects. Then, the favored attack of a raider was stock acquisition followed by a proxy contest. Various defensive tactics, which provided no benefit whatever to the raider, evolved. Thus, the use of corporate funds by management to counter a proxy battle was approved. Litigation, supported by corporate funds, aimed at the raider has long been a popular device.

More recently, as the sophistication of both raiders and targets has developed, a host of other defensive measures to counter such ever mounting threats has evolved and received judicial sanction. These include defensive charter amendments and other devices bearing some rather exotic, but apt, names: Crown Jewel, White Knight, Pac Man, and Golden Parachute. Each has highly selective features, the object of which is to deter or defeat the raider.

Thus, while the exchange offer is a form of selective treatment, given the nature of the threat posed here the response is neither unlawful nor unreasonable. If the board of directors is disinterested, has acted in good faith and with due care, its decision in the absence of an abuse of discretion will be upheld as a proper exercise of business judgment.

To this Mesa responds that the board is not disinterested, because the directors are receiving a benefit from the tender of their own shares, which because of the Mesa exclusion, does not devolve upon all stockholders equally. See *Aronson v. Lewis*, Del. Supr., 473 A.2d 805, 812 (1984). However, Mesa concedes that if the exclusion is valid, then the directors and all other stockholders share the same benefit. The answer of course is that the exclusion is valid, and the directors' participation in the exchange offer does not rise to the level of a disqualifying interest. . . .

Nor does this become an "interested" director transaction merely because certain board members are large stockholders. As this Court has previously noted, that fact alone does not create a disqualifying "personal pecuniary interest" to defeat the operation of the business judgment rule. *Cheff v. Mathes*, 199 A.2d at 554.

Mesa also argues that the exclusion permits the directors to abdicate the fiduciary duties they owe it. However, that is not so. The board continues to owe Mesa the duties of due care and loyalty. But in the face of the destructive threat Mesa's tender offer was perceived to pose, the board had a supervening duty to protect the corporate enterprise, which includes the other shareholders, from threatened harm.

Mesa contends that the basis of this action is punitive, and solely in response to the exercise of its rights of corporate democracy. Nothing precludes Mesa, as a stockholder, from acting in its own self-interest. However, Mesa, while pursuing its own interests, has acted in a manner which a board consisting of a majority of independent directors has reasonably determined to be contrary to the best interests of Unocal and its other shareholders. In this situation, there is no support in Delaware law for the proposition that, when responding to a perceived harm, a corporation must guarantee a benefit to a stockholder who is deliberately provoking the danger being addressed. There is no obligation of self-sacrifice by a corporation and its shareholders in the face of such a challenge.

Here, the Court of Chancery specifically found that the "directors' decision [to oppose the Mesa tender offer] was made in the good faith belief that the Mesa tender offer is inadequate." Given our standard of review under *Levitt v. Bouvier*, Del. Supr., 287 A.2d 671, 673 (1972), and *Application of Delaware Racing Association*, Del. Supr., 213 A.2d 203, 207 (1965), we are satisfied that Unocal's board has met its burden of proof. *Cheff v. Mathes*, 199 A.2d at 555.

VI.

In conclusion, there was directorial power to oppose the Mesa tender offer, and to undertake a selective stock exchange made in good faith and upon a reasonable investigation pursuant to a clear duty to protect the corporate enterprise. Further, the selective stock repurchase plan chosen by Unocal is reasonable in relation to the threat that the board rationally and reasonably believed was posed by Mesa's inadequate and coercive two-tier tender offer. Under those circumstances the board's action is entitled to be measured by the standards of the business judgment rule. Thus, unless it is shown by a preponderance of the evidence that the directors' decisions were primarily based on perpetuating themselves in office, or some other breach of fiduciary duty such as fraud, overreaching, lack of good faith, or being uninformed, a Court will not substitute its judgment for that of the board.

In this case that protection is not lost merely because Unocal's directors have tendered their shares in the exchange offer. Given the validity of the Mesa exclusion, they are receiving a benefit shared generally by all other stockholders except Mesa. In this circumstance the test of *Aronson v. Lewis*, 473 A.2d at 812, is satisfied. See also *Cheff v. Mathes*, 199 A.2d at 554. If the stockholders are displeased with the action of their elected representatives, the powers of corporate democracy are at their disposal to turn the board out. *Aronson v. Lewis*, Del. Supr., 473 A.2d 805, 811 (1984). See also 8 Del. C. §§ 141(k) and 211(b).

With the Court of Chancery's findings that the exchange offer was based on the board's good faith belief that the Mesa offer was inadequate, that the board's action was informed and taken with due care, that Mesa's prior activities justify a reasonable inference that its principle objective was greenmail, and implicitly, that the substance of the offer itself was reasonable and fair to the corporation and its stockholders if Mesa were included, we cannot say that the Unocal directors have acted in such a manner as to have passed an "unintelligent and unadvised judgment." *Mitchell v. Highland-Western Glass Co.*, Del. Ch., 167 A. 831, 833 (1933). The decision of the Court of Chancery is therefore REVERSED, and the preliminary injunction is VACATED.

QUESTIONS

1. What did Mesa offer Unocal shareholders in the tender offer?

2. How did Unocal respond?

3. What test applies to determine the validity of a board decision to implement a takeover defense in response to a takeover attempt?

4. Why isn't the decision simply reviewed under the business judgment rule?

5. Did the court uphold the decision of Unocal's board? Why or why not?

6. What is greenmail? What does it have to do with this case?

In 1986, the SEC amended Rule 13e-4(f)(8)(i) under the Exchange Act to provide that an issuer tender offer must be open to all security holders. This is known as the "all-holders" rule and would have prevented Unocal from excluding Mesa from its self-tender offer, had it been in effect. At the same time, the SEC also adopted Rule 14d-10, which includes an all-holders rule applicable to non-issuer tender offers.

The next case further fleshes out what is now known as enhanced scrutiny or the *Unocal* test.

UNITRIN, INC. v. AMERICAN GENERAL CORP.
Delaware Supreme Court
651 A.2d 1361 (1995)

HOLLAND, JUSTICE.

This is an appeal from the Court of Chancery's entry of a preliminary injunction on October 13, 1994, upon plaintiffs' motions in two actions: American General Corporation's ("American General") suit against Unitrin, Inc. ("Unitrin") and its directors; and a parallel class action brought by Unitrin stockholders. . . .

American General, which had publicly announced a proposal to merge with Unitrin for $2.6 billion at $50-⅜ per share, and certain Unitrin shareholder plaintiffs, filed suit in the Court of Chancery, *inter alia*, to enjoin Unitrin from repurchasing up to 10 million shares of its own stock (the "Repurchase Program"). After expedited discovery, briefing and argument, the Court of Chancery preliminarily enjoined Unitrin from making further repurchases on the ground that the Repurchase Program was a disproportionate response to the threat posed by American General's inadequate all cash for all shares offer, under the standard of this Court's holding in *Unocal Corp. v. Mesa Petroleum Co.*, Del. Supr., 493 A.2d 946 (1985) ("*Unocal*").

Unitrin's Contentions

Unitrin has raised several issues in this appeal. First, it contends that the Court of Chancery erred in assuming that the outside directors would subconsciously act contrary to their substantial financial interests as stockholders and, instead, vote in favor of a subjective desire to protect the "prestige and perquisites" of membership on Unitrin's Board of Directors. Second, it contends that the Court of Chancery erred in holding that the adoption of the Repurchase Program would materially affect the ability of an insurgent stockholder to win a proxy contest. According to Unitrin, that holding is unsupported by the evidence, is based upon a faulty mathematical analysis, and disregards the holding of *Moran v. Household Int'l, Inc.*, Del. Supr., 500 A.2d 1346, 1355 (1985). Furthermore, Unitrin argues that the Court of Chancery erroneously substituted its own judgment for that of Unitrin's Board, contrary to this Court's subsequent interpretations of *Unocal* in *Paramount Communications, Inc. v. QVC Network, Inc.*, Del. Supr., 637 A.2d 34, 45–46 (1994), and *Paramount Communications, Inc. v. Time, Inc.*, Del. Supr., 571 A.2d 1140 (1990). . . .

The Parties

American General is the largest provider of home service insurance. On July 12, 1994, it made a merger proposal to acquire Unitrin for $2.6 billion at $50-⅜ per share. Following a public announcement of this proposal, Unitrin shareholders filed suit seeking to compel a sale of the company. American General filed suit to enjoin Unitrin's Repurchase Program.

Unitrin is also in the insurance business. It is the third largest provider of home service insurance. The other defendants-appellants are the members of Unitrin's seven person Board of Directors (the "Unitrin Board" or "Board"). Two directors are employees, Richard C. Vie ("Vie"), the Chief Executive Officer, and Jerrold V. Jerome ("Jerome"), Chairman of the Board. The five remaining directors are not and have never been employed by Unitrin. . . .

The record reflects that the non-employee directors each receive a fixed annual fee of $30,000. They receive no other significant financial benefit from serving as directors. At the offering price proposed by American General, the value of Unitrin's non-employee directors' stock exceeded $450 million.

American General's Offer

In January 1994, James Tuerff ("Tuerff"), the President of American General, met with Richard Vie, Unitrin's Chief Executive Officer. Tuerff advised Vie that American General was considering acquiring other companies. Unitrin was apparently at or near the top of its list. Tuerff did not mention any terms for a potential acquisition of Unitrin. Vie replied that Unitrin had excellent prospects as an independent company and had never considered a merger. Vie indicated to Tuerff that Unitrin was not for sale.

According to Vie, he reported his conversation with Tuerff at the next meeting of the Unitrin Board in February 1994. The minutes of the full Board meeting do not reflect a discussion of Tuerff's proposition. Nevertheless, the parties agree that the Board's position in February was that Unitrin was not for sale. It was unnecessary to respond to American General because no offer had been made.

On July 12, 1994, American General sent a letter to Vie proposing a consensual merger transaction in which it would "purchase all of Unitrin's 51.8 million outstanding shares of common stock for $50-\frac{3}{8}$ per share, in cash" (the "Offer"). The Offer was conditioned on the development of a merger agreement and regulatory approval. The Offer price represented a 30% premium over the market price of Unitrin's shares. In the Offer, American General stated that it "would consider offering a higher price" if "Unitrin could demonstrate additional value." American General also offered to consider tax-free "[a]lternatives to an all cash transaction."

Unitrin's Rejection

Upon receiving the American General Offer, the Unitrin Board's Executive Committee . . . engaged legal counsel and scheduled a telephonic Board meeting for July 18. At the July 18 special meeting, the Board reviewed the terms of the Offer. The Board was advised that the existing charter and bylaw provisions might not effectively deter all types of takeover strategies. It was suggested that the Board consider adopting a shareholder rights plan and an advance notice provision for shareholder proposals.

The Unitrin Board met next on July 25, 1994 in Los Angeles for seven hours. All directors attended the meeting. The principal purpose of the meeting was to discuss American General's Offer.

Vie reviewed Unitrin's financial condition and its ongoing business strategies. The Board also received a presentation from its investment advisor, Morgan Stanley & Co. ("Morgan Stanley"), regarding the financial adequacy of American General's proposal. Morgan Stanley expressed its opinion that the Offer was financially inadequate. Legal counsel expressed concern that the combination of Unitrin and American General would raise antitrust complications due to the resultant decrease in competition in the home service insurance markets.

The Unitrin Board unanimously concluded that the American General merger proposal was not in the best interests of Unitrin's shareholders and voted to reject the Offer. The Board then received advice from its legal and financial advisors about a number of possible defensive measures it might adopt, including a shareholder rights plan ("poison pill") and an advance notice bylaw provision for shareholder proposals. Because the Board apparently thought that American General intended to keep its Offer private, the Board did not implement any defensive measures at that time.

On July 26, 1994, Vie faxed a letter to Tuerff, rejecting American General's Offer. That correspondence stated:

> As I told you back in January, when you first proposed acquiring our company, we are not for sale. The Board believed then, and believes even more strongly today, that the company's future as an independent enter-

prise is excellent and will provide greater long-term benefits to the
company, our stockholders and our other constituencies than pursuing a
sale transaction.

Accordingly, we don't view a combination with you as part of our future and
our Board is unanimous and unequivocal that we should not pursue it.

The Board has specifically directed me to say that we assume you do not
want to create an adversarial situation and that you agree with us it would
be counterproductive to do so. But our Board is very firm in its conclusion
about your offer and if our assumption about your intentions proves to be
incorrect, Unitrin has, as you know, the financial capacity to pursue all
avenues the Board considers appropriate.

Vie acknowledged during discovery that the latter portion of his letter referred, in
part, to the Repurchase Program.

American General's Publicity

Unitrin's Initial Responses

On August 2, 1994, American General issued a press release announcing its Offer
to Unitrin's Board to purchase all of Unitrin's stock for $50-⅜ per share. The press
release also noted that the Board had rejected American General's Offer. After that
public announcement, the trading volume and market price of Unitrin's stock
increased.

At its regularly scheduled meeting on August 3, the Unitrin Board discussed the
effects of American General's press release. The Board noted that the market
reaction to the announcement suggested that speculative traders or arbitrageurs
were acquiring Unitrin stock. The Board determined that American General's
public announcement constituted a hostile act designed to coerce the sale of Unitrin
at an inadequate price. The Board unanimously approved the poison pill and the
proposed advance notice bylaw that it had considered previously.

Beginning on August 2 and continuing through August 12, 1994, Unitrin issued
a series of press releases to inform its shareholders and the public market: first,
that the Unitrin Board believed Unitrin's stock was worth more than the $50-⅜
American General offered; second, that the Board felt that the price of American
General's Offer did not reflect Unitrin's long term business prospects as an
independent company; third, that "the true value of Unitrin [was] not reflected in
the [then] current market price of its common stock," and that because of its strong
financial position, Unitrin was well positioned "to pursue strategic and financial
opportunities;" fourth, that the Board believed a merger with American General
would have anticompetitive effects and might violate antitrust laws and various
state regulatory statutes; and fifth, that the Board had adopted a shareholder rights
plan (poison pill) to guard against undesirable takeover efforts.

Unitrin's Repurchase Program

The Unitrin Board met again on August 11, 1994. The minutes of that meeting indicate that its principal purpose was to consider the Repurchase Program. At the Board's request, Morgan Stanley had prepared written materials to distribute to each of the directors. Morgan Stanley gave a presentation in which alternative means of implementing the Repurchase Program were explained. Morgan Stanley recommended that the Board implement an open market stock repurchase. The Board voted to authorize the Repurchase Program for up to ten million shares of its outstanding stock.

On August 12, Unitrin publicly announced the Repurchase Program. The Unitrin Board expressed its belief that "Unitrin's stock is undervalued in the market and that the expanded program will tend to increase the value of the shares that remain outstanding." The announcement also stated that the director stockholders were not participating in the Repurchase Program, and that the repurchases "will increase the percentage ownership of those stockholders who choose not to sell."

Unitrin's August 12 press release also stated that the directors owned 23% of Unitrin's stock, that the Repurchase Program would cause that percentage to increase, and that Unitrin's certificate of incorporation included a supermajority voting provision. The following language from a July 22 draft press release revealing the antitakeover effects of the Repurchase Program was omitted from the final press release.

> Under the [supermajority provision], the consummation of the expanded repurchase program would enhance the ability of nonselling stockholders, including the directors, to prevent a merger with a greater-than-15% stockholder if they did not favor the transaction.

Unitrin sent a letter to its stockholders on August 17 regarding the Repurchase Program which stated:

> Your Board of Directors has authorized the Company to repurchase, in the open market or in private transactions, up to 10 million of Unitrin's 51.8 million outstanding common shares. This authorization is intended to provide an additional measure of liquidity to the Company's shareholders in light of the unsettled market conditions resulting from American General's unsolicited acquisition proposal. The Board believes that the Company's stock is undervalued and that this program will tend to increase the value of the shares that remain outstanding.

Between August 12 and noon on August 24, Morgan Stanley purchased nearly 5 million of Unitrin's shares on Unitrin's behalf. The average price paid was slightly above American General's Offer price.

Procedural Posture

It is important to begin our review by recognizing and emphasizing the procedural posture of this case in the Court of Chancery as well as in this Court. The Court of Chancery granted the plaintiffs' request for a preliminary injunction. After the Court of Chancery entered the preliminary injunction, it certified an appeal from that interlocutory ruling. Supr.Ct.R. 42. This Court accepted the interlocutory appeal and has expedited its review.

The legal paradigm which guides the Court of Chancery before entering a preliminary injunction is well established. First, the plaintiff must demonstrate a reasonable probability of success on the merits at trial. Second, the plaintiff must prove a reasonable probability of irreparable harm in the absence of such preliminary injunctive relief. Finally, the plaintiff must convince the Court of Chancery that, after balancing the relative hardships to the parties involved, the harm to the plaintiff if injunctive relief is denied outweighs the harm to the defendant if the relief is granted.

Nature of Proceeding
Determines Judicial Review

In this case, before the Court of Chancery could evaluate the reasonable probability of the plaintiffs' success on the merits, it had to determine the nature of the proceeding. When shareholders challenge directors' actions, usually one of three levels of judicial review is applied: the traditional business judgment rule, the *Unocal* standard of enhanced judicial scrutiny, or the entire fairness analysis.[16] "Because the effect of the proper invocation of the business judgment rule is so powerful and the standard of entire fairness so exacting, the determination of the appropriate standard of judicial review frequently is determinative of the outcome of [the] litigation." *Mills Acquisition Co. v. Macmillan, Inc.*, 559 A.2d at 1279 (*citing AC Acquisitions Corp. v. Anderson, Clayton & Co.*, Del. Ch., 519 A.2d 103, 111 (1986)). . . .

The plaintiffs . . . argued that the conduct of the Unitrin Board should be examined under the entire fairness standard. The Court of Chancery concluded that the Board's implementation of the poison pill and the Repurchase Program, in response to American General's Offer, did not constitute self-dealing that would require the Unitrin Board to demonstrate entire fairness. Consequently, the Court of Chancery addressed the plaintiffs' third alternative argument, that the Unitrin Board's actions should be examined under the standard of enhanced judicial scrutiny this Court set forth in *Unocal*.

Unitrin Board's Actions Defensive
Unocal is Proper Review Standard

Before a board of directors' action is subject to the *Unocal* standard of enhanced judicial scrutiny, the court must determine whether the particular conduct was defensive. The stockholder-plaintiffs asked the Court of Chancery to review both the poison pill and the Repurchase Program pursuant to the *Unocal* standard. American General requested the Court of Chancery to apply *Unocal* and enjoin the

---

[16] [n.7] The entire fairness standard applies "only if the presumption of the business judgment rule is defeated." Grobow v. Perot, Del. Supr., 539 A.2d 180, 187 (1988) (*citing* Aronson v. Lewis, Del. Supr., 473 A.2d 805, 812–17 (1984)). The entire fairness standard is exacting and requires judicial scrutiny regarding both "fair dealing" and "fair price." Mills Acquisition Co. v. Macmillan, Inc., Del. Supr., 559 A.2d 1261, 1280 (1989) (*citing* Weinberger v. UOP, Inc., Del. Supr., 457 A.2d 701, 711 (1983)).

Repurchase Program only. Unitrin acknowledged that the poison pill was subject to the enhanced scrutiny *Unocal* requires but argued that the Court of Chancery should evaluate the Repurchase Program under the business judgment rule.

According to the Unitrin Board, the Repurchase Program was enacted for a valid business purpose and, therefore, should not be evaluated as a defensive measure under *Unocal*. The Court of Chancery agreed that, had the Board enacted the Repurchase Program independent of a takeover proposal, its decision would be reviewed under the traditional business judgment rule. The Court of Chancery concluded, however, that the Unitrin Board perceived American General's Offer as a threat and, from the timing of the consideration and implementation of the Repurchase Program, adopted the Repurchase Program as one of several defensive measures in response to that threat. Unitrin does not dispute that conclusion for the purpose of this interlocutory appeal.

The Court of Chancery held that all of the Unitrin Board's defensive actions merited judicial scrutiny according to *Unocal*. The record supports the Court of Chancery's determination that the Board perceived American General's Offer as a threat and adopted the Repurchase Program, along with the poison pill and advance notice bylaw, as defensive measures in response to that threat. Therefore, the Court of Chancery properly concluded the facts before it required an application of *Unocal* and its progeny. . . .

This Court has recognized that directors are often confronted with an " 'inherent conflict of interest' during contests for corporate control '[b]ecause of the omnipresent specter that a board may be acting primarily in its own interests, rather than those of the corporation and its shareholders.' " *Id.* (quoting *Unocal*, 493 A.2d at 954). Consequently, in such situations, before the board is accorded the protection of the business judgment rule, and that rule's concomitant placement of the burden to rebut its presumption on the plaintiff, the board must carry its own initial two-part burden:

> First, a *reasonableness test*, which is satisfied by a demonstration that the board of directors had reasonable grounds for believing that a danger to corporate policy and effectiveness existed, and

> Second, a *proportionality test*, which is satisfied by a demonstration that the board of directors' defensive response was reasonable in relation to the threat posed.

Unocal, 493 A.2d at 955. The common law pronouncement in *Unocal* of enhanced judicial scrutiny, as a threshold or condition precedent to an application of the traditional business judgment rule, is now well known.

The enhanced judicial scrutiny mandated by *Unocal* is not intended to lead to a structured, mechanistic, mathematical exercise.[17] Conversely, it is not intended to

---

[17] [n.13] Efforts to relate *Unocal*'s inherently qualitative proportionality test to a quantitative formula have demonstrated the fallacy of such an exercise, e.g., the reasonableness test:

> the reasonableness test requires a court to engage in a "calculus" of harms: a factual determination of what course of action is in the shareholders' best interests. Set forth in terms of an equation, an antitakeover device is in the shareholders' best interests if (FV − TP)(pFV)

be an abstract theory. The *Unocal* standard is a flexible paradigm that jurists can apply to the myriad of "fact scenarios" that confront corporate boards. . . .

American General Threat
Reasonableness Burden Sustained

The first aspect of the *Unocal* burden, the reasonableness test, required the Unitrin Board to demonstrate that, after a reasonable investigation, it determined in good faith, that American General's Offer presented a threat to Unitrin that warranted a defensive response. This Court has held that the presence of a majority of outside independent directors will materially enhance such evidence. An "outside" director has been defined as a non-employee and non-management director, (e.g., Unitrin argues, five members of its seven-person Board). Independence "means that a director's decision is based on the corporate merits of the subject before the board rather than extraneous considerations or influences." *Aronson v. Lewis*, Del. Supr., 473 A.2d 805, 816 (1984).

The Unitrin Board identified two dangers it perceived the American General Offer posed: inadequate price and antitrust complications. The Court of Chancery characterized the Board's concern that American General's proposed transaction could never be consummated because it may violate antitrust laws and state insurance regulations as a "makeweight excuse" for the defensive measure. It determined, however, that the Board reasonably believed that the American General Offer was inadequate and also reasonably concluded that the Offer was a threat to Unitrin's uninformed stockholders.

The Court of Chancery held that the Board's evidence satisfied the first aspect or reasonableness test under *Unocal.* The Court of Chancery then noted, however, that the threat to the Unitrin stockholders from American General's inadequate opening bid was "mild," because the Offer was negotiable both in price and structure. The court then properly turned its attention to *Unocal's* second aspect, the proportionality test because "[i]t is not until both parts of the *Unocal* inquiry have been satisfied that the business judgment rule attaches to defensive actions of a board of directors." *Paramount Communications, Inc. v. Time, Inc.*, 571 A.2d at 1154.[17]

$- (TP - SV)(pSV) > 0$ where "FV" is a "full" value greater than the tender price, "TP" is the tender price, "pFV" is the probability of realizing this "full" value if the antitakeover device is maintained, "SV" is the subsequent value of the target's stock if the directors have not realized the "full" value and the tender offer is withdrawn or revised downwards, and "pSV" is the probability that SV shall occur. The only factor in the reasonableness equation which is precisely known is TP; the value of the other quantities may only be approximated.

George H. Kanter, Comment, *Judicial Review of Antitakeover Devices Employed in the Noncoercive Tender Offer Context: Making Sense of the Unocal Test*, 138 U.Pa.L.Rev., 225, 254–55 (1989) (footnote omitted).

Proportionality Burden
Chancery Approves Poison Pill

The second aspect or proportionality test of the initial *Unocal* burden required the Unitrin Board to demonstrate the proportionality of its response to the threat American General's Offer posed. The record reflects that the Unitrin Board considered three options as defensive measures: the poison pill, the advance notice bylaw, and the Repurchase Program. The Unitrin Board did not act on any of these options on July 25.

On August 2, American General made a public announcement of its offer to buy all the shares of Unitrin for $2.6 billion at $50-⅜ per share. The Unitrin Board had already concluded that the American General offer was inadequate. It also apparently feared that its stockholders did not realize that the long term value of Unitrin was not reflected in the market price of its stock.

On August 3, the Board met to decide whether any defensive action was necessary. The Unitrin Board decided to adopt defensive measures to protect Unitrin's stockholders from the inadequate American General Offer in two stages: first, it passed the poison pill and the advance notice bylaw; and, a week later, it implemented the Repurchase Program.

With regard to the second aspect or proportionality test of the initial *Unocal* burden, the Court of Chancery analyzed each stage of the Unitrin Board's defensive responses separately. Although the Court of Chancery characterized Unitrin's antitrust concerns as "makeweight," it acknowledged that the directors of a Delaware corporation have the prerogative to determine that the market undervalues its stock and to protect its stockholders from offers that do not reflect the long term value of the corporation under its present management plan. The Court of Chancery concluded that Unitrin's Board believed in good faith that the American General Offer was inadequate and properly employed a poison pill as a proportionate defensive response to protect its stockholders from a "low ball" bid. . . .

Proportionality Burden
Chancery Enjoins Repurchase Program

The Court of Chancery did not view either its conclusion that American General's Offer constituted a threat, or its conclusion that the poison pill was a reasonable response to that threat, as requiring it, *a fortiori*, to conclude that the Repurchase Program was also an appropriate response. The Court of Chancery then made two factual findings: first, the Repurchase Program went beyond what was "necessary" to protect the Unitrin stockholders from a "low ball" negotiating strategy; and second, it was designed to keep the decision to combine with American General within the control of the members of the Unitrin Board, as stockholders, under virtually all circumstances. Consequently, the Court of Chancery held that the Unitrin Board failed to demonstrate that the Repurchase Program met the second aspect or proportionality requirement of the initial burden *Unocal* ascribes to a board of directors.

The Court of Chancery framed the ultimate question before it as follows:

This case comes down to one final question: Is placing the decision to sell the company in the hands of stockholders who are also directors a disproportionate response to a low price offer to buy all the shares of the company for cash?

The Court of Chancery then answered that question:

I conclude that because the only threat to the corporation is the inadequacy of an opening bid made directly to the board, and the board has already taken actions that will protect the stockholders from mistakenly falling for a low ball negotiating strategy, a repurchase program that intentionally provides members of the board with a veto of any merger proposal is not reasonably related to the threat posed by American General's negotiable all shares, all cash offer.

In explaining its conclusion, the Court of Chancery reasoned that:

I have no doubt that a hostile acquiror can make an offer high enough to entice at least some of the directors that own stock to break ranks and sell their shares. Yet, these directors undoubtedly place a value, probably a substantial one, on their management of Unitrin, and will, at least subconsciously, reject an offer that does not compensate them for that value. . . . The prestige and perquisites that accompany managing Unitrin as a member of its Board of directors, even for the non-officer directors that do not draw a salary, may cause these stockholder directors to reject an excellent offer unless it includes this value in its "price parameter."

The Court of Chancery concluded that, although the Unitrin Board had properly perceived American General's inadequate Offer as a threat and had properly responded to that threat by adopting a "poison pill," the additional defensive response of adopting the Repurchase Program was unnecessary and disproportionate to the threat the Offer posed. Accordingly, it concluded that the plaintiffs had "established with reasonable probability that the [Unitrin Board] violated its duties under *Unocal* [by authorizing the Repurchase Program]" because the Board had not sustained its burden of demonstrating that the Repurchase Program was a proportionate response to American General's Offer. Therefore, the Court of Chancery held that the plaintiffs proved a likelihood of success on that issue and granted the motion to preliminarily enjoin the Repurchase Program.[18]

Proxy Contest
Supermajority Vote
Repurchase Program

Before the Repurchase Program began, Unitrin's directors collectively held approximately 23% of Unitrin's outstanding shares. Unitrin's certificate of incorpo-

---

[18] [n.18] We note that the directors' failure to carry their initial burden under *Unocal* does not, *ipso facto*, invalidate the board's actions. Instead, once the Court of Chancery finds the business judgment rule does not apply, the burden remains on the directors to prove "entire fairness." *See* Cede & Co. v. Technicolor, Inc., Del. Supr., 634 A.2d 345, 361 (1993); Grobow v. Perot, Del. Supr., 539 A.2d 180, 187 (1988) (*citing* Aronson v. Lewis, Del. Supr., 473 A.2d 805, 812–17 (1984)); Shamrock Holdings, Inc. v. Polaroid Corp., Del. Ch., 559 A.2d 257, 271 (1989).

ration already included a "shark-repellent" provision barring any business combination with a more–than–15% stockholder unless approved by a majority of
continuing directors or by a 75% stockholder vote ("Supermajority Vote"). Unitrin's
shareholder directors announced publicly that they would not participate in the
Repurchase Program and that this would result in a percentage increase of
ownership for them, as well as for any other shareholder who did not participate.

The Court of Chancery found that by not participating in the Repurchase
Program, the Board "expected to create a 28% voting block to support the Board's
decision to reject [a future] offer by American General." From this underlying
factual finding, the Court of Chancery concluded that American General might be
"chilled" in its pursuit of Unitrin:

> Increasing the board members' percentage of stock ownership, combined
> with the supermajority merger provision, does more than protect unin-
> formed stockholders from an inadequate offer, it chills any unsolicited
> acquiror from making an offer.

The parties are in substantial disagreement with respect to the Court of
Chancery's ultimate factual finding that the Repurchase Program was a disproportionate response under *Unocal*. Unitrin argues that American General or another
potential acquiror can theoretically prevail in an effort to obtain control of Unitrin
through a proxy contest. American General argues that the record supports the
Court of Chancery's factual determination that the adoption of the Repurchase
Program violated the principles of *Unocal*, even though American General acknowledges that the option of a proxy contest for obtaining control of Unitrin remained
theoretically available. The stockholder-plaintiffs argue that even if it can be said, as
a matter of law, that it is acceptable under certain circumstances to leave potential
bidders with a proxy battle as the sole avenue for acquiring an entity, the Court of
Chancery correctly determined, as a factual matter, that the Repurchase Program
was disproportionate to the threat American General's Offer posed. . . .

Takeover Strategy
Tender Offer/Proxy Contest

We begin our examination of Unitrin's Repurchase Program mindful of the
special import of protecting the shareholder's franchise within *Unocal's* requirement that a defensive response be reasonable and proportionate. For many years
the "favored attack of a [corporate] raider was stock acquisition followed by a proxy
contest." *Unocal*, 493 A.2d at 957. Some commentators have noted that the recent
trend toward tender offers as the preferable alternative to proxy contests appears
to be reversing because of the proliferation of sophisticated takeover defenses.
Lucian A. Bebchuk & Marcel Kahan, *A Framework for Analyzing Legal Policy
Towards Proxy Contests*, 78 Cal.L.Rev. 1071, 1134 (1990). In fact, the same
commentators have characterized a return to proxy contests as "the only alternative
to hostile takeovers to gain control against the will of the incumbent directors." *Id.*

The Court of Chancery, in the case *sub judice*, was obviously cognizant that the
emergence of the "poison pill" as an effective takeover device has resulted in such
a remarkable transformation in the market for corporate control that hostile

bidders who proceed when such defenses are in place will usually "have to couple proxy contests with tender offers." Joseph A. Grundfest, *Just Vote No: A Minimalist Strategy for Dealing with Barbarians Inside the Gates*, 45 Stan.L.Rev. 857, 858 (1993). The Court of Chancery concluded that Unitrin's adoption of a poison pill was a proportionate response to the threat its Board reasonably perceived from American General's Offer. Nonetheless, the Court of Chancery enjoined the additional defense of the Repurchase Program as disproportionate and "unnecessary."

The record reflects that the Court of Chancery's decision to enjoin the Repurchase Program is attributable to a continuing misunderstanding, i.e., that in conjunction with the longstanding Supermajority Vote provision in the Unitrin charter, the Repurchase Program would operate to provide the director shareholders with a "veto" to preclude a successful proxy contest by American General. The origins of that misunderstanding are three premises that are each without record support. Two of those premises are objective misconceptions and the other is subjective.

Directors' Motives
"Prestige and Perquisites"
Subjective Determination

The subjective premise was the Court of Chancery's *sua sponte* determination that Unitrin's outside directors, who are also substantial stockholders, would not vote like other stockholders in a proxy contest, i.e., in their own best economic interests. At American General's Offer price, the outside directors held Unitrin shares worth more than $450 million. Consequently, Unitrin argues the stockholder directors had the same interest as other Unitrin stockholders generally, when voting in a proxy contest, to wit: the maximization of the value of their investments.

In rejecting Unitrin's argument, the Court of Chancery stated that the stockholder directors would be "subconsciously" motivated in a proxy contest to vote against otherwise excellent offers which did not include a "price parameter" to compensate them for the loss of the "prestige and perquisites" of membership on Unitrin's Board. The Court of Chancery's subjective determination that the *stockholder directors* of Unitrin would reject an "excellent offer," unless it compensated them for giving up the "prestige and perquisites" of directorship, appears to be subjective and without record support. It cannot be presumed.

It must be the subject of proof that the Unitrin directors' objective in the Repurchase Program was to forego the opportunity to sell their stock at a premium. In particular, it cannot be presumed that the prestige and perquisites of holding a director's office or a motive to strengthen collective power prevails over a stockholder-director's economic interest. Even the shareholder-plaintiffs in this case agree with the legal proposition Unitrin advocates on appeal: stockholders are presumed to act in their own best economic interests when they vote in a proxy contest.

Without Repurchase Program
Actual Voting Power Exceeds 25%

The first objective premise relied upon by the Court of Chancery, unsupported by the record, is that the shareholder directors needed to implement the Repurchase Program to attain voting power in a proxy contest equal to 25%. The Court of Chancery properly calculated that if the Repurchase Program was completed, Unitrin's shareholder directors would increase their absolute voting power to 25%. It then calculated the odds of American General marshalling enough votes to defeat the Board and its supporters.

The Court of Chancery and all parties agree that proxy contests do not generate 100% shareholder participation. The shareholder plaintiffs argue that 80–85% may be a usual turnout. Therefore, *without* the Repurchase Program, the director shareholders' absolute voting power of 23% would already constitute *actual voting power greater than* 25% in a proxy contest with normal shareholder participation below 100%. *See Berlin v. Emerald Partners*, Del. Supr., 552 A.2d 482 (1989).

Supermajority Vote
No Realistic Deterrent

The second objective premise relied upon by the Court of Chancery, unsupported by the record, is that American General's ability to succeed in a proxy contest depended on the Repurchase Program being enjoined because of the Supermajority Vote provision in Unitrin's charter. Without the approval of a target's board, the danger of activating a poison pill renders it irrational for bidders to pursue stock acquisitions above the triggering level. Instead, "bidders intent on working around a poison pill must launch and win proxy contests to elect new directors who are willing to redeem the target's poison pill." Joseph A. Grundfest, *Just Vote No: A Minimalist Strategy for Dealing with Barbarians Inside the Gates*, 45 Stan.L.Rev. 857, 859 (1993).

As American General acknowledges, a less than 15% stockholder bidder need not proceed with acquiring shares to the extent that it would ever implicate the Supermajority Vote provision. In fact, it would be illogical for American General or any other bidder to acquire more than 15% of Unitrin's stock because that would not only trigger the poison pill, but also the constraints of 8 *Del. C.* § 203. If American General were to initiate a proxy contest *before* acquiring 15% of Unitrin's stock, it would need to amass only 45.1% of the votes assuming a 90% voter turnout. If it commenced a tender offer at an attractive price contemporaneously with its proxy contest, it could seek to acquire 50.1% of the outstanding voting stock.

The record reflects that institutional investors own 42% of Unitrin's shares. Twenty institutions own 33% of Unitrin's shares. It is generally accepted that proxy contests have re-emerged with renewed significance as a method of acquiring corporate control because "the growth in institutional investment has reduced the dispersion of share ownership." Lucian A. Bebchuk & Marcel Kahan, *A Framework for Analyzing Legal Policy Towards Proxy Contests*, 78 Cal.L.Rev. 1071, 1134 (1990). "Institutions are more likely than other shareholders to vote at all, more likely to vote against manager proposals, and more likely to vote for proposals by other shareholders." Bernard S. Black, *The Value of Institutional Investor Monitoring: The Empirical Evidence*, 39 UCLA L.Rev. 895, 925 (1992).

With Supermajority Vote
After Repurchase Program
Proxy Contest Appears Viable

The assumptions and conclusions American General sets forth in this appeal for a different purpose are particularly probative with regard to the effect of the institutional holdings in Unitrin's stock. American General's two predicate assumptions are a 90% stockholder turnout in a proxy contest and a bidder with 14.9% holdings, i.e., the maximum the bidder could own to avoid triggering the poison pill and the Supermajority Vote provision. American General also calculated the votes available to the Board or the bidder with and without the Repurchase Program:

> Assuming no Repurchase [Program], the [shareholder directors] would hold 23%, the percentage collectively held by the [directors] and the bidder would be 37.9%, and the percentage of additional votes available to either side would be 52.1%.

> Assuming the Repurchase [Program] is fully consummated, the [shareholder directors] would hold 28%, the percentage collectively held by the bidder and the [directors] would be 42.9%, and the percentage of additional votes available to either side would be 47.1%.

American General then applied these assumptions to reach conclusions regarding the votes needed for the 14.9% stockholder bidder to prevail: first, in an election of directors; and second, in the subsequent vote on a merger. With regard to the election of directors, American General made the following calculations:

> Assume 90% stockholder turnout. To elect directors, a plurality must be obtained; assuming no abstentions and only two competing slates, one must obtain the votes of 45.1% of the shares.

> The percentage of additional votes the bidder needs to win is: 45.1% − 14.9% (maximum the bidder could own and avoid the poison pill, § 203 and supermajority) = **30.2%**.

A merger requires approval of a majority of outstanding shares, 8 *Del. C.* § 251, not just a plurality. In that regard, American General made the following calculations:

> Assume 90% stockholder turnout. To approve a merger, one must obtain the favorable vote of 50.1% of the shares.

> The percentage of additional votes the bidder needs to win is 50.1% − 14.9% = **35.2%**.

Consequently, to prevail in a proxy contest with a 90% turnout, the percentage of additional shareholder votes a 14.9% shareholder bidder needs to prevail is 30.2% for directors and 35.2% in a subsequent merger. The record reflects that institutional investors held 42% of Unitrin's stock and 20 institutions held 33% of the stock. Thus, American General's own assumptions and calculations in the record support the Unitrin Board's argument that "it is hard to imagine a company more readily susceptible to a proxy contest concerning a pure issue of dollars."

The conclusion of the Court of Chancery that the Repurchase Program would make a proxy contest for Unitrin a "theoretical" possibility that American General could not realistically pursue may be erroneous and appears to be inconsistent with its own earlier determination that the "repurchase program strengthens the position of the Board of Directors to defend against a hostile bidder, but will not deprive the public stockholders of the 'power to influence corporate direction through the ballot.' " Even a complete implementation of the Repurchase Program, in combination with the pre-existing Supermajority Vote provision, would not appear to have a preclusive effect upon American General's ability successfully to marshall enough shareholder votes to win a proxy contest. A proper understanding of the record reflects that American General or any other 14.9% shareholder bidder could apparently win a proxy contest with a 90% turnout.

The key variable in a proxy contest would be the merit of American General's issues, not the size of its stockholdings. If American General presented an attractive price as the cornerstone of a proxy contest, it could prevail, irrespective of whether the shareholder directors' absolute voting power was 23% or 28%. In that regard, the following passage from the Court of Chancery's Opinion is poignant:

> Harold Hook, the Chairman of American General, admitted in his deposition that the repurchase program is not a "show stopper" because the directors that own stock will act in their own best interest if the price is high enough. (Hook Dep. at 86–87). Fayez Sarofim, one of the Unitrin directors that holds a substantial number of shares, testified that 'everything has a price parameter.' "

Consequently, a proxy contest apparently remained a viable alternative for American General to pursue notwithstanding Unitrin's poison pill, Supermajority Vote provision, and a fully implemented Repurchase Program.

Substantive Coercion
American General's Threat

This Court has recognized "the prerogative of a board of directors to resist a third party's unsolicited acquisition proposal or offer." *Paramount Communications, Inc. v. QVC Network, Inc.*, Del. Supr., 637 A.2d 34, 43 n. 13 (1994). The Unitrin Board did not have unlimited discretion to defeat the threat it perceived from the American General Offer by any draconian[19] means available. Pursuant to the *Unocal* proportionality test, the nature of the threat associated with a particular hostile offer sets the parameters for the range of permissible defensive tactics. Accordingly, the purpose of enhanced judicial scrutiny is to determine whether the Board acted reasonably in "relation . . . to the threat which a particular bid

---

[19] [n.34] Draconian, adj. Of or pert. to Draco, an archon and member of the Athenian eupatridae, or the code of laws which is said to have been framed about 621 B.C. by him as thesmothete. In them the penalty for most offenses was death, and to a later age they seemed so severe that they were said to be written in blood. Hence, barbarously severe; harsh; cruel. *Webster's New International Dictionary* 780 (2d ed. 1951).

allegedly poses to stockholder interests." *Mills Acquisition Co. v. Macmillan, Inc.*, Del. Supr., 559 A.2d 1261, 1288 (1989).

"The obvious requisite to determining the reasonableness of a defensive action is a clear identification of the nature of the threat." *Paramount Communications, Inc. v. Time, Inc.*, Del. Supr., 571 A.2d 1140, 1154 (1990). Courts, commentators and litigators have attempted to catalogue the threats posed by hostile tender offers. *Id.* at 1153. Commentators have categorized three types of threats:

> (i) *opportunity loss* . . . [where] a hostile offer might deprive target shareholders of the opportunity to select a superior alternative offered by target management [or, we would add, offered by another bidder]; (ii) *structural coercion,* . . . the risk that disparate treatment of non-tendering shareholders might distort shareholders' tender decisions; and (iii) *substantive coercion,* . . . the risk that shareholders will mistakenly accept an underpriced offer because they disbelieve management's representations of intrinsic value.

Id. at 1153 n. 17 (*quoting* Ronald J. Gilson & Reinier Kraakman, *Delaware's Intermediate Standard for Defensive Tactics: Is There Substance to Proportionality Review?*, 44 BUS. LAW. 247, 267 (1989)).

This Court has held that the "inadequate value" of an all cash for all shares offer is a "legally cognizable threat." *Paramount Communications, Inc. v. Time, Inc.*, 571 A.2d at 1153. In addition, this Court has specifically concluded that inadequacy of value is *not* the only legally cognizable threat from "an all-shares, all-cash offer at a price below what a target board in good faith deems to be the present value of its shares." *Id.* at 1152–53. In making that determination, this Court held that the Time board of directors had reasonably determined that inadequate value was not the only threat that Paramount's all cash for all shares offer presented, but was *also* reasonably concerned that the Time stockholders might tender to Paramount in ignorance or based upon a mistaken belief, i.e., yield to substantive coercion.

The record reflects that the Unitrin Board perceived the threat from American General's Offer to be a form of substantive coercion. The Board noted that Unitrin's stock price had moved up, on higher than normal trading volume, to a level slightly below the price in American General's Offer. The Board also noted that some Unitrin shareholders had publicly expressed interest in selling at or near the price in the Offer. The Board determined that Unitrin's stock was undervalued by the market at current levels and that the Board considered Unitrin's stock to be a good long-term investment. The Board also discussed the speculative and unsettled market conditions for Unitrin stock caused by American General's public disclosure. The Board concluded that a Repurchase Program would provide additional liquidity to those stockholders who wished to realize short-term gain, and would provide enhanced value to those stockholders who wished to maintain a long-term investment. Accordingly, the Board voted to authorize the Repurchase Program for up to ten million shares of its outstanding stock on the open market.

In *Unocal*, this Court noted that, pursuant to Delaware corporate law, a board of directors' duty of care required it to respond actively to protect the corporation and its shareholders from perceived harm. *Unocal*, 493 A.2d at 955. In *Unocal*, when describing the proportionality test, this Court listed several examples of concerns that boards of directors should consider in evaluating and responding to perceived threats. Unitrin's Board deemed three of the concerns exemplified in *Unocal* relevant in deciding to authorize the Repurchase Program: first, the inadequacy of the price offered; second, the nature and timing of American General's Offer; and third, the basic stockholder interests at stake, including those of short-term speculators whose actions may have fueled the coercive aspect of the Offer at the expense of the long-term investor.

The record appears to support Unitrin's argument that the Board's justification for adopting the Repurchase Program was its reasonably perceived risk of substantive coercion, i.e., that Unitrin's shareholders might accept American General's inadequate Offer because of "ignorance or mistaken belief" regarding the Board's assessment of the long-term value of Unitrin's stock. In this case, the Unitrin Board's letter to its shareholders specifically reflected those concerns in describing its perception of the threat from American General's Offer. The adoption of the Repurchase Program also appears to be consistent with this Court's holding that economic inadequacy is not the only threat presented by an all cash for all shares hostile bid, because the threat of such a hostile bid could be exacerbated by shareholder "ignorance or . . . mistaken belief." *Paramount Communications, Inc. v. Time, Inc.*, 571 A.2d at 1153.

Range of Reasonableness
Proper Proportionality Burden . . .

We have already noted that the Court of Chancery made a factual finding unsupported by the record, i.e., that the increase in the percentage of ownership by the stockholder directors from 23% to 28%, resulting from the completed Repurchase Program, would make it merely theoretically possible for an insurgent to win a proxy contest. That finding was based upon a hypothetical risk which originated from the Court of Chancery's attribution of subjective "prestige and perquisite" voting motives to Unitrin's outside shareholder directors. *See Stroud v. Grace*, Del. Supr., 606 A.2d 75, 82 (1992). In addition, that factual finding was based upon two objective mathematically erroneous calculations regarding the relative voting strength of American General and the stockholder directors.

The Court of Chancery applied an incorrect legal standard when it ruled that the Unitrin decision to authorize the Repurchase Program was disproportionate because it was "unnecessary." The Court of Chancery stated:

> Given that the Board had already implemented the poison pill and the advance notice provision, the repurchase program was unnecessary to protect Unitrin from an inadequate bid.

In *QVC*, this Court recently elaborated upon the judicial function in applying enhanced scrutiny, citing *Unocal* as authority, albeit in the context of a sale of control and the target board's consideration of one of several reasonable alternatives. That teaching is nevertheless applicable here:

> a court applying enhanced judicial scrutiny should be deciding whether the directors made *a reasonable* decision, not *a perfect* decision. If a board

selected one of several reasonable alternatives, a court should not second guess that choice even though it might have decided otherwise or subsequent events may have cast doubt on the board's determination. Thus, courts will not substitute their business judgment for that of the directors, but will determine if the directors' decision was, on balance, within a range of reasonableness. *See Unocal*, 493 A.2d at 955–56; *Macmillan*, 559 A.2d at 1288; *Nixon*, 626 A.2d at 1378.

Paramount Communications, Inc. v. QVC Network, Inc., Del. Supr., 637 A.2d 34, 45–46 (1994) (emphasis in original). The Court of Chancery did not determine whether the Unitrin Board's decision to implement the Repurchase Program fell within a "range of reasonableness."

The record reflects that the Unitrin Board's adoption of the Repurchase Program was an apparent recognition on its part that all shareholders are not alike. This Court has stated that distinctions among types of shareholders are neither inappropriate nor irrelevant for a board of directors to make, e.g., distinctions between long-term shareholders and short-term profit-takers, such as arbitrageurs, and their stockholding objectives. *Id.* In *Unocal* itself, we expressly acknowledged that "a board may reasonably consider the basic stockholder interests at stake, including those of short term speculators, whose actions may have fueled the coercive aspect of the offer at the expense of the long term investor." *Unocal*, 493 A.2d at 955–56.

The Court of Chancery's determination that the Unitrin Board's adoption of the Repurchase Program was unnecessary constituted a substitution of its business judgment for that of the Board, contrary to this Court's "range of reasonableness" holding in *Paramount Communications, Inc. v. QVC Network, Inc.*, 637 A.2d at 45–46. . . .

Draconian Defenses
Coercive or Preclusive
Range of Reasonableness

In assessing a challenge to defensive actions by a target corporation's board of directors in a takeover context, this Court has held that the Court of Chancery should evaluate the board's overall response, including the justification for each contested defensive measure, and the results achieved thereby. Where all of the target board's defensive actions are inextricably related, the principles of *Unocal* require that such actions be scrutinized collectively as a unitary response to the perceived threat. Thus, the Unitrin Board's adoption of the Repurchase Program, in addition to the poison pill, must withstand *Unocal* 's proportionality review.

In *Unocal*, the progenitor of the proportionality test, this Court stated that the board of directors' "duty of care extends to protecting the corporation and its [stockholders] from perceived harm whether a threat originates from third parties or other shareholders." *Unocal*, 493 A.2d at 955. We then noted that "such powers are not absolute." *Id.* Specifically, this Court held that the board "does not have unbridled discretion to defeat any perceived threat by any Draconian means available." *Id.* Immediately following those observations in *Unocal*, when exemplifying the parameters of a board's authority in adopting a restrictive stock repurchase, this Court held that "the directors may not have acted *solely* or *primarily* out of a desire to perpetuate themselves in office" (preclusion of the stockholders' corporate franchise right to vote) and, further, that the stock repurchase plan must not be inequitable. *Unocal*, 493 A.2d at 955 (emphasis added).[37]

An examination of the cases applying *Unocal* reveals a direct correlation between findings of proportionality or disproportionality and the judicial determination of whether a defensive response was draconian because it was either coercive or preclusive in character. In *Time*, for example, this Court concluded that the Time board's defensive response was reasonable and proportionate since it was not aimed at "cramming down" on its shareholders a management-sponsored alternative, i.e., was not coercive, and because it did not preclude Paramount from making an offer for the combined Time–Warner company, i.e., was not preclusive.

This Court also applied *Unocal's* proportionality test to the board's adoption of a "poison pill" shareholders' rights plan in *Moran v. Household Int'l, Inc.*, Del. Supr., 500 A.2d 1346 (1985). After acknowledging that the adoption of the rights plan was within the directors' statutory authority, this Court determined that the implementation of the rights plan was a proportionate response to the theoretical threat of a hostile takeover, in part, because it did not "strip" the stockholders of their right to receive tender offers *and* did not fundamentally restrict proxy contests, i.e., was not preclusive. *Id.* at 1357.

More than a century before *Unocal* was decided, Justice Holmes observed that the common law must be developed through its application and "cannot be dealt with as if it contained only the axioms and corollaries of a book of mathematics." Oliver Wendell Holmes, Jr., *The Common Law* 1 (1881). As common law applications of *Unocal's* proportionality standard have evolved, at least two characteristics of draconian defensive measures taken by a board of directors in responding to a threat have been brought into focus through enhanced judicial scrutiny. In the modern takeover lexicon, it is now clear that since *Unocal*, this Court has consistently recognized that defensive measures which are either preclusive or coercive are included within the common law definition of draconian.

If a defensive measure is not draconian, however, because it is not either coercive or preclusive, the *Unocal* proportionality test requires the focus of enhanced judicial scrutiny to shift to "the range of reasonableness." *Paramount Communications, Inc. v. QVC Network, Inc.*, Del. Supr., 637 A.2d 34, 45–46 (1994). Proper and proportionate defensive responses are intended and permitted to thwart perceived threats. When a corporation is not for sale, the board of directors is the defender of the metaphorical medieval corporate bastion and the protector of the corporation's shareholders. The fact that a defensive action must not be coercive or preclusive does not prevent a board from responding defensively before a bidder is at the corporate bastion's gate.[20]

---

[20] [n.38] This Court's choice of the term draconian in *Unocal* was a recognition that the law affords boards of directors substantial latitude in defending the perimeter of the corporate bastion against perceived threats. Thus, continuing with the medieval metaphor, if a board reasonably perceives that a

The *ratio decidendi* for the "range of reasonableness" standard is a need of the board of directors for latitude in discharging its fiduciary duties to the corporation and its shareholders when defending against perceived threats. The concomitant requirement is for judicial restraint. Consequently, if the board of directors' defensive response is not draconian (preclusive or coercive) and is within a "range of reasonableness," a court must not substitute its judgment for the board's.

This Case
Repurchase Program
Proportionate With Poison Pill

In this case, the initial focus of enhanced judicial scrutiny for proportionality requires a determination regarding the defensive responses by the Unitrin Board to American General's offer. We begin, therefore, by ascertaining whether the Repurchase Program, as an addition to the poison pill, was draconian by being either coercive or preclusive.

A limited nondiscriminatory self-tender, like some other defensive measures, may thwart a current hostile bid, but is not inherently coercive. Moreover, it does not necessarily preclude future bids or proxy contests by stockholders who decline to participate in the repurchase. A selective repurchase of shares in a public corporation on the market, such as Unitrin's Repurchase Program, generally does not discriminate because all shareholders can voluntarily realize the same benefit by selling. Here, there is no showing on this record that the Repurchase Program was coercive.

We have already determined that the record in this case appears to reflect that a proxy contest remained a viable (if more problematic) alternative for American General even if the Repurchase Program were to be completed in its entirety. Nevertheless, the Court of Chancery must determine whether Unitrin's Repurchase Program would only inhibit American General's ability to wage a proxy fight and institute a merger or whether it was, in fact, preclusive39 because American General's success would either be mathematically impossible or realistically unattainable. If the Court of Chancery concludes that the Unitrin Repurchase Program was not draconian because it was not preclusive, one question will remain to be answered in its proportionality review: whether the Repurchase Program was within a range of reasonableness?

The Court of Chancery found that the Unitrin Board reasonably believed that American General's Offer was inadequate and that the adoption of a poison pill was a proportionate defensive response. Upon remand, in applying the correct legal standard to the factual circumstances of this case, the Court of Chancery may conclude that the implementation of the limited Repurchase Program was also within a range of reasonable additional defensive responses available to the Unitrin Board. In considering whether the Repurchase Program was within a range of

---

threat is on the horizon, it has broad authority to respond with a panoply of individual or combined defensive precautions, e.g., staffing the barbican, raising the drawbridge, and lowering the portcullis. Stated more directly, depending upon the circumstances, the board may respond to a reasonably perceived threat by adopting individually or sometimes in combination: advance notice by-laws, supermajority voting provisions, shareholder rights plans, repurchase programs, etc.

reasonableness the Court of Chancery should take into consideration whether: (1) it is a statutorily authorized form of business decision which a board of directors may routinely make in a non-takeover context;40 (2) as a defensive response to American General's Offer it was limited and corresponded in degree or magnitude to the degree or magnitude of the threat, (i.e., assuming the threat was relatively "mild," was the response relatively "mild?"); (3) with the Repurchase Program, the Unitrin Board properly recognized that all shareholders are not alike, and provided immediate liquidity to those shareholders who wanted it.

The Court of Chancery's holding in *Shamrock*, cited with approval by this Court in *Time*, appears to be persuasive support for the proportionality of the multiple defenses Unitrin's Board adopted. In *Shamrock*, the Court of Chancery concluded that the Polaroid board had "a valid basis for concern that the Polaroid stockholders [like Unitrin's stockholders] will be unable to reach an accurate judgment as to the intrinsic value of their stock." *Shamrock Holdings, Inc. v. Polaroid Corp.*, 559 A.2d at 290. The Court of Chancery also observed, "the likely shift in the stockholder profile in favor of Polaroid" as a result of the repurchase plan "appears to be minimal." *Id.* Consequently, the Court of Chancery concluded that Polaroid's defensive response as a whole — the ESOP, the issuance of stock to a friendly third party and the stock repurchase plan — was not disproportionate to the Shamrock threat or improperly motivated, and "individually or collectively will [not] preclude the successful completion of Shamrock's tender offer." *Id.* at 288.

American General argues that the all cash for all shares offer in *Shamrock* is distinguishable because *Shamrock* involved a hostile tender offer, whereas this case involves a fully negotiable Offer to enter into a consensual merger transaction. Nevertheless, American General acknowledges that a determinative factor in *Shamrock* was a finding that the defensive responses had only an incidental effect on the stockholder profile for the purpose of a proxy contest, i.e., was not preclusive. *See id.* at 286–288. In *Shamrock*, the Court of Chancery's proportionality holding was also an implicit determination that the series of multiple defensive responses were within a "range of reasonableness."

Remand to Chancery

In this case, the Court of Chancery erred by substituting its judgment, that the Repurchase Program was unnecessary, for that of the Board. The Unitrin Board had the power and the duty, upon reasonable investigation, to protect Unitrin's shareholders from what it perceived to be the threat from American General's inadequate all-cash for all-shares Offer. *Unocal*, 493 A.2d at 958. The adoption of the poison pill *and* the limited Repurchase Program was not coercive and the Repurchase Program may not be preclusive. Although each made a takeover more difficult, individually and collectively, if they were not coercive or preclusive the Court of Chancery must determine whether they were within the range of reasonable defensive measures available to the Board.

If the Court of Chancery concludes that individually and collectively the poison pill and the Repurchase Program were proportionate to the threat the Board believed American General posed, the Unitrin Board's adoption of the Repurchase Program and the poison pill is entitled to review under the traditional business judgment rule. The burden will then shift "back to the plaintiffs who have the ultimate burden of persuasion [in a preliminary injunction proceeding] to show a breach of the directors' fiduciary duties." *Moran v. Household Int'l, Inc.*, Del. Supr., 500 A.2d 1346, 1356 (1985) (*citing Unocal*, 493 A.2d at 958). In order to rebut the protection of the business judgment rule, the burden on the plaintiffs will be to demonstrate, "by a preponderance of the evidence that the directors' decisions were *primarily* based on [(1)] perpetuating themselves in office or [(2)] some other breach of fiduciary duty such as fraud, overreaching, lack of good faith, or [(3)] being uninformed." *Unocal*, 493 A.2d at 958 (emphasis added). . . .

QUESTIONS

1. What is the proposed deal involved in the case?

2. What defensive measures did Unitrin adopt?

3. What is the anti-takeover effect of the Repurchase Program?

4. Why did the lower court enjoin the Repurchase Program?

5. How does the court clarify the reasonableness test?

6. How does the court clarify the proportionality test?

7. What did the lower court get wrong?

VERSATA ENTERPRISES, INC. v. SELECTICA, INC.
Delaware Supreme Court
5 A.3d 586 (2010)

HOLLAND, Justice:

This is an appeal from a final judgment entered by the Court of Chancery. On November 16, 2008 the Board of Directors of Selectica, Inc. ("Selectica") reduced the trigger of its "poison pill" Shareholder Rights Plan from 15% to 4.99% of Selectica's outstanding shares and capped existing shareholders who held a 5% or more interest to a further increase of only 0.5% (the "NOL Poison Pill"). Selectica's reason for taking such action was to protect the company's net operating loss carryforwards ("NOLs"). When Trilogy, Inc. ("Trilogy") subsequently purchased shares above this cap, Selectica filed suit in the Court of Chancery on December 21, 2008, seeking a declaration that the NOL Poison Pill was valid and enforceable. On January 2, 2009, Selectica implemented the dilutive exchange provision (the "Exchange") of the NOL Poison Pill, which reduced Trilogy's interest from 6.7% to 3.3%, and adopted another Rights Plan with a 4.99% trigger (the "Reloaded NOL Poison Pill"). Selectica then amended its complaint to seek a declaration that the Exchange and the Reloaded NOL Poison Pill were valid.

Trilogy and its subsidiary Versata Enterprises, Inc. ("Versata") counterclaimed that the NOL Poison Pill, the Reloaded NOL Poison Pill, and the Exchange were unlawful on the grounds that, before acting, the Board failed to consider that its NOLs were unusable or that the two NOL poison pills were unnecessary given Selectica's unbroken history of losses and doubtful prospects of annual profits. Trilogy and Versata also asserted that the NOL Poison Pill and the Reloaded NOL Poison Pill were impermissibly preclusive of a successful proxy contest for Board control, particularly when combined with Selectica's staggered director terms. After trial, the Court of Chancery held that the NOL Poison Pill, the Reloaded NOL Poison Pill, and the Exchange were all valid under Delaware law.

Trilogy and Versata now appeal and assert two claims of error. First, they contend that the Court of Chancery erred in applying the *Unocal* test for enhanced judicial scrutiny when confronting what they frame as a question of first impression. The issue (as framed by them) is: "what are the minimum requirements for a reasonable investigation before the board of a never-profitable company may adopt a [Rights Plan with a 4.99% trigger] for the ostensible purpose of protecting NOLs from an 'ownership change' under § 382 of the Internal Revenue Code?" Second, they submit that the Court of Chancery erred in holding that the two NOL poison pills, either individually or in combination with a charter-based classified Board, did not have a preclusive effect on the shareholders' ability to pursue a successful proxy contest for control of the Company's board. We conclude that both arguments are without merit. . . .

Facts

The Court of Chancery described this as a case about the value of net operating loss carryforwards ("NOLs") to a currently profitless corporation, and the extent to which such a corporation may fight to preserve those NOLs. The Court of Chancery also provided a helpful overview of the concepts surrounding NOLs, their calculation, and possible impairment.

NOLs are tax losses, realized and accumulated by a corporation, that can be used to shelter future (or immediate past) income from taxation.[21] If taxable profit has been realized, the NOLs operate either to provide a refund of prior taxes paid or to reduce the amount of future income tax owed. Thus, NOLs can be a valuable asset, as a means of lowering tax payments and producing positive cash flow. NOLs are considered a contingent asset, their value being contingent upon the firm's reporting a future profit or having an immediate past profit.

Should the firm fail to realize a profit during the lifetime of the NOL (twenty years), the NOL expires. The precise value of a given NOL is usually impossible to determine since its ultimate use is subject to the timing and amount of recognized profit at the firm. If the firm never realizes taxable income, at dissolution its NOLs, regardless of their amount, would have zero value.

In order to prevent corporate taxpayers from benefiting from NOLs generated by other entities, Internal Revenue Code § 382 establishes limitations on the use of NOLs in periods following an "ownership change." If § 382 is triggered, the law

---

[21] [n.2] NOLs may be carried backward two years and carried forward twenty years.

restricts the amount of prior NOLs that can be used in subsequent years to reduce the firm's tax obligations.[22] Once NOLs are so impaired, a substantial portion of their value is lost.

The precise definition of an "ownership change" under § 382 is rather complex. At its most basic, an ownership change occurs when more than 50% of a firm's stock ownership changes over a three-year period. Specific provisions in § 382 define the precise manner by which this determination is made. Most importantly for purposes of this case, the only shareholders considered when calculating an ownership change under § 382 are those who hold, or have obtained during the testing period, a 5% or greater block of the corporation's shares outstanding.

The Parties

Selectica, Inc. ("Selectica" or the "Company") is a Delaware corporation, headquartered in California and listed on the NASDAQ Global Market. It provides enterprise software solutions for contract management and sales configuration systems. Selectica is a micro-cap company with a concentrated shareholder base: the Company's seven largest investors own a majority of the stock, while fewer than twenty-five investors hold nearly two-thirds of the stock.

Trilogy, Inc. ("Trilogy") is a Delaware corporation also specializing in enterprise software solutions. Trilogy stock is not publicly traded, and its founder, Joseph Liemandt, holds over 85% of the stock. Versata Enterprises, Inc. ("Versata"), a Delaware corporation and a subsidiary of Trilogy, provides technology powered business services to clients.

Before the events giving rise to this action, Versata and Trilogy beneficially owned 6.7% of Selectica's common stock. After they intentionally triggered Selectica's Shareholder Rights Plan through the purchase of additional shares, Versata's and Trilogy's joint beneficial ownership was diluted from 6.7% to approximately 3.3%. . . .

Selectica's Historical Operating Difficulties

Since it became a public company in March 2000, Selectica has lost a substantial amount of money and failed to turn an annual profit, despite routinely projecting near-term profitability. Its IPO price of $30 per share has steadily fallen and now languishes below $1 per share, placing Selectica's market capitalization at roughly $23 million as of the end of March 2009. By Selectica's own admission, its value today "consists primarily in its cash reserves, its intellectual property portfolio, its customer and revenue base, and its accumulated NOLs." By consistently failing to achieve positive net income, Selectica has generated an estimated $160 million in NOLs for federal tax purposes over the past several years.

---

[22] [n.3] The annual limitation on the use of past period NOLs following a change-in-control is calculated as the value of the firm's equity at the time of the ownership change, multiplied by a published rate of return, the federal long term exemption rate.

Selectica's Relationship with Trilogy

Selectica has had a complicated and often adversarial relationship with Trilogy, stretching back at least five years. Both companies compete in the relatively narrow market space of contract management and sales configuration. In April 2004, a Trilogy affiliate sued Selectica for patent infringement and secured a judgment that required Selectica, among other things, to pay Trilogy $7.5 million. While their suit was pending, in January 2005 Trilogy made an offer to buy Selectica for $4 per share in cash — a 20% premium above the then-trading price — which Selectica's Board rejected. Nevertheless, during March and April of that year, a Trilogy affiliate acquired nearly 7% of Selectica's common stock through open market trades. In early fall 2005, Trilogy made another offer for Selectica's shares at a 16%–23% premium, which was also rejected.

In September 2006, a Trilogy-affiliated holder of Selectica stock sent a letter to the Board questioning whether certain stock option grants had been backdated. The following month, Trilogy filed another patent infringement lawsuit against Selectica. That action was settled in October 2007, when Selectica agreed to a one-time payment of $10 million, plus an additional amount of not more than $7.5 million in subsequent payments to be made quarterly. In late fall 2006, Trilogy sold down its holdings in Selectica.

Steel Partners

Steel Partners is a private equity fund that has been a Selectica shareholder since at least 2006 and is currently its largest shareholder. One of Steel Partners' apparent investment strategies is to invest in small companies with large NOLs with the intent to pair the failing company with a profitable business in order to reap the tax benefits of the NOLs. Steel Partners has actively worked with Selectica to calculate and monitor the Company's NOLs since the time of its original investment.

By early 2008, Steel Partners was advocating a quick sale of Selectica's assets, leaving a NOL shell that could be merged with a profitable operating company in order to shelter the profits of the operating company. In October 2008, Steel Partners informed members of Selectica's Board that it planned to increase its ownership position to 14.9% just below the 15% trigger of the 2003 Rights Plan, which it later did. Jack Howard, President of Steel Partners, lobbied for a Board seat twice in 2008, citing his experience dealing with NOLs, but was rebuffed.

Selectica Investigates Its NOLs

In 2006, at the urging of Steel Partners, Selectica directed Alan Chinn, its outside tax adviser, to perform a high-level analysis into whether its NOLs were subject to any limitations under § 382 of the Internal Revenue Code. Chinn concluded that five prior changes in ownership had caused the forfeiture of approximately $24.6 million in NOLs. Selectica provided the results of this study to Steel Partners, although not to any other Selectica shareholder.

In March 2007, again at Steel Partner's recommendation, Selectica retained a second accountant who specialized in NOL calculations, John Brogan of Burr Pilger

& Mayer, LLP, to analyze the Company's NOLs more carefully and report on Chinn's § 382 analysis. Brogan had previously analyzed the NOLs at other Steel Partners ventures. Brogan ultimately determined that Chinn's conclusions were erroneous.

The Company engaged Brogan to perform additional work on the topic of NOLs in June 2007. One of Steel Partners's employees, Avi Goodman, worked closely with Brogan on the matter, although Brogan was working for and being paid by Selectica and received no compensation from Steel Partners. Brogan's draft letter opinion, concluding that the Company had not undergone an "ownership change" for § 382 purposes since 1999, was shared with Steel Partners, although again not with any other outside investors.

In the fall of 2007, Brogan proposed a third, more detailed, § 382 study, which Selectica's then-CEO, Robert Jurkowski, opposed. In February 2008, the Board voted against spending $40,000–$50,000 to fund this § 382 study. By July, however, the Board asked Brogan to update his study. Brogan delivered the draft opinion that, as of March 31, 2008, the Company had approximately $165 million in NOLs. Brogan was later asked to advise the Board in the fall of 2008 on the updated status of its NOLs when the Board moved to amend its Rights Plan.

Lloyd Sems Elected Director

In April 2008, the Board began interviewing candidates for an open board seat, giving preference to the Company's large stockholders. Selectica investor Lloyd Sems had previously expressed interest in joining the Board and had sought support from certain shareholders, including Steel Partners, through Howard, and Lloyd Miller, another large Selectica shareholder not affiliated with Steel Partners. Both Miller and Howard wrote to the Board in support of Sems's appointment, although Sems was already favored by the Board by that time. In June 2008, Sems was appointed to the Board.

As large shareholders, Sems, Howard, and Miller had periodically discussed Selectica as early as October 2007. At that time, Sems had e-mailed Howard, stating, "I wanted to get your opinion of how or if you would like me to proceed with [Selectica]." Howard replied, "Lloyd [Miller] said he would call you about [Selectica]." Both before and after his appointment to the Board, Sems discussed with Howard and Miller a number of the proposals that Sems ultimately advocated as a director, including that Selectica should buy back its stock, that Selectica should consider selling its businesses, that the NOLs were important and should be preserved through the adoption of a Rights Plan with a 5% trigger, and that Jurkowski should be removed as CEO.

Selectica Restructures and Explores Alternatives

In early July 2008, after determining that the Company needed to change course, the Board terminated Jurkowski as CEO and eliminated several management positions in the sales configuration business. Later that month, prompted by the receipt of five unsolicited acquisition offers over the span of a few weeks, the Board announced that it was in the process of selecting an investment banker (ultimately,

Jim Reilly of Needham & Company) to evaluate strategic alternatives for the Company and to assist with a process that ultimately might result in the Company's sale. In view of the potential sale, the Board decided to forgo the expense of replacing Jurkowski and, instead, asked Zawatski and Thanos jointly to assume the title of Co–Chair and to perform operational oversight roles on an interim basis.

The Needham Process

Needham has actively carried out its task of evaluating Selectica's strategic options since its selection by the Board. Needham first discussed with the Board the various strategic choices that the Company could take. These included a merger of equals with a public company, a reverse IPO or other going-private transaction, the sale of certain assets, and the use of cash to acquire another company, as well as stock repurchases or the issuance of dividends if Selectica decided to continue as an independent public company in the absence of sufficient market interest for an acquisition.

In October 2008, Needham prepared an Executive Summary of the assets and operations of Selectica and subsequently reached out to potential buyers, keeping in touch with various interested parties throughout the remainder of the year and into the first part of 2009. By February 2009, at least half a dozen parties had come forward with letters of intent and were in the process of meeting with Selectica management and conducting due diligence in the Company, with Needham evaluating their various proposals for the purchase of all or part of Selectica's operations. As of April 2009, Selectica, through Needham, had signed a letter of intent and entered into exclusive negotiations with a potential buyer.

Trilogy's Offers Rejected

On July 15, 2008, Trilogy's President, Joseph Liemandt, called Zawatski to inquire generally about the possibility of an acquisition of Selectica by Trilogy. On July 29, Trilogy Chief Financial Officer Sean Fallon, Trilogy Director of Finance Andrew Price, and Versata Chief Executive Officer Randy Jacops participated in a conference call with Selectica Co–Chairs Zawatski and Thanos on the same topic. During the call, Thanos inquired as to how Trilogy would calculate a value for the Company's NOLs. Fallon replied that Trilogy, "really [did not] pursue them with as much vigor as other[s] might since that is not our core strategy."

The following evening, Fallon contacted Zawatski and outlined two proposals for Trilogy to acquire Selectica's business: (1) Trilogy's purchase of all of the assets of Selectica's sales configuration business in exchange for the cancellation of the $7.1 million in debt Selectica still owed under the October 2007 settlement with Trilogy; or (2) Trilogy's purchase of Selectica's entire operations for the cancellation of the debt plus an additional $6 million in cash. Fallon subsequently followed up with an email reiterating both proposals and suggesting that either proposal would allow Selectica to still make use of its NOLs through the later sale of its corporate entity.

Shortly thereafter, the Board rejected both proposals, made no counterproposal, and there were no follow-up discussions. On October 9, 2008, Trilogy made a second bid to acquire all of the Selectica's assets for $10 million in cash plus the cancellation of the debt, which the Board also rejected. Although Trilogy was invited to participate in the sale process being overseen by Needham, Trilogy was apparently unwilling to sign a non-disclosure agreement, which was a prerequisite for participation. Around this same time, Trilogy had begun making open-market purchases for Selectica stock, although the Board apparently was not aware of this fact at the time.

Trilogy Buys Selectica Stock

On the evening of November 10, Fallon contacted Zawatski and informed her that Trilogy had purchased more than 5% of Selectica's outstanding stock and would be filing a Schedule 13D shortly, which it did on November 13. On a subsequent call with Zawatski and Reilly, Fallon explained that Trilogy had begun buying because it believed that "the company should work quickly to preserve whatever share-holder value remained and that we were interested in seeing this process that they announced with Needham, that we were interested in seeing that accelerate. . . ." Within four days of its 13D filing, Trilogy had acquired more than 320,000 additional shares, representing an additional 1% of the Company's outstanding shares.

NOL Poison Pill Adopted

In the wake of Trilogy's decision to begin acquiring Selectica shares, the Board took actions to gauge the impact of these acquisitions, if any, on the Company's NOLs, and to determine whether anything needed to be done to mitigate their effects. Sems immediately asked Brogan to revise his § 382 analysis — which had not been formally updated since July — to take into account the recent purchases. The revised analysis was delivered to Sems and the Company's new CFO, Richard Heaps, on November 15. It showed that the cumulative acquisition of stock by shareholders over the past three years stood at 40%, which was roughly unchanged from the previous calculation, due to some double counting that occurred in the July analysis.

The Board met on November 16 to discuss the situation and to consider amending Selectica's Shareholder Rights Plan, which had been in place since February 2003. As with many Rights Plans employed as protection devices against hostile takeovers, Selectica's Rights Plan had a 15% trigger. The Board considered an amendment that would reduce that threshold trigger to 4.99% in order to prevent additional 5% owners from emerging and potentially causing a change-in-control event, thereby devaluing Selectica's NOLs. Also present at the meeting were Heaps, Brogan, and Reilly, along with Delaware counsel.

Heaps gave an overview of the Company's existing Shareholder Rights Plan and reviewed the stock price activity since Trilogy had filed its Schedule 13D, noting that shares totaling approximately 2.3% of the Company had changed hands in the two days following the filing. Brogan reviewed the § 382 ownership analysis that his firm had undertaken on behalf of the Company, noting that additional acquisitions of roughly 10% of the float by new or existing 5% holders would "result in a permanent limitation on use of the Company's net operating loss carryforwards and that, once an ownership change occurred, there would be no way to cure the use limitation on the net operating loss carryforwards." He further advised the Board that "net operating loss carryforwards were a significant asset" and that he generally advises companies to consider steps to protect their NOLs when they experience a 30% or greater change in beneficial ownership. Lastly, Brogan noted that, while he believed that the cumulative ownership change calculations would decline significantly over the next twelve months, "it would decline only modestly, if at all, over the next three to four months," meaning that "the Company would continue to be at risk of an ownership change over the near term."

Reilly discussed the Company's strategic alternatives and noted that Steel Partners and other parties had expressed interest in pursuing a transaction that would realize the value of Selectica's NOLs. He also reviewed potential transaction structures in which the Company might be able to utilize its NOLs. Responding to questions from the Board, Reilly noted that "it is difficult to value the Company's net operating loss carryforwards with greater precision, because their value depends, among other things, on the ability of the Company to generate profits." He confirmed that "existing stockholders may realize significant potential value" from the utilization of the Company's NOLs, which would be "significantly impaired" if a § 382 ownership change occurred.

At the request of the Board, Delaware counsel reviewed the Delaware law standards that apply for adopting and implementing measures that have an anti-takeover effect. The Board then discussed amending the existing Shareholder Rights Plan, and the possible terms of such an amendment. These included: the pros and cons of providing a cushion for preexisting 5% holders, the appropriate effective date of the new Shareholder Rights Plan, whether the Board should have authority to exclude purchases by specific stockholders from triggering the Rights Plan, and whether a review process should be implemented to determine periodically whether the Rights Plan should remain in effect.

The Board then unanimously passed a resolution amending Selectica's Shareholder Rights Plan, by decreasing the beneficial ownership trigger from 15% to 4.99%, while grandfathering in existing 5% shareholders and permitting them to acquire up to an additional 0.5% (subject to the original 15% cap) without triggering the NOL Poison Pill.

The Board resolution also established an Independent Director Evaluation Committee (the "Committee") as a standing committee of the Board to review periodically the rights agreement at the behest of the Board and to "determine whether the Rights [Plan] continues to be in the best interest of the Corporation and its stockholders." The Committee was also directed to review "the appropriate trigger percentage" of the Rights Plan based on corporate and shareholder developments, any broader developments relating to rights plans generally — including academic studies of rights plans and contests for corporate control — and any other factors it deems relevant. The Board set April 30, 2009, as the first date that the Committee should report its findings.

Trilogy Triggers NOL Poison Pill

The Board publicly announced the amendment of Selectica's Rights Plan on Monday, November 17. Early the following morning, Fallon e-mailed Trilogy's broker, saying "[W]e need to stop buying SLTC. They announced a new pill and we need to understand it." Fallon also sent Liemandt a copy of Selectica's 8–K containing the amended language of the NOL Poison Pill. Trilogy immediately sought legal advice about the NOL Poison Pill. The following morning, Liemandt e-mailed Price, with a copy to Fallon, asking, "What percentage of [Selectica] would we need to buy to ruin the tax attributes that [S]teel [P]artners is looking for?"[11] They concluded that they would need to acquire 23% to trigger a change-in-control event.

Later that week, Trilogy sent Selectica a letter asserting that a Selectica contract with Sun Microsystems constituted a breach of the October 2007 settlement and seeking an immediate meeting with Selectica purportedly to discuss the breach, even though members of Trilogy's management had been on notice of the contract as early as July. Fallon, Liemandt, and Jacops from Trilogy, along with Zawatski, Thanos, and Heaps from Selectica met on December 17. The parties' discussions at this meeting are protected by a confidentiality agreement that had been circulated in advance. However, Selectica contends that "based solely on statements and conduct outside that meeting, it is evident that Trilogy threatened to trigger the NOL Poison Pill deliberately unless Selectica agreed to Trilogy's renewed efforts to extract money from the Company."

On December 18, Trilogy purchased an additional 30,000 Selectica shares, and Trilogy management verified with Liemandt his intention to proceed with "buying through" the NOL Poison Pill. The following morning, Trilogy purchased an additional 124,061 shares of Selectica, bringing its ownership share to 6.7% and thereby becoming an "Acquiring Person" under the NOL Poison Pill. Liemandt testified that the rationale behind triggering the pill was to "bring accountability" to the Board and "expose" what Liemandt characterized as "illegal behavior" by the Board in adopting a pill with such a low trigger. Fallon asserted that the reason for triggering the NOL Poison Pill was to "bring some clarity and urgency" to their discussions with Selectica about the two parties' somewhat complicated relationship by "setting a time frame that might help accelerate discussions" on the direction of the business.

Fallon placed a telephone call to Zawatski on December 19 to advise her that Trilogy had bought through the NOL Poison Pill. During a return call by Zawatski later that evening, Fallon indicated that Trilogy felt, based on the conversations from December 17, that Selectica no longer wanted Trilogy as a shareholder or creditor. He then proposed that Selectica repurchase Trilogy's shares, accelerate the payment of its debt, terminate its license with Sun, and make a payment to Trilogy of $5 million "for settlement of basically all outstanding issues between our companies." Zawatski recalled that Fallon told her that Trilogy had triggered the pill "to get our attention and create a sense of urgency;" that, since the Board would have ten days to determine how to react to the pill trigger, "it would force the board to make a decision."

Board Considers Options and Requests a Standstill

The Selectica Board had a telephonic meeting on Saturday, December 20, to discuss Trilogy's demands and an appropriate response. The Board discussed "the desirability of taking steps to ensure the validity of the Shareholder Rights Plan," and ultimately passed a resolution authorizing the filing of this lawsuit, which occurred the following day. On December 22, Trilogy filed an amended Schedule 13D disclosing its ownership percentage and again the Selectica Board met telephonically to discuss the litigation. It eventually agreed to have a representative contact Trilogy to seek a standstill on any additional open market purchases while the Board used the ten-day clock under the NOL Poison Pill to determine whether to consider Trilogy's purchases "exempt" under the Rights Plan, and if not, how Selectica would go about implementing the pill.

The amended Rights Plan allowed the Board to declare Trilogy an "Exempt Person" during the ten-day period following the trigger, if the Board determined that Trilogy would not "jeopardize or endanger the availability to the Company of the NOLs. . . ." The Board could also decide during this window to exchange the rights (other than those held by Trilogy) for shares of common stock. If the Board did nothing, then after ten days the rights would "flip in" automatically, becoming exercisable for $36 worth of newly-issued common stock at a price of $18 per right.

The Board met again by telephone the following day, December 23, to discuss the progress of the litigation and to consider the potential impact of the various alternatives under the NOL Poison Pill. The Board agreed to meet in person the following Monday, December 29, along with the Company's financial, legal, and accounting advisors, to evaluate further the available options. The Board also voted to reduce the number of authorized directors from seven to five.

On Wednesday, December 24, the Board met once again by telephone upon learning that the Company's counsel had not succeeded in convincing Trilogy to agree to a standstill. The Board resolved that Zawatski should call Fallon to determine whether Trilogy was willing "to negotiate a standstill agreement that might make triggering the remedies available under the Shareholder Rights Plan, as amended, unnecessary at this time." Zawatski spoke with Fallon on the morning of December 26. Fallon stated that Trilogy did not want to agree to a standstill, that relief from the NOL Poison Pill was not Trilogy's goal, and that Trilogy expected that the NOL Poison Pill would apply to it. Fallon reiterated that the ten-day window would help "speed [the] course" towards a resolution of their claims.

The Board and its advisors met again on December 29. Thanos provided an update on recent developments at the Company, including financial results, management changes, and the Needham Process, as well as an overview of the make-up of the Company's shareholder base. Reilly then provided a more detailed report on the status of the Needham Process. Thereafter, Brogan presented his firm's updated analysis of Selectica's NOLs, which found that the Company had at least $160 million in NOLs and that there had been a roughly 40% ownership change by 5% holders over the three-year testing period. Since those were not expected to "roll off" in the near term, there was "a significant risk of a § 382 ownership change."

Brogan subsequently discussed the possible consequences of the two principal mechanisms for implementing the triggered NOL Poison Pill to the change-in-control analysis. He stated that employing a share exchange would not likely have a materially negative impact on the § 382 analysis. He expressed concern, however, about the uncertain effect of a flip-in pill on subsequent ownership levels (specifically, the possibility that a flip-in pill would, itself, trigger a § 382 ownership change). Reilly once again addressed the Board to explain the ways he believed the NOLs would be valuable to the Company in its ongoing exploration of strategic alternatives, and reiterated his opinion that an ownership change would "reduce the value of the Company."

The Board also discussed Trilogy's settlement demands. It found them "highly unreasonable" and "lack[ing] any reasonable basis in fact," and that "it [was] not in the best interests of the Company and its stockholders to accept Trilogy/Versata's settlement demands relating to entirely separate intellectual property disputes as a precondition to negotiating a standstill agreement to resolve this dispute." The Board discussed Trilogy's actions at some length, ultimately concluding that they "were very harmful to the Company in a number of respects," and that "implementing the exchange was reasonable in relation to the threat imposed by Trilogy." In particular, that was because (1) the NOLs were seen as "an important corporate asset that could significantly enhance stockholder value," and (2) Trilogy had intentionally triggered the NOL Poison Pill, publicly suggested it might purchase additional stock, and had refused to negotiate a standstill agreement, even though an additional 10% acquisition by a 5% shareholder would likely trigger an ownership change under § 382.

The Board then authorized Delaware counsel to contact Trilogy in writing, one final time, to seek a standstill agreement. It also passed resolutions delegating the full power of the Board to the Committee to determine whether or not to treat Trilogy or its acquisition as "exempt," and nominating Alan Howe as a new member of the Board. On the evening of December 29, Selectica's Delaware counsel e-mailed Trilogy's trial counsel at the Board's instruction, seeking a standstill agreement "so that the Board could consider either declaring them an 'Exempt Person' under the Rights Plan . . . or alternatively, settle the litigation altogether in exchange for a long term agreement relating to your clients' ownership of additional shares." The following afternoon, Trilogy's counsel responded that Trilogy was not willing to agree to the proposed standstill.

Two days later, on December 31, the Board met telephonically and was informed of Trilogy's latest rejection of a standstill agreement. The Board discussed its options with its legal advisors and ultimately concluded that the NOL Poison Pill should go into effect and that an exchange was the best alternative and should be implemented as soon as possible in order to protect the NOLs, even at the risk of disrupting common stock trading. The Board directed advisers to prepare a technical amendment to the NOL Poison Pill to clarify the time at which the exchange would become effective.

Board Adopts Reloaded Pill and Dilutes Trilogy Holdings

On January 2, the Board met telephonically once more, reiterating its delegation of authority to the Committee to make recommendations regarding the implementation of the NOL Poison Pill. The Board also passed a resolution expressly confirming that the Board's delegation of authority to the Committee included the power to effect an exchange of the rights under the NOL Poison Pill and to declare a new dividend of rights under an amended Rights Plan (the "Reloaded NOL Poison Pill"). The Board then adjourned and the Committee — comprised of Sems and Arnold — met with legal and financial advisors, who confirmed that there had been no new agreement with representatives from Trilogy, reiterated that the NOLs remained "a valuable corporate asset of the Company in connection with the Company's ongoing exploration of strategic alternatives," and advised the Committee members of their fiduciary obligations under Delaware law.

Reilly presented information to the Committee about the current takeover environment and the use of Rights Plans (specifically, the types of pills commonly employed and their triggering thresholds), and reviewed the Company's then-current anti-takeover defenses compared with those of other public companies. Reilly stated that "a so-called NOL rights plan with a 4.99% trigger threshold is designed to help protect against stock accumulations that would trigger an 'ownership change,'" and that "implementing appropriate protections of the Company's net operating loss carryforwards was especially important at present," given Trilogy's recent share acquisitions superimposed on the Company's existing § 382 ownership levels. Finally, Reilly reviewed the proposed terms and conditions of the Reloaded NOL Poison Pill, discussed the methodology for determining the exercise price of the new rights, and made recommendations. The Committee sought and obtained reconfirmed assurances by its financial and legal advisors that the NOLs were a valuable corporate asset and that they remained at a significant risk of being impaired.

The Committee concluded that Trilogy should not be deemed an "Exempt Person," that its purchase of additional shares should not be deemed an "Exempt Transaction," that an exchange of rights for common stock (the "Exchange") should occur, and that a new rights dividend on substantially similar terms should be adopted. The Committee passed resolutions implementing those conclusions, thereby adopting the Reloaded NOL Poison Pill and instituting the Exchange.

The Exchange doubled the number of shares of Selectica common stock owned by each shareholder of record, other than Trilogy or Versata, thereby reducing their beneficial holdings from 6.7% to 3.3%. The implementation of the Exchange led to a freeze in the trading of Selectica stock from January 5, 2009 until February 4, 2009, with the stock price frozen at $0.69. The Reloaded NOL Poison Pill will expire on January 2, 2012, unless the expiration date is advanced or extended, or unless these rights are exchanged or redeemed by the Board some time before.

ANALYSIS
Unocal *Standard Applies*

In *Unocal*, this Court recognized that "our corporate law is not static. It must grow and develop in response to, indeed in anticipation of, evolving concepts and needs."[23] The Court of Chancery concluded that the protection of company NOLs may be an appropriate corporate policy that merits a defensive response when they are threatened. We agree.

The *Unocal* two part test is useful as a judicial analytical tool because of the flexibility of its application in a variety of fact scenarios. Delaware courts have approved the adoption of a Shareholder Rights Plan as an antitakeover device, and have applied the *Unocal* test to analyze a board's response to an actual or potential hostile takeover threat. Any NOL poison pill's principal intent, however, is to prevent the inadvertent forfeiture of potentially valuable assets, not to protect against hostile takeover attempts. Even so, any Shareholder Rights Plan, by its nature, operates as an antitakeover device. Consequently, notwithstanding its primary purpose, a NOL poison pill must also be analyzed under *Unocal* because of its effect and its direct implications for hostile takeovers.

Threat Reasonably Identified

The first part of *Unocal* review requires a board to show that it had reasonable grounds for concluding that a threat to the corporate enterprise existed. The Selectica Board concluded that the NOLs were an asset worth preserving and that their protection was an important corporate objective. Trilogy contends that the Board failed to demonstrate that it conducted a reasonable investigation before determining that the NOLs were an asset worth protecting. We disagree.

The record reflects that the Selectica Board met for more than two and a half hours on November 16. The Court of Chancery heard testimony from all four directors and from Brogan, Reilly, and Heaps, who also attended that meeting and advised the Board. The record shows that the Board first analyzed the NOLs in September 2006, and sought updated § 382 analyses from Brogan in March 2007, June 2007, and July 2008. At the November 16 meeting, Brogan advised the Board that the NOLs were a "significant asset" based on his recently updated calculations of the NOLs' magnitude. Reilly, an investment banker, similarly advised the Board that the NOLs were worth protecting given the possibility of a sale of Selectica or its assets. Accordingly, the record supports the Court of Chancery's factual finding that the Board acted in good faith reliance on the advice of experts16 in concluding that "the NOLs were an asset worth protecting and thus, that their preservation was an important corporate objective."

The record also supports the reasonableness of the Board's decision to act promptly by reducing the trigger on Selectica's Rights Plan from 15% to 4.99%. At the November 16 meeting, Brogan advised the Board that the change-of-ownership calculation under § 382 stood at approximately 40%. Trilogy's ownership had climbed to over 5% in just over a month, and Trilogy intended to continue buying

---

[23] [n.12] Unocal Corp. v. Mesa Petroleum Co., 493 A.2d 946, 957 (Del. 1985).

more stock. There was nothing to stop others from acquiring stock up to the 15% trigger in the Company's existing Rights Plan. Once the § 382 limitation was tripped, the Board was advised it could not be undone.

At the November 16 meeting, the Board voted to amend Selectica's existing Rights Plan to protect the NOLs against a potential § 382 "change of ownership." It reduced the trigger of its Shareholders Rights Plan from 15% to 4.99% and provided that existing shareholders who held in excess of 4.99% would be subject to dilutive consequences if they increased their holdings by 0.5%. The Board also created the Review Committee (Arnold and Sems) with a mandate to conduct a periodic review of the continuing appropriateness of the NOL Poison Pill.

The Court of Chancery found the record "replete with evidence" that, based upon the expert advice it received, the Board was reasonable in concluding that Selectica's NOLs were worth preserving and that Trilogy's actions presented a serious threat of their impairment. The Court of Chancery explained those findings, as follows:

> The threat posed by Trilogy was reasonably viewed as qualitatively different from the normal corporate control dispute that leads to the adoption of a shareholder rights plan. In this instance, Trilogy, a competitor with a contentious history, recognized that harm would befall its rival if it purchased sufficient shares of Selectica stock, and Trilogy proceeded to act accordingly. It was reasonable for the Board to respond, and the timing of Trilogy's campaign required the Board to act promptly. Moreover, the 4.99% threshold for the NOL Poison Pill was driven by our tax laws and regulations; the threshold, low as it is, was measured by reference to an external standard, one created neither by the Board nor by the Court [of Chancery]. Within this context, it is not for the Court [of Chancery] to second-guess the Board's efforts to protect Selectica's NOLs.

Those findings are not clearly erroneous. They are supported by the record and the result of a logical deductive reasoning process. Accordingly, we hold that the Selectica directors satisfied the first part of the *Unocal* test by showing "that they had reasonable grounds for believing that a danger to corporate policy and effectiveness existed because of another person's stock ownership."[24]

Selectica Defenses Not Preclusive

The second part of the *Unocal* test requires an initial evaluation of whether a board's defensive response to the threat was preclusive or coercive and, if neither, whether the response was "reasonable in relation to the threat" identified. Under *Unitrin*, a defensive measure is disproportionate and unreasonable *per se* if it is draconian by being either coercive or preclusive. A coercive response is one that is "aimed at 'cramming down' on its shareholders a management-sponsored alternative."[25]

---

[24] [n.19] Unocal Corp. v. Mesa Petroleum Co., 493 A.2d at 955 (citing Cheff v. Mathes, 199 A.2d at 554–55).

[25] [n.22] Unitrin, Inc. v. Am. Gen. Corp., 651 A.2d at 1387 (citing Paramount Communications, Inc. v.

A defensive measure is preclusive where it "makes a bidder's ability to wage a successful proxy contest and gain control either 'mathematically impossible' or 'realistically unattainable.' "[26] A successful proxy contest that is mathematically impossible is, *ipso facto*, realistically unattainable. Because the "mathematically impossible" formulation in *Unitrin* is subsumed within the category of preclusivity described as "realistically unattainable," there is, analytically speaking, only one test of preclusivity: "realistically unattainable."

Trilogy claims that a Rights Plan with a 4.99% trigger renders the possibility of an effective proxy contest realistically unattainable. In support of that position, Trilogy argues that, because a proxy contest can only be successful where the challenger has sufficient credibility, the 4.99% pill trigger prevents a potential dissident from signaling its financial commitment to the company so as to establish such credibility. In addition, Professor Ferrell, Trilogy's expert witness, testified that the 5% cap on ownership exacerbates the free rider problem already experienced by investors considering fielding an insurgent slate of directors, and makes initiating a proxy fight an economically unattractive proposition.

This Court first examined the validity of a Shareholder Rights Plan in *Moran v. Household International, Inc.* In *Moran* the Rights Plan at issue had a 20% trigger. We recognized that, while a Rights Plan "does deter the formation of proxy efforts of a certain magnitude, it does not limit the voting power of individual shares." In *Moran*, we concluded that the assertion that a Rights Plan would frustrate proxy fights was "highly conjectural" and pointed to "recent corporate takeover battles in which insurgents holding less than 10% stock ownership were able to secure corporate control through a proxy contest or the threat of one."

The 5% trigger that is necessary for a NOL poison pill to serve its primary objective imposes a lower threshold than the Rights Plan thresholds that have traditionally been adopted and upheld as acceptable anti-takeover defenses by Delaware courts. Selectica submits that the distinguishing feature of the NOL Poison Pill and Reloaded NOL Poison Pill — the 5% trigger — is not enough to differentiate them from other Rights Plans previously upheld by Delaware courts, and that there is no evidence that a challenger starting below 5% could not realistically hope to prevail in a proxy contest at Selectica. In support of those arguments Selectica presented expert testimony from Professor John C. Coates IV and Peter C. Harkins.

Professor Coates identified more than fifty publicly held companies that have implemented NOL poison pills with triggers at roughly 5%, including several large, well-known corporations, some among the Fortune 1000. Professor Coates noted that 5% Rights Plans are customarily adopted where issuers have "ownership controlled" assets, such as the NOLs at issue in this case. Professor Coates also testified that Selectica's 5% Rights Plan trigger was narrowly tailored to protect the NOLs because the relevant tax law, § 382, measures ownership changes based on shareholders who own 5% or more of the outstanding stock.

Time, Inc., 571 A.2d at 1154–1155 (Del. 1990)). There are no allegations contended that the NOL Poison Pill, the Exchange, and the Reloaded NOL Poison Pill are coercive.

26 [n.23] Carmody v. Toll Bros., Inc., 723 A.2d 1180, 1195 (Del. Ch. 1998) (quoting Unitrin, Inc. v. Am. Gen. Corp., 651 A.2d at 1389).

Moreover, and as the Court of Chancery noted, shareholder advisory firm RiskMetrics Group now supports Rights Plans with a trigger below 5% on a case-by-case basis if adopted for the stated purpose of preserving a company's net operating losses. The factors RiskMetrics will consider in determining whether to support a management proposal to adopt a NOL poison pill are the pill's trigger, the value of the NOLs, the term of the pill, and any corresponding shareholder protection mechanisms in place, such as a sunset provision causing the pill to expire upon exhaustion or expiration of the NOLs.

Selectica expert witness Harkins of the D.F. King & Co. proxy solicitation firm analyzed proxy contests over the three-year period ending December 31, 2008. He found that of the fifteen proxy contests that occurred in micro-cap companies where the challenger controlled less than 5.49% of the outstanding shares, the challenger successfully obtained board seats in ten contests, five of which involved companies with classified boards. Harkins opined that Selectica's unique shareholder profile would considerably reduce the costs associated with a proxy fight, since seven shareholders controlled 55% of Selectica's shares, and twenty-two shareholders controlled 62%. Harkins testified that "if you have a compelling platform, which is critical, it would be easy from a logistical perspective; and from a cost perspective, it would be *de minimis* expense to communicate with those investors, among others." Harkins noted that to win a proxy contest at Selectica, one would need to gain only the support of owners of 43.2% plus one share.

The Court of Chancery concluded that the NOL Poison Pill and Reloaded NOL Poison Pill were not preclusive. For a measure to be preclusive, it must render a successful proxy contest realistically unattainable given the specific factual context. The record supports the Court of Chancery's factual determination and legal conclusion that Selectica's NOL Poison Pill and Reloaded NOL Poison Pill do not meet that preclusivity standard.

Our observation in *Unitrin* is also applicable here: "[I]t is hard to imagine a company more readily susceptible to a proxy contest concerning a pure issue of dollars." The key variable in a proxy contest would be the merit of the bidder's proposal and not the magnitude of its stockholdings. The record reflects that Selectica's adoption of a 4.99% trigger for its Rights Plan would not preclude a hostile bidder's ability to marshal enough shareholder votes to win a proxy contest.

Trilogy argues that, even if a 4.99% shareholder could realistically win a proxy contest "the preclusiveness question focuses on whether a challenger could realistically attain sufficient board control to remove the pill." Here, Trilogy contends, Selectica's charter-based classified board effectively forecloses a bid conditioned upon a redemption of the NOL Poison Pill, because it requires a proxy challenger to launch and complete two successful proxy contests in order to change control. Therefore, Trilogy argues that even if a less than 5% shareholder could win a proxy contest, Selectica's Rights Plan with a 4.99% trigger in combination with Selectica's charter-based classified board, makes a successful proxy contest for control of the board "realistically unattainable."

Trilogy's preclusivity argument conflates two distinct questions: first, is a successful proxy contest realistically attainable; and second, will a successful proxy contest result in gaining control of the board at the next election? Trilogy argues that unless both questions can be answered affirmatively, a Rights Plan and a classified board, viewed collectively, are preclusive. If that preclusivity argument is correct, then it would apply whenever a corporation has both a classified board and a Rights Plan, irrespective whether the trigger is 4.99%, 20%, or anywhere in between those thresholds.

Classified boards are authorized by statute and are adopted for a variety of business purposes. Any classified board also operates as an antitakeover defense by preventing an insurgent from obtaining control of the board in one election. More than a decade ago, in *Carmody*, the Court of Chancery noted "because only one third of a classified board would stand for election each year, a classified board would *delay — but not prevent — a hostile acquiror from obtaining control of the board*, since a determined acquiror could wage a proxy contest and obtain control of two thirds of the target board over a two year period, as opposed to seizing control in a single election."[27] The fact that a combination of defensive measures makes it more difficult for an acquirer to obtain control of a board does not make such measures realistically unattainable, i.e., preclusive.

In *Moran*, we rejected the contention "that the Rights Plan strips stockholders of their rights to receive tender offers, and that the Rights Plan fundamentally restricts proxy contests." We explained that "the Rights Plan will not have a severe impact upon proxy contests and it will not *preclude* all hostile acquisitions of Household." In this case, we hold that the combination of a classified board and a Rights Plan do not constitute a preclusive defense.

Range of Reasonableness

If a defensive measure is neither coercive nor preclusive, the *Unocal* proportionality test "requires the focus of enhanced judicial scrutiny to shift to 'the range of reasonableness.' "[28] Where all of the defenses "are inextricably related, the principles of *Unocal* require that such actions be scrutinized collectively as a unitary response to the perceived threat."[29] Trilogy asserts that the NOL Poison Pill, the Exchange, and the Reloaded NOL Poison Pill were not a reasonable collective response to the threat of the impairment of Selectica's NOLs.

The critical facts do not support that assertion. On November 20, within days of learning of the NOL Poison Pill, Trilogy sent Selectica a letter, demanding a conference to discuss an alleged breach of a patent settlement agreement between the parties. The parties met on December 17, and the following day, Trilogy resumed its purchases of Selectica stock.

Fallon testified that he and Liemandt had a discussion wherein Fallon advised Liemandt that Trilogy had purchased additional shares, but not enough to trigger the NOL Poison Pill. Fallon then asked if Liemandt really wanted to trigger the pill,

---

[27] [n.37] Carmody v. Toll Bros., Inc., 723 A.2d at 1186 n. 17 (emphasis added).

[28] [n.42] Unitrin, Inc. v. Am. Gen. Corp., 651 A.2d at 1388 (quoting Paramount Communications, Inc. v. QVC Network, Inc., 637 A.2d 34, 45–46 (Del. 1994)).

[29] [n.43] Unitrin, Inc. v. Am. Gen. Corp., 651 A.2d at 1387 (citing Gilbert v. El Paso Co., 575 A.2d 1131, 1145 (Del. 1990)).

and Liemandt expressly directed Fallon to proceed. On December 19, 2008, Trilogy bought a sufficient number of shares to become an "Acquiring Person" under the NOL Poison Pill. According to Fallon, this was done to " 'bring some clarity and urgency' to Trilogy's discussions with Selectica about the two parties' somewhat complicated relationship by 'setting a time frame that might help accelerate discussions' on the direction of the business."

Fallon described Trilogy's relationship with Selectica as a "three-legged stool," referring to Trilogy's status as a competitor, a creditor, and a stockholder of Selectica. The two companies had settled prior patent disputes in 2007 under terms that included a cross-license of intellectual property and quarterly payments from Selectica to Trilogy based on Selectica's revenues from certain products. Selectica argues that Trilogy took the unprecedented step of deliberately triggering the NOL Poison Pill — exposing its equity investment of under $2 million to dilution — primarily to extract substantially more value for the other two "legs" of the stool.

Trilogy's deliberate trigger started a ten business day clock under the terms of the NOL Poison Pill. If the Board took no action during that time, then the rights (other than those belonging to Trilogy) would "flip-in" and become exercisable for deeply discounted common stock. Alternatively, the Board had the power to exchange the rights (other than those belonging to Trilogy) for newly-issued common stock, or to grant Trilogy an exemption. Three times in the two weeks following the triggering, Selectica offered Trilogy an exemption in exchange for an agreement to stand still and to withdraw its threat to impair the value and usability of Selectica's NOLs. Three times Trilogy refused and insisted instead that Selectica repurchase its stock, terminate a license agreement with an important client, sign over intellectual property, and pay Trilogy millions of dollars. After three failed attempts to negotiate with Trilogy, it was reasonable for the Board to determine that they had no other option than to implement the NOL Poison Pill.

The Exchange employed by the Board was a more proportionate response than the "flip-in" mechanism traditionally envisioned for a Rights Plan. Because the Board opted to use the Exchange instead of the traditional "flip-in" mechanism, Trilogy experienced less dilution of its position than a Rights Plan is traditionally designed to achieve.

The implementation of the Reloaded NOL Poison Pill was also a reasonable response. The Reloaded NOL Poison Pill was considered a necessary defensive measure because, although the NOL Poison Pill and the Exchange effectively thwarted Trilogy's immediate threat to Selectica's NOLs, they did not eliminate the general threat of a § 382 change-in-control. Following implementation of the Exchange, Selectica still had a roughly 40% ownership change for § 382 purposes and there was no longer a Rights Plan in place to discourage additional acquisitions by 5% holders. Selectica argues that the decision to adopt the Reloaded NOL Poison Pill was reasonable under those circumstances. We agree.

The record indicates that the Board was presented with expert advice that supported its ultimate findings that the NOLs were a corporate asset worth protecting, that the NOLs were at risk as a result of Trilogy's actions, and that the steps that the Board ultimately took were reasonable in relation to that threat. Outside experts were present and advised the Board on these matters at both the

November 16 meeting at which the NOL Poison Pill was adopted and at the Board's December 29 meeting. The Committee also heard from expert advisers a third time at the January 2 meeting prior to instituting the Exchange and adopting the Reloaded NOL Poison Pill.

Under part two of the *Unocal* test, the Court of Chancery found that the combination of the NOL Poison Pill, the Exchange, and the Reloaded NOL Poison Pill was a proportionate response to the threatened loss of Selectica's NOLs. Those findings are not clearly erroneous.45 They are supported by the record and the result of a logical deductive reasoning process. Accordingly, we hold that the Selectica directors satisfied the second part of the *Unocal* test by showing that their defensive response was proportionate by being "reasonable in relation to the threat" identified.

Context Determines Reasonableness

Under a *Unocal* analysis, the reasonableness of a board's response is determined in relation to the "specific threat," at the time it was identified. Thus, it is the specific nature of the threat that "sets the parameters for the range of permissible defensive tactics" at any given time. The record demonstrates that a longtime competitor sought to increase the percentage of its stock ownership, not for the purpose of conducting a hostile takeover but, to intentionally impair corporate assets, or else coerce Selectica into meeting certain business demands under the threat of such impairment. Only in relation to that specific threat have the Court of Chancery and this Court considered the reasonableness of Selectica's response.

The Selectica Board carried its burden of proof under both parts of the *Unocal* test. Therefore, at this time, the Selectica Board has withstood the enhanced judicial scrutiny required by the two part *Unocal* test. That does not, however, end the matter.

As we held in *Moran*, the adoption of a Rights Plan is not absolute. In other cases, we have upheld the adoption of Rights Plans in specific defensive circumstances while simultaneously holding that it may be inappropriate for a Rights Plan to remain in place when those specific circumstances change dramatically. The fact that the NOL Poison Pill was reasonable under the specific facts and circumstances of this case, should not be construed as generally approving the reasonableness of a 4.99% trigger in the Rights Plan of a corporation with or without NOLs.

To reiterate *Moran*, "the ultimate response to an actual takeover bid must be judged by the Directors' actions at that time."53 If and when the Selectica Board "is faced with a tender offer and a request to redeem the [Reloaded NOL Poison Pill], they will not be able to arbitrarily reject the offer. They will be held to the same fiduciary standards any other board of directors would be held to in deciding to adopt a defensive mechanism."54 The Selectica Board has no more discretion in refusing to redeem the Rights Plan "than it does in enacting any defensive mechanism." Therefore, the Selectica Board's future use of the Reloaded NOL Poison Pill must be evaluated if and when that issue arises.

QUESTIONS

1. What are NOLs?

2. What defensive measures did Selectica adopt? Why?

3. Did the measures pass muster under the *Unocal* test? Why or why not?

4. How does "realistically unattainable" fit into the *Unocal* analysis?

5. What are Trilogy's arguments for why there is realistic unattainability here? Why does the court reject these arguments?

We close this subsection with a seminal case that applies a different sort of enhanced scrutiny to a board decision that negatively impacts the "shareholder franchise."

BLASIUS INDUSTRIES, INC. v. ATLAS CORP.
Delaware Chancery Court
564 A.2d 651 (1988)

ALLEN, Chancellor . . .

[This case] challenges the validity of board action taken at a telephone meeting of December 31, 1987 that added two new members to Atlas' seven member board. That action was taken as an immediate response to the delivery to Atlas by Blasius the previous day of a form of stockholder consent that, if joined in by holders of a majority of Atlas' stock, would have increased the board of Atlas from seven to fifteen members and would have elected eight new members nominated by Blasius.

As I find the facts of this first case, they present the question whether a board acts consistently with its fiduciary duty when it acts, in good faith and with appropriate care, for the primary purpose of preventing or impeding an unaffiliated majority of shareholders from expanding the board and electing a new majority. For the reasons that follow, I conclude that, even though defendants here acted on their view of the corporation's interest and not selfishly, their December 31 action constituted an offense to the relationship between corporate directors and shareholders that has traditionally been protected in courts of equity. As a consequence, I conclude that the board action taken on December 31 was invalid and must be voided. The basis for this opinion is set forth . . . below. . . .

I.

Blasius Acquires a 9% Stake in Atlas.

Blasius is a new stockholder of Atlas. It began to accumulate Atlas shares for the first time in July, 1987. On October 29, it filed a Schedule 13D with the Securities

Exchange Commission disclosing that, with affiliates, it then owed 9.1% of Atlas' common stock. It stated in that filing that it intended to encourage management of Atlas to consider a restructuring of the Company or other transaction to enhance shareholder values. It also disclosed that Blasius was exploring the feasibility of obtaining control of Atlas, including instituting a tender offer or seeking "appropriate" representation on the Atlas board of directors.

Blasius has recently come under the control of two individuals, Michael Lubin and Warren Delano, who after experience in the commercial banking industry, had, for a short time, run a venture capital operation for a small investment banking firm. Now on their own, they apparently came to control Blasius with the assistance of Drexel Burnham's well noted junk bond mechanism. Since then, they have made several attempts to effect leveraged buyouts, but without success.

In May, 1987, with Drexel Burnham serving as underwriter, Lubin and Delano caused Blasius to raise $60 million through the sale of junk bonds. A portion of these funds were used to acquire a 9% position in Atlas. According to its public filings with the SEC, Blasius' debt service obligations arising out of the sale of the junk bonds are such that it is unable to service those obligations from its income from operations.

The prospect of Messrs. Lubin and Delano involving themselves in Atlas' affairs, was not a development welcomed by Atlas' management. Atlas had a new CEO, defendant Weaver, who had, over the course of the past year or so, overseen a business restructuring of a sort. Atlas had sold three of its five divisions. It had just announced (September 1, 1987) that it would close its once important domestic uranium operation. The goal was to focus the Company on its gold mining business. By October, 1987, the structural changes to do this had been largely accomplished. Mr. Weaver was perhaps thinking that the restructuring that had occurred should be given a chance to produce benefit before another restructuring (such as Blasius had alluded to in its Schedule 13D filing) was attempted, when he wrote in his diary on October 30, 1987:

> 13D by Delano & Lubin came in today. Had long conversation w/MAH & Mark Golden [of Goldman, Sachs] on issue. All agree we must dilute these people down by the acquisition of another Co. w/stock, or merger or something else.

The Blasius Proposal of A Leverage Recapitalization Or Sale.

Immediately after filing its 13D on October 29, Blasius' representatives sought a meeting with the Atlas management. Atlas dragged its feet. A meeting was arranged for December 2, 1987 following the regular meeting of the Atlas board. Attending that meeting were Messrs. Lubin and Delano for Blasius, and, for Atlas, Messrs. Weaver, Devaney (Atlas' CFO), Masinter (legal counsel and director) and Czajkowski (a representative of Atlas' investment banker, Goldman Sachs).

At that meeting, Messrs. Lubin and Delano suggested that Atlas engage in a leveraged restructuring and distribute cash to shareholders. In such a transaction, which is by this date a commonplace form of transaction, a corporation typically raises cash by sale of assets and significant borrowings and makes a large one time cash distribution to shareholders. The shareholders are typically left with cash and an equity interest in a smaller, more highly leveraged enterprise. Lubin and Delano gave the outline of a leveraged recapitalization for Atlas as they saw it.

Immediately following the meeting, the Atlas representatives expressed among themselves an initial reaction that the proposal was infeasible. On December 7, Mr. Lubin sent a letter detailing the proposal. In general, it proposed the following: (1) an initial special cash dividend to Atlas' stockholders in an aggregate amount equal to (a) $35 million, (b) the aggregate proceeds to Atlas from the exercise of option warrants and stock options, and (c) the proceeds from the sale or disposal of all of Atlas' operations that are not related to its continuing minerals operations; and (2) a special non-cash dividend to Atlas' stockholders of an aggregate $125 million principal amount of 7% Secured Subordinated Gold-Indexed Debentures. The funds necessary to pay the initial cash dividend were to principally come from (i) a "gold loan" in the amount of $35,625,000, repayable over a three to five year period and secured by 75,000 ounces of gold at a price of $475 per ounce, (ii) the proceeds from the sale of the discontinued Brockton Sole and Plastics and Ready-Mix Concrete businesses, and (iii) a then expected January, 1988 sale of uranium to the Public Service Electric & Gas Company. (DX H.)

Atlas Asks Its Investment Banker to Study the Proposal.

This written proposal was distributed to the Atlas board on December 9 and Goldman Sachs was directed to review and analyze it.

The proposal met with a cool reception from management. On December 9, Mr. Weaver issued a press release expressing surprise that Blasius would suggest using debt to accomplish what he characterized as a substantial liquidation of Atlas at a time when Atlas' future prospects were promising. He noted that the Blasius proposal recommended that Atlas incur a high debt burden in order to pay a substantial one time dividend consisting of $35 million in cash and $125 million in subordinated debentures. Mr. Weaver also questioned the wisdom of incurring an enormous debt burden amidst the uncertainty in the financial markets that existed in the aftermath of the October crash.

Blasius attempted on December 14 and December 22 to arrange a further meeting with the Atlas management without success. During this period, Atlas provided Goldman Sachs with projections for the Company. Lubin was told that a further meeting would await completion of Goldman's analysis. A meeting after the first of the year was proposed.

The Delivery of Blasius' Consent Statement.

On December 30, 1987, Blasius caused Cede & Co. (the registered owner of its Atlas stock) to deliver to Atlas a signed written consent (1) adopting a precatory resolution recommending that the board develop and implement a restructuring proposal, (2) amending the Atlas bylaws to, among other things, expand the size of the board from seven to fifteen members-the maximum number under Atlas' charter, and (3) electing eight named persons to fill the new directorships. Blasius also filed suit that day in this court seeking a declaration that certain bylaws adopted by the board on September 1, 1987 acted as an unlawful restraint on the shareholders' right, created by § 228 of our corporation statute, to act through consent without undergoing a meeting.

The reaction was immediate. Mr. Weaver conferred with Mr. Masinter, the Company's outside counsel and a director, who viewed the consent as an attempt to take control of the Company. They decided to call an emergency meeting of the board, even though a regularly scheduled meeting was to occur only one week hence, on January 6, 1988. The point of the emergency meeting was to act on their conclusion (or to seek to have the board act on their conclusion) "that we should add at least one and probably two directors to the board . . .". A quorum of directors, however, could not be arranged for a telephone meeting that day. A telephone meeting was held the next day. At that meeting, the board voted to amend the bylaws to increase the size of the board from seven to nine and appointed John M. Devaney and Harry J. Winters, Jr. to fill those newly created positions. Atlas' Certificate of Incorporation creates staggered terms for directors; the terms to which Messrs. Devaney and Winters were appointed would expire in 1988 and 1990, respectively.

The Motivation of the Incumbent Board In Expanding the Board and Appointing New Members.

In increasing the size of Atlas' board by two and filling the newly created positions, the members of the board realized that they were thereby precluding the holders of a majority of the Company's shares from placing a majority of new directors on the board through Blasius' consent solicitation, should they want to do so. Indeed the evidence establishes that that was the principal motivation in so acting.

The conclusion that, in creating two new board positions on December 31 and electing Messrs. Devaney and Winters to fill those positions the board was principally motivated to prevent or delay the shareholders from possibly placing a majority of new members on the board, is critical to my analysis of the central issue posed . . . . If the board in fact was not so motivated, but rather had taken action completely independently of the consent solicitation, which merely had an incidental impact upon the possible effectuation of any action authorized by the shareholders, it is very unlikely that such action would be subject to judicial nullification. The board, as a general matter, is under no fiduciary obligation to suspend its active management of the firm while the consent solicitation process goes forward.

There is testimony in the record to support the proposition that, in acting on December 31, the board was principally motivated simply to implement a plan to expand the Atlas board that preexisted the September, 1987 emergence of Blasius as an active shareholder. I have no doubt that the addition of Mr. Winters, an expert in mining economics, and Mr. Devaney, a financial expert employed by the Company, strengthened the Atlas board and, should anyone ever have reason to review the wisdom of those choices, they would be found to be sensible and prudent. I cannot conclude, however, that the strengthening of the board by the addition of these men was the principal motive for the December 31 action. As I view this factual determination as critical, I will pause to dilate briefly upon the evidence that leads me to this conclusion.

The evidence indicates that CEO Weaver was acquainted with Mr. Winters prior to the time he assumed the presidency of Atlas. When, in the fall of 1986, Mr. Weaver learned of his selection as Atlas' future CEO, he informally approached Mr. Winters about serving on the board of the Company. Winters indicated a willingness to do so and sent to Mr. Weaver a copy of his *curriculum vitae.* Weaver, however, took no action with respect to this matter until he had some informal discussion with other board members on December 2, 1987, the date on which Mr. Lubin orally presented Blasius' restructuring proposal to management. At that time, he mentioned the possibility to other board members.

Then, on December 7, Mr. Weaver called Mr. Winters on the telephone and asked him if he would serve on the board and Mr. Winters again agreed.

On December 24, 1987, Mr. Weaver wrote to other board members, sending them Mr. Winters *curriculum vitae* and notifying them that Mr. Winters would be proposed for board membership at the forthcoming January 6 meeting. It was also suggested that a dinner meeting be scheduled for January 5, in order to give board members who did not know Mr. Winters an opportunity to meet him prior to acting on that suggestion. The addition of Mr. Devaney to the board was not mentioned in that memo, nor, so far as the record discloses, was it discussed at the December 2 board meeting.

It is difficult to consider the timing of the activation of the interest in adding Mr. Winters to the board in December as simply coincidental with the pressure that Blasius was applying. The connection between the two events, however, becomes unmistakably clear when the later events of December 30 and 31 are focused upon. As noted above, on the 30th, Atlas received the Blasius consent which proposed to shareholders that they expand the board from seven to fifteen and add eight new members identified in the consent. It also proposed the adoption of a precatory resolution encouraging restructuring or sale of the Company. Mr. Weaver immediately met with Mr. Masinter. In addition to receiving the consent, Atlas was informed it had been sued in this court, but it did not yet know the thrust of that action. At that time, Messrs. Weaver and Masinter "discussed a lot of [reactive] strategies and Edgar [Masinter] told me we really got to put a program together to go forward with this consent. . . . we talked about taking no action. We talked about adding one board member. We talked about adding two board members. We talked about adding eight board members. And we did a lot of looking at other and various and sundry alternatives. . . . They decided to add two board members and to hold an emergency board meeting that very day to do so. It is clear that the reason that Mr. Masinter advised taking this step immediately rather than waiting for the January 6 meeting was that he feared that the Court of Chancery might issue a temporary restraining order prohibiting the board from increasing its membership, since the consent solicitation had commenced. It is admitted that there was no fear that Blasius would be in a position to complete a public solicitation for consents prior to the January 6 board meeting.

In this setting, I conclude that, while the addition of these qualified men would, under other circumstances, be clearly appropriate as an independent step, such a step was in fact taken in order to impede or preclude a majority of the shareholders from effectively adopting the course proposed by Blasius. Indeed, while defendants never forsake the factual argument that that action was simply a continuation of business as usual, they, in effect, admit from time to time this overriding purpose. For example, everyone concedes that the directors understood on December 31 that the effect of adding two directors would be to preclude stockholders from effectively implementing the Blasius proposal. Mr. Weaver, for example, testifies as follows:

Q: Was it your view that by electing these two directors, Atlas was preventing Blasius from electing a majority of the board?

A: I think that is a component of my total overview. I think in the short term, yes, it did.

This candor is praiseworthy, but any other statement would be frankly incredible. The timing of these events is, in my opinion, consistent only with the conclusion that Mr. Weaver and Mr. Masinter originated, and the board immediately endorsed, the notion of adding these competent, friendly individuals to the board, not because the board felt an urgent need to get them on the board immediately for reasons relating to the operations of Atlas' business, but because to do so would, for the moment, preclude a majority of shareholders from electing eight new board members selected by Blasius. As explained below, I conclude that, in so acting, the board was not selfishly motivated simply to retain power.

There was no discussion at the December 31 meeting of the feasibility or wisdom of the Blasius restructuring proposal. While several of the directors had an initial impression that the plan was not feasible and, if implemented, would likely result in the eventual liquidation of the Company, they had not yet focused upon and acted on that subject. Goldman Sachs had not yet made its report, which was scheduled to be given January 6.

The January 6 Rejection of the Blasius Proposal.

On January 6, the board convened for its scheduled meeting. At that time, it heard a full report from its financial advisor concerning the feasibility of the Blasius restructuring proposal. The Goldman Sachs presentation included a summary of five year cumulative cash flows measured against a base case and the Blasius proposal, an analysis of Atlas' debt repayment capacity under the Blasius proposal, and pro forma income and cash flow statements for a base case and the Blasius proposal, assuming prices of $375, $475 and $575 per ounce of gold.

After completing that presentation, Goldman Sachs concluded with its view that if Atlas implemented the Blasius restructuring proposal (i) a severe drain on operating cash flow would result, (ii) Atlas would be unable to service its long-term debt and could end up in bankruptcy, (iii) the common stock of Atlas would have little or no value, and (iv) since Atlas would be unable to generate sufficient cash to service its debt, the debentures contemplated to be issued in the proposed restructuring could have a value of only 20% to 30% of their face amount. Goldman Sachs also said that it knew of no financial restructuring that had been undertaken by a company where the company had no chance of repaying its debt, which, in its judgment, would be Atlas' situation if it implemented the Blasius restructuring proposal. Finally, Goldman Sachs noted that if Atlas made a meaningful commercial discovery of gold after implementation of the Blasius restructuring proposal, Atlas would not have the resources to develop the discovery.

The board then voted to reject the Blasius proposal. Blasius was informed of that action. The next day, Blasius caused a second, modified consent to be delivered to Atlas. A contest then ensued between the Company and Blasius for the votes of Atlas' shareholders. . . .

II.

Plaintiff attacks the December 31 board action as a selfishly motivated effort to protect the incumbent board from a perceived threat to its control of Atlas. Their conduct is said to constitute a violation of the principle . . . that directors hold legal powers subjected to a supervening duty to exercise such powers in good faith pursuit of what they reasonably believe to be in the corporation's interest. The December 31 action is also said to have been taken in a grossly negligent manner, since it was designed to preclude the recapitalization from being pursued, and the board had no basis at that time to make a prudent determination about the wisdom of that proposal, nor was there any emergency that required it to act in any respect regarding that proposal before putting itself in a position to do so advisedly.

Defendants, of course, contest every aspect of plaintiffs' claims. They claim the formidable protections of the business judgment rule.

They say that, in creating two new board positions and filling them on December 31, they acted without a conflicting interest (since the Blasius proposal did not, in any event, challenge *their* places on the board), they acted with due care (since they well knew the persons they put on the board and did not thereby preclude later consideration of the recapitalization), and they acted in good faith (since they were motivated, they say, to protect the shareholders from the threat of having an impractical, indeed a dangerous, recapitalization program foisted upon them). Accordingly, defendants assert there is no basis to conclude that their December 31 action constituted any violation of the duty of the fidelity that a director owes by reason of his office to the corporation and its shareholders.

Moreover, defendants say that their action was fair, measured and appropriate, in light of the circumstances. Therefore, even should the court conclude that some level of substantive review of it is appropriate under a legal test of fairness, or under the intermediate level of review authorized by *Unocal Corp. v. Mesa Petroleum Co.*, Del. Supr., 493 A.2d 946 (1985), defendants assert that the board's decision must be sustained as valid in both law and equity.

III.

One of the principal thrusts of plaintiffs' argument is that, in acting to appoint two additional persons of their own selection, including an officer of the Company, to the board, defendants were motivated not by any view that Atlas' interest (or those of its shareholders) required that action, but rather they were motivated improperly, by selfish concern to maintain their collective control over the Company.

That is, plaintiffs say that the evidence shows there was no policy dispute or issue that really motivated this action, but that asserted policy differences were pretexts for entrenchment for selfish reasons. If this were found to be factually true, one would not need to inquire further. The action taken would constitute a breach of duty.

In support of this view, plaintiffs point to the early diary entry of Mr. Weaver, to the lack of any consideration at all of the Blasius recapitalization proposal at the December 31 meeting, the lack of any substantial basis for the outside directors to have had any considered view on the subject by that time-not having had any view from Goldman Sachs nor seen the financial data that it regarded as necessary to evaluate the proposal-and upon what it urges is the grievously flawed, slanted analysis that Goldman Sachs finally did present.

While I am satisfied that the evidence is powerful, indeed compelling, that the board was chiefly motivated on December 31 to forestall or preclude the possibility that a majority of shareholders might place on the Atlas board eight new members sympathetic to the Blasius proposal, it is less clear with respect to the more subtle motivational question: whether the existing members of the board did so because they held a good faith belief that such shareholder action would be self-injurious and shareholders needed to be protected from their own judgment.

On balance, I cannot conclude that the board was acting out of a self-interested motive in any important respect on December 31. I conclude rather that the board saw the "threat" of the Blasius recapitalization proposal as posing vital policy differences between itself and Blasius. It acted, I conclude, in a good faith effort to protect its incumbency, not selfishly, but in order to thwart implementation of the recapitalization that it feared, reasonably, would cause great injury to the Company.

The real question the case presents, to my mind, is whether, in these circumstances, the board, even if it *is* acting with subjective good faith (which will typically, if not always, be a contestable or debatable judicial conclusion), may validly act for the principal purpose of preventing the shareholders from electing a majority of new directors. The question thus posed is not one of intentional wrong (or even negligence), but one of authority *as between the fiduciary and the beneficiary* (not simply legal authority, i.e., as between the fiduciary and the world at large).

IV.

It is established in our law that a board may take certain steps-such as the purchase by the corporation of its own stock-that have the effect of defeating a threatened change in corporate control, when those steps are taken advisedly, in good faith pursuit of a corporate interest, and are reasonable in relation to a threat to legitimate corporate interests posed by the proposed change in control. Does this rule-that the reasonable exercise of good faith and due care generally validates, in equity, the exercise of legal authority even if the act has an entrenchment effect-apply to action designed for the primary purpose of interfering with the effectiveness of a stockholder vote? Our authorities, as well as sound principles, suggest that the central importance of the franchise to the scheme of corporate governance, requires that, in this setting, that rule not be applied and that closer scrutiny be accorded to such transaction.

1. *Why the deferential business judgment rule does not apply to board acts taken for the primary purpose of interfering with a stockholder's vote, even if taken advisedly and in good faith.*

A. *The question of legitimacy.*

The shareholder franchise is the ideological underpinning upon which the legitimacy of directorial power rests. Generally, shareholders have only two protections against perceived inadequate business performance. They may sell their stock (which, if done in sufficient numbers, may so affect security prices as to create an incentive for altered managerial performance), or they may vote to replace incumbent board members.

It has, for a long time, been conventional to dismiss the stockholder vote as a vestige or ritual of little practical importance. It may be that we are now witnessing the emergence of new institutional voices and arrangements that will make the stockholder vote a less predictable affair than it has been. Be that as it may, however, whether the vote is seen functionally as an unimportant formalism, or as an important tool of discipline, it is clear that it is critical to the theory that legitimates the exercise of power by some (directors and officers) over vast aggregations of property that they do not own. Thus, when viewed from a broad, institutional perspective, it can be seen that matters involving the integrity of the shareholder voting process involve consideration not present in any other context in which directors exercise delegated power.

B. *Questions of this type raise issues of the allocation of authority as between the board and the shareholders.*

The distinctive nature of the shareholder franchise context also appears when the matter is viewed from a less generalized, doctrinal point of view. From this point of view, as well, it appears that the ordinary considerations to which the business judgment rule originally responded are simply not present in the shareholder voting context.[30] That is, a decision by the board to act for the primary purpose of

---

[30] [n.2] Delaware courts have long exercised a most sensitive and protective regard for the free and effective exercise of voting rights. This concern suffuses our law, manifesting itself in various settings. For example, the perceived importance of the franchise explains the cases that hold that a director's fiduciary duty requires disclosure to shareholders asked to authorize a transaction of all material information in the corporation's possession, even if the transaction is not a self-dealing one. *See, e.g.,* Smith v. Van Gorkom, Del. Supr., 488 A.2d 858 (1985); In re Anderson Clayton Shareholders' Litigation, Del. Ch., 519 A.2d 669, 675 (1986).

A similar concern, for credible corporate democracy, underlies those cases that strike down board action that sets or moves an annual meeting date upon a finding that such action was intended to thwart a shareholder group from effectively mounting an election campaign. *See, e.g.,* Schnell v. Chris Craft, *supra*; Lerman v. Diagnostic Data, Inc., Del. Ch., 421 A.2d 906 (1980); Aprahamian v. HBO, Del. Ch., 531 A.2d 1204 (1987).

The cases invalidating stock issued for the primary purpose of diluting the voting power of a control block also reflect the law's concern that a credible form of corporate democracy be maintained. *See*

preventing the effectiveness of a shareholder vote inevitably involves the question who, as between the principal and the agent, has authority with respect to a matter of internal corporate governance. That, of course, is true in a very specific way in this case which deals with the question who should constitute the board of directors of the corporation, but it will be true in every instance in which an incumbent board seeks to thwart a shareholder majority. A board's decision to act to prevent the shareholders from creating a majority of new board positions and filling them does not involve the exercise of *the corporation's power* over its property, or with respect to *its* rights or obligations; rather, it involves allocation, between shareholders as a class and the board, of effective power with respect to governance of the corporation. This need not be the case with respect to other forms of corporate action that may have an entrenchment effect-such as the stock buybacks present in *Unocal, Cheff* or *Kors v. Carey.* Action designed principally to interfere with the effectiveness of a vote inevitably involves a conflict between the board and a shareholder majority. Judicial review of such action involves a determination of the legal and equitable obligations of an agent towards his principal. This is not, in my opinion, a question that a court may leave to the agent finally to decide so long as he does so honestly and competently; that is, it may not be left to the agent's business judgment.

2. *What rule does apply: per se invalidity of corporate acts intended primarily to thwart effective exercise of the franchise or is there an intermediate standard?*

Plaintiff argues for a rule of *per se* invalidity once a plaintiff has established that a board has acted for the primary purpose of thwarting the exercise of a shareholder vote. Our opinions in *Canada Southern Oils, Ltd. v. Manabi Exploration Co.*, Del. Ch., 96 A.2d 810 (1953) and *Condec Corporation v. Lunkenheimer Company*, Del. Ch., 230 A.2d 769 (1967) could be read as support for such a rule of *per se* invalidity. *Condec* is informative.

There, plaintiff had recently closed a tender offer for 51% of defendants' stock. It had announced no intention to do a follow-up merger. The incumbent board had earlier refused plaintiffs' offer to merge and, in response to its tender offer, sought alternative deals. It found and negotiated a proposed sale of all of defendants' assets for stock in the buyer, to be followed up by an exchange offer to the seller's shareholders. The stock of the buyer was publicly traded in the New York Stock Exchange, so that the deal, in effect, offered cash to the target's shareholders. As a condition precedent to the sale of assets, an exchange of authorized but unissued shares of the seller (constituting about 15% of the total issued and outstanding

---

Canada Southern Oils, Ltd. v. Manabi Exploration Co., Inc., Del. Ch., 96 A.2d 810 (1953); Condec Corporation v. Lunkenheimer Company, Del. Ch., 230 A.2d 769 (1967); Phillips v. Insituform of North America, Inc., Del. Ch., C.A. No. 9173, Allen, C., 1987 WL 16285 (August 27, 1987).

Similarly, a concern for corporate democracy is reflected (1) in our statutory requirement of annual meetings (8 *Del. C.* § 211), and in the cases that aggressively and summarily enforce that right. *See, e.g.*, Coaxial Communications, Inc. v. CNA Financial Corp., Del. Supr., 367 A.2d 994 (1976); Speiser v. Baker, Del. Ch., 525 A.2d 1001 (1987), and (2) in our consent statute (8 *Del. C.* § 228) and the interpretation it has been accorded. *See* Datapoint Corp. v. Plaza Securities Co., Del. Supr., 496 A.2d 1031 (1985) (order); Allen v. Prime Computer, Inc., Del. Supr., No. 26, 1988 [538 A.2d 1113 (table)] (Jan. 26, 1988); Frantz Manufacturing Company v. EAC Industries, Del. Supr., 501 A.2d 401 (1985).

shares after issuance) was to occur. Such issuance would, of course, negate the effective veto that plaintiffs' 51% stockholding would give it over a transaction that would require shareholder approval. Plaintiff sued to invalidate the stock issuance.

The court concluded, as a factual matter, that: ". . . the primary purpose of the issuance of such shares was to prevent control of Lunkenheimer from passing to Condec. . . ." 230 A.2d at 775. The court then implied that not even a good faith dispute over corporate policy could justify a board in acting for the primary purpose of reducing the voting power of a control shareholder:

> Nonetheless, I am persuaded on the basis of the evidence adduced at trial that the transaction here attacked unlike the situation involving the purchase of stock with corporate funds [the court having just cited *Bennett v. Propp*, Del. Supr., 187 A.2d 405, 409 (1962), and *Cheff v. Mathes*, Del. Supr., 199 A.2d 548 (1964)] was clearly unwarranted because it unjustifiably strikes at the very heart of corporate representation by causing a stockholder with an equitable right to a majority of corporate stock to have his right to a proportionate voice and influence in corporate affairs to be diminished by the simple act of an exchange of stock which brought no money into the Lunkenheimer treasury, was not connected with a stock option plan or other proper corporate purpose, and which was obviously designed for the primary purpose of reducing Condec's stockholdings in Lunkenheimer below a majority.

Id. at 777. A *per se* rule that would strike down, in equity, any board action taken for the primary purpose of interfering with the effectiveness of a corporate vote would have the advantage of relative clarity and predictability.[31] It also has the advantage of most vigorously enforcing the concept of corporate democracy. The disadvantage it brings along is, of course, the disadvantage a *per se* rule always has: it may sweep too broadly.

In two recent cases dealing with shareholder votes, this court struck down board acts done for the primary purpose of impeding the exercise of stockholder voting power. In doing so, a *per se* rule was not applied. Rather, it was said that, in such a case, the board bears the heavy burden of demonstrating a compelling justification for such action.

In *Aprahamian v. HBO & Company*, Del. Ch., 531 A.2d 1204 (1987), the incumbent board had moved the date of the annual meeting on the eve of that meeting when it learned that a dissident stockholder group had or appeared to have in hand proxies representing a majority of the outstanding shares. The court restrained that action and compelled the meeting to occur as noticed, even though the board stated that it had good business reasons to move the meeting date forward, and that that action was recommended by a special committee. The court concluded as follows:

---

[31] [n.4] While it must be admitted that any rule that requires for its invocation the finding of a subjective mental state (i.e., a primary purpose) necessarily will lead to controversy concerning whether it applies or not, nevertheless, once it is determined to apply, this *per se* rule would be clearer than the alternative discussed below.

The corporate election process, if it is to have any validity, must be conducted with scrupulous fairness and without any advantage being conferred or denied to any candidate or slate of candidates. In the interests of corporate democracy, those in charge of the election machinery of a corporation must be held to the highest standards of providing for and conducting corporate elections. The business judgment rule therefore does not confer any presumption of propriety on the acts of directors in postponing the annual meeting. Quite to the contrary. When the election machinery appears, at least facially, to have been manipulated those in charge of the election have the burden of persuasion to justify their actions.

Aprahamian, 531 A.2d at 1206–07.

In *Phillips v. Insituform of North America, Inc.*, Del. Ch., C.A. No. 9173, Allen, C. (Aug. 27, 1987), the court enjoined the voting of certain stock issued for the primary purpose of diluting the voting power of certain control shares [stating] . . .

I conclude that no justification has been shown that would arguably make the extraordinary step of issuance of stock for the admitted purpose of impeding the exercise of stockholder rights reasonable in light of the corporate benefit, if any, sought to be obtained. Thus, whether our law creates an unyielding prohibition to the issuance of stock for the primary purpose of depriving a controlling shareholder of control or whether, as *Unocal* suggests to my mind, such an extraordinary step might be justified in some circumstances, the issuance of the Leopold shares was, in my opinion, an unjustified and invalid corporate act.

Phillips v. Insituform of North America, Inc., supra at 26–27. Thus, in *Insituform*, it was unnecessary to decide whether a *per se* rule pertained or not.

In my view, our inability to foresee now all of the future settings in which a board might, in good faith, paternalistically seek to thwart a shareholder vote, counsels against the adoption of a *per se* rule invalidating, in equity, every board action taken for the sole or primary purpose of thwarting a shareholder vote, even though I recognize the transcending significance of the franchise to the claims to legitimacy of our scheme of corporate governance. It may be that some set of facts would justify such extreme action.[32] This, however, is not such a case.

---

[32] [n.5] Imagine the facts of *Condec* changed very slightly and coming up in today's world of corporate control transactions. Assume an acquiring company buys 25% of the target's stock in a small number of privately negotiated transactions. It then commences a public tender offer for 26% of the company stock at a cash price that the board, in good faith, believes is inadequate. Moreover, the acquiring corporation announces that it may or may not do a second-step merger, but if it does one, the consideration will be junk bonds that will have a value, when issued, in the opinion of its own investment banker, of no more than the cash being offered in the tender offer. In the face of such an offer, the board may have a duty to seek to protect the company's shareholders from the coercive effects of this inadequate offer. Assume, for purposes of the hypothetical, that neither newly amended § 203, nor any defensive device available to the target specifically, offers protection. Assume that the target's board turns to the market for corporate control to attempt to locate a more fairly priced alternative that would be available to all shareholders. And assume that just as the tender offer is closing, the board locates an all cash deal for all shares at a price materially higher than that offered by the acquiring corporation. Would the board of the target corporation be justified in issuing sufficient shares to the second acquiring corporation to dilute the 51% stockholder down so that it no longer had a practical veto over the merger or sale of assets

3. *Defendants have demonstrated no sufficient justification for the action of December 31 which was intended to prevent an unaffiliated majority of shareholders from effectively exercising their right to elect eight new directors.*

The board was not faced with a coercive action taken by a powerful shareholder against the interests of a distinct shareholder constituency (such as a public minority). It was presented with a consent solicitation by a 9% shareholder. Moreover, here it had time (and understood that it had time) to inform the shareholders of its views on the merits of the proposal subject to stockholder vote. The only justification that can, in such a situation, be offered for the action taken is that the board knows better than do the shareholders what is in the corporation's best interest. While that premise is no doubt true for any number of matters, it is irrelevant (except insofar as the shareholders wish to be guided by the board's recommendation) when the question is who should comprise the board of directors. The theory of our corporation law confers power upon directors as the agents of the shareholders; it does not create Platonic masters. It may be that the Blasius restructuring proposal was or is unrealistic and would lead to injury to the corporation and its shareholders if pursued. Having heard the evidence, I am inclined to think it was not a sound proposal. The board certainly viewed it that way, and that view, held in good faith, entitled the board to take certain steps to evade the risk it perceived. It could, for example, expend corporate funds to inform shareholders and seek to bring them to a similar point of view. But there is a vast difference between expending corporate funds to inform the electorate and exercising power for the primary purpose of foreclosing effective shareholder action. A majority of the shareholders, who were not dominated in any respect, could view the matter differently than did the board. If they do, or did, they are entitled to employ the mechanisms provided by the corporation law and the Atlas certificate of incorporation to advance that view. They are also entitled, in my opinion, to restrain their agents, the board, from acting for the principal purpose of thwarting that action.

I therefore conclude that, even finding the action taken was taken in good faith, it constituted an unintended violation of the duty of loyalty that the board owed to the shareholders. I note parenthetically that the concept of an unintended breach of the duty of loyalty is unusual but not novel. That action will, therefore, be set aside by order of this court. . . .

Judgment will be entered in favor of defendants. An appropriate form of order may be submitted on notice.

QUESTIONS

1. Why did Atlas increase its board size by two directors?

---

that the target board had arranged for the benefit of all shares? It is not necessary to now hazard an opinion on that abstraction. The case is clearly close enough, however, despite the existence of the *Condec* precedent, to demonstrate, to my mind at least, the utility of a rule that permits, in some extreme circumstances, an incumbent board to act in good faith for the purpose of interfering with the outcome of a contemplated vote. *See also* American International Rent-A-Car, Inc. v. Cross, *supra*, n. 3.

2. Why didn't this decision get business judgment rule protection? What standard did the court apply?

3. Did the court uphold the board's decision? Why or why not?

4. Would the case have come out differently if instead of increasing its board size, Atlas's board amended the corporation's bylaws to prohibit shareholder action by written consent?

---

b. *Revlon* Duties

If a board contemplates a "break-up" or "change of control" of the company, decisions and actions by the board as part of the sales process will be subject to enhanced scrutiny as described in the next case.

REVLON, INC. v. MACANDREWS
Delaware Supreme Court
506 A.2d 173 (1985)

MOORE, Justice.

In this battle for corporate control of Revlon, Inc. (Revlon), the Court of Chancery enjoined certain transactions designed to thwart the efforts of Pantry Pride, Inc. (Pantry Pride) to acquire Revlon. The defendants are Revlon, its board of directors, and Forstmann Little & Co. and the latter's affiliated limited partnership (collectively, Forstmann). The injunction barred consummation of an option granted Forstmann to purchase certain Revlon assets (the lock-up option), a promise by Revlon to deal exclusively with Forstmann in the face of a takeover (the no-shop provision), and the payment of a $25 million cancellation fee to Forstmann if the transaction was aborted. The Court of Chancery found that the Revlon directors had breached their duty of care by entering into the foregoing transactions and effectively ending an active auction for the company. The trial court ruled that such arrangements are not illegal per se under Delaware law, but that their use under the circumstances here was impermissible. We agree. *See MacAndrews & Forbes Holdings, Inc. v. Revlon, Inc.*, Del. Ch., 501 A.2d 1239 (1985). Thus, we granted this expedited interlocutory appeal to consider for the first time the validity of such defensive measures in the face of an active bidding contest for corporate control. Additionally, we address for the first time the extent to which a corporation may consider the impact of a takeover threat on constituencies other than shareholders. *See Unocal Corp. v. Mesa Petroleum Co.*, Del. Supr., 493 A.2d 946, 955 (1985).

In our view, lock-ups and related agreements are permitted under Delaware law where their adoption is untainted by director interest or other breaches of fiduciary duty. The actions taken by the Revlon directors, however, did not meet this standard. Moreover, while concern for various corporate constituencies is proper when addressing a takeover threat, that principle is limited by the requirement that there be some rationally related benefit accruing to the stockholders. We find no such benefit here.

Thus, under all the circumstances we must agree with the Court of Chancery that the enjoined Revlon defensive measures were inconsistent with the directors' duties to the stockholders. Accordingly, we affirm.

I.

The somewhat complex maneuvers of the parties necessitate a rather detailed examination of the facts. The prelude to this controversy began in June 1985, when Ronald O. Perelman, chairman of the board and chief executive officer of Pantry Pride, met with his counterpart at Revlon, Michel C. Bergerac, to discuss a friendly acquisition of Revlon by Pantry Pride. Perelman suggested a price in the range of $40-50 per share, but the meeting ended with Bergerac dismissing those figures as considerably below Revlon's intrinsic value. All subsequent Pantry Pride overtures were rebuffed, perhaps in part based on Mr. Bergerac's strong personal antipathy to Mr. Perelman.

Thus, on August 14, Pantry Pride's board authorized Perelman to acquire Revlon, either through negotiation in the $42-$43 per share range, or by making a hostile tender offer at $45. Perelman then met with Bergerac and outlined Pantry Pride's alternate approaches. Bergerac remained adamantly opposed to such schemes and conditioned any further discussions of the matter on Pantry Pride executing a standstill agreement prohibiting it from acquiring Revlon without the latter's prior approval.

On August 19, the Revlon board met specially to consider the impending threat of a hostile bid by Pantry Pride. At the meeting, Lazard Freres, Revlon's investment banker, advised the directors that $45 per share was a grossly inadequate price for the company. Felix Rohatyn and William Loomis of Lazard Freres explained to the board that Pantry Pride's financial strategy for acquiring Revlon would be through "junk bond" financing followed by a break-up of Revlon and the disposition of its assets. With proper timing, according to the experts, such transactions could produce a return to Pantry Pride of $60 to $70 per share, while a sale of the company as a whole would be in the "mid 50" dollar range. Martin Lipton, special counsel for Revlon, recommended two defensive measures: first, that the company repurchase up to 5 million of its nearly 30 million outstanding shares; and second, that it adopt a Note Purchase Rights Plan. Under this plan, each Revlon shareholder would receive as a dividend one Note Purchase Right (the Rights) for each share of common stock, with the Rights entitling the holder to exchange one common share for a $65 principal Revlon note at 12% interest with a one-year maturity. The Rights would become effective whenever anyone acquired beneficial ownership of 20% or more of Revlon's shares, unless the purchaser acquired all the company's stock for cash at $65 or more per share. In addition, the Rights would not be available to the acquiror, and prior to the 20% triggering event the Revlon board could redeem the rights for 10 cents each. Both proposals were unanimously adopted.

Pantry Pride made its first hostile move on August 23 with a cash tender offer for any and all shares of Revlon at $47.50 per common share and $26.67 per preferred share, subject to (1) Pantry Pride's obtaining financing for the purchase, and (2) the Rights being redeemed, rescinded or voided.

The Revlon board met again on August 26. The directors advised the stockholders to reject the offer. Further defensive measures also were planned. On August 29, Revlon commenced its own offer for up to 10 million shares, exchanging for each share of common stock tendered one Senior Subordinated Note (the Notes) of $47.50 principal at 11.75% interest, due 1995, and one-tenth of a share of $9.00 Cumulative Convertible Exchangeable Preferred Stock valued at $100 per share. Lazard Freres opined that the notes would trade at their face value on a fully distributed basis. Revlon stockholders tendered 87 percent of the outstanding shares (approximately 33 million), and the company accepted the full 10 million shares on a pro rata basis. The new Notes contained covenants which limited Revlon's ability to incur additional debt, sell assets, or pay dividends unless otherwise approved by the "independent" (non-management) members of the board.

At this point, both the Rights and the Note covenants stymied Pantry Pride's attempted takeover. The next move came on September 16, when Pantry Pride announced a new tender offer at $42 per share, conditioned upon receiving at least 90% of the outstanding stock. Pantry Pride also indicated that it would consider buying less than 90%, and at an increased price, if Revlon removed the impeding Rights. While this offer was lower on its face than the earlier $47.50 proposal, Revlon's investment banker, Lazard Freres, described the two bids as essentially equal in view of the completed exchange offer.

The Revlon board held a regularly scheduled meeting on September 24. The directors rejected the latest Pantry Pride offer and authorized management to negotiate with other parties interested in acquiring Revlon. Pantry Pride remained determined in its efforts and continued to make cash bids for the company, offering $50 per share on September 27, and raising its bid to $53 on October 1, and then to $56.25 on October 7.

In the meantime, Revlon's negotiations with Forstmann and the investment group Adler & Shaykin had produced results. The Revlon directors met on October 3 to consider Pantry Pride's $53 bid and to examine possible alternatives to the offer. Both Forstmann and Adler & Shaykin made certain proposals to the board. As a result, the directors unanimously agreed to a leveraged buyout by Forstmann. The terms of this accord were as follows: each stockholder would get $56 cash per share; management would purchase stock in the new company by the exercise of their Revlon "golden parachutes"; Forstmann would assume Revlon's $475 million debt incurred by the issuance of the Notes; and Revlon would redeem the Rights and waive the Notes covenants for Forstmann or in connection with any other offer superior to Forstmann's. The board did not actually remove the covenants at the October 3 meeting, because Forstmann then lacked a firm commitment on its financing, but accepted the Forstmann capital structure, and indicated that the outside directors would waive the covenants in due course. Part of Forstmann's plan was to sell Revlon's Norcliff Thayer and Reheis divisions to American Home Products for $335 million. Before the merger, Revlon was to sell its cosmetics and fragrance division to Adler & Shaykin for $905 million. These transactions would facilitate the purchase by Forstmann or any other acquiror of Revlon.

When the merger, and thus the waiver of the Notes covenants, was announced, the market value of these securities began to fall. The Notes, which originally traded near par, around 100, dropped to 87.50 by October 8. One director later reported (at the October 12 meeting) a "deluge" of telephone calls from irate noteholders, and on October 10 the Wall Street Journal reported threats of litigation by these creditors.

Pantry Pride countered with a new proposal on October 7, raising its $53 offer to $56.25, subject to nullification of the Rights, a waiver of the Notes covenants, and the election of three Pantry Pride directors to the Revlon board. On October 9, representatives of Pantry Pride, Forstmann and Revlon conferred in an attempt to negotiate the fate of Revlon, but could not reach agreement. At this meeting Pantry Pride announced that it would engage in fractional bidding and top any Forstmann offer by a slightly higher one. It is also significant that Forstmann, to Pantry Pride's exclusion, had been made privy to certain Revlon financial data. Thus, the parties were not negotiating on equal terms.

Again privately armed with Revlon data, Forstmann met on October 11 with Revlon's special counsel and investment banker. On October 12, Forstmann made a new $57.25 per share offer, based on several conditions. The principal demand was a lock-up option to purchase Revlon's Vision Care and National Health Laboratories divisions for $525 million, some $100-$175 million below the value ascribed to them by Lazard Freres, if another acquiror got 40% of Revlon's shares. Revlon also was required to accept a no-shop provision. The Rights and Notes covenants had to be removed as in the October 3 agreement. There would be a $25 million cancellation fee to be placed in escrow, and released to Forstmann if the new agreement terminated or if another acquiror got more than 19.9% of Revlon's stock. Finally, there would be no participation by Revlon management in the merger. In return, Forstmann agreed to support the par value of the Notes, which had faltered in the market, by an exchange of new notes. Forstmann also demanded immediate acceptance of its offer, or it would be withdrawn. The board unanimously approved Forstmann's proposal because: (1) it was for a higher price than the Pantry Pride bid, (2) it protected the noteholders, and (3) Forstmann's financing was firmly in place. The board further agreed to redeem the rights and waive the covenants on the preferred stock in response to any offer above $57 cash per share. The covenants were waived, contingent upon receipt of an investment banking opinion that the Notes would trade near par value once the offer was consummated.

Pantry Pride, which had initially sought injunctive relief from the Rights plan on August 22, filed an amended complaint on October 14 challenging the lock-up, the cancellation fee, and the exercise of the Rights and the Notes covenants. Pantry Pride also sought a temporary restraining order to prevent Revlon from placing any assets in escrow or transferring them to Forstmann. Moreover, on October 22, Pantry Pride again raised its bid, with a cash offer of $58 per share conditioned upon nullification of the Rights, waiver of the covenants, and an injunction of the Forstmann lock-up.

On October 15, the Court of Chancery prohibited the further transfer of assets, and eight days later enjoined the lock-up, no-shop, and cancellation fee provisions of the agreement. The trial court concluded that the Revlon directors had breached their duty of loyalty by making concessions to Forstmann, out of concern for their liability to the noteholders, rather than maximizing the sale price of the company for the stockholders' benefit.

II.

To obtain a preliminary injunction, a plaintiff must demonstrate both a reasonable probability of success on the merits and some irreparable harm which will occur absent the injunction. Additionally, the Court shall balance the conveniences of and possible injuries to the parties.

A.

We turn first to Pantry Pride's probability of success on the merits. The ultimate responsibility for managing the business and affairs of a corporation falls on its board of directors. In discharging this function the directors owe fiduciary duties of care and loyalty to the corporation and its shareholders. These principles apply with equal force when a board approves a corporate merger pursuant to 8 Del. C. § 251(b); and of course they are the bedrock of our law regarding corporate takeover issues. While the business judgment rule may be applicable to the actions of corporate directors responding to takeover threats, the principles upon which it is founded — care, loyalty and independence — must first be satisfied.

If the business judgment rule applies, there is a "presumption that in making a business decision the directors of a corporation acted on an informed basis, in good faith and in the honest belief that the action taken was in the best interests of the company." *Aronson v. Lewis*, 473 A.2d 805, 812 (1984). However, when a board implements anti-takeover measures there arises "the omnipresent specter that a board may be acting primarily in its own interests, rather than those of the corporation and its shareholders . . .". *Unocal Corp. v. Mesa Petroleum Co.*, 493 A.2d at 954. This potential for conflict places upon the directors the burden of proving that they had reasonable grounds for believing there was a danger to corporate policy and effectiveness, a burden satisfied by a showing of good faith and reasonable investigation. *Id.* at 955. In addition, the directors must analyze the nature of the takeover and its effect on the corporation in order to ensure balance — that the responsive action taken is reasonable in relation to the threat posed. *Id.*

B.

The first relevant defensive measure adopted by the Revlon board was the Rights Plan, which would be considered a "poison pill" in the current language of corporate takeovers — a plan by which shareholders receive the right to be bought out by the corporation at a substantial premium on the occurrence of a stated triggering event. By 8 Del. C. §§ 141 and 122(13), the board clearly had the power to adopt the measure. Thus, the focus becomes one of reasonableness and purpose.

The Revlon board approved the Rights Plan in the face of an impending hostile takeover bid by Pantry Pride at $45 per share, a price which Revlon reasonably concluded was grossly inadequate. Lazard Freres had so advised the directors, and had also informed them that Pantry Pride was a small, highly leveraged company bent on a "bust-up" takeover by using "junk bond" financing to buy Revlon cheaply, sell the acquired assets to pay the debts incurred, and retain the profit for itself. In adopting the Plan, the board protected the shareholders from a hostile takeover at a price below the company's intrinsic value, while retaining sufficient flexibility to address any proposal deemed to be in the stockholders' best interests.

To that extent the board acted in good faith and upon reasonable investigation. Under the circumstances it cannot be said that the Rights Plan as employed was unreasonable, considering the threat posed. Indeed, the Plan was a factor in causing Pantry Pride to raise its bids from a low of $42 to an eventual high of $58. At the time of its adoption the Rights Plan afforded a measure of protection consistent with the directors' fiduciary duty in facing a takeover threat perceived as detrimental to corporate interests. Far from being a "show-stopper," . . . the measure spurred the bidding to new heights, a proper result of its implementation.

Although we consider adoption of the Plan to have been valid under the circumstances, its continued usefulness was rendered moot by the directors' actions on October 3 and October 12. At the October 3 meeting the board redeemed the Rights conditioned upon consummation of a merger with Forstmann, but further acknowledged that they would also be redeemed to facilitate any more favorable offer. On October 12, the board unanimously passed a resolution redeeming the Rights in connection with any cash proposal of $57.25 or more per share. Because all the pertinent offers eventually equaled or surpassed that amount, the Rights clearly were no longer any impediment in the contest for Revlon. This mooted any question of their propriety under *Moran* or *Unocal*.

C.

The second defensive measure adopted by Revlon to thwart a Pantry Pride takeover was the company's own exchange offer for 10 million of its shares. The directors' general broad powers to manage the business and affairs of the corporation are augmented by the specific authority conferred under 8 Del. C. § 160(a), permitting the company to deal in its own stock. However, when exercising that power in an effort to forestall a hostile takeover, the board's actions are strictly held to the fiduciary standards outlined in *Unocal*. These standards require the directors to determine the best interests of the corporation and its stockholders, and impose an enhanced duty to abjure any action that is motivated by considerations other than a good faith concern for such interests.

The Revlon directors concluded that Pantry Pride's $47.50 offer was grossly inadequate. In that regard the board acted in good faith, and on an informed basis, with reasonable grounds to believe that there existed a harmful threat to the corporate enterprise. The adoption of a defensive measure, reasonable in relation to the threat posed, was proper and fully accorded with the powers, duties, and responsibilities conferred upon directors under our law.

D.

However, when Pantry Pride increased its offer to $50 per share, and then to $53, it became apparent to all that the break-up of the company was inevitable. The Revlon board's authorization permitting management to negotiate a merger or buyout with a third party was a recognition that the company was for sale. The duty of the board had thus changed from the preservation of Revlon as a corporate entity to the maximization of the company's value at a sale for the stockholders' benefit. This significantly altered the board's responsibilities under the *Unocal* standards. It no longer faced threats to corporate policy and effectiveness, or to the stockholders' interests, from a grossly inadequate bid. The whole question of defensive measures became moot. The directors' role changed from defenders of the corporate bastion to auctioneers charged with getting the best price for the stockholders at a sale of the company.

III.

This brings us to the lock-up with Forstmann and its emphasis on shoring up the sagging market value of the Notes in the face of threatened litigation by their holders. Such a focus was inconsistent with the changed concept of the directors' responsibilities at this stage of the developments. The impending waiver of the Notes covenants had caused the value of the Notes to fall, and the board was aware of the noteholders' ire as well as their subsequent threats of suit. The directors thus made support of the Notes an integral part of the company's dealings with Forstmann, even though their primary responsibility at this stage was to the equity owners.

The original threat posed by Pantry Pride — the break-up of the company — had become a reality which even the directors embraced. Selective dealing to fend off a hostile but determined bidder was no longer a proper objective. Instead, obtaining the highest price for the benefit of the stockholders should have been the central theme guiding director action. Thus, the Revlon board could not make the requisite showing of good faith by preferring the noteholders and ignoring its duty of loyalty to the shareholders. The rights of the former already were fixed by contract. The noteholders required no further protection, and when the Revlon board entered into an auction-ending lock-up agreement with Forstmann on the basis of impermissible considerations at the expense of the shareholders, the directors breached their primary duty of loyalty.

The Revlon board argued that it acted in good faith in protecting the noteholders because *Unocal* permits consideration of other corporate constituencies. Although such considerations may be permissible, there are fundamental limitations upon that prerogative. A board may have regard for various constituencies in discharging its responsibilities, provided there are rationally related benefits accruing to the stockholders. However, such concern for non-stockholder interests is inappropriate when an auction among active bidders is in progress, and the object no longer is to protect or maintain the corporate enterprise but to sell it to the highest bidder.

Revlon also contended that by *Gilbert v. El Paso Co.*, Del. Ch., 490 A.2d 1050, 1054-55 (1984), it had contractual and good faith obligations to consider the noteholders. However, any such duties are limited to the principle that one may not interfere with contractual relationships by improper actions. Here, the rights of the noteholders were fixed by agreement, and there is nothing of substance to suggest that any of those terms were violated. The Notes covenants specifically contemplated a waiver to permit sale of the company at a fair price. The Notes were accepted by the holders on that basis, including the risk of an adverse market effect stemming from a waiver. Thus, nothing remained for Revlon to legitimately protect, and no rationally related benefit thereby accrued to the stockholders. Under such circumstances we must conclude that the merger agreement with Forstmann was unreasonable in relation to the threat posed.

A lock-up is not per se illegal under Delaware law. Its use has been approved in an earlier case. *Thompson v. Enstar Corp.*, Del. Ch., [509] A.2d [578] (1984). Such options can entice other bidders to enter a contest for control of the corporation, creating an auction for the company and maximizing shareholder profit. Current economic conditions in the takeover market are such that a "white knight" like Forstmann might only enter the bidding for the target company if it receives some form of compensation to cover the risks and costs involved. However, while those lock-ups which draw bidders into the battle benefit shareholders, similar measures which end an active auction and foreclose further bidding operate to the shareholders' detriment. . . .

The Forstmann option had a . . . destructive effect on the auction process. Forstmann had already been drawn into the contest on a preferred basis, so the result of the lock-up was not to foster bidding, but to destroy it. The board's stated reasons for approving the transactions were: (1) better financing, (2) noteholder protection, and (3) higher price. As the Court of Chancery found, and we agree, any distinctions between the rival bidders' methods of financing the proposal were nominal at best, and such a consideration has little or no significance in a cash offer for any and all shares. The principal object, contrary to the board's duty of care, appears to have been protection of the noteholders over the shareholders' interests.

While Forstmann's $57.25 offer was objectively higher than Pantry Pride's $56.25 bid, the margin of superiority is less when the Forstmann price is adjusted for the time value of money. In reality, the Revlon board ended the auction in return for very little actual improvement in the final bid. The principal benefit went to the directors, who avoided personal liability to a class of creditors to whom the board owed no further duty under the circumstances. Thus, when a board ends an intense bidding contest on an insubstantial basis, and where a significant by-product of that action is to protect the directors against a perceived threat of personal liability for consequences stemming from the adoption of previous defensive measures, the action cannot withstand the enhanced scrutiny which *Unocal* requires of director conduct.

In addition to the lock-up option, the Court of Chancery enjoined the no-shop provision as part of the attempt to foreclose further bidding by Pantry Pride. The no-shop provision, like the lock-up option, while not per se illegal, is impermissible under the *Unocal* standards when a board's primary duty becomes that of an auctioneer responsible for selling the company to the highest bidder. The agreement to negotiate only with Forstmann ended rather than intensified the board's involvement in the bidding contest.

It is ironic that the parties even considered a no-shop agreement when Revlon had dealt preferentially, and almost exclusively, with Forstmann throughout the contest. After the directors authorized management to negotiate with other parties, Forstmann was given every negotiating advantage that Pantry Pride had been denied: cooperation from management, access to financial data, and the exclusive opportunity to present merger proposals directly to the board of directors. Favoritism for a white knight to the total exclusion of a hostile bidder might be justifiable when the latter's offer adversely affects shareholder interests, but when bidders make relatively similar offers, or dissolution of the company becomes inevitable, the directors cannot fulfill their enhanced *Unocal* duties by playing favorites with the contending factions. Market forces must be allowed to operate freely to bring the target's shareholders the best price available for their equity. Thus, as the trial court ruled, the shareholders' interests necessitated that the board remain free to negotiate in the fulfillment of that duty. . . .

IV.

Having concluded that Pantry Pride has shown a reasonable probability of success on the merits, we address the issue of irreparable harm. The Court of Chancery ruled that unless the lock-up and other aspects of the agreement were enjoined, Pantry Pride's opportunity to bid for Revlon was lost. The court also held that the need for both bidders to compete in the marketplace outweighed any injury to Forstmann. Given the complexity of the proposed transaction between Revlon and Forstmann, the obstacles to Pantry Pride obtaining a meaningful legal remedy are immense. We are satisfied that the plaintiff has shown the need for an injunction to protect it from irreparable harm, which need outweighs any harm to the defendants.

V.

In conclusion, the Revlon board was confronted with a situation not uncommon in the current wave of corporate takeovers. A hostile and determined bidder sought the company at a price the board was convinced was inadequate. The initial defensive tactics worked to the benefit of the shareholders, and thus the board was able to sustain its *Unocal* burdens in justifying those measures. However, in granting an asset option lock-up to Forstmann, we must conclude that under all the circumstances the directors allowed considerations other than the maximization of shareholder profit to affect their judgment, and followed a course that ended the auction for Revlon, absent court intervention, to the ultimate detriment of its shareholders. No such defensive measure can be sustained when it represents a breach of the directors' fundamental duty of care. In that context the board's action is not entitled to the deference accorded it by the business judgment rule. The measures were properly enjoined. The decision of the Court of Chancery, therefore, is AFFIRMED.

QUESTIONS

1.   What defenses did Revlon implement to ward off Pantry Pride?

2.   What test applies to determine the validity of the Revlon board's decisions to implement these defenses?

3.   What are *Revlon* duties? Why were they triggered here?

4.   What did the Revlon board do wrong?

5.   What is the policy behind *Revlon* duties?

The next case discusses, among other things, what a board has to do to fulfill its *Revlon* duties and how *Revlon* duties fit within the duty of care/duty of loyalty rubric.

LYONDELL CHEMICAL COMPANY v. RYAN
Delaware Supreme Court
970 A.2d 235 (2009)

BERGER, Justice.

We accepted this interlocutory appeal to consider a claim that directors failed to act in good faith in conducting the sale of their company. . . .

FACTUAL AND PROCEDURAL BACKGROUND

Before the merger at issue, Lyondell Chemical Company ("Lyondell") was the third largest independent, publicly traded chemical company in North America. Dan Smith ("Smith") was Lyondell's Chairman and CEO. Lyondell's other ten directors were independent and many were, or had been, CEOs of other large, publicly traded companies. Basell AF ("Basell") is a privately held Luxembourg company owned by Leonard Blavatnik ("Blavatnik") through his ownership of Access Industries. Basell is in the business of polyolefin technology, production and marketing.

In April 2006, Blavatnik told Smith that Basell was interested in acquiring Lyondell. A few months later, Basell sent a letter to Lyondell's board offering $26.50-$28.50 per share. Lyondell determined that the price was inadequate and that it was not interested in selling. During the next year, Lyondell prospered and no potential acquirors expressed interest in the company. In May 2007, an Access affiliate filed a Schedule 13D with the Securities and Exchange Commission disclosing its right to acquire an 8.3% block of Lyondell stock owned by Occidental Petroleum Corporation. The Schedule 13D also disclosed Blavatnik's interest in possible transactions with Lyondell.

In response to the Schedule 13D, the Lyondell board immediately convened a special meeting. The board recognized that the 13D signaled to the market that the company was "in play,"[33] but the directors decided to take a "wait and see" approach. A few days later, Apollo Management, L.P. contacted Smith to suggest a management-led LBO, but Smith rejected that proposal. In late June 2007, Basell announced that it had entered into a $9.6 billion merger agreement with Huntsman Corporation ("Huntsman"), a specialty chemical company. Basell apparently reconsidered, however, after Hexion Specialty Chemicals, Inc. made a topping bid for Huntsman. Faced with competition for Huntsman, Blavatnik returned his attention to Lyondell.

On July 9, 2007, Blavatnik met with Smith to discuss an all-cash deal at $40 per share. Smith responded that $40 was too low, and Blavatnik raised his offer to $44-$45 per share. Smith told Blavatnik that he would present the proposal to the board, but that he thought the board would reject it. Smith advised Blavatnik to give Lyondell his best offer, since Lyondell really was not on the market. The meeting ended at that point, but Blavatnik asked Smith to call him later in the day. When Smith called, Blavatnik offered to pay $48 per share. Under Blavatnik's proposal, Basell would require no financing contingency, but Lyondell would have to agree to a $400 million break-up fee and sign a merger agreement by July 16, 2007.

Smith called a special meeting of the Lyondell board on July 10, 2007 to review and consider Basell's offer. The meeting lasted slightly less than one hour, during which time the board reviewed valuation material that had been prepared by Lyondell management for presentation at the regular board meeting, which was scheduled for the following day. The board also discussed the Basell offer, the status of the Huntsman merger, and the likelihood that another party might be interested in Lyondell. The board instructed Smith to obtain a written offer from Basell and more details about Basell's financing.

Blavatnik agreed to the board's request, but also made an additional demand. Basell had until July 11 to make a higher bid for Huntsman, so Blavatnik asked Smith to find out whether the Lyondell board would provide a firm indication of interest in his proposal by the end of that day. The Lyondell board met on July 11, again for less than one hour, to consider the Basell proposal and how it compared to the benefits of remaining independent. The board decided that it was interested, authorized the retention of Deutsche Bank Securities, Inc. ("Deutsche Bank") as its financial advisor, and instructed Smith to negotiate with Blavatnik.

Basell then announced that it would not raise its offer for Huntsman, and Huntsman terminated the Basell merger agreement. From July 12-July 15 the parties negotiated the terms of a Lyondell merger agreement; Basell conducted due diligence; Deutsche Bank prepared a "fairness" opinion; and Lyondell conducted its regularly scheduled board meeting. The Lyondell board discussed the Basell proposal again on July 12, and later instructed Smith to try to negotiate better terms. Specifically, the board wanted a higher price, a go-shop provision[34], and a reduced break-up fee. As the trial court noted, Blavatnik was "incredulous." He had offered his best price, which was a substantial premium, and the deal had to be

---

[33] [n.1] On the day that the 13D was made public, Lyondell's stock went from $33 to $37 per share.

[34] [n.2] A "go-shop" provision allows the seller to seek other buyers for a specified period after the agreement is signed.

concluded on his schedule. As a sign of good faith, however, Blavatnik agreed to reduce the break-up fee from $400 million to $385 million.

On July 16, 2007, the board met to consider the Basell merger agreement. Lyondell's management, as well as its financial and legal advisers, presented reports analyzing the merits of the deal. The advisors explained that, notwithstanding the no-shop provision in the merger agreement, Lyondell would be able to consider any superior proposals that might be made because of the "fiduciary out" provision. In addition, Deutsche Bank reviewed valuation models derived from "bullish" and more conservative financial projections. Several of those valuations yielded a range that did not even reach $48 per share, and Deutsche Bank opined that the proposed merger price was fair. Indeed, the bank's managing director described the merger price as "an absolute home run." Deutsche Bank also identified other possible acquirors and explained why it believed no other entity would top Basell's offer. After considering the presentations, the Lyondell board voted to approve the merger and recommend it to the stockholders. At a special stockholders' meeting held on November 20, 2007, the merger was approved by more than 99% of the voted shares. . . .

DISCUSSION

The class action complaint challenging this $13 billion cash merger alleges that the Lyondell directors breached their "fiduciary duties of care, loyalty and candor . . . and . . . put their personal interests ahead of the interests of the Lyondell shareholders." Specifically, the complaint alleges that: 1) the merger price was grossly insufficient; 2) the directors were motivated to approve the merger for their own self-interest;[35] 3) the process by which the merger was negotiated was flawed; 4) the directors agreed to unreasonable deal protection provisions; and 5) the preliminary proxy statement omitted numerous material facts. The trial court rejected all claims except those directed at the process by which the directors sold the company and the deal protection provisions in the merger agreement.

The remaining claims are but two aspects of a single claim, under *Revlon v. MacAndrews & Forbes Holdings, Inc.*,[36] that the directors failed to obtain the best available price in selling the company. As the trial court correctly noted, *Revlon* did not create any new fiduciary duties. It simply held that the "board must perform its fiduciary duties in the service of a specific objective: maximizing the sale price of the enterprise."[37] The trial court reviewed the record, and found that Ryan might be able to prevail at trial on a claim that the Lyondell directors breached their duty of care. But Lyondell's charter includes an exculpatory provision, pursuant to 8 *Del. C.* § 102(b)(7), protecting the directors from personal liability for breaches of the duty of care. Thus, this case turns on whether any arguable shortcomings on the part of the Lyondell directors also implicate their duty of loyalty, a breach of which is not exculpated. Because the trial court determined that the board was independent and

---

[35] [n.5] The directors' alleged financial interest is the fact that they would receive cash for their stock options.

[36] [n.6] 506 A.2d 173, 182 (Del. 1986).

[37] [n.7] Malpiede v. Townson, 780 A.2d 1075, 1083 (Del. 2001).

was not motivated by self-interest or ill will, the sole issue is whether the directors are entitled to summary judgment on the claim that they breached their duty of loyalty by failing to act in good faith.

This Court examined "good faith"[38] in two recent decisions. In *In re Walt Disney Co. Deriv. Litig.*,[39] the Court discussed the range of conduct that might be characterized as bad faith, and concluded that bad faith encompasses not only an intent to harm but also intentional dereliction of duty:

> [A]t least three different categories of fiduciary behavior are candidates for the "bad faith" pejorative label. The first category involves so-called "subjective bad faith," that is, fiduciary conduct motivated by an actual intent to do harm. . . . [S]uch conduct constitutes classic, quintessential bad faith. . . .

> The second category of conduct, which is at the opposite end of the spectrum, involves lack of due care-that is, fiduciary action taken solely by reason of gross negligence and without any malevolent intent. . . . [W]e address the issue of whether gross negligence (including failure to inform one's self of available material facts), without more, can also constitute bad faith. The answer is clearly no. . . .

> That leaves the third category of fiduciary conduct, which falls in between the first two categories. . . . This third category is what the Chancellor's definition of bad faith-intentional dereliction of duty, a conscious disregard for one's responsibilities-is intended to capture. The question is whether such misconduct is properly treated as a non-exculpable, nonindemnifiable violation of the fiduciary duty to act in good faith. In our view, it must be. . . .[40]

The *Disney* decision expressly disavowed any attempt to provide a comprehensive or exclusive definition of "bad faith."

A few months later, in *Stone v. Ritter*,[41] this Court addressed the concept of bad faith in the context of an "oversight" claim. We adopted the standard articulated ten years earlier, in *In re Caremark Int'l Deriv. Litig.*[42]

> [W]here a claim of directorial liability for corporate loss is predicated upon ignorance of liability creating activities within the corporation . . . only a sustained or systematic failure of the board to exercise oversight-such as an utter failure to attempt to assure a reasonable information and reporting

---

[38] [n.8] Our corporate decisions tend to use the terms "bad faith" and "failure to act in good faith" interchangeably, although in a different context we noted that, "[t]he two concepts-bad faith and conduct not in good faith are not necessarily identical." 25 Massachusetts Avenue Property LLC v. Liberty Property Limited Partnership, Del. Supr., No. 188, 2008, Order at p. 5, (November 25, 2008). For purposes of this appeal, we draw no distinction between the terms.

[39] [n.9] 906 A.2d 27 (Del. 2006).

[40] [n.10] *Id.* at 64-66.

[41] [n.11] 911 A.2d 362 (Del. 2006).

[42] [n.12] 698 A.2d 959, 971 (Del. Ch. 1996).

system exists-will establish the lack of good faith that is a necessary condition to liability.

The *Stone* Court explained that the *Caremark* standard is fully consistent with the *Disney* definition of bad faith. *Stone* also clarified any possible ambiguity about the directors' mental state, holding that "imposition of liability requires a showing that the directors knew that they were not discharging their fiduciary obligations."[43]

The Court of Chancery recognized these legal principles, but it denied summary judgment in order to obtain a more complete record before deciding whether the directors had acted in bad faith. Under other circumstances, deferring a decision to expand the record would be appropriate. Here, however, the trial court reviewed the existing record under a mistaken view of the applicable law. Three factors contributed to that mistake. First, the trial court imposed *Revlon* duties on the Lyondell directors before they either had decided to sell, or before the sale had become inevitable. Second, the court read *Revlon* and its progeny as creating a set of requirements that must be satisfied during the sale process. Third, the trial court equated an arguably imperfect attempt to carry out Revlon duties with a knowing disregard of one's duties that constitutes bad faith.

Summary judgment may be granted if there are no material issues of fact in dispute and the moving party is entitled to judgment as a matter of law. The facts, and all reasonable inferences, must be considered in the light most favorable to the non-moving party. The Court of Chancery identified several undisputed facts that would support the entry of judgment in favor of the Lyondell directors: the directors were "active, sophisticated, and generally aware of the value of the Company and the conditions of the markets in which the Company operated." They had reason to believe that no other bidders would emerge, given the price Basell had offered and the limited universe of companies that might be interested in acquiring Lyondell's unique assets. Smith negotiated the price up from $40 to $48 per share-a price that Deutsche Bank opined was fair. Finally, no other acquiror expressed interest during the four months between the merger announcement and the stockholder vote.

Other facts, however, led the trial court to "question the adequacy of the Board's knowledge and efforts. . . ." After the Schedule 13D was filed in May, the directors apparently took no action to prepare for a possible acquisition proposal. The merger was negotiated and finalized in less than one week, during which time the directors met for a total of only seven hours to consider the matter. The directors did not seriously press Blavatnik for a better price, nor did they conduct even a limited market check. Moreover, although the deal protections were not unusual or preclusive, the trial court was troubled by "the Board's decision to grant considerable protection to a deal that may not have been adequately vetted under *Revlon.*"

The trial court found the directors' failure to act during the two months after the filing of the Basell Schedule 13D critical to its analysis of their good faith. The court pointedly referred to the directors' "two months of slothful indifference despite *knowing* that the Company was in play," and the fact that they "languidly awaited

---

[43] [n.13] *Stone*, 911 A.2d at 370.

overtures from potential suitors. . . ." In the end, the trial court found that it was this "failing" that warranted denial of their motion for summary judgment:

> [T]he Opinion clearly questions whether the Defendants "engaged" in the sale process. . . . This is where the 13D filing in May 2007 and the subsequent two months of (apparent) Board inactivity become critical. . . . [T]he Directors made *no apparent effort* to arm themselves with *specific knowledge* about the present value of the Company in the May through July 2007 time period, despite *admittedly knowing* that the 13D filing . . . effectively put the Company "in play," and, therefore, presumably, also knowing that an offer for the sale of the Company could occur at any time. It is these facts that raise the specter of "bad faith" in the present summary judgment record. . . .

The problem with the trial court's analysis is that *Revlon* duties do not arise simply because a company is "in play."[44] The duty to seek the best available price applies only when a company embarks on a transaction-on its own initiative or in response to an unsolicited offer-that will result in a change of control. Basell's Schedule 13D did put the Lyondell directors, and the market in general, on notice that Basell was interested in acquiring Lyondell. The directors responded by promptly holding a special meeting to consider whether Lyondell should take any action. The directors decided that they would neither put the company up for sale nor institute defensive measures to fend off a possible hostile offer. Instead, they decided to take a "wait and see" approach. That decision was an entirely appropriate exercise of the directors' business judgment. The time for action under *Revlon* did not begin until July 10, 2007, when the directors began negotiating the sale of Lyondell.

The Court of Chancery focused on the directors' two months of inaction, when it should have focused on the one week during which they considered Basell's offer. During that one week, the directors met several times; their CEO tried to negotiate better terms; they evaluated Lyondell's value, the price offered and the likelihood of obtaining a better price; and then the directors approved the merger. The trial court acknowledged that the directors' conduct during those seven days might not demonstrate anything more than lack of due care. But the court remained skeptical about the directors' good faith-at least on the present record. That lingering concern was based on the trial court's synthesis of the *Revlon* line of cases, which led it to the erroneous conclusion that directors must follow one of several courses of action to satisfy their *Revlon* duties.

There is only one *Revlon* duty-to "[get] the best price for the stockholders at a sale of the company."[45] No court can tell directors exactly how to accomplish that goal, because they will be facing a unique combination of circumstances, many of which will be outside their control. As we noted in *Barkan v. Amsted Industries, Inc.*, "there is no single blueprint that a board must follow to fulfill its duties."[46] That said, our courts have highlighted both the positive and negative aspects of

---

[44] [n.23] Paramount Communications, Inc. v. Time, Inc., 571 A.2d 1140, 1151 (Del. 1989).

[45] [n.26] *Revlon*, 506 A.2d at 182.

[46] [n.27] 567 A.2d 1279, 1286 (Del. 1989).

various boards' conduct under Revlon. The trial court drew several principles from those cases: directors must "engage actively in the sale process," and they must confirm that they have obtained the best available price either by conducting an auction, by conducting a market check, or by demonstrating "an impeccable knowledge of the market."

The Lyondell directors did not conduct an auction or a market check, and they did not satisfy the trial court that they had the "impeccable" market knowledge that the court believed was necessary to excuse their failure to pursue one of the first two alternatives. As a result, the Court of Chancery was unable to conclude that the directors had met their burden under *Revlon*. In evaluating the totality of the circumstances, even on this limited record, we would be inclined to hold otherwise. But we would not question the trial court's decision to seek additional evidence if the issue were whether the directors had exercised due care. Where, as here, the issue is whether the directors failed to act in good faith, the analysis is very different, and the existing record mandates the entry of judgment in favor of the directors.

As discussed above, bad faith will be found if a "fiduciary intentionally fails to act in the face of a known duty to act, demonstrating a conscious disregard for his duties."[47] The trial court decided that the *Revlon* sale process must follow one of three courses, and that the Lyondell directors did not discharge that "known set of [*Revlon*] 'duties'." But, as noted, there are no legally prescribed steps that directors must follow to satisfy their *Revlon* duties. Thus, the directors' failure to take any specific steps during the sale process could not have demonstrated a conscious disregard of their duties. More importantly, there is a vast difference between an inadequate or flawed effort to carry out fiduciary duties and a conscious disregard for those duties.

Directors' decisions must be reasonable, not perfect. "In the transactional context, [an] extreme set of facts [is] required to sustain a disloyalty claim premised on the notion that disinterested directors were intentionally disregarding their duties."[48] The trial court denied summary judgment because the Lyondell directors' "unexplained inaction" prevented the court from determining that they had acted in good faith. But, if the directors failed to do all that they should have under the circumstances, they breached their duty of care. Only if they knowingly and completely failed to undertake their responsibilities would they breach their duty of loyalty. The trial court approached the record from the wrong perspective. Instead of questioning whether disinterested, independent directors did everything that they (arguably) should have done to obtain the best sale price, the inquiry should have been whether those directors utterly failed to attempt to obtain the best sale price.

Viewing the record in this manner leads to only one possible conclusion. The Lyondell directors met several times to consider Basell's premium offer. They were generally aware of the value of their company and they knew the chemical company market. The directors solicited and followed the advice of their financial and legal advisors. They attempted to negotiate a higher offer even though all the evidence

---

47 [n.31] *Disney* at 67.

48 [n.34] In re Lear Corp. S'holder Litig., 2008 WL 4053221 at *11 (Del. Ch.).

indicates that Basell had offered a "blowout" price. Finally, they approved the merger agreement, because "it was simply too good not to pass along [to the stockholders] for their consideration." We assume, as we must on summary judgment, that the Lyondell directors did absolutely nothing to prepare for Basell's offer, and that they did not even consider conducting a market check before agreeing to the merger. Even so, this record clearly establishes that the Lyondell directors did not breach their duty of loyalty by failing to act in good faith. In concluding otherwise, the Court of Chancery reversibly erred.

CONCLUSION

Based on the foregoing, the decision of the Court of Chancery is reversed and this matter is remanded for entry of judgment in favor of the Lyondell directors. Jurisdiction is not retained.

QUESTIONS

1.   What did the Lyondell board allegedly do wrong?

2.   Lawyers refer to the triggering of *Revlon* duties as the board being in *Revlon* mode or *Revlon*-land. Was the Lyondell board in *Revlon* mode? Why or why not?

3.   What does the court say a board is required to do when in *Revlon* mode?

4.   Does a board's failure to meet *Revlon* duties constitute a breach of the duty of care? A breach of the duty of loyalty? What is the impact of an exculpation provision on the analysis?

As demonstrated by *Lyondell*, a key question concerning *Revlon* is under what circumstances a board's role changes "from defenders of the corporate bastion to auctioneers charged with getting the best price for the stockholders at a sale of the company." In *Arnold v. Society for Savings Bancorp, Inc.*, the Delaware Supreme Court answered this question as follows:

> The directors of a corporation "have the obligation of acting reasonably to seek the transaction offering the best value reasonably available to the stockholders," *Paramount Communications, Inc. v. QVC Network, Inc.*, Del. Supr., 637 A.2d 34, 43 (1994), in at least the following three scenarios: (1) "when a corporation initiates an active bidding process seeking to sell itself or to effect a business reorganization involving a clear break-up of the company," *Paramount Communications, Inc. v. Time Inc.*, Del. Supr., 571 A.2d 1140, 1150 (1990); (2) "where, in response to a bidder's offer, a target abandons its long-term strategy and seeks an alternative transaction involving the break-up of the company," *id.*; or (3) when approval of a transaction results in a "sale or change of control," *QVC*, 637 A.2d at 42–43, 47. In the latter situation, there is no "sale or change in control" when

" '[c]ontrol of both [companies] remain[s] in a large, fluid, changeable and changing market.' " *Id.* at 47.[49]

The effect of the last sentence of the above-quote is that (3) does not apply to a deal where target is to be acquired for bidder *stock* and neither target nor bidder has a controlling shareholder. In other words, both bidder and target are controlled by "a large, fluid, changeable and changing market."

I added emphasis to the word "stock" because several Chancery Court opinions have stated that (3) applies and thus *Revlon* is triggered when target is acquired for cash even if bidder does not have a controlling shareholder. Below is an excerpt from one such opinion, *In re Smurfit-Stone Container Corp. Shareholder Litigation*,[50] which addresses whether *Revlon* applies to a deal where target is acquired for a mix of cash and bidder stock by a bidder without a controlling shareholder.

> Under § 141(a) of the Delaware General Corporation Law, a corporation's board of directors is empowered to manage the business and affairs of the corporation.[51] The business judgment rule ("BJR"), a deferential standard of review, reflects the common law's recognition of § 141(a).[52] In short, it is a "presumption that in making a business decision the directors of a corporation acted on an informed basis, in good faith and in the honest belief that the action taken was in the best interests of the company."[53] This standard of review is respectful to director prerogatives to manage the business of a corporation; in cases where it applies, courts must give "great deference" to directors' decisions and, as long as the Court can discern a rational business purpose for the decision, it must "not invalidate the decision . . . examine its reasonableness, [or] substitute [its] views for those of the board. . . ."[54]
>
> In limited circumstances, however, the Delaware Supreme Court has imposed special obligations of reasonableness on boards of corporations

---

[49] 650 A.2d 1270, 1289-90 (Del. 1994).

[50] 2011 WL 2028076, *11–*16 (Del. Ch. 2011) (unpublished).

[51] [n.81] *See* 8 *Del. C.* § 141(a); see also *Revlon, Inc.*, 506 A.2d at 179.

[52] [n.82] *See MM Cos. v. Liquid Audio, Inc.*, 813 A.2d 1118, 1127–28 (Del.2003).

[53] [n.83] *See id.* (internal quotation marks omitted); *see also, e.g., Emerald P'rs v. Berlin*, 787 A.2d 85, 90–91 (Del.2001); *Revlon, Inc.*, 506 A.2d at 180; *Moran v. Household Int'l, Inc.*, 500 A.2d 1346, 1356 (Del.1985). Generally, the party challenging director action has the initial burden of adducing evidence to rebut this presumption. *See Liquid Audio, Inc.*, 813 A.2d at 1127–28; *Emerald P'rs*, 787 A.2d at 90–91. Plaintiffs can rebut the presumption by showing, among other things, that the board violated its fiduciary duties of care or loyalty in connection with a challenged transaction or committed fraud or self-dealing. *See, e.g., In re Walt Disney Co. Deriv. Litig.*, 907 A.2d 693, 746–47 (Del.Ch.2005), *aff'd*, 906 A.2d 27 (Del.2006). If the presumption properly is rebutted, the burden then shifts to the director defendants to establish that the challenged transaction was "entirely fair" to the corporation and its stockholders. *See, e .g., id.* If the plaintiffs fail to rebut the presumption, the board's decision will be upheld unless it cannot be attributed to any "rational business purpose." *See, e.g., id.; Emerald P'rs*, 787 A.2d at 90–91.

[54] [n.84] *Paramount Commc'ns Inc. v. QVC Network Inc.*, 637 A.2d 34, 45 n. 17 (Del.1994) (internal quotation marks omitted); *see also, e .g., Liquid Audio, Inc.*, 813 A.2d at 1127–28; *Emerald P'rs*, 787 A.2d at 90–91.

who oversee the sale of control of their corporation.[55] When a board leads its corporation into so-called *Revlon* territory, its subsequent actions will be reviewed by this Court not under the deferential BJR standard, but rather under the heightened standard of reasonableness. In addition, and as discussed in greater detail below, the Board's fiduciary obligations shift to obtaining the best value reasonably available to the target's stockholders.[56]

While the differences between directors' obligations under business judgment and *Revlon* review are not insignificant,[57] the standard of review is not necessarily outcome determinative. Nonetheless, "absent a limited set of circumstances as defined under *Revlon*, a board of directors, while always required to act in an informed manner, is not under any *per se* duty to maximize shareholder value in the short term . . . ."[58] Therefore, a question of much ongoing debate, and one to which the parties devoted much ink in this case, is *when* does a corporation enter *Revlon* mode such that its directors must act reasonably to maximize short-term value of the corporation for its stockholders.

The Delaware Supreme Court has determined that a board might find itself faced with such a duty in at least three scenarios: "(1) when a corporation initiates an active bidding process seeking to sell itself or to effect a business reorganization involving a clear break-up of the company[ ]; (2) where, in response to a bidder's offer, a target abandons its long-term strategy and seeks an alternative transaction involving the break-up of the company; or (3) when approval of a transaction results in a sale or change of control[.]"[59]

Here, Plaintiffs do not allege that the Board initiated an active bidding process to sell itself or effected a reorganization involving the break-up of Smurfit–Stone. Nor do they argue that the Board abandoned its long-term strategy in response to a bidder's offer and sought an alternative transac-

---

55 [n.85] *See, e.g., QVC Network Inc.*, 637 A.2d at 42; *Revlon, Inc. v. MacAndrews & Forbes Hldgs., Inc.*, 506 A.2d 173, 182 (Del.1986).

56 [n.86] *Revlon, Inc.*, 506 A.2d at 182–84; *QVC Network Inc.*, 637 A.2d at 44.

57 [n.87] *See In re Netsmart Techs., Inc. S'holders Litig.*, 924 A.2d 171, 192 (Del.Ch.2007) ("Unlike the bare rationality standard applicable to garden-variety decisions subject to the business judgment rule, the *Revlon* standard contemplates a judicial examination of the reasonableness of the board's decision-making process.").

58 [n.88] *Paramount Commc'ns, Inc. v. Time Inc.*, 571 A.2d 1140, 1150 (Del.1989); *Air Prods. & Chems., Inc. v. Airgas, Inc.*, 16 A.3d 48, 101–02 (Del.Ch.2011) ("It is not until the board is under *Revlon* that its duty 'narrow[s]' to getting the best price reasonably available for stockholders in a sale of the company."). In *Lyondell*, for example, the Supreme Court held that "*Revlon* duties do not arise simply because a company is 'in play.' "*Lyondell Chem. Co. v. Ryan*, 970 A.2d 235, 244 (Del.2009) ("The duty to seek the best available price applies only when a company embarks on a transaction — on its own initiative or in response to an unsolicited offer — that will result in a change of control."). Moreover, in *Paramount Communications v. Time*, the Supreme Court held that Time's board of directors did not enter *Revlon* mode solely by virtue of either entering into the initial merger agreement with Warner or adopting structural safety devices. *See Time Inc.*, 571 A.2d at 1142, 1151.

59 [n.89] *See, e.g., In re Santa Fe Pac. Corp. S'holder Litig.*, 669 A.2d 59, 71 (Del.1995) (citing *Paramount Commc'ns Inc. v. QVC Network Inc.*, 637 A.2d 34, 42–43, 47–48 (Del.1994) (internal quotation marks and citations omitted); *Arnold v. Soc'y for Sav. Bancorp, Inc.*, 650 A.2d 1270, 1289–90 (Del.1994).

tion involving the break-up of the Company. Rather, they allege that *Revlon* should apply to this case because the Merger Consideration was comprised of 50% cash and 50% stock at the time the parties entered into the Agreement, which qualifies the Proposed Transaction as a "change of control" transaction.[60] A question remains, however, as to when a mixed stock and cash merger constitutes a change of control transaction for *Revlon* purposes.

On the one hand, pure stock-for-stock transactions do not necessarily trigger *Revlon*. If, for example, the resulting entity has a controlling stockholder or stockholder group such that the target's stockholders are relegated to minority status in the combined entity, Delaware Courts have found a change of control would occur for *Revlon* purposes.[61] But, if ownership shifts from one large unaffiliated group of public stockholders to another, that alone does not amount to a change of control.[62] In this event, the target's stockholders' voting power will not be diminished to minority status and they are not foreclosed from an opportunity to obtain a control premium in a future change of control transaction involving the resulting entity.[63]

On the other hand, *Revlon* will govern a board's decision to sell a corporation where stockholders will receive cash for their shares.[64] *Revlon* applies in the latter instance because, among other things, there is no tomorrow for the corporation's present stockholders, meaning that they will forever be shut out from future profits generated by the resulting entity as well as the possibility of obtaining a control premium in a subsequent transaction.[65] Heightened scrutiny is appropriate because of an

---

[60] [n.90] POB 21–22. Alternatively, Plaintiffs seem to contend that even if the Proposed Transaction is held not to involve a "change of control" as defined in the relevant precedents, this 50/50 cash/stock scenario in the circumstances of this case still qualifies for *Revlon* review under an as yet unarticulated fourth *Revlon* category. *See* PRB 10 n.6.

[61] [n.91] *See Paramount Commc'ns Inc. v. QVC Network Inc.*, 637 A.2d 34, 42–23 (Del.1994) ("When a majority of a corporation's voting shares are acquired by a single person or entity, or by a cohesive group acting together, there is a significant diminution in the voting power of those who thereby become minority stockholders.").

[62] [n.92] *See, e.g., In re Santa Fe Pac. Corp.*, 669 A.2d at 71 (noting that a corporation does not undergo a change in control where control of the postmerger entity remains in a "large, fluid, changeable and changing market") (internal quotation marks omitted); *Arnold*, 650 A.2d at 1289–90 (same); *Time Inc.*, 571 A.2d at 1150; *Krim v. ProNet, Inc.*, 744 A.2d 523, 527 (Del.Ch.1999) (noting that *Revlon* "does not apply to stock-for-stock strategic mergers of publicly traded companies, a majority of the stock of which is dispersed in the market.").

[63] [n.93] *See Arnold*, 650 A.2d at 1290 ("[P]laintiff argues that there was a 'sale or change in control' of Bancorp because its former stockholders are now relegated to minority status in BoB, losing their opportunity to enjoy a control premium. As a continuing BoB stockholder, plaintiff's opportunity to receive a control premium is not foreclosed. Thus, plaintiff's claim that enhanced scrutiny is required under the circumstances of this case lacks merit. . . .").

[64] [n.94] *See, e.g., In re NYMEX S'holder Litig.*, 2009 WL 3206051, at *5 (Del.Ch. Sept.30, 2009); *In re Topps Co. S'holders Litig.*, 926 A.2d 58, 64 (Del.Ch.2007); *TW Servs., Inc. v. SWT Acq. Corp.*, 1989 WL 20290, at * 1184 (Del.Ch. Mar.2, 1989).

[65] [n.95] *See, e.g., Air Prods. & Chems., Inc. v. Airgas, Inc.*, 16 A .3d 48, 101–02 (Del.Ch.2011); *TW*

"omnipresent specter" that a board, which may have secured a continuing interest of some kind in the surviving entity, may favor its interests over those of the corporation's stockholders.[66]

The Supreme Court has not yet clarified the precise bounds of when *Revlon* applies in the situation where merger consideration consists of an equal or almost equal split of cash and stock. Thus, to make such a determination, I evaluate the circumstances of the Proposed Transaction based on its economic implications and relevant judicial precedent.

As to judicial precedent, I note that, on a few occasions, Delaware courts have provided guidance on this issue. In *In re Santa Fe Pacific Corp.*, for example, the Supreme Court considered on a motion to dismiss the plaintiffs' claim that *Revlon* should apply to a transaction in which Burlington would acquire up to 33% of Santa Fe common shares through a tender offer (*i.e.*, cash) and then acquire the balance of Santa Fe shares through a stock-for-stock exchange.[67] The Court declined to apply *Revlon* because it found that the plaintiffs failed to allege that the Santa Fe board decided to pursue a transaction, including the one finally settled upon, which would result in a sale of control of Santa Fe to Burlington.[68] Notably, the Court highlighted the plaintiffs' failure to describe Burlington's capital structure, which left it with little reason to doubt that "control of Burlington and Santa Fe after the merger would [ ] remain 'in a large, fluid, changeable and changing market.' "[69]

Similarly, in *In re Lukens Inc.*, Vice Chancellor Lamb considered a transaction in which Bethlehem Steel would acquire 100% of Lukens' common stock for a value of $25 per common share. Under the terms of the merger, which were subject to dispute on the defendants' motion to dismiss, "each Lukens shareholder would have the right to elect to receive the consideration in cash, subject to a maximum total cash payout equal to 62% of the total consideration."[70] As in *Santa Fe*, the parties disputed whether *Revlon* should control the transaction. While the Court did not have occasion to determine definitively whether *Revlon* should apply — it assumed that it did — it offered sage guidance on transactions involving both cash and stock merger consideration, which informs this Court's opinion here. Vice Chancellor Lamb opined that, though the Supreme

---

Servs., Inc., 1989 WL 20290, at *1184 (noting that "for the present shareholders [of a company that will be sold for cash], there is no long run. For them it does not matter that a buyer who will pay more cash plans to subject the corporation to a risky level of debt, or that a buyer who offers less cash will be a more generous employer for whom labor peace is more likely. The rationale for recognizing . . . the appropriateness of sacrificing achievable share value today in the hope of greater long term value, is not present when all of the current shareholders will be removed from the field by the contemplated transaction.").

66 [n.96] *See In re Lukens Inc. S'holders Litig.*, 757 A.2d 720, 732 n. 6 (Del.Ch.1999), *aff'd sub nom.*, *Walker v. Lukens, Inc.*, 757 A.2d 1278 (Del.2000).

67 [n.97] *In re Santa Fe Pac. Corp. S'holder Litig.*, 669 A.2d 59, 64–65 (Del.1995).

68 [n.98] *Id.* at 71.

69 [n.99] *Id.*

70 [n.100] *In re Lukens Inc.*, 757 A.2d at 725.

Court had not yet established a bright line rule for what percentage of merger consideration could be cash without triggering *Revlon*, he would find that under the circumstances of the *Lukens* case *Revlon* would apply.[71] In pertinent part, he explained as follows:

> I cannot understand how the Director Defendants were *not* obliged, in the circumstances, to seek out the best price reasonably available. The defendants argue that because over 30% of the merger consideration was shares of Bethlehem common stock, a widely held company without any controlling shareholder, *Revlon* and *QVC* do not apply. I disagree. Whether 62% or 100% of the consideration was to be in cash, the directors were obliged to take reasonable steps to ensure that the shareholders received the best price available because, in any event, for a substantial majority of the then-current shareholders, "there is no long run." . . . I do not agree with the defendants that *Santa Fe*, in which shareholders tendered 33% of their shares for cash and exchanged the remainder for common stock, controls a situation in which over 60% of the consideration is cash. . . . I take for granted . . . that a cash offer for 95% of a company's shares, for example, even if the other 5% will be exchanged for the shares of a widely held corporation, will constitute a change of corporate control. Until instructed otherwise, I believe that purchasing more than 60% achieves the same result.[72]

Thus far, this Court has not been instructed otherwise, and, while the stock portion of the Merger Consideration is larger than the portion in *Lukens*, I am persuaded that Vice Chancellor Lamb's reasoning applies here, as well. Defendants attempt to distinguish *Lukens* on its facts, arguing that "they offer no support to plaintiffs' position."[73] I disagree. While the factual scenarios are not identical, there are some material similarities. Most important of these is that the Court in *Lukens* was wary of the fact that a majority of holders of Lukens common stock potentially could have elected to cash out their positions entirely, subject to the 62% total cash consideration limit. In this case, Defendants emphasize that no Smurfit–Stone stockholder involuntarily or voluntarily can be cashed out completely and, after consummation of the Proposed Transaction, the stockholders will own slightly less than half of Rock–Tenn. While the facts of this case and *Lukens* differ slightly in that regard, Defendants lose sight of the fact that while no Smurfit–Stone stockholder will be cashed out 100%, 100% of its stockholders who elect to participate in the merger will see approximately 50% of their Smurfit–Stone investment cashed out. As such, like Vice Chancellor Lamb's concern that potentially there was no "tomor-

---

[71] [n.101] *Id.* at 732 n. 25; *see also In re NYMEX S'holder Litig.*, 2009 WL 3206051, at *5 (Del.Ch. Sept.30, 2009) (similarly noting that the Supreme Court has not established a bright line rule). In *In re NYMEX*, this Court considered a mixed consideration transaction consisting of 56% stock and 44% cash, but determined that it did not need to address whether *Revlon* applied. *See In re NYMEX*, 2009 WL 3206051, at *5–6.

[72] [n.102] *In re Lukens*, 757 A.2d at 732 n. 25.

[73] [n.103] DAB 26–27.

row" for a substantial majority of Lukens stockholders, the concern here is that there is no "tomorrow" for approximately 50% of each stockholder's investment in Smurfit–Stone. That each stockholder may retain a portion of her investment after the merger is insufficient to distinguish the reasoning of *Lukens*, which concerns the need for the Court to scrutinize under *Revlon* a transaction that constitutes an end-game for all or a substantial part of a stockholder's investment in a Delaware corporation.

Defendants' other arguments, while cogent, similarly are unavailing. Citing to *Arnold*,[74] they contend that because control of Rock–Tenn after closing will remain in a large, fluid, changing, and changeable market, Smurfit–Stone stockholders will retain the right to obtain a control premium in the future and, as such, the Proposed Transaction is not a change of control transaction under *Revlon*. As with their attempt to distinguish *Lukens*, Defendants assert that even though a significant part of the Merger Consideration is in cash, there is a "tomorrow" for the Company's stockholders because they will own approximately 45% of Rock–Tenn after the merger. They aver that "[h]olding that *Revlon* applies in this type of case would require directors to behave as if there is no long run for their shareholders when in fact there is, and to pretend that shareholders will not participate in the future of the combined entity when in fact they will."[75] This statement, however, is only half correct. While the Company's stockholders will see approximately half of their equity trans-formed into Rock–Tenn equity such that they potentially can benefit from Rock–Tenn's future value, the other half of their investment in Smurfit-–Stone will be cashed out. Even if Rock–Tenn has no controlling stock-holder and Smurfit–Stone's stockholders will not be relegated to a minority status in the postmerger entity, half of their investment will be liquidated.

Citing to *Santa Fe*, Defendants note that the Supreme Court did not suggest that cashing out 33% of shares out would transform Santa Fe's transaction with Burlington into a change of control transaction. As the Court noted, the plaintiffs in that case did not allege that control of Burlington would not remain in a large, fluid, changing, and changeable market postmerger. The approximately 50% being cashed out of each stockholder's investment in Smurfit–Stone obviously falls between the 33% cash out that the Supreme Court held did not trigger *Revlon* in *Santa Fe* and the 62% proportion of cash consideration that Vice Chancellor Lamb determined would trigger *Revlon* in *Lukens*. Mathematically, this situation is closer to *Lukens*, but only marginally.[76] Thus, assuming the Court's

---

[74] [n.104] 650 A.2d 1270.

[75] [n.105] DAB 24.

[76] [n.106] Indeed, Defendants also argue that, because there is no collar on the stock portion of the Merger Consideration, Smurfit–Stone stockholders can benefit from the market's anticipation of future synergies. Moreover, because Rock–Tenn's share price has risen since the announcement of the Transaction, the Merger Consideration now stands at 56% stock and 44% cash. In my view, a more logical and workable analysis here focuses on the relative proportion of cash and stock as of the time the parties entered into the Merger Agreement, which was 50/50 cash and stock. Accepting Defendants' position would require the Court to base its determination as to whether to apply *Revlon* on its best guess as to

analysis in *Lukens* was correct, as I do, this case is necessarily approaching a limit in relation to the Supreme Court's holdings in *Santa Fe* and *Arnold*, which, again, involved a stock-for-stock transaction. As previously noted, however, my conclusion that *Revlon* applies here is not free from doubt.

Finally, I note that factors identified by Plaintiffs and Defendants as having been considered by Delaware courts in determining whether to apply *Revlon* review in cases like *QVC* and others are important to a robust analysis of the issue.[77] In *QVC*, for example, the Supreme Court noted the importance of considering whether a target's stockholder's voting rights would be relegated to minority status in the surviving entity of a merger and whether such stockholders still could obtain a control premium in future transactions as part of the postmerger entity in determining whether a "change of control" had occurred.[78] But, the fact that control of Rock–Tenn after consummation will remain in a large pool of unaffiliated stockholders, while important, neither addresses nor affords protection to the portion of the stockholders' investment that will be converted to cash and thereby be deprived of its long-run potential.

Based on the foregoing, therefore, I conclude that Plaintiffs are likely to succeed on their argument that the approximately 50% cash and 50% stock consideration here triggers *Revlon.*

c.　Deal Protection Devices

As we discussed in Chapter 5, deal protection devices are provisions of an acquisition agreement designed to protect bidder from losing the deal to a competing bidder. As discussed in the next case, a target board's decision to sign-off on such devices is subject to enhanced scrutiny, even if target is not in *Revlon* mode.

---

the price of Rock–Tenn's stock as of the date the Transaction closes. Leaving this determination up to the vagaries of the stock market is not a workable method and potentially may lead to inequitable results. Therefore, I consider Plaintiffs' claims in light of the 50% cash and 50% stock Merger Consideration that was in effect as of the date the parties entered into the Merger Agreement.

77 [n.107] *See* DAB 27 ("Taken together, these cases suggest the questions that should inform the applicability of *Revlon* in a mixed cash/stock deal: Does control of the post-merger company remain in a large, fluid, and changeable market? Do the target's shareholders retain a significant economic interest in the combined company? Must the directors, in considering the transaction, exercise their business judgment, or is price the only question they must consider to protect shareholders' interest? Do the shareholders retain the future opportunity to receive a control premium? Is there a "long run" for every target shareholder in the combined company?"); POB 23–24 & PRB 10 n.6 (urging the Court to consider the fact that Moore and Hunt will collect "change of control" bonuses in the range of $19 million if the Proposed Transaction closes as supporting the proposition that the Transaction represents a change of control). While the Board's treatment of certain of its management's change of control bonuses arguably may be relevant to the Court's analysis, the subjective beliefs of the Board members are not sufficient alone to invoke *Revlon. See Paramount Commc'ns, Inc. v. Time Inc.,* 571 A.2d 1140, 1151 (Del.1989).

78 [n.108] *See Paramount Commc'ns Inc. v. QVC Network Inc.,* 637 A.2d 34, 42–43 (Del.1994).

OMNICARE, INC. v. NCS HEALTHCARE, INC.
Delaware Supreme Court
818 A.2d 914 (2003)

HOLLAND, Justice, for the majority:

NCS Healthcare, Inc. ("NCS"), a Delaware corporation, was the object of competing acquisition bids, one by Genesis Health Ventures, Inc. ("Genesis"), a Pennsylvania corporation, and the other by Omnicare, Inc. ("Omnicare"), a Delaware corporation. The proceedings before this Court were expedited due to exigent circumstances, including the pendency of the stockholders' meeting to consider the NCS/Genesis merger agreement. . . .

Overview of Opinion

The board of directors of NCS, an insolvent publicly traded Delaware corporation, agreed to the terms of a merger with Genesis. Pursuant to that agreement, all of the NCS creditors would be paid in full and the corporation's stockholders would exchange their shares for the shares of Genesis, a publicly traded Pennsylvania corporation. Several months after approving the merger agreement, but before the stockholder vote was scheduled, the NCS board of directors withdrew its prior recommendation in favor of the Genesis merger.

In fact, the NCS board recommended that the stockholders reject the Genesis transaction after deciding that a competing proposal from Omnicare was a superior transaction. The competing Omnicare bid offered the NCS stockholders an amount of cash equal to more than twice the then current market value of the shares to be received in the Genesis merger. The transaction offered by Omnicare also treated the NCS corporation's other stakeholders on equal terms with the Genesis agreement.

The merger agreement between Genesis and NCS contained a provision authorized by § 251(c) of Delaware's corporation law. It required that the Genesis agreement be placed before the corporation's stockholders for a vote, even if the NCS board of directors no longer recommended it. At the insistence of Genesis, the NCS board also agreed to omit any effective fiduciary clause from the merger agreement. In connection with the Genesis merger agreement, two stockholders of NCS, who held a majority of the voting power, agreed unconditionally to vote all of their shares in favor of the Genesis merger. Thus, the combined terms of the voting agreements and merger agreement guaranteed, *ab initio*, that the transaction proposed by Genesis would obtain NCS stockholder's approval.

The Court of Chancery ruled that the voting agreements, when coupled with the provision in the Genesis merger agreement requiring that it be presented to the stockholders for a vote pursuant to 8 *Del. C.* § 251(c), constituted defensive measures within the meaning of *Unocal Corp. v. Mesa Petroleum Co.*[79] After

---

[79] [n.2] Unocal Corp. v. Mesa Petroleum Co., 493 A.2d 946 (Del. 1985). *See also* Unitrin, Inc. v. Am. Gen. Corp., 651 A.2d 1361, 1386–89 (Del. 1995).

applying the *Unocal* standard of enhanced judicial scrutiny, the Court of Chancery held that those defensive measures were reasonable. We have concluded that, in the absence of an effective fiduciary out clause, those defensive measures are both preclusive and coercive. Therefore, we hold that those defensive measures are invalid and unenforceable.

The Parties

The defendant, NCS, is a Delaware corporation headquartered in Beachwood, Ohio. NCS is a leading independent provider of pharmacy services to long-term care institutions including skilled nursing facilities, assisted living facilities and other institutional healthcare facilities. NCS common stock consists of Class A shares and Class B shares. The Class B shares are entitled to ten votes per share and the Class A shares are entitled to one vote per share. The shares are virtually identical in every other respect.

The defendant Jon H. Outcalt is Chairman of the NCS board of directors. Outcalt owns 202,063 shares of NCS Class A common stock and 3,476,086 shares of Class B common stock. The defendant Kevin B. Shaw is President, CEO and a director of NCS. At the time the merger agreement at issue in this dispute was executed with Genesis, Shaw owned 28,905 shares of NCS Class A common stock and 1,141,134 shares of Class B common stock. . . .

The defendant Genesis is a Pennsylvania corporation with its principal place of business in Kennett Square, Pennsylvania. It is a leading provider of healthcare and support services to the elderly. The defendant Geneva Sub, Inc., a wholly owned subsidiary of Genesis, is a Delaware corporation formed by Genesis to acquire NCS.

The plaintiffs in the class action own an unspecified number of shares of NCS Class A common stock. They represent a class consisting of all holders of Class A common stock. As of July 28, 2002, NCS had 18,461,599 Class A shares and 5,255,210 Class B shares outstanding.

Omnicare is a Delaware corporation with its principal place of business in Covington, Kentucky. Omnicare is in the institutional pharmacy business, with annual sales in excess of $2.1 billion during its last fiscal year. Omnicare purchased 1000 shares of NCS Class A common stock on July 30, 2002.

PROCEDURAL BACKGROUND

This is a consolidated appeal from orders of the Court of Chancery in two separate proceedings. One proceeding is brought by Omnicare seeking to invalidate a merger agreement between NCS and Genesis on fiduciary duty grounds. In that proceeding, Omnicare also challenges Voting Agreements between Genesis and Jon H. Outcalt and Kevin B. Shaw, two major NCS stockholders, who collectively own over 65% of the voting power of NCS stock. The Voting Agreements irrevocably commit these stockholders to vote for the merger. . . .

The other proceeding is a class action brought by NCS stockholders. That action seeks to invalidate the merger primarily on the ground that the directors of NCS violated their fiduciary duty of care in failing to establish an effective process designed to achieve the transaction that would produce the highest value for the NCS stockholders. . . .

FACTUAL BACKGROUND

The parties are in substantial agreement regarding the operative facts. They disagree, however, about the legal implications. This recitation of facts is taken primarily from the opinion by the Court of Chancery.

NCS Seeks Restructuring Alternatives

Beginning in late 1999, changes in the timing and level of reimbursements by government and third-party providers adversely affected market conditions in the health care industry. As a result, NCS began to experience greater difficulty in collecting accounts receivables, which led to a precipitous decline in the market value of its stock. NCS common shares that traded above $20 in January 1999 were worth as little as $5 at the end of that year. By early 2001, NCS was in default on approximately $350 million in debt, including $206 million in senior bank debt and $102 million of its 5 ¾ % Convertible Subordinated Debentures (the "Notes"). After these defaults, NCS common stock traded in a range of $0.09 to $0.50 per share until days before the announcement of the transaction at issue in this case.

NCS began to explore strategic alternatives that might address the problems it was confronting. As part of this effort, in February 2000, NCS retained UBS Warburg, L.L.C. to identify potential acquirers and possible equity investors. UBS Warburg contacted over fifty different entities to solicit their interest in a variety of transactions with NCS. UBS Warburg had marginal success in its efforts. By October 2000, NCS had only received one non-binding indication of interest valued at $190 million, substantially less than the face value of NCS's senior debt. This proposal was reduced by 20% after the offeror conducted its due diligence review.

NCS Financial Deterioration

In December 2000, NCS terminated its relationship with UBS Warburg and retained Brown, Gibbons, Lang & Company as its exclusive financial advisor. During this period, NCS's financial condition continued to deteriorate. In April 2001, NCS received a formal notice of default and acceleration from the trustee for holders of the Notes. As NCS's financial condition worsened, the Noteholders formed a committee to represent their financial interests (the "Ad Hoc Committee"). At about that time, NCS began discussions with various investor groups regarding a restructuring in a "pre-packaged" bankruptcy. NCS did not receive any proposal that it believed provided adequate consideration for its stakeholders. At that time, full recovery for NCS's creditors was a remote prospect, and any recovery for NCS stockholders seemed impossible.

Omnicare's Initial Negotiations

In the summer of 2001, NCS invited Omnicare, Inc. to begin discussions with Brown Gibbons regarding a possible transaction. On July 20, Joel Gemunder,

Omnicare's President and CEO, sent Shaw a written proposal to acquire NCS in a bankruptcy sale under § 363 of the Bankruptcy Code. This proposal was for $225 million subject to satisfactory completion of due diligence. NCS asked Omnicare to execute a confidentiality agreement so that more detailed discussions could take place.

In August 2001, Omnicare increased its bid to $270 million, but still proposed to structure the deal as an asset sale in bankruptcy. Even at $270 million, Omnicare's proposal was substantially lower than the face value of NCS's outstanding debt. It would have provided only a small recovery for Omnicare's Noteholders and no recovery for its stockholders. In October 2001, NCS sent Glen Pollack of Brown Gibbons to meet with Omnicare's financial advisor, Merrill Lynch, to discuss Omnicare's interest in NCS. Omnicare responded that it was not interested in any transaction other than an asset sale in bankruptcy.

There was no further contact between Omnicare and NCS between November 2001 and January 2002. Instead, Omnicare began secret discussions with Judy K. Mencher, a representative of the Ad Hoc Committee. In these discussions, Omnicare continued to pursue a transaction structured as a sale of assets in bankruptcy. In February 2002, the Ad Hoc Committee notified the NCS board that Omnicare had proposed an asset sale in bankruptcy for $313,750,000.

NCS Independent Board Committee

In January 2002, Genesis was contacted by members of the Ad Hoc Committee concerning a possible transaction with NCS. Genesis executed NCS's standard confidentiality agreement and began a due diligence review. Genesis had recently emerged from bankruptcy because, like NCS, it was suffering from dwindling government reimbursements.

Genesis previously lost a bidding war to Omnicare in a different transaction. This led to bitter feelings between the principals of both companies. More importantly, this bitter experience for Genesis led to its insistence on exclusivity agreements and lock-ups in any potential transaction with NCS.

NCS Financial Improvement

NCS's operating performance was improving by early 2002. As NCS's performance improved, the NCS directors began to believe that it might be possible for NCS to enter into a transaction that would provide some recovery for NCS stockholders' equity. In March 2002, NCS decided to form an independent committee of board members who were neither NCS employees nor major NCS stockholders (the "Independent Committee"). The NCS board thought this was necessary because, due to NCS's precarious financial condition, it felt that fiduciary duties were owed to the enterprise as a whole rather than solely to NCS stockholders.

Sells and Osborne were selected as the members of the committee, and given authority to consider and negotiate possible transactions for NCS. The entire four member NCS board, however, retained authority to approve any transaction. The

Independent Committee retained the same legal and financial counsel as the NCS board.

The Independent Committee met for the first time on May 14, 2002. At that meeting Pollack suggested that NCS seek a "stalking-horse merger partner" to obtain the highest possible value in any transaction. The Independent Committee agreed with the suggestion.

Genesis Initial Proposal

Two days later, on May 16, 2002, Scott Berlin of Brown Gibbons, Glen Pollack and Boake Sells met with George Hager, CFO of Genesis, and Michael Walker, who was Genesis's CEO. At that meeting, Genesis made it clear that if it were going to engage in any negotiations with NCS, it would not do so as a "stalking horse." As one of its advisors testified, "We didn't want to be someone who set forth a valuation for NCS which would only result in that valuation . . . being publicly disclosed, and thereby creating an environment where Omnicare felt to maintain its competitive monopolistic positions, that they had to match and exceed that level." Thus, Genesis "wanted a degree of certainty that to the extent [it] w[as] willing to pursue a negotiated merger agreement . . . , [it] would be able to consummate the transaction [it] negotiated and executed."

In June 2002, Genesis proposed a transaction that would take place outside the bankruptcy context. Although it did not provide full recovery for NCS's Noteholders, it provided the possibility that NCS stockholders would be able to recover something for their investment. As discussions continued, the terms proposed by Genesis continued to improve. On June 25, the economic terms of the Genesis proposal included repayment of the NCS senior debt in full, full assumption of trade credit obligations, an exchange offer or direct purchase of the NCS Notes providing NCS Noteholders with a combination of cash and Genesis common stock equal to the par value of the NCS Notes (not including accrued interest), and $20 million in value for the NCS common stock. Structurally, the Genesis proposal continued to include consents from a significant majority of the Noteholders as well as support agreements from stockholders owning a majority of the NCS voting power.

Genesis Exclusivity Agreement

NCS's financial advisors and legal counsel met again with Genesis and its legal counsel on June 26, 2002, to discuss a number of transaction-related issues. At this meeting, Pollack asked Genesis to increase its offer to NCS stockholders. Genesis agreed to consider this request. Thereafter, Pollack and Hager had further conversations. Genesis agreed to offer a total of $24 million in consideration for the NCS common stock, or an additional $4 million, in the form of Genesis common stock.

At the June 26 meeting, Genesis's representatives demanded that, before any further negotiations take place, NCS agree to enter into an exclusivity agreement with it. As Hager from Genesis explained it: "[I]f they wished us to continue to try to move this process to a definitive agreement, that they would need to do it on an exclusive basis with us. We were going to, and already had incurred significant expense, but we would incur additional expenses . . . , both internal and external, to bring this transaction to a definitive signing. We wanted them to work with us on an exclusive basis for a short period of time to see if we could reach agreement." On June 27, 2002, Genesis's legal counsel delivered a draft form of exclusivity agreement for review and consideration by NCS's legal counsel.

The Independent Committee met on July 3, 2002, to consider the proposed exclusivity agreement. Pollack presented a summary of the terms of a possible Genesis merger, which had continued to improve. The then-current Genesis proposal included (1) repayment of the NCS senior debt in full, (2) payment of par value for the Notes (without accrued interest) in the form of a combination of cash and Genesis stock, (3) payment to NCS stockholders in the form of $24 million in Genesis stock, plus (4) the assumption, because the transaction was to be structured as a merger, of additional liabilities to trade and other unsecured creditors.

NCS director Sells testified, Pollack told the Independent Committee at a July 3, 2002 meeting that Genesis wanted the Exclusivity Agreement to be the first step towards a completely locked up transaction that would preclude a higher bid from Omnicare:

> A. [Pollack] explained that Genesis felt that they had suffered at the hands of Omnicare and others. I guess maybe just Omnicare. I don't know much about Genesis [sic] acquisition history. But they had suffered before at the 11:59:59 and that they wanted to have a pretty much bulletproof deal or they were not going to go forward.
>
> Q. When you say they suffered at the hands of Omnicare, what do you mean?
>
> A. Well, my expression is that that was related to — a deal that was related to me or explained to me that they, Genesis, had tried to acquire, I suppose, an institutional pharmacy, I don't remember the name of it. Thought they had a deal and then at the last minute, Omnicare outbid them for the company in a like 11:59 kind of thing, and that they were unhappy about that. And once burned, twice shy.

After NCS executed the exclusivity agreement, Genesis provided NCS with a draft merger agreement, a draft Noteholders' support agreement, and draft voting agreements for Outcalt and Shaw, who together held a majority of the voting power of the NCS common stock. Genesis and NCS negotiated the terms of the merger agreement over the next three weeks. During those negotiations, the Independent Committee and the Ad Hoc Committee persuaded Genesis to improve the terms of its merger.

The parties were still negotiating by July 19, and the exclusivity period was automatically extended to July 26. At that point, NCS and Genesis were close to executing a merger agreement and related voting agreements. Genesis proposed a short extension of the exclusivity agreement so a deal could be finalized. On the morning of July 26, 2002, the Independent Committee authorized an extension of the exclusivity period through July 31.

Omnicare Proposes Negotiations

By late July 2002, Omnicare came to believe that NCS was negotiating a transaction, possibly with Genesis or another of Omnicare's competitors, that would potentially present a competitive threat to Omnicare. Omnicare also came to believe, in light of a run-up in the price of NCS common stock, that whatever transaction NCS was negotiating probably included a payment for its stock. Thus, the Omnicare board of directors met on the morning of July 26 and, on the recommendation of its management, authorized a proposal to acquire NCS that did not involve a sale of assets in bankruptcy.

On the afternoon of July 26, 2002, Omnicare faxed to NCS a letter outlining a proposed acquisition. The letter suggested a transaction in which Omnicare would retire NCS's senior and subordinated debt at par plus accrued interest, and pay the NCS stockholders $3 cash for their shares. Omnicare's proposal, however, was expressly conditioned on negotiating a merger agreement, obtaining certain third party consents, and completing its due diligence.

Mencher saw the July 26 Omnicare letter and realized that, while its economic terms were attractive, the "due diligence" condition substantially undercut its strength. In an effort to get a better proposal from Omnicare, Mencher telephoned Gemunder and told him that Omnicare was unlikely to succeed in its bid unless it dropped the "due diligence outs." She explained this was the only way a bid at the last minute would be able to succeed. Gemunder considered Mencher's warning "very real," and followed up with his advisors. They, however, insisted that he retain the due diligence condition "to protect [him] from doing something foolish." Taking this advice to heart, Gemunder decided not to drop the due diligence condition.

Late in the afternoon of July 26, 2002, NCS representatives received voicemail messages from Omnicare asking to discuss the letter. The exclusivity agreement prevented NCS from returning those calls. In relevant part, that agreement precluded NCS from "engag[ing] or particpat[ing] in any discussions or negotiations with respect to a Competing Transaction or a proposal for one." The July 26 letter from Omnicare met the definition of a "Competing Transaction."

Despite the exclusivity agreement, the Independent Committee met to consider a response to Omnicare. It concluded that discussions with Omnicare about its July 26 letter presented an unacceptable risk that Genesis would abandon merger discussions. The Independent Committee believed that, given Omnicare's past bankruptcy proposals and unwillingness to consider a merger, as well as its decision to negotiate exclusively with the Ad Hoc Committee, the risk of losing the Genesis proposal was too substantial. Nevertheless, the Independent Committee instructed Pollack to use Omnicare's letter to negotiate for improved terms with Genesis.

Genesis Merger Agreement And Voting Agreements

Genesis responded to the NCS request to improve its offer as a result of the Omnicare fax the next day. On July 27, Genesis proposed substantially improved terms. First, it proposed to retire the Notes in accordance with the terms of the indenture, thus eliminating the need for Noteholders to consent to the transaction. This change involved paying all accrued interest plus a small redemption premium.

Second, Genesis increased the exchange ratio for NCS common stock to one-tenth of a Genesis common share for each NCS common share, an 80% increase. Third, it agreed to lower the proposed termination fee in the merger agreement from $10 million to $6 million. In return for these concessions, Genesis stipulated that the transaction had to be approved by midnight the next day, July 28, or else Genesis would terminate discussions and withdraw its offer.

The Independent Committee and the NCS board both scheduled meetings for July 28. The committee met first. Although that meeting lasted less than an hour, the Court of Chancery determined the minutes reflect that the directors were fully informed of all material facts relating to the proposed transaction. After concluding that Genesis was sincere in establishing the midnight deadline, the committee voted unanimously to recommend the transaction to the full board.

The full board met thereafter. After receiving similar reports and advice from its legal and financial advisors, the board concluded that "balancing the potential loss of the Genesis deal against the uncertainty of Omnicare's letter, results in the conclusion that the only reasonable alternative for the Board of Directors is to approve the Genesis transaction." The board first voted to authorize the voting agreements with Outcalt and Shaw, for purposes of § 203 of the Delaware General Corporation Law ("DGCL"). The board was advised by its legal counsel that "under the terms of the merger agreement and because NCS shareholders representing in excess of 50% of the outstanding voting power would be *required* by Genesis to enter into stockholder voting agreements contemporaneously with the signing of the merger agreement, and would agree to vote their shares in favor of the merger agreement, shareholder approval of the merger would be assured even if the NCS Board were to withdraw or change its recommendation. *These facts would prevent NCS from engaging in any alternative or superior transaction in the future.*" (emphasis added).

After listening to a *summary* of the merger terms, the board then resolved that the merger agreement and the transactions contemplated thereby were advisable and fair and in the best interests of all the NCS stakeholders. The NCS board further resolved to recommend the transactions to the stockholders for their approval and adoption. A definitive merger agreement between NCS and Genesis and the stockholder voting agreements were executed later that day. The Court of Chancery held that it was not a *per se* breach of fiduciary duty that the NCS board never read the NCS/Genesis merger agreement word for word.

NCS/Genesis Merger Agreement

Among other things, the NCS/Genesis merger agreement provided the following:

- NCS stockholders would receive 1 share of Genesis common stock in exchange for every 10 shares of NCS common stock held;
- NCS stockholders could exercise appraisal rights under *8 Del. C. § 262;*
- NCS would redeem NCS's Notes in accordance with their terms;

- NCS would submit the merger agreement to NCS stockholders regardless of whether the NCS board continued to recommend the merger;

- NCS would not enter into discussions with third parties concerning an alternative acquisition of NCS, or provide non-public information to such parties, unless (1) the third party provided an unsolicited, *bona fide* written proposal documenting the terms of the acquisition; (2) the NCS board believed in good faith that the proposal was or was likely to result in an acquisition on terms superior to those contemplated by the NCS/Genesis merger agreement; and (3) before providing non-public information to that third party, the third party would execute a confidentiality agreement at least as restrictive as the one in place between NCS and Genesis; and

- If the merger agreement were to be terminated, under certain circumstances NCS would be required to pay Genesis a $6 million termination fee and/or Genesis's documented expenses, up to $5 million.

Voting Agreements

Outcalt and Shaw, in their capacity as NCS stockholders, entered into voting agreements with Genesis. NCS was also required to be a party to the voting agreements by Genesis. Those agreements provided, among other things, that:

- Outcalt and Shaw were acting in their capacity as NCS stockholders in executing the agreements, not in their capacity as NCS directors or officers;

- Neither Outcalt nor Shaw would transfer their shares prior to the stockholder vote on the merger agreement;

- Outcalt and Shaw agreed to vote all of their shares in favor of the merger agreement; and

- Outcalt and Shaw granted to Genesis an irrevocable proxy to vote their shares in favor of the merger agreement.

- The voting agreement was specifically enforceable by Genesis.

The merger agreement further provided that if either Outcalt or Shaw breached the terms of the voting agreements, Genesis would be entitled to terminate the merger agreement and potentially receive a $6 million termination fee from NCS. Such a breach was impossible since Section 6 provided that the voting agreements were specifically enforceable by Genesis.

Omnicare's Superior Proposal

On July 29, 2002, hours after the NCS/Genesis transaction was executed, Omnicare faxed a letter to NCS restating its conditional proposal and attaching a draft merger agreement. Later that morning, Omnicare issued a press release publicly disclosing the proposal.

On August 1, 2002, Omnicare filed a lawsuit attempting to enjoin the NCS/ Genesis merger, and announced that it intended to launch a tender offer for NCS's shares at a price of $3.50 per share. On August 8, 2002, Omnicare began its tender offer. By letter dated that same day, Omnicare expressed a desire to discuss the terms of the offer with NCS. Omnicare's letter continued to condition its proposal on satisfactory completion of a due diligence investigation of NCS.

On August 8, 2002, and again on August 19, 2002, the NCS Independent Committee and full board of directors met separately to consider the Omnicare tender offer in light of the Genesis merger agreement. NCS's outside legal counsel and NCS's financial advisor attended both meetings. The board was unable to determine that Omnicare's expressions of interest were likely to lead to a "Superior Proposal," as the term was defined in the NCS/Genesis merger agreement. On September 10, 2002, NCS requested and received a waiver from Genesis allowing NCS to enter into discussions with Omnicare without first having to determine that Omnicare's proposal was a "Superior Proposal."

On October 6, 2002, Omnicare irrevocably committed itself to a transaction with NCS. Pursuant to the terms of its proposal, Omnicare agreed to acquire all the outstanding NCS Class A and Class B shares at a price of $3.50 per share in cash. As a result of this irrevocable offer, on October 21, 2002, the NCS board withdrew its recommendation that the stockholders vote in favor of the NCS/Genesis merger agreement. NCS's financial advisor withdrew its fairness opinion of the NCS/Genesis merger agreement as well.

Genesis Rejection Impossible

The Genesis merger agreement permits the NCS directors to furnish non-public information to, or enter into discussions with, "any Person in connection with an unsolicited bona fide written Acquisition Proposal by such person" that the board deems likely to constitute a "Superior Proposal." That provision has absolutely no effect on the Genesis merger agreement. Even if the NCS board "changes, withdraws or modifies" its recommendation, as it did, it must still submit the merger to a stockholder vote.

A subsequent filing with the Securities and Exchange Commission ("SEC") states: "the NCS independent committee and the NCS board of directors have determined to withdraw their recommendations of the Genesis merger agreement and recommend that the NCS stockholders vote against the approval and adoption of the Genesis merger." In that same SEC filing, however, the NCS board explained why the success of the Genesis merger had already been predetermined. "Notwithstanding the foregoing, the NCS independent committee and the NCS board of directors recognize that (1) the existing contractual obligations to Genesis currently prevent NCS from accepting the Omnicare irrevocable merger proposal; and (2) the existence of the voting agreements entered into by Messrs. Outcalt and Shaw, whereby Messrs. Outcalt and Shaw agreed to vote their shares of NCS Class A common stock and NCS Class B common stock in favor of the Genesis merger, ensure NCS stockholder approval of the Genesis merger." This litigation was commenced to prevent the consummation of the inferior Genesis transaction.

LEGAL ANALYSIS

Business Judgment or Enhanced Scrutiny

The "defining tension" in corporate governance today has been characterized as "the tension between deference to directors' decisions and the scope of judicial review."[80] The appropriate standard of judicial review is dispositive of which party has the burden of proof as any litigation proceeds from stage to stage until there is a substantive determination on the merits. Accordingly, identification of the correct analytical framework is essential to a proper judicial review of challenges to the decision-making process of a corporation's board of directors. . . .

The prior decisions of this Court have identified the circumstances where board action must be subjected to enhanced judicial scrutiny before the presumptive protection of the business judgment rule can be invoked. One of those circumstances was described in *Unocal:* when a board adopts defensive measures in response to a hostile takeover proposal that the board reasonably determines is a threat to corporate policy and effectiveness. In *Moran v. Household*, we explained why a *Unocal* analysis also was applied to the adoption of a stockholder's rights plan, even in the absence of an immediate threat. Other circumstances requiring enhanced judicial scrutiny give rise to what are known as *Revlon* duties, such as when the board enters into a merger transaction that will cause a change in corporate control, initiates an active bidding process seeking to sell the corporation, or makes a break up of the corporate entity inevitable.

Merger Decision Review Standard

The first issue decided by the Court of Chancery addressed the standard of judicial review that should be applied to the decision by the NCS board to merge with Genesis. This Court has held that a board's decision to enter into a merger transaction that does not involve a change in control is entitled to judicial deference pursuant to the procedural and substantive operation of the business judgment rule. When a board decides to enter into a merger transaction that will result in a change of control, however, enhanced judicial scrutiny under *Revlon* is the standard of review.

The Court of Chancery concluded that, because the stock-for-stock merger between Genesis and NCS did not result in a change of control, the NCS directors' duties under *Revlon* were not triggered by the decision to merge with Genesis. The Court of Chancery also recognized, however, that *Revlon* duties are imposed "when a corporation initiates an active bidding process seeking to sell itself."[81] The Court of Chancery then concluded, alternatively, that *Revlon* duties had not been

---

80 [n.5] E. Norman Veasey, *The Defining Tension in Corporate Governance in America*, 52 Bus. Law. 393, 403 (1997).

81 [n.21] Arnold v. Soc'y for Sav. Bancorp, Inc., 650 A.2d 1270, 1290 (Del. 1994) (quoting Paramount Communications, Inc. v. Time Inc., 571 A.2d 1140, 1150 (Del. 1989)); *see also* Mills Acquisition Co. v. Macmillan, Inc., 559 A.2d at 1287; McMullin v. Beran, 765 A.2d 910, 919–20 (Del. 2000) (finding *Revlon* duties were implicated where the board agreed to sell the entire company, even though the merger did not involve a "change of control").

triggered because NCS did not start an active bidding process, and the NCS board "abandoned" its efforts to sell the company when it entered into an exclusivity agreement with Genesis.

After concluding that the *Revlon* standard of enhanced judicial review was completely inapplicable, the Court of Chancery then held that it would examine the decision of the NCS board of directors to approve the Genesis merger pursuant to the business judgment rule standard. After completing its business judgment rule review, the Court of Chancery held that the NCS board of directors had not breached their duty of care by entering into the exclusivity and merger agreements with Genesis. The Court of Chancery also held, however, that "even applying the more exacting *Revlon* standard, the directors acted in conformity with their fiduciary duties in seeking to achieve the highest and best transaction that was reasonably available to [the stockholders]."

The appellants argue that the Court of Chancery's *Revlon* conclusions are without factual support in the record and contrary to Delaware law for at least two reasons. First, they submit that NCS did initiate an active bidding process. Second, they submit that NCS did not "abandon" its efforts to sell itself by entering into the exclusivity agreement with Genesis. The appellants contend that once NCS decided "to initiate a bidding process seeking to maximize short-term stockholder value, it cannot avoid enhanced judicial scrutiny under *Revlon* simply because the bidder it selected [Genesis] happens to have proposed a merger transaction that does not involve a change of control."

The Court of Chancery's decision to review the NCS board's decision to merge with Genesis under the business judgment rule rather than the enhanced scrutiny standard of *Revlon* is not outcome determinative for the purposes of deciding this appeal. We have assumed arguendo that the business judgment rule applied to the decision by the NCS board to merge with Genesis. We have also assumed arguendo that the NCS board exercised due care when it: abandoned the Independent Committee's recommendation to pursue a stalking horse strategy, without even trying to implement it; executed an exclusivity agreement with Genesis; acceded to Genesis' twenty-four hour ultimatum for making a final merger decision; and executed a merger agreement that was summarized but never completely read by the NCS board of directors.

Deal Protection Devices Require Enhanced Scrutiny

The dispositive issues in this appeal involve the defensive devices that protected the Genesis merger agreement. The Delaware corporation statute provides that the board's management decision to enter into and recommend a merger transaction can become final only when ownership action is taken by a vote of the stockholders. Thus, the Delaware corporation law expressly provides for a balance of power between boards and stockholders which makes merger transactions a shared enterprise and ownership decision. Consequently, a board of directors' decision to adopt defensive devices to protect a merger agreement may implicate the stockholders' right to effectively vote contrary to the initial recommendation of the board in favor of the transaction.

It is well established that conflicts of interest arise when a board of directors acts to prevent stockholders from effectively exercising their right to vote contrary to the will of the board. The "omnipresent specter" of such conflict may be present whenever a board adopts defensive devices to protect a merger agreement. The stockholders' ability to effectively reject a merger agreement is likely to bear an inversely proportionate relationship to the structural and economic devices that the board has approved to protect the transaction.

In *Paramount v. Time*, the original merger agreement between Time and Warner did not constitute a "change of control."[82] The plaintiffs in *Paramount v. Time* argued that, although the original Time and Warner merger agreement did not involve a change of control, the use of a lock-up, no-shop clause, and "dry-up" provisions violated the Time board's *Revlon* duties. This Court held that "[t]he adoption of structural safety devices alone does not trigger *Revlon*. Rather, as the Chancellor stated, *such devices are properly subject to a Unocal analysis.*"[83]

In footnote 15 of *Paramount v. Time*, we stated that legality of the structural safety devices adopted to protect the original merger agreement between Time and Warner were not a central issue on appeal. That is because the issue on appeal involved the "Time's board [decision] to recast its consolidation with Warner into an outright cash and securities acquisition of Warner by Time."[84] Nevertheless, we determined that there was substantial evidence on the record to support the conclusions reached by the Chancellor in applying a *Unocal* analysis to each of the structural devices contained in the original merger agreement between Time and Warner.

There are inherent conflicts between a board's interest in protecting a merger transaction it has approved, the stockholders' statutory right to make the final decision to either approve or not approve a merger, and the board's continuing responsibility to effectively exercise its fiduciary duties at all times after the merger agreement is executed. These competing considerations require a threshold determination that board-approved defensive devices protecting a merger transaction are within the limitations of its statutory authority and consistent with the directors' fiduciary duties. Accordingly, in *Paramount v. Time*, we held that the business judgment rule applied to the Time board's original decision to merge with Warner. We further held, however, that defensive devices adopted by the board to protect the original merger transaction must withstand enhanced judicial scrutiny under the *Unocal* standard of review, even when that merger transaction does not result in a change of control.

Enhanced Scrutiny Generally

In *Paramount v. QVC*, this Court identified the key features of an enhanced judicial scrutiny test. The first feature is a "judicial determination regarding the adequacy of the decisionmaking process employed by the directors, including the

---

[82] [n.28] Paramount Communications, Inc. v. Time Inc., 571 A.2d at 1150.

[83] [n.29] *Id.* at 1151 (footnote omitted) (emphasis added).

[84] [n.31] *Id.* at 1148.

information on which the directors based their decision."[85] The second feature is "a judicial examination of the reasonableness of the directors' action in light of the circumstances then existing."[86] We also held that "the directors have the burden of proving that they were adequately informed and acted reasonably."[87]

In *QVC*, we explained that the application of an enhanced judicial scrutiny test involves a judicial "review of the reasonableness of the substantive merits of the board's actions."[88] In applying that standard, we held that "a court should not ignore the complexity of the directors' task" in the context in which action was taken.[89] Accordingly, we concluded that a court applying enhanced judicial scrutiny should not decide whether the directors made a perfect decision but instead should decide whether "the directors' decision was, on balance, within a range of reasonableness."[90]

In *Unitrin*, we explained the "*ratio decidendi* for the 'range of reasonableness' standard"[91] when a court applies enhanced judicial scrutiny to director action pursuant to our holding in *Unocal*. It is a recognition that a board of directors needs "latitude in discharging its fiduciary duties to the corporation and its shareholders when defending against perceived threats."[92] "The concomitant requirement is for judicial restraint."[93] Therefore, if the board of directors' collective defensive responses are not draconian (preclusive or coercive) and are "within a 'range of reasonableness,' a court must not substitute its judgment for the board's [judgment]."[94] The same *ratio decidendi* applies to the "range of reasonableness" when courts apply *Unocal's* enhanced judicial scrutiny standard to defensive devices intended to protect a merger agreement that will not result in a change of control.

A board's decision to protect its decision to enter a merger agreement with defensive devices against uninvited competing transactions that may emerge is analogous to a board's decision to protect against dangers to corporate policy and effectiveness when it adopts defensive measures in a hostile takeover contest. In applying *Unocal's* enhanced judicial scrutiny in assessing a challenge to defensive actions taken by a target corporation's board of directors in a takeover context, this Court held that the board "does not have unbridled discretion to defeat perceived threats by any Draconian means available".[95] Similarly, just as a board's statutory power with regard to a merger decision is not absolute, a board does not have unbridled discretion to defeat any perceived threat to a merger by protecting it with any draconian means available.

---

[85] [n.35] Paramount Communications Inc. v. QVC Network Inc., 637 A.2d 34, 45 (Del. 1993).

[86] [n.36] *Id.*

[87] [n.37] *Id.*

[88] [n.38] *Id.* (footnote omitted).

[89] [n.39] *Id.*

[90] [n.40] *Id.* (citations omitted).

[91] [n.41] Unitrin, Inc. v. Am. Gen. Corp., 651 A.2d at 1388.

[92] [n.43] *Id.*

[93] [n.44] *Id.*

[94] [n.45] *Id.* (citation omitted); *see also* Unocal Corp. v. Mesa Petroleum Co., 493 A.2d at 949, 954–57.

[95] [n.46] Unocal Corp. v. Mesa Petroleum Co., 493 A.2d at 955.

Since *Unocal*, "this Court has consistently recognized that defensive measures which are either preclusive or coercive are included within the common law definition of draconian."[96] In applying enhanced judicial scrutiny to defensive actions under *Unocal*, a court must "evaluate the board's overall response, including the justification for each contested defensive measure, and the results achieved thereby."[97] If a "board's defensive actions are inextricably related, the principles of *Unocal* require that such actions be scrutinized collectively as a unitary response to the perceived threat."[98]

Therefore, in applying enhanced judicial scrutiny to defensive devices designed to protect a merger agreement, a court must first determine that those measures are not preclusive or coercive *before* its focus shifts to the "range of reasonableness" in making a proportionality determination. If the trial court determines that the defensive devices protecting a merger are not preclusive or coercive, the proportionality paradigm of *Unocal* is applicable. The board must demonstrate that it has reasonable grounds for believing that a danger to the corporation and its stockholders exists if the merger transaction is not consummated. That burden is satisfied "by showing good faith and reasonable investigation."[99] Such proof is materially enhanced if it is approved by a board comprised of a majority of outside directors or by an independent committee.

When the focus of judicial scrutiny shifts to the range of reasonableness, *Unocal* requires that any defensive devices must be proportionate to the perceived threat to the corporation and its stockholders if the merger transaction is not consummated. Defensive devices taken to protect a merger agreement executed by a board of directors are intended to give that agreement an advantage over any subsequent transactions that materialize before the merger is approved by the stockholders and consummated. This is analogous to the favored treatment that a board of directors may properly give to encourage an initial bidder when it discharges its fiduciary duties under *Revlon*.

Therefore, in the context of a merger that does not involve a change of control, when defensive devices in the executed merger agreement are challenged *vis-à-vis* their effect on a subsequent competing alternative merger transaction, this Court's analysis in *Macmillan* is didactic. In the context of a case of defensive measures taken against an existing bidder, we stated in *Macmillan*:

> In the face of disparate treatment, the trial court must first examine whether the directors properly perceived that shareholder interests were enhanced. In any event the board's action must be reasonable in relation to the advantage sought to be achieved [by the merger it approved], or conversely, to the threat which a [competing transaction] poses to stockholder interests. If on the basis of this enhanced *Unocal* scrutiny the trial

---

[96] [n.47] Unitrin, Inc. v. Am. Gen. Corp., 651 A.2d at 1387.

[97] [n.48] *Id.*

[98] [n.49] *Id.* (citation omitted).

[99] [n.52] Unocal Corp. v. Mesa Petroleum Co., 493 A.2d at 955 (citations omitted).

court is satisfied that the test has been met, then the directors' actions necessarily are entitled to the protections of the business judgment rule.[100]

The latitude a board will have in either maintaining or using the defensive devices it has adopted to protect the merger it approved will vary according to the degree of benefit or detriment to the stockholders' interests that is presented by the value or terms of the subsequent competing transaction.

Genesis' One Day Ultimatum

The record reflects that two of the four NCS board members, Shaw and Outcalt, were also the *same* two NCS stockholders who combined to control a majority of the stockholder voting power. Genesis gave the four person NCS board less than twenty-four hours to vote in favor of its proposed merger agreement. Genesis insisted the merger agreement include a § 251(c) clause, mandating its submission for a stockholder vote even if the board's recommendation was withdrawn. Genesis further insisted that the merger agreement omit any effective fiduciary out clause.

Genesis also gave the two stockholder members of the NCS board, Shaw and Outcalt, the same accelerated time table to personally sign the proposed voting agreements. These voting agreements committed them irrevocably to vote their majority power in favor of the merger and further provided in Section 6 that the voting agreements be specifically enforceable. Genesis also required that NCS execute the voting agreements.

Genesis' twenty-four hour ultimatum was that, *unless both* the merger agreement and the voting agreements were signed with the terms it requested, its offer was going to be withdrawn. According to Genesis' attorneys, these "were unalterable conditions to Genesis' willingness to proceed." Genesis insisted on the execution of the interlocking voting rights and merger agreements because it feared that Omnicare would make a superior merger proposal. The NCS board signed the voting rights and merger agreements, without any effective fiduciary out clause, to expressly guarantee that the Genesis merger would be approved, even if a superior merger transaction was presented from Omnicare or any other entity.

Deal Protection Devices

Defensive devices, as that term is used in this opinion, is a synonym for what are frequently referred to as "deal protection devices." Both terms are used interchangeably to describe any measure or combination of measures that are intended to protect the consummation of a merger transaction. Defensive devices can be economic, structural, or both.

Deal protection devices need not all be in the merger agreement itself. In this case, for example, the § 251(c) provision in the merger agreement was combined with the separate voting agreements to provide a structural defense for the Genesis merger agreement against any subsequent superior transaction. Genesis made the NCS board's defense of its transaction absolute by insisting on the omission of any

---

[100] [n.55] Mills Acquisition Co. v. Macmillan Inc., 559 A.2d 1261, 1288 (Del. 1988) (citation omitted).

effective fiduciary out clause in the NCS merger agreement.

Genesis argues that stockholder voting agreements cannot be construed as deal protection devices taken by a board of directors because stockholders are entitled to vote in their own interest. Genesis cites *Williams v. Geier*[101] and *Stroud v. Grace*[102] for the proposition that voting agreements are not subject to the *Unocal* standard of review. Neither of those cases, however, holds that the operative effect of a voting agreement must be disregarded *per se* when a *Unocal* analysis is applied to a comprehensive and combined merger defense plan.

In this case, the stockholder voting agreements were inextricably intertwined with the defensive aspects of the Genesis merger agreement. In fact, the voting agreements with Shaw and Outcalt were the linchpin of Genesis' proposed tripartite defense. Therefore, Genesis made the execution of those voting agreements a non-negotiable condition precedent to its execution of the merger agreement. In the case before us, the Court of Chancery held that the acts which locked-up the Genesis transaction were the § 251(c) provision and "the execution of the *voting agreement* by Outcalt and Shaw."

With the assurance that Outcalt and Shaw would irrevocably agree to exercise their majority voting power in favor of its transaction, Genesis insisted that the merger agreement reflect the other two aspects of its concerted defense, i.e., the inclusion of a § 251(c) provision and the omission of any effective fiduciary out clause. Those dual aspects of the merger agreement would not have provided Genesis with a complete defense in the absence of the voting agreements with Shaw and Outcalt.

These Deal Protection Devices Unenforceable

In this case, the Court of Chancery correctly held that the NCS directors' decision to adopt defensive devices to *completely* "lock up" the Genesis merger mandated "special scrutiny" under the two-part test set forth in *Unocal*. That conclusion is consistent with our holding in *Paramount v. Time* that "safety devices" adopted to protect a transaction that did not result in a change of control are subject to enhanced judicial scrutiny under a *Unocal* analysis. The record does not, however, support the Court of Chancery's conclusion that the defensive devices adopted by the NCS board to protect the Genesis merger were reasonable and proportionate to the threat that NCS perceived from the potential loss of the Genesis transaction.

Pursuant to the judicial scrutiny required under *Unocal's* two-stage analysis, the NCS directors must first demonstrate "that they had reasonable grounds for believing that a danger to corporate policy and effectiveness existed . . . ."[103] To satisfy that burden, the NCS directors are required to show they acted in good faith after conducting a reasonable investigation. The threat identified by the NCS board

---

[101] [n.57] Williams v. Geier, 671 A.2d 1368 (Del. 1996).

[102] [n.58] Stroud v. Grace, 606 A.2d 75 (Del. 1992).

[103] [n.61] Unocal Corp. v. Mesa Petroleum Co., 493 A.2d 946, 955 (Del. 1985) (citation omitted).

was the possibility of losing the Genesis offer and being left with no comparable alternative transaction.

The second stage of the *Unocal* test requires the NCS directors to demonstrate that their defensive response was "reasonable in relation to the threat posed."[104] This inquiry involves a two-step analysis. The NCS directors must first establish that the merger deal protection devices adopted in response to the threat were not "coercive" or "preclusive," and then demonstrate that their response was within a "range of reasonable responses" to the threat perceived.[105] In *Unitrin*, we stated:

- A response is "coercive" if it is aimed at forcing upon stockholders a management-sponsored alternative to a hostile offer.

- A response is "preclusive" if it deprives stockholders of the right to receive all tender offers or precludes a bidder from seeking control by fundamentally restricting proxy contests or otherwise.

This aspect of the *Unocal* standard provides for a disjunctive analysis. If defensive measures are either preclusive or coercive they are draconian and impermissible. In this case, the deal protection devices of the NCS board were *both* preclusive and coercive.

This Court enunciated the standard for determining stockholder coercion in the case of *Williams v. Geier*.[106] A stockholder vote may be nullified by wrongful coercion "where the board or some other party takes actions which have the effect of causing the stockholders to vote in favor of the proposed transaction for some reason other than the merits of that transaction."[107] In *Brazen v. Bell Atlantic Corporation*, we applied that test for stockholder coercion and held "that although the termination fee provision may have influenced the stockholder vote, there were 'no structurally or situationally coercive factors' that made an otherwise valid fee provision impermissibly coercive" under the facts presented.[108]

In *Brazen*, we concluded "the determination of whether a particular stockholder vote has been robbed of its effectiveness by impermissible coercion depends on the facts of the case."[109] In this case, the Court of Chancery did not expressly address the issue of "coercion" in its *Unocal* analysis. It did find as a fact, however, that NCS's public stockholders (who owned 80% of NCS and overwhelmingly supported Omnicare's offer) will be forced to accept the Genesis merger because of the structural defenses approved by the NCS board. Consequently, the record reflects that any stockholder vote would have been robbed of its effectiveness by the impermissible coercion that predetermined the outcome of the merger without regard to the merits of the Genesis transaction at the time the vote was scheduled to be taken. Deal protection devices that result in such coercion cannot withstand

---

[104] [n.63] *Id.*

[105] [n.64] Unitrin, Inc. v. Am. Gen. Corp., 651 A.2d 1361, 1387–88 (Del. 1995).

[106] [n.67] Williams v. Geier, 671 A.2d 1368 (Del. 1996).

[107] [n.68] *Id.* at 1382–83 (citations omitted).

[108] [n.69] Brazen v. Bell Atl. Corp., 695 A.2d 43, 50 (Del. 1997).

[109] [n.70] Brazen v. Bell Atl. Corp., 695 A.2d at 50 (quoting Williams v. Geier, 671 A.2d at 1383).

Unocal's enhanced judicial scrutiny standard of review because they are not within the range of reasonableness.

Although the minority stockholders were not forced to vote for the Genesis merger, they were required to accept it because it was *a fait accompli.* The record reflects that the defensive devices employed by the NCS board are preclusive and coercive in the sense that they accomplished *a fait accompli.* In this case, despite the fact that the NCS board has withdrawn its recommendation for the Genesis transaction and recommended its rejection by the stockholders, the deal protection devices approved by the NCS board operated in concert to have a preclusive and coercive effect. Those tripartite defensive measures — the § 251(c) provision, the voting agreements, and the absence of an effective fiduciary out clause — made it "mathematically impossible" and "realistically unattainable" for the Omnicare transaction or any other proposal to succeed, no matter how superior the proposal.

The deal protection devices adopted by the NCS board were designed to coerce the consummation of the Genesis merger and preclude the consideration of any superior transaction. The NCS directors' defensive devices are not within a reasonable range of responses to the perceived threat of losing the Genesis offer because they are preclusive and coercive. Accordingly, we hold that those deal protection devices are unenforceable.

Effective Fiduciary Out Required

The defensive measures that protected the merger transaction are unenforceable not only because they are preclusive and coercive but, alternatively, they are unenforceable because they are invalid as they operate in this case. Given the specifically enforceable irrevocable voting agreements, the provision in the merger agreement requiring the board to submit the transaction for a stockholder vote and the omission of a fiduciary out clause in the merger agreement completely prevented the board from discharging its fiduciary responsibilities to the minority stockholders when Omnicare presented its superior transaction. "To the extent that a [merger] contract, or a provision thereof, purports to require a board to act or not act in such a fashion as to limit the exercise of fiduciary duties, it is invalid and unenforceable."[110]

In *QVC,*[111] this Court recognized that "[w]hen a majority of a corporation's voting shares are acquired by a single person or entity, or by *a cohesive group acting together* [as in this case], there is a significant diminution in the voting power of those who thereby become minority stockholders."[112] Therefore, we acknowledged that "[i]n the absence of devices protecting the minority stockholders,

---

[110] [n.74] Paramount Communications Inc. v. QVC Network Inc., 637 A.2d 34, 51 (Del. 1993) (citation omitted). *Restatement (Second) of Contracts* § 193 explicitly provides that a "promise by a fiduciary to violate his fiduciary duty *or a promise that tends to induce such a violation is unenforceable on grounds of public policy.*" The comments to that section indicate that "[d]irectors and other officials of a corporation act in a fiduciary capacity and are subject to the rule stated in this Section." Restatement (Second) of Contracts § 193 (1981) (emphasis added).

[111] [n.75] Paramount Communications Inc. v. QVC Network Inc., 637 A.2d 34 (Del. 1993).

[112] [n.76] *Id.* at 42 (emphasis added).

stockholder votes are likely to become mere formalities," where a cohesive group acting together to exercise majority voting powers have already decided the outcome.[113] Consequently, we concluded that since the minority stockholders lost the power to influence corporate direction through the ballot, "minority stockholders must rely for protection solely on the fiduciary duties owed to them by the directors."[114]

Under the circumstances presented in this case, where a cohesive group of stockholders with majority voting power was irrevocably committed to the merger transaction, "[e]ffective representation of the financial interests of the minority shareholders imposed upon the [NCS board] an affirmative responsibility to protect those minority shareholders' interests."[115] The NCS board could not abdicate its fiduciary duties to the minority by leaving it to the stockholders alone to approve or disapprove the merger agreement because two stockholders had already combined to establish a majority of the voting power that made the outcome of the stockholder vote a foregone conclusion.

The Court of Chancery noted that § 251(c) of the Delaware General Corporation Law now permits boards to agree to submit a merger agreement for a stockholder vote, even if the Board later withdraws its support for that agreement and recommends that the stockholders reject it. The Court of Chancery also noted that stockholder voting agreements are permitted by Delaware law. In refusing to certify this interlocutory appeal, the Court of Chancery stated "it is simply nonsensical to say that a board of directors abdicates its duties to manage the 'business and affairs' of a corporation under § 141(a) of the DGCL by agreeing to the inclusion in a merger agreement of a term authorized by § 251(c) of the same statute."

Taking action that is otherwise legally possible, however, does not *ipso facto* comport with the fiduciary responsibilities of directors in all circumstances. The synopsis to the amendments that resulted in the enactment of § 251(c) in the Delaware corporation law statute specifically provides: "the amendments are not intended to address the question of whether such a submission requirement is appropriate in any particular set of factual circumstances." Section 251 provisions, like the no-shop provision examined in QVC, are "presumptively valid in the abstract."[116] Such provisions in a merger agreement may not, however, "validly define or limit the directors' fiduciary duties under Delaware law or prevent the [NCS] directors from carrying out their fiduciary duties under Delaware law."[117]

Genesis admits that when the NCS board agreed to its merger conditions, the NCS board was seeking to assure that the NCS creditors were paid in full and that the NCS stockholders received the highest value available for their stock. In fact, Genesis defends its "bulletproof" merger agreement on that basis. We hold that the

---

[113]   [n.77] *Id.* (footnote omitted).

[114]   [n.78] *Id.* at 43.

[115]   [n.79] McMullin v. Beran, 765 A.2d 910, 920 (Del. 2000).

[116]   [n.82] Paramount Communications Inc. v. QVC Network Inc., 637 A.2d at 48.

[117]   [n.83] *Id.*

NCS board did not have authority to accede to the Genesis demand for an absolute "lock-up."

The directors of a Delaware corporation have a continuing obligation to discharge their fiduciary responsibilities, as future circumstances develop, after a merger agreement is announced. Genesis anticipated the likelihood of a superior offer after its merger agreement was announced and demanded defensive measures from the NCS board that *completely* protected its transaction. Instead of agreeing to the absolute defense of the Genesis merger from a superior offer, however, the NCS board was required to negotiate a fiduciary out clause to protect the NCS stockholders if the Genesis transaction became an inferior offer. By acceding to Genesis' ultimatum for complete protection *in futuro*, the NCS board disabled itself from exercising its own fiduciary obligations at a time when the board's own judgment is most important, i.e. receipt of a subsequent superior offer.

Any board has authority to give the proponent of a recommended merger agreement reasonable structural and economic defenses, incentives, and fair compensation if the transaction is not completed. To the extent that defensive measures are economic and reasonable, they may become an increased cost to the proponent of any subsequent transaction. Just as defensive measures cannot be draconian, however, they cannot limit or circumscribe the directors' fiduciary duties. Notwithstanding the corporation's insolvent condition, the NCS board had no authority to execute a merger agreement that subsequently prevented it from effectively discharging its ongoing fiduciary responsibilities.

The stockholders of a Delaware corporation are entitled to rely upon the board to discharge its fiduciary duties at all times. The fiduciary duties of a director are unremitting and must be effectively discharged in the specific context of the actions that are required with regard to the corporation or its stockholders as circumstances change. The stockholders with majority voting power, Shaw and Outcalt, had an absolute right to sell or exchange their shares with a third party at any price. This right was not only known to the other directors of NCS, it became an integral part of the Genesis agreement. In its answering brief, Genesis candidly states that its offer "came with a condition — Genesis would not be a stalking horse and would not agree to a transaction to which NCS's controlling shareholders were not committed."

The NCS board was required to contract for an effective fiduciary out clause to exercise its continuing fiduciary responsibilities to the minority stockholders. The issues in this appeal do not involve the general validity of either stockholder voting agreements or the authority of directors to insert a § 251(c) provision in a merger agreement. In this case, the NCS board combined those two otherwise valid actions and caused them to operate in concert as an absolute lock up, in the absence of an effective fiduciary out clause in the Genesis merger agreement.

In the context of this preclusive and coercive lock up case, the protection of Genesis' contractual expectations must yield to the supervening responsibility of the directors to discharge their fiduciary duties on a continuing basis. The merger agreement and voting agreements, as they were combined to operate in concert in this case, are inconsistent with the NCS directors' fiduciary duties. To that extent, we hold that they are invalid and unenforceable. . . .

QUESTIONS

1.   What deal protection devices did NCS implement with respect to the Genesis deal? Why did the NCS board feel they were necessary?

2.   Why did NCS's board initially decide to go with the Genesis deal and not the deal offered by Omnicare? Why did it later withdraw its recommendation of the Genesis deal?

3.   What did the court mean when it said that the Genesis deal was completely locked-up?

4.   Did NCS enter *Revlon*-land? Was the issue critical to the court's analysis?

5.   Why is a board's decision to implement deal protection devices subject to enhanced scrutiny?

6.   Did NCS's deal protection devices pass muster under *Unocal*? Why or why not?

7.   What is a fiduciary out? What was the court's reasoning for requiring a fiduciary out in the Genesis deal?

ORMAN v. CULLMAN
Delaware Chancery Court
2004 Del. Ch. LEXIS 150 (Oct. 20, 2004)

CHANDLER, J.

This case is about a merger transaction in which one tobacco company, Swedish Match AB, purchased an equity stake in another tobacco company, General Cigar Holdings, Inc. Members of the Cullman family are the controlling shareholders of General Cigar. Swedish Match did not purchase control of General Cigar, as it wanted the Cullmans to continue managing the company after the merger.

Although Swedish Match paid a significant premium above the market price for the public shares in General Cigar, plaintiff Joseph Orman sued the General Cigar board of directors for breach of their fiduciary duties in negotiating the merger terms. . . . Defendants contend that a fully informed vote of a majority of the public shareholders in favor of the merger operates to extinguish plaintiff's claim. This contention raises the following question: Were the General Cigar public shareholders impermissibly coerced to vote for the merger because of a lock-up provision required by Swedish Match as part of the transaction? . . .

I. BACKGROUND

General Cigar Holdings, Inc. was founded in 1906 by the Cullman family. General Cigar became a public company through an IPO in February 1997 at an IPO price of $18.00 per share. The prospectus issued in connection with the IPO informed potential investors that certain members of the Cullman and Ernst families (the "Cullmans") would "have substantial control over the Company and may have the power . . . to approve any action requiring stockholder approval, including . . . approving mergers." The Cullmans' control over General Cigar was by virtue of their exclusive power over the Company's Class B common stock, which is entitled to ten votes per share. Following the IPO, the Company's stock traded as high as $33.25 per share. Throughout 1998 and 1999, however, the stock traded as low as $5.50 per share.

At the end of April 1999, General Cigar sold part of its business to Swedish Match AB. Later that year, Swedish Match contacted the Company to discuss "acquiring a significant stake" in General Cigar's business. In November 1999, the Company's board authorized management to pursue discussions with Swedish Match. On December 2, 1999, Edgar Cullman Sr., General Cigar's chairman, informed the board that he and Edgar Cullman Jr., the Company's CEO, were meeting with a representative of Swedish Match in London to discuss an acquisition. At the early December meeting in London, Swedish Match expressed a high level of interest in making an equity investment in General Cigar. Swedish Match also indicated that "they wanted Edgar M. Cullman, Sr. and Edgar M. Cullman, Jr. to maintain management responsibility and day-to-day control of General Cigar." Swedish Match's interest, and desire to have the Cullmans remain in control of General Cigar, was reaffirmed at meetings in New York from December 19–21, 1999. At these meetings, General Cigar made their management available in order to permit Swedish Match to begin their due diligence process.

Given the continuing interest of Swedish Match, General Cigar's board created a special committee to advise and make recommendations to the full board concerning any transaction with Swedish Match. The special committee consisted of Dan Lufkin, Thomas Israel, and Francis Vincent, Jr. The chairman of the special committee, Lufkin, believed it was the committee's responsibility to ensure that the public shareholders were "fairly represented." Although the special committee was charged with advising the board regarding any transaction with Swedish Match, it was not authorized to solicit offers by third parties. The special committee also did not negotiate directly with Swedish Match. Instead, the negotiations were conducted primarily by Peter J. Solomon Company Limited, an investment company owned by a member of the Company's board, Peter Solomon. The special committee retained Wachtell, Lipton, Rosen & Katz ("Wachtell") to serve as legal counsel to the committee. The special committee also retained Deutsche Bank Securities Inc. ("Deutsche Bank") to render a fairness opinion on any proposals made by Swedish Match.

During the negotiations that led to the merger, Swedish Match required that the Cullmans enter into a stockholders' voting agreement. "Under that agreement, the Cullmans agreed not to sell their shares, and to vote their shares against any alternative acquisition proposal for a specified period following any termination of the merger between Swedish Match and General Cigar." According to Swedish Match's CFO:

A central purpose of the voting agreement was to protect Swedish Match against the risk that the Cullmans or General Cigar would "shop" Swedish Match's offer to other potential bidders. Because the Cullmans held a controlling interest in General Cigar, the voting agreement would prevent an alternative bidder from acquiring control of General Cigar during the specified period if the merger did not go forward. This protection was particularly important to Swedish Match because the merger agreement did not contain a termination fee or expense reimbursement provision.

Swedish Match originally asked that the Cullmans agree to a restricted period of three years. This was rejected. The restricted period was later negotiated down to one year.

Drafts of the merger agreement and the voting agreement were sent to the Cullmans and the special committee on January 18, 2000. These drafts reflected a potential transaction structure in which the Cullmans would sell approximately one third of their equity interest to Swedish Match at a price of $15.00 per share followed by a merger into a Swedish Match subsidiary in which public shareholders would also receive $15.00 per share. The voting agreement circulated on January 18 contained a requirement that the Cullmans not sell their shares, and to vote their shares against any alternative acquisition proposal, for one year following any termination of the merger agreement between Swedish Match and General Cigar. Following the merger, General Cigar would be owned 64% by Swedish Match and 36% by the Cullmans. The Cullmans, specifically Edgar Cullman Sr. and Edgar Cullman Jr., however, would remain in control of the Company.

The special committee met on January 19, 2000. Wachtell and Deutsche Bank attended the meeting. At this meeting, Lufkin informed the full committee that Swedish Match agreed to increase the price paid to the public shareholders to $15.25 per share. In exchange for this slightly higher offer, Swedish Match required the Cullmans to increase the restricted period under the voting agreement from twelve to eighteen months. Deutsche Bank made a presentation at the meeting and opined that from a financial point of view the offer price of $15.25 per share was fair to the public shareholders. After Deutsche Bank's presentation, discussion ensued, and the special committee voted unanimously to recommend that the full board approve the merger. After the special committee's meeting, the full board met, approved the merger, and the relevant documents were signed by all parties on the evening of January 19, 2000. A public announcement was made the following day.

As noted earlier, the voting agreement between the Cullmans and Swedish Match required that the Cullmans vote their Class B shares, constituting a majority of the voting power of the Company, in favor of the merger and against any alternative acquisition of the Company for eighteen months after termination of the merger agreement. The voting agreement, however, reveals that the Cullmans were bound only in their capacities as shareholders and that nothing in the voting agreement limits or affects their actions as officers or directors of General Cigar. Moreover, the merger agreement permitted General Cigar's board to entertain unsolicited acquisition proposals from potential acquirors if the board, upon recommendation by the special committee, concluded that such a proposal was *bona fide* and would be more favorable to the public shareholders than the proposed merger with Swedish Match. The agreement also permitted the board to withdraw its recommendation of the merger with Swedish Match if the board concluded, upon consultation with outside counsel, that its fiduciary duties so required.

On April 10, 2000, almost three months after the public announcement of the Swedish Match transaction, General Cigar filed the proxy statement relating to the shareholder vote on the proposed merger. As expected, the proxy statement attached the merger agreement, the voting agreement, and contained the background relating to the proposed merger. The proxy statement also revealed (1) that the merger could not occur without the approval of the merger by the Class A shareholders and (2) that the Cullmans agreed to vote their shares of Class A common stock held by them pro rata in accordance with the vote of the Class A public shareholders. In other words, the merger could not proceed without approval by a "majority of the minority." The shareholder meeting was held on May 8, 2000. The public shareholders, i.e., a majority of the minority, overwhelmingly approved the merger.

II. ANALYSIS . . .

2. *The Voting Agreement*

[P]laintiff . . . argues that members of the Cullman and Ernst families on General Cigar's board breached their fiduciary duties "by entering into the voting agreement." Plaintiff's argument, which rests on a misapplication of *Paramount Communications, Inc. v. QVC Network, Inc.*[118] and *Omnicare, Inc. v. NCS Healthcare Inc.*,[119] is without merit.

In *Paramount*, the Supreme Court noted that "[t]o the extent that a contract, or a provision thereof, purports to require a board to act in such a fashion as to limit the exercise of fiduciary duties, it is invalid and unenforceable."[120] In *Omnicare*, the Supreme Court made a similar observation.[121] I do not question the general validity of these statements, but they have no application here because in both cases the challenged action was the directors' entering into a contract in their capacity *as directors* . The Cullmans entered into the voting agreement *as shareholders.* Nothing in the voting agreement prevented the Cullmans from exercising their duties *as officers and directors.* For example, the Cullmans could have voted, as directors, to withdraw their recommendation that the public shareholders approve the merger. This factual distinction from *Paramount* and *Omnicare* is meaningful.

In *Bershad v. Curtiss–Wright Corporation*,[122] the Supreme Court held that "a majority stockholder is under no duty to sell its holdings in a corporation, even if it is a majority shareholder, merely because the sale would profit the minority."[123]

---

[118] [n.58] 637 A.2d 34 (Del. 1994).

[119] [n.59] 818 A.2d 914 (Del. 2003).

[120] [n.60] *Paramount*, 637 A.2d at 51.

[121] [n.61] Contract provisions "cannot limit or circumscribe the directors' fiduciary duties." *Omnicare*, 818 A.2d at 938.

[122] [n.62] 535 A.2d 840 (Del. 1987).

[123] [n.63] *Id.* at 845.

This principle of Delaware law was more recently recognized in *Peter Schoenfeld Asset Management, LLC v. Shaw*,[124] where this Court observed:

> A majority shareholder has discretion as to when to sell his stock and to whom, a discretion that comes from the majority shareholder's rights *qua* shareholder. This is true even when a proposed transaction would result in the minority sharing in a control premium.[125]

Nothing in *Paramount* or *Omnicare* displaces this longstanding principle. In fact, *Omnicare* found that "[t]he stockholders with majority voting power . . . had an *absolute right* to sell or exchange their shares with a third party at any price."[126]

Plaintiff's challenge both to the voting and merger agreement's deal protection mechanisms are more properly analyzed *vis-a-vis* the board's decision to recommend that the Company's public shareholders approve the merger and whether the shareholders' ensuing vote was improperly coerced. This is the task to which I now turn.

3. *The Deal Protection Mechanisms*

Although the parties have framed the Court's inquiry as relating only to the issue whether the deal protection mechanisms "coerced" the shareholder vote, plaintiff suggests that *Omnicare* requires a more taxing process of judicial review. Whether the deal protection devices were "coercive" now appears to be but one part of a larger analytical framework.

In *Omnicare*, the board of directors of NCS Healthcare, Inc. approved a merger with Genesis Health Ventures, Inc. The deal was "protected" with a three-part defense that included: (1) the inclusion of a § 251(c) provision in the merger agreement;[127] (2) the absence of any effective fiduciary out clause; and (3) a voting agreement between two shareholders and Genesis which ensured that a majority of shareholders voted in favor of the transaction. After the merger was approved by the board another suitor, Omnicare, Inc., forwarded a superior proposal. The NCS board then reversed course, recommending that the NCS shareholders vote against the Genesis merger. The NCS board's change of heart had no practical effect, however, because the three deal protection mechanisms, working in tandem, "guaranteed . . . that the transaction proposed by Genesis would obtain NCS stockholder's approval."[128] "Because of the structural defenses approved by the NCS board," the Genesis merger was "a *fait accompli.*"[129]

---

[124] [n.64] 2003 Del. Ch. LEXIS 79, 2003 WL 21649926 (Del. Ch. July 10, 2003), *aff'd*, 2003 Del. LEXIS 624, 2003 WL 22998806 (Del. Dec. 17, 2003) (ORDER).

[125] [n.65] *Id.* at *9 (internal punctuation and citations omitted).

[126] [n.66] 818 A.2d at 938 (emphasis added). *Omnicare* did not address the "general validity" of stockholder voting agreements. *Id.* at 939.

[127] [n.67] Such a provision requires that a merger agreement be placed before a corporation's stockholders for a vote, even if the corporation's board of directors no longer recommends it. 8 *Del. C.* § 251(c).

[128] [n.68] 818 A.2d at 918.

[129] [n.69] *Id.* at 936.

A bare majority of the Supreme Court found that the tripartite deal protection mechanism was invalid. The majority concluded that deal protection devices, even when those devices protect a proposed merger that does not result in a change of control, require enhanced scrutiny.[130] Specifically, the *Omnicare* majority applied the two-stage analysis of *Unocal Corp. v. Mesa Petroleum Co.*[131] . . . [T]he majority held that the deal protection devices were coercive and preclusive because they accomplished a *fait accompli*, i.e., they "made it 'mathematically impossible' and 'realistically unattainable' for . . . any other proposal to succeed, no matter how superior the proposal."[132] The *Unocal* inquiry ended there. But the *Omnicare* majority held "alternatively" that the NCS board was required to negotiate a fiduciary out clause into the merger agreement because the voting agreement and the § 251(c) provision, in the absence of a fiduciary out clause, resulted in an absolute lock-up of the Genesis transaction.[133] . . .

Applying the first stage of the *Unocal* analysis is simple in this case. During the negotiations that led to the merger, Swedish Match "required" some form of deal protection.[134] If the special committee and full board had not approved the inclusion of the deal protection devices, they risked losing the Swedish Match transaction and being left with no comparable alternative transaction. As in *Omnicare* itself, this is reasonable grounds for believing that a danger to corporate policy and effectiveness existed.

Applying the second stage of the *Unocal* analysis is also straightforward. *Williams v. Geier*[135] provides the standard for determining if deal protection measures are coercive.[136] The measures are improper if they "have the effect of causing the stockholders to vote in favor of the proposed transaction for some reason other than the merits of that transaction."[137] An example of such impermissible coercion was found in *Lacos Land Company v. Arden Group, Inc.*[138] In *Lacos Land*, Arden's principal shareholder and CEO made "an explicit threat . . . that unless [certain] proposed amendments were approved, he would use his power (and not simply his power *qua* shareholder) to block transactions that may be in the best interests of [Arden]."[139] The threat to block transactions in the best interest of Arden was unrelated to the merits of the proposed amendments under consider-

---

[130] [n.70] *Id.* at 930.

[131] [n.71] 493 A.2d 946 (Del. 1985). The dissents in *Omnicare* by former Chief Justice Veasey and current Chief Justice Steele argue that *Unocal* should not have applied, but rather the business judgment rule. 818 A.2d at 943 (Veasey, C.J.), at 947 (Steele, J.).

[132] [n.76] *Id.* at 936.

[133] [n.77] *Id.*

[134] [n.79] Declaration of Sven Hindrikes ("Hindrikes Dec.") ¶ 2. *See also* Cullman Aff. ¶ 4 ("Swedish Match insisted upon some form of deal protection"); Lufkin Dep. at 84 ("there would have been no merger without the lockup").

[135] [n.80] 671 A.2d 1368 (Del. 1995).

[136] [n.81] Plaintiff does not argue that the deal protection measures were "preclusive" under *Unocal*; only "coercion" is at issue.

[137] [n.82] Williams v. Geier, 671 A.2d at 1382–83 (citations omitted).

[138] [n.83] 517 A.2d 271 (Del. Ch. 1986).

[139] [n.84] *Id.* at 276.

ation by the shareholders and constituted impermissible coercion. The basic teaching of *Lacos Land*, as discussed in *Williams*, is that fiduciaries cannot threaten stockholders so as to cause the vote to turn on factors extrinsic to the merits of the transaction.[140]

Now, compare *Lacos Land* with *Brazen v. Bell Atlantic Corporation*.[141] In *Brazen*, Bell Atlantic and NYNEX Corporation negotiated a merger agreement with a $550 million termination fee provision that could be triggered if Bell Atlantic's shareholders voted not to approve merger.[142] The Supreme Court found that the termination fee was "an integral part of the merits of the transaction."[143] The Court further stated "although the termination fee provision may have influenced the stockholder vote, there were 'no structurally or situationally coercive factors' that made an otherwise valid fee provision impermissibly coercive in this setting."[144]

Here, like *Brazen*, the deal would not have occurred without the inclusion of deal protection mechanisms, i.e., the deal protection mechanisms were "an integral part of the merits of the transaction."[145] But the circumstances here are distinguishable from *Lacos Land* because General Cigar's public shareholders were not encouraged to vote in favor of the Swedish Match transaction for reasons unrelated to the transaction's merits. Instead, the "lock-up" negotiated in this case is similar to the termination fee found permissible by the Supreme Court in *Brazen*.[146] That is, nothing in this record suggests that the lock-up had the effect of causing General Cigar's stockholders to vote in favor of the proposed transaction for some reason other than the merits of that transaction. Furthermore, unlike the situation in *Omnicare*, the deal protection mechanisms at issue in this case were not tantamount to "*a fait accompli.*" The public shareholders were free to reject the proposed deal, even though, permissibly, their vote may have been influenced by the existence of the deal protection measures.[147] Because General Cigar's public

---

[140] [n.85] *See Williams*, 671 A.2d at 1383 (explaining and distinguishing *Lacos Land*). In *Williams*, the Supreme Court found that a shareholder vote was not impermissibly coerced where the shareholders were informed (accurately) that failure to vote for a transaction could lead to the corporation's stock being de-listed from the NYSE. *Id.*

[141] [n.86] 695 A.2d 43 (Del. 1997).

[142] [n.87] *Id.* at 46.

[143] [n.88] *Id.* at 50.

[144] [n.89] *Id.* (quoting Brazen v. Bell Atlantic Corp., 1997 Del. Ch. LEXIS 44, 1997 WL 153810 (Del. Ch. Mar. 19, 1997) (Chandler, C.)).

[145] [n.90] *Id.*

[146] [n.91] Plaintiff also appears to argue that the board breached its fiduciary duty by failing to negotiate for a break-up fee in lieu of the voting agreement lock-up. First, voting agreements, of course, are perfectly legal. And nothing in the record indicated that Swedish Match would have agreed to a different provision, such as a break-up fee. Second, there is no preference in the law for one form of deal protection device over another. And third, how would a board determine, in advance, that one particular form of defensive device, would be the "least coercive" of any array of devices? Ultimately, this argument, in my opinion, leads nowhere.

[147] [n.92] Plaintiff never addresses the deeper question of how it is fair to say that a minority was coerced by a voting and ownership structure that was fully disclosed to the minority before they bought into a corporation whose capital structure was so organized. In fact, the coercion of which plaintiff

shareholders retained the power to reject the proposed transaction with Swedish Match, the fiduciary out negotiated by General Cigar's board was a meaningful and effective one — it gave the General Cigar board power to recommend that the shareholders veto the Swedish Match deal. That is to say, had the board determined that it needed to recommend that General Cigar's shareholders reject the transaction, the shareholders were fully empowered to act upon that recommendation because the public shareholders (those not "locked-up" in the voting agreement) retained the power to reject the proposed merger.[148] For these reasons, I conclude as a matter of law that the deal protection mechanisms present here were not impermissibly coercive.[149]

The last step of the *Unocal* analysis is a determination of whether the deal protection devices were within a range of reasonable responses to the danger to corporate policy and effectiveness.[150] As mentioned, the danger in this case was the risk of losing the Swedish Match transaction and being left with no comparable alternative transaction. In fact, without the deal protection mechanisms "there would have been no merger."[151] General Cigar's shareholders could have lost the significant premium that Swedish Match's offer carried, no small concern given the uncertain future of the tobacco business.[152] In addition, "[t]he latitude a board will have in either maintaining or using the defensive devices it has adopted to protect the merger it approved will vary according to the degree of benefit or detriment to the stockholders' interests that is presented by the value or terms of the subsequent competing transaction."[153] Notably, there was no competing bid for General Cigar; no alternative transaction was available to its shareholders. General Cigar's board should therefore be afforded the maximum latitude regarding its decision to recommend the Swedish Match merger.

In sum, the argument that *Omnicare* applies in the circumstances here is misplaced. The General Cigar board retained a fiduciary out, allowing it to consider superior proposals and recommend against the Swedish Match deal. Importantly, a majority of the nonaffiliated public shareholders could have rejected the deal on its

---

complains is more properly understood as the coercion resulting from the fact that the Cullmans owned a controlling interest. Surely it cannot be the case that whenever a controlling stockholder can vote against a sale the out voted minority can assert a coercion claim.

148 [n.93] Moreover, there was nothing in either the merger agreement or the voting agreement to prevent a third party from making a tender offer for the publicly-held shares that Swedish Match sought to acquire.

149 [n.94] The relevant question "is not whether a [proposal] is coercive, but whether it is actionably coercive." Weiss v. Samsonite Corp., 741 A.2d 366, 372 (Del. Ch.), *aff'd*, 746 A.2d 277 (Del. 1999) (TABLE). "For the word [coercion] to have much meaning for purposes of legal analysis, it is necessary in each case that a normative judgment be attached to the concept ('inappropriately coercive' or 'wrongfully coercive,' etc.)." Lacos Land, 517 A.2d at 277. The line between "coercion" and "actionable coercion" is whether the vote to approve turned on factors extrinsic to the merits of the transaction.

150 [n.95] *Omnicare* at 935 (quoting *Unocal* at 955).

151 [n.96] Lufkin Dep. at 83–84.

152 [n.97] *Id.*

153 [n.98] *Omnicare*, 818 A.2d at 933. I pass over the practical difficulty implied by this balancing test: how can a board know, at the time of adopting defensive devices, the terms of a transaction that emerges at a later time? As formulated, the test would appear to result in judicial invalidation of negotiated contractual provisions based on the advantages of hindsight.

merits. Unlike *Omnicare*, nothing in the merger or stockholder agreements made it "mathematically certain" that the transaction would be approved. If the shareholders believed $15.25 per share (a 75% premium over the market price) did not reflect General Cigar's intrinsic value (and the market also misunderstood that value), they could have said, "no thanks, I would rather make an investment bet on the long term prospects of this company." These shareholders were fully informed about the offer. They knew that no other offer or potential buyer had appeared, although nothing prevented it. They knew that no termination fee would be paid if they rejected the proposal. It is true, as plaintiffs repeatedly point out, that the Cullman vote against any future, hypothetical deal was "locked-up" for 18 months. It was this deal or nothing, at least for that period of time.[154] Again, however, no other suitor was waiting in the wings. And, assuming a shareholder believed that General Cigar's long term intrinsic value was greater than $15.25 per share, was an 18 month delay a meaningful "cost" that could be said realistically to "coerce" the shareholders' vote? The Cullman lock-up hardly seems unreasonable, given the absence of other deal protection devices in this particular transaction and given the buyer's understandable concern about transaction costs and market uncertainties. Unless being in a voting minority automatically means that the shareholder is coerced (because the minority shareholder's investment views or hopes have been precluded by a majority), plaintiff's concept of coercion is far more expansive than *Omnicare* or any other decisional authority brought to my attention. As a matter of law, therefore, the approval of the Swedish Match proposal by a fully informed majority of the minority public shareholders was not impermissibly coerced. As a result of that ratifying vote, plaintiff's remaining fiduciary duty claim is extinguished. . . .

QUESTIONS

1. What is the deal involved in this case?

2. What deal protection devices did General Cigar implement?

3. Did General Cigar's deal protection devices pass muster under *Unocal*? Why or why not?

4. How is this case distinguishable from *Omnicare*?

The below article is included to you give a sense for fiduciary duty litigation in the M&A context so you know what's at stake in advising the board on fiduciary duty compliance.

---

[154] [n.99] A third party could nonetheless have made a tender offer for the public shares. In addition, the Cullman's could have waited out the 18 month delay, or the Cullmans could have breached and put Swedish Match in the position of proving its non-speculative damages from a breach of the no-sale clause.

Douglas J. Clark & Marcia Kramer Mayer,[155]
Anatomy of a Merger Litigation
https://www.boardmember.com/WorkArea/
DownloadAsset.aspx?id=7319 (Feb. 6, 2012)[156]

When a press release gives official notice that a public company is to be sold, a lawsuit objecting to the deal is soon filed. There are exceptions to this rule, but as a basic principle, it is a pretty sound one. The lawsuit names as defendants the target company, its board of directors, and the purchaser. The operative theory is that the target is being sold for too little and that the directors breached their fiduciary duties by agreeing to the sale, with the insidious help of the purchaser. The lawsuit seeks to stop the transaction from proceeding on the terms announced.

This article will take the reader on a journey through a particular litigated merger, Broadcom Corporation's purchase of NetLogic Microsystems, Inc., from start to finish. There's nothing exceptional or unique about the deal, the litigation that ensued, or the outcome of that litigation. This is a well-worn path. This journey will be taken with a minimum of commentary or criticism. At the end, the reader can draw his or her own conclusions as to whether this activity creates value for stockholders or advances the cause of corporate governance.

The Announcement

At 7 a.m. EDT on September 12, 2011, NetLogic and Broadcom issued a press release announcing that they had entered into a definitive merger agreement. Under the agreement, NetLogic stockholders would receive $50 per share, a 57% premium over the prior day's closing price. The transaction value was $3.7 billion. The deal was well received by the market, although some analysts intimated that Broadcom may have overpaid. *The Wall Street Journal* stated that "[a]nalysts noted that Broadcom is paying a lot for [NetLogic]. NetLogic's shares have never traded above $44. And the company has mainly reported losses under generally accepted accounting principles, in large part because of charges associated with past acquisitions."

The definitive agreement contained standard terms and conditions, such as the transaction being contingent on obtaining regulatory approvals. The merger also would have to be approved by NetLogic's stockholders.

---

[155] [n.1] Douglas J. Clark is a Partner at Wilson Sonsini Goodrich & Rosati and Co-managing Partner of the firm. Marcia Kramer Mayer, Ph.D., is a Senior Vice President of NERA Economic Consulting and Chair of the firm's Global Securities and Finance Practice. The data referenced in this paper was compiled by Svetlana Starykh of NERA and Molly Arico of Wilson Sonsini. Using the MergerStat database, they identified 731 mergers and acquisitions that were announced from 2006 through 2010, completed by February 2011, involved a U.S. public company target, and had an announced value of at least $100 million. From RiskMetrics, they identified securities class actions objecting to these deals in state or federal court. From RiskMetrics and court dockets, they learned the outcomes of these cases through June 2011. Filing dates and allegations were obtained from RiskMetrics and the complaints.

[156] Copyright © 2012. All rights reserved. Reprinted by permission.

Finding a Plaintiff

At 10:18 a.m. EDT the same morning, a plaintiffs' securities class action law firm issued a press release concerning the transaction. The text of the release stated:

> Bernstein Leibhard LLP is investigating whether the Board of Directors of NetLogic Microsystems, Inc. ("NetLogic Microsystems" or the "Company") (NASDAQ: NETL) breached its fiduciary duty to its shareholders in agreeing to sell NetLogic Microsystems to Broadcom Corporation.
>
> Under the terms of the agreement, NetLogic Microsystems shareholders will receive $50 in cash for each share they own. The investigation is focused on the potential unfairness of the price to NetLogic Microsystems shareholders and the process by which the NetLogic Microsystems Board of Directors considered and approved the transaction.

The purpose of this press release was simple: the law firm was looking for a client. Despite the considerable ingenuity of plaintiffs' lawyers, they have not yet figured out how to file a lawsuit without a client. Bernstein Leibhard was the first firm to issue a release, but it was far from the last. The following firms issued press releases seeking plaintiffs to protest the potential unfairness of a sale paying a 57% premium over the prior close, its offer price $6 per share higher than the stock had ever traded.

9/12
Bernstein Liebhard LLP
Kendall Law Group
Levi & Korsinsky, LLP
Briscoe Law Firm
Powers Taylor, LLP
Glancy Binkow & Goldberg LLP
Finkelstein Thompson LLP
Holzer Holzer & Fistel
Brower Piven
Robbins Umeda LLP
Law Offices of Vincent Wong

9/13
Ryan & Maniskas, LLP
Law Offices of Howard G. Smith
Murray Frank LLP
Joseph Klein
Faruqi & Faruqi, LLP

9/14 and Beyond
Brodsky & Smith, LLC
Bull & Lifshitz, LLP
Goldfarb Branham Law Firm LLP
Levi & Korsinsky, LLP

So, within hours of the announcement of the transaction, an avalanche of law-firm press releases ensued. Notably, the releases started before NetLogic filed additional information concerning the transaction with the SEC, including the definitive agreement. That occurred at 10:24 a.m. EDT on September 12. With so many law firms looking for a plaintiff, it was all but inevitable that a lawsuit would be filed.

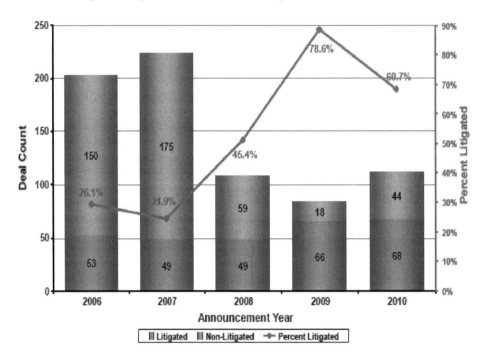

From 2006 through 2010, the percentage of eventually completed $100 million-plus transactions that were challenged in stockholder class actions increased sharply. Practitioners now routinely advise public company clients involved in a public/public sale transaction that a lawsuit will be filed questioning the deal regardless of the terms.

Lawsuit(s) Filed

The first complaint attacking the NetLogic transaction was filed on September 16, 2011, four days after the transaction was announced. The complaint was filed in Santa Clara County Superior Court in San Jose, California. While NetLogic is a Delaware corporation, it is headquartered in Santa Clara, the heart of Silicon Valley. Notably, the complaint — which objected to the deal's announced terms, as discussed in more detail below — was filed before the preliminary proxy was filed (October 5, 2011). That SEC filing contains highly pertinent information, such as the background of the transaction and a summary of the fairness opinion and financial analysis supporting the valuation and the board's decision to sell the company. Is such haste unusual?

Time from Announcement of Deal to Filing of First Class Action

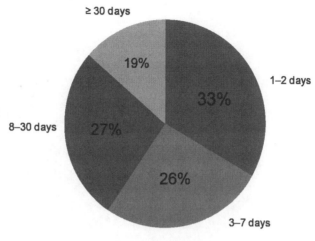

N = 257 Litigated Deals

Not at all. A review of complaints objecting to public company sales announced from 2006 through 2010 with announced values of at least $100 million shows that 59% were filed within seven days of the transaction's announcement.

A second complaint was filed in Delaware Chancery Court on September 16, 2011. It's not crazy to ask why a second suit, in a second location. The answer: A different plaintiffs' firm wanted in on the game. Were this firm to have filed in Santa Clara County, the second complaint would have been consolidated into the first and the attorneys for the second plaintiff would have had little leverage to negotiate separately with defendants for a settlement or anything else. The other choices in this situation were the state of incorporation (Delaware) or a United States district court. State courts are more popular for this type of case because the primary relief sought is injunctive and they tend to move faster than federal courts. That is particularly true of the First State, Delaware. Speed matters because if plaintiffs want to stop a deal, they need to do so before it closes. Another consideration prompting plaintiffs to prefer state court is that it allows them to avoid the tougher standards of federal law, which also entail some unique and time-consuming provisions for class actions.

So, now there were two complaints on file, in two different states. Is this unusual?

Popularity of Delaware in Litigated Deals with a State Filing

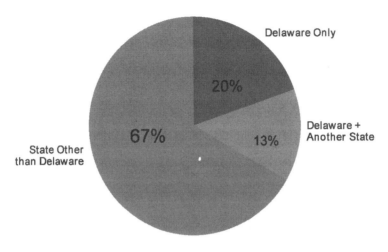

N = 277 Litigated Deals

It is not. Among $100 million-plus transactions that were announced from 2006 through 2010 and challenged in state court, 33 percent were litigated in Delaware. For 13 percent of the state-litigated deals, Delaware was not the only state addressing the transaction. If the Delaware numbers seem lower than expected, keep a few factors in mind. First, while most companies are incorporated in Delaware, not all are. Second, the Delaware Chancery Court is the most sophisticated and experienced judiciary when it comes to governance questions and that may make it unattractive for a plaintiff with a weak case. Third, the Chancery Court takes a rigorous approach to analyzing the fairness of consideration going to stockholders when granting attorneys' fees after a settlement, further marring its appeal to such plaintiffs.

The Initial Complaints

The California complaint was filed by the New Jersey Carpenters pension fund. A cursory check revealed this was not the Carpenters' first rodeo. They were the plaintiff in a merger litigation assailing InfoGroup, Inc.'s sale, as well as in class actions against NVIDIA Corporation, Residential Capital, and Hansen Natural Corporation.

As is customary in such matters, the Carpenters complaint named as defendants the target, NetLogic, its board of directors, and the buyer, Broadcom. It made three sets of substantive allegations: (1) the merger agreement contained preclusive deal terms (i.e., would inhibit higher offers) such as a break-up fee and a non-solicitation clause; (2) the merger agreement afforded inadequate consideration in light of NetLogic's recent financial results; and (3) the NetLogic board engaged in self-dealing involving such things as acceleration of stock appreciation rights. The complaint asserted two causes of action for breach of fiduciary duty against the NetLogic defendants and a cause of action against Broadcom for aiding and abetting those breaches of duty.

The Delaware complaint was identical in structure and leveled the same substantive allegations. The plaintiff, Vincent Anthony Danielo, does not appear to have served as a class representative prior to this case.

The Litigation

There is no story of an epic court battle to be told as part of this saga. Very able lawyers on both sides filed a number of well-crafted procedural motions in the two pending matters.

The complaints in both matters were amended, as they always are, to include allegations based on the target's disclosures in its preliminary proxy statement. The California plaintiff amended its complaint on October 7, 2011 (two days after the preliminary proxy was filed) "adding allegations that the preliminary proxy statement . . . contained inadequate and misleading disclosures under Delaware law by failing to provide additional and more detailed disclosure regarding the events leading up to the merger, the analysis and opinion of Qatalyst Partners LP [the target's banker], and the NetLogic financial forecasts." The Delaware complaint was amended on October 19, 2011, to add similar claims.

Defendants moved to stay the California case in lieu of the Delaware matter and moved to dismiss both cases. Those motions were never heard. Plaintiffs sought expedited discovery in California. That request was denied. On October 27, 2011, the California plaintiff moved to enjoin the transaction. Defendants opposed that motion. The motion was never heard.

Such sparse litigation is not unusual. Vice Chancellor J. Travis Laster of the Delaware Chancery Court described the "Kabuki dance" of litigation in these types of cases: "[A] controller made a merger proposal. A series of actions were filed with a brief flurry of activity until the [plaintiff] leadership structure was settled. Real litigation activity then ceased."

Guess What?

The cases settled. Most $100 million-plus litigated deals announced from 2006 through 2010 had settled by June 2011. So, settling is not unusual and this was not an unusual settlement.

On November 11, 2011, NetLogic announced that both litigations had been resolved and issued a Report on Form 8-K summarizing the settlement. The terms of settlement required: (1) additional disclosures concerning the "Selected Companies Analysis" and "Selected Transactions Analysis" in the summary of the fairness opinion; (2) an additional line of disclosure relating to the discounted cash flow analysis; (3) dismissal of the pending litigations; and (4) an agreement that plaintiffs' counsel could seek fees of up to $795,000 in the California action.

Very standard stuff. The vast majority of merger cases settle for disclosure, as opposed to monetary consideration such as an increase in deal price. The following chart illustrates this point.

Beneficiaries of Settled Litigated Deals

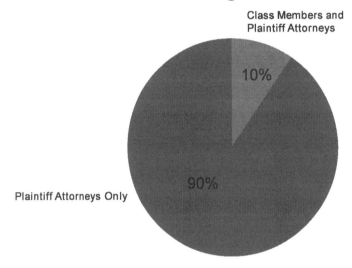

Class Members and Plaintiff Attorneys

10%

Plaintiff Attorneys Only

90%

N = 162 Settled Litigated Deals

So, to put it bluntly, it's not unusual that the only people getting paid in the settlement of a merger case are plaintiff lawyers. Nor is the amount of the payment to them in this case unusual.

Settled Litigated Deals
by Total Settlement Amount
N = 160 Settled Litigated Deals

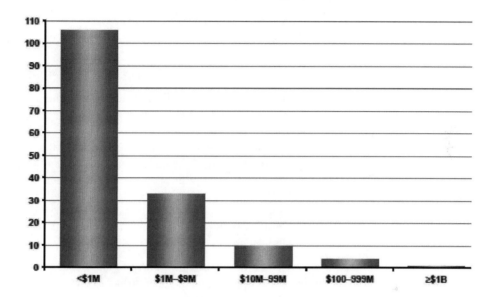

Conclusion

That's what happens in a typical merger litigation. The final step (pending as of this writing) will be judicial approval of the settlement, after notice to the class (owners of NetLogic stock at the time of the merger). Outside of Delaware, as will no doubt be the case in this matter, settlements in this type of litigation — including the attorneys' fees — are approved without controversy. Even in Delaware, settlements are usually approved without substantial objection.

A return to a question raised at the beginning of this article is worthwhile. Does this type of litigation provide any real benefit to stockholders, the cause of good corporate governance, or society as a whole? We think the facts speak for themselves, but defer to readers to form their own opinions.

B.   CONTROLLING SHAREHOLDER FIDUCIARY DUTIES

It is well established under corporate common law that a controlling shareholder of a corporation owes the corporation's other shareholders a duty of loyalty. The issue comes up most often when a controlling shareholder enters into a transaction with the corporation it controls. A second-step merger between target and a bidder subsidiary following a successful tender offer by bidder provides a classic example in the M&A context. Specifically, post-tender offer bidder will be the controlling shareholder of target and thus the second-step merger will essentially be between target and its controlling shareholder. The concern is that bidder will use its influence as controlling shareholder to cause target to sign off on low, or unfair, merger consideration in the deal. Thus, as discussed in the next case, such a conflict of interest transaction is generally subject to entire fairness review.

KAHN v. LYNCH COMMUNICATION SYSTEMS, INC.
Delaware Supreme Court
638 A.2d 1110 (1994)

HOLLAND, Justice:

This is an appeal by the plaintiff-appellant, Alan R. Kahn ("Kahn"), from a final judgment of the Court of Chancery which was entered after a trial. The action, instituted by Kahn in 1986, originally sought to enjoin the acquisition of the defendant-appellee, Lynch Communication Systems, Inc. ("Lynch"), by the defendant-appellee, Alcatel U.S.A. Corporation ("Alcatel"), pursuant to a tender offer and cash-out merger. Kahn amended his complaint to seek monetary damages after the Court of Chancery denied his request for a preliminary injunction. The Court of Chancery subsequently certified Kahn's action as a class action on behalf of all Lynch shareholders, other than the named defendants, who tendered their stock in the merger, or whose stock was acquired through the merger.

A three-day trial was held April 13–15, 1993. Kahn alleged that Alcatel was a controlling shareholder of Lynch and breached its fiduciary duties to Lynch and its shareholders. According to Kahn, Alcatel dictated the terms of the merger; made false, misleading, and inadequate disclosures; and paid an unfair price.

The Court of Chancery concluded that Alcatel was, in fact, a controlling shareholder that owed fiduciary duties to Lynch and its shareholders. It also concluded that Alcatel had not breached those fiduciary duties. Accordingly, the Court of Chancery entered judgment in favor of the defendants.

Kahn has raised three contentions in this appeal. Kahn's first contention is that the Court of Chancery erred by finding that "the tender offer and merger were negotiated by an independent committee," and then placing the burden of persuasion on the plaintiff, Kahn. Kahn asserts the uncontradicted testimony in the record demonstrated that the committee could not and did not bargain at arm's length with Alcatel. Kahn's second contention is that Alcatel's Offer to Purchase was false and misleading because it failed to disclose threats made by Alcatel to the effect that if Lynch did not accept its proposed price, Alcatel would institute a hostile tender offer at a lower price. Third, Kahn contends that the merger price was unfair. Alcatel contends that the Court of Chancery was correct in its findings, with the exception of concluding that Alcatel was a controlling shareholder.

This Court has concluded that the record supports the Court of Chancery's finding that Alcatel was a controlling shareholder. However, the record does not support the conclusion that the burden of persuasion shifted to Kahn. Therefore, the burden of proving the *entire* fairness of the merger transaction remained on Alcatel, the controlling shareholder. Accordingly, the judgment of the Court of Chancery is reversed. The matter is remanded for further proceedings in accordance with this opinion.

Facts

Lynch, a Delaware corporation, designed and manufactured electronic telecommunications equipment, primarily for sale to telephone operating companies. Alcatel, a holding company, is a subsidiary of Alcatel (S.A.), a French company involved in public telecommunications, business communications, electronics, and optronics. Alcatel (S.A.), in turn, is a subsidiary of Compagnie Generale d'Electricite ("CGE"), a French corporation with operations in energy, transportation, telecommunications and business systems.

In 1981, Alcatel acquired 30.6 percent of Lynch's common stock pursuant to a stock purchase agreement. As part of that agreement, Lynch amended its certificate of incorporation to require an 80 percent affirmative vote of its shareholders for approval of any business combination. In addition, Alcatel obtained proportional representation on the Lynch board of directors and the right to purchase 40 percent of any equity securities offered by Lynch to third parties. The agreement also precluded Alcatel from holding more than 45 percent of Lynch's stock prior to October 1, 1986. By the time of the merger which is contested in this action, Alcatel owned 43.3 percent of Lynch's outstanding stock; designated five of the eleven members of Lynch's board of directors; two of three members of the executive committee; and two of four members of the compensation committee.

In the spring of 1986, Lynch determined that in order to remain competitive in the rapidly changing telecommunications field, it would need to obtain fiber optics technology to complement its existing digital electronic capabilities. Lynch's management identified a target company, Telco Systems, Inc. ("Telco"), which possessed both fiber optics and other valuable technological assets. The record reflects that Telco expressed interest in being acquired by Lynch. Because of the supermajority voting provision, which Alcatel had negotiated when it first purchased its shares, in order to proceed with the Telco combination Lynch needed Alcatel's consent. In June 1986, Ellsworth F. Dertinger ("Dertinger"), Lynch's CEO and chairman of its board of directors, contacted Pierre Suard ("Suard"), the chairman of Alcatel's parent company, CGE, regarding the acquisition of Telco by Lynch. Suard expressed Alcatel's opposition to Lynch's acquisition of Telco. Instead, Alcatel proposed a combination of Lynch and Celwave Systems, Inc. ("Celwave"), an indirect subsidiary of CGE engaged in the manufacture and sale of telephone wire, cable and other related products.

Alcatel's proposed combination with Celwave was presented to the Lynch board at a regular meeting held on August 1, 1986. Although several directors expressed interest in the original combination which had been proposed with Telco, the Alcatel representatives on Lynch's board made it clear that such a combination would not be considered before a Lynch/Celwave combination. According to the minutes of the August 1 meeting, Dertinger expressed his opinion that Celwave would not be of interest to Lynch if Celwave was not owned by Alcatel.

At the conclusion of the meeting, the Lynch board unanimously adopted a resolution establishing an Independent Committee, consisting of Hubert L. Kertz ("Kertz"), Paul B. Wineman ("Wineman"), and Stuart M. Beringer ("Beringer"), to negotiate with Celwave and to make recommendations concerning the appropriate terms and conditions of a combination with Celwave. On October 24, 1986, Alcatel's investment banking firm, Dillon, Read & Co., Inc. ("Dillon Read") made a presentation to the Independent Committee. Dillon Read expressed its views concerning the benefits of a Celwave/Lynch combination and submitted a written proposal of an exchange ratio of 0.95 shares of Celwave per Lynch share in a stock-for-stock merger.

However, the Independent Committee's investment advisors, Thomson McKinnon Securities Inc. ("Thomson McKinnon") and Kidder, Peabody & Co. Inc. ("Kidder Peabody"), reviewed the Dillon Read proposal and concluded that the 0.95 ratio was predicated on Dillon Read's overvaluation of Celwave. Based upon this advice, the Independent Committee determined that the exchange ratio proposed by Dillon Read was unattractive to Lynch. The Independent Committee expressed its unanimous opposition to the Celwave/Lynch merger on October 31, 1986.

Alcatel responded to the Independent Committee's action on November 4, 1986, by withdrawing the Celwave proposal. Alcatel made a simultaneous offer to acquire the entire equity interest in Lynch, constituting the approximately 57 percent of Lynch shares not owned by Alcatel. The offering price was $14 cash per share.

On November 7, 1986, the Lynch board of directors revised the mandate of the Independent Committee. It authorized Kertz, Wineman, and Beringer to negotiate the cash merger offer with Alcatel. At a meeting held that same day, the Independent Committee determined that the $14 per share offer was inadequate. The Independent's Committee's own legal counsel, Skadden, Arps, Slate, Meagher & Flom ("Skadden Arps"), suggested that the Independent Committee should review alternatives to a cash-out merger with Alcatel, including a "white knight" third party acquiror, a repurchase of Alcatel's shares, or the adoption of a shareholder rights plan.

On November 12, 1986, Beringer, as chairman of the Independent Committee, contacted Michiel C. McCarty ("McCarty") of Dillon Read, Alcatel's representative in the negotiations, with a counteroffer at a price of $17 per share. McCarty responded on behalf of Alcatel with an offer of $15 per share. When Beringer informed McCarty of the Independent Committee's view that $15 was also insufficient, Alcatel raised its offer to $15.25 per share. The Independent Committee also rejected this offer. Alcatel then made its final offer of $15.50 per share.

At the November 24, 1986 meeting of the Independent Committee, Beringer advised its other two members that Alcatel was "ready to proceed with an unfriendly tender at a lower price" if the $15.50 per share price was not recommended by the Independent Committee and approved by the Lynch board of directors. Beringer also told the other members of the Independent Committee that the alternatives to a cash-out merger had been investigated but were impracticable.[157] After meeting with its financial and legal advisors, the Independent Committee voted unanimously to recommend that the Lynch board of directors

---

[157] [n.3] The minutes reflect that Beringer told the Committee the "white knight" alternative "appeared impractical with the 80% approval requirement"; the repurchase of Alcatel's shares would produce a "highly leveraged company with a lower book value" and was an alternative "not in the least encouraged by Alcatel"; and a shareholder rights plan was not viable because of the increased debt it would entail.

approve Alcatel's $15.50 cash per share price for a merger with Alcatel. The Lynch board met later that day. With Alcatel's nominees abstaining, it approved the merger.

Alcatel Dominated Lynch Controlling Shareholder Status

This Court has held that "a shareholder owes a fiduciary duty only if it owns a majority interest in or *exercises control* over the business affairs of the corporation." *Ivanhoe Partners v. Newmont Mining Corp.*, Del. Supr., 535 A.2d 1334, 1344 (1987) (emphasis added). With regard to the exercise of control, this Court has stated:

> [A] shareholder who owns less than 50% of a corporation's outstanding stocks does not, without more, become a controlling shareholder of that corporation, with a concomitant fiduciary status. For a dominating relationship to exist in the absence of controlling stock ownership, a plaintiff must allege domination by a minority shareholder through actual control of corporation conduct.

Citron v. Fairchild Camera & Instrument Corp., Del. Supr., 569 A.2d 53, 70 (1989) (quotations and citation omitted).

Alcatel held a 43.3 percent minority share of stock in Lynch. Therefore, the threshold question to be answered by the Court of Chancery was whether, despite its minority ownership, Alcatel exercised control over Lynch's business affairs. Based upon the testimony and the minutes of the August 1, 1986 Lynch board meeting, the Court of Chancery concluded that Alcatel did exercise control over Lynch's business decisions. . . .

The record supports the Court of Chancery's factual finding that Alcatel dominated Lynch. . . .

At the August 1 meeting, Alcatel opposed the renewal of compensation contracts for Lynch's top five managers. According to Dertinger, Christian Fayard ("Fayard"), an Alcatel director, told the board members, "[y]ou must listen to us. We are 43 percent owner. You have to do what we tell you." The minutes confirm Dertinger's testimony. They recite that Fayard declared, "you are pushing us very much to take control of the company. Our opinion is not taken into consideration."

Although Beringer and Kertz, two of the independent directors, favored renewal of the contracts, according to the minutes, the third independent director, Wineman, admonished the board as follows:

> Mr. Wineman pointed out that the vote on the contracts is a "watershed vote" and the motion, due to Alcatel's "strong feelings," might not carry if taken now. Mr. Wineman clarified that "you [management] might win the battle and lose the war." With Alcatel's opinion so clear, Mr. Wineman questioned "if management wants the contracts renewed under these circumstances." He recommended that management "think twice." Mr. Wineman declared: "I want to keep the management. I can't think of a better management." Mr. Kertz agreed, again advising consideration of the "critical" period the company is entering.

The minutes reflect that the management directors left the room after this statement. The remaining board members then voted not to renew the contracts.

At the same meeting, Alcatel vetoed Lynch's acquisition of the target company, which, according to the minutes, Beringer considered "an immediate fit" for Lynch. Dertinger agreed with Beringer, stating that the "target company is extremely important as they have the products that Lynch needs now." Nonetheless, Alcatel prevailed. The minutes reflect that Fayard advised the board: "Alcatel, with its 44% equity position, would not approve such an acquisition as . . . it does not wish to be diluted from being the main shareholder in Lynch." From the foregoing evidence, the Vice Chancellor concluded:

> . . . Alcatel did control the Lynch board, at least with respect to the matters under consideration at its August 1, 1986 board meeting. The interplay between the directors was more than vigorous discussion, as suggested by defendants. The management and independent directors disagreed with Alcatel on several important issues. However, when Alcatel made its position clear, and reminded the other directors of its significant stockholdings, Alcatel prevailed. Dertinger testified that Fayard "scared [the non-Alcatel directors] to death." While this statement undoubtedly is an exaggeration, it does represent a first-hand view of how the board operated. I conclude that the non-Alcatel directors deferred to Alcatel because of its position as a significant stockholder and not because they decided in the exercise of their own business judgment that Alcatel's position was correct [citation omitted].

The record supports the Court of Chancery's underlying factual finding that "the non-Alcatel [independent] directors deferred to Alcatel because of its position as a significant stockholder and not because they decided in the exercise of their own business judgment that Alcatel's position was correct." The record also supports the subsequent factual finding that, notwithstanding its 43.3 percent minority shareholder interest, Alcatel did exercise actual control over Lynch by dominating its corporate affairs. The Court of Chancery's legal conclusion that Alcatel owed the fiduciary duties of a controlling shareholder to the other Lynch shareholders followed syllogistically as the logical result of its cogent analysis of the record.

Entire Fairness Requirement Dominating Interested Shareholder

A controlling or dominating shareholder standing on both sides of a transaction, as in a parent-subsidiary context, bears the burden of proving its entire fairness. The demonstration of fairness that is required was set forth by this Court in *Weinberger*:

> The concept of fairness has two basic aspects: fair dealing and fair price. The former embraces questions of when the transaction was timed, how it was initiated, structured, negotiated, disclosed to the directors, and how the approvals of the directors and the stockholders were obtained. The latter aspect of fairness relates to the economic and financial considerations of the proposed merger, including all relevant factors: assets, market value, earnings, future prospects, and any other elements that affect the intrinsic

or inherent value of a company's stock. However, the test for fairness is not a bifurcated one as between fair dealing and price. All aspects of the issue must be examined as a whole since the question is one of entire fairness.

Weinberger v. UOP, Inc., 457 A.2d at 711 (citations omitted).

The logical question raised by this Court's holding in *Weinberger* was what type of evidence would be reliable to demonstrate entire fairness. That question was not only anticipated but also initially addressed in the *Weinberger* opinion. *Id.* at 709–10 n. 7. This Court suggested that the result "could have been entirely different if UOP had appointed an independent negotiating committee of its outside directors to deal with Signal at arm's length," because "fairness in this context can be equated to conduct by a theoretical, wholly independent, board of directors." *Id.* Accordingly, this Court stated, "a showing that the action taken was as though each of the contending parties had in fact exerted its bargaining power against the other at arm's length is strong *evidence* that the transaction meets the test of fairness." *Id.* (emphasis added).

In this case, the Vice Chancellor noted that the Court of Chancery has expressed "differing views" regarding the effect that an approval of a cash-out merger by a special committee of disinterested directors has upon the controlling or dominating shareholder's burden of demonstrating entire fairness. One view is that such approval shifts to the plaintiff the burden of proving that the transaction was unfair. The other view is that such an approval renders the business judgment rule the applicable standard of judicial review. . . .

Entire fairness remains the proper focus of judicial analysis in examining an interested merger, irrespective of whether the burden of proof remains upon or is shifted away from the controlling or dominating shareholder, because the unchanging nature of the underlying "interested" transaction requires careful scrutiny. The policy rationale for the exclusive application of the entire fairness standard to interested merger transactions has been stated as follows:

> Parent subsidiary mergers, unlike stock options, are proposed by a party that controls, and will continue to control, the corporation, whether or not the minority stockholders vote to approve or reject the transaction. The controlling stockholder relationship has the potential to influence, however subtly, the vote of [ratifying] minority stockholders in a manner that is not likely to occur in a transaction with a noncontrolling party.

> Even where no coercion is intended, shareholders voting on a parent subsidiary merger might perceive that their disapproval could risk retaliation of some kind by the controlling stockholder. For example, the controlling stockholder might decide to stop dividend payments or to effect a subsequent cash out merger at a less favorable price, for which the remedy would be time consuming and costly litigation. At the very least, the potential for that perception, and its possible impact upon a shareholder vote, could never be fully eliminated. Consequently, in a merger between the corporation and its controlling stockholder — even one negotiated by disinterested, independent directors — no court could be certain whether the transaction terms fully approximate what truly independent parties

would have achieved in an arm's length negotiation. Given that uncertainty, a court might well conclude that even minority shareholders who have ratified a . . . merger need procedural protections beyond those afforded by full disclosure of all material facts. One way to provide such protections would be to adhere to the more stringent entire fairness standard of judicial review.

Citron v. E.I. Du Pont de Nemours & Co., 584 A.2d at 502.

Once again, this Court holds that the exclusive standard of judicial review in examining the propriety of an interested cash-out merger transaction by a controlling or dominating shareholder is entire fairness. The initial burden of establishing entire fairness rests upon the party who stands on both sides of the transaction. However, an approval of the transaction by an independent committee of directors or an informed majority of minority shareholders shifts the burden of proof on the issue of fairness from the controlling or dominating shareholder to the challenging shareholder-plaintiff. Nevertheless, even when an interested cash-out merger transaction receives the informed approval of a majority of minority stockholders or an independent committee of disinterested directors, an entire fairness analysis is the only proper standard of judicial review. *See id.*

Independent Committees Interested Merger Transactions

It is a now well-established principle of Delaware corporate law that in an interested merger, the controlling or dominating shareholder proponent of the transaction bears the burden of proving its entire fairness. It is equally well-established in such contexts that any shifting of the burden of proof on the issue of entire fairness must be predicated upon this Court's decisions in *Rosenblatt v. Getty Oil Co.*, Del. Supr., 493 A.2d 929 (1985) and *Weinberger v. UOP, Inc.*, Del. Supr., 457 A.2d 701 (1983). In *Weinberger*, this Court noted that "[p]articularly in a parent-subsidiary context, a showing that the action taken was as though each of the contending parties had *in fact* exerted its bargaining power against the other at arm's length is strong evidence that the transaction meets the test of fairness." 457 A.2d at 709–10 n. 7 (emphasis added). *Accord Rosenblatt v. Getty Oil Co.*, 493 A.2d at 937–38 & n. 7. In *Rosenblatt*, this Court pointed out that "[an] independent bargaining structure, while not conclusive, is strong evidence of the fairness" of a merger transaction. *Rosenblatt v. Getty Oil Co.*, 493 A.2d at 938 n. 7.

The same policy rationale which requires judicial review of interested cash-out mergers exclusively for entire fairness also mandates careful judicial scrutiny of a special committee's real bargaining power before shifting the burden of proof on the issue of entire fairness. A recent decision from the Court of Chancery articulated a two-part test for determining whether burden shifting is appropriate in an interested merger transaction. *Rabkin v. Olin Corp.*, Del. Ch., C.A. No. 7547 (Consolidated), Chandler, V.C., 1990 WL 47648, slip op. at 14–15 (Apr. 17, 1990), *reprinted in* 16 Del.J.Corp.L. 851, 861–62 (1991), *aff'd*, Del. Supr., 586 A.2d 1202 (1990). In *Olin*, the Court of Chancery stated:

> The mere existence of an independent special committee . . . does not itself shift the burden. At least two factors are required. First, the majority

shareholder must not dictate the terms of the merger. *Rosenblatt v. Getty Oil Co.*, Del. Supr., 493 A.2d 929, 937 (1985). Second, the special committee must have real bargaining power that it can exercise with the majority shareholder on an arms length basis.

Id., slip op. at 14–15, 16 Del.J.Corp.L. at 861–62.[158] This Court expressed its agreement with that statement by affirming the Court of Chancery decision in *Olin* on appeal.

Lynch's Independent Committee

In the case *sub judice*, the Court of Chancery observed that although "Alcatel did exercise control over Lynch with respect to the decisions made at the August 1, 1986 board meeting, it does not necessarily follow that Alcatel also controlled the terms of the merger and its approval." This observation is theoretically accurate, as this opinion has already stated. *Weinberger v. UOP, Inc.*, 457 A.2d at 709–10 n. 7. However, the performance of the Independent Committee merits careful judicial scrutiny to determine whether Alcatel's demonstrated pattern of domination was effectively neutralized so that "each of the contending parties had in fact exerted its bargaining power against the other at arm's length." *Id.* The fact that the same independent directors had submitted to Alcatel's demands on August 1, 1986 was part of the basis for the Court of Chancery's finding of Alcatel's domination of Lynch. Therefore, the Independent Committee's ability to bargain at arm's length with Alcatel was suspect from the outset.

The Independent Committee's original assignment was to examine the merger with Celwave which had been proposed by Alcatel. The record reflects that the Independent Committee effectively discharged that assignment and, in fact, recommended that the Lynch board reject the merger on Alcatel's terms. Alcatel's response to the Independent Committee's adverse recommendation was not the pursuit of further negotiations regarding its Celwave proposal, but rather its response was an offer to buy Lynch. That offer was consistent with Alcatel's August 1, 1986 expressions of an intention to dominate Lynch, since an acquisition would effectively eliminate once and for all Lynch's remaining vestiges of independence.

The Independent Committee's second assignment was to consider Alcatel's proposal to purchase Lynch. The Independent Committee proceeded on that task with full knowledge of Alcatel's demonstrated pattern of domination. The Independent Committee was also obviously aware of Alcatel's refusal to negotiate with it on the Celwave matter.

---

[158] [n.6] In *Olin*, the Court of Chancery concluded that because the special committee had been given "the narrow mandate of determining the monetary fairness of a non-negotiable offer," and because the majority shareholder "dictated the terms" and "there were no arm's-length negotiations," the burden of proof on the issue of entire fairness remained with the defendants. *Id.*, slip op. at 15, 16 Del.J.Corp.L. at 862. In making that determination, the Court of Chancery pointed out that the majority shareholder "could obviously have used its majority stake to effectuate the merger" regardless of the committee's or the board's disapproval, and that the record demonstrated that the directors of both corporations were "acutely aware of this fact." *Id.*, slip op. at 13, 16 Del.J.Corp.L. at 861.

Burden of Proof Shifted Court of Chancery's Finding

The Court of Chancery began its factual analysis by noting that Kahn had "attempted to shatter" the image of the Independent Committee's actions as having "appropriately simulated" an arm's length, third-party transaction. The Court of Chancery found that "to some extent, [Kahn's attempt] was successful." The Court of Chancery gave credence to the testimony of Kertz, one of the members of the Independent Committee, to the effect that he did not believe that $15.50 was a fair price but that he voted in favor of the merger because he felt there was no alternative.

The Court of Chancery also found that Kertz understood Alcatel's position to be that it was ready to proceed with an unfriendly tender offer at a lower price if Lynch did not accept the $15.50 offer, and that Kertz perceived this to be a threat by Alcatel. The Court of Chancery concluded that Kertz ultimately decided that, "although $15.50 was not fair, a tender offer and merger at that price would be better for Lynch's stockholders than an unfriendly tender offer at a significantly lower price." The Court of Chancery determined that "Kertz failed either to satisfy himself that the offered price was fair or oppose the merger."

In addition to Kertz, the other members of the Independent Committee were Beringer, its chairman, and Wineman. Wineman did not testify at trial.[159] Beringer was called by Alcatel to testify at trial. Beringer testified that at the time of the Committee's vote to recommend the $15.50 offer to the Lynch board, he thought "that *under the circumstances*, a price of $15.50 was fair and should be accepted" (emphasis added).

Kahn contends that these "circumstances" included those referenced in the minutes for the November 24, 1986 Independent Committee meeting: "Mr. Beringer added that Alcatel is 'ready to proceed with an unfriendly tender at a lower price' if the $15.50 per share price is not recommended to, and approved by, the Company's Board of Directors." In his testimony at trial, Beringer verified, albeit reluctantly, the accuracy of the foregoing statement in the minutes: "[Alcatel] *let us know* that they were giving serious consideration to making an unfriendly tender" (emphasis added).

The record reflects that Alcatel was "ready to proceed" with a hostile bid. This was a conclusion reached by Beringer, the Independent Committee's chairman and spokesman, based upon communications to him from Alcatel. Beringer testified that although there was no reference to a particular price for a hostile bid during his discussions with Alcatel, or even specific mention of a "lower" price, "the implication

---

[159] [n.7] Based upon inferences from Kertz's testimony, the Court of Chancery noted that "Wineman apparently agreed" that $15.50 was a fair price. However, the record also reflects that it was Wineman who urged the other independent directors to yield to Alcatel's demands at the August 1, 1986 meeting.

Wineman's failure to testify also permits both this Court and the Court of Chancery to draw the inference adverse to Alcatel, that Alcatel dictated the outcome of the November 24, 1986 meeting. As we have previously noted, the production of weak evidence when strong is, or should have been, available can lead only to the conclusion that the strong would have been adverse. *See Smith v. Van Gorkom, Del. Supr., 488 A.2d 858, 878 (1985).*

was clear to [him] that it probably would be at a lower price."[160]

According to the Court of Chancery, the Independent Committee rejected three lower offers for Lynch from Alcatel and then accepted the $15.50 offer "after being advised that [it] was fair and after considering the absence of alternatives." The Vice Chancellor expressly acknowledged the impracticability of Lynch's Independent Committee's alternatives to a merger with Alcatel:

> Lynch was not in a position to shop for other acquirors, since Alcatel could block any alternative transaction. Alcatel also made it clear that it was not interested in having its shares repurchased by Lynch. The Independent Committee decided that a stockholder rights plan was not viable because of the increased debt it would entail.

Nevertheless, based upon the record before it, the Court of Chancery found that the Independent Committee had "appropriately simulated a third-party transaction, where negotiations are conducted at arms-length and there is no compulsion to reach an agreement." The Court of Chancery concluded that the Independent Committee's actions "as a whole" were "sufficiently well informed . . . and aggressive to simulate an arms-length transaction," so that the burden of proof as to entire fairness shifted from Alcatel to the contending Lynch shareholder, Kahn. The Court of Chancery's reservations about that finding are apparent in its written decision.

The Power to Say No, The Parties' Contentions, Arm's Length Bargaining

The Court of Chancery properly noted that limitations on the alternatives to Alcatel's offer did not mean that the Independent Committee should have agreed to a price that was unfair:

> The power to say no is a significant power. It is the duty of directors serving on [an independent] committee to approve only a transaction that is in the best interests of the public shareholders, to say no to any transaction that is not fair to those shareholders and is not the best transaction available. It is not sufficient for such directors to achieve the best price that a fiduciary will pay if that price is not a fair price.

(Quoting *In re First Boston, Inc. Shareholders Litig.*, Del. Ch., C.A. 10338 (Consolidated), Allen, C., 1990 WL 78836, slip op. at 15–16 (June 7, 1990)).

The Alcatel defendants argue that the Independent Committee exercised its "power to say no" in rejecting the three initial offers from Alcatel, and that it therefore cannot be said that Alcatel dictated the terms of the merger or precluded the Independent Committee from exercising real bargaining power.[161] The Alcatel defendants contend, alternatively, that "even assuming that such a threat [of a

---

[160] [n.8] On the other hand, Dertinger, an officer and director of Lynch, testified that he was informed by Alcatel that the price of an unfriendly tender offer would indeed be lower and would in fact be $12 per share.

[161] [n.9] Alcatel also points to the fairness opinions of two investment banking firms employed by the Committee, Kidder Peabody and Thomson McKinnon, and the involvement of independent legal counsel, Skadden Arps, in considering and rejecting alternatives to the Alcatel cash offers.

hostile takeover] could have had a coercive effect on the [Independent] Committee," the willingness of the Independent Committee to reject Alcatel's initial three offers suggests that "the alleged threat was either nonexistent or ineffective." *Braunschweiger v. American Home Shield Corp.*, Del. Ch., C.A. No. 10755, Allen, C., 1991 WL 3920, slip op. at 13 (Jan. 7, 1991), *reprinted in* 17 Del.J.Corp.L. 206, 219 (1991).

Kahn contends the record reflects that the conduct of Alcatel deprived the Independent Committee of an effective "power to say no." Kahn argues that Alcatel not only threatened the Committee with a hostile tender offer in the event its $15.50 offer was not recommended and approved, but also directed the affairs of Lynch for Alcatel's benefit in such a way as to make it impossible for Lynch to continue as a public company under Alcatel's control without injury to itself and its minority shareholders. In support of this argument, Kahn relies upon another proceeding wherein the Court of Chancery has been previously presented with factual circumstances comparable to those of the case *sub judice*, albeit in a different procedural posture. *See American Gen. Corp. v. Texas Air Corp.*, Del. Ch., C.A. Nos. 8390, 8406, 8650 & 8805, Hartnett, V.C., 1987 WL 6337 (Feb. 5, 1987), *reprinted in* 13 Del.J.Corp.L. 173 (1987).

In *American General*, in the context of an application for injunctive relief, the Court of Chancery found that the members of the Special Committee were "truly independent and . . . performed their tasks in a proper manner," but it also found that "at the end of their negotiations with [the majority shareholder] the Committee members were issued an ultimatum and told that they must accept the $16.50 per share price or [the majority shareholder] would proceed with the transaction without their input." *Id.*, slip op. at 11–12, 13 Del.J.Corp.L. at 181. The Court of Chancery concluded based upon this evidence that the Special Committee had thereby lost "its ability to negotiate in an arms-length manner" and that there was a reasonable probability that the burden of proving entire fairness would remain on the defendants if the litigation proceeded to trial. *Id.*, slip op. at 12, 13 Del.J.Corp.L. at 181.

Alcatel's efforts to distinguish *American General* are unpersuasive. Alcatel's reliance on *Braunschweiger* is also misplaced. In *Braunschweiger*, the Court of Chancery pointed out that "[p]laintiffs do not allege that [the management-affiliated merger partner] ever used the threat of a hostile takeover to influence the special committee." *Braunschweiger v. American Home Shield Corp.*, slip op. at 13, 17 Del.J.Corp.L. at 219. Unlike *Braunschweiger*, in this case the coercion was extant and directed to a specific price offer which was, in effect, presented in the form of a "take it or leave it" ultimatum by a controlling shareholder with the capability of following through on its threat of a hostile takeover.

Alcatel's Entire Fairness Burden Did Not Shift to Kahn

A condition precedent to finding that the burden of proving entire fairness has shifted in an interested merger transaction is a careful judicial analysis of the factual circumstances of each case. Particular consideration must be given to evidence of whether the special committee was truly independent, fully informed, and had the freedom to negotiate at arm's length. *Weinberger v. UOP, Inc.*, Del. Supr., 457 A.2d 701, 709–10 n. 7 (1983). *See also American Gen. Corp. v. Texas Air*

Corp., Del. Ch., C.A. Nos. 8390, 8406, 8650 & 8805, Hartnett, V.C., 1987 WL 6337, slip op. at 11 (Feb. 5, 1987), *reprinted in* 13 Del.J.Corp.L. 173, 181 (1988). "Although perfection is not possible," unless the controlling or dominating shareholder can demonstrate that it has not only formed an independent committee but also replicated a process "as though each of the contending parties had in fact exerted its bargaining power at arm's length," the burden of proving entire fairness will not shift. *Weinberger v. UOP, Inc.*, 457 A.2d at 709–10 n. 7. *See also Rosenblatt v. Getty Oil Co.*, Del. Supr., 493 A.2d 929, 937–38 (1985).

Subsequent to *Rosenblatt*, this Court pointed out that "the use of an independent negotiating committee of outside directors may have significant advantages to the majority stockholder in defending suits of this type," but it does not *ipso facto* establish the procedural fairness of an interested merger transaction. *Rabkin v. Philip A. Hunt Chem. Corp.*, Del. Supr., 498 A.2d 1099, 1106 & n. 7 (1985). In reversing the granting of the defendants' motion to dismiss in *Rabkin*, this Court implied that the burden on entire fairness would not be shifted by the use of an independent committee which concluded its processes with "what could be considered a quick surrender" to the dictated terms of the controlling shareholder.[162] *Id.* at 1106. This Court concluded in *Rabkin* that the majority stockholder's "attitude toward the minority," coupled with the "apparent absence of any meaningful negotiations as to price," did not manifest the exercise of arm's length bargaining by the independent committee. *Id.*

The Court of Chancery's determination that the Independent Committee "appropriately simulated a third-party transaction, where negotiations are conducted at arm's-length and there is no compulsion to reach an agreement," is not supported by the record. Under the circumstances present in the case *sub judice*, the Court of Chancery erred in shifting the burden of proof with regard to entire fairness to the contesting Lynch shareholder-plaintiff, Kahn. The record reflects that the ability of the Committee effectively to negotiate at arm's length was compromised by Alcatel's threats to proceed with a hostile tender offer if the $15.50 price was not approved by the Committee and the Lynch board. The fact that the Independent Committee rejected three initial offers, which were well below the Independent Committee's estimated valuation for Lynch and were not combined

---

[162] [n.10] A "surrender" need not occur at the outset of the negotiation process in order to deny a controlling shareholder the burden-shifting function which might otherwise follow from establishing an independent committee bargaining structure. *See* Freedman v. Restaurant Assocs. Indus., Inc., Del. Ch., C.A. No. 9212, Allen, C., 1990 WL 135923 (Sept. 19, 1990), *reprinted in* 16 Del.J.Corp.L. 1462 (1990). *See also* Block, Barton & Radin, *The Business Judgment Rule: Fiduciary Duties of Corporate Directors* 170–72 (4th ed. 1993). In *Freedman*, finding that there was no "fully functional" independent committee, the Court of Chancery stated:

> [F]acts are alleged that would establish that [the] special committee was not given the opportunity to select from among the range of alternatives that an independent, disinterested board would have had available to it; it was, in effect, 'hemmed in' by the management group's actions. Under these circumstances, where, according to the allegations contained in the amended complaint, the management group could (and did) veto any action of the special committee that was not agreeable to the conflicted interests of the management directors it would be formalistically perverse to afford the special committee's action the effect of burden shifting of which that device is capable.

Freedman v. Restaurant Assocs. Indus., Inc., slip op. at 17–18, 16 Del.J.Corp.L. at 1475.

with an explicit threat that Alcatel was "ready to proceed" with a hostile bid, cannot alter the conclusion that any semblance of arm's length bargaining ended when the Independent Committee surrendered to the ultimatum that accompanied Alcatel's final offer.

Conclusion

Accordingly, the judgment of the Court of Chancery is reversed. This matter is remanded for further proceedings consistent herewith, including a redetermination of the entire fairness of the cash-out merger to Kahn and the other Lynch minority shareholders with the burden of proof remaining on Alcatel, the dominant and interested shareholder.

QUESTIONS

1.   What is the deal involved in the case?

2.   What is the test for determining whether someone is a controlling shareholder? Is Alcatel a controlling shareholder of Lynch? Why or why not?

3.   What is the effect of being labeled a controlling shareholder?

4.   What standard of review applies to a transaction between a corporation and its controlling shareholder?

5.   What is the effect of approval of a controlling shareholder transaction by an independent and disinterested board committee? How does this differ from the effect of such approval of a conflict of interest transaction between one or more directors and the corporation? Why the difference?

6.   Was the burden regarding entire fairness shifted to Lynch here? Why or why not?

7.   In hindsight, what should Alcatel have done differently?

KAHN v. M & F WORLDWIDE CORP.
Delaware Supreme Court
88 A.3d 635 (2014)

HOLLAND, Justice:

This is an appeal from a final judgment entered by the Court of Chancery in a proceeding that arises from a 2011 acquisition by MacAndrews & Forbes Holdings, Inc. ("M & F" or "MacAndrews & Forbes") — a 43% stockholder in M & F Worldwide Corp. ("MFW") — of the remaining common stock of MFW (the "Merger"). From the outset, M & F's proposal to take MFW private was made contingent upon two stockholder-protective procedural conditions. First, M & F required the Merger to be negotiated and approved by a special committee of independent MFW directors (the "Special Committee"). Second, M & F required that the Merger be approved by a majority of stockholders unaffiliated with M & F. The Merger closed in December 2011, after it was approved by a vote of 65.4% of MFW's minority stockholders.

The Appellants initially sought to enjoin the transaction. They withdrew their request for injunctive relief after taking expedited discovery, including several depositions. The Appellants then sought post-closing relief against M & F, Ronald O. Perelman, and MFW's directors (including the members of the Special Committee) for breach of fiduciary duty. Again, the Appellants were provided with extensive discovery. The Defendants then moved for summary judgment, which the Court of Chancery granted.

Court of Chancery Decision

The Court of Chancery found that the case presented a "novel question of law," specifically, "what standard of review should apply to a going private merger conditioned upfront by the controlling stockholder on approval by both a properly empowered, independent committee and an informed, uncoerced majority-of-the-minority vote." The Court of Chancery held that business judgment review, rather than entire fairness, should be applied to a very limited category of controller mergers. That category consisted of mergers where the controller voluntarily relinquishes its control — such that the negotiation and approval process replicate those that characterize a third-party merger.

The Court of Chancery held that, rather than entire fairness, the business judgment standard of review should apply "if, *but only if:* (i) the controller conditions the transaction on the approval of both a Special Committee and a majority of the minority stockholders; (ii) the Special Committee is independent; (iii) the Special Committee is empowered to freely select its own advisors and to say no definitively; (iv) the Special Committee acts with care; (v) the minority vote is informed; and (vi) there is no coercion of the minority."

The Court of Chancery found that those prerequisites were satisfied and that the Appellants had failed to raise any genuine issue of material fact indicating the contrary. The court then reviewed the Merger under the business judgment standard and granted summary judgment for the Defendants.

Appellants' Arguments

The Appellants raise two main arguments on this appeal. First, they contend that the Court of Chancery erred in concluding that no material disputed facts existed regarding the conditions precedent to business judgment review. The Appellants submit that the record contains evidence showing that the Special Committee was not disinterested and independent, was not fully empowered, and was not effective. The Appellants also contend, as a legal matter, that the majority-of-the-minority provision did not afford MFW stockholders protection sufficient to displace entire fairness review.

Second, the Appellants submit that the Court of Chancery erred, as a matter of law, in holding that the business judgment standard applies to controller freeze-out mergers where the controller's proposal is conditioned on both Special Committee approval and a favorable majority-of-the-minority vote. Even if both procedural protections are adopted, the Appellants argue, entire fairness should be retained as the applicable standard of review.

Defendants' Arguments

The Defendants argue that the judicial standard of review should be the business judgment rule, because the Merger was conditioned *ab initio* on two procedural protections that together operated to replicate an arm's-length merger: the employment of an active, unconflicted negotiating agent free to turn down the transaction; and a requirement that any transaction negotiated by that agent be approved by a majority of the disinterested stockholders. The Defendants argue that using and *establishing* pretrial that both protective conditions were extant renders a going private transaction analogous to that of a third-party arm's-length merger under Section 251 of the Delaware General Corporation Law. That is, the Defendants submit that a Special Committee approval in a going private transaction is a proxy for board approval in a third-party transaction, and that the approval of the unaffiliated, noncontrolling stockholders replicates the approval of all the (potentially) adversely affected stockholders.

FACTS

MFW and M & F

MFW is a holding company incorporated in Delaware. Before the Merger that is the subject of this dispute, MFW was 43.4% owned by MacAndrews & Forbes, which in turn is entirely owned by Ronald O. Perelman. MFW had four business segments. Three were owned through a holding company, Harland Clarke Holding Corporation ("HCHC"). They were the Harland Clarke Corporation ("Harland"), which printed bank checks; Harland Clarke Financial Solutions, which provided technology products and services to financial services companies; and Scantron Corporation, which manufactured scanning equipment used for educational and other purposes. The fourth segment, which was not part of HCHC, was Mafco Worldwide Corporation, a manufacturer of licorice flavorings.

The MFW board had thirteen members. They were: Ronald Perelman, Barry Schwartz, William Bevins, Bruce Slovin, Charles Dawson, Stephen Taub, John Keane, Theo Folz, Philip Beekman, Martha Byorum, Viet Dinh, Paul Meister, and Carl Webb. Perelman, Schwartz, and Bevins were officers of both MFW and MacAndrews & Forbes. Perelman was the Chairman of MFW and the Chairman and CEO of MacAndrews & Forbes; Schwartz was the President and CEO of MFW and the Vice Chairman and Chief Administrative Officer of MacAndrews & Forbes; and Bevins was a Vice President at MacAndrews & Forbes.

The Taking MFW Private Proposal

In May 2011, Perelman began to explore the possibility of taking MFW private. At that time, MFW's stock price traded in the $20 to $24 per share range. MacAndrews & Forbes engaged a bank, Moelis & Company, to advise it. After preparing valuations based on projections that had been supplied to lenders by MFW in April and May 2011, Moelis valued MFW at between $10 and $32 a share.

On June 10, 2011, MFW's shares closed on the New York Stock Exchange at $16.96. The next business day, June 13, 2011, Schwartz sent a letter proposal ("Proposal") to the MFW board to buy the remaining MFW shares for $24 in cash. The Proposal stated, in relevant part:

> The proposed transaction would be subject to the approval of the Board of Directors of the Company [*i.e.*, MFW] and the negotiation and execution of mutually acceptable definitive transaction documents. It is our expectation that the Board of Directors will appoint a special committee of independent directors to consider our proposal and make a recommendation to the Board of Directors. *We will not move forward with the transaction unless it is approved by such a special committee. In addition, the transaction will be subject to a non-waivable condition requiring the approval of a majority of the shares of the Company not owned by M & F or its affiliates* . . . .
>
> In considering this proposal, you should know that in our capacity as a stockholder of the Company we are interested only in acquiring the shares of the Company not already owned by us and that in such capacity we have no interest in selling any of the shares owned by us in the Company nor would we expect, in our capacity as a stockholder, to vote in favor of any alternative sale, merger or similar transaction involving the Company. If the special committee does not recommend or the public stockholders of the Company do not approve the proposed transaction, such determination would not adversely affect our future relationship with the Company and we would intend to remain as a long-term stockholder. . . .
>
> In connection with this proposal, we have engaged Moelis & Company as our financial advisor and Skadden, Arps, Slate, Meagher & Flom LLP as our legal advisor, and we encourage the special committee to retain its own legal and financial advisors to assist it in its review.

MacAndrews & Forbes filed this letter with the U.S. Securities and Exchange Commission ("SEC") and issued a press release disclosing substantially the same information.

The Special Committee Is Formed

The MFW board met the following day to consider the Proposal. At the meeting, Schwartz presented the offer on behalf of MacAndrews & Forbes. Subsequently, Schwartz and Bevins, as the two directors present who were also directors of MacAndrews & Forbes, recused themselves from the meeting, as did Dawson, the CEO of HCHC, who had previously expressed support for the proposed offer.

The independent directors then invited counsel from Willkie Farr & Gallagher — a law firm that had recently represented a Special Committee of MFW's independent directors in a potential acquisition of a subsidiary of MacAndrews & Forbes — to join the meeting. The independent directors decided to form the Special Committee, and resolved further that:

> [T]he Special Committee is empowered to: (i) make such investigation of the Proposal as the Special Committee deems appropriate; (ii) evaluate the terms of the Proposal; (iii) negotiate with Holdings [*i.e.*, MacAndrews & Forbes] and its representatives any element of the Proposal; (iv) negotiate the terms of any definitive agreement with respect to the Proposal (it being understood that the execution thereof shall be subject to the approval of the Board); (v) report to the Board its recommendations and conclusions with respect to the Proposal, including a determination and *recommendation as to whether the Proposal is fair and in the best interests of the stockholders of the Company other than Holdings* and its affiliates and should be approved by the Board; and (vi) determine to elect not to pursue the Proposal . . . .

> [T]he Board shall not approve the Proposal without a prior favorable recommendation of the Special Committee. . . .

> [T]he Special Committee [is] empowered to retain and employ legal counsel, a financial advisor, and such other agents as the Special Committee shall deem necessary or desirable in connection with these matters. . . .

The Special Committee consisted of Byorum, Dinh, Meister (the chair), Slovin, and Webb. The following day, Slovin recused himself because, although the MFW board had determined that he qualified as an independent director under the rules of the New York Stock Exchange, he had "some current relationships that could raise questions about his independence for purposes of serving on the Special Committee."

ANALYSIS

What Should Be The Review Standard?

Where a transaction involving self-dealing by a controlling stockholder is challenged, the applicable standard of judicial review is "entire fairness," with the defendants having the burden of persuasion. In other words, the defendants bear the ultimate burden of proving that the transaction with the controlling stockholder was entirely fair to the minority stockholders. In *Kahn v. Lynch Communication Systems, Inc.*,[163] however, this Court held that in "entire fairness" cases, the defendants may shift the burden of persuasion to the plaintiff if either (1) they show that the transaction was approved by a well-functioning committee of independent directors; **or** (2) they show that the transaction was approved by an informed vote of a majority of the minority stockholders.

---

[163] [n.6] *Kahn v. Lynch Comc'n Sys., Inc.*, 638 A.2d 1110 (Del.1994).

This appeal presents a question of first impression: what should be the standard of review for a merger between a controlling stockholder and its subsidiary, where the merger is conditioned *ab initio* upon the approval of **both** an independent, adequately-empowered Special Committee that fulfills its duty of care, and the uncoerced, informed vote of a majority of the minority stockholders. The question has never been put directly to this Court.

Almost two decades ago, in *Kahn v. Lynch*, we held that the approval by *either* a Special Committee *or* the majority of the noncontrolling stockholders of a merger with a buying controlling stockholder would shift the burden of proof under the entire fairness standard from the defendant to the plaintiff. *Lynch* did not involve a merger conditioned by the controlling stockholder on both procedural protections. The Appellants submit, nonetheless, that statements in *Lynch* and its progeny could be (and were) read to suggest that even if both procedural protections were used, the standard of review would remain entire fairness. However, in *Lynch* and the other cases that Appellants cited, *Southern Peru* and *Kahn v. Tremont*, the controller did not give up its voting power by agreeing to a non-waivable majority-of-the-minority condition. That is the vital distinction between those cases and this one. The question is what the legal consequence of that distinction should be in these circumstances.

The Court of Chancery held that the consequence should be that the business judgment standard of review will govern going private mergers with a controlling stockholder that are conditioned *ab initio* upon (1) the approval of an independent and fully-empowered Special Committee that fulfills its duty of care and (2) the uncoerced, informed vote of the majority of the minority stockholders.

The Court of Chancery rested its holding upon the premise that the common law equitable rule that best protects minority investors is one that encourages controlling stockholders to accord the minority both procedural protections. A transactional structure subject to both conditions differs fundamentally from a merger having only one of those protections, in that:

> By giving controlling stockholders the opportunity to have a going private transaction reviewed under the business judgment rule, a strong incentive is created to give minority stockholders much broader access to the transactional structure that is most likely to effectively protect their interests. . . . That structure, it is important to note, is critically different than a structure that uses only *one* of the procedural protections. The "or" structure does not replicate the protections of a third-party merger under the DGCL approval process, because it only requires that one, and not both, of the statutory requirements of director and stockholder approval be accomplished by impartial decisionmakers. The "both" structure, by contrast, replicates the arm's-length merger steps of the DGCL by "requir-[ing] two independent approvals, which it is fair to say serve independent integrity-enforcing functions."[164]

Before the Court of Chancery, the Appellants acknowledged that "this transac-

---

[164] [n.10] *In re MFW Shareholders Litigation*, 67 A.3d 496, 528 (Del.Ch.2013) (citing *In re Cox Commc'ns, Inc. S'holders Litig.*, 879 A.2d 604, 618 (Del.Ch.2005)).

tional structure is the optimal one for minority shareholders." Before us, however, they argue that neither procedural protection is adequate to protect minority stockholders, because "possible ineptitude and timidity of directors" may undermine the special committee protection, and because majority-of-the-minority votes may be unduly influenced by arbitrageurs that have an institutional bias to approve virtually any transaction that offers a market premium, however insubstantial it may be. Therefore, the Appellants claim, these protections, even when combined, are not sufficient to justify "abandon[ing]" the entire fairness standard of review.

With regard to the Special Committee procedural protection, the Appellants' assertions regarding the MFW directors' inability to discharge their duties are not supported either by the record or by well-established principles of Delaware law. As the Court of Chancery correctly observed:

> Although it is possible that there are independent directors who have little regard for their duties or for being perceived by their company's stockholders (and the larger network of institutional investors) as being effective at protecting public stockholders, the court thinks they are likely to be exceptional, and certainly our Supreme Court's jurisprudence does not embrace such a skeptical view.

Regarding the majority-of-the-minority vote procedural protection, as the Court of Chancery noted, "plaintiffs themselves do not argue that minority stockholders will vote against a going private transaction because of fear of retribution." Instead, as the Court of Chancery summarized, the Appellants' argued as follows:

> [Plaintiffs] just believe that most investors like a premium and will tend to vote for a deal that delivers one and that many long-term investors will sell out when they can obtain most of the premium without waiting for the ultimate vote. But that argument is not one that suggests that the voting decision is not voluntary, it is simply an editorial about the motives of investors and does not contradict the premise that a majority-of-the-minority condition gives minority investors a free and voluntary opportunity to decide what is fair for themselves.

Business Judgment Review Standard Adopted

We hold that business judgment is the standard of review that should govern mergers between a controlling stockholder and its corporate subsidiary, where the merger is conditioned *ab initio* upon both the approval of an independent, adequately-empowered Special Committee that fulfills its duty of care; and the uncoerced, informed vote of a majority of the minority stockholders. We so conclude for several reasons.

First, entire fairness is the highest standard of review in corporate law. It is applied in the controller merger context as a substitute for the dual statutory protections of disinterested board and stockholder approval, because both protections are potentially undermined by the influence of the controller. However, as this case establishes, that undermining influence does not exist in every controlled merger setting, regardless of the circumstances. The simultaneous deployment of the procedural protections employed here create a countervailing, offsetting influence of equal — if not greater — force. That is, where the controller irrevocably and publicly disables itself from using its control to dictate the outcome of the negotiations and the shareholder vote, the controlled merger then acquires the shareholder-protective characteristics of third-party, arm's-length mergers, which are reviewed under the business judgment standard.

Second, the dual procedural protection merger structure optimally protects the minority stockholders in controller buyouts. As the Court of Chancery explained:

> [W]hen these two protections are established up-front, a potent tool to extract good value for the minority is established. From inception, the controlling stockholder knows that it cannot bypass the special committee's ability to say no. And, the controlling stockholder knows it cannot dangle a majority-of-the-minority vote before the special committee late in the process as a deal-closer rather than having to make a price move.

Third, and as the Court of Chancery reasoned, applying the business judgment standard to the dual protection merger structure:

> . . . is consistent with the central tradition of Delaware law, which defers to the informed decisions of impartial directors, especially when those decisions have been approved by the disinterested stockholders on full information and without coercion. Not only that, the adoption of this rule will be of benefit to minority stockholders because it will provide a strong incentive for controlling stockholders to accord minority investors the transactional structure that respected scholars believe will provide them the best protection, a structure where stockholders get the benefits of independent, empowered negotiating agents to **bargain for the best price and say no** if the agents believe the deal is not advisable for any proper reason, plus the critical ability to determine for themselves whether to accept any deal that their negotiating agents recommend to them. A transactional structure with both these protections is fundamentally different from one with only one protection.

Fourth, the underlying purposes of the dual protection merger structure utilized here and the entire fairness standard of review both converge and are fulfilled at the same critical point: **price.** Following *Weinberger v. UOP, Inc.*, this Court has consistently held that, although entire fairness review comprises the dual components of fair dealing and fair price, in a non-fraudulent transaction "price may be the preponderant consideration outweighing other features of the merger."[165] The dual protection merger structure requires two price-related pretrial determinations: first, that a fair price was achieved by an empowered, independent committee that acted with care; and, second, that a fully-informed, uncoerced majority of the minority stockholders voted in favor of the price that was recommended by the independent committee.

---

[165] [n.12] *Weinberger v. UOP, Inc.*, 457 A.2d 701, 711 (Del.1983).

The New Standard Summarized

To summarize our holding, in controller buyouts, the business judgment standard of review will be applied *if and only if:* (i) the controller conditions the procession of the transaction on the approval of both a Special Committee and a majority of the minority stockholders; (ii) the Special Committee is independent; (iii) the Special Committee is empowered to freely select its own advisors and to say no definitively; (iv) the Special Committee meets its duty of care in negotiating a fair price; (v) the vote of the minority is informed; and (vi) there is no coercion of the minority.[166]

If a plaintiff that can plead a reasonably conceivable set of facts showing that any or all of those enumerated conditions did not exist, that complaint would state a claim for relief that would entitle the plaintiff to proceed and conduct discovery. If, after discovery, triable issues of fact remain about whether either or both of the dual procedural protections were established, or if established were effective, the case will proceed to a trial in which the court will conduct an entire fairness review.

This approach is consistent with *Weinberger, Lynch* and their progeny. A controller that employs and/or establishes only one of these dual procedural protections would continue to receive burden-shifting within the entire fairness standard of review framework. Stated differently, unless *both* procedural protections for the minority stockholders are established *prior to trial*, the ultimate judicial scrutiny of controller buyouts will continue to be the entire fairness standard of review.

Having articulated the circumstances that will enable a controlled merger to be reviewed under the business judgment standard, we next address whether those circumstances have been established as a matter of undisputed fact and law in this case.

Dual Protection Inquiry

To reiterate, in this case, the controlling stockholder conditioned its offer upon the MFW Board agreeing, *ab initio*, to both procedural protections, *i.e.*, approval by a Special Committee and by a majority of the minority stockholders. For the combination of an effective committee process and majority-of-the-minority vote to qualify (jointly) for business judgment review, each of these protections must be effective singly to warrant a burden shift.

---

[166] [n.14] The Verified Consolidated Class Action Complaint would have survived a motion to dismiss under this new standard. First, the complaint alleged that Perelman's offer "value[d] the company at just four times" MFW's profits per share and "five times 2010 pre-tax cash flow," and that these ratios were "well below" those calculated for recent similar transactions. Second, the complaint alleged that the final Merger price was two dollars per share *lower* than the trading price only about two months earlier. Third, the complaint alleged particularized facts indicating that MWF's share price was depressed at the times of Perelman's offer and the Merger announcement due to short-term factors such as MFW's acquisition of other entities and Standard & Poor's downgrading of the United States' creditworthiness. Fourth, the complaint alleged that commentators viewed both Perelman's initial $24 per share offer and the final $25 per share Merger price as being surprisingly low. These allegations about the sufficiency of the price call into question the adequacy of the Special Committee's negotiations, thereby necessitating discovery on all of the new prerequisites to the application of the business judgment rule.

We begin by reviewing the record relating to the independence, mandate, and process of the Special Committee. In *Kahn v. Tremont Corp.*, this Court held that "[t]o obtain the benefit of burden shifting, the controlling stockholder must do more than establish a perfunctory special committee of outside directors."[167]

Rather, the special committee must "function in a manner which indicates that the controlling stockholder did not dictate the terms of the transaction and that the committee exercised real bargaining power 'at an arms-length.' "[168] As we have previously noted, deciding whether an independent committee was effective in negotiating a price is a process so fact-intensive and inextricably intertwined with the merits of an entire fairness review (fair dealing and fair price) that a pretrial determination of burden shifting is often impossible. Here, however, the Defendants have successfully established a record of independent committee effectiveness and process that warranted a grant of summary judgment entitling them to a burden shift prior to trial.

We next analyze the efficacy of the majority-of-the-minority vote, and we conclude that it was fully informed and not coerced. That is, the Defendants also established a pretrial majority-of-the-minority vote record that constitutes an independent and alternative basis for shifting the burden of persuasion to the Plaintiffs.

The Special Committee Was Independent

The Appellants do not challenge the independence of the Special Committee's Chairman, Meister. They claim, however, that the three other Special Committee members — Webb, Dinh, and Byorum — were beholden to Perelman because of their prior business and/or social dealings with Perelman or Perelman-related entities.

The Appellants first challenge the independence of Webb. They urged that Webb and Perelman shared a "longstanding and lucrative business partnership" between 1983 and 2002 which included acquisitions of thrifts and financial institutions, and which led to a 2002 asset sale to Citibank in which Webb made "a significant amount of money." The Court of Chancery concluded, however, that the fact of Webb having engaged in business dealings with Perelman nine years earlier did not raise a triable fact issue regarding his ability to evaluate the Merger impartially. We agree.

Second, the Appellants argued that there were triable issues of fact regarding Dinh's independence. The Appellants demonstrated that between 2009 and 2011, Dinh's law firm, Bancroft PLLC, advised M & F and Scientific Games (in which M & F owned a 37.6% stake), during which time the Bancroft firm earned $200,000 in fees. The record reflects that Bancroft's limited prior engagements, which were

---

[167] *Kahn v. Tremont Corp.*, 694 A.2d 422, 429 (Del.1997) (citation omitted). *See Emerald Partners v. Berlin*, 726 A.2d 1215, 1222–23 (Del.1999) (describing that the special committee must exert "real bargaining power" in order for defendants to obtain a burden shift); *see also Beam v. Stewart*, 845 A.2d 1040, 1055 n. 45 (Del.2004) (citing *Kahn v. Tremont Corp.*, 694 A.2d 422, 429–30 (Del.1997)) (noting that the test articulated in *Tremont* requires a determination as to whether the committee members "*in fact*" functioned independently).

[168] [n.19] *Kahn v. Tremont Corp.*, 694 A.2d at 429 (citation omitted).

inactive by the time the Merger proposal was announced, were fully disclosed to the Special Committee soon after it was formed. The Court of Chancery found that the Appellants failed to proffer any evidence to show that compensation received by Dinh's law firm was material to Dinh, in the sense that it would have influenced his decisionmaking with respect to the M & F proposal. The only evidence of record, the Court of Chancery concluded, was that these fees were "*de minimis*" and that the Appellants had offered no contrary evidence that would create a genuine issue of material fact.

The Court of Chancery also found that the relationship between Dinh, a Georgetown University Law Center professor, and M & F's Barry Schwartz, who sits on the Georgetown Board of Visitors, did not create a triable issue of fact as to Dinh's independence. No record evidence suggested that Schwartz could exert influence on Dinh's position at Georgetown based on his recommendation regarding the Merger. Indeed, Dinh had earned tenure as a professor at Georgetown before he ever knew Schwartz.

The Appellants also argue that Schwartz's later invitation to Dinh to join the board of directors of Revlon, Inc. "illustrates the ongoing personal relationship between Schwartz and Dinh." There is no record evidence that Dinh expected to be asked to join Revlon's board at the time he served on the Special Committee. Moreover, the Court of Chancery noted, Schwartz's invitation for Dinh to join the Revlon board of directors occurred months after the Merger was approved and did not raise a triable fact issue concerning Dinh's independence from Perelman. We uphold the Court of Chancery's findings relating to Dinh.

Third, the Appellants urge that issues of material fact permeate Byorum's independence and, specifically, that Byorum "had a business relationship with Perelman from 1991 to 1996 through her executive position at Citibank." The Court of Chancery concluded, however, the Appellants presented no evidence of the nature of Byorum's interactions with Perelman while she was at Citibank. Nor was there evidence that after 1996 Byorum had an ongoing economic relationship with Perelman that was material to her in any way. Byorum testified that any interactions she had with Perelman while she was at Citibank resulted from her role as a senior executive, because Perelman was a client of the bank at the time. Byorum also testified that she had no business relationship with Perelman between 1996 and 2007, when she joined the MFW Board.

The Appellants also contend that Byorum performed advisory work for Scientific Games in 2007 and 2008 as a senior managing director of Stephens Cori Capital Advisors ("Stephens Cori"). The Court of Chancery found, however, that the Appellants had adduced no evidence tending to establish that the $100,000 fee Stephens Cori received for that work was material to either Stephens Cori or to Byoru personally. Stephens Cori's engagement for Scientific Games, which occurred years before the Merger was announced and the Special Committee was convened, was fully disclosed to the Special Committee, which concluded that "it was not material, and it would not represent a conflict." We uphold the Court of Chancery's findings relating to Byorum as well.

To evaluate the parties' competing positions on the issue of director independence, the Court of Chancery applied well-established Delaware legal principles. To show that a director is not independent, a plaintiff must demonstrate that the director is "beholden" to the controlling party "or so under [the controller's] influence that [the director's] discretion would be sterilized."[169] Bare allegations that directors are friendly with, travel in the same social circles as, or have past business relationships with the proponent of a transaction or the person they are investigating are not enough to rebut the presumption of independence.

A plaintiff seeking to show that a director was not independent must satisfy a materiality standard. The court must conclude that the director in question had ties to the person whose proposal or actions he or she is evaluating that are sufficiently substantial that he or she could not objectively discharge his or her fiduciary duties. Consistent with that predicate materiality requirement, the existence of some financial ties between the interested party and the director, without more, is not disqualifying. The inquiry must be whether, applying a subjective standard, those ties were *material*, in the sense that the alleged ties could have affected the impartiality of the individual director.

The Appellants assert that the materiality of any economic relationships the Special Committee members may have had with Mr. Perelman "should not be decided on summary judgment." But Delaware courts have often decided director independence as a matter of law at the summary judgment stage. In this case, the Court of Chancery noted, that despite receiving extensive discovery, the Appellants did "nothing . . . to compare the actual circumstances of the [challenged directors] to the ties [they] contend affect their impartiality" and "fail[ed] to proffer any real evidence of their economic circumstances." . . .

The Court of Chancery found that to the extent the Appellants claimed the Special Committee members, Webb, Dinh, and Byorum, were beholden to Perelman based on prior economic relationships with him, the Appellants never developed or proffered evidence showing the materiality of those relationships:

> Despite receiving the chance for extensive discovery, the plaintiffs have done nothing . . . to compare the actual economic circumstances of the directors they challenge to the ties the plaintiffs contend affect their impartiality. In other words, the plaintiffs have ignored a key teaching of our Supreme Court, requiring a showing that a specific director's independence is compromised by factors material to her. As to each of the specific directors the plaintiffs challenge, the plaintiffs fail to proffer any real evidence of their economic circumstances.

The record supports the Court of Chancery's holding that none of the Appellants' claims relating to Webb, Dinh or Byorum raised a triable issue of material fact concerning their individual independence or the Special Committee's collective independence.

---

[169] [n.27] *Rales v. Blasband*, 634 A.2d 927, 936 (Del.1993) (citing *Aronson v. Lewis*, 473 A.2d 805, 815 (Del.1984)).

The Special Committee Was Empowered

It is undisputed that the Special Committee was empowered to hire its own legal and financial advisors, and it retained Willkie Farr & Gallagher LLP as its legal advisor. After interviewing four potential financial advisors, the Special Committee engaged Evercore Partners ("Evercore"). The qualifications and independence of Evercore and Willkie Farr & Gallagher LLP are not contested.

Among the powers given the Special Committee in the board resolution was the authority to "report to the Board its recommendations and conclusions with respect to the [Merger], including a determination and recommendation as to whether the Proposal is fair and in the best interests of the stockholders. . . ." The Court of Chancery also found that it was "undisputed that the [S]pecial [C]ommittee was empowered not simply to 'evaluate' the offer, like some special committees with weak mandates, but to negotiate with [M & F] over the terms of its offer to buy out the noncontrolling stockholders. This negotiating power was accompanied by the clear authority to say no definitively to [M & F]" and to "make that decision stick." MacAndrews & Forbes promised that it would not proceed with any going private proposal that did not have the support of the Special Committee. Therefore, the Court of Chancery concluded, "the MFW committee did not have to fear that if it bargained too hard, MacAndrews & Forbes could bypass the committee and make a tender offer directly to the minority stockholders."

The Court of Chancery acknowledged that even though the Special Committee had the authority to negotiate and "say no," it did not have the authority, as a practical matter, to sell MFW to other buyers. MacAndrews & Forbes stated in its announcement that it was not interested in selling its 43% stake. Moreover, under Delaware law, MacAndrews & Forbes had no duty to sell its block, which was large enough, again as a practical matter, to preclude any other buyer from succeeding unless MacAndrews & Forbes decided to become a seller. Absent such a decision, it was unlikely that any potentially interested party would incur the costs and risks of exploring a purchase of MFW.

Nevertheless, the Court of Chancery found, "this did not mean that the MFW Special Committee did not have the leeway to get advice from its financial advisor about the strategic options available to MFW, including the potential interest that other buyers might have *if MacAndrews & Forbes was willing to sell.*" The undisputed record shows that the Special Committee, with the help of its financial advisor, did consider whether there were other buyers who might be interested in purchasing MFW, and whether there were other strategic options, such as asset divestitures, that might generate more value for minority stockholders than a sale of their stock to MacAndrews & Forbes.

The Special Committee Exercised Due Care

The Special Committee insisted from the outset that MacAndrews (including any "dual" employees who worked for both MFW and MacAndrews) be screened off from the Special Committee's process, to ensure that the process replicated arm's-length negotiations with a third party. In order to carefully evaluate M & F's offer, the Special Committee held a total of eight meetings during the summer of 2011.

From the outset of their work, the Special Committee and Evercore had projections that had been prepared by MFW's business segments in April and May 2011. Early in the process, Evercore and the Special Committee asked MFW management to produce new projections that reflected management's most up-to-date, and presumably most accurate, thinking. Consistent with the Special Committee's determination to conduct its analysis free of any MacAndrews influence, MacAndrews — including "dual" MFW/MacAndrews executives who normally vetted MFW projections — were excluded from the process of preparing the updated financial projections. Mafco, the licorice business, advised Evercore that all of its projections would remain the same. Harland Clarke updated its projections. On July 22, 2011, Evercore received new projections from HCHC, which incorporated the updated projections from Harland Clarke. Evercore then constructed a valuation model based upon all of these updated projections.

The updated projections, which formed the basis for Evercore's valuation analyses, reflected MFW's deteriorating results, especially in Harland's check-printing business. Those projections forecast EBITDA for MFW of $491 million in 2015, as opposed to $535 million under the original projections.

On August 10, Evercore produced a range of valuations for MFW, based on the updated projections, of $15 to $45 per share. Evercore valued MFW using a variety of accepted methods, including a discounted cash flow ("DCF") model. Those valuations generated a range of fair value of $22 to $38 per share, and a premiums paid analysis resulted in a value range of $22 to $45. MacAndrews & Forbes's $24 offer fell within the range of values produced by each of Evercore's valuation techniques.

Although the $24 Proposal fell within the range of Evercore's fair values, the Special Committee directed Evercore to conduct additional analyses and explore strategic alternatives that might generate more value for MFW's stockholders than might a sale to MacAndrews. The Special Committee also investigated the possibility of other buyers, *e.g.*, private equity buyers, that might be interested in purchasing MFW. In addition, the Special Committee considered whether other strategic options, such as asset divestitures, could achieve superior value for MFW's stockholders. Mr. Meister testified, "The Committee made it very clear to Evercore that we were interested in any and all possible avenues of increasing value to the stockholders, including meaningful expressions of interest for meaningful pieces of the business."

The Appellants insist that the Special Committee had "no right to solicit alternative bids, conduct any sort of market check, or even consider alternative transactions." But the Special Committee did just that, even though MacAndrews' stated unwillingness to sell its MFW stake meant that the Special Committee did not have the practical ability to market MFW to other buyers. The Court of Chancery properly concluded that despite the Special Committee's inability to solicit alternative bids, it *could* seek Evercore's advice about strategic alternatives, including *values that might be available if MacAndrews was willing to sell.*

Although the MFW Special Committee considered options besides the M & F Proposal, the Committee's analysis of those alternatives proved they were unlikely to achieve added value for MFW's stockholders. The Court of Chancery summarized the performance of the Special Committee as follows:

> [t]he special committee did consider, with the help of its financial advisor, whether there were other buyers who might be interested in purchasing MFW, and whether there were other strategic options, such as asset divestitures, that might generate more value for minority stockholders than a sale of their stock to MacAndrews & Forbes.

On August 18, 2011, the Special Committee rejected the $24 a share Proposal, and countered at $30 per share. The Special Committee characterized the $30 counteroffer as a negotiating position. The Special Committee recognized that $30 per share was a very aggressive counteroffer and, not surprisingly, was prepared to accept less.

On September 9, 2011, MacAndrews & Forbes rejected the $30 per share counteroffer. Its representative, Barry Schwartz, told the Special Committee Chair, Paul Meister, that the $24 per share Proposal was now far less favorable to MacAndrews & Forbes — but more attractive to the minority — than when it was first made, because of continued declines in MFW's businesses. Nonetheless, MacAndrews & Forbes would stand behind its $24 offer. Meister responded that he would not recommend the $24 per share Proposal to the Special Committee. Later, after having discussions with Perelman, Schwartz conveyed MacAndrews's "best and final" offer of $25 a share.

At a Special Committee meeting the next day, Evercore opined that the $25 per share *price was fair* based on generally accepted valuation methodologies, including DCF and comparable companies analyses. At its eighth and final meeting on September 10, 2011, the Special Committee, although empowered to say "no," instead unanimously approved and agreed to recommend the Merger at a price of $25 per share.

Influencing the Special Committee's assessment and acceptance of M & F's $25 a share price were developments in both MFW's business and the broader United States economy during the summer of 2011. For example, during the negotiation process, the Special Committee learned of the underperformance of MFW's Global Scholar business unit. The Committee also considered macroeconomic events, including the downgrade of the United States' bond credit rating, and the ongoing turmoil in the financial markets, all of which created financing uncertainties.

In scrutinizing the Special Committee's execution of its broad mandate, the Court of Chancery determined there was no "evidence indicating that the independent members of the special committee did not meet their duty of care. . . ." To the contrary, the Court of Chancery found, the Special Committee "met frequently and was presented with a rich body of financial information relevant to whether and at what *price* a going private transaction was advisable." The Court of Chancery ruled that "the plaintiffs d[id] not make any attempt to show that the MFW Special Committee failed to meet its duty of care. . . ." Based on the undisputed record, the Court of Chancery held that, "there is no triable issue of fact regarding whether the

[S]pecial [C]ommittee fulfilled its duty of care." In the context of a controlling stockholder merger, a pretrial determination that the *price* was negotiated by an empowered independent committee that acted with care would shift the burden of persuasion to the plaintiffs under the entire fairness standard of review.

Majority of Minority Stockholder Vote

We now consider the second procedural protection invoked by M & F — the majority-of-the-minority stockholder vote. Consistent with the second condition imposed by M & F at the outset, the Merger was then put before MFW's stockholders for a vote. On November 18, 2011, the stockholders were provided with a proxy statement, which contained the history of the Special Committee's work and recommended that they vote in favor of the transaction at a price of $25 per share.

The proxy statement disclosed, among other things, that the Special Committee had countered M & F's initial $24 per share offer at $30 per share, but only was able to achieve a final offer of $25 per share. The proxy statement disclosed that the MFW business divisions had discussed with Evercore whether the initial projections Evercore received reflected management's latest thinking. It also disclosed that the updated projections were lower. The proxy statement also included the five separate price ranges for the value of MFW's stock that Evercore had generated with its different valuation analyses.

Knowing the proxy statement's disclosures of the background of the Special Committee's work, of Evercore's valuation ranges, and of the analyses supporting Evercore's *fairness opinion*, MFW's stockholders — representing more than 65% of the minority shares — approved the Merger. In the controlling stockholder merger context, it is settled Delaware law that an uncoerced, informed majority-of-the-minority vote, without any other procedural protection, is itself sufficient to shift the burden of persuasion to the plaintiff under the entire fairness standard of review. The Court of Chancery found that "the plaintiffs themselves do not dispute that the majority-of-the-minority vote was fully informed and uncoerced, because they fail to allege any failure of disclosure or any act of coercion."

Both Procedural Protections Established

Based on a highly extensive record, the Court of Chancery concluded that the procedural protections upon which the Merger was conditioned — approval by an independent and empowered Special Committee and by a uncoerced informed majority of MFW's minority stockholders — had *both* been undisputedly established *prior to trial*. We agree and conclude the Defendants' motion for summary judgment was properly granted on all of those issues.

Business Judgment Review Properly Applied

We have determined that the business judgment rule standard of review applies to this controlling stockholder buyout. Under that standard, the claims against the Defendants must be dismissed unless no rational person could have believed that the merger was favorable to MFW's minority stockholders. In this case, it cannot be credibly argued (let alone concluded) that no rational person would find the Merger favorable to MFW's minority stockholders.

———————

QUESTIONS

1.   What is the deal involved in this case?

2.   Why did MacAndrews & Forbes condition going forward with the deal on approval by (i) an MFW independent special committee, and (ii) a vote of a majority of MFW stockholders unaffiliated with MacAndrews & Forbes? Was MacAndrews & Forbes legally required to impose these conditions on itself?

3.   What is the test for determining director independence? Were the members of the MFW special committee independent? Why or why not?

4.   How is this case distinguishable from *Lynch*?

5.   What is the legal effect of having a controlling shareholder transaction approved by an independent and disinterested special committee of the board and a vote of a majority of minority shareholders? What is the policy behind giving those actions such an effect?

———————

Appendix

BUSINSESS ORGANIZATIONS LAW REFRESHER

Below is a brief refresher of concepts you likely covered in your business organizations course. It focuses mostly on corporate law because this book focuses mostly on M&A in the corporate law context. However, there is some discussion of unincorporated entities at the end of this refresher.

A. CORPORATIONS

1. Formation

You form, or incorporate, a corporation by filing "articles of incorporation" or a similarly named document (e.g., Delaware and New York use the term "certificate of incorporation") with the secretary of state of the state in which the client wants the corporation incorporated. The state's corporate law statute will specify what must be included in the articles/certificate of incorporation (this document is often called a "charter" for short, regardless of the term used by the applicable state). See subsection 3 below for a sample charter.

In addition to a charter, a corporation is required to have bylaws. A corporation's bylaws specify rules regarding the governance of the corporation. These rules address, among other things, notice and quorum requirements for board and shareholder meetings, number and qualifications of directors, voting standards, proxy voting, appointment of officers, and stock certificates. See subsection 3 below for sample bylaws. Bylaws are normally drafted by the attorney retained to handle the incorporation of a business. In terms of hierarchy, the corporate law statute trumps the charter which trumps the bylaws.[1] In other words, if a bylaw provision is inconsistent with the statute or the charter, the statute or the charter controls. Similarly, if a charter provision is inconsistent with the statute, the statute controls.

2. Governing Law

Pursuant to the internal affairs doctrine,[2] a corporation is governed by the law of the state in which it is incorporated. Each state has its own corporate law statute.

---

[1] *See, e.g.*, Gaskill v. Gladys Belle Oil Co., 146 A. 337, 340 (Del. Ch. 1929) ("[W]ith respect to corporations, the law of their being is characterized by gradation of authority. That which is superior over-rides all below it in rank. The by-laws must succumb to the superior authority of the charter; the charter if it conflicts with the statute must give way; and the statute, if it conflicts with the Constitution, is void.").

[2] The internal affairs doctrine is a choice of law rule that applies to all business entities, e.g., corporations, LLCs, partnerships. It provides that a business entity is governed by the business entity statute of the state in which it is organized (or incorporated). It is called the internal affairs doctrine because business entity statutes generally address the internal governance of the business entity, that is, the rights and duties of owners and managers. In *Vantage Point Partners v. Examen, Inc.*, 871 A.2d 1109 (Del. 2005), the Delaware Supreme Court explained the policy behind the internal affairs doctrine, at least in the corporate context, as follows:

The following 32 states have corporate law statutes based on some form of the Model Business Corporation Act (MBCA): Alabama, Alaska, Arizona, Arkansas, Connecticut, Florida, Georgia, Hawaii, Idaho, Indiana, Iowa, Kentucky, Maine, Massachusetts, Mississippi, Montana, Nebraska, New Hampshire, New Mexico, North Carolina, Oregon, Rhode Island, South Carolina, South Dakota, Tennessee, Utah, Vermont, Virginia, Washington, West Virginia, Wisconsin, and Wyoming. The remaining 18 states developed their own statutes, although many of them have adopted select provisions of the Model Business Corporation Act (MBCA).

The MBCA was promulgated in 1950 by what is now the Section of Business Law of the American Bar Association (ABA). The Section has amended the MBCA on numerous occasions throughout the years and promulgated a complete revision in 1984 (sometimes referred to as the Revised Model Business Corporation Act or RMBCA). From time to time, the Section puts out a new edition of the MBCA that incorporates all amendments adopted since the last edition. The latest edition is the fourth, which the ABA published in 2007. As is the case with all business entity statutes, you should not assume that a state has adopted the MBCA verbatim. States are free to make changes or not adopt amendments. Thus, in practice, when a corporate law issue comes up with respect to a corporation incorporated in an MBCA state, you should consult the applicable state's corporate law statute and not the MBCA (although you may want to look at the official MBCA commentary on the particular provision at issue). For non-MBCA states, you should likewise consult the applicable state's corporate law statute.

Delaware is unquestionably the most important non-MBCA state, because it by far attracts the most incorporations by out-of-state businesses and is the state of incorporation for over 50 percent of U.S. publicly traded companies. Delaware's corporate law statute is titled the Delaware General Corporation Law (DGCL).

3. Governing Documents

As mentioned above, a corporation is required to have a charter and bylaws. These documents are collectively referred to as a corporation's governing (or organic) documents. Other governing documents include shareholders' agreements and corporate governance principles. Various provisions of corporate law statutes provide default rules that a corporation can vary or opt out of by including appropriate language in one or more of its governing documents. These documents

---

The internal affairs doctrine developed on the premise that, in order to prevent corporations from being subjected to inconsistent legal standards, the authority to regulate a corporation's internal affairs should not rest with multiple jurisdictions. It is now well- established that only the law of the state of incorporation governs and determines issues relating to a corporation's internal affairs. By providing certainty and predictability, the internal affairs doctrine protects the justified expectations of the parties with interests in the corporation. The internal affairs doctrine applies to those matters that pertain to the relationships among or between the corporation and its officers, directors, and shareholders. The Restatement (Second) of Conflict of Laws § 301 provides: "application of the local law of the state of incorporation will usually be supported by those choice-of-law factors favoring the need of the interstate and international systems, certainty, predictability and uniformity of result, protection of the justified expectations of the parties and ease in the application of the law to be applied." Accordingly, the conflicts practice of both state and federal courts has consistently been to apply the law of the state of incorporation to "the entire gamut of internal corporate affairs."

do not necessarily address or mention default rules that a corporation does not want to vary or mandatory rules that the statute does not permit a corporation to alter. Thus, it is critical to consult a corporation's organic documents *and* the applicable corporate law statute when advising a corporation on a corporate law issue.

A corporation's charter, among other things, specifies the corporation's name, the types of stock (e.g., common stock and preferred stock) it is authorized to issue, the rights and preference of any preferred stock, and an office and agent for the service of process in the state of incorporation. The initial charter of most corporations is pretty bare-bones and is oftentimes only one or two pages long. The following is the certificate of incorporation of Zipcar in effect prior to its acquisition by Avis Budget. It is a bit longer than two pages in part because Zipcar was a public company and therefore its charter included various anti-takeover provisions (we discuss anti-takeover charter provisions in Chapter 6).

EIGHTH RESTATED
CERTIFICATE OF INCORPORATION
OF
ZIPCAR, INC.
(originally incorporated on January 11, 2000)

FIRST: The name of the Corporation is Zipcar, Inc.

SECOND: The address of the Corporation's registered office in the State of Delaware is Corporation Trust Center, 1209 Orange Street, in the City of Wilmington, County of New Castle. The name of its registered agent at that address is The Corporation Trust Company.

THIRD: The nature of the business or purposes to be conducted or promoted by the Corporation is to engage in any lawful act or activity for which corporations may be organized under the General Corporation Law of the State of Delaware.

FOURTH: The total number of shares of all classes of stock which the Corporation shall have authority to issue is five hundred ten million (510,000,000) shares, consisting of (i) five hundred million (500,000,000) shares of Common Stock, $.001 par value per share ("Common Stock"), and (ii) ten million (10,000,000) shares of Preferred Stock, $.001 par value per share ("Preferred Stock").

The following is a statement of the designations and the powers, privileges and rights, and the qualifications, limitations or restrictions thereof in respect of each class of capital stock of the Corporation.

A. COMMON STOCK

1. General. The voting, dividend and liquidation rights of the holders of the Common Stock are subject to and qualified by the rights of the holders of the Preferred Stock of any series as may be designated by the Board of Directors upon any issuance of the Preferred Stock of any series.

2. Voting. The holders of the Common Stock shall have voting rights at all meetings of stockholders, each such holder being entitled to one vote for each share thereof held by such holder; provided, however, that, except as

otherwise required by law, holders of Common Stock shall not be entitled to vote on any amendment to this Certificate of Incorporation (which, as used herein, shall mean the certificate of incorporation of the Corporation, as amended from time to time, including the terms of any certificate of designations of any series of Preferred Stock) that relates solely to the terms of one or more outstanding series of Preferred Stock if the holders of such affected series are entitled, either separately or together as a class with the holders of one or more other such series, to vote thereon pursuant to this Certificate of Incorporation. There shall be no cumulative voting.

The number of authorized shares of Common Stock may be increased or decreased (but not below the number of shares thereof then outstanding) by the affirmative vote of the holders of a majority of the stock of the Corporation entitled to vote, irrespective of the provisions of § 242(b)(2) of the General Corporation Law of the State of Delaware.

3. Dividends. Dividends may be declared and paid on the Common Stock from funds lawfully available therefor as and when determined by the Board of Directors and subject to any preferential dividend or other rights of any then outstanding Preferred Stock.

4. Liquidation. Upon the dissolution or liquidation of the Corporation, whether voluntary or involuntary, holders of Common Stock will be entitled to receive all assets of the Corporation available for distribution to its stockholders, subject to any preferential or other rights of any then outstanding Preferred Stock.

B. PREFERRED STOCK

Preferred Stock may be issued from time to time in one or more series, each of such series to have such terms as stated or expressed herein and in the resolution or resolutions providing for the issue of such series adopted by the Board of Directors of the Corporation as hereinafter provided. Any shares of Preferred Stock which may be redeemed, purchased or acquired by the Corporation may be reissued except as otherwise provided by law.

Authority is hereby expressly granted to the Board of Directors from time to time to issue the Preferred Stock in one or more series, and in connection with the creation of any such series, by adopting a resolution or resolutions providing for the issuance of the shares thereof and by filing a certificate of designations relating thereto in accordance with the General Corporation Law of the State of Delaware, to determine and fix the number of shares of such series and such voting powers, full or limited, or no voting powers, and such designations, preferences and relative participating, optional or other special rights, and qualifications, limitations or restrictions thereof, including without limitation thereof, dividend rights, conversion rights, redemption privileges and liquidation preferences, as shall be stated and expressed in such resolutions, all to the full extent now or hereafter permitted by the General Corporation Law of the State of Delaware. Without limiting the generality of the foregoing, the resolutions providing for issuance of any series of Preferred Stock may provide that such series shall be superior or rank equally or be junior to any other series of Preferred Stock to the extent permitted by law.

The number of authorized shares of Preferred Stock may be increased or decreased (but not below the number of shares then outstanding) by the affirmative vote of the holders of a majority of the voting power of the capital stock of the Corporation entitled to vote thereon, voting as a single class, irrespective of the provisions of § 242(b)(2) of the General Corporation Law of the State of Delaware.

FIFTH: Except as otherwise provided herein, the Corporation reserves the right to amend, alter, change or repeal any provision contained in this Certificate of Incorporation, in the manner now or hereafter prescribed by statute and this Certificate of Incorporation, and all rights conferred upon stockholders herein are granted subject to this reservation.

SIXTH: In furtherance and not in limitation of the powers conferred upon it by the General Corporation Law of the State of Delaware, and subject to the terms of any series of Preferred Stock, the Board of Directors shall have the power to adopt, amend, alter or repeal the By-laws of the Corporation by the affirmative vote of a majority of the directors present at any regular or special meeting of the Board of Directors at which a quorum is present. The stockholders may not adopt, amend, alter or repeal the By-laws of the Corporation, or adopt any provision inconsistent therewith, unless such action is approved, in addition to any other vote required by this Certificate of Incorporation, by the affirmative vote of the holders of at least seventy-five percent (75%) of the votes that all the stockholders would be entitled to cast in any annual election of directors or class of directors. Notwithstanding any other provisions of law, this Certificate of Incorporation or the By-laws of the Corporation, and notwithstanding the fact that a lesser percentage may be specified by law, the affirmative vote of the holders of at least seventy-five percent (75%) of the votes that all the stockholders would be entitled to cast in any annual election of directors or class of directors shall be required to amend or repeal, or to adopt any provision inconsistent with, this Article SIXTH.

SEVENTH: Except to the extent that the General Corporation Law of the State of Delaware prohibits the elimination or limitation of liability of directors for breaches of fiduciary duty, no director of the Corporation shall be personally liable to the Corporation or its stockholders for monetary damages for any breach of fiduciary duty as a director, notwithstanding any provision of law imposing such liability. No amendment to or repeal of this provision shall apply to or have any effect on the liability or alleged liability of any director of the Corporation for or with respect to any acts or omissions of such director occurring prior to such amendment or repeal. If the General Corporation Law of the State of Delaware is amended to permit further elimination or limitation of the personal liability of directors, then the liability of a director of the Corporation shall be eliminated or limited to the fullest extent permitted by the General Corporation Law of the State of Delaware as so amended.

EIGHTH: The Corporation shall provide indemnification as follows . . . .

NINTH: This Article NINTH is inserted for the management of the business and for the conduct of the affairs of the Corporation.

1. General Powers. The business and affairs of the Corporation shall be managed by or under the direction of the Board of Directors.

2. Number of Directors; Election of Directors. Subject to the rights of holders of any series of Preferred Stock to elect directors, the number of directors of the Corporation shall be established by the Board of Directors. Election of directors need not be by written ballot, except as and to the extent provided in the By-laws of the Corporation.

3. <u>Classes of Directors</u>. Subject to the rights of holders of any series of Preferred Stock to elect directors, the Board of Directors shall be and is divided into three classes, designated Class I, Class II and Class III. Each class shall consist, as nearly as may be possible, of one-third of the total number of directors constituting the entire Board of Directors. The Board of Directors is authorized to assign members of the Board of Directors already in office to Class I, Class II or Class III at the time such classification becomes effective.

4. <u>Terms of Office</u>. Subject to the rights of holders of any series of Preferred Stock to elect directors, each director shall serve for a term ending on the date of the third annual meeting of stockholders following the annual meeting of stockholders at which such director was elected; <u>provided</u> that each director initially assigned to Class I shall serve for a term expiring at the Corporation's first annual meeting of stockholders held after the effectiveness of this Restated Certificate of Incorporation; each director initially assigned to Class II shall serve for a term expiring at the Corporation's second annual meeting of stockholders held after the effectiveness of this Restated Certificate of Incorporation; and each director initially assigned to Class III shall serve for a term expiring at the Corporation's third annual meeting of stockholders held after the effectiveness of this Restated Certificate of Incorporation; <u>provided further</u>, that the term of each director shall continue until the election and qualification of his or her successor and be subject to his or her earlier death, resignation or removal.

5. <u>Quorum</u>. The greater of (a) a majority of the directors at any time in office and (b) one-third of the number of directors fixed pursuant to Section 2 of this Article NINTH shall constitute a quorum of the Board of Directors. If at any meeting of the Board of Directors there shall be less than such a quorum, a majority of the directors present may adjourn the meeting from time to time without further notice other than announcement at the meeting, until a quorum shall be present.

6. <u>Action at Meeting</u>. Every act or decision done or made by a majority of the directors present at a meeting duly held at which a quorum is present shall be regarded as the act of the Board of Directors unless a greater number is required by law or by this Certificate of Incorporation.

7. <u>Removal</u>. Subject to the rights of holders of any series of Preferred Stock, directors of the Corporation may be removed only for cause and only by the affirmative vote of the holders of at least seventy-five percent (75%) of the votes that all the stockholders would be entitled to cast in any annual election of directors or class of directors.

8. <u>Vacancies</u>. Subject to the rights of holders of any series of Preferred Stock, any vacancy or newly created directorship in the Board of Directors, however occurring, shall be filled only by vote of a majority of the directors then in office, although less than a quorum, or by a sole remaining director and shall not be filled by the stockholders. A director elected to fill a vacancy shall hold office until the next election of the class for which such director shall have been chosen, subject to the election and qualification of a successor and to such director's earlier death, resignation or removal.

9. <u>Stockholder Nominations and Introduction of Business, Etc.</u> Advance notice of stockholder nominations for election of directors and other business to be brought by stockholders before a meeting of stockholders shall be given in the manner provided by the By-laws of the Corporation.

10. <u>Amendments to Article</u>. Notwithstanding any other provisions of law, this Certificate of Incorporation or the By-laws of the Corporation, and notwithstanding the fact that a lesser percentage may be specified by law, the affirmative vote of the holders of at least seventy-five percent (75%) of the votes which all the stockholders would be entitled to cast in any annual election of directors or class of directors shall be required to amend or repeal, or to adopt any provision inconsistent with, this Article NINTH.

TENTH: Stockholders of the Corporation may not take any action by written consent in lieu of a meeting. Notwithstanding any other provisions of law, this Certificate of Incorporation or the By-laws of the Corporation, and notwithstanding the fact that a lesser percentage may be specified by law, the affirmative vote of the holders of at least seventy-five percent (75%) of the votes that all the stockholders would be entitled to cast in any annual election of directors or class of directors shall be required to amend or repeal, or to adopt any provision inconsistent with, this Article TENTH.

ELEVENTH: Special meetings of stockholders for any purpose or purposes may be called at any time by only the Board of Directors, the Chairman of the Board or the Chief Executive Officer, and may not be called by any other person or persons. Business transacted at any special meeting of stockholders shall be limited to matters relating to the purpose or purposes stated in the notice of meeting. Notwithstanding any other provisions of law, this Certificate of Incorporation or the By-laws of the Corporation, and notwithstanding the fact that a lesser percentage may be specified by law, the affirmative vote of the holders of at least seventy-five percent (75%) of the votes that all the stockholders would be entitled to cast in any annual election of directors or class of directors shall be required to amend or repeal, or to adopt any provision inconsistent with, this Article ELEVENTH.

IN WITNESS WHEREOF, this Eighth Restated Certificate of Incorporation, which restates, integrates and amends the certificate of incorporation of the Corporation, and which has been duly adopted in accordance with §§ 228, 242 and 245 of the General Corporation Law of the State of Delaware, has been executed by its duly authorized officer this 19th day of April, 2011.

ZIPCAR, INC.
By: /s/ Scott W. Griffith

Name: Scott W. Griffith
Title: Chief Executive Officer

As mentioned above, a corporation's bylaws specify rules regarding the governance of the corporation. The following are sample bylaws for a Delaware corporation.

SHOE CO. BYLAWS

ARTICLE I
Offices

1.01 Offices. The address of the registered office of Shoe Co. (the "**Corporation**") in the State of Delaware is at 1209 Orange Street, Wilmington, New Castle County, Delaware 19801. The Corporation may have other offices, both within and without the State of Delaware, as the board of directors of the Corporation (the "**Board of Directors**") from time to time shall determine or the business of the Corporation may require.

1.02 Books and Records. Any records maintained by the Corporation in the regular course of its business, including its stock ledger, books of account and minute books, may be maintained on any information storage device or method; *provided that* the records so kept can be converted into clearly legible paper form within a reasonable time. The Corporation shall so convert any records so kept upon the request of any person entitled to inspect such records pursuant to applicable law.

ARTICLE II
Meetings of the Stockholders

2.01 Place of Meetings. All meetings of the stockholders shall be held at such place, if any, either within or without the State of Delaware, as shall be designated from time to time by resolution of the Board of Directors and stated in the notice of meeting.

2.02 Annual Meeting. The annual meeting of the stockholders for the election of directors and for the transaction of such other business as may properly come before the meeting shall be held at such date, time and place, if any, as shall be determined by the Board of Directors and stated in the notice of the meeting.

2.03 Special Meetings. Special meetings of stockholders for any purpose or purposes shall be called pursuant to a resolution approved by the Board of Directors and may not be called by any other person or persons. The only business which may be conducted at a special meeting shall be the matter or matters set forth in the notice of such meeting.

2.04 Adjournments. Any meeting of the stockholders, annual or special, may be adjourned from time to time to reconvene at the same or some other place, if any, and notice need not be given of any such adjourned meeting if the time, place, if any, thereof and the means of remote communication, if any, are announced at the meeting at which the adjournment is taken. At the adjourned meeting, the Corporation may transact any business which might have been transacted at the original meeting. If the adjournment is for more than 30 days, a notice of the adjourned meeting shall be given to each stockholder of record entitled to vote at the meeting. If after the adjournment a new record date is fixed for stockholders entitled to vote at the adjourned meeting, the Board of Directors shall fix a new record date for notice of the adjourned meeting and shall give notice of the adjourned meeting to each stockholder of record entitled to vote at the adjourned meeting as of the record date fixed for notice of the adjourned meeting.

2.05 Notice of Meetings. Notice of the place, if any, date, hour, the record date for determining the stockholders entitled to vote at the meeting (if such date is different from the record date for stockholders entitled to notice of the meeting) and means of remote communication, if any, of every meeting of stockholders shall be given by the Corporation not less than ten days nor more than 60 days before the meeting (unless a different time is specified by law) to every stockholder entitled to vote at the meeting as of the record date for determining the stockholders entitled to notice of the meeting. Notices of special meetings shall also specify the purpose or purposes for which the meeting has been called. Except as otherwise provided herein or permitted by applicable law, notice to stockholders shall be in writing and delivered personally or mailed to the stockholders at their address appearing on the books of the Corporation. Without limiting the manner by which notice otherwise may be given effectively to stockholders, notice of meetings may be given to stockholders by means of electronic transmission in accordance with applicable law. Notice of any meeting need not be given to any stockholder who shall, either before or after the meeting, submit a waiver of notice or who shall attend such meeting, except when the stockholder attends for the express purpose of objecting, at the beginning of the meeting, to the transaction of any business because the meeting is not lawfully called or convened. Any stockholder so waiving notice of the meeting shall be bound by the proceedings of the meeting in all respects as if due notice thereof had been given.

2.06 List of Stockholders. The officer of the Corporation who has charge of the stock ledger shall prepare a complete list of the stockholders entitled to vote at any meeting of stockholders (provided, however, if the record date for determining the stockholders entitled to vote is less than ten days before the date of the meeting, the list shall reflect the stockholders entitled to vote as of the tenth day before the meeting date), arranged in alphabetical order, and showing the address of each stockholder and the number of shares of each class of capital stock of the Corporation registered in the name of each stockholder at least ten days before any meeting of the stockholders.

2.07 Quorum. Unless otherwise required by law, the Corporation's Certificate of Incorporation (the "**Certificate of Incorporation**") or these bylaws, at each meeting of the stockholders, a majority in voting power of the shares of the Corporation entitled to vote at the meeting, present in person or represented by proxy, shall constitute a quorum. If, however, such quorum shall not be present or represented at any meeting of the stockholders, the stockholders entitled to vote thereat, present in person or represented by proxy, shall have power, by the affirmative vote of a majority in voting power thereof, to adjourn the meeting from time to time, in the manner provided in **Section 2.04**, until a quorum shall be present or represented. A quorum, once established, shall not be broken by the subsequent withdrawal of enough votes to leave less than a quorum. At any such adjourned meeting at which there is a quorum, any business may be transacted that might have been transacted at the meeting originally called.

2.08 Conduct of Meetings. The Board of Directors may adopt by resolution such rules and regulations for the conduct of the meeting of the stockholders as it shall deem appropriate.

2.09 Voting; Proxies. Unless otherwise required by law or the Certificate of Incorporation the election of directors shall be by written ballot and shall be decided by a plurality of the votes cast at a meeting of the stockholders by the holders of stock entitled to vote in the election. Unless otherwise required by law, the Certificate of Incorporation or these bylaws, any matter, other than the election of directors, brought before any meeting of stockholders shall be decided by the affirmative vote of the majority of shares present in person or represented by proxy at the meeting and entitled to vote on the matter. Each stockholder entitled to vote at a meeting of stockholders or to express consent to corporate action in writing without a meeting may authorize another person or persons to act for such stockholder by proxy, but no such proxy shall be voted or acted upon after three years from its date, unless the proxy provides for a longer period. A proxy shall be irrevocable if it states that it is irrevocable and if, and only as long as, it is coupled with an interest sufficient in law to support an irrevocable power. A stockholder may revoke any proxy which is not irrevocable by attending the meeting and voting in person or by delivering to the secretary of the Corporation a revocation of the proxy or a new proxy bearing a later date. Voting at meetings of stockholders need not be by written ballot.

2.10 Written Consent of Stockholders Without a Meeting. Any action to be taken at any annual or special meeting of stockholders may be taken without a meeting, without prior notice and without a vote, if a consent or consents in writing, setting forth the action to be so taken, shall be signed by the holders of outstanding stock having not less than the minimum number of votes that would be necessary to authorize or take such action at a meeting at which all shares entitled to vote thereon were present and voted and shall be delivered (by hand or by certified or registered mail, return receipt requested) to the Corporation by delivery to its registered office in the State of Delaware, its principal place of business or an officer or agent of the Corporation having custody of the book in which proceedings of meetings of stockholders are recorded. Every written consent shall bear the date of signature of each stockholder who signs the consent, and no written consent shall be effective to take the corporate action referred to therein unless, within 60 days of the earliest dated consent delivered in the manner required by this **Section 2.10**, written consents signed by a sufficient number of holders to take action are delivered to the Corporation as aforesaid. Prompt notice of the taking of the corporate action without a meeting by less than unanimous written consent shall, to the extent required by applicable law, be given to those stockholders who have not consented in writing, and who, if the action had been taken at a meeting, would have been entitled to notice of the meeting if the record date for notice of such meeting had been the date that written consents signed by a sufficient number of holders to take the action were delivered to the Corporation.

2.11 Fixing the Record Date.

(a) In order that the Corporation may determine the stockholders entitled to notice of or to vote at any meeting of stockholders or any adjournment thereof, the Board of Directors may fix a record date, which record date shall not precede the date upon which the resolution fixing the record date is adopted by the Board of Directors, and which record date shall not be more than 60 nor less than ten days before the date of such meeting. If the Board of Directors so fixes a date, such date shall also be the record date for determining the stockholders entitled to vote at such meeting unless the Board of Directors determines, at the time it fixes such record date, that a later date on or before the date of the meeting shall be the date for making such determination. If no record date is fixed by the Board of Directors, the record date for determining stockholders entitled to notice of or to vote at a meeting of stockholders shall be at the close of business on the day next preceding the day on which notice is given, or, if notice is waived, at the close of business on the day next preceding the day on which the meeting is held. A determination of stockholders of record entitled to notice of or to vote at a meeting of stockholders shall apply to any adjournment of the meeting; *provided, however*, that the Board of Directors may fix a new record date for the determination of stockholders entitled to vote at the adjourned meeting and in such case shall also fix as the record date for stockholders entitled to notice of such adjourned meeting the same or an earlier date as that fixed for the determination of stockholders entitled to vote therewith at the adjourned meeting.

(b) In order that the Corporation may determine the stockholders entitled to consent to corporate action in writing without a meeting, the Board of Directors may fix a record date, which record date shall not precede the date upon which the resolution fixing the record date is adopted by the Board of Directors, and which record date shall not be more than ten days after the date upon which the resolution fixing the record date is adopted by the Board of Directors. If no record date has been fixed by the Board of Directors, the record date for determining stockholders entitled to consent to corporate action in writing without a meeting: (i) when no prior action by the Board of Directors is required by law, the record date for such purpose shall be the first date on which a signed written consent setting forth the action taken or proposed to be taken is delivered to the Corporation by delivery (by hand, or by certified or registered mail, return receipt requested) to its registered office in the State of Delaware, its principal place of business, or an officer or agent of the Corporation having custody of the book in which proceedings of meetings of stockholders are recorded and (ii) if prior action by the Board of Directors is required by law, the record date for such purpose shall be at the close of business on the day on which the Board of Directors adopts the resolution taking such prior action.

(c) In order that the Corporation may determine the stockholders entitled to receive payment of any dividend or other distribution or allotment of any rights or the stockholders entitled to exercise any rights in respect of any change, conversion or exchange of stock, or for the purpose of any other lawful action, the Board of Directors may fix a record date, which record date shall not precede the date upon which the resolution fixing the record date is adopted, and which record date shall be not more than 60 days prior to such action. If no record date is fixed, the record date for determining stockholders for any such purpose shall be at the close of business on the day on which the Board of Directors adopts the resolution relating thereto.

ARTICLE III
Board of Directors

3.01 General Powers. The business and affairs of the Corporation shall be managed by or under the direction of the Board of Directors. The Board of Directors may adopt such rules and procedures, not inconsistent with the Certificate of Incorporation, these bylaws or applicable law, as it may deem proper for the conduct of its meetings and the management of the Corporation.

3.02 Number; Term of Office. The Board of Directors shall consist of five members. Each director shall hold office until a successor is duly elected and qualified or until the director's earlier death, resignation, disqualification or removal.

3.03 Newly Created Directorships and Vacancies. Any newly created directorships resulting from an increase in the authorized number of directors and any vacancies occurring in the Board of Directors, shall be filled solely by the affirmative votes of a majority of the remaining members of the Board of Directors, although less than a quorum, or by a sole remaining director. A director so elected shall be elected to hold office until the earlier of the expiration of the term of office of the director whom he or she has replaced, a successor is duly elected and qualified or the earlier of such director's death, resignation or removal.

3.04 Resignation. Any director may resign at any time by notice given in writing or by electronic transmission to the Corporation. Such resignation shall take effect at the date of receipt of such notice by the Corporation or at such later time as is therein specified.

3.05 Removal. Except as prohibited by applicable law or the Certificate of Incorporation, the stockholders entitled to vote in an election of directors may remove any director from office at any time, with or without cause, by the affirmative vote of a majority in voting power thereof.

3.06 Regular Meetings. Regular meetings of the Board of Directors may be held without notice at such times and at such places as may be determined from time to time by the Board of Directors or its chairman.

3.07 Special Meetings. Special meetings of the Board of Directors may be held at such times and at such places as may be determined by the chairman or the Chief Executive Officer on at least 24 hours' notice to each director given by one of the means specified in **Section 3.10** of these Bylaws other than by mail or on at least three days' notice if given by mail. Special meetings shall be called by the chairman or the Chief Executive Officer in like manner and on like notice on the written request of any two or more directors.

3.08 Telephone Meetings. Board of Directors or Board of Directors committee meetings may be held by means of telephone conference or other communications equipment by means of which all persons participating in the meeting can hear each other and be heard. Participation by a director in a meeting pursuant to this **Section 3.08** shall constitute presence in person at such meeting.

3.09 Adjourned Meetings. A majority of the directors present at any meeting of the Board of Directors, including an adjourned meeting, whether or not a quorum is present, may adjourn and reconvene such meeting to another time and place. At least 24 hours notice of any adjourned meeting of the Board of Directors shall be given to each director whether or not present at the time of the adjournment, if such notice shall be given by one of the means specified in **Section 3.10** hereof other than by mail, or at least three days notice if by mail. Any business may be transacted at an adjourned meeting that might have been transacted at the meeting as originally called.

3.10 Notices. Subject to **Section 3.07, Section 3.09** and **Section 3.11** hereof, whenever notice is required to be given to any director by applicable law, the Certificate of Incorporation or these bylaws, such notice shall be deemed given effectively if given in person or by telephone, mail addressed to such director at such director's address as it appears on the records of the Corporation, facsimile, e-mail or by other means of electronic transmission.

3.11 Waiver of Notice. Whenever notice to directors is required by applicable law, the Certificate of Incorporation or these bylaws, a waiver thereof, in writing signed by, or by electronic transmission by, the director entitled to the notice, whether before or after such notice is required, shall be deemed equivalent to notice. Attendance by a director at a meeting shall constitute a waiver of notice of such meeting except when the director attends a meeting for the express purpose of objecting, at the beginning of the meeting, to the transaction of any business on the ground that the meeting was not lawfully called or convened. Neither the business to be transacted at, nor the purpose of, any regular or special Board of Directors or committee meeting need be specified in any waiver of notice.

3.12 Organization. At each meeting of the Board of Directors, the chairman or, in his or her absence, another director selected by the Board of Directors shall preside. The secretary shall act as secretary at each meeting of the Board of Directors. If the secretary is absent from any meeting of the Board of Directors, an assistant secretary shall perform the duties of secretary at such meeting; and in the absence from any such meeting of the secretary and all assistant secretaries, the person presiding at the meeting may appoint any person to act as secretary of the meeting.

3.13 Quorum of Directors. The presence of a majority of the Board of Directors shall be necessary and sufficient to constitute a quorum for the transaction of business at any meeting of the Board of Directors.

3.14 Action By Majority Vote. Except as otherwise expressly required by these bylaws, the Certificate of Incorporation or by applicable law, the vote of a majority of the directors present at a meeting at which a quorum is present shall be the act of the Board of Directors.

3.15 Action Without Meeting. Unless otherwise restricted by the Certificate of Incorporation or these bylaws, any action required or permitted to be taken at any meeting of the Board of Directors or of any committee thereof may be taken without a meeting if all directors or members of such committee, as the case may be, consent thereto in writing or by electronic transmission, and the writings or electronic transmissions are filed with the minutes of proceedings of the Board of Directors or committee in accordance with applicable law.

3.16 Committees of the Board of Directors. The Board of Directors may designate one or more committees, each committee to consist of one or more of the directors of the Corporation. The Board of Directors may designate one or more directors as alternate members of any committee, who may replace any absent or disqualified member at any meeting of the committee. If a member of a committee shall be absent from any meeting, or disqualified from voting thereat, the remaining member or members present at the meeting and not disqualified from voting, whether or not such member or members constitute a quorum, may unanimously appoint another member of the Board of Directors to act at the meeting in the place of any such absent or disqualified member. Any such committee, to the extent permitted by applicable law, shall have and may exercise all the powers and authority of the Board of Directors in the management of the business and affairs of the Corporation and may authorize the seal of the Corporation to be affixed to all papers that may require it to the extent so authorized by the Board of Directors. Unless the Board of Directors provides otherwise, at all meetings of such committee, a majority of the then authorized members of the committee shall constitute a quorum for the transaction of business, and the vote of a majority of the members of the committee present at any meeting at which there is a quorum shall be the act of the committee. Each committee shall keep regular minutes of its meetings. Unless the Board of Directors provides otherwise, each committee designated by the Board of Directors may make, alter and repeal rules and procedures for the conduct of its business. In the absence of such rules and procedures each committee shall conduct its business in the same manner as the Board of Directors conducts its business pursuant to this Article III.

ARTICLE IV
Officers

4.01   Positions and Election. The officers of the Corporation shall be elected by the Board of Directors and shall include a president, a treasurer and a secretary. The Board of Directors, in its discretion, may also elect a chairman (who must be a director), one or more vice chairmen (who must be directors) and one or more vice presidents, assistant treasurers, assistant secretaries and other officers. Any two or more offices may be held by the same person.

4.02   Term. Each officer of the Corporation shall hold office until such officer's successor is elected and qualified or until such officer's earlier death, resignation or removal. Any officer elected or appointed by the Board of Directors may be removed by the Board of Directors at any time with or without cause by the majority vote of the members of the Board of Directors then in office. The removal of an officer shall be without prejudice to his or her contract rights, if any. The election or appointment of an officer shall not of itself create contract rights. Any officer of the Corporation may resign at any time by giving written notice of his or her resignation to the president or the secretary. Any such resignation shall take effect at the time specified therein or, if the time when it shall become effective shall not be specified therein, immediately upon its receipt. Unless otherwise specified therein, the acceptance of such resignation shall not be necessary to make it effective. Should any vacancy occur among the officers, the position shall be filled for the unexpired portion of the term by appointment made by the Board of Directors.

4.03   The President. The president shall have general supervision over the business of the Corporation and other duties incident to the office of president, and any other duties as may be from time to time assigned to the president by the Board of Directors and subject to the control of the Board of Directors in each case.

4.04 Vice Presidents. Each vice president shall have such powers and perform such duties as may be assigned to him or her from time to time by the chairman of the Board of Directors or the president.

4.05 The Secretary. The secretary shall attend all sessions of the Board of Directors and all meetings of the stockholders and record all votes and the minutes of all proceedings in a book to be kept for that purpose, and shall perform like duties for committees when required. He or she shall give, or cause to be given, notice of all meetings of the stockholders and meetings of the Board of Directors, and shall perform such other duties as may be prescribed by the Board of Directors or the president. The secretary shall keep in safe custody the seal of the Corporation and have authority to affix the seal to all documents requiring it and attest to the same.

4.06 The Treasurer. The treasurer shall have the custody of the corporate funds and securities, except as otherwise provided by the Board of Directors, and shall keep full and accurate accounts of receipts and disbursements in books belonging to the Corporation and shall deposit all moneys and other valuable effects in the name and to the credit of the Corporation in such depositories as may be designated by the Board of Directors. The treasurer shall disburse the funds of the Corporation as may be ordered by the Board of Directors, taking proper vouchers for such disbursements, and shall render to the president and the directors, at the regular meetings of the Board of Directors, or whenever they may require it, an account of all his or her transactions as treasurer and of the financial condition of the Corporation.

4.07 Duties of Officers May be Delegated. In case any officer is absent, or for any other reason that the Board of Directors may deem sufficient, the president or the Board of Directors may delegate for the time being the powers or duties of such officer to any other officer or to any director.

ARTICLE V
Stock Certificates and Their Transfer

5.01 Certificates Representing Shares. The shares of stock of the Corporation shall be represented by certificates; provided that the Board of Directors may provide by resolution or resolutions that some or all of any class or series shall be uncertificated shares that may be evidenced by a book-entry system maintained by the registrar of such stock. If shares are represented by certificates, such certificates shall be in the form, other than bearer form, approved by the Board of Directors. The certificates representing shares of stock of each class shall be signed by, or in the name of, the Corporation by the chairman, any vice chairman, the president or any vice president, and by the secretary, any assistant secretary, the treasurer or any assistant treasurer. Any or all such signatures may be facsimiles. Although any officer, transfer agent or registrar whose manual or facsimile signature is affixed to such a certificate ceases to be such officer, transfer agent or registrar before such certificate has been issued, it may nevertheless be issued by the Corporation with the same effect as if such officer, transfer agent or registrar were still such at the date of its issue.

5.02 Transfers of Stock. Stock of the Corporation shall be transferable in the manner prescribed by law and in these bylaws. Transfers of stock shall be made on the books of the Corporation only by the holder of record thereof, by such person's attorney lawfully constituted in writing and, in the case of certificated shares, upon the surrender of the certificate thereof, which shall be cancelled before a new certificate or uncertificated shares shall be issued. No transfer of stock shall be valid as against the Corporation for any purpose until it shall have been entered in the stock records of the Corporation by an entry showing from and to whom transferred. To the extent designated by the president or any vice president or the treasurer of the Corporation, the Corporation may recognize the transfer of fractional uncertificated shares, but shall not otherwise be required to recognize the transfer of fractional shares.

5.03   Transfer Agents and Registrars. The Board of Directors may appoint, or authorize any officer or officers to appoint, one or more transfer agents and one or more registrars.

5.04   Lost, Stolen or Destroyed Certificates. The Board of Directors may direct a new certificate or uncertificated shares to be issued in place of any certificate theretofore issued by the Corporation alleged to have been lost, stolen or destroyed upon the making of an affidavit of that fact by the owner of the allegedly lost, stolen or destroyed certificate. When authorizing such issue of a new certificate or uncertificated shares, the Board of Directors may, in its discretion and as a condition precedent to the issuance thereof, require the owner of the lost, stolen or destroyed certificate, or the owner's legal representative to give the Corporation a bond sufficient to indemnify it against any claim that may be made against the Corporation with respect to the certificate alleged to have been lost, stolen or destroyed or the issuance of such new certificate or uncertificated shares.

ARTICLE VI
General Provisions

6.01   Seal. The seal of the Corporation shall be in such form as shall be approved by the Board of Directors. The seal may be used by causing it or a facsimile thereof to be impressed or affixed or reproduced or otherwise, as may be prescribed by law or custom or by the Board of Directors.

6.02   Checks, Notes, Drafts, Etc. All checks, notes, drafts or other orders for the payment of money of the Corporation shall be signed, endorsed or accepted in the name of the Corporation by such officer, officers, person or persons as from time to time may be designated by the Board of Directors or by an officer or officers authorized by the Board of Directors to make such designation.

6.03   Dividends. Subject to applicable law and the Certificate of Incorporation, dividends upon the shares of capital stock of the Corporation may be declared by the Board of Directors at any regular or special meeting of the Board of Directors. Dividends may be paid in cash, in property or in shares of the Corporation's capital stock, unless otherwise provided by applicable law or the Certificate of Incorporation.

6.04   Conflict   With   Applicable   Law   or   Certificate   of Incorporation. These bylaws are adopted subject to any applicable law and the Certificate of Incorporation. Whenever these bylaws may conflict with any applicable law or the Certificate of Incorporation, such conflict shall be resolved in favor of such law or the Certificate of Incorporation.

ARTICLE VII
Amendments

These bylaws may be amended, altered, changed, adopted and repealed or new bylaws adopted by the Board of Directors. The stockholders may make additional bylaws and may alter and repeal any bylaws whether such bylaws were originally adopted by them or otherwise.

Shareholders' agreements are common for closely held corporations and may address a myriad of issues. Typical provisions include stock transfer restrictions, employment of shareholders, board representation, and buy-sell rights with respect to the corporation's shares.

Corporate governance principles are common for publicly held corporations. They typically address, among other things, director responsibilities, board committees, content and frequency of board and committee meetings, and director compensation.

4. Management

Corporate law statutes vest ultimate management authority in a corporation's board of directors.[3] The number of people on the board is set by the corporation, and its shareholders elect the directors. This structure is referred to as centralized management because the authority to manage the corporation is centralized in the board of directors as opposed to decentralized among the business's owners. A corporation's shareholders have no statutory authority to manage the corporation.

Typically, a board of directors does not make day-to-day decisions with respect to a corporation's business. Instead, it appoints officers to run the business, subject to board oversight. In a closely held corporation, it is common for all shareholders to be on the board of directors and to serve as officers. Thus, they wear three hats simultaneously: shareholder, director, and officer. Such a structure obviously frays the concept of centralized management, but oftentimes makes sense for a closely held corporation. Conversely, at public corporations, the overwhelming majority of shareholders are neither on the board nor officers of the corporation. Below is a brief discussion of shareholders, directors, and officers.

a. Shareholders

Shareholders[4] are regarded as the owners of a corporation but, reflecting the centralized management structure of corporate law, get a say in only a limited number of matters, a say that they express through voting. In that regard, corporate law statutes provide shareholders a vote on the following matters only:

---

[3] *See, e.g.*, MBCA § 8.01(b); DGCL § 141(a).

[4] The MBCA uses the term "shareholder," while the DGCL uses the term "stockholder." The terms are synonymous, but I have decided to go with "shareholder" even when referring to the DGCL. Some attorneys, however, make a point to use the term "shareholder" when talking about a corporation incorporated in an MBCA state and the term "stockholder" when talking about a Delaware corporation, and will call others on it who do not do the same. You can do it, too, if you want, but I think it is kind of silly.

(1) election and removal of directors,

(2) amendments to the corporation's charter,

(3) shareholder (as opposed to board) initiated amendments to the corporation's bylaws,

(4) dissolution of the corporation,

(5) a merger of the corporation, and

(6) a sale of all (or substantially all) of the corporation's assets.

The board may choose to put additional matters to a shareholder vote (e.g., approval of a conflict of interest transaction) even though it is not required to under state corporate law. Furthermore, a corporation's charter or bylaws may specify additional matters on which shareholders get to vote, but expanding the list is fairly uncommon except with respect to voting by holders of preferred stock.

i. Shareholders' Meetings and Voting

Shareholder voting is done through the mechanism of a shareholders' meeting. There are two types of shareholders' meetings, annual and special. An annual meeting is a regularly scheduled meeting held by a corporation each year so that shareholders can vote on the election of directors. Corporate law statutes require corporations to hold annual meetings, unless the corporation's directors are elected by written consent (discussed below). Shareholders may also be asked to vote on other matters at the annual meeting, for example, a proposed merger.

A special meeting is one held between annual meetings to have shareholders vote on a matter or matters that cannot wait until the next annual meeting. For example, say the board has approved the sale of all of the corporation's assets, and the buyer wants to close the transaction as soon as possible. As noted above, the sale of all of a corporation's assets is one of the few matters that require shareholder approval. Assume the corporation had held its annual meeting the previous month. Instead of waiting the eleven months until its next annual meeting, the corporation can call and hold a special meeting on fairly short notice so that shareholders can vote on the proposed sale of assets.

For a vote at a meeting to be valid, (1) a corporation must provide its shareholders with notice of the meeting (subject to waiver[5]), and (2) a quorum of shares must be present at the meeting. As for notice, both the MBCA and the DGCL require a corporation to notify its shareholders of the date, time, and place of the meeting at least 10 but not more than 60 days prior to the meeting.[6] For a special meeting, the notice must include a description of the purpose or purposes for which the meeting is called.[7]

In the shareholder voting context, a quorum is the minimum number of shareholder votes that must be represented at a shareholders' meeting. It is *not* the number of shareholders that must be present, because shareholder voting is

---

[5] *See* MBCA § 7.06; DGCL § 229.

[6] *See* MBCA § 7.05; DGCL § 222.

[7] *See id.*

based on votes per share, not headcount. The default rule under both the MBCA and the DGCL is that a quorum is a majority of the corporation's outstanding votes.[8]

ii. Proxies

A shareholder does not have to physically attend a shareholders' meeting for his or her shares to be considered present for purposes of a quorum and voted. Instead, the shareholder can appoint a person who will be attending the meeting to serve as the shareholder's "proxy" at the meeting. In this context, a proxy is an agent appointed by a shareholder to whom the shareholder gives express actual authority to vote the shareholder's shares at a shareholders' meeting. Corporate law statutes specify the rules for a valid appointment of a proxy.[9] Among other things, the appointment must be reflected in a written or electronic transmission.

Any corporation with more than a handful of shareholders routinely solicits its shareholders to appoint the proxy chosen by the corporation for a particular shareholders' meeting. The corporation does this to ensure that enough shares are present at the meeting in person or by proxy to meet the quorum requirement. Proxy solicitation by public companies is subject to regulation under federal proxy rules. We discuss these rules in Chapter 3.

iii. Written Consents

A vote at a formal shareholders' meeting is not the only way a corporation can obtain shareholder approval of a matter. Corporate law statutes also provide for shareholder approval through written consent.[10] For example, MBCA § 7.04(a) provides:

> Action required or permitted by this Act to be taken at a shareholders' meeting may be taken without a meeting if the action is taken by all the shareholders entitled to vote on the action. The action must be evidenced by one or more written consents bearing the date of signature and describing the action taken, signed by all the shareholders entitled to vote on the action, and delivered to the corporation for inclusion in the minutes or filing with the corporate records.

Basically, instead of holding a shareholders' meeting, a corporation can secure shareholder approval by having its shareholders sign a piece of paper indicating their approval.

iv. Voting Requirements

A voting requirement refers to the minimum number of votes a matter must receive to pass. The default MBCA shareholder voting requirement for matters other than the election of directors is what I call a "more votes for than against" requirement. Specifically, § 7.25(c) provides that "unless the articles of incorporation or this Act require a greater number of affirmative votes," a matter passes if

---

[8] *See* MBCA § 7.25(a); DGCL § 216.

[9] *See* MBCA § 7.22; DGCL § 212.

[10] *See* MBCA § 7.04; DGCL § 228.

"the votes cast . . . favoring the action exceed the votes cast opposing the action." The default DGCL shareholder voting requirement is higher. It is what I call a "majority of a quorum" requirement. Specifically, § 216 provides that unless a different requirement is set forth in another section of the DGCL or the corporation's charter or bylaws, "the affirmative vote of the majority of shares present in person or represented by proxy at the meeting and entitled to vote on the subject matter shall be the act of the stockholders."[11] Note that corporate law statutes typically provide for a higher voting requirement for a shareholder vote on an M&A transaction, such as a merger. For example, DGCL § 251(c) sets the voting standard at a majority of outstanding stock for shareholder approval of a merger.

b. Directors

The default corporate law rule is that ultimate managerial authority resides in a corporation's board of directors. In that regard, MBCA § 8.01(b) provides:

> All corporate powers shall be exercised by or under the authority of the board of directors of the corporation, and the business and affairs of the corporation shall be managed by or under the direction, and subject to the oversight, of its board of directors. . . .

The analogous provision under the DGCL is § 141(a). Typically, a board of directors does not make day-to-day decisions with respect to a corporation's business. Instead, it elects officers to run the business, subject to board oversight. This arrangement is contemplated by the "by or under" phraseology used in the above provision.

i. Board Action

Similar to shareholders, boards take action by voting at a board meeting. There must be a quorum present at a meeting for a board to act. Under the default rule, the presence of a majority of directors constitutes a quorum (a director participating by phone or similar means is considered present).[12] An item must receive the affirmative vote of a majority of directors present at the meeting to pass.[13]

A board can also act through written consent. For example, MBCA § 8.21(a) provides:

> Except to the extent that the articles of incorporation or bylaws require that action by the board of directors be taken at a meeting, action required or permitted by this Act to be taken by the board of directors may be taken without a meeting if each director signs a consent describing the action to be taken and delivers it to the corporation.

Basically, instead of holding a board meeting, a corporation can secure board approval by having all of its directors sign a piece of paper indicating their approval. Section 141(f) is the analogous DGCL provision.

---

[11] DGCL § 216.

[12] *See* MBCA §§ 8.20(b) and 8.24(a); DGCL § 141(b) and (i).

[13] *See* MBCA § 8.24(c); DGCL § 141(b).

ii. Elections

The default rule under the MBCA and the DGCL is that shareholders elect directors using straight voting.[14] Under straight voting, each shareholder can cast the number of votes he or she has (assuming one vote per share, this would correspond to the number of shares the shareholder owns) on her preferred candidates for the board seats up for election. The default voting standard for the election of directors is plurality.[15] In this context, plurality means that the director candidates who receive the largest number of votes are elected, up to the maximum number of director slots up for election. For example, if five individuals are running for three slots, the top three vote-getters would win.

iii. Terms

Under the default rule, a director's term is generally one year. I say generally because a director's term technically lasts until the next election, which is normally a year later, but could be sooner or later than that.[16]

A corporation can instead choose to stagger, or classify, its board, meaning the terms of only a portion of its directors expire in a particular year. For example, DGCL § 141(d) provides:

> The directors of any corporation organized under this chapter may, by the certificate of incorporation or by an initial bylaw, or by a bylaw adopted by a vote of the stockholders, be divided into 1, 2 or 3 classes; the term of office of those of the first class to expire at the first annual meeting held after such classification becomes effective; of the second class 1 year thereafter; of the third class 2 years thereafter; and at each annual election held after such classification becomes effective, directors shall be chosen for a full term, as the case may be, to succeed those whose terms expire. The certificate of incorporation or bylaw provision dividing the directors into classes may authorize the board of directors to assign members of the board already in office to such classes at the time such classification becomes effective.[17]

We talk more about staggered boards in Chapter 6.

c. Officers

Officers oversee the day-to-day management of the corporation and are elected by the board or appointed by more senior officers. Corporate law statutes have few specifics regarding them, leaving it to a corporation to specify the titles and duties of its officers in its bylaws or through a board resolution.[18] In the M&A context, it is normally an officer that signs the various deal documents, e.g., merger agreement, articles of merger, escrow agreement. Thus, in the board resolutions

---

[14] *See* MBCA § 7.28(a); DGCL § 216(3).

[15] *See* MBCA § 7.28(a); DGCL § 216(3).

[16] *See* MBCA § 8.05(b); DGCL § 141(b).

[17] The analogous MBCA provision is § 8.06.

[18] *See* MBCA § 8.40(a); DGCL § 142(a).

approving the transaction will be resolutions authorizing one or more officers to sign these documents on behalf of the corporation. In agency law terms, the resolutions provide the officers with express actual authority to bind the corporation.

B. UNINCORPORATED ENTITIES

Unincorporated entities include limited liability companies (LLCs), limited liability partnerships (LLPs), and limited partnerships (LPs). Each state has a separate statute governing these entities. Thus, for example, if target is a Nevada LLC, i.e. an LLC organized under the laws of Nevada (regardless of where it is headquartered), you would examine the Nevada limited liability company statute (Nevada Revised Statutes Chapter 86).

Note that the statute applicable to an LLP is a state's general partnership statute. This is because states created the limited liability partnership form by adding LLP provisions to their general partnership statutes. An LLP is simply a general partnership that has elected LLP status under the applicable provisions of the general partnership statute. Conversely, all states have a separate limited partnership (LP) statute.

An unincorporated entity will normally have a written agreement signed by each owner that addresses, among other things, management structure, allocation of profits and losses among the owners, owner taxation, admission and withdrawal of owners, and dissolution. The name of the agreement varies by entity, i.e., an LLP calls it a limited liability partnership agreement, an LP calls it a limited partnership agreement, and an LLC calls it a limited liability company agreement or operating agreement. It is important to understand that unincorporated entity statutes are composed largely of default rules that the entity can alter or opt out of through appropriate language in its partnership or LLC agreement. In other words, a partnership/LLC agreement allows the owners to tailor the rules to their specific needs and preference. As a result, the starting point for providing advice to an unincorporated entity on unincorporated law issues is usually a review of the partnership/LLC agreement and not the applicable statute. The statute does, however, remain relevant because it contains some rules that owners cannot contract around and rules that apply if the partnership/LLC agreement is silent on a particular matter.

TABLE OF CASES

[References are to pages]

[References are to pages]

[References are to pages]

[References are to pages]

INDEX

[References are to sections.]

A

ACQUISITION AGREEMENTS
Generally . . . 5[E]
Asset purchase
    Excluded assets . . . 5[E][4][a][1]
    Included and excluded assets . . . 5[E][4][a][1]
    Liabilities, assumption of . . . 5[E][4][a][2]
    Price, purchase . . . 5[E][4][a][3]
Bidder's reps . . . 5[E][9][d]
Closing
    Conditions . . . 5[E][11]
    Mechanics . . . 5[E][8]
Covenants
    Generally . . . 5[E][10]
    Post-closing . . . 5[E][10][b]
    Pre-closing . . . 5[E][10][a]
Definitions . . . 5[E][3]
Disclosure schedules . . . 5[E][14]
Earnouts . . . 5[E][7]
Exchange ratios . . . 5[E][5]
Indemnification . . . 5[E][13]
Merger . . . 5[E][4][c]
Non-reliance provisions . . . 5[E][9][e]
Post-closing purchase price adjustment . . . 5[E][6]
Preamble . . . 5[E][1]
Purchase and sale/merger
    Generally . . . 5[E][4]
    Asset purchase (See subhead: Asset purchase)
    Merger . . . 5[E][4][c]
    Stock purchase . . . 5[E][4][b]
Qualifiers . . . 5[E][9][b]
Recitals . . . 5[E][2]
Representations and warranties
    Generally . . . 5[E][9][a]
    Bidder's reps . . . 5[E][9][d]
    Non-reliance provisions . . . 5[E][9][e]
    Qualifiers . . . 5[E][9][b]
    Target's reps . . . 5[E][9][c]
Stock purchase . . . 5[E][4][b]
Target's reps . . . 5[E][9][c]
Termination . . . 5[E][12]
Warranties, representations and (See subhead: Representations and warranties)

AGREEMENTS
Acquisition (See ACQUISITION AGREEMENTS)
Confidentiality agreement . . . 5[B]

APPRAISAL RIGHTS
Delaware General Corporation Law (DGCL) (See DELAWARE GENERAL CORPORATION LAW (DGCL), subhead: Appraisal rights)
Mergers and acquisitions (M&A) deal . . . 4[E]
Model Business Corporations Act (MBCA) (See MODEL BUSINESS CORPORATIONS ACT (MBCA), subhead: Appraisal rights)

ASSET PURCHASE
Generally . . . 1[A][1]
Acquisition agreements (See ACQUISITION AGREEMENTS, subhead: Asset purchase)
Delaware General Corporation Law (DGCL) (See DELAWARE GENERAL CORPORATION LAW (DGCL), subhead: Asset purchase)
Model Business Corporations Act (MBCA) (See MODEL BUSINESS CORPORATIONS ACT (MBCA), subhead: Asset purchase)

B

BIDDERS
Generally . . . 1[D]
Acquisition agreements, reps in . . . 5[E][9][d]
Asset purchase
    Appraisal rights
        Delaware General Corporation Law (DGCL) . . . 2[A][1][b][3]
        Model Business Corporations Act (MBCA) . . . 2[A][1][a][3][b]
    Shareholder approval
        Delaware General Corporation Law (DGCL) . . . 2[A][1][b][2][b]
        Model Business Corporations Act (MBCA) . . . 2[A][1][a][2][b]
No indemnification in public target deals . . . 5[G][2]
Reps in acquisition agreements . . . 5[E][9][d]
Shareholder approval
    Model Business Corporations Act (MBCA)
        Asset purchase . . . 2[A][1][a][2][b]
        Stock purchase . . . 2[A][2][a][2][b]
    Stock purchase . . . 2[A][2][a][2][b]

C

CONFIDENTIALITY AGREEMENT
Generally . . . 5[B]

CORPORATIONS
Generally . . . App.A

COVENANTS (See ACQUISITION AGREEMENTS, subhead: Covenants)

D

DELAWARE GENERAL CORPORATION LAW (DGCL)
Appraisal rights
    Asset purchase . . . 2[A][1][b][3]
    Direct merger . . . 2[A][3][b][3]
    Forward triangular merger . . . 2[A][4][b][3]
    Reverse triangular merger . . . 2[A][5][b][3]
Asset purchase
    Appraisal rights . . . 2[A][1][b][3]
    Board approval . . . 2[A][1][b][1]

[References are to sections.]

[References are to sections.]